Theatre Profiles 6

THEATRE COMMUNICATIONS GROUP

Theatre Profiles 6

The Illustrated Reference Guide to America's
Nonprofit Professional Theatres

Edited by Laura Ross

NEW YORK • 1984

ACKNOWLEDGEMENTS

TCG gratefully acknowledges the generous support of the following foundations, corporations and government agencies: Actors' Equity Foundation, Alcoa Foundation, American Telephone & Telegraph Company, Atlantic Richfield Foundation, Robert Sterling Clark Foundation, Dayton Hudson Foundation, The Equitable Life Assurance Society of the United States, Exxon Corporation, The Ford Foundation, The General Electric Foundation, Home Box Office, Inc., The Andrew W. Mellon Foundation, Metropolitan Life Foundation, National Endowment for the Arts, The New York Community Trust, New York State Council on the Arts, The Scherman Foundation and Warner Theatre Productions, Inc.

The editor wishes to thank the following people for their support, advice and assistance during the editorial process: Gregory Leaming, Paul Pierson, Frances Robertson and Joe Freedman. Special thanks are also extended to the staff members at all of the participating theatres who took the time and care to help make this volume as comprehensive and accurate as possible.

Copyright © 1984, Theatre Communications Group, Inc.
Theatre Profiles is published biennially by Theatre Communications Group, 355 Lexington Ave., New York, NY 10017. All rights reserved. No part of this book may be reproduced in any manner whatsoever without written permission from the publisher, except in the case of brief quotations embodied in critical articles and reviews.

Design and typography: Joe Marc Freedman

Typesetting: Village Type & Graphics

Mechanicals: Soho Studio

Printing: McNaughton & Gunn

ISBN 0-930452-33-X cloth
ISBN 0-930452-34-8 paper
LCCN 76-641618

Cover: James Maronek's set design for *The Threepenny Opera,* produced by the Goodman Theatre, 1970. Maronek is professor of design at the Depaul/Goodman School of Drama.

Frontis: Manhattan Theatre Club. Alvin Epstein and Paul McCrane in *Crossing Niagara.* Photo. Gerry Goodstein.

TENNESSEE WILLIAMS 1911-1983

This volume is dedicated to the memory of Tennessee Williams, whose graceful, vulnerable, shatteringly human characters have touched us all, and will be with us always. Had America not produced any other playwright, our contribution to world drama would have been great. Williams continues to be our most frequently produced playwright, and a glance through these pages reveals what many of us already knew: that it was in the nonprofit professional theatre that he found his most enduring home.

As important as the plays he has given us is the influence Williams exerted on an entire generation of playwrights—many of whom can also be found between these covers. The following few pages can only serve to remind us—more eloquently than words could hope to—of the Tennessee Williams who is still very much alive and in our presence.

GERARD MALANGA

Amanda: Laura, come here and make a wish on the moon!
Laura: Moon?
Amanda: A little silver slipper of a moon. Look over your left shoulder, Laura, and make a wish! Now! Now, darling, wish.
Laura: What shall I wish for, Mother?
Amanda: Happiness! And just a little bit of good fortune!   THE GLASS MENAGERIE

The Glass Menagerie, clockwise from right.
Portland Stage Company, 1981. John Griesemer and Derek Hoxby. Photo: Dean Abramson.
The Guthrie Theater, 1964. Ellen Geer and Ed Flanders. Photo: Dan Nordstrom.
The American Stage Company, 1983. Marjorie Greenwood and Ariel Bock. Photo: David G. MacLean.

Blanche: Yes, yes, magic! I try to give that to people. I do misrepresent things to them. I don't tell the truth, I tell what *ought* to be the truth. And if that's a sin, then let me be damned for it!

A STREETCAR NAMED DESIRE

Asolo State Theater, 1976. Steven Ryan and Barbara Reid. Photo: Gary W. Sweetman.

Milwaukee Repertory Theater, 1980. Tom Berenger, Jahni Brenn and Peggy Cowles. Photo: Mark Avery.

Margaret: Oh, you weak, beautiful people who give up with such grace. What you need is someone to take hold of you—gently, with love, and hand your life back to you, like something gold you let go of—and I can! I'm determined to do it—and nothing's more determined than a cat on a tin roof—is there? Is there, baby?

———— CAT ON A HOT TIN ROOF

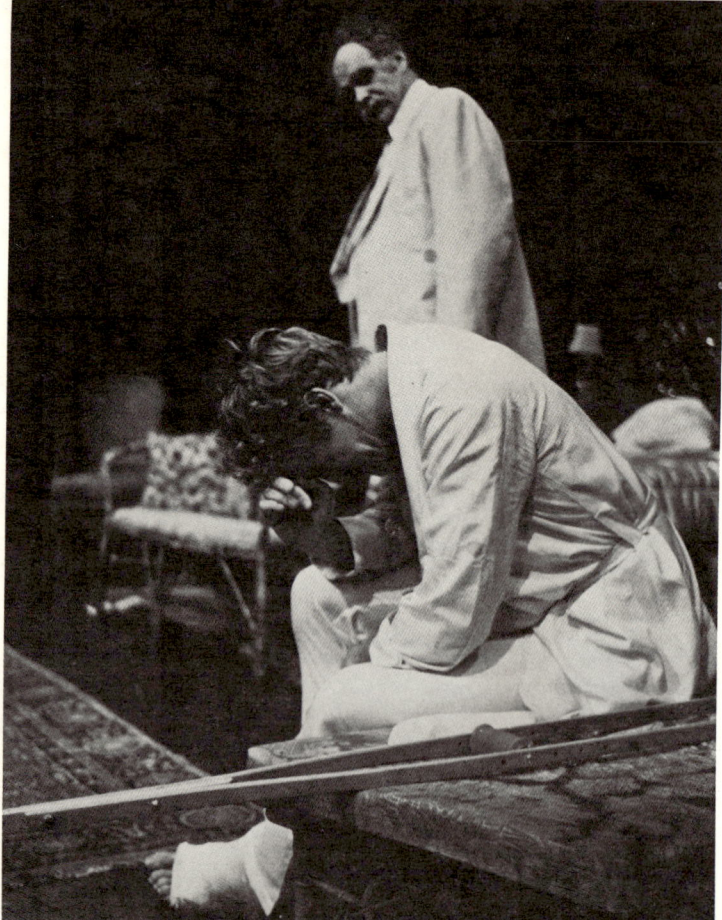

Cat on a Hot Tin Roof, clockwise from left:

Round House Theatre, 1982. Greta Lambert and Alessandro Cima. Photo: Brian Eggleston.

The Guthrie Theater, 1976. Christopher Pennock and Tony Mockus. Photo: Steve Rouch.

Syracuse Stage, 1982. Kate Mulgrew and Robert Gentry. Photo: Susan Piper Kublick.

Hannah: I still say that I'm not a bird, Mr. Shannon. I'm a human being and when a member of that fantastic species builds a nest in the heart of another, the question of permanence isn't the first or even the last thing that's considered . . . NIGHT OF THE IGUANA

Circle in the Square, 1952. Geraldine Page and Lee Richardson in *Summer and Smoke*. Photo: Roy Schatt.

Circle in the Square, 1976. Richard Chamberlain and Dorothy McGuire in *Night of the Iguana*. Photo: Martha Swope.

Prudence: Now we dismiss young lovers with skins of silk and eyes like a child's first prayer, we put them away as lightly as we put away white gloves meant only for summer, and pick up a pair of black ones, suitable for winter.   CAMINO REAL

The Cleveland Play House, 1943. Reigh Walston and Florence Healy in *You Touched Me*.
Alley Theatre, 1971. *Camino Real*. Photo: Richard Pipes.

Long Wharf Theatre, 1977. Emery Battis and Rita Moreno in *The Rose Tattoo*. Photo: Bill Smith.

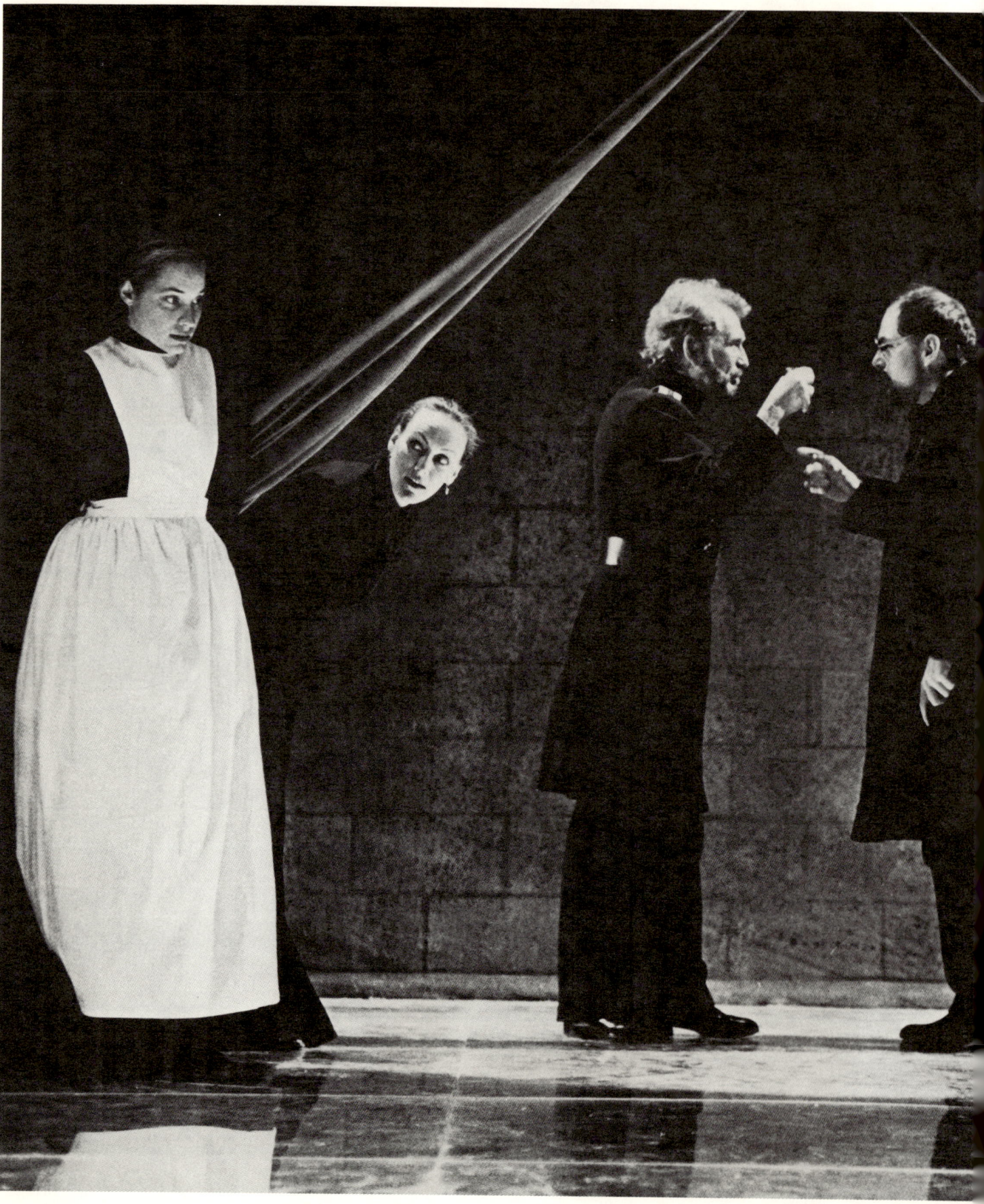

Contents

FOREWORD xv

USING THIS BOOK xvi

THEATRES xix

THEATRE PROFILES 2

THEATRE CHRONOLOGY 232

REGIONAL INDEX 234

INDEX OF NAMES 237

INDEX OF TITLES 255

ABOUT TCG 264

American Repertory Theatre. Marianne Owen, Alvin Epstein and Richard Grusin in *The Three Sisters*. Photo: Richard Feldman.

Foreword

Twenty-three years ago, when TCG was new, it was a fairly simple matter to know one's way around the American professional theatre. Even 12 years ago, when the *Theatre Profiles* series was born, visiting all of the existing companies was not an insurmountable task (there were fewer than 100 listed in *Theatre Profiles 1*). Today, the task would be quite an ambitious one. The 174 theatres represented in this volume are widespread in location, multifarious in philosophy and diverse in size, wealth and repertoire.

Theatre Profiles, now something of an institution among arts references, attempts the paradoxical: While opening up its readers' eyes to the vast number and variety of theatres around the country, it simultaneously makes a *smaller* world out of an ever-expanding one, affording easy access to an enormous amount of eclectic information.

Of course it's not possible to cram the life and vitality of thousands of artists, hundreds of productions between the covers of any one book — or even a series of books. What *Theatre Profiles* does offer is an "armchair" visit to all of those theatres that have become so difficult to visit in fact, as well as an evocation and a reminder of those companies with which one is already familiar. It is a kind of relief map of our nation's theatres, complete with a feeling for their particular climates and contours.

What's more, with each successive volume, the series has grown to constitute a historical document, charting the development of both institutions and repertoires.

A young artist beginning his professional career in the theatre is joining a family—but he is also very much alone in a difficult, competitive world—facing a tremendous number of tough questions. Shall I join a company? What theatres employ resident playwrights? Are there enough theatres in Seattle to provide me a living there? Just what kind of plays do they produce at the Guthrie, anyway? And, *how do I get in touch with these theatres?*

It's *Theatre Profiles'* job to answer questions, and over the years — with the help of its responsive audience — it has evolved to try to answer more questions better.

These pages provide a record of where we in the American theatre have been during the past two years, as well as who we are today. Perhaps if scrutinized carefully, they may also have something to reveal about where we're going.

LAURA ROSS
November 1983

The Children's Theatre Company and School. Elizabeth Fink, Gary Briggle and Annie Enneking in *Alice in Wonderland*. Photo: George Heinrich.

Using This Book

All of the theatres included in *Theatre Profiles 6* are Constituents of Theatre Communications Group, the national organization for the nonprofit professional theatre. Information was requested in the spring of 1983, and the text of this volume is based on materials submitted by the 174 theatres included.

The following notes provide an element-by-element guide to the use of this book.

Personnel

Current artistic and managing directors, as well as board presidents, are listed for each theatre. This information does not necessarily reflect the theatres' leadership during the 1981-82 and 1982-83 seasons. Where there has been a recent change in artistic leadership, the former artistic director is noted near the production lists, with an indication of which season(s) he or she was responsible for.

Founding

The founding date represents the beginning of public performances, or, in a few cases, the conceptual or legal establishment of the institution.

Season

The months listed indicate the opening and closing dates of the theatre's major performing season. "Year-round" indicates that the company performs throughout the year, often without formal opening or closing dates. "Variable" indicates a changeable or unstructured season. In such cases, current season information can be obtained directly from the theatre.

Schedule

Evening and matinee performance days are listed for theatres which have established regular performing schedules for the run of each production. Wherever possible, this edition also includes variable performance days (e.g., "selected Saturdays"). Specific information on variable schedules should be requested directly from the theatre; please note that even regular schedule information is subject to change and should always be verified with the theatre in advance of attendance.

Facilities

Seating capacities and types of stages are included only for those theatres that own, rent or regularly use a specific performing space or spaces. Theatre facility names and addresses are included when they differ from the institutional name and/or business mailing address. The information is current as of publication, and does not necessarily reflect the two seasons highlighted in the book.

For the sake of clarity, a common terminology for types of stages has been adopted, eliminating idiosyncratic nomenclature in favor of the following general designations:

PROSCENIUM

The traditional, picture-window stage, which the audience views from a single "fourth wall" perspective.

THRUST

All types of stage arrangements in which the audience sits on three sides of the playing area.

MODIFIED THRUST

Also called a "modified proscenium," it utilizes a jutting or fan-shaped apron on which action can take place. The audience still maintains a basic "fourth wall" relationship to the action.

ARENA

The audience completely surrounds the playing space.

FLEXIBLE

All types of stages and spaces which can be altered or converted from one category to another. Also included in this designation are "environmental" spaces or stages created to meet the demands of individual productions.

CABARET

A simple performance platform.

Finances

Financial figures reflect the fiscal year most recently completed when the information for *Theatre Profiles* was gathered. All figures (operating expenses, earned income and grants/contributions) have been rounded to the nearest thousand dollars. While most are based on precise, audited figures, their purpose in this book is to provide a general sense of the relationship between expenses and income, and the overall size of the theatre operation.

Audience

The estimated total annual attendance for the most recently completed season is provided, in addition to the number of subscribers for that season. The attendance figure includes all activities, including touring.

The Guthrie Theater. Caitlin Clarke and David Warrilow in *The Marriage of Figaro*. Photo: Joe Giannetti.

Touring contact

For the convenience of potential sponsoring organizations, specific names are listed for theatres offering major touring and residency programs.

Booked-in events

Many theatres regularly sponsor other arts events or rent their facilities to other performing groups and individual artists. Interests in specific types of events are indicated to assist other companies and performers seeking performance spaces or bookings.

Equity contracts

Information on Actors' Equity Association contracts is included for each theatre employing actors under union jurisdiction. Please note that the League of Resident Theatres (LORT) contract has four categories (A, B, C and D), based on the number of seats in the theatre. For more specific information on these and other contracts listed, contact Actors' Equity Assoc., 165 West 46th St., New York, NY 10036.

Artistic statement

All theatres were invited to submit an artistic statement of any length up to 250 words, reflecting their current philosophy and goals, performance activities and community relationship. While most have been edited for style and clarity, every attempt has been made by the editor to retain the individuality and unique flavor of these diverse statements.

Programs and services

Because of the increasing importance of theatres not only as producing units but also as local cultural resources, descriptions of programs and services outside of regular theatrical production are listed.

Production lists

Productions from the 1981-82 and 1982-83 seasons (1982 and 1983, for theatres with summer operations) are listed with authors, translators, adaptors, composers and lyricists, along with the source of literary adaptations, as provided by the theatres. In the case of revivals, only the title of the production is repeated in the second listing. For the first time in this edition, directors' names are also listed along with each production.

Designers

Scenic, costume and lighting designers are listed alphabetically under each theatre, for both seasons combined.

Photographs

Photographs were selected to convey the range and diversity of production activity, and to best represent the nature of each company's work. Individual performers are identified when appearing in groups of five or less, and special prominence is given to photographs of high visual quality.

Regional Index

To readily identify theatres located in individual states, a geographical listing is included.

Theatre Chronology

The "time line" history of the nonprofit professional theatres included in this volume is intended to demonstrate the amazing growth and decentralization of the American theatre over the past 75 years.

Index of Names

All playwrights, composers, artistic and administrative directors, stage directors, designers and theatre founders appearing in this edition are listed in the name index.

Index of Titles

For the reader's convenience, all titles of dramatic works are listed in this separate index.

Theatres

Academy Theatre
A Contemporary Theatre
The Acting Company
Actors Theatre of Louisville
Actors Theatre of St. Paul
Alabama Shakespeare Festival
Alaska Repertory Theatre
Alley Theatre
Alliance Theatre Company/
    Atlanta Children's Theatre
AMAS Repertory Theatre
American Conservatory Theatre
The American Jewish Theatre of
    the 92nd St. Y
The American Place Theatre
American Repertory Theatre
The American Stage Company
American Stage Festival
American Theatre Arts
American Theatre Company
The American Theater Company in
    Aspen
Arena Stage
Arizona Theatre Company
Arkansas Repertory Theatre
Asolo State Theater
The Attic Theatre
Barter Theatre
Berkeley Repertory Theatre
Berkeley Shakespeare Festival
Berkeley Stage Company
Berkshire Theatre Festival
BoarsHead: Michigan Public Theater
The Body Politic Theatre

Boston Shakespeare Company
Caldwell Playhouse
Capital Repertory Company
Center Stage
The Changing Scene
The Children's Theatre Company
    and School
Cincinnati Playhouse in the Park
Circle in the Square
Circle Repertory Company
The Clarence Brown Company
The Cleveland Play House
Coconut Grove Playhouse
Cocteau Repertory
The Cricket Theatre
Crossroads Theatre Company
CSC Repertory
Cumberland County Playhouse
Dallas Theater Center
Delaware Theatre Company
Dell'Arte Players Company
Denver Center Theatre Company
Detroit Repertory Theatre
Dorset Theatre Festival
East West Players
El Teatro Campesino
Empire State Institute for the
    Performing Arts
The Empty Space
Ensemble Studio Theatre
Eureka Theatre Company
Fairmount Theatre of the Deaf
The First All Children's Theatre
Florida Studio Theatre

Folger Theatre
George Street Playhouse
Germinal Stage Denver
GeVa Theatre
Goodman Theatre
The Great-American Children's
    Theatre Company
The Great Lakes Shakespeare Festival
The Guthrie Theater
Hartford Stage Company
The Hartman Theatre
Hippodrome State Theatre
Honolulu Theatre for Youth
Horse Cave Theatre
Hudson Guild Theatre
Huntington Theatre Company
Illusion Theater
The Independent Eye
Indiana Repertory Theatre
INTAR
Interart Theatre
Intiman Theatre Company
Jewish Repertory Theatre
The Julian Theatre
L.A. Public Theatre
L.A. Stage Co.
L.A. Theatre Works
Living Stage Theatre Company
Long Wharf Theatre
Looking Glass Theatre
Los Angeles Actors' Theatre
Mabou Mines
Magic Theatre
Manhattan Punch Line

Asolo State Theater. Karl Redcoff and Viveca Parker in *A Midsummer Night's Dream*.
Photo: Gary W. Sweetman.

Manhattan Theatre Club
Mark Taper Forum
McCarter Theatre Company
Medicine Show Theatre Ensemble
Merrimack Regional Theatre
Milwaukee Repertory Theater
Missouri Repertory Theatre
Music-Theatre Group/
    Lenox Arts Center
Nassau Repertory Theatre
National Black Theatre
Nebraska Theatre Caravan
New American Theater
New Dramatists
New Federal Theatre
New Jersey Shakespeare Festival
New Playwrights' Theatre
New York Shakespeare Festival
North Carolina Shakespeare Festival
North Light Repertory
Odyssey Theatre Ensemble
The Old Creamery Theatre Company
Old Globe Theatre
Omaha Magic Theatre
One Act Theatre Company of
    San Francisco
O'Neill Theater Center
Ontological-Hysteric Theatre

Oregon Shakespearean Festival
Organic Theater Company
Paper Mill Playhouse
Pennsylvania Stage Company
The People's Light and Theatre
    Company
Periwinkle Productions
Philadelphia Drama Guild
Pittsburgh Public Theater
Playhouse on the Square
PlayMakers Repertory Company
The Playwrights' Center
Playwrights Horizons
Portland Stage Company
Puerto Rican Traveling Theatre
    Company
Repertorio Español
The Repertory Theatre of St. Louis
The Road Company
Roadside Theater
Roundabout Theatre Company
Round House Theatre
San Diego Repertory Theatre
San Jose Repertory Company
Seattle Repertory Theatre
The Second Stage
Soho Repertory Theatre
South Coast Repertory

Stage One: The Louisville Children's
    Theatre
StageWest
Steppenwolf Theatre Company
The Street Theater
Studio Arena Theatre
Syracuse Stage
Tacoma Actors Guild
Theatre by the Sea
Theater for the New City
Theater of the Open Eye
Theatre Project Company
Theatre Three
Theatre West Virginia
Theatre X
Trinity Square Repertory Company
Victory Gardens Theater
Virginia Museum Theatre
Virginia Stage Company
Westport Country Playhouse
The Whole Theatre Company
Williamstown Theatre Festival
Wisdom Bridge Theatre
The Wooster Group
Worcester Foothills Theatre Company
WPA Theatre
Yale Repertory Theatre

Theatre Profiles 6

Arena Stage. *Buried Child*. Photo: Joan Marcus.

Academy Theatre

FRANK WITTOW
Producing Director

JOHN E. BLIZZARD
Managing Director

LAWRENCE L. GELLERSTEDT, III
Board President

Box 77070
Atlanta, GA 30357
(404) 873-2518 (business)
(404) 892-0880 (box office)

FOUNDED 1956
Frank Wittow

SEASON
September-May

SCHEDULE

Evenings
Wednesday-Saturday

Matinees
Theatre for Youth
Monday-Saturday
Mainstage
Sunday

FACILITIES
1137 Peachtree St., NE

Mainstage
Seating capacity: 420
Stage: thrust

First Stage
Seating capacity: 90
Stage: arena

FINANCES
August 1, 1982-July 31, 1983
$498,000 operating expenses
$258,000 earned income
$234,000 grants/contributions

AUDIENCE
Annual attendance: 150,000
Subscribers: 2,200

TOURING CONTACT
John E. Blizzard

BOOKED-IN EVENTS
Theatre, music, dance

Academy Theatre. Fiddler's Rock. Photo: Charles M. Rafshoon.

Founded by current producing director Frank Wittow, the Academy Theatre is built around a resident company whose annual performing season is concurrent with, and inseparable from, a continuing program of theatre training for professional actors and students.

The concept of regional theatre as a playwrights' theatre provides the Academy's artistic thrust. The ensemble approach to creative dramatic expression is key: a laboratory environment is created in which actors teach, teachers act, directors act and actors direct. Consequently, the Academy has, during its first quarter-of-a-century, produced more than 100 original or company-developed works in addition to an equal number of classics and contemporary plays.

Annually, approximately 15 actors are selected for the resident Mainstage company, and 15 each fill the First Stage company and Apprentice Program rosters. For some 45 actors, the Academy provides a versatile training atmosphere with the opportunity to build careers in Atlanta and the Southeast.

For its primarily rural region, the Academy provides a showcase for new works and new talent, plus a full complement of thought-provoking dramatic work. The Mainstage season includes a four-play subscription series, plus the Academy's own version of the holiday classic *A Christmas Carol*. These plays also provide a repertoire for touring and other nonsubscription performances. The First Stage season includes production of three new works and one company-developed play under the direction of Wittow. Plays-in-progress by southeastern playwrights, or those addressing regional themes are solicited for inclusion in this series.

The Academy Theatre for Youth produces three original children's plays plus a regional artists-in-schools residency program. Each season a new play on a current theme for teenagers is created from subject contributions by high school students across the state. The Academy School of Performing Arts offers professional training for the First Stage and Apprentice Companies, as well as producing a Laboratory Theatre series of four productions per season.

Now that the Academy has settled in its permanent home in the heart of Atlanta's theatre district, the company will enhance its emphasis on the development of new regional work for the stage.

Programs and services

Children's theatre; artists-in-schools program; School of Performing Arts; touring; internships; apprenticeships.

PRODUCTIONS 1981-82

A Lesson from Aloes, Athol Fugard; dir: Frank Wittow

A Christmas Carol, adapt: Adrian Hall and Richard Cumming, from Charles Dickens; dir: Margaret Ferguson

A Contemporary Theatre

The Effect of Gamma Rays on Man-in-the-Moon-Marigolds, Paul Zindel; dir: Frank Wittow
Candida, George Bernard Shaw; dir: Margaret Ferguson
Fiddler's Rock, Frank Wittow; dir: Frank Wittow
A Moon for the Misbegotten, Eugene O'Neill; dir: Frank Wittow
Beauty and the Beast, adapt: Jill Clements; dir: Jill Clements
Canterbury Tales!, Arnold Wengrow; dir: Frank Wittow
Dear Dragon, John Stephens; dir: John Stephens
International Folk Tales, Judith Ahrens; dir: Rosemary Newcott
Starting Tomorrow, company-developed; dir: Frank Wittow

PRODUCTIONS 1982-83

The Miss Firecracker Contest, Beth Henley; dir: Frank Wittow
A Christmas Carol, adapt: John Stephens, from Charles Dickens; dir: John Stephens
The Rope Dancers, Morton Wishengrad; dir: Frank Wittow
The Flowering Peach, Clifford Odets; dir: Margaret Ferguson
The Glass Menagerie, Tennessee Williams; dir: Margaret Ferguson
Witches, John Stephens; dir: John Stephens
Tales of Scheherazade, Jill Clements; dir: Rosemary Newcott
Companions of the Crossed Swords, Judith Ahrens; dir: Judith Ahrens
High & Dry, company-developed; dir: Frank Wittow
The Last Vision of Paddy O'Sheen, John Stephens; dir: John Stephens

DESIGNERS

Sets: Judith Ahrens, Randall J. Bailey, Jill Clements, Fred Fonner, Steven Fryar, Michael Halpern, Anthony Loadholt, John Stephens, James Wasson, Robert West.
Costumes: Ann Boylan, Madeline Keeling, Jo Weinstein, Judy Winograd, Pam Wofford.
Lights: Cullen Clark, Keith Crofford, Paul Lasakow, Brian Rehlkopf, Charles Rickett, James Wasson.

GREGORY A. FALLS
Producing Director

SUSAN TRAPNELL MORITZ
Administrative Manager

AUBREY DAVIS
Board President

100 West Roy St.
Seattle, WA 98119
(206) 285-3220 (business)
(206) 285-5110 (box office)

FOUNDED 1965
Gregory A. Falls

SEASON

Mainstage
May-October

Young ACT Company
January-April

SCHEDULE

Evenings
Tuesday-Sunday

Matinees
Saturday, Sunday, first Wednesday

FACILITIES

Mainstage
Seating capacity: 454
Stage: thrust

Backstage
Seating capacity: 100
Stage: flexible

FINANCES
January 1, 1982 - December 31, 1982
$1,115,000 operating expenses
$ 890,000 earned income
$ 290,000 grants/contributions

AUDIENCE
Annual attendance: 114,391
Subscribers: 7,390

TOURING CONTACT
Anne-Denise Ford

BOOKED-IN EVENTS
Theatre

AEA LORT (C) contract

A Contemporary Theatre. J. Kenneth Campbell, Jerry Harper and Maureen Kilmurry in Whose Life Is It Anyway? *Photo: Chris Bennion.*

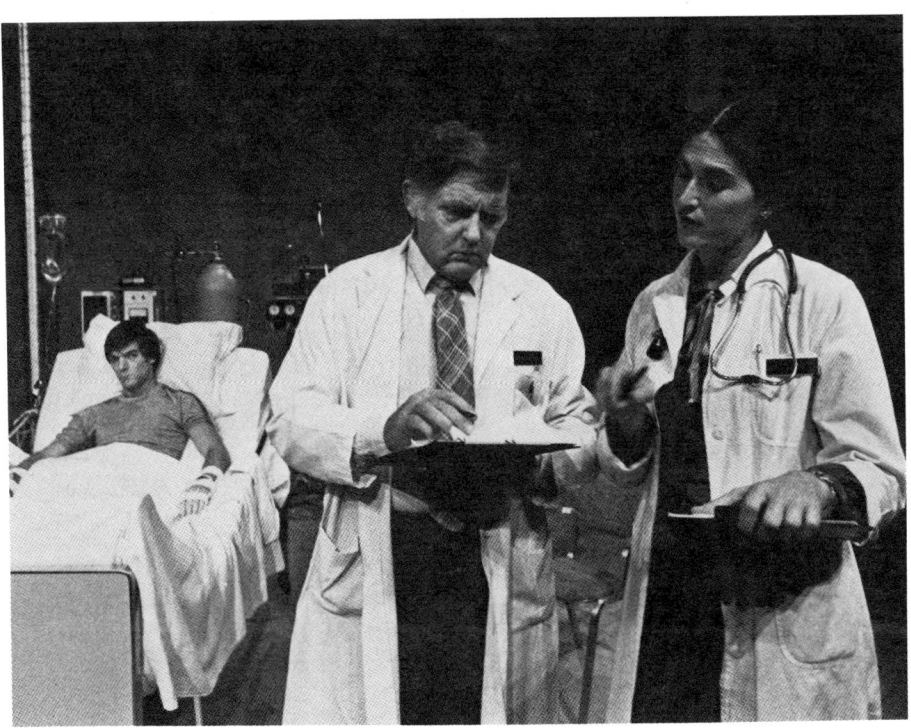

A Contemporary Theatre opened nearly two decades ago as Seattle's second resident professional theatre, dedicated to presenting "the important plays of our time." Since then, ACT has become one of the state's six major cultural institutions and the place where Northwest audiences numbering more than one million have seen their first professional productions of works by Albee, Ayckbourn, Brecht, Fugard, Kopit, Ionesco, Stoppard, Weller and many others.

ACT has also presented several notable American and world premieres, including Brian Moore's *Catholics*, N. Richard Nash's *Echos*, Michael Neville's *Ballymurphy*, Barry Dinerman's *Quiet Caravans* and Alexander Buzo's *Makassar Reef*. In all, ACT has produced an average of one new script each year.

ACT's commitment to high-quality, professional theatre also extends to young people, through its Young ACT Company, the oldest Equity company of its kind on the West Coast. For 18 years, its original productions—performed by adult actors—have toured the western United States and Alaska, and have been seen at international festivals and the Kennedy Center. In 1980, the company received the Jennie Heiden Award, and is on the brink of expanding to a full series of family-oriented productions beginning in early 1984, in addition to its annual holiday productions.

ACT Backstage programming helps fulfill the theatre's commitment to expanding the opportunities and resources of American theatre with the talent and skill available in the Northwest. A unique Backstage project called "Songworks" brings together composers, lyricists and librettists in a professional environment to actively encourage the development of new music for the theatre.

ACT aims for stimulating, sometimes controversial, always challenging theatre in its year-round programming. In addition to new plays, its six-play mainstage season is often highlighted by an international exchange of actors, or by guest directors and designers.

Programs and services

Post-play discussions; creative dramatics for children; discount performances; newsletters and annual reports; administrative and technical assistantships/internships; school tours; lecture/dialogue series; Songworks new music workshops.

PRODUCTIONS 1982

Da, Hugh Leonard; dir: Richard Edwards
Fridays, Andrew Johns; dir: Clayton Corzatte
Waiting for the Parade, John Murrell; dir: Richard Edwards
The Gin Game, D.L. Coburn; dir: Joy Carlin
The Greeks, adapt: John Barton and Kenneth Cavander, from Euripides, Sophocles, Aeschylus and Homer; dir: Gregory A. Falls
A Christmas Carol, adapt: Gregory A. Falls, from Charles Dickens; dir: Eileen MacRae Murphy
Aladdin and the Magic Lamp, adapt: Gregory A. Falls; dir: Anne-Denise Ford

PRODUCTIONS 1983

The Dresser, Ronald Harwood; dir: Jay Broad
The Dining Room, A.R. Gurney, Jr.; dir: Lou Salerni
Crimes of the Heart, Beth Henley; dir: M. Burke Walker
Educating Rita, Willy Russell; dir: Sharon Ott
A Soldier's Play, Charles Fuller; dir: Douglas Turner Ward (Negro Ensemble Company production)
Cloud 9, Caryl Churchill; dir: Jeff Steitzer

DESIGNERS

Sets: Robert Dahlstrom, Thomas M. Fichter, Alison Ford, William Forrester, Karen Gjelsteen, Bill Raoul, Shelley Henze Schermer, Scott Weldin.
Costumes: Nanrose Buchman, Marian Cottrell, Shay Cunliffe, Alison Ford, Julie James, Susan Min, Sally Richardson, Shelley Henze Schermer.
Lights: Randall G. Chiarelli, Christopher Beardslee, Jody Briggs, Donna Grout, Phil Schermer.

The Acting Company

JOHN HOUSEMAN
Producing Artistic Director

MICHAEL KAHN
ALAN SCHNEIDER
Artistic Directors

MARGOT HARLEY
Executive Producer

MARY BETH CARROLL
General Manager

EDGAR LANSBURY
Board President

Box 898, Times Square Station
New York, NY 10108
(212) 564-3510

FOUNDED 1972
John Houseman, Margot Harley

SEASON
August–July

FINANCES
July 1, 1982–June 3, 1983
$1,970,000 operating expenses
$1,227,000 earned income
$ 743,000 grants/contributions

AUDIENCE
Annual attendance: 150,000

TOURING CONTACT
Rob Hill

AEA LORT (B) and (C) contracts

Now functioning as the touring arm of the Kennedy Center for the Performing Arts, The Acting Company was founded for and is dedicated to the development of American actors.

In 1972, John Houseman, then head of the Drama Division of the Juillard School in New York, saw in his first graduating class a group of actors so talented that he felt they should not disband. Together with Margot Harley, now the company's executive producer, he organized the graduates into a professional company which made its debut as the dramatic wing of the Saratoga Performing Arts Festival in New York State.

The company now consists of 15 inten-

The Acting Company. Richard S. Iglewski and Megan Gallagher in Tartuffe. *Photo: Diane Gorodnitzki.*

sively trained actors selected from America's finest professional schools, conservatories and resident theatres. Once chosen, they rehearse in the ensemble tradition of the company, taking on a variety of roles which they perform in repertory on tour throughout the United States. The performers sustain a rigorous schedule over an extended period, playing in vastly differing theatres week after week. This experience allows them further to test and develop themselves into the outstanding professionals for which The Acting Company has become known.

The second and equally important commitment of the company is to tour professional productions of both classical and contemporary plays to theatres across America. To date, The Acting Company has performed a repertoire of 49 plays in 235 cities, in 44 states, before more than one million people, and has traveled more than 250,000 miles.

A number of the company's productions have received prestigious awards and nominations, including two Antoinette Perry ("Tony") awards and an Obie Special Citation for Outstanding Achievement. Numerous company members have gone on to successful careers in theatre, films and television.

With the presentation of its first Alumni production, Marc Blitzstein's *The Cradle Will Rock* in May 1983, The Acting Company took its first step toward the development of a permanent, organic repertory company. Under the direction of John Houseman, the production was cast entirely from former members of The Acting Company — but it did more than simply draw together old friends and associates for a show. It launched a new era for the company and, it is hoped, the American theatre as well.

Programs and services

Workshops in voice, theatre games, mask demonstration, stage fighting, stage management, text to performance, movement, auditioning, improvisation, costuming and makeup; summer theatre school in Chautauqua, N.Y.

PRODUCTIONS 1981-82

Il Campiello—a Venetian Comedy, Carlo Goldoni; adapt: Richard Nelson; dir: Liviu Ciulei
Waiting for Godot, Samuel Beckett; dir: Alan Schneider
A Midsummer Night's Dream, William Shakespeare; dir: David Chambers and Christopher J. Markle
The Country Wife, William Wycherley; dir: Garland Wright
Twelfth Night, William Shakespeare; dir: Michael Langham

PRODUCTIONS 1982-83

The Country Wife
Twelfth Night
Tartuffe, Molière; trans: Richard Wilbur; dir: Brian Murray
Pericles, William Shakespeare; dir: Toby Robertson
Play and Other Plays, Samuel Beckett; dir: Alan Schneider

DESIGNERS

Sets: Jack Barkla, Radu Boruzescu, Franco Colavecchia, Mark Fitzgibbons, Desmond Heeley, Heidi Landesman, Michael Yeargan.
Costumes: Miruna Boruzescu, Judith Dolan, Jane Greenwood, Desmond Heeley, Carol Oditz, John David Ridge.
Lights: John Michael Deegan, Greg MacPherson, Dennis Parichy.

Actors Theatre of Louisville

JON JORY
Producing Director

ALEXANDER SPEER
Administrative Director

MARILEE HEBERT-SLATER
Associate Director

WILLIAM C. BALLARD, JR.
Board President

316-320 West Main St.
Louisville, KY 40202
(502) 584-1265 (business)
(502) 584-1205 (box office)

FOUNDED 1964
Richard Block, Ewel Cornett

SEASON
September-June

SCHEDULE
Evenings
Tuesday-Sunday

Matinees
Wednesday, Saturday, Sunday

FACILITIES
Pamela Brown Auditorium
Seating capacity: 637
Stage: thrust

Victor Jory Theatre
Seating capacity: 179
Stage: thrust

Starving Artist Cabaret
Seating capacity: 100
Stage: cabaret

FINANCES
June 1, 1982-May 31, 1983
$3,236,000 operating expenses
$1,864,000 earned income
$1,379,000 grants/contributions

AUDIENCE
Annual attendance: 246,432
Subscribers: 17,000

TOURING CONTACT
Marilee Hebert-Slater

AEA LORT (B) contract

Actors Theatre of Louisville is a frontrunner in the development and production of new plays by emerging American writers. In addition to presenting a general repertoire, over the course of its nine-month season ATL produces new work by dozens of playwrights, many in its two major festivals.

The Humana Festival of New American Plays — almost a season in itself — has become a significant, much awaited event on the American theatre scene, and plays premiering there have moved quickly into the national and international repertoire. ATL's Shorts Festival is devoted entirely to new one-act works.

Actors Theatre has also toured nationally and internationally, appearing in Israel, Belgrade, Dublin, Toronto, Baltimore and Sydney, Australia.

Programs and services

Acting apprenticeships; management and technical internships; regional and international touring.

PRODUCTIONS 1981-82

Lone Star, James McLure; dir: L. Susan Rowland
Chug, Ken Jenkins; dir: Jon Jory and Ken Jenkins
The Three Musketeers, adapt: Peter Raby, from Alexandre Dumas; dir: Jon Jory
Shorts Festival:
 Clara's Play, John Olive; dir: Patrick Tovatt
 A Pale Lion, Michael Neville; dir: Ray Fry
 The Boy Who Ate the Moon, Jane Martin; dir: Jon Jory
 Damn Everything But the Circus, Terri Wagener; dir: Jon Jory
 The New Girl, Vaughn McBride; dir: Jon Jory
 The Eye of the Beholder, Kent Broadhurst; dir: Larry Deckel
 The Groves of Academe, Mark Stein; dir: Steven D. Albrezzi
 Singles: Clear Glass Marbles, 15 Minutes, Handler, Marks, Rodeo, Scraps and *Twirler*, Jane Martin; dir: Jon Jory; *Cemetery Man* and *Rupert's Birthday*, Ken Jenkins; dir: Jon Jory

 Gun for the Roses, Patrick Tovatt and Jim Wann; dir: Ken Jenkins
 In Between Time, Ara Watson; dir: Adale O'Brien
 Intermission, Robert Schenkkan; dir: Frazier W. Marsh
 Lunch Break, Robert Schenkkan; dir: Steven D. Albrezzi
 Merry-Go-Round, Wendy Kesselman; dir: Adale O'Brien
 Private Showing, Jeffrey Sweet; dir: Bekki Jo Schneider
 The Saint of the Day, Judy Romberger; dir: Jon Jory
 Wash, Rinse, Spin, Dry, Richard Whelan; dir: Larry Deckel
Humana Festival:
 The Informer, adapt: Thomas Murphy, from Liam O'Flaherty; dir: Jon Jory
 Clara's Play, John Olive; dir: Patrick Tovatt
 The Grapes of Wrath, adapt: Terrence Shank, from John Steinbeck; dir: Terrence Shank
 Oldtimer's Game, Lee Blessing; dir: Patrick Tovatt
 Full Hookup, Conrad Bishop and Elizabeth Fuller; dir: Jon Jory
 Cemetery Man and *Rupert's Birthday*
 The New Girl
 The Eye of the Beholder
 The Groves of Academe
 Solo: The Subject Animal, Larry Atlas; *Sidekick*, Jim Beaver; *Butterfly, Marguerite, Norma . . . And Irma Jean*, Trish Johnson; *The Survivalist*, Robert Schenkkan; dir: Michael Hankins; *Slow Drag, Mama*, Dare Clubb and Isabell Monk; dir: Steven D. Albrezzi; *Rubert's Birthday*
 Talking With: Clear Glass Marbles, 15 Minutes, Handler, Marks, Rodeo, Scraps, Twirler, Maps, Cul de Sac, Dragons and *Audition*, Jane Martin; dir: Jon Jory
 A Different Moon, Ara Watson; dir: Sam Blackwell
The Gift of the Magi, adapt: Peter Ekstrom, from O. Henry; dir: Larry Deckel
The Spider's Web, Agatha Christie; dir: Adale O'Brien
The Arabian Nights, Richard Burton and company; dir: Jon Jory
Tintypes, music and lyrics: various; adapt: Mary Kyte, Mel Marvin and Gary Pearle; dir: Larry Deckel

Actors Theatre of Louisville. Mary McDonnell, Randle Mell and William Mesnick in A Weekend Near Madison. *Photo: David S. Talbott.*

Billy Bishop Goes to War, John Gray and Eric Peterson; dir: Amy Saltz

The Oldest Living Graduate, Preston Jones; dir: Ken Jenkins

PRODUCTIONS 1982-83

Julius Caesar, William Shakespeare; dir: Norris Houghton

Shorts Festival:
 I Love You, I Love You Not, Wendy Kesselman; dir: Frazier W. Marsh
 The Cameo, Ray Fry; dir: Frazier W. Marsh
 In the Bag, Lezley Havard; dir: Frazier W. Marsh
 Bartok as Dog, Patrick Tovatt; dir: Frazier W. Marsh
 The Happy Worker, Stephen Feinberg; dir: Dierk Torsek
 Partners, Dave Higgins; dir: Robert Spera
 Good Old Boy, Vaughn McBride; dir: Vaughn McBride
 A Tantalizing, William Mastrosimone; dir: Emily Mann
 The Value of Names, Jeffrey Sweet; dir: Emily Mann
 The Habitual Acceptance of the Near Enough, Kent Broadhurst; dir: Adale O'Brien
 Flight Lines, Barbara Schneider; dir: Vaughn McBride
 I Want to Be an Indian, William Borden; dir: Adale O'Brien
 Coup, Jane Martin; dir: Jon Jory
 Clucks, Jane Martin; dir: Jon Jory
 Mine, David Epstein; dir: Frazier W. Marsh
 The Art of Self Defense, Trish Johnson; dir: Larry Deckel
 Nice People Dancing to Good Country Music, Lee Blessing; dir: Larry Deckel

A Christmas Carol, adapt; Barbara Field, from Charles Dickens; dir: Ray Fry

The Gift of the Magi

Murder at the Vicarage, Agatha Christie; dir: Larry Deckel

Misalliance, George Bernard Shaw; dir: Thomas Bullard

Mass Appeal, Bill C. Davis; dir: Russell Treyz

Humana Festival:
 Eden Court, Murphy Guyer; dir: Ken Jenkins
 A Weekend Near Madison, Kathleen Tolan; dir: Kathleen Tolan
 Neutral Countries, Barbara Field; dir: Robert Falls
 Courage, John Pielmeier; dir: Susan Gregg
 Food from Trash, Gary Leon Hill; dir: Jon Jory
 In a Northern Landscape, Timothy Mason; dir: Frazier W. Marsh
 Sand Castles, Adele Edling Shank; dir: Theodore Shank
 Thanksgiving, James McLure; dir: Jon Jory
 Fathers and Daughters: A Tantalizing, William Mastrosimone; and *The Value of Names,* Jeffrey Sweet; dir: Emily Mann

The Hasty Heart, John Patrick; dir: Adale O'Brien

Key Exchange, Kevin Wade; dir: Larry Deckel

Wuthering Heights, adapt: Randolph Carter, from Emily Bronte; dir: Jon Jory

DESIGNERS

Sets: Karen Gerson, Grady Larkins, Paul Owen, Richard Wilcox.
Costumes: Karen Gerson, Jess Goldstein, Paul Owen, Kurt Wilhelm.
Lights: Karl Haas, Jeff Hill, Paul Owen.

Actors Theatre of St. Paul

MICHAEL ANDREW MINER
Artistic Director

JAN MINER
Managing Director

GEORGE S. HAGE
Board President

2115 Summit Ave.
St. Paul, MN 55105
(612) 227-0040 (business)
(612) 227-0050 (box office)

FOUNDED 1977
Michael Andrew Miner

SEASON
October-May

SCHEDULE

Evenings
Wednesday-Sunday

Matinees
Saturday, selected Thursdays

FACILITIES
Foley Theatre
Seating capacity: 260
Stage: proscenium

FINANCES
July 1, 1982-June 30, 1983
$426,000 operating expenses
$174,000 earned income
$254,000 grants/contributions

AUDIENCE
Annual attendance: 38,000
Subscribers: 1,850

BOOKED-IN EVENTS
Theatre

AEA LORT (D) contract

Actors Theatre of St. Paul is committed to developing a cohesive ensemble approach to a stylistically varied repertoire of contemporary and classical plays. At the heart of its aesthetic is a resident professional acting company responsive to the unique demands of ensemble acting. Every aspect of the theatre's program is formulated, organized, measured and modified in light of that goal.

Although the theatre is not organized as a collective, the company participates extensively in script selection, working with the artistic director to identify plays offering growth opportunities for individual artists and stylistic challenges to the company as a whole. From its inception, ATSP has eagerly embraced the responsibility of developing new writers and new works for the stage. The theatre has consistently assisted writers through both seasonal and production-length residencies, readings, productions, and representation at national playwriting conferences and festivals.

In recent seasons, ATSP produced new works commissioned by the theatre for its resident company including *Outlanders* by Amlin Gray, *Gift of the Magi* by John Olive and Libby Larson, and *Old Explorers* by James Cada and Mark Keller.

ATSP's three-year liason with the Caribbean/U.S. Theatre Exchange (CARIBUSTE) has included exchanges of technical production personnel as well as the engagement of Trinidadian actor Wilbert Holder to appear in *Pantomime* by Derek Walcott.

Plans for the 1983-84 season include continued emphasis on company development, work on a new collaborative theatre piece, improvements of a variety of production resources available to designers, and production of a new script by local playwright Lee Blessing.

Actors Theatre has begun work on its first long-term collaborative developmental piece involving the acting company and distinguished artists crossing multiple disciplines. In this way, the theatre hopes to become a "context for collaboration," seeking to be more in the business of creating theatre than recreating it. It is hoped that this context will provide increased dimensionality for the growth and expansion of its artists while providing substance and depth for the audiences they serve.

Programs and services

Technical, artistic and administrative internships; humanities discussion series; apprenticeships; touring.

Actors Theatre of St. Paul. Vada Russell, Louise Goetz, Paul Eiding, Sally Wingert and Barbara Kingsley in The Increased Difficulty of Concentration. *Photo: Connie Britzius Jerome.*

PRODUCTIONS 1981-82

Old Explorers, James Cada and Mark Keller; dir: Michael Andrew Miner
Hedda Gabler, Henrik Ibsen; dir: Michael Andrew Miner
Absurd Person Singular, Alan Ayckbourn; dir: Robert Mailand
How I Got That Story, Amlin Gray; dir: Jon Cranney
Waiting for the Parade, John Murrell; dir: Michael Andrew Miner
The Subject Was Roses, Frank D. Gilroy; dir: Jeff Steitzer
The Increased Difficulty of Concentration, Vaclav Havel; trans: Vera Blackwell; dir: James Cada
Tartuffe, Molière; dir: Jeff Steitzer

Alabama Shakespeare Festival

PRODUCTIONS 1982-82

The Seagull, Anton Chekhov; dir: Michael Andrew Miner
Fallen Angels, Noel Coward; dir: David Parrish
Sea Marks, Gardner McKay; dir: Michael Andrew Miner
Disability: a Comedy, Ron Whyte; dir: David Ira Goldstein
Angel Stret, Patrick Hamilton; dir: James Cada
Pantomime, Derek Wolcott; dir: Michael Andrew Miner
Have You Anything to Declare?, Maurice Hennequin and Pierre Veber; dir: Sharon Ott

DESIGNERS

Sets: James Guenther, Chris Johnson, Larry Kaushansky, Dick Leerhoff, Arthur Ridley, Don Yunker.
Costumes: Jill Hamilton, Michael L. Hansen, Chris Johnson, Nayna Ramey, Arthur Ridley, Don Yunker.
Lights: Chris Johnson, Paul Scharfenberger, Michael Vennerstrom, Don Yunker.

Alabama Shakespeare Festival. Michele Farr, Charles Antalosky and Kermit Brown in Twelfth Night. *Photo: Michael Doege.*

MARTIN L. PLATT
Artistic Director

JIM VOLZ
Managing Director

Box 141
Anniston, AL 36202
(205) 236-7503 (business)
(205) 237-2332 (box office)

FOUNDED 1972
Martin L. Platt

SEASON
Mainstage
July - August

Touring
September - November

SCHEDULE
Evenings
Tuesday - Sunday

Matinees
Thursday - Sunday

FACILITIES
Festival Theatre
12th and Woodstock Sts.
Seating capacity: 950
Stage: thrust

ACT Playhouse
1020 Noble St.
Seating capacity: 100
Stage: modified thrust

St. Michael and All Angels
18th and Cobb Sts.
Seating capacity: 450
Stage: modified thrust

FINANCES
January 1, 1982 - December 31, 1982
$695,000 operating expenses
$432,000 earned income
$245,000 grants/contributions

AUDIENCES
Annual attendance: 80,000
Subscribers: 2,100

TOURING CONTACT
Carol Ogus

BOOKED-IN EVENTS
Theatre, chamber music, musical artists

AEA LORT (B) contract

The Alabama Shakespeare Festival is a classical repertory company dedicated to serving the people of Alabama and the region. The concept of a resident, professional acting company and staff, producing in rotating repertory, is central to the theatre's purpose. By performing in this manner, actors and audience alike are challenged to take part in a variety of theatrical styles, constantly alert to the shifting values and demands of disparate works.

At the very core of the work that ASF does, of course, is Shakespeare: the richness of his language, world and characters are constant food for the Festival's growth, and ASF is dedicated to a continual re-examination of his works. Shakespeare demands much from an audience: that it imagine, that it enter into his world, and above all that it listen. By remaining true to the text rather than imposing concepts from without — by challenging audiences to enter into another world where they must listen to learn—ASF can expand their experience and their lives, as well as the lives of the artists.

To complement the works of Shakespeare, ASF's repertoire includes classics of Western theatre, those works which withstand the test of time. Wycherley, Wilde, Stoppard, Coward, Ibsen, Chekhov, Shaw, Goldoni and Moliere, among others, have

Alaska Repertory Theatre

graced the Festival's stages in past seasons. These classics find parallels in our time, striking responsive chords in the conscious and subconscious minds of the audience and actors, forcing them to better understand their lives in relation to those who have lived in other times.

The full purpose of ASF—which includes actor training, extensive regional touring and music programs — leads back to the principal artistic goal of the theatre: to interpret and present a playwright's ideas, characters and philosophy to the audience through his text, making it truly a playwright's theatre.

Programs and services

Conservatory; chamber music series; fall tour; technical and management internships; lecture series; after-theatre discussions; artists-in-education program.

PRODUCTIONS 1982

Uncle Vanya, Anton Chekhov; adapt: Martin L. Platt; dir: Martin L. Platt
Twelfth Night, William Shakespeare; dir: Sanford Robbins
Hamlet, William Shakespeare; dir: Martin L. Platt
Romeo and Juliet, William Shakespeare; dir: Martin L. Platt

PRODUCTIONS 1983

King Lear, William Shakespeare; dir: Martin L. Platt
All's Well That Ends Well, William Shakespeare; dir: Martin L. Platt
The Taming of the Shrew, William Shakespeare; dir: Allen R. Belknap
The Comedy of Errors, William Shakespeare; dir: John-Frederick Jones
Mass Appeal, Bill C. Davis; dir: Martin L. Platt
Arms and the Man, George Bernard Shaw; dir: Martin L. Platt

DESIGNERS

Sets: Charles Kilian, Michael Stauffer.
Costumes: Susan Cox, April Parke, Susan Rheaume, Michael Stauffer.
Lights: Lauren Miller, Paul Valoris.

ROBERT J. FARLEY
Artistic Director

PAUL BROWN
Producing Director

LOREN LOUNSBURY
Board President

705 West 6th Avenue, #201
Anchorage, AK 99501
(907) 276-2327 (business)
(907) 276-5500 (box office)

FOUNDED 1976
Alaska State Council on the Arts

SEASON
October–April

SCHEDULE
Evenings
Tuesday–Saturday

Matinee
Saturday, Sunday

FACILITIES

Sydney Laurence Auditorium
6th Ave. and F St.
Seating capacity: 626
Stage: proscenium

University of Alaska Fine Arts Theatre
University of Fairbanks
Seating capacity: 481
Stage: proscenium

Juneau Douglas Little Theatre
Seating capacity: 144
Stage: proscenium

FINANCES
July 1, 1982–June 30, 1983
$2,911,000 operating expenses
$ 697,000 earned income
$2,082,000 grants/contributions

Alaska Repertory Theatre. Elizabeth McGovern and Emery Battis in Major Barbara. Photo: Arend.

AUDIENCE
Annual attendance: 74,722
Subscribers: 10,661

TOURING CONTACT
Hugh F. Hall

AEA LORT (B) contract

Alaska Repertory Theatre strives to provide the highest quality professional theatre to Alaskans from the smallest villages to the largest population centers. Founded in 1976, Alaska Rep is the state's oldest and largest professional performing arts institution. The realization of the theatre's statewide mandate in the vast geography of Alaska continues to be a unique challenge.

Guided by the partnership of artistic director Robert J. Farley and producing director Paul Brown—and aided by the uncompromising support of the staff and statewide board of directors—Alaska Rep maintains its commitment to offer productions and services of the highest order. Whether Shakespeare or Lanford Wilson, Fats Waller or George Bernard Shaw, each of the theatre's productions has the spirit of a world premiere. This feeling arises from a special and highly charged relationship between artist and audience which extends not only to mainstage productions in Anchorage and Fairbanks but to statewide touring productions as well. Through its season of plays and other services, Alaska Rep serves the five varying cultures which comprise the state: the Aleuts, the Athabascan Indians, the Inuits, the Yupiks as well as the Western culture.

Through the revolutionary and nationally recognized cross-cultural Playmaking Program, Alaska Rep reaches rural communities. A creative collaboration between the traditional and the contemporary, Playmaking is now in its fourth season.

Despite its geographic isolation from other regional theatres, Alaska Rep strives to keep abreast of national theatre activity. Its most visible ongoing links to the national theatre community are associate artistic directors Walton Jones and John Going, both of whom are based in New York City. In the future, the theatre hopes to increase the quantity and scope of programs and services on a statewide level. Plans for fulfillment of this goal include a permanent touring company which would perform in rotating repertory.

Programs and services

Statewide touring; internships; Playmaking Program: residencies in rural Alaska; workshops and consultations; accessibility program for the handicapped and disadvantaged; pre-play discussions; equipment loans to other state arts organizations; creative dramatics; backstage tours; student matinees.

PRODUCTIONS 1981-82

The Man Who Came to Dinner, George S. Kaufman and Moss Hart; dir: John Going
A Christmas Carol, adapt. Martin L. Platt, from Charles Dickens; dir: Robert J. Farley and Dan Sedgwick
An Enemy of the People, Henrik Ibsen; adapt: Arthur Miller; dir: Irene Lewis
The Hot l Baltimore, Lanford Wilson; dir: Robert J. Farley
Fools, Neil Simon; dir: Walton Jones

PRODUCTIONS 1982-83

Nightingale, adapt: Charles Strouse, from Hans Christian Andersen; dir: Meridee Stein
Major Barbara, George Bernard Shaw; dir: John Going
Ain't Misbehavin', music and lyrics: Fats Waller, et al.; adapt: Richard Maltby, Jr.; dir: Murray Horwitz

DESIGNERS

Sets: Jamie Greenleaf, Hugh Landwehr, Ron Placzek, Kevin Rupnik, William Schroder.
Costumes: Randy Barcelo, Nanrose Buchman, Linda Fisher, James Berton Harris, Dunya Ramicova, Kurt Wilhelm.
Lights: Pat Collins, Lauren MacKenzie Miller, Spencer Mosse, Judy Rasmuson, James E. Sale, Victor En Yu Tan.

Alley Theatre

PAT BROWN
Artistic Director

TOM SPRAY
Managing Director

MRS. DUDLEY C. SHARP
Board President

615 Texas Ave.
Houston, TX 77002
(713) 228-9341 (business)
(713) 228-8421 (box office)

FOUNDED 1947
Nina Vance

SEASON
October – September

SCHEDULE
Evenings
Tuesday – Sunday

Matinees
Saturday, Sunday

FACILITIES
Large Stage
Seating capacity: 798
Stage: thrust

Arena Stage
Seating capacity: 296
Stage: arena

FINANCES
October 1, 1981 – September 30, 1982
$3,320,000 operating expenses
$2,025,000 earned income
$1,048,000 grants/contributions

AUDIENCE
Annual attendance: 306,000
Subscribers: 20,723

BOOKED-IN EVENTS
Theatre

AEA LORT (B) contract

Alley Theatre is one of the oldest resident professional theatres in the nation, founded to fulfill Nina Vance's artistic mission of innovation and excellence. Now, two years of growth under the dynamic leadership of

Pat Brown have tested and proven the theatre's constitutional strength, its vitality and vision, and have seen its production schedule grow. During 1982-83, the Alley produced a total of 21 events, the nucleus of which was a season of 11 plays on two stages. The programming addressed the need for an emphasis on strong and pertinent contemporary plays with a wide scope of themes and categories, and included two large-scale classics.

A permanent acting ensemble has long been a dream of resident theatres, one to which the Alley has given much time and careful attention. The result is a singularly talented company of 14 actors showing great range, dexterity in style and cohesiveness. Eighteen members of the Young Company, selected from the best professional training programs in the nation, guarantee the company's future.

Four Southwest premieres were included in the 1982-83 season, and Sheridan's *The Rivals* used the full resources of the Alley's revitalized technical departments, to present the work with style and elegance. Lunchtime Theatre developed the downtown corporate audience, and Monday Night Live readings — devoted to new playwrights' works — were offered four times during the season, free to subscribers. Year-round activity was completed with the production of a summer mystery, presented in rotation with the 15th season of film classics.

A substantial number of the Alley's large subscription audience are second-generation theatregoers who have been nurtured on 25 years of the theatre's unrivaled professional children's theatre. In the last season, an adaptation of Mark Twain's *The Prince and the Pauper* played to more than 20,000 youngsters, from toddlers through high schoolers.

In June 1983, the Alley completed its landmark exchange of resident professional companies from the United States and the United Kingdom when the company appeared at Alan Ayckbourn's Stephen Joseph Theatre in the Round, in Scarborough England, for a five-week run.

Programs and services

Merry-Go-Round children's school; Monday Night Live new play readings; children's theatre; summer classic film festival.

PRODUCTIONS 1981-82

Cyrano de Bergerac, Edmond Rostand; trans: Brian Hooker; dir: B.H. Barry and John Vreeke

you know Al he's a funny guy, Jerry Mayer; dir: John Pynchon Holms

Bedtime Story, Sean O'Casey; dir: John Vreeke

The Red Bluegrass Western Flyer Show, book and lyrics: Conn Fleming; music: Clint Ballard, Jr.; dir: Pat Brown

The House of Blue Leaves, John Guare; dir: Ivan Rider, Jr.

The Elephant Man, Bernard Pomerance; dir: Beth Sanford

"and if that Mockingbird don't sing . . .", William M. Whitehead; dir: Neil Havens

Paradise, Monty Philip Holamon; dir: Beth Sanford

Way Upstream, Alan Ayckbourn; dir: Alan Ayckbourn

Absent Friends, Alan Ayckbourn; dir: Alan Ayckbourn

Heidi, adapt: Donald Antrim, from Johanna Spyri; music: Stephen Houtz; dir: John Vreeke

Talley's Folly, Lanford Wilson; dir: Beth Sanford

Pinocchio: Evviva!, book: Vance G. Ormes; music and lyrics: Stephen Houtz; dir: Vance G. Ormes

The Unexpected Guest, Agatha Christie; dir: John Vreeke

The Wall, adapt: Millard Lampell, from John Hersey; dir: Pat Brown

Mother Figure and *Between Mouthfuls*, Alan Ayckbourn; dir: John Vreeke

PRODUCTIONS 1982-83

Scenes from American Life, A.R. Gurney, Jr.; dir: Beth Sanford

Pvt. Wars, James McLure; dir: Michael LaGue

Close Ties, Elizabeth Diggs; dir: Pat Brown

The Prince and the Pauper, adapt: John Vreeke, from Charlotte E. Chorpenning; dir: John Vreeke

The Rivals, Richard Brinsley Sheridan; dir: John Going

5th of July, Lanford Wilson; dir: Neil Havens

Nuts, Tom Topor; dir: Charles Abbott

Family Business, Dick Goldberg; dir: George Anderson

The Visit, Friedrich Duërrenmatt; adapt: Maurice Valency; dir: Beth Sanford and John Vreeke

The American Dream, Edward Albee; dir: John Vreeke

How I Got That Story, Amlin Gray; dir: Pat Brown

Alley Theatre. Robin Moseley and John Strano in Nuts. *Photo: Carl Davis.*

Alliance Theatre Company/ Atlanta Children's Theatre

The Dining Room, A.R. Gurney, Jr.; dir: Beth Sanford
Wait Until Dark, Frederick Knott; dir: John Vreeke
Taking Steps, Alan Ayckbourn; dir: Robert Graham
Holy Ghosts, Romulus Linney; dir: Romulus Linney

DESIGNERS

Sets: Keith Belli, Robert Blackman, William Bloodgood, John Bos, Dennis Bradford, James F. Franklin, Matthew Grant, Keith Hein, John Jensen, Edward Lipscomb, Arthur Meister, Michael Miller, Michael Olich, John Carver Sullivan, Dale White.
Costumes: Robert Blackman, Ainslie G. Bruneau, Deborah M. Dryden, Rosemary Ingham, Edward Lipscomb, Tom McKinley, Elizabeth Poindexter, Tom Rasmussen, Debbie Smithee, John Carver Sullivan, Mariann Verheyen, Linn Vercheski, Ann Wallace.
Lights: Tom Dean, Richard Devin, Jonathan Duff, James F. Franklin, Matthew Grant, Francis Lynch, Sean Murphy, Al Oster, Penny Remsen, James Sale, Greg Sullivan.

Alliance Theatre Company/Atlanta Children's Theatre. A Little Night Music. *Photo: Michael Siede.*

FRED CHAPPELL
Artistic Director

ANDREW M. WITT
Managing Director

LAURA HARDMAN
Board President

1280 Peachtree St., NW
Atlanta, GA 30309
(404) 898-1132 (business)
(404) 892-2414 (box office)

FOUNDED 1969
Atlanta Arts Alliance

SEASON
September – June

SCHEDULE
Evenings
Tuesday – Sunday

Matinees
Saturday, Sunday

FACILITIES
Alliance Theatre
Seating capacity: 868
Stage: proscenium

Studio Theatre
Seating capacity: 200
Stage: flexible

FINANCES
August 1, 1982 – July 31, 1983
$2,700,000 operating expenses
$2,700,000 earned income
$ 902,000 grants/contributions

AUDIENCE
Annual attendance: 335,000
Subscribers: 21,100

TOURING CONTACT
Debbie Shelton

BOOKED-IN EVENTS
Theatre, music, dance

AEA LORT (B), (D) and Theatre for Young Audiences contracts

A dynamic evolution at the Alliance Theatre has firmly established the company as a vital part of Atlanta's cultural community, as well as that of Georgia and the southeastern United States.

The first phase of this evolution began in 1977, when the theatre had 3,600 mainstage subscribers and an operating budget of $800,000. At that time, the Alliance set a two-fold goal: to provide a mainstage season of the highest professional artistic and technical quality; and to build a loyal, broad-based subscription audience that would create the strong fiscal foundation necessary

for continued artistic growth. Now, five years later, the mainstage season consists of works by new playwrights, musical theatre, and selections from the contemporary and classical repertoire. Subscriptions have grown to 21,000 with a 70 percent renewal rate.

While the mainstage season was evolving, other programs were also being developed. The Atlanta Children's Theatre plays to more than 130,000 school children on the mainstage each year; the Umbrella Players, an in-school touring company, travels all over the Southeast and to Bermuda; and the adult Studio season offers four innovative plays. In addition, a professional new play reading series provides an opportunity to explore new scripts and discover new playwrights while the Alliance Theatre School provides training and internships for promising young artists, and produces a popular series of lunchtime theatre events.

In the midst of this growth, the guiding principle for the Alliance has remained constant: a theatre's identity is shaped by those artists and craftsmen who create the work. Toward this end, the theatre has committed itself to offering fine artists a chance to do their best work before an eager and enlightened audience.

Programs and services

Professional and non-professional training programs; internship and apprenticeship programs; staged readings of new plays; lunchtime theatre; children's theatre; programs-in-schools.

PRODUCTIONS 1981-82

Whose Life Is It Anyway?, Brian Clark; dir: Fred Chappell
Brigadoon, book and lyrics: Alan J. Lerner; music: Frederick Loewe; dir: Charles Abbott
Private Lives, Noel Coward; dir: Fred Chappell
Loose Ends, Michael Weller; dir: Kent Stephens
Cabaret, book: Joe Masteroff; music: John Kander; lyrics: Fred Ebb; dir: Fred Chappell
A Midsummer Night's Dream, William Shakespeare; dir: Charles Abbott
Billy Bishop Goes to War, John Gray and Eric Peterson; dir: Charles Abbott
Sons and Fathers of Sons, Ray Aranha; dir: Ray Aranha
A Coupla White Chicks Sitting Around Talking, John Ford Noonan; dir: Billings LaPierre
The Diviners, Jim Leonard, Jr.; dir: Fred Chappell
Dungeons and Gryphons, Linden Petersen; dir: Charles Abbott
Sneakers, Judith Weinstein and Arnold Somers; dir: Charles Abbott

PRODUCTIONS 1982-83

Cotton Patch Gospel, book: Tom Key and Russell Treyz; music and lyrics: Harry Chapin; dir: Russell Treyz
Another Part of the Forest, Lillian Hellman; dir: Fred Chappell
Chekhov in Yalta, John Driver and Jeffrey Haddow; dir: Fred Chappell
Mame, book: Jerome Lawrence and Robert E. Lee; music and lyrics: Jerry Herman; dir: Russell Treyz
5th of July, Lanford Wilson; dir: Kent Stephens
A Little Night Music, book: Hugh Wheeler; music and lyrics: Stephen Sondheim; dir: Fred Chappell
Twelfth Night, William Shakespeare; dir: Kent Stephens
My Sister in This House, Wendy Kesselman; dir: Fred Chappell
Immorality Play, James Yaffee; dir: David McKenna
Home, Samm-Art Williams; dir: Walter Dallas
Educating Rita, Willy Russell; adapt: Ntozake Shange; dir: Fred Chappell
The Emperor's New Clothes, Larry Shue; dir: Kent Stephens
The Pirates of Penzance, book and lyrics: W.S. Gilbert; music: Arthur Sullivan; dir: Kent Stephens

DESIGNERS

Sets: Mark Morton, Michael Stauffer.
Costumes: Thom Coates, Susan Hirschfeld, Fannie Schubert, Stanley Simmons.
Lights: William B. Duncan, Michael Stauffer, Michael Orris Watson.

AMAS Repertory Theatre

ROSETTA LeNOIRE
Artistic Director

GARY HALCOTT
JERRY LAPIDUS
Administrators

1 East 104th St.
New York, NY 10029
(212) 369-8000

FOUNDED 1968
Rosetta LeNoire, Gerta Grunen, Mara Kim

SEASON
October – August

SCHEDULE
Evenings
Thursday – Saturday

Matinees
Sunday

FACILITIES
Experimental Theatre
Seating capacity: 99
Stage: modified thrust

Eubie Blake Children's Theatre
Seating capacity: 75
Stage: proscenium

FINANCES
July 1, 1982 – June 30, 1983
$225,000 operating expenses
$ 61,000 earned income
$164,000 grants/contributions

AUDIENCE
Annual attendance: 15,000

TOURING CONTACT
Rosetta LeNoire

AEA Showcase code

AMAS Repertory Theatre is a multiracial performing arts organization devoted to the development of original musical theatre and new musical theatre artists. Now entering its 16th season under the continued artistic guidance of its founder Rosetta LeNoire, AMAS (which means "you love" in Latin) is

AMAS Repertory Theatre. Joseph Fugett and Robert Lydiard in Five Points. *Photo: JWL.*

dedicated to bringing all people—regardless of race, color, creed, religion or economic background—together through the creative arts.

AMAS is perhaps best known for its showcase program, presenting premiere professional productions of new musicals. In creating and developing these works, special emphasis is placed on biographies of individuals, both famous and unknown, whose lives have enriched us all. AMAS' best-known works include *Bojangles, Come Laugh and Cry with Langston Hughes, Miss Waters, to You* and *Dunbar*. Among the musicals that have gone on to be produced elsewhere is the internationally acclaimed *Bubbling Brown Sugar*, as well as *Jam, Ragtime* and *Before the Flood*.

Despite its showcase status, AMAS has received the Kennedy Center Playwrights Award and numerous AUDELCO (Audience Development Committee) Awards for excellence in musical theatre. In the past two seasons alone, such distinguished artists as Luther Henderson, Mabel Robinson, Billie Allen, Colderidge Taylor Perkinson, Judy Dearing, William Michael Maher and Keith Rozie have collaborated on AMAS productions.

The theatre is equally proud of its extensive training and outreach programs. The award-winning Eubie Blake Children's Theatre is an integral part of the overall program, offering comprehensive professional training in singing, dancing and acting to young people ages 9 through 16. The Children's Theatre presents two full-scale productions (often original) each season, and performs at special events around the City. (In 1983, for example, the troupe was part of the Eubie Blake 100th Birthday celebration.) The AMAS Summer Tour brings an original musical revue to senior citizen centers, nursing homes and various other public sites throughout the five boroughs of New York, free of charge.

Programs and services

Children's theatre productions and classes; summer touring; adult workshops; performances in schools; free summer classes; internships.

PRODUCTIONS 1981-82

Will They Ever Love Us on Broadway?, book, music and lyrics: Osayande Baruti; dir: Mabel Robinson

The Winds of Change, book: Franklin C. Tramutola; music: Joseph D'Agostino; lyrics: Gary Romero; dir: William Michael Maher

Five Points, book: Laurence Holder; music and lyrics: John Braden; dir: William Michael Maher

Langston Speaks, adapt: Rosetta LeNoire; dir: Rosetta LeNoire and Bob Brooker

A Local Dilemma, book: Frederick McKinnon; music: Fred Lederman; lyrics: Alan Baboff; dir: Frederick McKinnon and Rosetta LeNoire

The Mikado, book and lyrics: W.S. Gilbert; music: Arthur Sullivan; dir: Margaret Bynum and Rosetta LeNoire

PRODUCTIONS 1982-83

Louisiana Summer, book: Robert and Bradley Wexler; music: Rocky Stone; lyrics: Robert Wexler; dir: Robert Stark

Miss Waters, to You, concept: Rosetta LeNoire; book: Loften Mitchell; special material: Luther Henderson; music and lyrics: various; dir: Billie Allen

Opening Night, book, music and lyrics: Corliss Taylor-Dunn and Sandra Reaves-Phillips; dir: William Michael Maher

Langston Speaks

The Nightingale, book, music and lyrics: Charles Strouse; dir: Rosetta LeNoire

Pippin, book: Roger O. Hirson; music and lyrics: Stephen Schwartz; dir: Fred Tuso and Rosetta LeNoire

DESIGNERS

Sets: Tom Barnes, Larry Fulton, Ed Goetz, Robert Lewis Smith.
Costumes: Gabriel Berry, Judy Dearing, Jeff Mazor, Eiko Yamaguchi, Mary Hays.
Lights: John Enea, Gregg Marriner, Ron McIntyre, Deborah Tulchin.

American Conservatory Theatre

WILLIAM BALL
General Director/Board President

JAMES B. McKENZIE
Executive Producer

450 Geary St.
San Francisco, CA 94102
(415) 771-3880 (business)
(415) 673-6440 (box office)

FOUNDED 1965
William Ball

SEASON
October - May

SCHEDULE

Evenings
Monday - Saturday

Matinees
Wednesday, Saturday

FACILITIES

Geary Theatre
415 Geary St.
Seating capacity: 1,364
Stage: proscenium

FINANCES
June 1, 1982 - May 31, 1983
$5,981,000 operating expenses
$4,337,000 earned income
$1,700,000 grants/contributions

AUDIENCE
Annual attendance: 251,600
Subscribers: 16,660

TOURING CONTACT
Benjamin Moore

BOOKED-IN EVENTS
Theatre, dance

AEA LORT (A) contract

American Conservatory Theatre. Bruce Williams, George Deloy, Sally Smythe and Ray Reinhardt in Loot. *Photo: Larry Merkle.*

In its beginning, American Conservatory Theatre was an experiment in allowing actors to govern themselves and liberate creative genius. When William Ball founded the company in 1965, he was reaching for a new level of theatre in this country by establishing an organization where training would be ongoing and inseparable from performance. Now, far beyond the experimental stage, ACT has fostered a company which remains passionately dedicated to these ideals after 17 years.

ACT's traditional side is evident in its focus on the classics, both in repertory productions and Conservatory curriculum. This grounding is essential for both audiences and actors when facing the challenges of new works. The tools artists and audiences bring to a contemporary performance must be sharpened by historical understanding, and in the search for new enlightenment in great drama, ACT believes that "classical" should never be viewed merely as "traditional."

ACT's 17th season in San Francisco's Geary Theatre—which it owns—ran for 33 weeks, presenting 267 performances of 8 plays to a collective audience of more than 300,000. The rotating repertory approach offers the audience a unique opportunity to see as many as three separate productions during a single week. Regional and national touring, including the 11th annual Hawaii residency and a two-week engagement in Los Angeles, completed its performance activities. During that time, the theatre employed 200 people, including 36 professional actors, 9 directors, 10 designers and 17 Conservatory trainers.

ACT is the only professional performing arts institution empowered to grant a Master of Fine Arts degree. The Conservatory instructed more than 750 students during the 1982-83 academic year in its Advanced Training Program, Summer Training Congress, Evening Academy and Young Conservatory.

Programs and services

Plays-in-Progress playreading series; administrative and technical internships; Concert Van touring productions; Prologue public lecture series; student matinees; signed performances; ticket discounts for senior citizens, the military, students and the handicapped.

American Jewish Theatre of the 92nd St. Y

PRODUCTIONS 1981-82

Richard II, William Shakespeare; dir: Elizabeth Huddle
I Remember Mama, John Van Druten; dir: Allen Fletcher
The Three Sisters, Anton Chekhov; dir: Tom Moore
The Admirable Crichton, James M. Barrie; dir: Michael Winters
A Christmas Carol, adapt: Dennis Powers and Laird Williamson, from Charles Dickens; dir: Laird Williamson
Happy Landings, William Hamilton; dir: Edward Hastings
Two one-acts:
  Black Comedy, Peter Shaffer; dir: James Edmondson
  The Browning Version, Terence Rattigan; dir: James Edmondson
Mourning Becomes Electra, Eugene O'Neill; dir: Allen Fletcher
Cat Among the Pigeons, Georges Feydeau; trans: John Mortimer; dir: Nagle Jackson
Another Part of the Forest, Lillian Hellman; dir: Allen Fletcher

PRODUCTIONS 1982-83

The Gin Game, D.L. Coburn; dir: James Edmondson
Dear Liar, Jerome Kilty; dir: James Edmondson
The Chalk Garden, Enid Bagnold; dir: Dakin Matthews
A Christmas Carol
Uncle Vanya, Anton Chekhov; trans: Pam Gems; dir: Helen Burns and Michael Langham
Loot, Joe Orton; dir: Ken Ruta
Morning's at Seven, Paul Osborn; dir: Allen Fletcher
The Holdup, Marsha Norman; dir: Edward Hastings

DESIGNERS

Sets: Robert Blackman, Ralph Funicello, Richard L. Hay, Richard Seger.
Costumes: Robert Blackman, Martha Burke, Michael Casey, Robert Morgan, Michael Olich.
Lights: Joseph Appelt, Mark Bosch, Dirk Epperson, Robert Peterson, James Sale, Duane Schuler.

STANLEY BRECHNER
Artistic Director

OMUS HIRSHBEIN
Director of Performing Arts

STEVEN L. OSTERWEIS
Board President

92nd St. Y
1395 Lexington Ave.
New York, NY 10028
(212) 427-6000, ext. 220 (business)
(212) 427-4410 (box office)

FOUNDED 1974
Stanley Brechner

SEASON
September-June

SCHEDULE

Evenings
Tuesday-Thursday, Saturday, Sunday

Matinees
Sunday

FACILITIES
Studio Theatre
Seating capacity: 90
Stage: flexible

FINANCES
July 1, 1982-June 30, 1983
$289,000 operating expenses
$160,000 earned income
$ 57,000 grants/contributions

AUDIENCE
Annual attendance: 16,000
Subscribers: 1,800

TOURING CONTACT
Norman Golden

AEA Mini contract and Showcase code

The American Jewish Theatre presents plays in English dealing with Jewish themes. These works fall into three basic categories: new translations of Yiddish plays, revivals of established classics, and contemporary works by both established and new playwrights. The American Jewish Theatre is also dedicated to the preservation of Jewish theatre.

Yiddish-language theatre, the most vibrant artistic expression of Jewish life in the United States and Europe until the Second World War, was the primary form of Jewish theatre for over a century. The end of World War II brought the destruction of millions, and the ultimate extinction of Yiddish as a language. Whereas there were 32 Yiddish-speaking theatres in New York alone in 1920, by 1945 there were only four: an entire theatrical tradition simply evaporated. The American Jewish Theatre was founded to bring the Jewish theatrical tradition alive again.

Finally, the American Jewish Theatre is dedicated to heightening Jewish consciousness by presenting provocative new works dealing with the inexorable realities of anti-

American Jewish Theatre. Art Burns and Albert Sinkys in The Man in the Glass Booth. *Photo: Gerry Goodstein.*

The American Place Theatre

semitism, Jewish feminism, Jewish violence, Christian America, Israel and the secular versus the religious Jew, as well as many other issues. In all, the American Jewish Theatre seeks to serve as a forum where all aspects of the Jewish experience are explored through theatre.

Programs and services

New play readings; Yiddish play translation program; touring; administrative and production internships.

PRODUCTIONS 1981-82

In the Matter of J. Robert Oppenheimer, Heinar Kipphardt; dir: Robert Brink
House Music, Hans Sahl; dir: Geoffrey Sherman
The Price, Arthur Miller; dir: Dan Held
The Keymaker, Nathan Teitel; dir: Stanley Brechner
The Raspberry Picker, Fritz Hochwalder; dir: Dan Held

PRODUCTIONS 1982-83

The Tenth Man, Paddy Chayefsky; dir: Robert Brink
David and Paula, Howard Fast; dir: Stanley Brechner
The Man in the Glass Booth, Robert Shaw; dir: Dan Held
The Rise of David Levinsky, book and lyrics: Isaiah Sheffer; music: Bobby Paul; dir: Sue Lawless
Two for the Seesaw, William Gibson; dir: Dan Held

DESIGNERS

Sets: Tony Castrigno, Paul Dale, Ken Foy, Keith Gonzales, Peter Wingate, Paul Wonsek.
Costumes: Kathy Blake, Claudia Brown, Richard Hornung, Karen Hummel, Barbara Weiss.
Lights: Greg Chabay, Helen Gatling, Martha Gibson, Paul Wonsek, Ann Wrightsen.

WYNN HANDMAN
Director

JULIA MILES
Associate Director

111 West 46th St.
New York, NY 10036
(212) 246-3730 (business)
(212) 247-0393 (box office)

FOUNDED 1964
Wynn Handman, Michael Tolan, Sidney Lanier, Myrna Loy

SEASON
September-June

SCHEDULE

Evenings
Tuesday-Saturday

Matinees
Variable

FACILITIES

Mainstage
Seating capacity: 299
Stage: flexible thrust

Subplot Cabaret
Seating capacity: 74
Stage: flexible

Basement Space
Seating capacity: 74
Stage: flexible

FINANCES
July 1, 1982-June 30, 1983
$900,000 operating expenses
$593,000 earned income
$311,000 grants/contributions

AUDIENCE
Annual attendance: 48,000
Subscribers: 1,584

TOURING CONTACT
Julia Miles

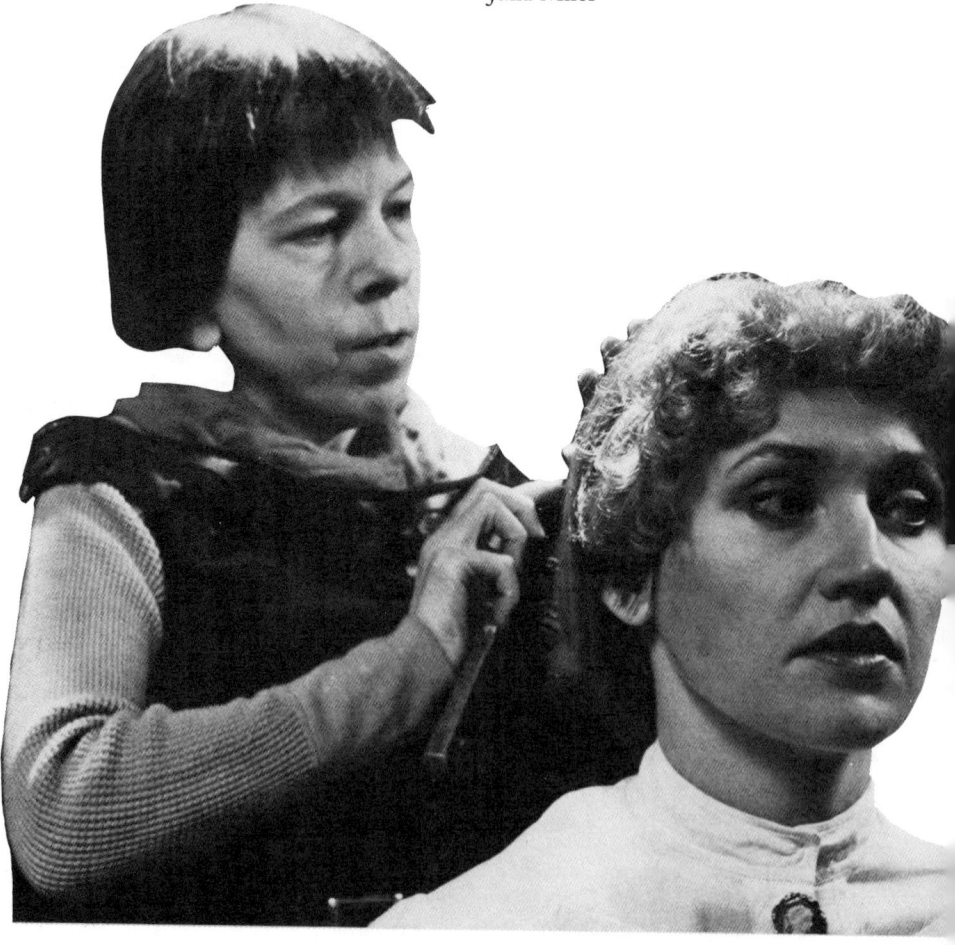

American Repertory Theatre

BOOKED-IN EVENTS
Theatre, music, dance

AEA Special Production contract

The American Place Theatre is in its 20th season of producing new works by living Americans. Its continuing purpose is to be a force for the advancement of theatre, by actively responding to the contemporary theatre's needs. Toward that end, it provides a creative environment and facilities free of commercial considerations for talented American writers; its innovative, original programming opens the way for increased public awareness and enrichment of the mainstream of the nation's theatre.

In order to promote and encourage new work of various genres with differing production needs, the American Place has several ongoing programs in addition to its mainstage series. These include The Women's Project: affiirmative action that is specifically designed to encourage, develop and produce women playwrights and directors; and the American Humorist Series, which creates entertainments drawn from the writings of past American humorists, as well as providing a stage for new American humorist performers.

The artistic emphasis of the American Place has recently been expanded as it becomes further involved in theatrical styles and materials drawn from the American past, presented either in their original form — as in the case of a recent recreation of a medicine show — or filtered through a contemporary sensibility and interpretation.

Programs and services

Directors' and dramaturgs' workshops; internship/residency program for directing, stage management, design, literary management and theatre administration; post-play discussions; study materials; workshop productions; staged readings.

The American Place Theatre. Linda Hunt and Caroline Kava in Little Victories. *Photo: Martha Holmes.*

PRODUCTIONS 1981-82

Grace, Jane Stanton Hitchcock; dir: Peter Thompson
Behind the Broken Words, various authors; dir: Anthony Zerbe and Roscoe Lee Browne
The Regard of Flight, Bill Irwin, with Doug Skinner and Michael O'Connor
The Death of a Miner, Paul Cizmar; dir: Barbara Rosoff
The Brothers, Kathleen Collins; dir: Billie Allen
Serious Bizness, various authors; dir: Sue Lawless
A Crowd of Two, Lisa Loomer and Rita Nachtmann; dir: Miriam Fond

PRODUCTIONS 1982-83

Do Lord Remember Me, James de Jongh; dir: Regge Life
Speakeasy: An Evening Out with Dorothy Parker, adapt: Michael Feingold; dir: Michael Feingold
Buck, Ronald Ribman; dir: Elinor Renfield
The Stage That Walks, Bruce D. Schwartz; dir: Bruce D. Schwartz
Great Days, Donald Barthelme; dir: J Ranelli
Little Victories, Lavonne Mueller; dir: Bryna Wortman
Territorial Rites, Carol Mack; dir: Josephine Abady
Heart of a Dog, Terry Galloway; dir: Suzanne Bennett

DESIGNERS

Sets: John Arnone, William Barclay, Maxine Klein, Brian Martin, David Potts, Leslie Taylor, Julie Taymor, Christina Weppner.
Costumes: Judy Dearing, K.L. Fredericks, Heide Hollmann, Mimi Maxmen, David Woolard.
Lights: Joan Arhelger, Frances Aronson, Arden Fingerhut, Phil Monet, Sandra Ross, Joni Wong, Christine Woppat, Ann Wrightson.

ROBERT BRUSTEIN
Artistic Director

ROBERT J. ORCHARD
Managing Director

ANTONIA CHAYES
Board Chairman

64 Brattle St.
Cambridge, MA 02138
(617) 495-2668 (business)
(617) 547-8300 (box office)

FOUNDED 1980
Robert Brustein

SEASON
November-June

SCHEDULE
Evenings
Tuesday-Sunday

Matinees
Saturday, Sunday

FACILITIES
Loeb Drama Center
Seating capacity: 556
Stage: flexible

Hasty Pudding Theatre
12 Holyoke St.
Seating capacity: 353
Stage: proscenium

FINANCES
July 1, 1982-June 30, 1983
$2,577,000 operating expenses
$1,353,000 earned income
$1,224,000 grants/contributions

AUDIENCE
Annual attendance: 141,800
Subscribers: 8,166

TOURING CONTACT
Robert J. Orchard

BOOKED-IN EVENTS
Theatre, music, dance

AEA LORT (B) contract

American Repertory Theatre. Kathy Bates and Anne Pitoniak in 'night Mother. Photo: Richard Feldman.

The American Repertory Theatre, a professional company in residence at Harvard University's Loeb Drama Center, was founded in 1980 by Robert Brustein and his associates, many of whom had been colleagues during his previous 13 years as founder and artistic director of the Yale Repertory Theatre. The resident ensemble of 14 to 18 actors, some of whom have been together for as many as 17 years, perform five to seven productions in rotating repertory during the 40-week season.

ART is specifically dedicated to the production of works in three categories: classics, respecting the integrity of the original text while attempting to create a sense of freshness and immediacy that speaks to contemporary audiences; neglected works of the past (frequently involving music) which have particular interest to current audiences; and new works, primarily American, which reach beyond traditional theatrical conventions. In recent seasons, Andrei Serban's production of *Three Sisters,* Peter Sellars' staging of Handel's *Orlando* and the premiere of Marsha Norman's Pulitzer Prize-winning *'night Mother* have been representative of the company's artistic thrust.

Other activities of the theatre include a Monday Series of staged readings, debates, lectures and special events; and productions of primarily new plays at the Hasty Pudding Theatre. In addition to extensive regional and national touring with its principal company, the ART went on an 11-week tour of Europe and the Middle East in the fall of 1982, performing at the Avignon, Edinburgh, Israel, BITEF and Asti Festivals, and in Amsterdam and Rotterdam. That tour ended with performances at the Duke of York's Theatre in London, where one of the productions was taped for British television.

In the fall of 1982, moreover, the Musical Theatre Lab moved its operations from the Kennedy Center in Washington, DC to Cambridge, and is now a joint project of the Stuart Ostrow Foundation, the ART and Radcliffe College.

In addition to its performing activities, the ART is also dedicated to identifying and training talent for the theatre. Presently, the company teaches 12 theatre-related courses for academic credit in the Harvard undergraduate curriculum, and offers a comprehensive program in professional theatre training in all disciplines through the Harvard School of Continuing Education and Harvard Summer School. A program of specialized workshops is also offered to secondary schools periodically throughout the academic year.

Programs and services

Undergraduate, graduate and extension courses; internships; Monday Series of staged readings, lectures, films and special events; touring; student and senior citizen ticket discounts.

PRODUCTIONS 1981-82

Sgnararelle, and Evening of Molière Farces, Molière; trans; Albert Bermel; dir: Andrei Serban

Orlando, George Friedrich Handel; dir: Peter Sellars and Craig Smith

The Journey of the Fifth Horse, Ronald Ribman; dir: Adrian Hall

Ghosts, Henrik Ibsen; adapt: Robert Brustein; dir: Robert Brustein

The American Stage Company

(FORMERLY PALISADES THEATRE COMPANY)

Orchids in the Moonlight, Carlos Fuentes; dir: Joann Green
True West, Sam Shepard; dir: David Wheeler
Rundown, Robert Auletta; dir: Bill Foeller

PRODUCTIONS 1982-83

The Three Sisters, Anton Chekhov; trans: Jean-Claude van Itallie; dir: Andrei Serban
'night Mother, Marsha Norman; dir: Tom Moore
Waiting for Godot, Samuel Beckett; dir: Andrei Belgrader
The Boys from Syracuse, book: George Abbott, from William Shakespeare; music: Richard Rodgers; lyrics: Lorenz Hart; dir: Alvin Epstein and Paul Schierhorn
The School for Scandal, Richard Brinsley Sheridan; dir: Jonathan Miller
Baby with the Bathwater, Christopher Durang; dir: Mark-Linn Baker
Three one-acts:
  Hughie, Eugene O'Neill; dir: Bill Foeller
  Footfall and Rockaby, Samuel Beckett; dir: John Grant-Phillips

DESIGNERS

Sets: Kate Edmunds, Heidi Landesman, Tom Lynch, Beni Montresor, Patrick Robertson, Kevin Rupnick, Don Soule, Elaine Spatz-Rabinowitz, Tony Straiges, Michael Yeargan.
Costumes: Nan Cibula, Lynn Jeffrey, Heidi Landesman, Beni Montresor, Liz Perlman, Dunya Ramicova, Kevin Rupnik, Rita Ryack, Nancy Thun, Rosemary Vercoe.
Lights: James F. Ingalls, Beni Montresor, Jennifer Tipton.

The American Stage Company. Tim Saukiavicus, Ariel Bock, Dennis Krausnick and Marjorie Greenwood in A Touch of the Poet. *Photo: David MacLean.*

JOHN A. BERGLUND
Managing Director

VICTORIA HOLLOWAY
Consulting Artistic Director

WILLIAM J. FLYNN
Board President

Box 1560
St. Petersburg, FL 33731
(813) 823-1600 (business)
(813) 822-8814 (box office)

FOUNDED 1979
Richard Hopkins and Bobbie Seifer

SEASON
October-May

SCHEDULE
Evenings
Wednesday-Saturday

Matinees
Saturday, Sunday

FACILITIES
175 Central Ave.
Seating capacity: 176
Stage: thrust

FINANCES
July 1, 1982-June 30, 1983
$135,000 operating expenses
$ 68,000 earned income
$ 67,000 grants/contributions

AUDIENCE
Annual attendance: 12,000
Subscribers: 638

AEA letter of agreement

The American Stage Company, formerly the Palisades Theatre of Florida, began touring throughout the southeastern United States in 1974 with a repertoire of children's classics. The assistance of the Junior League of St. Petersburg in 1979 and additional federal funding through the Comprehensive Education and Training Act (CETA) enabled the company to expand its programming and establish a resident theatre.

The withdrawal of that funding in 1981 altered the course of the company: the touring component was disbanded and emphasis was placed on maintaining a professional regional theatre for the Tampa Bay Area. Core company members reside within the Bay Area, although additional artists are drawn from both within and without the region.

The company operates under an Equity letter of agreement, and draws heavily from the theatre departments of several local colleges for design and technical assistance. The artistic vision of the company centers on the production of American classics, contemporary works and new works by American playwrights. Theatre as education is also emphasized and the company produces two plays each season geared toward the local school systems. Artist-in-Education pro-

American Stage Festival

gramming, acting workshops for nonprofessionals and in-class workshops are offered throughout the year.

The American Stage Company is supported by the region it serves, and the participation of Florida artists and playwrights is actively encouraged.

Programs and services

Professional and non-professional training workshops; Artist-in-Education programs; staged readings; administrative and production internships.

Note: During the 1981-82 season, Bobbie Seifer served as artistic director. During the 1982-83 season, Dennis Krausnick served as consulting artistic director.

PRODUCTIONS 1981-82

A Delicate Balance, Edward Albee; dir: Kevin Coleman
Table Settings, James Lapine; dir: Dennis Krausnick
The Sea Horse, Edward Moore; dir: Alfred Gingold
Two for the Seesaw, William Gibson; dir: Dennis Krausnick
Little Eyolf, Henrik Ibsen; dir: Nancy Cole
archy and mehitabel, Joe Darion and Mel Brooks; dir: Alfred Gingold

PRODUCTIONS 1982-83

Awake and Sing!, Clifford Odets; dir: Dennis Krausnick
A Christmas Carol, adapt: Kevin Coleman, from Charles Dickens; dir: Kevin Coleman
The Gin Game, D.L. Coburn; dir: Victoria Holloway
A Touch of the Poet, Eugene O'Neill; dir: Kevin Coleman
The Glass Menagerie, Tennessee Williams; dir: Dennis Krausnick

DESIGNERS

Sets: Brian A. Anstedt, James R. Carlson, Sandy Eppling, Paul Gralen.
Costumes: Victoria Holloway, Joanne Johnson.
Lights: Brian A. Anstedt, Paul Gralen.

LARRY CARPENTER
Artistic Director

JEFF SMULL
Managing Director

NORMAN P. SOLOWAY
Board President

Box 225
Milford, NH 03055
(603) 673-3143 (business)
(603) 673-7515 (box office)

FOUNDED 1975
Terry C. Lorden and local citizens

SEASON
June-August

SCHEDULE
Evenings
Tuesday-Sunday

Matinees
Wednesday

FACILITIES
Route 13N (Mont Vernon St.)
Seating capacity: 480
Stage: proscenium

FINANCES
November 1, 1981-October 31, 1982
$338,000 operating expenses
$199,000 earned income
$143,000 grants/contributions

AUDIENCE
Annual attendance: 40,000
Subscribers: 2,600

BOOKED-IN EVENTS
Children's theatre, arts & crafts

AEA Council on Resident Stock Theatre contract

The American Stage Festival stands on a nine-acre peninsula of woods and fields on New Hampshire's Souhegan River. Its year-round administrative staff produces a 10-week summer season, drawing its audiences

American Stage Festival. Carol Mayo Jenkins, Kurt Knudsen, Julia MacKenzie and Jana Schneider in Hobson's Choice. *Photo: Tom Bloom.*

primarily from its home state and northern Massachusetts. In its ninth season, ASF has grown to be one of New Hampshire's largest professional arts organizations.

The Festival's artistic mandate is to provide the highest quality, most diverse arts programming for its exurban family audience. In practice, this goal involves mixing what might be considered unusual choices from the established repertoire with a great deal of new work. The five-play season has over the years tended to adhere to a format of one classic, one musical, a murder-mystery, a period comedy and a contemporary comedy. The company aims for appropriate renderings of the literature in striking stagings, using the best talent available from all areas of theatre.

In addition to presenting plays, ASF maintains a rounded cultural trusteeship for its community by producing a children's workshop series, weekly art gallery exhibits, a special events series including such groups as the New Hampshire Symphony and the Hartford Ballet, play discussion seminars, a twice-weekly farmers' market and an annual arts and crafts fair.

ASF maintains a strong commitment to the training of young theatre artists and has adopted a conservatory approach to its apprentice and intern companies that mixes professional seminars and working exposure to acting, singing, dance, improvisation, design, production and administration.

Programs and services

Production and administrative internships; children's workshops; art gallery exhibits; special events series; post-play discussions; farmers' market; arts and crafts fair.

PRODUCTIONS 1982

Side by Side by Sondheim, music and lyrics: Stephen Sondheim, et al.; adapt: Ned Sherrin; dir: Robert Brink
Corpse, Gerald Moon; dir: John Tillinger
Inherit the Wind, Jerome Lawrence and Robert E. Lee; dir: William Woodman
Squabbles, Marshall Karp; dir: Larry Carpenter
Sullivan and Gilbert, Kenneth Ludwig; music: Arthur Sullivan; lyrics: W.S. Gilbert; dir: Larry Carpenter

PRODUCTIONS 1983

Same Time, Next Year, Bernard Slade; dir: William Woodman
Dramatic License, Kenneth Ludwig; dir: Larry Carpenter
The Importance of Being Earnest, Oscar Wilde; dir: Charles Karshmer
Ladyhouse Blues, Kevin O'Morrison; dir: Barbara Rosoff
Ain't Misbehavin', music and lyrics: Fats Waller, et al.; adapt: Richard Maltby, Jr.; dir: Alan Weeks

DESIGNERS

Sets: Dennis Bradford, Edward Cesaitis, John Falabella, Marjorie Bradley Kellogg, Karen Sparks Mellon, Jim Steere, Patricia Woodbridge.
Costumes: Amanda Aldridge, Barbara Beccio, Gail Grassard, Lowell Detweiler, Sam Fleming, David Murin.
Lights: William Armstrong, Jeff Davis, John Gisondi, Margaret Lee, Clarke W. Thornton, Richard Winkler.

American Theatre Arts

DON EITNER
Artistic Director

JOHN TERRY BELL
Executive Director

EDITH LASHLEY
Board President

6240 Hollywood Blvd.
Hollywood, CA 90028
(213) 466-2462

FOUNDED 1976
Don Eitner

SEASON
October-September

SCHEDULE
Evenings
Thursday-Sunday

Matinees
Sunday

FACILITIES
Borelli Theatre
Seating capacity: 70
Stage: flexible

Thornton Theatre
Seating capacity: 60
Stage: proscenium

FINANCES
January 1, 1982-December 31, 1982
$170,000 operating expenses
$ 88,000 earned income
$ 70,000 grants/contributions

AUDIENCE
Annual attendance: 10,760
Subscribers: 329

AEA 99-seat waiver

American Theatre Arts is a conservatory theatre interrelating professional productions and professional training. At the heart of ATA's artistic commitment is the development of an ensemble which epitomizes the life-blood of theatre. To quote Harold Clurman, "It's a group art entirely dependent on team work."

Such a commitment requires intensive study by the developing actors and continuing creative interaction among the professionals, evolving and refining every member of the company, providing new fields of study for ATA artists and much needed "workouts" for voice and body.

Developing new ensemble plays and meeting the challenges of new playwrights' work are also ATA goals that have been realized through the production of several world premieres. Among these is *The Gin Game,* which later won the Pulitzer Prize for drama and has been produced throughout the country at nonprofit professional theatres as well as on Broadway and internationally. In conjunction with new works, American Theatre Arts revives little known plays by major playwrights, such as Shaw's *In Good King Charles' Golden Days,* in order to return them to the mainstream of theatrical literature.

Programs and services

Acting for the Deaf program including signed performances; second stage/conservatory productions.

PRODUCTIONS 1981-82

Riverwind, book, music and lyrics: John Jennings; dir: Diane Haak
After the Rain, John Bowen; dir: Don Eitner
Catsplay, Istvan Orkeny; trans: Clara Gyorgyey; dir: James J. Agazzi
Ten Times Table, Alan Ayckbourn; dir: Diane Haak
Towards Zero, Agatha Christie; dir: Bill Cort
Body to Light, Doraine Poretz; dir: Betty Ferber
Embarcadero Fugue, Thomas Strehlich; dir: Buck Skelton

PRODUCTIONS 1982-83

A Murder Is Announced; Agatha Christie; dir: Joseph Ruskin
Absent Friends, Alan Ayckbourn; dir: Don Eitner
Private Life of the Master Race, Bertolt Brecht; trans: Kenneth Tigar and Clayton Koelb; music: Bruce Ewen; dir: Diane Haak
Period of Adjustment, Tennessee Williams; dir: Gene Nelson

DESIGNERS

Sets: James J. Agazzi, Don Eitner, Robert Green, Robert Smitherman, Dale Barnhart.
Costumes: Darlene Morgan, Jo McLachlan, Edouard Johnson, Mara Holland, Nancy Washington, Ruby K. Manis.
Lights: Nancy J. Shaffer, Robert Smitherman, Marc Haniuk.

American Theatre Arts. After the Rain.

American Theatre Company

KITTY ROBERTS
Producing Director

JERALD D. POPE
Artistic Director

C.S. LEWIS, III
Board Chairman

Box 1265
Tulsa, OK 74101
(918) 747-9494 (business, box office: Brook Theatre)
(918) 592-7111 (box office: Williams Theatre)

FOUNDED 1970
Kitty Roberts, Jerald Pope, Robert L. Odle, Richard Ellis

SEASON
October-June

SCHEDULE

Evenings
Tuesday-Saturday

Matinees
Sunday

FACILITIES

John H. Williams Theatre
2nd and Cincinnati Sts.
Seating capacity: 429
Stage: proscenium

Brook Theatre
3405 Peoria St.
Seating capacity: 529
Stage: flexible

FINANCES
January 1, 1982-December 31, 1982
$400,000 operating expenses
$235,000 earned income
$165,000 grants/contributions

AUDIENCE
Annual attendance: 65,575
Subscribers: 2,300

TOURING CONTACT
Robert L. Odle

BOOKED-IN EVENTS
Theatre

AEA Guest Artist contract

American Theatre Company is a frontier theatre in the buckle of the Bible Belt. Under pressure to survive, ATC has established a beachhead for professional theatre in Oklahoma by developing a network which criss-crosses the entire state with an education program and summer tour.

As the official resident theatre of the Tulsa Performing Arts Center, ATC presents its six mainstage productions there, while also programming a 2nd Stage cabaret nearby. Cross-over between the two stages is an important developmental aspect of the ATC philosophy. The generally younger 2nd Stage crowd is encouraged to reach out and sample the more serious traditional fare at the mainstage, while the traditional theatregoer is provided a more varied palette of programming by visiting the cabaret.

ATC is currently concentrating on ways to achieve its long-standing goal: to present a diversified repertoire which includes classics, the best work of contemporary playwrights and original work. Hence, ATC is bringing in guest actors, directors, and designers while at the same time searching for new ensemble members.

In addition, the company has established a technical internship program accredited by the Tulsa Public Schools and the local Junior College. ATC is also the only performing arts organization in the state with a fulltime Scholar-in-Residence funded by the Oklahoma Humanities Committee.

Under the same producing leadership since its founding in 1970, the American Theatre Company is a strong, exciting example of what talent and persistence can accomplish. The only professional stage company in a 300-mile radius of Tulsa, in a state which achieved statehood only 75 years ago, ATC survives and is stimulated by the challenges of the cultural frontier.

Programs and services

Professional training program; touring; programs-in-schools; workshops; lectures; film series; internships.

American Theatre Company. Karl Krause and Alex Johnson in Frankenstein. Photo: Dennis Fry.

The American Theater Company in Aspen (FORMERLY PILGRIM THEATER)

PRODUCTIONS 1981-82

Frankenstein, adapt: Robert F. Gross and Jerald D. Pope, from Mary Shelley; dir: James E. Runyan

Peter Pan, book: James M. Barrie; music: Mark Charlap and Jule Styne; lyrics: Carolyn Leigh, Betty Comden and Adolph Green; dir: Kerry Hauger

Terra Nova, Ted Tally; dir: James E. Runyan

The Merchant of Venice, William Shakespeare; dir: Jerald D. Pope

The Gin Game, D.L. Coburn; dir: James E. Runyan

You Can't Take It with You, Moss Hart and George S. Kaufman; dir: James E. Runyan

PRODUCTIONS 1982-83

Rain, John Colton and Clemence Randolph; dir: Jerald D. Pope

A Christmas Carol, adapt: Robert L. Odle, from Charles Dickens; music: Richard Averill; lyrics: Robert L. Odle and Richard Averill; dir: Kerry Hauger

Hedda Gabler, Henrik Ibsen; adapt: William Fears; dir: William Fears

A Coupla White Chicks Sitting Around Talking, John Ford Noonan; dir: Richard Gwartney

The Dresser, Ronald Harwood; dir: Harold W. Barrows

Division Street, Steve Tesich; dir: Richard Gwartney

DESIGNERS

Sets: Richard Ellis, Michael Bautista, David Morong, Ricky G. Newkirk, Jerald D. Pope, Eduardo Sicangco.

Costumes: Jo McClelland, Eduardo Sicangco, Gene Bernhardt.

Lights: Michael Bautista, Joe Leggett, David Morong, Richard Wilson.

WILLIAM SHORR
Artistic Director

R. THOMAS WARD
Executive Director

BONNIE B. BISHOP
Board President

Box 9438
Aspen, CO 81612
(303) 925-4752 (business)
(303) 925-6041 (box office)

FOUNDED 1978
William Shorr, Steve and Linda Carmichael

SEASON
July-August, January-March

SCHEDULE
Evenings
Monday-Saturday

FACILITIES
The Wheeler Opera House
Seating capacity: 400
Stage: proscenium

The Snowmass Theater
Snowmass Village, CO
Seating capacity: 280
Stage: thrust

FINANCES
October 1, 1981-September 30, 1982
$255,000 operating expenses
$129,000 earned income
$112,000 grants/contributions

AUDIENCE
Annual attendance: 8,274

BOOKED-IN EVENTS
Theatre

AEA LORT (C) contract

The American Theater Company in Aspen is committed to the development of new plays and the encouragement of American playwrights. The company's most important program is the Aspen Playwrights Conference, which in six seasons has presented 17 new plays by playwrights from around the country. The work of the Conference is guided each year by a playwright- or critic-in-residence. In 1982 Jules Feiffer served this function, and in 1983 the task fell to Jack Gelber. The Conference is complemented by workshops in playwriting and acting.

At the same time, the American Theater Company produces the Snowmass Festival,

American Theater Company. Charles Durning and John Travolta in Mass Appeal. Photo: Jeffrey Aaronson.

Arena Stage

where in three seasons six plays have been fully produced, including the premiere of Mark Medoff's *The Majestic Kid*.

The company also collaborates with the University of Denver to present staged readings of Colorado playwrights' works at least once a year. Eleven plays have been presented in Denver as part of this program. The American Theater Company in Aspen's goal is to provide the western slope of Colorado with a professional regional theatre which emphasizes the best of the American theatre, both old and—most importantly—new.

Programs and services

Classes in acting, auditioning and playwriting; children's theatre; staged readings; technical and administrative internships; school tours.

PRODUCTIONS 1982

The Voice of the Turtle, John Van Druten; dir: Paul Blake
Mass Appeal, Bill C. Davis; dir: Paul Blake
Tricycle Trail, Larry Ketron; dir: Alice Spivak
Chinese Coffee, Ira Lewis; dir: William Shorr

PRODUCTIONS 1983

The Majestic Kid, Mark Medoff; dir: Frank Condon
The Glass Menagerie, Tennessee Williams; dir: Roger Hendricks Simon
Unicorn Song, Laura Shamus; dir: David Hay
Weehawken Castle, Lewis Gardner; dir: Susan Einhorn
The Unauthorized Autobiography of "Kid Purple" Schwartz, David Wollner; dir: Roger Hendricks Simon

DESIGNERS

Sets: Linda Carmichael, Robert Fletcher, Russel Pyle, John Scheffler.
Costumes: Linda Carmichael, Robert Fletcher, Kim Simon.
Lights: Michael Olsen, Christopher Sackett.

ZELDA FICHANDLER
Producing Director

THOMAS C. FICHANDLER
Executive Director

LEE G. RUBENSTEIN
Board President

6th and Maine Ave., SW
Washington, D.C. 20024
(202) 554-9066 (business)
(202) 488-3300 (box office)

FOUNDED 1950
Zelda Fichandler, Thomas C. Fichandler, Edward Mangum

SEASON
September-June

SCHEDULE

Evenings
Tuesday-Sunday

Matinees
Saturday, Sunday

FACILITIES

The Arena
Seating capacity: 827
Stage: arena

The Kreeger Theater
Seating capacity: 514
Stage: modified thrust

The Old Vat Room
Seating capacity: 180
Stage: cabaret

The Scene Shop
Seating capacity: 130
Stage: flexible

FINANCES
July 1, 1982-June 30, 1983
$4,335,000 operating expenses
$3,168,000 earned income
$1,181,000 grants/contributions

AUDIENCE
Annual attendance: 300,000
Subscribers: 18,000

TOURING CONTACT
Catherine Irwin

BOOKED-IN EVENTS
Theatre, musical theatre

AEA LORT (B) contract

Since its beginning 33 years ago, Arena Stage's artistic and philosophical viewpoint has been molded by its co-founder and producing director, Zelda Fichandler, who built the company with Thomas C. Fichandler to provide a regular source of theatre art for the people of the Washington metropolitan community. "Our aim is no less than this," says Fichandler, "to bring life to life. And by doing so we are indissolubly connected to the world we live in and the people we live for . . . We live to illuminate life and make it more enjoyable."

The idea behind Arena Stage has proved extraordinarily fertile, for not only has Arena attracted the enthusiastic support of its community and experienced a long and steady growth, but it has also served as one of the progenitors of the nationwide resident professional theatre movement and remains a pioneer, a leader among American theatres.

Throughout the years, Arena's artistic staff and resident acting company have devoted themselves to the entire spectrum of theatrical literature, presenting new American plays, premieres of important European works, classics reborn in vivid new interpretations, new musicals and recent plays which undeservedly failed in commercial forums. Among the company's many firsts are the original productions of *The Great White Hope, Indians, Moonchildren, A History of the American Film, Tintypes* and *The Madness of God*. The Arena Stage production of the mountain climbing epic *K2* enjoyed a run on Broadway, garnering an Antoinette Perry ("Tony") award for its designer, Arena veteran Ming Cho Lee.

Arena Stage's home is a handsome theatre complex in Southwest Washington designed by Harry Weese. It was the first theatre center in the country built from direct experience to serve the needs of an existing company. It includes the 827-seat Arena built in 1961 and the 514-seat fan-shaped Kreeger Theater built in 1971. An intimate 180-seat cabaret was added in 1976 and, in 1983, Arena converted a rehearsal hall into its fourth performance space, The Scene

Shop, with 130 seats. The Scene Shop will be used as schedules permit to provide a special place for the innovative, exploratory and unexpected. This new space, combined with Arena's "Play Lab" series of staged readings, reconfirms the company's commitment to developing new American plays.

Programs and services

Artistic, administrative and technical/production internships; students performances; student and senior citizen ticket discounts; free ticket distribution; The Living Stage national touring company; post-performance discussions; Associates lecture series; The Actors Lab professional training program; The Play Lab staged readings; volunteer auxiliary; theatre rentals.

PRODUCTIONS 1981-82

Major Barbara, George Bernard Shaw; dir: Martin Fried
A Lesson from Aloes, Athol Fugard; dir: Douglas C. Wager
A Midsummer Night's Dream, William Shakespeare; dir: David Chambers
Tomfoolery, adapt: Cameron Mackintosh and Robin Ray; music and lyrics: Tom Lehrer; dir: Douglas C. Wager
A Delicate Balance, Edward Albee; dir: Zelda Fichandler
Undiscovered Country, Arthur Schnitzler; adapt: Tom Stoppard; dir: Garland Wright
K2, Patrick Meyers; dir: Jacques Levy
Animal Crackers, book: George S. Kaufman and Morrie Ryskind; music and lyrics: Bert Kalmar and Harry Ruby; dir: Douglas C. Wager

PRODUCTIONS 1982-83

On The Razzle, Tom Stoppard; dir: Douglas C. Wager
Cymbeline, William Shakespeare; dir: David Chambers
The Imaginary Invalid, Moliere; trans: John Wood; dir: Garland Wright
Screenplay, Istvan Orkeny; adapt: Gitta Honegger and Zelda Fichandler; dir: Zelda Fichandler
Geniuses, Jonathan Reynolds; dir: Gary Pearle
Buried Child, Sam Shepard; dir: Gilbert Moses
Candide, book adapt: Hugh Wheeler, from Voltaire; music: Leonard Bernstein; lyrics: Richard Wilbur, Stephen Sondheim and John Latouche; dir: Douglas C. Wager
Still Life, Emily Mann; dir: James Nicola

DESIGNERS

Sets: John Arnone, Zack Brown, Karl Eigsti, Heidi Landesman, Ming Cho Lee, Adrianne Lobel, Tom Lynch, Tony Straiges.
Costumes: Noel Broden, Marie Anne Chiment, Ann Hould-Ward, Mary Ann Powell, Marjorie Slaiman.
Lights: Frances Aronson, Arden Fingerhut, Allen Lee Hughes, Hugh Lester, William Mintzer, Nancy Shertler.

Arena Stage. Stephen McHattie and Stanley Anderson in K2. Photo: Joan Marcus.

Arizona Theatre Company

GARY GISSELMAN
Artistic Director

DAVID HAWKANSON
Managing Director

ARNOLD KRAUS
Board President

120 West Broadway
Tucson, AZ 85701
(602) 884-8210 (business)
(602) 622-2823 (box office)
(602) 234-2892 (Phoenix business)
(602) 279-0534 (Phoenix box office)

FOUNDED 1966
Sandy Rosenthal

SEASON
October-June

SCHEDULE

Evenings
Tuesday-Sunday

Matinees
Wednesday, Sunday

FACILITIES

Tucson Community Center Theatre
Seating capacity: 518
Stage: modified thrust

Phoenix College Theatre
1202 West Thomas Road, Phoenix, AZ
Seating capacity: 307
Stage: thrust

Scottsdale Center for the Arts
Scottsdale Mall, Scottsdale, AZ
Seating capacity: 700
Stage: modified thrust

FINANCES
July 1, 1982-June 30, 1983
$1,295,000 operating expenses
$ 737,000 earned income
$1,412,000 grants/contributions

AUDIENCE
Annual attendance: 100,000
Subscribers: 9,111

AEA LORT (C) contract

Arizona Theatre Company. Ken Ruta and Katerine Ferrand in Uncle Vanya. *Photo: Tim Fuller.*

While the Arizona Theatre Company has been in existence for 16 years, it is only 8 years old as a fully professional theatre, and is thus an emerging professional company in a southwestern state which is growing and shifting ground rapidly—literally and metaphorically. ATC serves a combined population of more than 1.5 million people in two cities: Tucson and Phoenix. While the theatre is headquartered in Tucson, Phoenix constitutes its second permanent home.

Arizona's geography determines the theatre's character in many ways. As the only professional theatre in the area, it is obligated to serve, attract and build as broadly based an audience as possible, serving no particular political polemic, playwright or patron. The company seeks to develop new audiences for theatre and to enlarge their sense of reality through its repertoire and styles of production.

The theatre is committed to developing a company of actors, artists and craftsmen willing to work together over a significant period of time, seeking to create a climate for artists rather than careers.

ATC is also committed to building its programming around a classical repertoire, neither excluding the new nor becoming obsessed with it. As Michael Langham once wrote, "If we are to represent in our communities, a crucible in which all forces reaffirming meaning to life or death can interact, then we should keep one boot in the treasure house of the past, reminding us that we are inescapably part of the human continuum, while the other boot slithers about in a contemporary maelstrom."

Arkansas Repertory Theatre

Programs and services

Training program; speaker's bureau; seminars; workshops for teachers, the handicapped and minorities; career guidance sessions; performances for students and the hearing-impaired.

PRODUCTIONS 1981-82

The Rainmaker, N. Richard Nash; dir: Michael Maggio

A Christmas Carol, adapt: Frederick Gaines, from Charles Dickens; dir: Gary Gisselman

Waiting for Godot, Samuel Beckett; dir: Gary Gisselman

Misalliance, George Bernard Shaw; dir: Michael Maggio

As You Like It, William Shakespeare; dir: Gary Gisselman

The Gin Game, D.L. Coburn; dir: Jon Cranney

Tintypes, music and lyrics: various; adapt: Mary Kyte, Mel Marvin and Gary Pearle; dir: Gary Gisselman and Lewis Whitlock

PRODUCTIONS 1982-83

What the Butler Saw, Joe Orton; dir: Gary Gisselman

A Christmas Carol

Journey's End, R.C. Sherriff; dir: Jon Cranney

Mass Appeal, Bill C. Davis; dir: Jay Broad

Uncle Vanya, Anton Chekhov; dir: Gary Gisselman

The Dining Room, A.R. Gurney, Jr.; dir: Jon Cranney

A Funny Thing Happened on the Way to the Forum, book: Bert Shevelove and Larry Gelbart; music and lyrics: Stephen Sondheim; dir: Gary Gisselman

DESIGNERS

Sets: Jack Barkla, Gene Davis Buck, Peter Davis, Kent Dorsey, Don Yunker.

Costumes: Jared Aswegan, Jack Barkla, Christopher Beesely, Gene Davis Buck, Sally Cleveland, Bobbi Culbert, David Kay Mickelsen.

Lights: Don Darnutzer, Kent Dorsey, John B. Forbes, Steven B. Peterson, Michael Vennerstrom.

CLIFF F. BAKER
Artistic Director

LYNN FRAZIER
Acting General Manager

CAROLINE PUGH
Board President

712 East 11th St.
Little Rock, AR 72202
(501) 378-0405

FOUNDED 1976
Cliff F. Baker

SEASON
September-June

SCHEDULE

Evenings
Tuesday-Sunday

Matinees
Sunday

FACILITIES
Seating capacity: 112
Stage: flexible

FINANCES
July 1, 1982-June 30, 1983
$351,000 operating expenses
$190,000 earned income
$160,000 grants/contributions

AUDIENCE
Annual attendance: 40,000
Subscribers: 1,500

TOURING CONTACT
Guy Couch

BOOKED-IN EVENTS
Theatre, dance

The Arkansas Repertory Theatre is committed to creative performance and innovative program development. Now entering its eighth season, Arkansas Rep exemplifies the phenomenal growth and success which a resident theatre can enjoy with a responsive public, an emphasis on artistic quality and sound management.

The Rep presents a five-production mainstage season balancing contemporary works, classics and original pieces. Each year two productions are selected for statewide touring, as well as regional touring through Mid-America Arts Alliance. A workshop theatre series, New Stage, consists of two productions each season of an experimental nature, or original works.

Both Arkansas Rep and its founding director Cliff F. Baker are committed to the development of programs serving people not traditionally considered "culture consumers." The largest of these is an artists-in-schools program which yearly provides hundreds of performances and workshops to Arkansas students and teachers. An innovative workshop program involving gifted high school students on a semester-long basis has also been developed.

The actors and actresses who compose the resident company bring a variety of talents and experience to Arkansas Rep and have been drawn from across the nation. In order to increase the opportunities for professional training in Arkansas, an internship/apprenticeship program has been established.

Arkansas Rep's primary goals during the coming year are audience development, an increased subscription base and development of a capital campaign for renovation. Education and touring programs reflect the theatre's statewide commitment and provide important cultural opportunities for thousands of Arkansans. The underlying concept of "ensemble" is very important and affects all facets of the organization. Arkansas Rep looks for works that challenge the company and the audiences. A varied season, growing outreach programs and a versatile company have made Arkansas Rep a major institution in the state.

Arkansas Repertory Theatre. Becke Wilenski, Caroline Pugh and Ronald Aulgur in Hay Fever. *Photo: Andrew Kilgore.*

Programs and services

Artists-in-Schools program; state and regional touring; internships.

PRODUCTIONS 1981-82

Starting Here, Starting Now, music: David Shire; lyrics: Richard Maltby, Jr.; dir: Cliff F. Baker
Scapino, adapt: Frank Dunlop and Jim Dale; dir: Montgomery Kuklenski
America Hurrah, Jean-Claude van Itallie; dir: Cliff F. Baker
The Subject Was Roses, Frank D. Gilroy; dir: Montgomery Kuklenski
Oh, What a Lovely War, adapt: Joan Littlewood; dir: Cliff F. Baker

PRODUCTIONS 1982-83

The Gin Game, D.L. Coburn; dir: Cliff F. Baker
Bonjour, là, Bonjour, Michel Tremblay; trans: John Van Burek and Bill Glassco; dir: Cliff F. Baker
A Lesson from Aloes, Athol Fugard; dir: Montgomery Kuklenski
A Christmas Carol, adapt: Tom Markus, from Charles Dickens; dir: Montgomery Kuklenski
The Workroom, Jean-Claude Grumberg; adapt and trans: Daniel A. Stein and Sara O'Connor; dir: Cliff F. Baker
Hay Fever, Noel Coward; dir: Cliff F. Baker
Can Can, book: Abe Burrows; music and lyrics: Cole Porter; dir: Cliff F. Baker

DESIGNERS

Sets: Kathy Gray, Michael Murray, Mike Nichols, Michael Smith, Robert Lewis Smith, Don Yanik.
Costumes: Cyndy Campbell, Morgan James, Maggie Luypers.
Lights: Kathy Gray.

Asolo State Theater

JOHN ULMER
Artistic Director

RICHARD G. FALLON
Executive Director

DAVID S. LEVENSON
Managing Director

WENTON STEWART
Board President

Postal Drawer E
Sarasota, FL 33578
(813) 355-7115 (business)
(813) 355-2771 (box office)

FOUNDED 1960
Arthur Dorlang, Richard G. Fallon, Eberle Thomas, Robert Strane

SEASON
December-July

SCHEDULE
Evenings
Tuesday-Sunday

Matinees
Wednesday, Sunday

FACILITIES
Asolo Theater
Ringling Museums
5401 Bayshore Road
Seating capacity: 320
Stage: proscenium

FINANCES
October 1, 1981-September 30, 1982
$1,483,000 operating expenses
ff   944,000 earned income
ff   602,000 grants/contributions

AUDIENCE
Annual attendance: 214,667
Subscribers: 2,225

TOURING CONTACT
Linda M. DiGabriele

AEA LORT (C) contract

The Asolo State Theater's three-fold program (Mainstage Company, Acting Conservatory, educational and other touring ac-

Asolo State Theater. Isa Thomas, Elizabeth Harrell and Alan Brooks in Picnic. *Photo: Gary W. Sweetman.*

tivities) radiates from a clear and central artistic vision focusing on the highest quality in all areas: acting, directing, design and technical theatre. Seasons are formulated by a play committee composed of staff members from all departments of the theatre and new plays are read by the artistic staff as well as a larger resident committee. Research and surveys have been completed to determine the popularity and quality of works as well as their marketing feasibility.

The Asolo was founded as an actor's theatre, where the presence, scope and versatility of the actor are expressed in a variety of roles from classical to contemporary. Similarly, the actor's impact is felt in formal and informal programs with the Acting Conservatory through workshops, understudy activities and class visits. Rehearsals for the Mainstage Company begin in mid-November for a season which closes in July and is divided into various combinations of rotating repertory and straight-run productions. Within the repertory segments of the season, shows are cast with productive use of the company in mind.

Since tourism is a major industry, the schedule is planned so that Asolo audiences may see as many as three plays during a short visit to Sarasota, and every effort is made to ensure diversity in the season's makeup. Consequently, the typical Asolo season is eclectic. A second facility is now in the planning stages and will be used primarily as the site for Conservatory productions, workshops and classes; new and experimental plays; and world premieres planned specifically for the facility.

Programs and services

Acting Conservatory; internships in stage management, lighting, costuming, directing and management; school tours; staged readings; student productions; newsletter; volunteer activities; lectures.

Note: During the 1981-82 season, Stuart Vaughan served as artistic advisor.

PRODUCTIONS 1982

A Midsummer Night's Dream, William Shakespeare; dir: Gregory Abels
Mrs. Warren's Profession, George Bernard Shaw; dir: Donald Madden
The Show-Off, George Kelly; dir: Thomas Gruenewald
The All Night Strut!, adapt: Fran Charnas; music and lyrics: various; dir: Jim Hoskins
Charley's Aunt, Brandon Thomas; dir: Stuart Vaughan
The Male Animal, James Thurber and Elliott Nugent; dir: Jonathan Bolt
Girl of the Golden West, David Belasco; dir: Stuart Vaughan

PRODUCTIONS 1983

The Dining Room, A.R. Gurney, Jr.; dir: Isa Thomas
A View from the Bridge, Arthur Miller; dir: John Ulmer
Misalliance, George Bernard Shaw; dir: Norris Houghton
Man with a Load of Mischief, book: Ben Tarver; music: John Clifton; lyrics: John Clifton and Ben Tarver; dir: Jim Hoskins
Sherlock Holmes, William Gillette and Arthur Conan Doyle; dir: John Ulmer
The Winslow Boy, Terence Rattigan; dir: James Kirkland
Dark of the Moon, Howard Richardson and William Berney; dir: Sheldon Epps

DESIGNERS

Sets: Bennett Averyt, Sam Bagarella, Peter Dean Beck, Thomas Cariello, Jeff Dean, John Doepp, John Ezell, Gordon Micunis.
Costumes: Catherine King, Sally Kos, Vicki Holden.
Lights: Martin Petlock.

The Attic Theatre

LAVINIA MOYER
Artistic Director

DANIEL YURGAITIS
Managing Director

JOSEPH GILLIS
Board Chairman

525 East Lafayette
Detroit, MI 48226
(313) 963-7750 (business)
(313) 963-7789 (box office)

FOUNDED 1976
Lavinia Moyer, Divina Cook, Nancy Shaynes, Herbert Ferrer, James Moran

SEASON
Year-round

SCHEDULE
Evenings
Thursday-Sunday

FACILITIES
Seating capacity: 175-200
Stage: thrust

FINANCES
October 1, 1981-September 30, 1982
$153,000 operating expenses
$140,000 earned income
$ 59,000 grants/contributions

AUDIENCE
Annual attendance: 28,000
Subscribers: 335

TOURING CONTACT
Daniel Yurgaitis

BOOKED-IN EVENTS
Theatre

AEA letter of agreement

The Attic Theatre is now in its eighth year of bringing top quality theatre productions to Detroit audiences. As Detroit's only year-round professional resident theatre, the Attic presents seven contemporary plays annually, performed by professional actors in an intimate, 190-seat space.

Most plays at the Attic are new to Michigan; some are world premieres. The Attic has showcased the work of more than a thousand local artists, and has been praised by local, state and national media for its adventurous, challenging programming. The repertoire arises from social concern and literary mission: the main criterion in play selection is that it present a unique theatrical experience for both the audience and the ensemble of actors.

In addition to the mainstage season, the Attic's services extend to some 23,000 people throughout the community through various educational and community outreach programs designed to develop both talent and audiences. In moving its artists into the field, the Attic presents quality performances and instruction to people young and old who might not otherwise experience professional theatre. Through its New Playwrights Forum in particular, the Attic is able to foster the development of new works; on several occasions, mainstage productions by area playwrights have resulted.

The Attic believes that the arts are important to the economy of the city of Detroit, in addition to enhancing the overall culture and appeal of the city's life. Its goal is to make resident arts entertainment a major attraction, a viable industry that thrives in a city traditionally known as a blue collar industrial town.

Programs and services

New Playwrights Forum of monthly staged readings; Oldsters Performing Troupe: senior citizen improvisational company; Midnight Theatre Showcases; arts workshops.

PRODUCTIONS 1981-82

Macbeth, William Shakespeare; dir: James Smith
Watch on the Rhine, Lillian Hellman; dir: Yolanda Fleisher
A Coupla White Chicks Sitting Around Talking, John Ford Noonan; dir: Nora Chester
Cisterns, Julie Jensen; dir: Martin LaPlatney

The Attic Theatre. Catrina Ganey and Roosevelt Johnson in Warp. *Photo: Eric Smith.*

Barter Theatre

Spokesong, book and lyrics: Stewart Parker; music: Jimmy Kennedy; dir: Elisabeth Orion

Working, book adapt: Stephen Schwartz, from Studs Terkel; music and lyrics: Stephen Schwartz, et al.; dir: Daniel Yurgaitis

The Diviners, James Leonard, Jr.; dir: Lavinia Moyer

PRODUCTIONS 1982-83

March of the Falsettos, William Finn; dir: Daniel Yurgaitis

To Grandmother's House We Go, Joanna M. Glass; dir: Randall Forte

Zastrozzi, George F. Walker; dir: Martin LaPlatney

Translations, Brian Friel; dir: James Richards

Between Daylight and Boonville, Matt Williams; dir: Richard Buzinski

Warp I: My Battlefield, My Body!, book: Bury St. Edmund and Stuart Gordon; music: William J. Norris and Richard Fire; dir: William J. Norris

Warp II: Unleashed, Unchained!, book: Bury St. Edmund and Stuart Gordon; music: William J. Norris and Richard Fire; dir: Richard Buzinski

Warp III; To Die . . . Alive!, book: Bury St. Edmund and Stuart Gordon; music: William J. Norris and Richard Fire; dir: Richard Buzinski

DESIGNERS

Sets: Michael Brooks, Gary Decker, Jeff Guzik, Rick Paul, Sam Pollak, James Smith, P.C. Vandenburg, Daniel Yurgaitis, Joe Zubrick.

Costumes: Martha Butler, Deni Deyonker, Johanna Forte, Cookie Gluck, Barbara Holcomb, Katherine S. Holkeboer, Paula Kalevas, Helen King, Barbara Olexzczuk, Bernadine Vida.

Lights: Paul Brohan, Gary Decker, Paul Epton, Jeff Guzik, Rich Latta.

REX PARTINGTON
Producing Director

FILLMORE McPHERSON
Board President

Abingdon, VA 24210
(703) 628-2281 (business)
(703) 628-3991 (box office)

FOUNDED 1933
Robert Porterfield

SEASON
April-March

SCHEDULE

Evenings
Tuesday-Sunday

Matinees
Wednesday, Saturday

FACILITIES

Barter Theatre
Seating capacity: 380
Stage: proscenium

Harris Theatre
George Mason University
4400 University Drive
Fairfax, VA
Seating capacity: 533
Stage: proscenium

FINANCES
November 1, 1981-October 31, 1982
$1,014,000 operating expenses
$ 562,000 earned income
$ 299,000 grants/contributions

AUDIENCE
Annual attendance: 92,799
Subscribers: 8,037

TOURING CONTACT
Pearl Hayter

AEA Lort (C) contract

On June 10, 1983, the Barter Theatre celebrated the completion of 50 years of professional theatre.

The Barter was founded during the height of the Depression by an enterprising young actor named Robert Porterfield. His unique idea was to allow patrons to exchange food for theatre tickets, thus allowing the region's principal inhabitants, the farmers, an opportunity to see live theatre. It also allowed the 22 actors in his company to act and eat. So, in the summer of 1933, this "barter system" gave the theatre its name.

In 1946, Barter became the first State Theatre in the nation. Assisted by an appropriation from the Virginia legislature, the Barter Players toured throughout the Commonwealth, providing Virginia residents with professional theatre. Three years later, the Barter production of *Hamlet* was chosen to represent the United States at Kronberg Castle in Elsinore, Denmark.

When the grand old Empire Theatre in New York City was torn down in 1953, Barter received much of the interior to redecorate the former Abingdon City Hall (circa 1830) which houses the theatre.

Following Robert Porterfield's death in 1971, Rex Partington became the theatre's producing director. In addition to its six-month resident season in Abingdon and a lengthy tour throughout Virginia and the neighboring states, the Barter Players are now in residence December through mid-March at George Mason University, in Fairfax, Virginia.

Barter Theatre is dedicated to presenting quality productions of important plays, classic and contemporary. Ideally, the plays, whether brand new or 2,500 years old, comedy or drama, will have relevance for the Barter's audiences.

Programs and services

Student performances and study materials; student ticket discounts; post-performance discussions; artistic, administrative and technical internships; apprentice program; state and national touring; children's theatre; workshop productions and staged readings; newsletter.

PRODUCTIONS 1981-82

The Corn Is Green, Emlyn Williams; dir: Rex Partington
Deathtrap, Ira Levin; dir: John Olon
On Golden Pond, Ernest Thompson; dir: Fred Chappell
Talley's Folly, Lanford Wilson; dir: Lawrence Kornfeld

The Heiress, Ruth and Augustus Goetz; dir: John Olon
Love's Labour's Lost, William Shakespeare; dir: Ada Brown Mather
You Can't Take It with You, George S. Kaufman and Moss Hart; dir: Thomas Gruenewald
Hedda Gabler, Henrik Ibsen; adapt: John Osborne; dir: Paul Berman
The Matchmaker, Thorton Wilder; dir: Rex Partington
Tintypes, music and lyrics: various; adapt: Mary Kyte, Mel Marvin and Gary Pearle; dir: Pamela Hunt
I Ought to Be in Pictures, Neil Simon; dir: Ken Costigan
The Mousetrap, Agatha Christie; dir: Dorothy Marie Robinson

PRODUCTIONS 1982-83

Hedda Gabler
The Matchmaker
The Mousetrap
Hay Fever, Noel Coward; dir: Dorothy Marie Robinson
Tintypes
Bus Stop, William Inge; dir: Ken Costigan
Fallen Angels, Noel Coward; dir: Harry Ellerby
Da, Hugh Leonard; dir: Ken Costigan
The Dining Room, A.R. Gurney, Jr.: dir: William Van Keyser
Dial M for Murder, Frederick Knott; dir: Harry Ellerby
Side by Side by Sondheim, music and lyrics: Stephen Sondheim, et al; adapt: Ned Sherrin; dir: Pamela Hunt

DESIGNERS

Sets: Bennett Averyt, Daniel H. Ettinger, John C. Larrance, Lynn Pecktal, Bob Phillips.
Costumes: Nancy Atkinson, Georgia Baker, Barbara Forbes, C.L. Hundley, Sigrid Insull, Rachel Kurland, Judianna Makovsky.
Lights: Charles Beatty, Daniel H. Ettinger, Al Oster, Tony Partington, Christopher H. Shaw.

Barter Theatre. Cleo Holladay, George Hosmer and Gerry Goodman in The Matchmaker. Photo: Bill Adams.

Berkeley Repertory Theatre

MICHAEL W. LEIBERT
Producing Director

MITZI SALES
Managing Director

NARSAI DAVID
Board President

2025 Addison St.
Berkeley, CA 94704
(415) 841-6108 (business)
(415) 845-4700 (box office)

FOUNDED 1968
Michael W. Leibert

SEASON
September-August

SCHEDULE
Evenings
Tuesday-Sunday

Matinees
Thursday, Saturday, Sunday

FACILITIES
Mainstage
Seating capacity: 401
Stage: thrust

Second Stage
Seating capacity: 70
Stage: flexible

FINANCES
September 1, 1982-August 31, 1983
$1,344,000 operating expenses
$1,084,000 earned income
$ 260,000 grants/contributions

AUDIENCE
Annual attendance: 118,000
Subscribers: 10,852

AEA LORT (C) contract

Berkeley Repertory Theatre is committed to presenting superior productions of classical, contemporary and new plays. Plays are selected for their ability to affect the way we think, feel and act in our individual lives. In recognition of the fact that theatre must captivate and entertain, the Rep seeks to create on stage a world which evokes an aesthetic

Berkeley Repertory Theatre. Heartbreak House. *Photo: Ken Friedman.*

response and illluminates the human condition.

Berkeley Rep uses many voices to reach its audiences. A diverse repertoire has kept the theatre dynamic and interesting; a recent focus on the development of new work for mainstage productions stems from the desire to find plays that are relevant and timely, plays that speak directly to the Rep's audiences and concerns.

The vitality of Berkeley Rep springs from the energy of its artistic company. This energy is nurtured through a strong commitment to the ensemble: material is chosen to stretch each artist while promoting the collaborative effort. Actors, directors, designers and technicians are encouraged to work closely together in order to synthesize a fresh vision. Above all, Berkeley Rep seeks to create a supportive environment for its theatre artists.

The Berkeley Rep believes that the theatre should be responsive to the philosophical and social concerns of its community. Artistic decisions and the development of audience services and outreach programs reflect this conviction.

Programs and services

Technical internships; Playworks staged readings; Lives in the Theatre lectures; newsletters; signed performances; Sennheiser Infrared Listening System; student matinees; community outreach presentations.

PRODUCTIONS 1981-82

The Cherry Orchard, Anton Chekhov; dir: James Moll
The Belle of Amherst, William Luce; dir: Michael W. Leibert
As You Like It, William Shakespeare; dir: Gregory Boyd
Savages, Christopher Hampton; dir: Tony Amendola
After the Fall, Arthur Miller; dir: Peter Layton
Heartbreak House, George Bernard Shaw; dir: Albert Takazauckas
The Diary of Anne Frank, Francis Goodrich and Albert Hackett; dir: Joy Carlin
Tonight at 8:30, Noel Coward; dir: Alex Kinney and Larry Berthelot

PRODUCTIONS 1982-83

Happy End, book and lyrics: Bertolt Brecht; music: Kurt Weill; adapt: Michael Feingold; dir: Michael W. Leibert
Chekhov In Yalta, John Driver and Jeffrey Haddow; dir: Albert Takazauckas
The Glass Menagerie, Tennessee Williams; dir: Michael W. Leibert
The Show-Off, George Kelly; dir: John Raymond Freimann
Beyond Therapy, Christopher Durang; dir: Joy Carlin
A Lesson from Aloes, Athol Fugard; dir: Ann Bowen
U.S.A., John Dos Passos and Paul Shyre; dir: Joy Carlin
Geoff Hoyle Meets Keith Terry, Geoff Hoyle and Keith Terry; dir: Joy Carlin

DESIGNERS

Sets: Mark Donnelly, Karen Gjelsteen, Jesse Hollis, Henry May, Richard G. Norgard, Ron Pratt, Gene Angell, Tom Rasmussen, Victoria Smith, Warren Travis, Bernard Vyzga.
Costumes: Robert Blackman, William P. Brewer II, Deborah Brothers-Lowry, Jeannie Davidson, Deborah Dryden, Lorraine Forman, Toni Lovaglia, Robert Morgan, Tom Rasmussen, Warren Travis, Walter Watson.
Lights: Joan Arhelger, Mark Bosch, Derek Duarte, Barbara DuBois, Larry French, Robert Peterson, Tom Rusika, Betty Schneider, Greg Sullivan.

Berkeley Shakespeare Festival

DAKIN MATTHEWS
Artistic Director

CAROL ZIMMERMAN
Administrative Director

BRAD BUNNIN
Board President

Box 969
Berkeley, CA 94701
(415) 548-3422

FOUNDED 1974
Bay Area actors

SEASON
June-December

SCHEDULE

Evenings
Wednesday-Sunday

Matinees
Wednesday, Sunday

FACILITIES

John Hinkel Park
Southampton and San Diego Roads
Seating capacity: 350
Stage: thrust

Veteran's Memorial Auditorium
1931 Center St.
Seating capacity: 450
Stage: flexible

FINANCES
January 1, 1982-December 31, 1982
$382,000 operating expenses
$261,000 earned income
$ 89,000 grants/contributions

AUDIENCE
Annual attendance: 35,000
Subscribers: 2,500

TOURING CONTACT
Carol Zimmerman

AEA LORT (D) contract

A Shakespeare company whose performances strive to entrance children and the uninitiated, while satisfying the most discerning critic: that's the Berkeley Shakespeare Festival. Situated outdoors in charming John Hinkel Park, utilizing a simple platform stage and semi-circular seating arrangement on a steep, terraced hillside, the Festival creates a direct, intimate relationship between players and audience.

The Festival's approach places primary emphasis on the clarity of the spoken word and on a strong, lucid, interpretive line of movement through the text. The company maintains a strong commitment to producing difficult or lesser-known plays, and developing production and performance styles that are swift, direct and eloquent.

BSF's 10th anniversary season in 1983 was a celebration of that peculiarly Shakespearean power to present characters from multiple points of view, offering clear visions from shifting perspectives. Complementary plays were chosen from each genre and performed in repertory to illustrate the wide range of Shakespeare's responses to his world.

From 1979 to 1982, the Festival experienced tremendous growth in most aspects of its operations. Ticket sales reached over 90 percent of capacity, and with the addition of a winter production to the schedule in 1981, the annual number of performances increased from 60 to 105. In 1983, the paid staff included 61 artists, technicians and administrators, augmented by 10 student interns and more than 40 community volunteers.

Begun in 1979, the Festival's Educational Institute offers classes, lectures and work-

Berkeley Shakespeare Festival. Lura Dolas, Annette Bening and Anne McNaughton in Romeo and Juliet. *Photo: Allen Nomura.*

shops for students at all levels. An apprentice program was added in 1983 to provide on-stage experience and intensive training for young professionals.

Dakin Matthews, the Festival's new artistic director, is an actor, director and dramaturg who brings extensive experience in resident professional theatre to his role.

Programs and services

Apprentice program; internships; Educational Institute; newsletter; post-performance discussions; classes for teachers of Shakespeare.

Note: During the 1982 season, Peter Layton served as executive producer.

PRODUCTIONS 1982

Antony and Cleopatra, William Shakespeare; dir: Patrick Tucker
All's Well That Ends Well, William Shakespeare; dir: Albert Takazauckas
The Winter's Tale, William Shakespeare; dir: Dakin Matthews
Hamlet, William Shakespeare; dir: Richard E.T. White

PRODUCTIONS 1983

Romeo and Juliet, William Shakespeare; dir: Richard E.T. White
Two Gentlemen of Verona, William Shakespeare; dir: Anne McNaughton
King John, William Shakespeare; dir: Julian Lopez-Morillas
Ivanhoe, company-adapt from Walter Scott; dir: Dakin Matthews
Much Ado About Nothing, William Shakespeare; dir: Anne McNaughton
Macbeth, William Shakespeare; dir: Richard E.T. White

DESIGNERS

Sets: Gene Angell, Michael Cook, Ewald Hackler, Jesse Hollis, Eric Landisman, Peggy McDonald, Ron Pratt, Roger Sherman III, Warren Travis.
Costumes: Barbara Bush, Eliza Shugg, Cathleen Edwards, Douglas Russel, Warren Travis.
Lights: James Brentano, Derek Duarte, Kurt Landisman.

Berkeley Stage Company

ANGELA PATON
Artistic Director

JIM ROYCE
Producing Director

DAVID MALCOLM
Board President

Box 2327
Berkeley, CA 94702
(415) 548-4728

FOUNDED 1974
Angela Paton, Robert W. Goldsby, Drury Pifer

SEASON
October-July

SCHEDULE
Evenings
Tuesday-Saturday

Matinees
Sunday

FACILITIES
Seating capacity: 108
Stage: flexible

FINANCES
October 1, 1981-September 30, 1982
$235,000 operating expenses
$ 88,000 earned income
$120,000 grants/contributions

AUDIENCE
Annual attendance: 18,000
Subscribers: 700

TOURING CONTACT
Jim Royce

BOOKED-IN EVENTS
Theatre, performance art

AEA letter of agreement

Berkeley Stage Company is a theatre where the future is the focus: a training ground where talents are found and nurtured, and a springboard in the research and development of drama. New forms, new voices and—in these precarious times—new means of expression emerge on its flexible stage.

The visual artist and composer join the dramatist in a theatrical and passionate presentation of ideas, questions and problems that engage and baffle the contemporary mind. The artistic emphasis is on a truly *living* theatre.

Programs and services

Staged readings; touring; Speakeasies: public discussions after performances.

Berkeley Stage Company. Helen Hughes and Robert Goldsby in Seascape. Photo: Jerry Morse.

Berkshire Theatre Festival

PRODUCTIONS 1981-82

Laughter in the Far Dark, John Allen; dir: Martin Berman
Elizabeth Dead, George W.S. Trow; dir: Robert W. Goldsby
Damien, Aldyth Morris; dir: Nola Hague
Paul Robeson, Phillip Hayes Dean; dir: Luther James
Letters Home, adapt: Rose Leiman Goldemberg, from Sylvia Plath; dir: Anne McNaughton
Mother Courage and Her Children, Bertolt Brecht; trans: Ralph Manheim; dir: Robert MacDougall
Continental Drift, Elizabeth Wray; dir: Ron Pratt
The Maids, Jean Genet; dir: Anne McNaughton
The Needle's Eye, Robert MacDougall; dir: Robert MacDougall
Maledetto, Ken Gaburo; dir: Robert MacDougall
I/O: A Ritual for 23 Performers, Roger Reynolds; dir: Robert MacDougall

PRODUCTIONS 1982-83

The Vienna Notes, Richard Nelson; dir: Angela Paton
Seascape, Edward Albee; dir: Robert W. Goldsby
Starz, Stripes . . . Forever, Stephan Regina-Thon; dir: Robert MacDougall
Sea Marks, Gardner McKay; dir: Angela Paton
Passione, Albert Innaurato; dir: Robert W. Goldsby
Theatre Festival of New Music I, various authors; dir: Robert MacDougall

DESIGNERS

Sets: Gene Angell, Loy Arcenas, Ariel, William Eddelman, Ewald Hackler, Peggy McDonald, Ron Pratt, James Sims, Warren Travis.
Costumes: Loy Arcenas, Ariel, Barbara Bush, Celia McCarthy, Jill Neff, Celestine Ranney, James Sims, Warren Travis, Roberta Yuen.
Lights: Kurt Landisman, Doug Nelson, Jeff Schuenke.

JOSEPHINE R. ABADY
Artistic Director

JOAN STEIN
Managing Director

JANE P. FITZPATRICK
Board President

Box 218
Stockbridge, MA 01262
(413) 298-5536 (business)
(413) 298-5576 (box office)

FOUNDED 1928
Mabel Choate, Walter Clark, Daniel Chester, Austin Riggs

SEASON
June-September

SCHEDULE
Evenings
Tuesday-Saturday
Matinees
Thursday, Saturday

Berkshire Theatre Festival. George Grizzard and Joyce Krempel in Harvey. *Photo: Walter Scott.*

FACILITIES

Berkshire Playhouse
Seating capacity: 429
Stage: proscenium

Unicorn Theatre
Seating capacity: 100
Stage: thrust

Unicorn Courtyard
Seating capacity: 100
Stage: flexible

FINANCES
September 1, 1981–August 31, 1982
$525,000 operating expenses
$345,000 earned income
$186,000 grants/contributions

AUDIENCE
Annual attendance: 26,202
Subscribers: 476

AEA Council on Resident Stock Theatre contract

Now looking forward to its 56th season, the Berkshire Theatre Festival in Stockbridge, Mass. is dedicated exclusively to the presentation and preservation of American theatre art. Since 1928, the historic Stockbridge Playhouse—the Festival's mainstage—has been providing a home where America's most talented players and most respected plays come alive each summer. The Festival is maintaining the swiftly fading traditions of summer stock, a vital link in our nation's artistic heritage.

The Festival sees itself not only as a link with America's theatrical past, but as a living bridge to its future. Its theatre training program is the oldest of its kind in the country, offering young people the opportunity to learn from and work side-by-side with experienced, dedicated and gifted professionals. In a community of interchange and interdependence, generations come together within the tradition of the theatre.

The BTF's Children's Theatre is dedicated to developing mature and appreciative audiences necessary to guarantee the survival of the American theatre of the future.

The Berkshire Theatre Festival's goals are to continue and to grow, ever expanding its audiences and producing American plays of quality on all three of its stages. It intends to maintain its programs in theatre training, new play development—including the full-scale production of new plays as well as a playreading series—and young audience development.

Programs and services

Playreading series; Greenroom Chats post-play discussions; Friday Night Live showcase presentations by apprentices; apprenticeships; internships.

PRODUCTIONS 1981-82

A View from the Bridge, Arthur Miller; dir: Josephine R. Abady
House of Blue Leaves, John Guare; dir: A.J. Antoon
A Safe Place, Carol Mack; dir: Josephine R. Abady
Two for the Seesaw, William Gibson; dir: Ted Weiant
In Celebration of Ruth Draper, Ruth Draper; dir: David Kaplan
Whatchamacallums & Thingamajigs, Peter Frisch; dir: Peter Frisch

PRODUCTIONS 1982-83

Sunrise at Campobello, Dore Schary; dir: Josephine R. Abady
The Animal Kingdom, Philip Barry; dir: John Wulp
A Thousand Clowns, Herb Gardner; dir: Josephine R. Abady
The Palace of Amateurs, John Faro PiRoman; dir: A.J. Antoon
Waiting for Lefty, Clifford Odets; dir: Peter Frisch
Class, John Lipsky and Steven Wangh; dir: Peter Frisch
The Broken and the Beautiful, adapt: Peter Frisch, from Hans Christian Andersen; dir: Peter Frisch

DESIGNERS

Sets: James Leonard Joy, John Kasarda, Susan Peterson, David Potts, Steve Saklad, Patricia Woodbridge.
Costumes: Roberta Brown, Zoe Brown, Linda Fisher, Del Risberg, Ann Roth, Christa Scholtz.
Lights: Jeff Davis, Stuart Duke.

BoarsHead:

RICHARD THOMSEN
Artistic Director

JOHN PEAKES
Producing Director

BARBARA CARLISLE
Managing Director

JANE WILENSKY
Board Chair

425 South Grand Ave.
Lansing, MI 48933
(517) 484-7800 (business)
(517) 484-7805 (box office)

FOUNDED 1970
Richard Thomsen, John Peakes

SEASON
October–August

SCHEDULE
Evenings
Thursday–Sunday

Matinees
Saturday, Sunday

FACILITIES
Center for the Arts
Seating capacity: 249
Stage: thrust

FINANCES
October 1, 1981–September 30, 1982
$326,000 operating expenses
$207,000 earned income
$106,000 grants/contributions

AUDIENCE
Annual attendance: 48,000
Subscribers: 1,500

TOURING CONTACT
Barbara Carlisle

AEA LORT (D) contract, letter of agreement

BoarsHead: Michigan Public Theater exists as the center for theatre in its region and must, therefore, function as both museum and laboratory, presenting a season balanced between established and new works. The

Michigan Public Theater

focus remains the audience. Each production must be accessible, must address the concerns of the time—and then, it is hoped, remain with its audience beyond the moment.

The resident company remains committed to the idea of an expanding theatre, reaching into the community and the state on several levels. New works tour statewide; new pieces are developed by area writers; designs are commissioned from area artists. The effort to involve new talent and find new audiences is central.

The theatre exists for the company as well, providing time and space for individual growth and development within an identifiable community. As a provincial company, BoarsHead constantly works toward development of a style, a voice, a place within the national theatre.

At its core, then, is the theatre's determination to give dramatic shape to the needs of a particular people at this time, in the belief that only the particular can make a universal statement.

Programs and services

Production and management internships; artist-in-schools residencies; Michigan Young Playwrights Festival; college-accredited summer apprentice program; residency at Blue Lake Fine Arts Camp; spring tour; All Peoples Theater troupe for the handicapped.

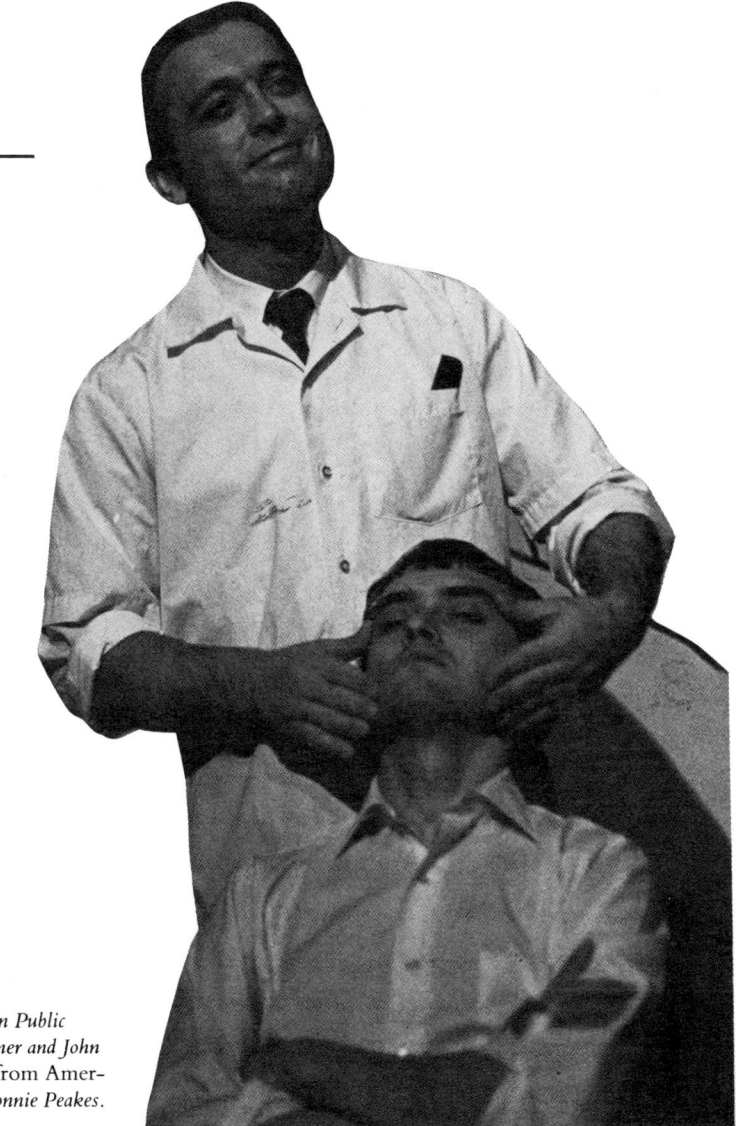

BoarsHead: Michigan Public Theater. Buck Schirner and John Bowman in Scenes from American Life. *Photo: Connie Peakes.*

PRODUCTIONS 1981-82

The Elephant Man, Bernard Pomerance; dir: John Peakes
The Chinese Viewing Pavillion, Gus Kaikkonen; dir: Richard Thomsen
Fridays, Andrew Johns; dir: Gus Kaikkonen
The Gin Game, D.L. Coburn; dir: Maggie Thatcher
Talley's Folly, Lanford Wilson; dir: John Peakes
Holy Mary, John Faro PiRoman; dir: Richard Thomsen
Strange Snow, Stephen Metcalfe; dir: Claude File
A Coupla White Chicks Sitting Around Talking, John Ford Noonan; dir: Barbara Carlisle
White Linen, Stephen Metcalfe; dir: Richard Thomsen
Feathers, Jeanne Darnelle; dir: John Peakes
I'm Almost Famous, Bob Baldori and Mike Steinberg; dir: Richard Thomsen
The Hypochondriac, Dennis Kennedy; dir: Claude File
A Christmas Carol, adapt: Richard Thomsen, from Charles Dickens; dir: Richard Thomsen
Songs of a Mermaid, Rob Gardner; dir: Claude File

PRODUCTIONS 1982-83

Sister Mary Ignatius Explains It All for You and *The Actor's Nightmare,* Christopher Durang; dir: Richard Thomsen
Second Prize: Two Months in Leningrad, Trish Johnson; dir: Gus Kaikkonen
Scenes from American Life, A.R. Gurney, Jr; dir: Claude File
REO/Internal Combustion, Dennis Kennedy; dir: Bob Hall
How I Got That Story, Amlin Gray; dir: Richard Thomsen
The Miss Firecracker Contest, Beth Henley; dir: John Peakes
Half A Lifetime, Stephen Metcalfe; dir: Nancy Kammer
Josh, Peter Link; dir: Peter Link
Burnish Me Bright, Julia Cunningham; adapt: Jim Burton; dir: Jim Burton
On Golden Pond, Ernest Thompson; dir: Barbara Carlisle
Kenneth and Barbara's Musical Dreamhouse, Nancy Kammer and Claude File; dir: John Peakes
The Sea Horse, Edward J. Moore; dir: Richard Thomsen

DESIGNERS

Sets: Fred Engelgau, Gordon Phetteplace, Tim Stapleton.
Costumes: Patricia K. Smith.
Lights: Gordon Phetteplace.

The Body Politic Theatre

JAMES O'REILLY
Artistic Director

SHARON PHILLIPS
Managing Director

CAROL NIE
Board President

2261 North Lincoln Ave.
Chicago, IL 60614
(312) 348-7901 (business)
(312) 871-3000 (box office)

FOUNDED 1969
Community Arts Foundation

SEASON
February-November

SCHEDULE
Evenings
Thursday-Sunday

Matinees
Sunday

FACILITIES
Seating capacity: 182
Stage: thrust

FINANCES
January 1, 1982-December 31, 1982
$239,000 operating expenses
$111,000 earned income
$ 59,000 grants/contributions

AUDIENCE
Annual attendance: 24,000
Subscribers: 1,600

BOOKED-IN EVENTS
Theatre, music

AEA Chicago Off Loop Theatre contract

The Body Politic Theatre. Lucy Childs and John Reeger in The Taming of the Shrew.
Photo: Jennifer Girard.

The missions of The Body Politic Theatre are to produce seasons of thought-provoking plays from the best of dramatic literature; to provide opportunities for growth to the Chicago-based actor, director, designer and playwright; to pursue outreach into the community; and to maintain accessibility to the general public.

The commitment is to plays of substance, of language—to plays that challenge the imagination. The season reflects this with its emphasis on the classics (particularly Shakespeare), on intriguing new works, and on an occasional revival.

A Body Politic play makes a statement about the human condition. With a penchant for highly theatrical material, there is a constant effort to be honest: to let the plays happen in a clear and straightforward manner. The intimacy of the theatre space—a large thrust with most of the seating on the sides—demands this honesty from the actors. It also demands the participation of the audience. The growth of the theatre's subscriber base indicates an appreciation of this sense of involvement.

There is also a commitment to the actor to provide an experience which stretches his talent and exercises his skills. An immediate and ongoing goal of Body Politic is to develop its own company. Artistic director James O'Reilly identifies the "company actor" as an intelligent, versatile, creative, imaginative player who understands the

Boston Shakespeare Company

balance between ego and ensemble. O'Reilly looks forward to selecting a season *for* a company of actors who trust the playwright, the director and each other. The ultimate goal is to identify a resident playwright who will write for and with this ensemble. As proven by the companies of Shakespeare, Molière and Chekhov, when the artistic mission is so shared, not only the immediate audience benefits, but the audience of the future as well.

Programs and services

Student matinee program; high school internships; signed performances; Bible Story Theatre; lobby gallery; annual street festival.

PRODUCTIONS 1981-82

The Taming of the Shrew, William Shakespeare; dir: James O'Reilly
Eve, adapt: Larry Fineberg, from Constance Beresford-Howe; dir: Susan Dafoe
Confusions, Alan Ayckbourn; dir: Pauline Brailsford
Translations, Brian Friel; dir: James O'Reilly

PRODUCTIONS 1982-83

The Playboy of the Western World, John Millington Synge; dir: James O'Reilly
Zastrozzi, George F. Walker; dir: James O'Reilly
Taking Steps, Alan Ayckbourn; dir: Pauline Brailsford
The Dresser, Ronald Harwood; dir: James O'Reilly

DESIGNERS

Sets: Jeffrey Bauer, Michael Merritt, James O'Reilly, Chris Phillips, John Rodriguez, John Storey.
Costumes: Elizabeth Bailey, Kerry Fleming, Elizabeth Passman, Nan Zabriskie.
Lights: Mary M. Badger, Robert James, Chris Phillips, Michael Rourke, Lynn Ziehe.

Boston Shakespeare Company. Henry Woronicz in Hamlet.

PETER SELLARS
Artistic Director

CHARLES MARZ
Executive Director

HERBERT EISENBERG
Board President

52 St. Botolph St.
Boston, MA 02116
(617) 267-5630 (business)
(617) 267-5600 (box office)

FOUNDED 1975
William Cain, Norman Frisch, Janet Buchwald

SEASON
October-May

SCHEDULE
Evenings
Tuesday-Sunday

Matinees
Sunday

FACILITIES
Mainstage
Seating capacity: 450
Stage: flexible

Downstairs
Seating capacity: 100
Stage: flexible

FINANCES
July 1, 1982-June 30, 1983
$400,000 operating expenses
$320,000 earned income
$ 80,000 grants/contributions

AUDIENCE
Annual attendance: 135,000
Subscribers: 3,000

TOURING CONTACT
Margaret Cleveland

BOOKED-IN EVENTS
Theatre, music, dance

In 1778 Goethe titled his new journal *Propylaen,* after the gateway of the Acropolis: "The youth who begins to feel the attraction of nature and art believes that a serious effort alone will enable him to penetrate to their inner sanctuary; but the *man* discovers that even after lengthy wanderings up and down, he is still in the forecourt.

"This is what has given rise to our title; the step, the door, the entrance, the antechamber, the space between the inner and

the outer, the sacred and the profane, this is the place we choose as the meeting ground for exchanges with our friends."

Named after Shakespeare, the company's plans for the new season under the direction of Peter Sellars include renaissance, restoration, rehabilitation, research, development. Means include family entertainment, operas, plays, films, concerts, civic occasions and environmental events.

In the words of T.S. Mayer, "High wit and tragedy, these are your aspirations. And sometimes you achieve them. But farce and melodrama are the facts. They always were."

The special topic under exploration at the Shakespeare Company in 1983-84 is the Search for True Comedy.

Programs and services

Touring; programs-in-schools; staged readings; internships; concert and film series; signed performances.

Note: During the 1981-82 season, William Cain served as artistic director; during the 1982-83 season, Gavin Cameron-Webb served as artistic director.

PRODUCTIONS 1981-82

Hamlet, William Shakespeare; dir: William Cain

Rosencrantz and Guildenstern Are Dead, Tom Stoppard; dir: Tom West

Falstaff, adapt: William Cain and Grey Johnson, from William Shakespeare's *Henry IV, Parts I and II;* dir: Grey Johnson

Much Ado About Nothing, William Shakespeare; dir: William Cain

Saint Joan, George Bernard Shaw; dir: William Cain

Othello, William Shakespeare; dir: Tom West

A Lesson from Aloes, Athol Fugard; dir: Henry Woronicz

PRODUCTIONS 1982-83

Romeo and Juliet, William Shakespeare; dir: Gavin Cameron-Webb

Private Lives, Noel Coward; dir: John Hickok

Twelfth Night, William Shakespeare; dir: Kent Thompson

One Flew Over the Cuckoo's Nest, adapt: Dale Wasserman, from Ken Kesey; dir: Gavin Cameron-Webb

Julius Caesar, William Shakespeare; dir: Gavin Cameron-Webb

The Importance of Being Earnest, Oscar Wilde; dir: Francis Cullinan

DESIGNERS

Sets: Charles Cameron, Don Clark, Richard Isaackes, Ned Lyon, Larry Sammons, Pat Trapp, Tom Tutino, Michael Franklin White.

Costumes: Dru Minton Clark, Baker Smith, Craig Sonnenberg.

Lights: Alain Brown, Marcus Dilliard, Nancy Goldstein, William O'Donnell.

Caldwell Playhouse

MICHAEL P. HALL
Managing and Artistic Director

LEON R. DeLIETO
Board Presdient

Box 277
Boca Raton, FL 33432
(305) 368-7611 (business)
(305) 368-7509 (box office)

FOUNDED 1975
James R. Caldwell

SEASON
November-April, July-August

SCHEDULE

Evenings
Tuesday-Sunday

Matinees
Wednesday, Sunday

FACILITIES
Boca Raton Mall
286 North Federal Hwy.
Seating capacity: 245
Stage: proscenium

FINANCES
June 1, 1982–May 31, 1983
$528,000 operating expenses
$393,000 earned income
$110,000 grants/contributions

AUDIENCE
Annual attendance: 50,000
Subscribers: 6,200

AEA LORT (C) contract

Caldwell Playhouse was the inspiration of the late James R. Caldwell, founder of the Rubbermaid Corporation and a prominent Boca Raton civic leader who felt that his city needed a resident theatre company as an addition or alternative to the several road-show houses in South Florida. Under the guidance of director Michael Hall and designer Frank Bennett, the Caldwell Playhouse began production in 1975 as a project of the College of Boca Raton. When the theatre outgrew its campus location, private donations exceeding $250,000 allowed the company to incorporate and build a 245-seat theatre inside a downtown shopping mall. The new facility opened in November 1980 with 6,000 subscribers.

Currently the Caldwell produces six shows a year, combining classics with new works and world premieres. Particularly successful are costume dramas (*The Heiress*), period pieces (*The Barretts of Wimpole Street*) and revivals of outstanding American plays (*The Hasty Heart*). In 1982 the theatre's "Friends," a support organization, sponsored a nationwide playwriting competition with a prize of $1,000 and full production at the Caldwell. The winning play, Lee and Marilyn Nestor's *Even in Laughter*, received so much acclaim that annual competitions are planned. The "Stars for Caldwell," another support group, raises money to offset the cost of company housing.

In 1981 and 1982 the Caldwell won the South Florida Entertainment Writers' Carbonell Awards for Best Play (*Mass Appeal*), Best Director (Michael Hall) and Best Supporting Actress (Barbara Bradshaw). In the past three years, annual attendance has grown from 30,000 to 50,000. Summer seasons were added in 1981 to considerable success.

Caldwell's goal is to present productions of plays of literary merit using a small resident company and numerous guest artists. Strong attention is paid to the importance of the spoken word and to period production details. The theatre's location inside the Boca Raton Mall has created a vibrant cultural atmosphere for one of the nation's fastest-growing areas.

Programs and services

Children's theatre classes; lecture series; playwriting competition; internships; workshops.

PRODUCTIONS 1981-82

Vanities, Jack Heifner
The Elephant Man, Bernard Pomerance
Waltz of the Toreadors, Jean Anouilh
The Heiress, Ruth and Augustus Goetz
Five Finger Exercise, Peter Shaffer
Absence of a Cello, Ira Wallach

PRODUCTIONS 1982-83

Once Upon a Mattress, book; Jay Thompson, et al; music; Mary Rodgers; lyrics; Marshall Barer
Mass Appeal, Bill C. Davis
Even in Laughter, Lee and Marilyn Nestor
The Barretts of Wimpole Street, Rudolf Besier
Light Up the Sky, Moss Hart
Misalliance, George Bernard Shaw

All productions directed by Michael P. Hall

DESIGNERS

Sets: Frank Bennett, Marion Kolsby.
Costumes: Bridget Bartlett.
Lights: Craig R. Ferraro, Joyce Fleming, Jas Myers.

Caldwell Playhouse. Curry Worsham and Barbara Bradshaw in Waltz of the Toreadors. *Photo: Mike Bady.*

Capital Repertory Company

BRUCE BOUCHARD
PETER H. CLOUGH
Producing Directors

DONALD D. O'DOWD
Board Chairman

Box 72
Albany, NY 12201
(518) 462-4531 (business)
(518) 462-4534 (box office)

FOUNDED 1980
Oakley Hall III, Michael Van Landingham

SEASON
October-April

SCHEDULE
Evenings
Tuesday-Saturday

Matinees
Wednesday, Sunday

FACILITIES
Market Theatre
111 North Pearl St.
Seating capacity: 258
Stage: thrust

FINANCES
July 1, 1982-June 30, 1983
$406,000 operating expenses
$229,000 earned income
$177,000 grants/contributions

AUDIENCE
Annual attendance: 25,000
Subscribers: 1,950

AEA LORT (D) contract

Formerly known as the Lexington Conservatory Theatre, in 1980 Capital Repertory Company became the only resident professional theatre in New York's capital district. The first season, while artistically successful, failed to generate the necessary financial support — but led by two new producing directors, Bruce Bouchard and Peter H. Clough, the theatre's subsequent survival was made possible through an alliance of the city of Albany, area businesses, the membership of 10 labor unions and a new board of directors. Capital Rep is now in its third season at the Market Theatre.

The purpose of Capital Rep is to produce classics, contemporary and new plays, each with a strong relevance to the current human condition, promoting dialogue between the theatre and its community. Productions emphasize the vision of the playwright and the actor/director relationship, rather than state-of-the-art technology, in order to give that vision an accessible form and style.

Capital Rep continues its long-standing commitment to new American plays, particularly those by women. The theatre has premiered full productions or readings of such works as *Close Ties* by Elizabeth Diggs, *My Sister in This House* by Wendy Kesselman, *Death of a Miner* by Paula Cizmar and *Territorial Rights* by Carol K. Mack. During each six-play season, the Rep produces at least one new play. The continuing search for new work is carried out by a panel of readers, led by the theatre's staff literary manager.

Plans for the future include playwrights in residence, a regular schedule of staged readings and workshop productions of new plays, and an expansion of the regular performance schedule from three-and-a-half weeks to five weeks per play.

Programs and services

New play readings; student matinees; programs-in-schools; artistic, management and technical internships; discussion series.

PRODUCTIONS 1981-82

Table Manners, Alan Ayckbourn; dir: Michael J. Hume

A Streetcar Named Desire, Tennessee Williams; dir: Louis Schaeffer

Feathers, Jeanne Darnell; dir: Susan Lehman

Frankenstein, adapt: Oakley Hall III and Kathleen Masterson, from Mary Shelley; dir: Peter H. Clough

PRODUCTIONS 1982-83

Sea Marks, Gardner McKay; dir: Gloria Muzio Thayer

Tartuffe, Molière; trans: Richard Wilbur; dir: Bruce Bouchard

True West, Sam Shepard; dir: Pamela Berlin

The Mound Builders, Lanford Wilson; dir: Peter H. Clough

Homesteaders, Nina Shengold; dir: June Stein

The Skin of Our Teeth, Thornton Wilder; dir: Michael J. Hume

DESIGNERS

Sets: Dale F. Jordan, Neil Prince, Ray Recht, Leslie Taylor, Robert Thayer.
Costumes: Barbara Forbes, Heidi Hollmann, Leslie Taylor, Cinthia Waas, Lloyd K. Waiwaiole.
Lights: Mark Di Quinzio, Dale F. Jordan, Lary Opitz, Malcolm Sturchio, Robert Thayer.

Capital Repertory Company. Terry VandenBosch, Shelley Wyant, Jane Jones, Jamey Sheridan and Keith Langsdale in Homesteaders.

Center Stage

STAN WOJEWODSKI, JR.
Artistic Director

PETER W. CULMAN
Managing Director

JOSEPH M. LANGMEAD
Board President

700 North Calvert St.
Baltimore, MD 21202
(301) 685-3200 (business)
(301) 332-0033 (box office)

FOUNDED 1963
Community Arts Committee

SEASON
September-June

SCHEDULE
Evenings
Tuesday-Sunday

Matinees
Wednesday, Saturday, Sunday

FACILITIES
Seating capacity: 541
Stage: modified thrust

FINANCES
July 1, 1982-June 30, 1983
$1,974,000 operating expenses
$1,360,000 earned income
$ 681,000 grants/contributions

AUDIENCE
Annual attendance: 180,000
Subscribers: 15,083

TOURING CONTACT
Victoria Nolan

AEA LORT (B) contract

"Art is not technology and cannot be mastered," wrote Shirley Hazzard in a recent *New York Times* article. "It is an endless access to revelatory states of mind." At Center Stage this "access" is examined through the emergence/evolution of the theatre's directorate and the implementation of the First Stage developmental series as a conduit to full mainstage production.

Seasons emerge in response to specific artistic goals: expanded pre-production research focusing on production and design history of often-produced plays; a more

Center Stage. Savages. Photo: Richard Anderson.

regular investigation of little known work by major playwrights and the collected work of lesser-known authors; comparative readings/analyses of extant translations and the initiation of new translations and adaptations; the search for new sources of contemporary foreign literature; and collective work on textual analyses of established texts —both pre-production and in rehearsal—in the search for solutions to problems in tone.

The search for and development of new scripts and their authors is done within the context of the First Stage program. Its goal is to provide readings, staged readings and workshop productions tailored by the directorate to suit the needs of individual plays and playwrights. Though concerned primarily with new scripts, the secondary goals of First Stage are: the investigation of fresh conceptual approaches to established texts; readings of new translations and adaptations; and the establishment of a laboratory for the discovery of the ambience (production style, appropriate talents, etc.) required by emerging contemporary forms.

The expansion of the directorate and the intensification of the First Stage process is an attempt not only to restate and re-evaluate artistic goals, but, most important, to plan the majority of the repertoire for several seasons through the identification, evolution and support of projects over 12 to 36 months.

Center Stage structures its seasons to include masterworks (both classic and contemporary) and recent work of both American and foreign playwrights. Scripts, both proven and unproven, are chosen to challenge theatre artists and audiences alike.

Programs and services

Technical and administrative internships; First Stage script development program; Noontime Lectures; Humanities Series.

PRODUCTIONS 1981-82

A Lesson from Aloes, Athol Fugard; dir: Jackson Phippin
Much Ado About Nothing, William Shakespeare; dir: Stan Wojewodski, Jr.
The Amen Corner, James Baldwin; dir: Walter Dallas
The Workroom, Jean-Claude Grumberg; adapt: Daniel A. Stein and Sara O'Connor; dir: Stan Wojewodski, Jr.
Terra Nova, Ted Tally; dir: Stan Wojewodski, Jr.
Savages, Christopher Hampton; dir: Jackson Phippin
Griffin! Griffin!, adapt: Russell Davis, from Frank Stockton; dir: Lenore Blank

PRODUCTIONS 1982-83

Last Looks, Grace McKeaney; dir: Jackson Phippin
The Miser, Moliere; adapt: Miles Malleson; dir: Stan Wojewodski, Jr.
Division Street, Steve Tesich; dir: Stan Wojewodski, Jr.
Wings, Arthur Kopit; dir: Stan Wojewodski, Jr.
The Woman, Edward Bond; dir: Jackson Phippin
Love's Labour's Lost, William Shakespeare; dir: Stan Wojewodski, Jr.
Yes, I Can!, Edward Stone; dir: Edward Stone

DESIGNERS

Sets: Wally Cobert, Richard R. Goodwin, Hugh Landwehr, Tony Straiges, Ed Wittstein.
Costumes: Linda Fisher, Dona Granata, Walter Pickette, Del W. Risberg, Lesley Skannal, Jacqueline Watts, Robert Wojewodski.
Lights: Bonnie Ann Brown, Arden Fingerhut, Craig Miller, Judy Rasmuson, Donald Edmund Thomas, John Tissot, Ann G. Wrightson.

The Changing Scene

ALFRED BROOKS
President

1527 1/2 Champa St.
Denver, CO 80202
(303) 893-5775

FOUNDED 1968
Maxine Munt, Alfred Brooks

SEASON
Year-round

SCHEDULE
Evenings
Thursday-Sunday

FACILITIES
Seating capacity: 76
Stage: flexible

FINANCES
January 1, 1982-December 31, 1982
$88,000 operating expenses
$23,000 earned income
$63,000 grants/contributions

AUDIENCE
Annual attendance: 25,000

The Changing Scene is an innovative, alternative theatre founded and still operated by the husband-and-wife team of Alfred Brooks and Maxine Munt. Even after producing 179 premiere plays (38 of which have gone on to subsequent productions in New York), the operating policy of the theatre includes dance, poetry, films, music and developmental works created through and by members of Brooks' Visual Theatre Workshop.

With a small budget and limited seating capacity, The Changing Scene has been able to take enormous risks in programming. Now, having received grants in the "presenter category," the theatre is planning a season of collaborative productions with, for example, the Denver Film Society (to screen a series of Fassbinder films not previously shown in Denver); L'Alliance & Co. (to produce plays in French); and a series of dance concerts featuring not only area choreographers but guest artists-in-residence such as Marleen Pennison, Tamar

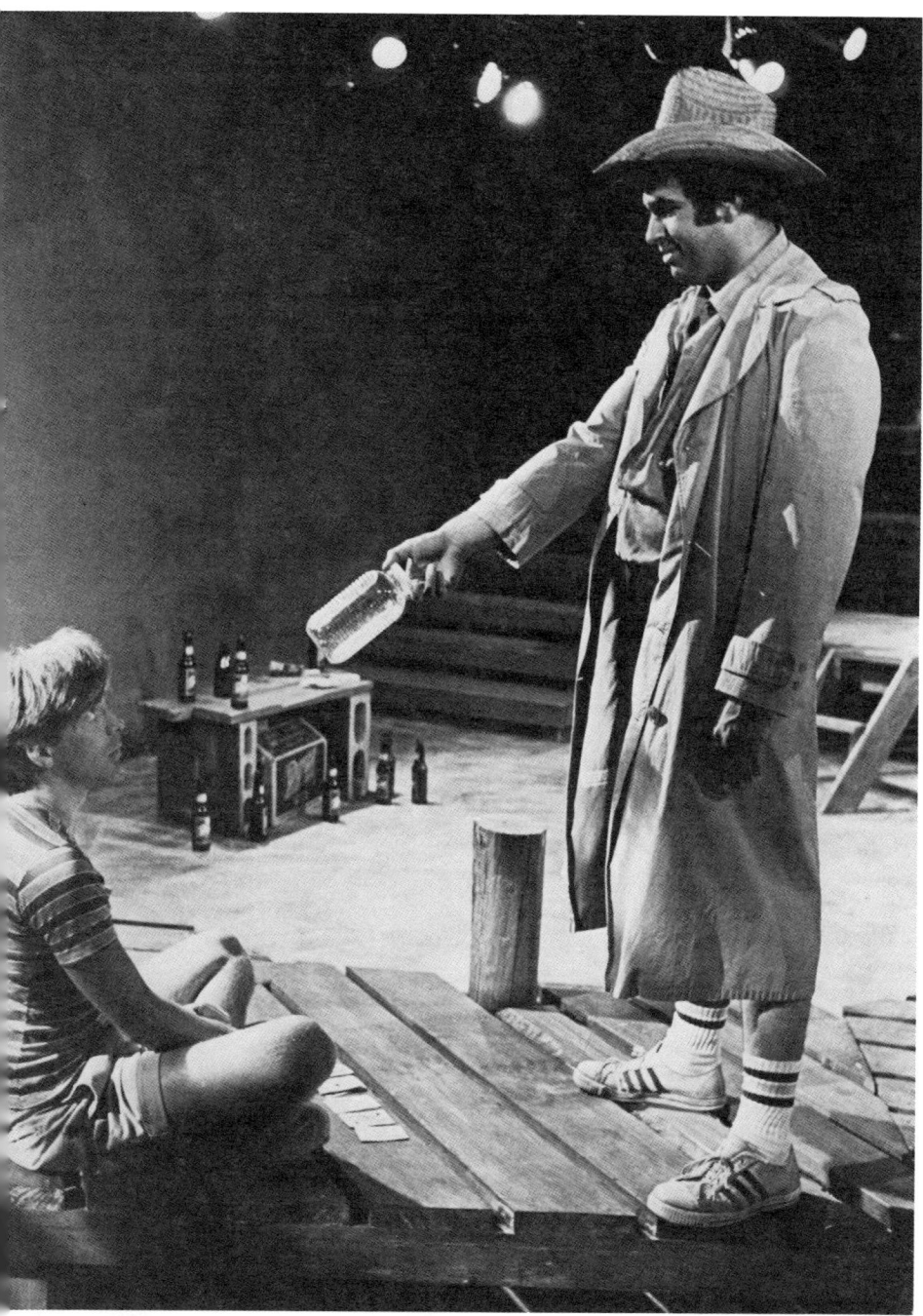

The Changing Scene. Joseph McDonald and Michael Mancuso in Last Night's Lightning. *Photo: Van Emden Henson.*

Programs and services

Staged readings by local playwrights; guest-artist workshops.

PRODUCTIONS 1982

A New Client, Lucille Hauser; dir: Michelle O. Serries
The Last of Hitler, Joan Schenkar; dir: Michelle O. Serries
The Last Slumber Party, Laura Shamas; dir: Doug Smith
The Last Prostitute, William Borden; dir: Michelle O. Serries
Last Night's Lightning, David Michael Erickson; dir: Van Emden Henson
False Colors, Eugene Drabent; dir: Andrea Edwards
Tu-Be, company-developed; dir: Alfred Brooks and John Osburn

PRODUCTIONS 1983

The Death of Galatea, Michael Hulett; dir: Margaret Mancinelli
Trojanshorse and Other Conundrums, Tom Baer; dir: Alfred Brooks and John Osburn

DESIGNERS

Sets: Ron Carter, Ben Fulgenzi, Van Emden Henson, Jerry Johnson, Michael Miller, Glenn Noe, Robert Schnautz, Paul Sehnert, Michelle O. Serries.
Costumes: William Gornel, Robin Klingensmith.
Lights: Mark Cole, Van Emden Henson.

Kotoske, Kim Arrow and John Wilson who create new works using Denver performers.

The spirit of support for artistic ventures in new and untried realms prevails. Readings by poets such as Diane di Prima, Anne Waldman or the Denver Street Poets challenge Changing Scene audiences. Staged readings are given for area playwrights to assist them in the development of their work. Scholarship dance classes are provided for minority teenagers, and all productions are cast from open auditions.

As an urban arts center, The Changing Scene continues to provide a forum for new ideas from both young aspirants and more mature artists in need of a place to present their work.

The Children's Theatre Company

JOHN CLARK DONAHUE
Artistic Director

SARAH LAWLESS
Executive Director

A.L. POWELL, JR.
Board President

2400 Third Ave. South
Minneapolis, MN 55404
(612) 874-0500 (business)
(612) 874-0400 (box office)

FOUNDED 1961
Beth Linnerson

SEASON
September-June

SCHEDULE
Evenings
Wednesday-Saturday

Matinees
Tuesday-Sunday

FACILITIES
Mainstage
Seating capacity: 746
Stage: proscenium

Studio Theatre
Seating capacity: 50-90
Stage: flexible

FINANCES
July 1, 1982-June 30, 1983
$2,685,000 operating expenses
$1,873,000 earned income
$ 834,000 grants/contributions

AUDIENCE
Annual attendance: 213,000
Subscribers: 8,960

TOURING CONTACT
Tony Steblay

BOOKED-IN EVENTS
Theatre, dance music, lectures, symposia

The Children's Theatre Company and School is a resident repertory theatre and training center, and has become the nation's largest professional organization of its kind. Through direct exposure to—and participation in—the performing arts, CTC provides the highest level of cultural and educational enrichment for a broad constituency of young people and adults. Under the leadership and inspiration of artistic director John Clark Donahue, the company has maintained and continues to develop innovative theatre for young audiences while simultaneously providing academic and performing arts training for the 120 elementary through secondary school students enrolled in The Children's Theatre School.

CTC employs a resident artistic staff of more than 20 people who are dynamically involved in the creation and performance of the company's mainstage season. This core staff of playwrights, composers, designers, directors and performers is joined by some 200 guest artists and students in presenting over 270 performances of six-to-eight original productions annually. An exciting and innovative repertoire drawn from the rich legacy of literary classics, folktales and fantasies, and completely original plays is frequently complemented by active collaboration with contemporary children's authors, resulting in adaptations of their works. The policy of producing only company-created adaptations, translations and original works in the mainstage season has produced more than 85 new scripts since 1965, earning CTC and Donahue the American Theatre Critics Association's 1980 Margo Jones Award for achievement and development of new plays and playwrights.

CTC maintains a Studio Theatre in response to the desire to explore adult classics, experimental and original works. CTC also continues to explore the medium of video, having produced five properties distributed by MCA/Universal for cable network and home purchase; this is considered a unique opportunity to expand CTC's audience while offering another facet in the education of its young students, technicians and artistic staff.

The nine-month Children's Theatre School, providing academic training within an arts-conscious and supportive environment, and the five-week residential Summer Theatre Institute, offer the dedicated theatre student a rare opportunity to learn surrounded by the stimulating daily activity of a professional theatre dedicated to the artists and audiences of tomorrow.

Programs and services

Children's Theatre School; Summer Theatre Institute; dance classes; residencies; touring; internships.

PRODUCTIONS 1981-82

Kidnapped in London, adapt: Timothy Mason, from John Bennett; music: Steven M. Rydberg; dir: Charles Nolte

Puss in Boots, adapt: Sharon Holland, from Charles Perrault; music: Hiram Titus; lyrics: Sharon Holland; dir: John Clark Donahue

The Little Match Girl, adapt: John Clark Donahue, from Hans Christian Andersen; dir: Bain Boehlke

The Cookie Jar, John Clark Donahue; music: Roberta Carlson; lyrics: John Clark Donahue and Roberta Carlson; dir: John Clark Donahue
Phantom of the Opera, adapt: George Muschamp and Thomas W. Olson, from Gaston Leroux; music: Steven M. Rydberg; dir: John Clark Donahue
Alice in Wonderland, adapt: Sharon Holland, from Lewis Carroll; music: Hiram Titus; dir: John Clark Donahue
The Maids, Jean Genet; dir: Myron Johnson
The Woods, David Mamet; dir: David Samuelson
Lids, John Clark Donahue; dir: Patrick McNellis
D'Art, Frank Pike; dir: David Samuelson
Ned and Jack, Sheldon Rosen; dir: Gary Briggle and Patrick McNellis

Night of January 16th, Ayn Rand; dir: Debbi Goldstein and Ginny Roethler
Album, David Rimmer; dir: Jason McLean

PRODUCTIONS 1982-83

The 500 Hats of Bartholomew Cubbins, adapt and lyrics: Timothy Mason, from Theodor Geisel (Dr. Seuss); music: Hiram Titus; dir: John Clark Donahue
Pippi Longstocking, Astrid Lindgren; trans: Thomas W. Olson and Truda Stockenstrom; music: Roberta Carlson; lyrics: Roberta Carlson and Thomas W. Olson; dir: Myron Johnson
Mr. Pickwick's Christmas, adapt: Thomas W. Olson and George Muschamp, from Charles Dickens; music: Hiram Titus; dir: John Clark Donahue
The Clown of God, adapt: John B. Davidson and John Clark Donahue, from Tomie dePaola; music: Steven M. Rydberg; dir: John Clark Donahue
The Adventures of Tom Sawyer, adapt: Timothy Mason, from Mark Twain; music: Peter Ostroushko; dir: John Clark Donahue
The Wind in the Willows, adapt: Sharon Holland, from Kenneth Grahame; dir: Myron Johnson
Erma's Dream, Warren G. Green; dir: Loren Johnson
The Indian Wants the Bronx, Israel Horovitz; dir: Loren Johnson
Hand in Hand, Leslye Orr; dir: Leslye Orr
The Unseen Hand, Sam Shepard; dir: Binky Wood
Trial by Jury, lyrics: W.S. Gilbert; music: Arthur Sullivan; dir: John Davidson
Desert in Flower, Marisha Chamberlain; music: Hiram Titus; dir: John Clark Donahue
Merely Players, Sharon Holland; music: Richard Dworsky; dir: David Samuelson
The Great American Family, John Davidson; music: James O. Martin; dir: John Davidson

DESIGNERS

Sets: Jack Barkla, Gene Davis Buck, Jay Bush, Tom Butsch, Dahl Delu, Tomie dePaola, John Clark Donahue, Ronald Scott Fry, Tanya Moiseiwitsch, Don Yunker.
Costumes: Jared Aswegan, Christopher Beesley, Gene Davis Buck, Judith Cooper, Dahl Delu, Tomie dePaola, Scott Martin, Tanya Moiseiwitsch, Barry Robison, Marsha Weist-Hines, Cate Whittemore, Christopher Williams.
Lights: Robert S. Hutchings, Jr., Karlis Ozols, Doug Pipan, Paul Scharfenberger, Duane Schuler, Michael Vennerstrom.

The Children's Theatre Company. Stephen Boe, Rana Haugen, Gaby Zuckerman and Molly Atwood in The Red Shoes. *Photo: George Heinrich.*

Cincinnati Playhouse in the Park

MICHAEL MURRAY
Producing Director

BAYLOR LANDRUM
Managing Director

CHARLES O. CAROTHERS
Board President

Box 6537
Cincinnati, OH 45206
(513) 421-5440 (business)
(513) 421-3888 (box office)

FOUNDED 1960
Community members

SEASON
September-June

SCHEDULE
Evenings
Tuesday-Sunday

Matinees
Wednesday, Sunday

FACILITIES
962 Mt. Adams Circle
Robert S. Marx Theatre
Seating capacity: 629
Stage: modified thrust

Thompson Shelterhouse
Seating capacity: 219
Stage: thrust

FINANCES
September 1, 1982-August 31, 1983
$1,994,000 operating expenses
$1,587,000 earned income
$ 561,000 grants/contributions

AUDIENCE
Annual attendance: 200,000
Subscribers: 18,100

BOOKED-IN EVENTS
Various

AEA LORT (B) and (D) contracts

Cincinnati Playhouse in the Park. Robert Pescovitz and Gerry Bamman in Macbeth.
Photo: Sandy Underwood.

The professional theatre for a three-state region of the Ohio River Valley, Cincinnati Playhouse in the Park was founded in 1960 in a 100-year-old shelterhouse, a Victorian fieldstone structure in a hilltop park overlooking downtown Cincinnati and, across the river, Kentucky.

The innovative 629-seat Robert S. Marx Theatre was built in 1968 to complement the refurbished Thompson Shelterhouse. In the fall of 1980, work was completed on the Vontz Theatre Center which encompasses both theatre structures, new offices and an atrium containing a bar and restaurant.

The Playhouse schedule includes two subscription series as well as the seasonal transformation of the Marx stage into a summer cabaret and the site of occasional concerts and special productions. Each season's schedule is designed for variety, challenge and high-quality entertainment. Plays are drawn from the entire spectrum of dramatic literature with special emphasis on those works whose human values create a bond between the performers and the audience. At least two new works and one musical are included among the 12 productions each season.

Productions are cast individually, and the directors and designers engaged are among the finest freelance artists in the country.

Programs and services

Acting, directing, stage management, technical and administrative internships; student performances; Dark Night Specials: new play readings; Critic's Corner: public forum with local critics; Prologue: subscriber newsletter; Playhouse Prompters: volunteer organization.

PRODUCTIONS 1981-82

Born Yesterday, Garson Kanin; dir: Ron Lagamarsino
Peter Pan, book: James M. Barrie; music: Mark Charlap and Jule Styne; lyrics: Carolyn Leigh, Betty Comden and Adolph Green; dir: George Bunt
Betrayal, Harold Pinter; dir: Michael Hankins
Macbeth, William Shakespeare; dir: Michael Murray
Ten Little Indians, Agatha Christie; dir: Donald MacKechnie
Talley's Folly, Lanford Wilson; dir: Michael Murray
Home, Samm-Art Williams; dir: Woodie King
A Coupla White Chicks Sitting Around Talking, John Ford Noonan; dir: Josephine Abady
A Lesson from Aloes, Athol Fugard; dir: Thomas Bullard
A Life in the Theatre, David Mamet; dir: James Milton

PRODUCTIONS 1982-83

Inherit the Wind, Jerome Lawrence and Robert E. Lee; dir: John Going
The Wizard of Oz, adapt: Frank Gabrielson, from L. Frank Baum; music and lyrics: Harold Arlen and E.Y. Harburg; dir: Worth Gardner
The Dresser, Ronald Harwood; dir: Josephine Abady
Medea, Euripides; dir: Amy Saltz
The Price, Arthur Miller; dir: Michael Hankins
The Importance of Being Earnest, Oscar Wilde; dir: Michael Murray
Mass Appeal, Bill C. Davis; dir: Don Toner
Sweet Basil, Lloyd Gold; dir: Leonard Mozzi
Strange Snow, Stephen Metcalfe; dir: Stephen Metcalfe
I'm Getting My Act Together and Taking It on the Road, Gretchen Cryer and Nancy Ford; dir: David Holdgriewe

DESIGNERS

Sets: David Ariosa, Lowell Detweiler, Karl Eigsti, Alison Ford, John Jensen, Alan Kimmel, David Potts, Paul Shortt, Robert D. Soule.
Costumes: Elizabeth Covey, Ann Firestone, James Berton Harris, William Schroder, Rebecca Senske, Paul Shortt, Caley Summers, Kurt Wilhelm.
Lights: Barry Arnold, Jay Depenbrock, F. Mitchell Dana, Jeff Davis, Neil Peter Jampolis, William Mintzer, Spencer Mosse, Victor En Yu Tan.

Circle in the Square

THEODORE MANN
Artistic Director

PAUL LIBIN
Managing Director

JOHN RUSSELL
Board Chairman

1633 Broadway
New York, NY 10019
(212) 581-3270 (business)
(212) 581-0720 (box office)

FOUNDED 1951
Theodore Mann, Aileen Cramer, Edward Mann, Jose Quintero, Emily Stevens, Jason Wingreen

SEASON
Year-round

SCHEDULE
Evenings
Tuesday-Saturday

Matinees
Wednesday, Saturday, Sunday

FACILITIES
Circle in the Square Uptown
Seating capacity: 600-681
Stage: arena

FINANCES
July 1, 1982-June 30, 1983
$5,130,000 operating expenses
$4,723,000 earned income
$ 484,000 grants/contributions

AUDIENCE
Annual attendance: 125,181
Subscribers: 12,854

AEA LORT (A) contract

In 1951, Circle in the Square Theatre, New York's oldest company, sparked the beginning of the Off Broadway theatre movement. In the past three decades, Circle in the Square has presented more than 125 productions, and has reached nearly two million audience members since 1972.

Circle in the Square is first and foremost an American classical theatre, physically

Circle in the Square. Brian Bedford and Mary Beth Hurt in The Misanthrope. *Photo: Martha Swope.*

conceived and artistically committed to the art of acting. This commitment is manifested in the intimacy of the theatre, where no seat is further than 55 feet from the stage, encouraging close interaction between the actor and audience.

Most important, this commitment forms the cornerstone of Circle's artistic policy. The season is selected from great works of dramatic literature, including recently *The Bacchae, Macbeth, The Misanthrope* and *Death of a Salesman.* Circle also searches for plays that deserve a re-examination, such as *Summer and Smoke, The Iceman Cometh, Major Barbara, The Queen and the Rebels* and *Present Laughter.* These plays—classics and potential classics — provide opportunities for the major actors who often work at Circle to stretch their talent. Circle offers these artists the opportunity to take on the challenge of the great roles in an atmosphere dedicated to developing the plays through a comfortable rehearsal and preview period.

The commitment to acting is further demonstrated by the existence of the Circle in the Square Theatre School, which is one of only two non-academic professional theatre training institutions in the country accredited by the U.S. government. At 22, the school is one of the oldest such conservatories in America, and provides rigorous, highly personalized training in acting, singing, voice production and dance, drawing upon the finest acting and directing talents in New York for its faculty. The school also offers a four-year Bachelor of Fine Arts program in conjunction with New York University.

Programs and services

Circle and the Schools: study guides, backstage tours, post-performance seminars and half-price tickets; Circle in the City: free ticket distribution to health organizations, senior citizens and service organizations; administrative internships; newsletter.

PRODUCTIONS 1981-82

Candida, George Bernard Shaw; dir: Michael Cristofer
Macbeth, William Shakespeare; dir: Nicol Williamson
Eminent Domain, Percy Granger; dir: Paul Austin

PRODUCTIONS 1982-83

Present Laughter, Noel Coward; dir: George C. Scott
The Queen and the Rebels, Ugo Betti; trans: Henry Reed; dir: Waris Hussein
The Misanthrope, Moliere; trans: Richard Wilbur; dir: Stephen Porter

DESIGNERS

Sets: Kenneth Foy, David Jenkins, Marjorie Bradley Kellogg, Michael Miller.
Costumes: Jane Greenwood, Richard Hornung, Ann Roth, Jennifer von Mayrhauser, Julie Weiss.
Lights: Lowell Achziger, William Armstrong, Paul Gallo, John McLain, Richard Nelson.

Circle Repertory Company

MARSHALL W. MASON
Artistic Director

B. RODNEY MARRIOTT
Acting Artistic Director

RICHARD FRANKEL
Managing Director

CHARLES D. WEBB
Board President

161 Ave. of the Americas
New York, NY 10013
(212) 691-3210 (business)
(212) 924-7100 (box office)

FOUNDED 1969
Marshall W. Mason, Lanford Wilson,
Tanya Berezin, Robert Thirkield

SEASON
October-June

SCHEDULE
Evenings
Tuesday-Sunday

Matinees
Saturday, Sunday

FACILITIES
Sheridan Square Playhouse
99 Seventh Ave. South
Seating capacity: 160
Stage: flexible

FINANCES
October 1, 1982-September 30, 1983
$1,165,000 operating expenses
$ 480,000 earned income
$ 763,000 grants/contributions

AUDIENCE
Annual attendance: 60,000
Subscribers: 5,300

TOURING CONTACT
Richard Frankel

BOOKED-IN EVENTS
Theatre, music

AEA Off Broadway contract

Circle Repertory Company, a permanent ensemble of actors, playwrights and designers, was founded in 1969 in a loft on upper Broadway by directors Marshall W. Mason and Rob Thirkield, playwright Lanford Wilson and actress Tanya Berezin. Today, Circle Rep is distinguished by its major playwrights in residence who create roles for specific actors. Circle Rep is a national resource: plays born in the company's developmental programs have been presented in 96 professional and 944 other productions in all 50 states and 11 foreign countries.

For a decade, Circle Rep has led in the rediscovery of lyric realism as the native voice of the American theatre. The company has been honored with 90 major awards including the Pulitzer Prize, two Antoinette Perry ("Tony") Awards, two New York Drama Critics' Awards, 27 Obies and 13 Drama Desk Awards. Among its 75 world premieres are such landmark productions as the 1980 Pulitzer Prize-winning *Talley's Folly* as well as *Angels Fall, 5th of July, A Tale Told, The Hot l Baltimore, Knock Knock, When You Comin' Back Red Ryder?* and *The Sea Horse*. Circle Rep has produced the New York premieres of Sam Shepard's *Suicide in B Flat* and *Fool for Love*,

Circle Repertory Company. Nancy Snyder and Fritz Weaver in Angels Fall. *Photo: Gerry Goodstein.*

David Storey's *The Farm* and Tennessee Williams' *Battle of Angels*. The company's production of *Gemini* became one of the longest running plays on Broadway.

In 1974, Circle Rep moved to its present location on Sheridan Square, where it offers a mainstage subscription season and a Projects-in-Progress series. The company also operates the Circle Lab where projects can develop free of commercial and critical pressure. The Lab holds play readings, playwright and director's units, actor training workshops and other services.

Through the interaction of its company (which now boasts 63 actors, 20 playwrights, 11 directors, 9 designers and stage managers), Circle Rep strives to bring the scripts of its resident writers to life so that the action of the plays becomes the experience of the audience.

Programs and services

Projects-in-Progress series of staged readings; Circle Repertory Lab; Extended Readings series of special event readings; Friday Readings; internships; signed performances; summer residency at Saratoga Performing Arts Festival; playwrights' weekends.

PRODUCTIONS 1981-82

Threads, Jonathan Bolt; dir: B. Rodney Marriott
Three one-acts:
   Thymus Vulgaris, Lanford Wilson; dir: June Stein
   Am I Blue, Beth Henley; dir: Stuart White
   Confluence, John Bishop; dir: B. Rodney Marriott
Richard II, William Shakespeare; dir: Marshall W. Mason
Great Grandson of Jedidiah Kohler, John Bishop; dir: Marshall W. Mason and John Manulis
Snow Orchid, Joe Pintauro; dir: Tony Giordano
A Think Piece, Jules Feiffer; dir: Caymichael Patton
Johnny Got His Gun, Dalton Trumbo; adapt: Bradley Rand Smith; dir: Elinor Renfield

First Annual Young Playwrights Festival:
   Bluffing, Peter Murphy; dir: Carole Rothman
   Present Tense, John McNamara; dir: Marshall W. Mason
   The Rennings Children, Kenneth Lonergan; dir: Marshall W. Mason
   It's Time for a Change, Adam Berger; dir: Elinor Renfield
   The Bronx Zoo, Lynette Serrano; dir: Gerald Chapman
   Half Fare, Shoshana Marchand; dir: Arthur Laurents

The Hold Up, Marsha Norman; dir: B. Rodney Marriott
Angels Fall, Lanford Wilson; dir: Marshall W. Mason

PRODUCTIONS 1982-83

Angels Fall
Black Angel, Michael Cristofer; dir: Gordon Davidson
What I Did Last Summer, A.R. Gurney, Jr.; dir: B. Rodney Marriott
Domestic Issues, Corinne Jacker; dir: Eve Merriam

Second Annual Young Playwrights Festival:
   A New Approach to Human Sacrifice, Peter Getty; dir: Garland Wright
   Third Street, Richard Colman; dir: Michael Bennett
   I'm Tired and I Want to Go to Bed, David Torbett; dir: Gerald Chapman
   The Birthday Present, Charlie Schulman; dir: John Ferraro

Fool for Love, Sam Shepard; dir: Sam Shepard (Magic Theatre production)
The Seagull, Anton Chekhov; trans: Jean-Claude van Itallie; dir: Elinor Renfield

DESIGNERS

Sets: John Arnone, John Lee Beatty, Karl Eigsti, Sally Jacobs, Hugh Landwehr, Kert Lundell, Bob Phillips, David Potts, Andy Stacklin.
Costumes: Laura Crow, Ardyss L. Golden, Sally Jacobs, Patricia McGourty, David Murin, Miriam Nieves, Danise Romano, Ann Roth, Jennifer von Mayrhauser, Joan E. Weiss.
Lights: John Gleason, Kurt Landisman, Craig Miller, Dennis Parichy, Mal Sturchio.

The Clarence Brown Company

WANDALIE HENSHAW
Artistic Director

BASHIE CURFMAN
Managing Director

FRANK COMUNALE
Board President

University of Tennessee
Box 8450
Knoxville, TN 37996
(615) 974-3447 (business)
(615) 974-5161 (box office)

FOUNDED 1974
Ralph G. Allen, Anthony Quayle

SEASON
January-June

SCHEDULE
Evenings
Monday-Saturday

Matinees
Thursday, Saturday

FACILITIES
Clarence Brown Theatre
1714 Andy Holt Ave.
Seating capacity: 604
Stage: proscenium

Lab Theatre
Seating capacity: 130
Stage: thrust

Carousel Theatre
1710 Andy Holt Ave.
Seating capacity: 425
Stage: arena

FINANCES
June 1, 1982-May 31, 1983
$211,000 operating expenses
$137,000 earned income
$110,000 grants/contributions

AUDIENCE
Annual attendance: 40,000
Subscribers: 5,200

TOURING CONTACT
John Ruch

AEA LORT (B) and Theatre for Young Audiences contracts

The Clarence Brown Company. Doctor Faustus. *Photo: Marc Engel.*

Founded in 1974 by Ralph Allen and Anthony Quayle, the Clarence Brown Company is named for the noted film director who is its major benefactor. From its beginning, the company's primary emphasis has been on organically conceived, fully mounted productions of the classics, "the great plays." Its basic premise is that the more completely and richly the dramatist's world is evoked for an audience, the more clearly that audience will perceive for itself the drama's relevance to the world of the here and now. Production elements as well as performances are intended to serve the text as faithfully, integrally and dynamically as possible.

The Clarence Brown Company is an affiliate of the University of Tennessee's College of Liberal Arts. It shares a modern, well-equipped three-theatre facility and a number of staff members with the Department of Speech and Theatre, and works in close cooperation with them to provide a classical cultural resource for the university, city and region, and to provide training, professional models and contacts for students majoring in theatre.

In 1982, an outreach program called "Shakespeare for Young Audiences" was initiated whereby fully produced programs go on tour to students too poor or far away to attend regular performances.

Every two or three years the company launches a production which makes its way to the Kennedy Center or Broadway, such as the early version of *Sugar Babies* and a production of *Medea* featuring Zoe Caldwell and Judith Anderson.

Yearly auditions are personally conducted by the artistic director. Casting is on a show-by-show basis, but actors often stay on for two or more productions in a season.

Programs and services

Shakespeare to the Schools; Theatre Outreach Program, including cable interview programs, study guides, tours and lectures; student seminars and workshops with professional actors, designers and directors; student apprenticeships.

PRODUCTIONS 1982

Medea, Euripides; adapt: Robinson Jeffers; dir: Robert Whitehead
Two Gentlemen of Verona, William Shakespeare; dir: Jeffrey Huberman
The Mikado, book and lyrics: W.S. Gilbert; music: Arthur Sullivan; dir: Wandalie Henshaw

PRODUCTIONS 1983

Doctor Faustus, Christopher Marlowe; dir: Wandalie Henshaw
Julius Caesar, William Shakespeare; dir: Thomas Cooke
The Importance of Being Earnest, Oscar Wilde; dir: Albert J. Harris

DESIGNERS

Sets: Robert Cothran, Ben Edwards.
Costumes: Bill Black, Marianne Custer, Jane Greenwood.
Lights: Martin Aronstein, L.J. DeCuir, Leonard Harman.

The Cleveland Play House

RICHARD OBERLIN
Artistic Director

JANET WADE
Managing Director

WILLIAM M. JONES
Board President

Box 1989
Cleveland, OH 44106
(216) 795-7000

FOUNDED 1915
Raymond O'Neil

SEASON
October-May

SCHEDULE

Evenings
Wednesday-Saturday

Matinees
Thursday, Saturday, Sunday

FACILITIES
8500 Euclid Ave.

Francis E. Drury Theatre
Seating capacity: 515
Stage: proscenium

Charles S. Brooks Theatre
Seating capacity: 160
Stage: proscenium

Bolton Theatre
Seating capacity: 650
Stage thrust

FINANCES
July 1, 1981-June 30, 1982
$2,187,000 operating expenses
$1,177,000 earned income
$ 791,000 grants/contributions

AUDIENCE
Annual attendance: 161,759
Subscribers: 11,275

TOURING CONTACT
Richard Oberlin, Janet Wade

BOOKED-IN EVENTS
Theatre

AEA LORT (C) contract

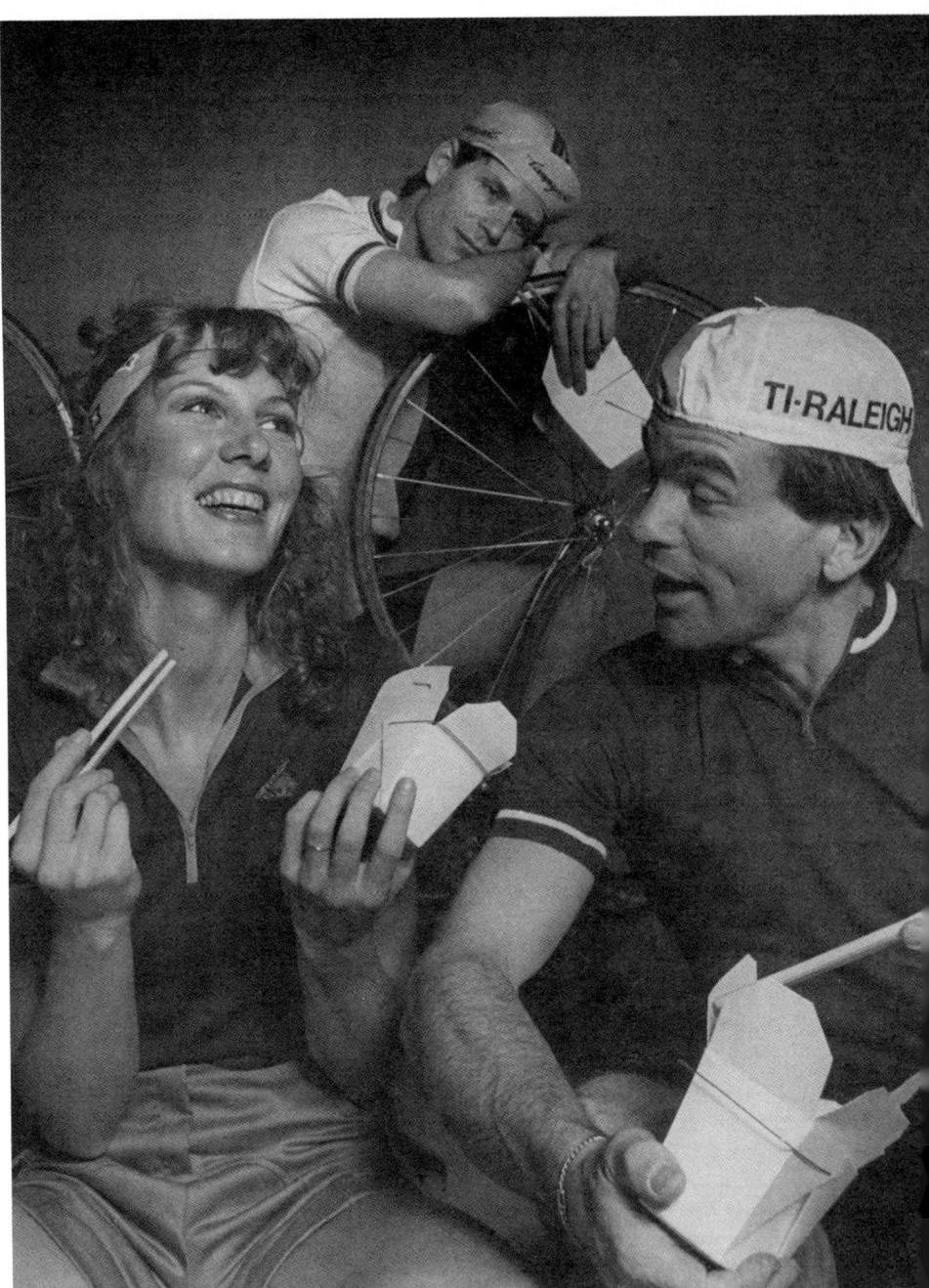

The Cleveland Play House. Lisa Kittrell, Anthony Kittrell and William Rhys in Key Exchange. *Photo: Mike Edwards.*

The Cleveland Play House, America's oldest resident theatre, is now in its 68th consecutive season. Two of its principal aims are to produce a challenging, eclectic variety of theatre works for an audience drawn from all over northeastern Ohio; and to nourish theatre arts and artists working in its three-theatre complex over a production season of 40 weeks.

The Play House employs a resident company and staff now numbering over 130, augmented by guest actors, directors and designers. Its season of 17 productions includes eight mainstage plays, a seven-play

Studio Theatre Series and two off-series events. The audience of more than 170,000 participates in quality productions of the classics, revivals of well-crafted plays of the immediate past, contemporary works, plays with music, new plays, adaptations and American premieres of foreign plays.

The whole range of theatre made available to the Play House's diverse community is custom built in its own shops and rehearsal halls, now encompassing a 12-acre theatre village, part of Cleveland's University Circle area, which also includes the Cleveland Orchestra and the Cleveland Art Museum.

The fall of 1983 marked the opening of a new 650-seat theatre with an extended apron stage designed by noted architect Philip Johnson, a native Clevelander who received his first taste of theatre as a young man attending the Cleveland Play House. The new Bolton Theatre now complements and adjoins the existing Drury and Brooks Theatres and their support spaces, along with a new 200,000-square foot production center embracing all shops, storage, rehearsal halls, administrative offices and a private subscriber club/restaurant.

A complete range of ancillary activities and programs enhances one of the most exciting and varied theatres in America.

Programs and services

Youtheatre children's classes; Play House Comes to School: workshops and lectures; fellowships; Quintessence: Monday series of lecture/performances.

PRODUCTIONS 1981-82

Tintypes, music and lyrics: various; adapt: Mary Kyte, Mel Marvin and Gary Pearle; dir: William Rhys
Translations, Brian Friel; dir: Kenneth Albers
Daughters, John Morgan Evans; dir: Edward Stern
A Christmas Carol, adapt: Doris Baizley, from Charles Dickens; dir: William Rhys
Sherlock Holmes and the Curse of the Sign of Four, adapt: Dennis Rosa, from Arthur Conan Doyle; dir: Paul Lee
Romeo and Juliet, William Shakespeare; dir: William Rhys
Betrayal, Harold Pinter; dir: Dennis Zacek
Pantomime, Derek Walcott; dir: David Connell
Talley's Folly, Lanford Wilson; dir: Evie McElroy
Cole, adapt: Benny Green and Alan Strachen; music and lyrics: Cole Porter; dir: Judith Haskell
Chekhov in Yalta, John Driver and Jeffrey Haddow; dir: Kenneth Albers
Trespassers Will Be Prosecuted, Peter Kenna; dir: Harper Jane McAdoo

PRODUCTIONS 1982-83

Appear and Show Cause, Stephen Taylor; dir: Woodie King, Jr.
The Middle Ages, A.R. Gurney, Jr.; dir: Harper Jane McAdoo
5th of July, Lanford Wilson; dir: Michael Maggio
Black Coffee, Agatha Christie; dir: Paul Lee
A Christmas Carol
Tomfoolery, adapt; Cameron MacIntosh and Robin Ray; music and lyrics: Tom Lehrer; dir: William Roudebush
A Tale of Two Cities, adapt: Mark Fitzgibbons, from Charles Dickens; dir: William Rhys
Sea Marks, Gardner McKay; dir: Tom Riccio
Key Exchange, Kevin Wade; dir: Dennis Zacek
Ten Times Table, Alan Ayckbourn; dir: Paul Lee
The Robber Bridegroom, book and lyrics: Alfred Uhry; music: Robert Waldman; dir: Michael Maggio
The Potsdam Quartet, David Pinner; dir: William Roudebush

DESIGNERS

Sets: Charles Berliner, Gary Eckhart, Richard Gould, James Irwin, Wayne Merritt.
Costumes: Larry Bauman, Charles Berliner, Frances Blau, Mary Carey, Richard Gould, Colleen Muscha, Estelle Painter, Jeffrey M. Smart, Elizabeth A. Streeter, Kim A. Trotter.
Lights: Richard Gould, James Irwin, Wayne Merritt.

Coconut Grove Playhouse

JOSE FERRER
Artistic Advisor

G. DAVID BLACK
Managing Director

PHILLIP T. GEORGE
Board Chairman

Box 616
Miami, FL 33133
(305) 442-2662 (business)
(305) 442-4000 (box office)

FOUNDED 1977
Thomas Spencer, Gerald Pulver

SEASON
October-May

SCHEDULE
Evenings
Tuesday-Sunday

Matinees
Wednesday, Saturday, Sunday

FACILITIES
3500 Main Highway, Coconut Grove
Seating capacity: 796
Stage: proscenium

FINANCES
July 1, 1982-June 30, 1983
$1,782,000 operating expenses
$ 952,000 earned income
$ 855,000 grants/contributions

AUDIENCE
Annual attendance: 102,600
Subscribers: 9,200

TOURING CONTACT
Barry Steinman

BOOKED-IN EVENTS
Theatre, dance

AEA LORT (B) contract

In April 1983, Players State Theatre took on the name of the historic building that had been its home for six years, becoming the

Coconut Grove Playhouse. Mel Johnson, Jr., Barbara Montgomery, Peter Francis-James and Samuel E. Wright in Oedipus Rex. *Photo: Henry Friedman.*

Coconut Grove Playhouse, a State Theatre of Florida. Along with the name change, major steps have also been taken toward strengthening the theatre's identity. A stroke of circumstance brought the highly respected theatre artistry of Jose Ferrer to the Playhouse, to help with this task, and he has become the company's artistic advisor.

Unlike most of its contemporaries, the Playhouse is closer in size and structure to a Broadway theatre, and calls for a production style that fills the space. It strives to present the best in American comedy, musical theatre and drama, reminding its audiences of our country's rich, enjoyable theatrical heritage—as well as its current wealth of new work. To match the quality of the selections, it attempts to bring the finest actors, directors and designers to its stage. Coconut Grove, as the largest nonprofit theatre in South Florida, is on a path of growth and development to match that of the region it serves.

Because of the area's unique mixture of peoples and cultures, the Playhouse has entered into a close involvement with its Hispanic and black communities. Through its outreach programs, its revivals from the world's repertoire, and its encouragement of the new playwright, the Playhouse is looking to achieve a national and international image for itself and for the city it serves.

Programs and services

Burger King Touring Company bilingual touring; Summer Tour of black theatre to local parks.

Note: During the 1981-82 season, David Robert Kanter served as artistic director.

PRODUCTIONS 1981-82

Da, Hugh Leonard; dir: David Robert Kanter

Oedipus Rex, Sophocles; adapt: Charles Nolte; dir: Charles Nolte

A Christmas Carol, adapt: David Robert Kanter, from Charles Dickens; dir: David Robert Kanter

The Summer People, Charles Nolte; dir: Charles Nolte

A Moon for the Misbegotten, Eugene O'Neill; dir: Lou Salerni

Talley's Folly, Lanford Wilson; dir: James Riley

Black Coffee, Agatha Christie; dir: David Robert Kanter

PRODUCTIONS 1982-83

The Dresser, Ronald Harwood; dir: Douglas Seale

5th of July, Lanford Wilson; dir: Kent Stephens

A Coupla White Chicks Sitting Around Talking, John Ford Noonan; dir: James Riley

Fallen Angels, Noel Coward; dir: Frith Banbury

A Destiny with Half Moon Street, Paul Zindel; dir: Jose Ferrer

Witness for the Prosecution, Agatha Christie; dir: Douglas Seale

DESIGNERS

Sets: Ron Fondaw, Marsha Hardy, Kenneth N. Kurtz, H. Paul Mazer, David Trimble.

Costumes: Barbara A. Bell, Barbara Forbes, Claire Gatrell, Steve Lambert, Maria Marrero, Ellis Tillman, David Trimble, Jill Young Zuckerman.

Lights: David Goodman, David Martin Jacques, Kenneth N. Kurtz, Michael Newton-Brown, James Riley, Pat Simmons, Stephen Welsh.

Cocteau Repertory

EVE ADAMSON
Artistic Director

BEN CARNEY
Managing Director

EDMUND SCHWESINGER
Board President

330 Bowery
New York, NY 10012
(212) 677-0060

FOUNDED 1971
Eve Adamson

SEASON
August-May

SCHEDULE
Evenings
Thursday-Sunday

Matinees
Saturday, Sunday

FACILITIES
Bouwerie Lane Theatre
Seating capacity: 140
Stage: modified thrust

FINANCES
July 1, 1982-June 30, 1983
$165,000 operating expenses
$ 90,000 earned income
$ 75,000 grants/contributions

AUDIENCE
Annual attendance: 20,000
Subscribers: 1,500

BOOKED-IN EVENTS
Theatre, dance, music, mime

Now in its 12th season, the Cocteau is a resident company of artists performing the great works of world theatre in a rotating repertory format. This scheduling enables the theatregoer to see two-to-five different productions during a single week.

The company is committed to Jean Cocteau's theory of "poetry of the theatre" in which all elements of production—performance, design, music—fuse into a unified whole that illumines the heart of the play and elevates it into a "dramatic poem." Whether approaching an established classic, a neglected piece by a well known writer, or a new work of provocative content and structure, the Cocteau strives to create that unique production style appropriate to each play which will engage the audience intellectually and emotionally.

Meeting this artistic challenge in the face of the logistical considerations created by rotating repertory requires a disciplined and flexible resident acting company as well as imaginative and resourceful designers and directors. Towards that end, the Cocteau continues to develop and nurture a growing community of repertory-oriented theatre artists.

Cocteau Repertory. Patrick Boyington, Craig Cook, Harris Berlinksy, Lynn Treveal and John Arndt in Swanwhite. *Photo: Gerry Goodstein.*

Programs and services

Student matinees; production and administrative internships.

PRODUCTIONS 1981-82

Something Cloudy, Something Clear, Tennessee Williams; dir: Eve Adamson
The Two Noble Kinsmen, William Shakespeare and John Fletcher; dir: Eve Adamson
The Revenger's Tragedy, Cyril Tourneur; dir: Toby Robertson
The Golem, H. Leivick; trans: Joseph C. Landis; dir: Eve Adamson
The Count of Monte Cristo, book adapt: Douglas McKeown, from Alexandre Dumas; music: Gene Mayer; lyrics: Dennis Green; dir: Douglas McKeown

PRODUCTIONS 1982-83

The Condemned of Altona, Jean Paul Sartre; trans: Sylvia and George Leeson; dir: Eve Adamson
Swanwhite, August Strindberg; trans: Susan Flakes; dir: Susan Flakes
Saint Joan, George Bernard Shaw; dir: Eve Adamson
The School for Scandal, Richard Brinsley Sheridan; dir: Robert Moss
Don Carlos, Friedrich von Schiller; trans: Charles E. Passage; dir: Eve Adamson
Philoctetes, Sophocles; adapt: Karen Sunde; dir: Karen Sunde

DESIGNERS

Sets: Rick Dennis, Karen Gerson, Gregory W. Laird, Christopher Martin, Douglas McKeown, David Robinson, Robert Joel Schwartz, Karen Sunde.
Costumes: Judith de Bruyn, Fotini Dimou, Karen Gerson, Thomas Carl Hansen, Christopher Martin, Douglas McKeown, David Robinson.
Lights: Giles Hogya, Gregory W. Laird, Christopher Martin, Toby Robertson, Craig Smith, Jack Stewart.

The Cricket Theatre

LOU SALERNI
Artistic Director

ROSSI SNIPPER
Managing Director

WILLIAM JOYCE
Board Chairman

Hennepin Center for the Arts
528 Hennepin Ave.
Minneapolis, MN 55403
(612) 333-5241 (business)
(612) 333-2401 (box office)

FOUNDED 1971
William H. Semans

SEASON
October-May

SCHEDULE
Evenings
Tuesday-Saturday

Matinees
Sunday

FACILITIES
Seating capacity: 384
Stage: modified thrust

FINANCES
July 1, 1982-June 30, 1983
$673,000 operating expenses
$236,000 earned income
$412,000 grants/contributions

AUDIENCE
Annual attendance: 41,000
Subscribers: 1,075

TOURING CONTACT
Rossi Snipper

AEA LORT (C) contract

It is the Cricket Theatre's mission to develop significant additions to American dramatic literature. It carries out this mission in two ways: by presenting superior productions of American plays which emphasize the exploration of the human spirit; and by actively seeking emerging playwrights of consequence and creating a network of professional artists and production resources in support and development of the playwright's craft.

The theatre's focus is on the contemporary American playwright, complemented by selective productions from the body of international dramatic literature. During Lou Salerni's seven years of artistic direction, the Cricket has become particularly known for its compelling presentation of American lyric realism.

At the same time, the theatre's Works-in-Progress program—under the direction of Sean Michael Dowse—offers emerging writers aid and support in developing their scripts for professional production.

In support of its mission, the Cricket recognizes its reponsibility to serve and develop its audience as well. It is known for its contributions to the rich and diverse cultural environment of Minneapolis/St. Paul, wherein the arts are patronized, appreciated and given the freedom to be innovative. The theatre offers Twin Cities theatregoers a variety of area and world premieres. Since its first full season in 1971, the Cricket has produced a total of 84 plays, of which 16 have been world premieres and 56 have been area premieres.

In 1979 the theatre moved into the renovated Hennepin Center for the Arts in downtown Minneapolis. Listed as a landmark building in the National Historic Register, the former Masonic Temple has been restored as a cultural center housing the Minnesota Dance Theatre and several smaller organizations in addition to the Cricket. The 384-seat theatre was specially designed to meet the Cricket's needs and is now its permanent home.

Programs and services

Works-in-Progress program: workshops leading to staged readings; artistic and administrative internships; touring; collaboration with local colleges on productions from Works-in-Progress program.

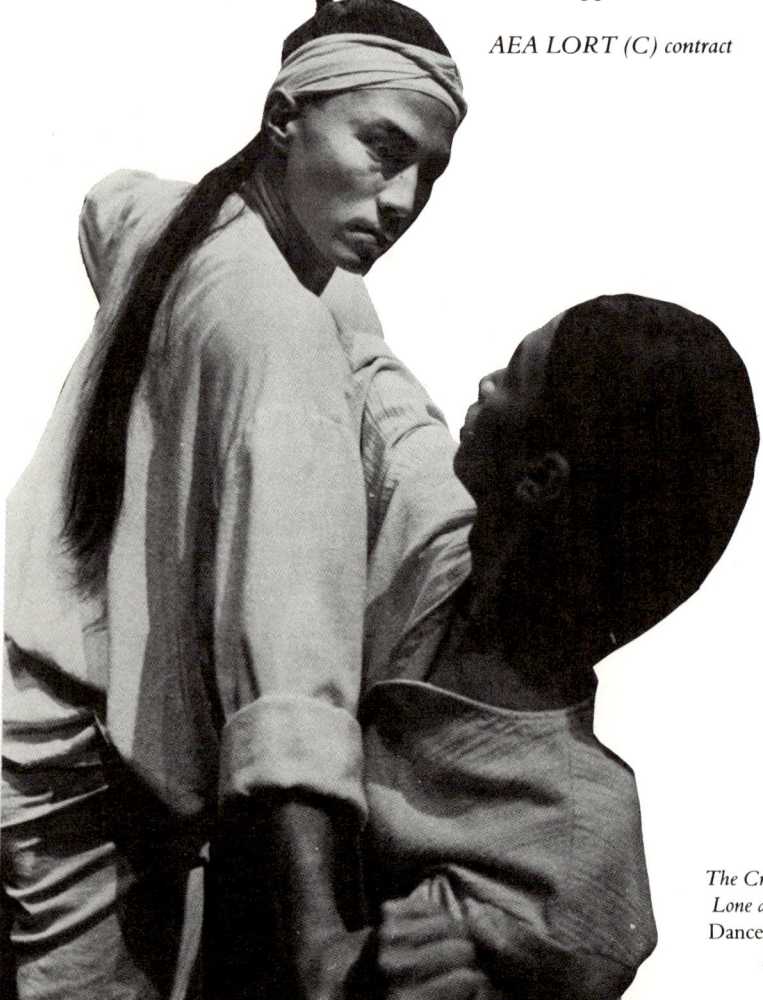

The Cricket Theatre. John Lone and Tzi Ma in The Dance and the Railroad. *Photo: Pat Boemer.*

Crossroads Theatre Company

PRODUCTIONS 1981-82

The Gin Game, D.L.Coburn; dir: Lou Salerni
Tintypes, music and lyrics: various; adapt: Mary Kyte, Mel Marvin and Gary Pearle; dir: Lewis Whitloch
Betrayal, Harold Pinter; dir: Lou Salerni
Childe Byron, Romulus Linney; dir: Steven Pearson
True West, Sam Shepard; dir: Lou Salerni
Dear Ruth, Norman Krasna; dir: Robert Moss

PRODUCTIONS 1982-83

Clarence Darrow, David W. Rintell; dir: Lou Salerni
The Dance and the Railroad, David Henry Hwang; dir: John Lone
Terra Nova, Ted Talley; dir: Lou Salerni
Billy Bishop Goes to War, John Gray and Eric Peterson; dir: James Lawless
American Buffalo, David Mamet; dir: Lou Salerni
The Constant Wife, W. Somerset Maugham; dir: Nicholas Kepros

DESIGNERS

Sets: Vera Polovko-Mednikov, Karen Schulz, Jerry Williams.
Costumes: Christopher Beesley, James Berton Harris, Vera Polovko-Mednikov, Karen Schulz, Colin Tugwell, Jerry Williams.
Lights: Lisa Johnson, Michael Vennerstrom.

L. KENNETH RICHARDSON
Artistic Director

RICK KHAN
Executive Director

CHERYL WALL
Board President

320 Memorial Pkwy.
New Brunswick, NJ 08901
(201) 249-5625 (business)
(201) 249-5560 (box office)

FOUNDED 1978
L. Kenneth Richardson, Rick Khan

SEASON
September-May

SCHEDULE
Evenings
Wednesday-Sunday

Matinees
Saturday, Sunday

FACILITIES
Seating capacity: 150
Stage: arena

FINANCES
July 1, 1982-June 30, 1983
$319,000 operating expenses
$166,000 earned income
$137,000 grants/contributions

AUDIENCE
Annual attendance: 31,825
Subscribers: 1,100

TOURING CONTACT
Rick Khan

AEA letter of agreement

Crossroads Theatre Company. Bingo Johnson, Neil Ross and Wilhelmina Rochester in The Trials and Tribulations of Staggerlee Booker T. Brown. *Photo: Harry Rubel.*

Crossroads Theatre Company was founded in 1978 by Rick Khan and Lee Richardson, associates since they met at Rutgers University during the late '60s. It was a time when economic frustration coupled with racial misunderstanding produced an uncontrollable tension which was in real need of adequate expression. The emergence of "angry black folk" on stage seemed to define for America what most still consider to be black theatre. In fact, black theatre, like black life, spans a wide spectrum of emotions and experiences both positive and negative. A fuller, more accurate reflection of this life was needed, and so Crossroads Theatre Company was established to present positive and diverse images of black life, assuring that people of all ages and backgrounds might have a more complete experience in theatre.

Crossroads presents contemporary plays as well as classics in black literature, hoping that one day these classics will be considered *American* classics, not just black classics. At Crossroads there is a special focus on developing new writers. In an effort to increase the interest in new works, Crossroads has conducted playwriting contests, staged readings and fully mounted productions of the best scripts; each season the theatre presents at least one original premiere. The program has been highly successful: one of the new scripts, *One Monkey Don't Stop No Show* by Don Evans, moved on to a New York production, and the Crossroads premiere of *A Lovesong for Miss Lydia* was taped and aired on both Public Television and ARTS, the ABC cable channel.

Located in the fast-growing city of New Brunswick (less than one hour from New York), Crossroads plans to move from its intimate loft space to a larger facility within the next few years. A more extensive touring schedule is planned for 1984, and a playwrights' workshop/new play festival for 1985.

Highlights of recent seasons include *Paul Robeson* with Avery Brooks and *Raisin* with Sandra Reeves-Phillips, choreographed by Al Perryman. Crossroads produces a six-play season with special discounts for groups, students and senior citizens.

Programs and services

Touring; artist-in-schools program; technical internships; free performances for senior citizens and young people; consultancies for schools and community groups.

PRODUCTIONS 1981-82

No Place to Be Somebody, Charles Gordone; dir: Rick Khan
Norman, Is That You?, Ron Clark and Sam Bobrick; dir: L. Kenneth Richardson
The Amen Corner, James Baldwin; dir: Rick Khan
Paul Robeson, Phillip Hayes Dean; dir: Harold Scott
A Lovesong for Miss Lydia, Don Evans; dir: L. Kenneth Richardson
Home, Samm-Art Williams; dir: Regge Life

PRODUCTIONS 1982-83

Meetings, Mustapha Matura; dir: Rick Khan
The Sty of the Blind Pig, Phillip Hayes Dean; dir: Harold Scott
Raisin, book adapt: Robert Nemiroff and Charlotte Zaltzberg, from Lorraine Hansberry; music: Judd Woldin; lyrics: Robert Britton; dir: Rick Khan
To Be Young, Gifted and Black, adapt: Robert Nemiroff, from Lorraine Hansberry; dir: L. Kenneth Richardson
The Blood Knot, Athol Fugard; dir: Samuel Barton
The Trials and Tribulations of Staggerlee Booker T. Brown, Don Evans; dir: L. Kenneth Richardson

DESIGNERS

Sets: Brian Martin, Michael Massee, Bill Motyka, Dan Proett.
Costumes: Valerie Charles, Judy Dearing, Judith Hart, Michael Massee.
Lights: Gary Fassler, Jaclyn Ferraro, Shirley Prendergast, Dan Proett, Dan Stratman, Bob Scheeler.

CSC Repertory

(CITY STAGE COMPANY)

CHRISTOPHER MARTIN
Artistic Director

DAN J. MARTIN
Managing Director

ARTHUR COHEN
Board President

136 East 13th St.
New York, NY 10003
(212) 674-4205 (business)
(212) 677-4210 (box office)

FOUNDED 1967
Christopher Martin

SEASON
September-May

SCHEDULE
Evenings
Tuesday-Sunday

Matinees
Saturday, Sunday

FACILITIES
Seating capacity: 199
Stage: thrust

FINANCES
July 1, 1982-June 30, 1983
$410,000 operating expenses
$228,000 earned income
$186,000 grants/contributions

AUDIENCE
Annual attendance: 31,000
Subscribers: 2,500

AEA Off Broadway contract

Accessible—and alive! That is the artistic imperative of CSC Repertory founder and artistic director Christopher Martin, now in his 16th year of bringing world classics and important contemporary plays to New York audiences. In this international city, the company aims not to express American life but to confront American society with the rest of the world so as to better understand America's cultural position.

What began as an artistic impulse has required careful political, sociological and cultural study of a text which is then

CSC Repertory. Peer Gynt. *Photo: Gerry Goodstein.*

delivered in direct, intimate ensemble performance illuminated by provocative, expressionist design—all in order to render difficult works exciting and immediate for contemporary audiences. Recent productions such as Goethe's *Faust Part One* and *Faust Part Two,* the uncut *Peer Gynt,* Sophocles' *Oedipus Cycle* and Yeats' *Cuchulain Plays* have caused CSC to be identified as "those people who do the un-doable."

The company is a permanent ensemble employed for an entire season, performing in rotating repertory (six plays were in active rep in 1982-83), evolving toward a collective of actors and staff maintaining a living library of works, and reworking productions (for example, *Faust* was reworked for touring).

After endeavoring to speak to the present through the past, the contemporary via the classics, Martin and company are now increasingly drawn toward contemporary plays that address world audiences and issues in a classic style, such as Roger Planchon's *Gilles de Rais,* Karen Sunde's *Balloon* and Botho Strauss' *Big and Little.*

In support of their goal to "build a bridge between societies," Martin and dramaturg Karen Sunde maintain a dialogue with CSC's European models and counterparts: Planchon at the Theatre National Populaire and Peter Stein at the Schaubuhne am Lehniner Platz, among others. Invitations to perform in western and eastern Europe at a number of international theatre festivals have led to major tour preparations for 1984.

Programs and services

Professional training program; administrative, technical and artistic internships.

PRODUCTIONS 1981-82

Peer Gynt, Henrik Ibsen; trans: Rolf Fjelde; dir: Christopher Martin
The Cherry Orchard, Anton Chekhov; trans: Alex Szogyi; dir: Rene Buch
King Lear, William Shakespeare; dir: Christopher Martin
Ghost Sonata, August Strindberg; trans: Christopher Martin; dir: Christopher Martin and Karen Sunde

PRODUCTIONS 1982-83

Faust, Pts. I and II, Johann Wolfgang Von Goethe; trans: Philip Wayne; dir: Christopher Martin
Ghost Sonata
Wild Oats, John O'Keeffe; dir: Christopher Martin
Balloon, Karen Sunde; dir: Karen Sunde and Christopher Martin
Danton's Death, Georg Buchner; trans: Christopher Martin; dir: Christopher Martin

DESIGNERS

Sets: Robert Weber Federico, Christopher Martin.
Costumes: Christopher Martin, Miriam Nieves.
Lights: Rick Butler, Christopher Martin.

Cumberland County Playhouse

MARY CRABTREE
JAMES R. CRABTREE
Producing Directors

PAT GUTHRIE
Board President

Box 484
Crossville, TN 38555
(615) 484-2300 (business)
(615) 484-5000 (box office)

FOUNDED 1965
Paul Crabtree, Margaret Keyes Harrison, Moses Dorton

SEASON
March–November

SCHEDULE
Evenings
Friday–Sunday (spring, fall)
Tuesday–Sunday (summer)

Matinees
Saturday, Sunday

FACILITIES
Highway 70 South
Seating capacity: 485
Stage: flexible

Theater-in-the-Woods
Seating capacity: 225
Stage: outdoor arena

Fairfield Glade Showroom
Seating capacity: 165
Stage: thrust

FINANCES
January 1, 1982–December 31, 1982
$328,000 operating expenses
$283,000 earned income
$ 39,000 grants/contributions

AUDIENCE
Annual attendance: 48,500
Subscribers: 1,150

AEA Guest Artist contract

Cumberland County Playhouse. Marc Powers and Mary Crabtree in Elizabeth the Queen. Photo: Jeff Mosser.

The Cumberland County Playhouse carries out a dual mission as both professional and community theatre, serving the rural Upper Cumberland area and the greater Knoxville/Nashville/Chattanooga region.

Founded in 1965 by the late Paul Crabtree and a group of visionary local citizens, the Playhouse has been managed and directed by members of the Crabtree family since its inception, and now serves an annual audience eight times the size of its hometown of Crossville (pop. 6,000). As "Tennessee's Family Theatre" the Playhouse strives to present a broad and challenging repertoire in a style that can be enjoyed by the entire family, and to serve as a regional cultural resource through several outreach and enrichment programs.

New works have always been an important part of the Playhouse's programming, beginning with Paul Crabtree's *Tennessee, USA!*, which has been seen in nine editions since 1965. Recent seasons have included five world premieres. Each season runs 36 to 40 weeks and includes six to eight productions. As of 1983, an outdoor theatre and a dinner theatre augment the proscenium playhouse.

Though it is Tennessee's largest professional theatre, volunteers remain an integral part of the Playhouse's entire operation. Through annual auditions in Crossville, Knoxville, Nashville, Atlanta and New York, a diversified company is selected with emphasis on people with ties to Tennessee and the Southeast. Performers include non-union professionals, Equity guest artists, local and regional volunteers, apprentices and performing interns. Rehearsals generally last three-and-a-half weeks, with performances running 5 to 10 weekends.

The Playhouse owns its well-equipped, 485-seat proscenium facility and has no accumulated deficit: since 1965, 88 percent of all revenues have been from earned income.

Programs and services

The Children's Creativity Center: classes and workshops; administrative and artistic internships; summer apprentice program; Sightlines newsletter; film series; children's theatre.

PRODUCTIONS 1981-82

110 in the Shade, Tom Jones and Harvey Schmidt; dir: James R. Crabtree
All the Way Home, Tad Mosel, dir: James R. Crabtree
An Introduction to Paperwork Management, Hal Corley; dir: James R. Crabtree
Guys and Dolls, book: Jo Swerling and Abe Burrows; music and lyrics: Frank Loesser; dir: James R. Crabtree
Cole, adapt: Alan Strachan and Benny Green; music and lyrics: Cole Porter; dir: Mary Crabtree
The Belle of Amherst, William Luce; dir: James R. Crabtree

Dallas Theater Center

Ladies in Retirement, Edward Percy and Reginald Denham; dir: Mary Crabtree

Cowboys!, book: Paul Mroczka; music and lyrics: John Briggs; dir: James R. Crabtree

Carnival, book and lyrics: Bob Merrill; music: Michael Stewart; dir: James R. Crabtree

The Glass Menagerie, Tennessee Williams; dir: James R. Crabtree

Two by Two, book: Peter Stone; music: Richard Rodgers; lyrics: Martin Charnin; dir: Mary Crabtree

PRODUCTIONS 1982-83

Tennessee, USA!, book, music and lyrics: Paul Crabtree; dir: James R. Crabtree

The Silver Screen, book: James and Mary Crabtree; music: Herb Bushnell; lyrics: James Crabtree; dir: James R. Crabtree

American Primitive, William Gibson; dir: James R. Crabtree

Arsenic and Old Lace, Joseph Kesselring; dir: Mary Crabtree

Temperance!, book and lyrics: James Crabtree; music: Ann Crabtree; dir: James R. Crabtree

The Crucible, Arthur Miller; dir: James R. Crabtree

Pippin, book: Roger Hirson; music and lyrics: Stephen Schwartz; dir: James R. Crabtree

Bye Bye Birdie, book: Michael Stewart; music: Charles Strouse; lyrics: Lee Adams; dir: Mary Crabtree

A Midsummer Night's Dream, William Shakespeare; dir: James R. Crabtree

Blithe Spirit, Noel Coward; dir: Mary Crabtree

Annie Get Your Gun, book: Herbert and Dorothy Fields; music and lyrics: Irving Berlin; dir: James R. Crabtree

DESIGNERS

Sets: Nathan Kwame Broun, Reagan Cook, James R. Crabtree, Brian Jackins, Karen Sparks Mellon, Caroyln D. Ott, Raymond C. Recht, John Scheffler.

Costumes: Laura Brookhart, Don Bolinger, Amelie Crabtree, Mary Crabtree, Brenda Schwab, Terry Schwab.

Lights: Scott Leathers, John Partyka, Steve Woods, Carolyn D. Ott, Raymond C. Recht, John Scheffler.

ADRIAN HALL
Artistic Director

ALBERT MILANO
General Manager

WILLIAM A. CUSTARD
Board President

3636 Turtle Creek Blvd.
Dallas, TX 75219
(214) 526-8210 (business)
(214) 526-8857 (box office)

FOUNDED 1959
Robert D. Stecker, Sr., Beatrice Handel, Paul Baker, Dallas citizens

SEASON
September-August

SCHEDULE

Evenings
Tuesday-Saturday

Matinees
Wednesday, Saturday

FACILITIES

Kalita Humphreys Theater
Seating capacity: 516
Stage: modified thrust

Down Center Stage
Seating capacity: 56
Stage: proscenium

FINANCES
September 1, 1982-August 31, 1983
$3,263,000 operating expenses
$2,024,000 earned income
$1,201,000 grants/contributions

AUDIENCE
Annual attendance: 175,000
Subscribers: 14,000

TOURING CONTACT
Carol Miles

BOOKED-IN EVENTS
Theatre

AEA LORT (C) contract

Dallas Theater Center began a new chapter in its history in the spring of 1983 when Adrian Hall, founder and artistic director of Trinity Square Repertory Company in Providence, R.I., was appointed artistic director. While continuing his association with Trinity Rep, Hall is working to provide Dallas playgoers with outstanding theatrical fare and to assemble an acting company of the highest quality.

Since its opening in 1959, Dallas Theater Center has presented more than 8,000 performances for adult audiences and children, both in its resident facility — designed by Frank Lloyd Wright — and on tour. Each season, DTC presents a balanced selection of classics, contemporary plays and world premieres. Prominent designers, directors, actors and writers from throughout the world come to the Theater Center to work, augmenting its resident company of professional theatre artists.

A past recipient of the Margo Jones Award for new play production, DTC has premiered more than 100 scripts, both by new writers and by established dramatists such as Mark Medoff, Robert Anderson, Paddy Chayefsky, and Jerome Lawrence and Robert E. Lee. Adrian Hall has also received the Margo Jones Award for his work with new American plays.

The Center focuses strongly on presenting professional productions, while not forgetting its commitment to enrich the lives of the citizens of Dallas and Texas through outreach and community service programs.

Programs and services

Teen-Children's Theater; community outreach and touring; Eugene McKinney New Play Reading Series; artistic, production and management internships.

Note: During the 1981-82 season, Paul Baker served as artistic director; during the 1982-83 season, Mary Sue Jones served as interim artistic director.

PRODUCTIONS 1981-82

Deathtrap, Ira Levin; dir: Christopher Pennywitt

War and Peace, adapt: Robert David MacDonald, Alfred Neumann, Erwin

Dallas Theater Center. Jenny Pichanick, James Hurdle and Paul Winfield in A Lesson from Aloes. *Photo: Linda Blase.*

Piscator and Guntram Prufer, from Leo Tolstoy; dir: Joan Vail Thorne
Tintypes, music and lyrics: various; adapt: Mary Kyte, Mel Marvin and Gary Pearle; dir: David Pursley
Of Mice and Men, John Steinbeck; dir: Anton Rodgers
Tartuffe, Molière; trans: Barnett Shaw; dir: Paul Baker
Black Coffee, Agatha Christie; dir: Walter Learning
The Gin Game, D. L. Coburn; dir: Karl Guttmann
Under Distant Skies, Jeffrey Kinghorn; dir: Randy Bonifay
Pigeons on the Walk, Andrew Johns; dir: Candy Buckley
The Wisteria Bush, Jo Vander Voort; dir: Michael Scudday

Beowulf—Nocturnal Solstice, Jim Marvin; dir: Robyn Flatt
The Miracle Worker, William Gibson; dir: Robyn Flatt
Macbeth, William Shakespeare; dir: Robyn Flatt
A Christmas Carol, adapt: Sally Netzel and John Filgmiller, from Charles Dickens; dir: Judith Davis
The Magic Turtle Series:
  Oz—Land of Magic, book and lyrics adapt: Jim Marvin, from L. Frank Baum; music: Randolph Tallman and Joe Cox; dir: Paul Munger
  Puss N. Boots, Ruth Cantrell; dir: Dennis Vincent
  The Legend of Sleepy Hollow, adapt: Frederick Gaines, from Washington Irving; dir: Peter Lynch

  Hansel and Gretel, Glenn Allen Smith; dir: Carol Miles
  Merlin and Arthur, Eleanor Lindsay; dir: Dennis Vincent

PRODUCTIONS 1982-83

The Three Musketeers, adapt: Peter Raby, from Alexandre Dumas; dir: David Pursley
A Murder Is Announced, adapt: Leslie Darbon, from Agatha Christie; dir: Robyn Flatt
A Lesson from Aloes, Athol Fugard; dir: Judith Davis
The Threepenny Opera, book and lyrics: Bertolt Brecht; music: Kurt Weill; trans: Marc Blitzstein; dir: Ivan Rider

Delaware Theatre Company

The Dresser, Ronald Harwood; dir: Mary Sue Jones
Talley's Folly, Lanford Wilson; dir: Robyn Flatt
Embarcadero Fugue, Thomas Strelich; dir: Kaki Dowling Hopkins
Topeka Scuffle, Paul Munger; dir: Dennis Vincent
The Pride of the Brittons, Kenneth Robbins; dir: Randy Bonifay
Angel and Dragon, Sally Netzel; dir: B. Jack Jones
A Christmas Carol

The Magic Turtle Series:

The Lion, the Witch and the Wardrobe, adapt from C.S. Lewis; dir: Eleanor Lindsay
Jane Eyre, adapt: John Logan, from Charlotte Bronte; dir: Mary Lou Hoyle
Step on a Crack, Suzan Zeder; dir: Kenneth Hill
Oz—Land of Magic

DESIGNERS

Sets: Yoichi Aoki, Sally Askins, Virgil Beavers, Irene Corey, Felecia Denney, Cheryl Denson, Robert Duffy, Zak Herring, Mary Sue Jones, John Landon, Peter Lynch, Stella McCord, David Pursley, Norman D. Schultz.
Costumes: Sally Askins, Virgil Beavers, Kathy Byrne, Irene Corey, Felecia Denney, Robert Duffy, Deborah Kinghorn, Scott L. Hammer, Tim Haynes, Russell Henderson, John Henson, Kenneth Hill, Mary Lou Hoyle, Ken Hudson, Stella McCord, Lynn Moon, Carol Miles, David Pursley, Ann Stephens, John Vigna.
Lights: Linda Blase, Randy Bonifay, Terrie Clark, Robert Duffy, Robyn Flatt, Raynard Harper, Zak Herring, Allen Hibbard, Ken Hudson, John Landon, Peter Lynch, Stella McCord, Randy Moore, Barbara Sanderson, John Vigna.

CLEVELAND MORRIS
Artistic Director

RAYMOND BONNARD
Managing Director

CHARLES F. RICHARDS, JR.
Board Chairman

303 French St.
Wilmington, DE 19801
(302) 658-6488 (business)
(302) 658-6445 (box office)

FOUNDED 1979
Peter DeLaurier, Cleveland Morris, Ceal Phelan

SEASON
October-March

SCHEDULE
Evenings
Tuesday-Saturday

Matinees
Wednesday, Saturday

FACILITIES
Mainstage
Seating capacity: 180
Stage: arena

Second Stage
808 Market St. Mall
Seating capacity: 60
Stage: thrust

FINANCES
September 1, 1982-August 31, 1983
$276,000 operating expenses
$103,000 earned income
$177,000 grants/contributions

AUDIENCE
Annual attendance: 16,900
Subscribers: 2,078

BOOKED-IN EVENTS
Theatre

AEA letter of agreement

The Delaware Theatre Company is the state's only resident professional theatre and is, like the state it serves, small but unique. Not viewing its size as a liability, the company seeks to do a limited number of things extremely well. Its annual subscription season of five productions is presented in a made-over firehouse and produced for a transverse stage (with the audience on two sides). Because of the informality and intimacy of the theatre itself, a highly detailed and subtle style of production has emerged and is evidenced in design and directorial technique, as well as acting.

As the state's unique professional theatre resource, the Theatre Company strives to present a diverse selection of plays, illustrating the range of the dramatic repertoire. Its small-cast, single-set productions are selected to emphasize the theatrical tradition that language is a powerful and effective technique of communication, and is society's principal method of developing and perpetuating thought. The theatre's programs strive to underscore the continuity of classical humanism, investigating the notion that an unreflective life is of inconsequential substance. In all programs, the theatre seeks to illustrate that entertainment can elicit a wide range of active responses.

Delaware Theatre Company maintains a fundamental sense of dual responsibility to both its artists and its audiences, in the hope that both can best be served through the production of first-quality theatre crafted expressly for the community.

Programs and services

Training program; artists-in-schools program; internships; lunchtime theatre; Tressler Forums: post-performance discussions led by a clinical psychologist.

PRODUCTIONS 1981-82

The Misanthrope, Molière; trans: Richard Wilbur; dir: Cleveland Morris
The Innocents, adapt: William Archibald, from Henry James; dir: Cleveland Morris
A Christmas Carol, adapt: Peter DeLaurier, from Charles Dickens; dir: Peter DeLaurier
Gemini, Albert Innaurato; dir: Frank Girardeau

Delaware Theatre Company. Ceal Phelan, Mary Cooper and Drucie McDaniel in Grand's Finale. *Photo: Richard Carter.*

Crime on Goat Island, Ugo Betti; dir: Richard Harden

Peg O' My Heart, J. Hartley Manners; dir: Cleveland Morris

PRODUCTIONS 1982-83

Tintypes, music and lyrics: various; adapt: Mary Kyte, Mel Marvin and Gary Pearle; dir: Derek Wolshonak

A Lesson from Aloes, Athol Fugard; dir: Bill Thompson

Talley's Folly, Lanford Wilson; dir: Peter DeLaurier

The Philoctetes, Sophocles; trans: Kenneth Cavander; dir: Cleveland Morris

Grand's Finale, Casey Kelly; dir: Cleveland Morris

The Gift of the Magi, adapt: Thomas Hischak, from O. Henry; dir: Peter De Laurier

The Undefeated Rhumba Champ, Charles Leipart; dir: Charles Gilbert, Jr.

Russian Strip, Drury Pifer; dir: Peter DeLaurier

Village Wooing, George Bernard Shaw; dir: Charles Gilbert, Jr.

Chinamen, Michael Frayn; dir: Sam Blackwell

DESIGNERS

Sets: Howard P. Beals, Jr., Robert McBroom, Thomas H. Schraeder, Dennis M. Size.

Costumes: Teri Beals, Barbara Forbes, Kenneth M. Yount.

Lights: Rachel Budin, Peter Reader, Harry Sangmeister, Thomas H. Schraeder, Dennis M. Size.

Dell'Arte Players Company

MICHAEL FIELDS
Managing Director

JOAN SCHIRLE
Board President

Box 816
Blue Lake, CA 95525
(707) 668-5411

FOUNDED 1971
Alain Schons, Joan Schirle, Michael Fields, Jael Weisman, Jon' Paul Cook, Carlo and Jane Mazzone-Clementi

SEASON
Year-round touring

FINANCES
October 1, 1981–September 30, 1982
$137,000 operating expenses
$ 73,000 earned income
$ 84,000 grants/contributions

AUDIENCE
Annual attendance: 25,000

TOURING CONTACT
Michael Fields

AEA letter of agreement

The Dell'Arte Players Company is an ensemble of professional actors and musicians inspired by commedia dell'arte, combining traditional acting values with highly developed skills in mask, acrobatics, juggling, etc. Based in rural Blue Lake, Calif., they have dramatized such subjects as the search for "Bigfoot," the medical profession and California water wars.

Themes derived from a rural lifestyle achieve universality in the hands of this touring company, and when combined with high performing standards (all company members are full-time, salaried professionals), a unique and exciting style results. In 1980, the Players were guests of the Italian government, the only American company to perform at the 1980 Venice Biennale.

The company unveils only one or two major works each year, after a long process of creation and investigation. Works are toured, rewritten and toured again, with continuous refinement of style, idea and execution. Each play is meant to be both entertaining and relevant to the lives of the company and its community. *Intrigue at Ah-Pah*, a mystery-comedy about the future of California's ecology, used the movie-detective genre with a private eye heroine; in *Whiteman Meets Bigfoot*, the legendary beast came to life from the pages of an R. Crumb

Dell'Arte Players Company. Donald Forrest, Joan Schirle and Michael Fields in Performance Anxiety. *Photo: Michael Rothman.*

Denver Center Theatre Company

comic book adapted for the stage with music.

Residencies and workshops are a major part of each touring itinerary, which includes rural towns, colleges, community centers and extended runs in major West Coast cities.

The company is associated with the Dell'Arte School of Mime and Comedy in Blue Lake, a professional training school emphasizing physical performance skills in a year-long program. Programs-in-schools, outreach through community service agencies and children's theatre are additional services of Dell'Arte.

Programs and services

Dell'Arte School of Mime and Comedy: full-time professional training; summer workshops in mask, cabaret and commedia; residencies, including lecture demonstrations, classes and performances.

PRODUCTIONS 1981-82

Performance Anxiety, company-developed; dir: Jael Weisman
Intrigue at Ah-Pah, company-developed; dir: Jael Weisman

PRODUCTIONS 1982-83

Performance Anxiety
You Can Be Replaced, company-developed; dir: Jael Weisman
A Child's Christmas in Humboldt County, company-developed; dir: Michael Fields
Malpractice, or Love Is the Best Doctor, company-adapt, from Molière; dir: Jael Weisman

DESIGNERS

Sets: Alain Schons.
Costumes: Cindy Claymore, Mimi Mace, Marianne Scozzari Raaberg.
Lights: Alain Schons, Ted Vukovich.

DONOVAN MARLEY
Artistic Director

GULLY STANFORD
Managing Director

DONALD R. SEAWELL
Board Chairman

1050 13th St.
Denver, CO 80204
(303) 893-4200 (business)
(303) 893-4100 (box office)

FOUNDED 1980
Denver Center for the Performing Arts

SEASON
November-June

SCHEDULE
Evenings
Monday-Saturday

Matinees
Saturday

FACILITIES
The Stage
Seating capacity: 650
Stage: thrust

The Space
Seating capacity: 450-465
Stage: flexible

The Lab
Seating capacity: 99
Stage: flexible

Denver Center Theatre Company. Quilters. *Photo: Nicholas De Sciose.*

FINANCES
July 1, 1982–June 30, 1983
$3,118,000 operating expenses
$1,276,000 earned income
$1,842,000 grants/contributions

AUDIENCE
Annual attendance: 175,000
Subscribers: 10,400

TOURING CONTACT
Eleanor Glover

BOOKED-IN EVENTS
Theatre, music, dance, lectures, fashion shows

AEA LORT (B) and Theatre for Young Audiences contracts

The Denver Center Theatre Company, which opened its doors on New Year's Eve 1979, is the only professional resident repertory theatre in the Rocky Mountain area. DCTC offers a seven-play season featuring the acting company in a variety of roles. Four plays operate on a rotating schedule in two different theatres throughout the season. It is regional theatre in the truest sense of the word, successfully serving the people of the entire Rocky Mountain region.

The Theatre presents classics re-interpreted for the contemporary audience, as well as works by the best current playwrights. It is also dedicated to presenting works by local playwrights, and has commissioned several plays exploring life in Colorado and the West. By making available the classics and the contemporary, as well as devoting a space to the creation of new works, the Theatre has achieved a distinctive presence in the American theatre.

DCTC mounts an annual regional tour of mainstage works in addition to its popular school tours. In August 1983, the Company traveled to the Edinburgh and Dublin Festivals with *Quilters,* a play created at the Center and given its world premiere during the 1982-83 season.

A division of the Denver Center for the Performing Arts, the theatre complex was designed by Kevin Roche and John Dinkeloo, and has been called "the crown jewel of Denver."

Programs and services

Subscriber magazine; high school ushers' workshop; student matinees; post-performance discussions; classes; signed performances; student internships.

Note: During the 1981-82 and 1982-83 seasons, Edward Payson Call served as artistic director.

PRODUCTIONS 1981-82

Androcles and the Lion, George Bernard Shaw; dir: Edward Payson Call
Tartuffe, Molière; trans: Richard Wilbur; dir: Richard Russell Ramos
An Enemy of the People, Henrik Ibsen; adapt: Arthur Miller; dir: Michael Lessac

The World of Sam Shepard:
  Patti's Poem to Sam, Sam Shepard and Patti Smith; dir: Mark Cuddy
  Suicide in B Flat, Sam Shepard; dir: Mark Cuddy

Antigone, Jean Anouilh; trans: Lewis Galantiere; dir: Larry Arrick
Much Ado About Nothing, William Shakespeare; dir: Edward Payson Call
A Double Play:
  Yanks 3, Detroit 0, Top of the Seventh, Jonathan Reynolds; dir: George Touliatos
  What the Babe Said, Martin Halpern; dir: George Touliatos

PRODUCTIONS 1982-83

Quilters, Molly Newman and Barbara Damashek; music and lyrics: Barbara Damashek; dir: Barbara Damashek
The Tempest, William Shakespeare; dir: Edward Payson Call
The Hostage, Brendan Behan; dir: Donovan Marley
Arms and the Man, George Bernard Shaw; dir: Edward Hastings
Of Mice and Men, John Steinbeck; dir: Richard Owen Geer
The Three Sisters, Anton Chekhov; trans: Tyrone Guthrie and Claude Kipnis; dir: Edward Payson Call
The Taming of the Shrew, William Shakespeare; dir: Barbara Damashek

DESIGNERS

Sets: Ursula Belden, Robert Blackman, Peter A. Davis, Lowell Detweiler, Christina Haatainen, Michael Stauffer, Thomas A. Walsh.
Costumes: Robert Blackman, Lowell Detweiler, Robert Fletcher, Christina Haatainen, Elizabeth P. Palmer, John David Ridge.
Lights: Dawn Chiang, Kent Dorsey, Allen Lee Hughes, Danny Ionazzi, Robert Jared, Duane Shuler, Greg Sullivan.

Detroit Repertory Theatre

BRUCE E. MILLAN
Artistic Director

ROBERT WILLIAMS
Executive Director

DOROTHY J. BROWN
Board Chairman

13103 Woodrow Wilson Ave.
Detroit, MI 48238
(313) 868-1347

FOUNDED 1957
Bruce E. Millan, Barbara Busby, T.O. Andrus

SEASON
September–June

SCHEDULE

Evenings
Thursday–Sunday

Matinees
Saturday

FACILITIES
Seating capacity: 196
Stage: proscenium

FINANCES
January 1, 1982–December 31, 1982
$155,000 operating expenses
$101,000 earned income
$131,000 grants/contributions

AUDIENCE
Annual attendance: 15,700
Subscribers: 552

AEA letter of agreement

Detroit Repertory Theatre. Peggy J. Woods, Wilton Hurtt, The American Tourist Puppets and William Paul Unger in The Man Who Killed the Buddha. *Photo: Bruce E. Millan.*

The Detroit Repertory Theatre was founded in 1957 under the name of the Millan Theatre Company, a touring company of adult professional actors performing music-dramas for children. Over a 10-year period the group originated seven music-dramas, many of which were subsequently produced by other children's theatres throughout the nation.

From the beginning, the Millan Theatre Company cast its racially mixed company without regard to race. When the 1967 riots hit metropolitan Detroit, there seemed to be no place for a company that stood fast on its principle of amalgamation. Funds for the touring program dried up and the children's theatre company became less wleecome both in the heart of the city and in suburban communities.

Artistic director Bruce E. Millan, as much for reasons of survival as aesthetics, made the decision to convert the rehearsal space at 13103 Woodrow Wilson into a small proscenium stage, and the company began performing adult theatre open to the public. The name Detroit Repertory Theatre was adopted to reflect the new direction of the Millan Theatre Company.

Some 15 years, 60 productions and 1,800 performances later, the Detroit Repertory Theatre is one of the few professional theatres in the country to remain staunchly dedicated to its neighborhood, and has become a living testimonial that perseverance, dedication and artistic excellence have cultural impact far beyond a physical location.

Today, plays are still made on Woodrow Wilson Avenue because of a burning compulsion to reflect and project, in artistic terms, the contours and content of human experience. The DRT is possessed by an endless need to search for meaning, truths and purposes to guide us all in the business of living

Programs and services

Cultural Fellowship Program; acting workshops; Michigan Playwrights Program; Repertory Gallery exhibits.

PRODUCTIONS 1981-82

A Lesson from Aloes, Athol Fugard; dir: Bruce E. Millan
The Captivity of Pixie Shedman, Romulus Linney; dir: Barbara Busby

Dorset Theatre Festival

An Enemy of the People, Henrik Ibsen; trans: Rolf Fjelde; dir: Barbara Busby
Byron's Ghost, Paul Simpson; dir: Bruce E. Millan

PRODUCTIONS 1982-83

Holy Ghosts, Romulus Linney; dir: Barbara Busby
2 by South, Frank South; dir: Bruce E. Millan:
   Precious Blood
   Rattlesnake in a Cooler
Two Pieces of Silver, Bruce E. Millan; dir: Bruce E. Millan and Ruth A. Palmer:
   Belder and the Bloom
   The Fisherman and His Wife
The Man Who Killed the Buddha, Martin Epstein; dir: Dee Andrus

DESIGNERS

Sets: Patrick Czeski, Bruce E. Millan.
Costumes: Anne-Kristiine Flones-Gzeski, Anne Saunders, Bernadine Vida-Darrell.
Lights: Steve Dambach, Kenneth R. Hewitt, Jr., Marylynn Kacir, Jeffrey Shabazz, Dick Smith.

JILL CHARLES
Artistic Director/Board President

JOHN NASSIVERA
Producing Director

Box 519
Dorset, VT 05251
(802) 867-2223 (business)
(802) 867-5777 (box office)

FOUNDED 1976
Jill Charles, John Nassivera

SEASON
June-October

SCHEDULE
Evenings
Tuesday-Sunday

Matinees
Saturday

FACILITIES
Cheney Road
Seating capacity: 218
Stage: proscenium

FINANCES
January 1, 1982-December 31, 1982
$160,000 operating expenses
$116,000 earned income
$ 41,000 grants/contributions

AUDIENCE
Annual attendance: 13,000
Subscribers: 200

AEA letter of agreement

Professional theatre has been a tradition at the Dorset Playhouse since the 1930s, shortly after the building was assembled from two pre-Revolutionary barns in the picturesque village of Dorset. The current structure of the Dorset Theatre Festival was established in 1976, and since that time the budget has more than tripled, the season has increased in length and the Colony House for Writers has opened its doors.

The artistic thrust of the Festival is to offer seasons of outstanding theatre with an interesting mixture of plays. In recent seasons, the Festival's trend has been toward American revivals such as *Sweeney Todd,* adapted from several 19th century versions of the play; *Little Women; Peg O' My Heart;* and a special production of the "rediscovered" Cole Porter musical *You Never Know*.

Another feature which distinguishes the Dorset Theatre Festival from many other companies operating on a short production season is its interest in new plays and in the nurturing of new American playwrights. To that end, the Dorset Colony House was founded in 1980, as a project of the Theatre Festival. The Colony House, which serves as a residence for the production company from June through September, is converted to a writers' colony for the remainder of the year. Playwrights can obtain residencies from one week to two months in duration to work on scripts in the seclusion of the 10-bedroom retreats. It is expected that writers using the Colony House will become a source of new scripts for production by the Festival. Each season the Festival has produced from one to three new plays or adaptations in its summer-fall season.

The Green Mountain region of southern

Dorset Theatre Festival. Janice Lynde and June Stein in The Miss Firecracker Contest. *Photo: Silvio Calabi.*

East West Players

Vermont has been known for more than a century as a retreat for artists and writers, and an area of outstanding New England culture. Through its professional productions and residency program, the Dorset Theatre Festival and Colony House helps to maintain this tradition.

Programs and services

Management internships; college apprenticeships; Colony House residencies, workshops and retreats.

PRODUCTIONS 1981-82

Deathtrap, Ira Levin; dir: John Morrison
Little Women, adapt: Marian de Forest, from Louisa May Alcott; dir: Jill Charles
Harvey, Mary Chase; dir: Edgar Lansbury
The Last of Mrs. Lincoln, James Prideaux; dir: John Morrison
You Never Know, book: Rowland Leigh; music and lyrics: Cole Porter; dir: Paul Lazarus
The Miss Firecracker Contest, Beth Henley; dir: Stuart White
The Belle of Amherst, William Luce; dir: John Morrison

PRODUCTIONS 1982-83

Sleuth, Anthony Shaffer; dir: John Morrison
Peg O' My Heart, J. Hartley Manners; dir: Jill Charles
A Moon for the Misbegotten, Eugene O'Neill; dir: John Morrison
On Borrowed Time, Paul Osborn; dir: Jill Charles
You Never Know
A Hard Look at Old Times, John Nassivera; dir: Jill Charles

DESIGNERS

Sets: William John Aupperlee, Keith Gonzales, James Katen.
Costumes: Emily Ellis, Heather Lee Vassar.
Lights: James Katen.

East West Players. Shizuko Hoshi, Jim Ishida and Jim Saito in The Dream of Kitamura. *Photo: James Young.*

MAKO
Artistic Director

JANET MITSUI
Administrator

ANDREW WONG
Board President

4424 Santa Monica Blvd.
Los Angeles, CA 90029
(213) 660-0366 (business)
(213) 660-0366, -0867 (box office)

FOUNDED 1965
Mako, James Hong, June Kim, Guy Lee, Pat Li, Yet Lock, Beulah Quo

SEASON
October-June

SCHEDULE
Evenings
Tuesday-Sunday

FACILITIES
Seating capacity: 99
Stage: flexible

FINANCES
July 1, 1981-June 30, 1982
$175,000 operating expenses
$ 98,000 earned income
$ 85,000 grants/contributions

AUDIENCE
Annual attendance: 60,000
Subscribers: 700

TOURING CONTACT
Janet Mitsui

AEA 99-seat waiver

The East West Players was formed in 1965 when seven Asian American actors representing the Japanese, Chinese and Korean communities joined to create an acting company—the first Asian American theatre in the country.

The avowed purpose of East West Players is to acknowledge and celebrate the Asian/Pacific American experience. The company addresses the frustration of people who, despite their accomplishments and contributions to American society, remain largely an invisible minority or, perhaps worse, are consistently locked into stereotypical roles.

The company provides a forum where Asian and Pacific artists—both performers and writers—can create true and meaningful additions to American theatre, express and preserve the cultural heritage of their community and, perhaps most importantly, bridge cultural understanding between East and West through the performing arts.

In line with its goals, East West Players presents an annual season of primarily origi-

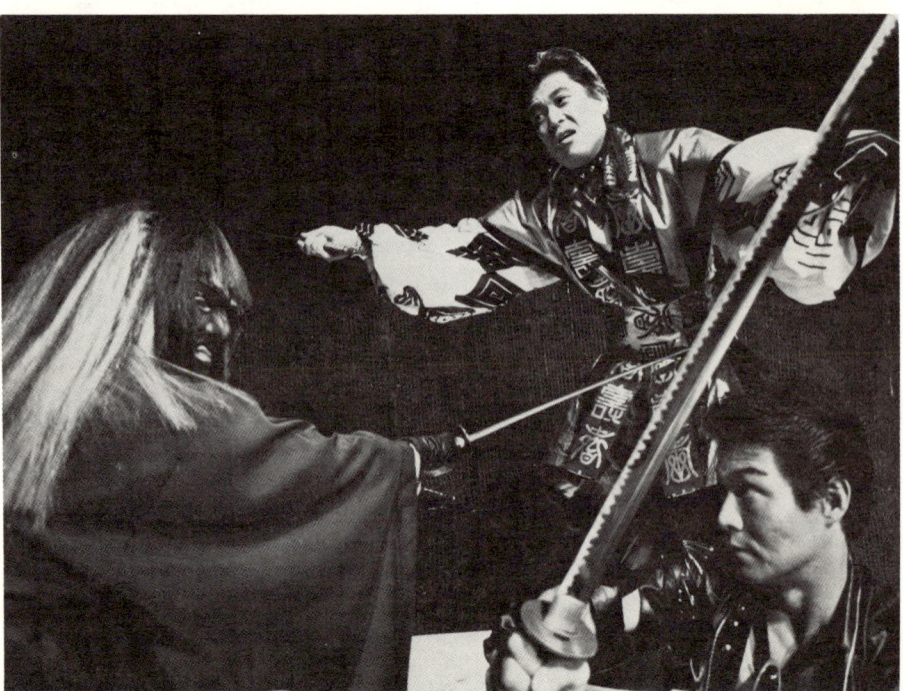

El Teatro Campesino

nal works at its East Hollywood facility, showcases Asian/Pacific musicians and dancers in regularly scheduled recitals and concerts, and schedules tours to disseminate its unique theatrical vision.

Programs and services

Summer acting workshop; foreign language tour; programs-in-schools; staged readings.

PRODUCTIONS 1981-82

Station J: An American Epic, Richard France; dir: Mako and Alberto Isaac
Christmas in Camp, Dom Magwili; concept: Mako; dir: Mako and Shizuko Hoshi
12-1-A, Wakako Yamauchi; dir: Saburo
Pilgrimmage, Edward Sakamoto; dir: Mako and Shizuko Hoshi

PRODUCTIONS 1982-83

Imperial Valley, Margaret De Priest; dir: Mako and Shizuko Hoshi
Have You Heard, Soon-Teck Oh, with Kwang Lim Kim and Sukman Kim; dir: Shizuko Hoshi, Mako and Soon-Teck Oh
Yamashita, Roger Pulvers; dir: Alberto Isaac and Betty Muramoto
The Dream of Kitamura, Philip Kan Gotanda; dir: Mako
No Smile for Strangers, Harold Heifetz; dir: Mako and Dana Lee
Yellow Fever, R.A. Shiomi; dir: Alberto Isaac

DESIGNERS

Sets: Fred Chuang, Rae Creevey, Shizuko Herrera, Mako.
Costumes: Rodney Kageyama, Terrence Tam Soon, Shigeru Yaji.
Lights: Rae Creevey, Shizuko Herrera.

LUIS VALDEZ
Artistic Director/Board Chairman

GLORIAMALIA FLORES PEREZ
Executive Director

Box 1240
San Juan Bautista, CA 95045
(408) 623-4505 (business)
(408) 623-2444 (box office)

FOUNDED 1965
Luis Valdez

SEASON
Year-round

SCHEDULE
Evenings
Wednesday-Saturday

Matinees
Saturday, Sunday

FACILITIES
705 Fourth St.
Seating capacity: 150
Stage: flexible

FINANCES
October 1, 1981-September 30, 1982
$380,000 operating expenses
$ 56,000 earned income
$325,000 grants/contributions

AUDIENCE
Annual attendance: 39,500

TOURING CONTACT
Phil Esparza

AEA letter of agreement

El Teatro Campesino looks back on many years of growth and accomplishment as a contributing force in the Chicano cultural, sociological and political renaissance.

Ever expanding, the theatre's aesthetic now encompasses a vision of the world which correlates urban and rural realities; thus it is serving more and more as a cross-cultural bridge between Chicanos and other ethnic and cultural groups which form the fabric of the new American society. The organic evolution of the Campesino aesthetic has been rooted from the beginning in the

El Teatro Campesino. Socorro Valdez, Bel Hernandez and Jorge Galvan in Dona Elena y el Frances. *Photo: Joe Ramos.*

Empire State Institute for the Performing Arts

indigenous culture of Mexican farmworkers.

Another mission of this professional company is to create, produce and present in its own resident theatre in San Juan Bautista, "popular" theatre and dance; then to tour nationally and internationally those productions with proven, broad audience appeal.

A last but basic objective is to provide a unique institution in a rural setting for gifted aspiring artists — from large urban areas, small towns or farm labor camps—to train, work and develop professional skills in the performing arts.

Programs and services

Touring; artistic and administrative internships; sale of films, publications, records and tapes.

PRODUCTIONS 1981-82

Bandido!, Luis Valdez; dir: Luis Valdez
Los Corridos, Luis Valdez; dir: Luis Valdez
Soldierboy, Severo and Judith Perez; dir: Luis Valdez
La Virgen del Tepeyac, adapt: Luis Valdez; dir: Socorro Valdez

PRODUCTIONS 1982-83

Los Corridos
The Rogue of Seville, Tirso de Molina; adapt: Michael Griggs; dir: Michael Griggs
La Pastorela, traditional; dir: Socorro Valdez

DESIGNERS

Sets: Gary Daines, Eddie Martinez, Russell Pyle, Luis Valdez.
Costumes: Diane Rodriguez, Frances Romero, Kim Simons, Elaine Yokoyama.
Lights: Jose Lopez, Randy Kone, Russell Pyle.

PATRICIA B. SNYDER
Producing Director

ROBERT J. MORGADO
Board President

FOUNDED 1976
Empire State Youth Theatre Institute and Governor Nelson A. Rockefeller Empire State Plaza Performing Arts Center Corporation

Empire State Plaza
Albany, NY 12223
(518) 474-1199 (business)
(518) 473-3750 (box office)

SEASON
September-June

SCHEDULE
Evenings
Friday, Saturday

Matinees
Monday-Friday, Sunday

FACILITIES
Mainstage
Seating capacity: 883
Stage: flexible

Recital Hall
Seating capacity: 450
Stage: thrust

FINANCES
April 1, 1982-March 31, 1983
$669,000 operating expenses
$887,000 earned income
$ 18,000 grants/contributions

AUDIENCE
Annual attendance: 82,000
Subscribers: 578

TOURING CONTACT
Renee Hariton

BOOKED-IN EVENTS
Dance, music, theatre

The program of the Empire State Institute for the Performing Arts focuses on the creation and presentation of top-quality music, dance and theatre productions designed for the widest possible family audience. These productions combine the highest professional and artistic standards with a dedication to educational and community involvement, thus encouraging audiences to know and appreciate artists and their work.

To protect the long-range goals and high purpose of this venture, ESIPA has built upon the firm foundation established by the Empire State Youth Theatre Institute of the State University of New York, and the experience of the Nelson A. Rockefeller Empire State Plaza Performing Arts Center Corporation.

Over the past six seasons the Youth Theatre has provided a unique and carefully designed program of performances which are significantly integrated with pre- and post-performance education activities. Each production of the Youth Theatre has generated research material and in-service presentations for teachers and members of the community. This arts-in-education policy has built a new generation of discerning audiences who understand the importance of supporting top-quality theatre.

The artistic, educational and community service mission of the Youth Theatre has been expanded by the work of the Empire State Institute for the Performing Arts. The home base of these activities is the appropriately dramatic, architecturally striking theatre designed by Wallace Harrison which is the centerpiece of the Nelson A. Rockefeller Empire State Plaza in Albany, and has been affectionately dubbed "The Egg" by the community. Since the egg is the beginning of life, it is appropriate that this designation has stuck. The Empire State Institute for the Performing Arts hopes that The Egg will be the source of a new artistic vitality in the Albany community, the educational system of New York State, and the world of professional theatre.

Empire State Institute for the Performing Arts.
Nightingale. *Photo: Fred Ricard.*

Programs and services

Guest Artists Series; New Play Program: staged readings, workshops and fellowships for playwrights; residencies; college and high school internships; research materials; theatre arts school; Straw Hat Summer Program for high school and college students; Dance Ensemble; master classes and symposia; accessibility program.

PRODUCTIONS 1981-82

Beauty and the Beast, Ray Bono; dir: W.A. Frankonis
The Swan, Ferenc Molnar; trans: Benjamin F. Glazer; dir: Rose Deak
The Wizard of Oz, adapt from L. Frank Baum; music: Harold Arlen; lyrics: E.Y. Harburg; dir: Patricia B. Snyder
Antigone, Sophocles; dir: Shela Xoregos
Fiddler on the Roof, book: Joseph Stein; music: Jerry Bock; lyrics: Sheldon Harnick; dir: Joseph Balfior
The Thwarting of Baron Bolligrew, Robert Bolt; dir: W.A. Frankonis

PRODUCTIONS 1982-83

The All-Time Good-Time Knickerbocker Follies, book: Hugh Wheeler; music and lyrics: various; dir: Patricia Birch
Romeo and Juliet, William Shakespeare; dir: W.A. Frankonis
The Wizard of Oz
The Wind in the Willows, book adapt and lyrics: John Jakes, from Kenneth Grahame; music: Claire Strauch; dir: Edmund Waterstreet
You Can't Take It with You, Moss Hart and George S. Kaufman; dir: John Going
Nightingale, Charles Strouse; dir: Joseph Balfior

DESIGNERS

Sets: Marcia Louis Eck, Richard Finkelstein, Klaus Holm, Penny Kurtz, Dan Leigh, Tom Lynch, Stuart Wurtzel.
Costumes: Robert Anton, Marcia Louis Eck, Karen Kammer, Fanny Kemenes, Penny Kurtz, Elaine Yokoyama Roos, Hilary Rosenfeld, Fred Voelpel, Patrizia von Brandenstein, Sally Whitmore.
Lights: Ed Effron, Toni Goldin, Richard Nelson, Lary Opitz, Lloyd S. Riford III.

The Empty Space

M. BURKE WALKER
Artistic Director

KEVIN M. HUGHES
Managing Director

WILLIAM STALZER
Board President

919 East Pike St.
Seattle, WA 98122
(206) 325-4444 (business)
(206) 325-4443 (box office)

FOUNDED 1970
M. Burke Walker, Charles Younger, Julian Schembri, James Royce

SEASON
October-June

SCHEDULE
Evenings
Tuesday-Sunday

Matinees
Sunday

FACILITIES
Seating capacity: 99
Stage: flexible

FINANCES
July 1, 1982-June 30, 1983
$535,000 operating expenses
$321,000 earned income
$243,000 grants/contributions

AUDIENCE
Annual attendance: 30,000
Subscribers: 3,011

AEA letter of agreement

Founded in 1970, the Empty Space has evolved from an all-volunteer theatre lab into a fully professional company of artists, technicians and managers whose philosophy has remained consistent through 13 years: to produce works of significance from the writers of our generation. The production of new works is complemented with occasional contemporary or classic revivals, and excursions into the too-often-neglected world of low comedy.

The Space has worked actively with local

Empty Space Theatre. Rebecca Wells, Rex Rabold, Kevin Field and Gwen Jackson in Sister Mary Ignatius Explains It All for You. *Photo: Chris Bennion.*

writers and performers to develop and produce new works for the mainstage. This emphasis on regional playwrights has taken on added importance with the beginning of the New Playwrights Forum in 1978, the Northwest Playwrights Conference in 1981 and the One-Act Play Commission Project in 1982.

The theatre extended its development work at the national level in 1982 when Mabou Mines' Lee Breuer was in residence, developing his play *Red Beads*. In 1983, as participants in the first round of the CBS/FDG New Play Program, the Empty Space produced Richard Nelson's *The Return of Pinocchio*. Direct contact, commissions and collaboration with artists of national stature will continue in upcoming seasons.

The Space's focus on new playwrights took an international turn in 1980-81 when a decision was made to expand programming beyond its American/British/Canadian bias. Productions of Jean-Claude Grumberg's *The Workroom* and Dario Fo's *We Won't Pay! We Won't Pay!* were followed by the English language premieres of Franz Xaver Kroetz' *Mensch Meier* in 1982 and *Through the Leaves* in 1983. Through an active program of translation commissions, the Empty Space is further expanding that program.

These initiatives in production, development and translation have one shared goal: to provide new texts for the Space's artists and audiences which can then be shared with other theatres nationally and internationally.

Programs and services

Administrative and technical internships; script commissions; staged and non-staged readings; workshops; newsletter; volunteer auxiliary.

PRODUCTIONS 1981-82

Bent, Martin Sherman; dir: John Kauffman
Talley's Folly, Lanford Wilson; dir: M. Burke Walker
Fefu and Her Friends, Maria Irene Fornes; dir: M. Burke Walker and John Kauffman
Mensch Meier, Franz Xaver Kroetz; trans: Roger Downey; dir: M. Burke Walker
The Clown Show, Diane Schenker, Kurt Beattie, Megan Dean, Lori Larsen, Robert Wright and Kathryn Sestrap; dir: Diane Schenker and John Kauffman

PRODUCTIONS 1982-83

Sister Mary Ignatius Explains It All for You and *The Actor's Nightmare,* Christopher Durang; dir: M. Burke Walker
Tartuffe, Molière; adapt: Roger Downey; dir: Jeff Steitzer
Through the Leaves, Franz Xaver Kroetz; trans: Roger Downey; dir: Emily Mann
Woza Albert!, Percy Mtwa, Mbongeni Ngema and Barney Simon; dir: Barney Simon
The Return of Pinocchio, Richard Nelson; dir: M. Burke Walker
Filthy Rich, George F. Walker; dir: Jeff Steitzer

DESIGNERS

Sets: William Bloodgood, Bill Forrester, Karen Gjelsteen, Barney Simon, Scott Weldin.
Costumes: Sheryl Collins, Celeste Cleveland, Laura Crow, Ron Erickson, Michael Murphy, Sally Richardson.
Lights: Michael Davidson, Rick Kennedy-Paulsen, Mannie Manim, Jeff Robbins, Jim Royce.

Ensemble Studio Theatre

CURT DEMPSTER
Artistic Director

DAVID S. ROSENAK
Managing Director

G.H. DENNISTON, JR.
Board Chairman

549 West 52nd St.
New York, NY 10019
(212) 247-4982

FOUNDED 1971
Curt Dempster

SEASON
October-June

SCHEDULE

Evenings
Tuesday-Sunday

Matinees
Sunday

FACILITIES

Mainstage
Seating capacity: 98
Stage: flexible

Workshop
Seating capacity: 50
Stage: flexible

Workshop
Seating capacity: 40
Stage: flexible

FINANCES
July 1, 1982-June 30, 1983
$444,000 operating expenses
$104,000 earned income
$309,000 grants/contributions

AUDIENCE
Annual attendance: 18,300
Subscribers: 250

AEA letter of agreement

The Ensemble Studio Theatre was founded in 1971 as a membership organization of theatre professionals and today is composed of more than 300 playwrights, actors, directors, designers, technicians and administrators. Dedicated to nurturing the resources of professional theatre, EST has an active, ongoing program of developing new works for the stage, and providing artistic and financial support for EST artist members, who can work among their peers in a stimulating and supportive environment free from commercial pressures.

For the past six years, EST has celebrated its commitment to the one-act form by presenting an annual spring festival of 12 to 16 new one-acts by new and established writers. A season at EST includes three new American plays, the one-act Marathon, and New Voices, a series of staged readings of full-length plays in development. Ongoing series of readings and workshops focus on the development of new work by member artists and selected non-members.

In 1982-83, EST was one of five theatres in the country selected to participate in the first FDG/CBS New Plays Program. The theatre also received the 1982 Brandeis University Creative Arts Award, citing it as a "rich environment for the creation and nurturing of new American plays."

EST encourages its members to pursue more than one theatrical discipline: typically, actors will write or direct; playwrights will direct or act; resulting in the development of a multi-talented ensemble. An annual summer conference provides a retreat where members have an opportunity to develop ideas and new work for the coming season within a relaxed artistic community.

The theatre occupies two-and-a-half floors of a city-owned warehouse, housing two flexible performing spaces, offices, dressing rooms and a scene shop. An annex at 12 West End Ave. provides space for the literary department, the Institute and two classroom/workshop/rehearsal studios.

Ensemble Studio Theatre, Robert Joy and June Stein in Welcome to the Moon. *Photo: Carol Rosegg.*

Eureka Theatre Company

ANTHONY TACCONE
Artistic Director

MARY MASON
General Manager

PAUL W. FAGIN
Board President

2730 16th St.
San Francisco, CA 94103
(415) 558-9811

FOUNDED 1972
Robert Woodruff, Chris Silva

SEASON
October-August

SCHEDULE
Evenings
Wednesday-Sunday

FACILITIES
Seating capacity: 200
Stage: flexible

FINANCES
October 1, 1982-September 30, 1983
$214,000 operating expenses
$ 40,000 earned income
$175,000 grants/contributions

AUDIENCE
Annual attendance: 6,000
Subscribers: 900

TOURING CONTACT
Mary Mason

AEA letter of agreement

Eureka Theatre Company retains a strong commitment to producing contemporary plays that attempt to interpret the political and social contradictions of our world. Regardless of the wide range of styles which these plays and their authors employ, each seeks to penetrate the myriad of moral, psychological and historical assumptions we, as Americans living in the 1980s, make about the world in which we reside.

Each mainstage project in the 1983 season was a reflection of this idea. The company worked extensively, for example, with Amlin Gray, author of *How I Got That Story*, on resetting his highly successful play about

Programs and services

Workshop series; Octoberfest: two-week festival of workshops and staged readings; New Voices: spring series of full-length staged readings; weekly literary department readings; playwrights' unit; summer conference; Institute for Professional Training: classes in acting, directing, playwriting and screenwriting; internships in production, stage management, casting, administration, development and marketing.

PRODUCTIONS 1981-82

Best of the Marathon:
  A Sermon, David Mamet; dir: David Mamet
  Dumping Ground, Elizabeth Diggs; dir: Pamela Berlin
  The Lady or the Tiger, Shel Silverstein; dir: Art Wolff
  Open Admissions, Shirely Lauro; dir: Elinor Renfield

The House Across the Street, Darrah Cloud; dir: Bruce Levitt
Bella Figura, Brother Jonathan, O.S.F.; dir: John Schwab
Marathon '82:
  Fog, Conrad Bromberg; dir: Marilyn Rockafellow
  Appearances, Tina Howe; dir: Douglas Johnson
  The Undefeated Rhumba Champ, Charles Leipart; dir: Charles I. Karchmer
  The Forest Lawn Diet, James G. Richardson; dir: Raymond Singer
  The Fisher Wedding, Carol Hall; dir: Marcia Haufrecht
  The Fortress of Solitude, Jeffrey M. Jones; dir: James A. Simpson
  Goodbye, Howard, Romulus Linney; dir: Art Wolff
  The Self-Begotten, John Weldman; dir: Pamela Berlin
  Buddies, Mary Gallagher; dir: Mary B. Robinson
  Ord-Way, Ames-Gay, Susan Vick; dir: Pamela Berlin
  Rosario and the Gypsies, book and lyrics: Eduardo Machado; music: Rick Vartorella; dir: Shirley Kaplan
  Kilo, Marc B. Berman; dir: Risa Bramon
  Class Reunion, Kermit Frazier; dir: Madeline Thornton Sherwood
  Many Happy Returns, Willie Reale; dir: June Stein
  Routed, Jeffrey Sweet; dir: Charles I. Karchmer

PRODUCTIONS 1982-83

Welcome to the Moon, John Patrick Shanley; dir: Douglas Aibel
The Modern Ladies of Guanabacoa, Eduardo Machado; dir: James Hammerstein
The House of Ramon Iglesia, Jose Rivera; dir: Jack Gelber
Marathon '83:
  Touch Black, Bill Bozzone; dir: Risa Bramon
  The Survivalist, Robert Schenkkan; dir: Steven Albrezzi
  The Dolphin Position, Percy Granger; dir: Jack Gelber
  Five Unrelated Pieces, David Mamet; dir: Curt Dempster
  Postcards, Carol K. Mack; dir: Joan Micklin Silver
  Poisoner of the Wells, Brother Jonathan, O.S.F.; dir: James A. Simpson
  Pastoral or Recollections of Country Life, Peter Maloney; dir: John Schwab
  Tender Offer, Wendy Wasserstein; dir: Jerry Zaks
  Eulogy, James G. Richardson; dir: Heidi Helen Davis
  Cash, Stuart Spencer; dir: Charles I. Karchmer
  I Love You, I Love You Not, Wendy Kesselman; dir: Julianne Boyd
  Delusions of a Government Witness, Louis Lippa; dir: Pamela Berlin
  Fast Woman, Willie Reale, dir: W.H. Macy
  Two Hot Dogs with Everything, William Wise; dir: Richard Russell Ramos

DESIGNERS

Sets: Bennet Averyt, Dana Hasson, Dale Jordan, Brian Martin, Johniene Papandreas, Evelyn Sakash, Leslie Taylor.
Costumes: Gail Brassard, Madeline Cohen, Martha Hally, Nina Moser, Isis Mussenden, Deborah Shaw.
Lights: Geoffrey Dunbar, Todd Elmer, Richard Lund, Mal Sturchio, Cheryl Thacker.

Eureka Theatre Company. Luis Oropeza and Charles Jenkins in How I Got That Story. *Photo: Allen Nomura.*

Vietnam to reflect the current situation in Central America. Eureka commissioned Emily Mann, with whom it had built a strong relationship during production of her *Still Life*, to write a play dealing with the shocking assassinations of former San Francisco mayor George Moscone and supervisor Harvey Milk by supervisor Dan White. Eureka produced the English premiere of *Neither Fish nor Fowl*, the newest play by Germany's Franz Xaver Kroetz, which deals with the effects of automation and corporate modernization on the lives of two families. Finally, it produced Caryl Churchill's enormously popular *Cloud 9*, which probes the formation of a culture's basic values toward sexuality.

Taken together, these plays represent Eureka's current interests and project an accurate blueprint for the theatre's aspirations. The emphasis is on working with leading American and international playwrights, all of whom have a strong social conscience and proven level of skill in the creation, translation and/or application of their work to the concerns of artists and audiences in the San Francisco Bay Area.

Programs and services

Touring; readings; internships; acting classes.

PRODUCTIONS 1981-82

The Jail Diary of Albie Sachs, David Edgar; dir: Anthony Taccone and Oskar Eustis
A Mad World, My Masters, Barrie Keeffe; dir: Richard E. T. White and Oskar Eustis
Still Life, Emily Mann; dir: Anthony Taccone
Lucky Lindy, Dick D. Zigun; dir: David Ostwald

PRODUCTIONS 1982-83

How I Got That Story, Amlin Gray; dir: Anthony Taccone
Neither Fish nor Fowl, Franz Xaver Kroetz; trans: Oskar Eustis; dir: Susan Marsden
Cloud 9, Caryl Churchill; dir: Richard Seyd

DESIGNERS

Sets: Gene Angell, Jeffrey Beecroft, Ed Botts, William Eddelman, Peggy McDonald, Ron Pratt, Randy Richards.
Costumes: Vivian Altmann, Barbara Bush, Eliza Chugg, William Eddelman.
Lights: Rhonda Birnbaum, James Brentano, Stephanie Johnson, Kurt Landisman, Jackie Manassee.

Fairmount Theatre of the Deaf

MICHAEL G. REGNIER
Acting Artistic Director

PEGGY SHUMATE
Administrative Director

MARY JOHNSON KNERLY
Board President

11206 Euclid Ave.
Cleveland, OH 44106
(216) 231-8787, ext. 262, 265, 231
(business)
(216) 795-7000 (box office)

FOUNDED 1975
Brian Kilpatrick, Charles St. Clair

SEASON
December-May

SCHEDULE
Evenings
Wednesday-Saturday

Matinees
Saturday, Sunday

FACILITIES
Brooks Theatre
2040 East 86th St.
Seating capacity: 160
Stage: proscenium

FINANCES
July 1, 1982-June 30, 1983
$230,000 operating expenses
$ 54,000 earned income
$176,000 grants/contributions

AUDIENCE
Annual attendance: 40,000

TOURING CONTACT
Peggy Shumate

Fairmount Theatre of the Deaf is America's only resident professional sign language and voice theatre. The board of trustees and the company are dedicated to the following purposes:

1) To produce professional (published and original) dramatic works, and creatively integrate the spoken word with sign language and other theatrical techniques, thereby

The First All

creating theatre that is accessible both to the hearing and deaf person.

2) To increase and enhance public awareness of the world of deafness, and to enrich the lives of hearing and deaf persons by uniting them in a shared theatrical experience which exposes hearing audiences to the beauty of the languages of deaf persons, while exposing the realm of theatre arts to the deaf and hearing-impaired.

3) To offer career opportunities and training in theatre arts to both deaf and hearing persons.

4) To create and produce educational programming for hearing and deaf elementary, secondary and college students, senior citizens and the general public. At present, outreach programming includes full-length performances; residencies; programs-in-schools; slide shows; lecture/demonstrations; showcase performances and workshops.

5) To create, provide and produce touring and/or media productions for the Greater Cleveland area, the state, the country and other countries.

6) To nurture playwrights and aid in the creation of sign language-translated scripts.

Programs and services

Residencies; FTD-in-the-Schools program; slide shows and lecture demonstrations; workshops in sign language theatre, sign language, sign and song, creative dramatics and mime; touring; volunteers.

Note: During the 1981-82 season, Robert Tolaro served as artistic director.

PRODUCTIONS 1981-82

Dracula, adapt: Don Bangs and Robert Tolaro, from Bram Stoker; dir: Robert Tolaro
The Odd Couple, Neil Simon; dir: Benjamin Strout
Circus of Signs, Adrian Blue and Deborah Taylor; dir: Adrian Blue
Story Theatre, Paul Sills; dir: Robert Tolaro

PRODUCTIONS 1982-83

Circus of Signs, dir: Chuck Sidlow
The Amorous Flea, book: Jerry Devine; music and lyrics: Bruce Montgomery; dir: Word Baker and Roderic Kates

DESIGNERS

Sets: Donald McBride.
Costumes: Harriet Cone, Jackie Kilpatrick, Reggie Ray, Debbie Rennie, Robert Tolaro.
Lights: Dennie Fyffe, Bruce Keller.

MERIDEE STEIN
Artistic Director

LISA LOOSEMORE
Business Manager

ROBERT HARSHAW
Board President

37 West 65th St.
New York, NY 10023
(212) 873-6400

FOUNDED 1969
Meridee Stein

SEASON
October-June

SCHEDULE
Evenings
Variable

Matinees
Saturday, Sunday

FACILITIES
Seating capacity: 125
Stage: thrust

The Samantha Difiris Theatre
Seating capacity: 50
Stage: thrust

FINANCES
September 1, 1982-August 31, 1983
$340,000 operating expenses
$177,000 earned income
$163,000 grants/contributions

AUDIENCE
Annual attendance: 22,450

TOURING CONTACT
Lisa Loosemore

Founded in 1969, The First All Children's Theatre is a repertory company dedicated to presenting theatre of the highest artistic quality performed by young people ages 8 through 22. The company continues to serve as a training center for young perform-

Fairmount Theatre of the Deaf. The Amorous Flea. *Photo: Michael Zaremba.*

Children's Theatre

ers, a catalyst for writers and composers engaged in creating original musical works for family audiences and a means of inspiring and cultivating a youthful audience's awareness of theatre's ability to excite, challenge and reveal.

Each season the company produces four original musicals commissioned by First ACT, one of which is a world premiere developed over a two- to three-year period. The company has performed at the New York Shakespeare Festival, Annenberg Center, Beacon Theatre, Alaska Repertory Theatre and in annual benefits on Broadway. It has also appeared on all three major television networks and in a TV film about teamwork in America entitled *Nobody Does It Better Than You, America,* featuring Ed Asner.

Over the past several years the company has emerged as a national resource for child arts. In this capacity, First ACT was chosen to represent the United States on the satellite telecast officially launching the United Nations International Year of the Child. The Company has also been part of two international exchanges: as host to the Flemish Children's Theatre of Ghent at Lincoln Center in New York, at the Smithsonian Institution in Washington, DC and as part of the All China Youth Federation Exchange Program to the People's Republic of China.

Artistry has been and shall remain First ACT's primary objective, but its commitment to the growth of young people has brought about a host of community outreach programs in addition to its performing schedule.

The First All Children's Theatre. John Schuck and company member in Nightingale. *Photo: Anthony Stein.*

Programs and services

Workshops; teacher training seminars; free and discounted tickets for the disadvantaged and handicapped; programs-in-schools.

PRODUCTIONS 1981-82

Medusa, Robert Pridham; dir: Meridee Stein

Guess Again, book and lyrics: Benjamin Goldstein; music: Philip Namanworth; dir: Linda Reiff

The Children's Crusade, book and lyrics: Kenneth Cavander; music: Richard Peaslee; dir: Meridee Stein

Nightingale, book, music and lyrics: Charles Strouse; dir: Meridee Stein

PRODUCTIONS 1982-83

The Incredible Feeling Show, book, music and lyrics: Elizabeth Swados; dir: Meridee Stein

Nightingale

The Children's Crusade

The Trip, book adapt: Anthony Stein, from Ezra Jack Keats; music and lyrics: Stephen Schwartz; dir: Meridee Stein

DESIGNERS

Sets: Marjorie Bradley Kellogg, Oliver Smith, Mavis Smith, Ezra Jack Keats.
Costumes: Christine Andrews, Eloise Lowry, Ezra Jack Keats.
Lights: Victor En Yu Tan, Joshua White, Stan Pressner.

Florida Studio Theatre

RICHARD HOPKINS
Artistic Director

PATRICIA BALDWIN
Managing Director

ROBERT DRABIK
Board President

1241 North Palm Ave.
Sarasota, FL 33577
(813) 366-9017 (business)
(813) 366-9796 (box office)

FOUNDED 1973
Jon Spelman

SEASON
November–April

SCHEDULE
Evenings
Tuesday–Sunday

Matinees
Friday, Saturday

FACILITIES
Seating capacity: 165
Stage: modified thrust

FINANCES
July 1, 1982–June 30, 1983
$170,000 operating expenses
$ 85,000 earned income
$ 85,000 grants/contributions

AUDIENCE
Annual attendance: 21,000
Subscribers: 1,950

TOURING CONTACT
Lach Adair

BOOKED-IN EVENTS
Theatre, music, dance, puppetry

AEA letter of agreement

Three years of path-finding have grown into a solid philosophy and a unified approach to the work at Florida Studio Theatre. That philosophy is best reflected in James Joyce's statement that the purpose of the artist is "to create the uncreated conscience of the race." The theatre interprets this to mean that its objective is to lead the audience down those dark corridors too frightening to tread alone. To reveal ourselves to ourselves. To conjure up the greater reality that lies beneath the surface reality. It can happen in comedy or drama, classics or contemporary works.

The aesthetics of FST are best served by a small, intimate atmosphere where the artist can explore the inner reaches of his being; an artistic environment where the truth of humanity can rise to the surface. It is that universality of human truth that Florida Studio Theatre seeks to bring to its audience.

Staying small is key: FST feels that its size bears a direct relationship to its adaptability to a rapidly changing society. Smallness also allows the theatre to remain in direct contact with all of its artists and personnel. This intimacy and the resulting flexibility have become the hallmarks of Florida Studio Theatre.

FST intends to remain an alternative to the larger theatres; to keep its "Off Broadway" feel; to stay at the cutting edge in order to serve best the artist and the public. The theatre promises talent, thought and feeling. And most of all, it promises emotional and artistic honesty in all of its work.

Programs and services

Touring; new play development program; film festival; new play festival; internships; audience education program.

Florida Studio Theatre. 5th of July. Photo: Stan Gerry.

PRODUCTIONS 1981-82

Betrayal, Harold Pinter; dir: Richard Hopkins
I Ought to Be in Pictures, Neil Simon; dir: John Bennett
Talley's Folly, Lanford Wilson; dir: Richard Hopkins
The Gin Game, D.L. Coburn; dir: Lach Adair
Relatively Speaking, Alan Ayckbourn; dir: Richard Hopkins

PRODUCTIONS 1982-83

Key Exchange, Kevin Wade; dir: Roger Danforth
La Ronde, Arthur Schnitzler; dir: Richard Hopkins
Mass Appeal, Bill C. Davis; dir: Roger Danforth
A Coupla White Chicks Sitting Around Talking, John Ford Noonan; dir: Daniel Irvine
5th of July, Lanford Wilson; dir: Richard Hopkins

DESIGNERS

Sets: David S.S. Davis, David Johnson, Kevin Lock.
Costumes: Robin Bisha, Vicki Holden, Brad Russell.
Lights: David S.S. Davis, Kevin Lock.

Folger Theatre

JOHN NEVILLE-ANDREWS
Artistic Producer

MARY ANN DE BARBIERI
Managing Director

WILLIAM DAVIS
Board Chairman

201 East Capitol St., S.E.
Washington, D.C. 20003
(202) 547-3230 (business)
(202) 546-4000 (box office)

FOUNDED 1970
O.B. Hardison, Richmond Crinkley

SEASON
September-June

SCHEDULE
Evenings
Tuesday-Sunday

Matinees
Variable, twice weekly

FACILITIES
Seating capacity: 233
Stage: thrust

FINANCES
July 1, 1982-June 30, 1983
$1,152,000 operating expenses
$ 755,000 earned income
$ 396,000 grants/contributions

AUDIENCE
Annual attendance: 59,109
Subscribers: 4,325

AEA LORT (D) contract

Folger Theatre. Mikel Lambert, Paul Norwood and Brian Petchey in Marriage à la Mode. *Photo: Valerie Hanlon.*

The Folger Theatre is a division of the internationally known Folger Shakespeare Memorial Library. The theatre stages Shakespeare and other classics on a beautiful evocation of an Elizabethan stage, located inside the library in Washington, D.C. In its 13 seasons, the Folger has developed a distinctly American approach to Shakespeare, relying on the text itself rather than any arbitrary imposition of time, place or style. The Folger enjoys a reputation for verbal clarity, innovative production values and the creative use of its small but authentic playing space.

Perceiving a need for a national classic theatre—and having the production expertise required to undertake its creation—the Folger began to concentrate solely on classics in 1982. (For the theatre's purposes, the classics are defined as anything written before 1800.) During the 1983 season, *A Medieval Christmas Pageant* and a new adaptation of Dryden's *Marriage à la Mode* were presented, among other works.

For the first time, in 1983 the theatre had a resident company, consisting of 12 actors and established in order to create the ensemble cohesion so necessary for classical productions. Workshops and classes in voice and movement are now held to improve and expand the company's skills.

In an effort to establish a pool of talented actors from which to draw, the Folger has instituted an acting conservatory. Classes are taught by the company members as well as outside specialists. The theatre also has a young people's conservatory for students between the ages of 10 and 16, to open young minds to the joys of Shakespeare and other classical playwrights.

Programs and services

Conservatory; young people's conservatory; technical consultancies.

Note: Louis W. Scheeder served as producer until October 31, 1981.

PRODUCTIONS 1981-82

Julius Caesar, William Shakespeare; dir: Louis W. Scheeder
The Rover, Aphra Behn; adapt: Michael Diamond; dir: Michael Diamond
The Tempest, William Shakespeare; dir: Roger Hendricks Simon
The Comedy of Errors, William Shakespeare; dir: John Neville-Andrews

PRODUCTIONS 1982-83

The Merchant of Venice, William Shakespeare; dir: John Neville-Andrews
A Medieval Christmas Pageant, various authors; dir: Ross Allen
She Stoops to Conquer, Oliver Goldsmith; dir: Davey Marlin Jones
Marriage à la Mode, John Dryden; adapt: Giles Havergal; dir: Giles Havergal
All's Well That Ends Well, William Shakespeare; dir: John Neville-Andrews

DESIGNERS

Sets: Lewis Folden, Hugh Lester, Hugh McKay, Russell Metheny.
Costumes: Kay Haskle, Bary Allen Odom.
Lights: Hugh Lester, Richard Winkler.

George Street Playhouse

ERIC KREBS
Producing Director

GEOFFREY COHEN
General Manager

ANTHONY L. MARCHETTA
Board President

391 George St.
New Brunswick, NJ 08901
(201) 846-2895 (business)
(201) 246-7717 (box office)

FOUNDED 1974
Eric Krebs, John Herochik

SEASON
October-May

SCHEDULE

Evenings
Tuesday-Sunday

Matinees
Wednesday, Saturday, Sunday

FACILITIES
9 Livingston Ave.

Stage One
Seating capacity: 352
Stage: thrust

Stage II
Seating capacity: 186
Stage: flexible

Stage III/Cabaret
Seating capacity: 125
Stage: cabaret

FINANCES
July 1, 1982-June 31, 1983
$530,000 operating expenses
$330,000 earned income
$200,000 grants/contributions

AUDIENCE
Annual attendance: 60,000
Subscribers: 4,200

TOURING CONTACT
Sharon Rothe

AEA LORT (D) contract

The George Street Playhouse produces new scripts, classics and popular contemporary works. Each season includes two premieres developed by the producing director in collaboration with commissioned writers and musicians. These new productions often focus on current social and moral issues.

Because of the theatre's proximity to New York City and that city's resources, no attempt has been made to form a permanent company, but a pool of actors dedicated to working at the Playhouse constitutes an unofficial company. In addition to a subscription season, the Playhouse produces children's theatre and has been instrumental in the creation of Crossroads, New Jersey's first black Equity theatre.

The Playhouse offers apprenticeships with small stipends and internships for college credit to those interested in working with a professional company.

Programs and services

Children's theatre; school touring; playreading series; free ticket distribution; career day.

PRODUCTIONS 1981-82

Betrayal, Harold Pinter; dir: Paul Austin
Vanities, Jack Heifner; dir: Sue Lawless
Tintypes, music and lyrics: various; adapt: Mary Kyte, Mel Marvin and Gary Pearle; dir: Eric Krebs
Out of the Night, adapt: Eric Krebs, from Jan Valtin; dir: Eric Krebs
Loot, Joe Orton; dir: Bob Hall
Lorenzo, book: Judd Woldin and Richard Engquist; music: Judd Woldin; lyrics: Richard Engquist; dir: Fran Soeder

PRODUCTIONS 1982-83

Of Mice and Men, John Steinbeck; dir: Paul Austin
Mass Appeal, Bill C. Davis; dir: Maureen Heffernan
Raisin, book adapt: Robert Nemiroff and Charlotte Zaltzberg, from Lorraine Hansberry; music: Judd Woldin; lyrics: Robert Brittan; dir: Rick Khan
The Doctor in Spite of Himself, Molière; adapt: John Pynchon Holms; dir: John Pynchon Holms
Cemetary Man, Chug and Rupert's Birthday, Ken Jenkins; dir: Bob Hall
Sleuth, Anthony Shaffer; dir: Maureen Heffernan

DESIGNERS

Sets: Bill Barclay, Gary Fassler, Gary Kechely, Daniel Proett, Nancy Thun, Dean Tschetter.
Costumes: Pat Adshead, Judy Dearing, Linda Reynolds.
Lights: David Gotwald, Natasha Katz, Phil Monat, Shirley Prendergast, Daniel Proett, Daniel Stratman.

George Street Playhouse. The Doctor in Spite of Himself. *Photo: Suzanne Karp Krebs.*

Germinal Stage Denver

ED BAIERLEIN
Director/Manager

1820 Market St.
Denver, CO 80202
(303) 296-1192

FOUNDED 1974
Ed Baierlein, Sallie Diamond, Ginger Valone, Jack McKnight

SEASON
October-July

SCHEDULE
Evenings
Thursday-Sunday

FACILITIES
Seating capacity: 132
Stage: thrust

FINANCES
August 1, 1981-July 31, 1982
$56,000 operating expenses
$44,000 earned income
$17,000 grants/contributions

AUDIENCE
Annual attendance: 8,384
Subscribers: 995

Germinal Stage Denver's purpose has always been to present plays of substance in an exciting and intimate atmosphere. "Plays of substance" refers to those works of comedy, drama, musical theatre or tragedy which show evidence of serious inquiry into philosophy, sociology, psychology, language, style or the nature of the theatre experience. "Exciting" defines the psychic environment that exists when playwright, director, actors and audience are experiencing the play as a vehicle for enhancing their own personal understanding of the universe. "Intimate" refers to the optimum space for achieving actor/audience communion. The point at which an actor begins to view the audience as an abstract unit rather than as individuals gathered to share a common experience is the point at which intimacy has been lost. With this in mind, GSD recently reduced its seating by 40, to reclaim intimacy.

The essential tension of the organization has always been based on its desire to be both outrageous and popular. The many artistic phases through which it has moved over the past nine years are clearly points on this continuum, although even the production of more traditional plays has been marked by the investigation of unusual and sometimes bizarre performance techniques.

The 1981-82 season found Germinal Stage Denver attempting—with mixed success—to synthesize Greek, Elizabethan and Japanese forms into a new, popular, non-representational form. The effort has helped to clarify GSD's position in the Denver theatre community as a company committed to continuing postmodern experimentation. The 1983 production of *Hedda Gabler,* for example, was a fusion of Ibsen with the techniques of German experimental dramatist Peter Handke.

On September 9, 1982, Colorado governor Richard D. Lamm presented Germinal Stage Denver with a 1982 Governor's Award for Excellence in the Arts, recognizing "the artistic quality of the theatre work produced, and for having made a major contribution to the culture of the area over a sustained period of time."

Programs and services

Administrative internships; post-performance discussions.

PRODUCTIONS 1981-82

Othello, William Shakespeare
Drinks before Dinner, E.L. Doctorow
The Good Woman of Setzuan, Bertolt Brecht; adapt: Eric Bentley
Goodbye, Radiant Meadows, Seyril Schochen
Don Juan in Hell, George Bernard Shaw

PRODUCTIONS 1982-83

Habeas Corpus, Alan Bennett
J.B., Archibald MacLeish
Hedda Gabler, Henrik Ibsen; adapt: Ed Baierlein
Years Ago, Ruth Gordon

All productions directed by Ed Baierlein.

DESIGNERS

Sets: Ed Baierlein.
Costumes: Sallie Diamond, Penny Stames, Hilleary Watters.
Lights: Ed Baierlein.

Germinal Stage Denver. Ed Baierlein, Teresa Wickersham and Brandon Leigh in Othello. *Photo: Ed Baierlein.*

GeVa Theatre

HOWARD J. MILLMAN
Producing Director

TIMOTHY C. NORLAND
General Manager

HERBERT L. REES
Board President

168 Clinton Ave. South
Rochester, NY 14604
(716) 232-1366 (business)
(716) 232-1363 (box office)

FOUNDED 1972
William and Cynthia Selden

SEASON
October-April

SCHEDULE

Evenings
Tuesday-Sunday

Matinees
Saturday, Sunday

FACILITIES
Seating capacity: 230
Stage: thrust

FINANCES
July 1, 1982-June 30, 1983
$750,000 operating expenses
$380,000 earned income
$370,000 grants/contributions

AUDIENCE
Annual attendance: 40,000
Subscribers: 5,350

BOOKED-IN EVENTS
Mime, theatre, benefits

AEA LORT (D) contract

GeVa Theatre, founded as the Genesee Valley Arts Foundation and located in the heart of Rochester, is in the process of undergoing significant and far-reaching changes. A new theatre facility is in the planning stages with the goal of starting the 1984-85 season in a newly renovated historical naval armory building. The new facility will be directly across the street from GeVa's present facility, and the theatre will continue to serve outlying communities while making a major contribution to the revitalization of downtown Rochester.

Within this charged atmosphere of change and rapid growth, GeVa's basic objectives remain solid: to stage high-quality productions for its community; to make available training in all aspects of the theatre; and to foster the commitment to artistic integrity and the appreciation of professional theatre in the Rochester/Monroe County area.

As the only resident professional theatre in the vicinity, GeVa selects plays based on three considerations: first, a dedication to new plays and playwrights; second, a commitment to bringing to the audience the best of the world's theatrical literature of the past; and third, a belief in the continuing need to expose audiences to contemporary writing, particularly those plays that deserve a much wider audience than they have received in the past.

While individual casts and production teams are currently assembled for each of the six mainstage productions, the theatre is attempting to build a resident company of actors who will make GeVa Theatre their home base.

Programs and services

Workshops for teenagers and adults; college and high school internships; programs-in-schools; lectures; newsletter.

Goodman Theatre

Note: During the 1981-82 season, Gideon Y. Schein served as producing director.

PRODUCTIONS 1981-82

The Passion of Dracula, Bob Hall and David Richmond; dir: Gideon Y. Schein
Pantomime, Derek Walcott; dir: Ben Levit
She Stoops to Conquer, Oliver Goldsmith; dir: Beth Dixon
How I Got That Story, Amlin Gray; dir: Stephen Katz
Artichoke, Joanna M. Glass; dir: Sharon Ott
Constance and the Musician, book and lyrics: Caroline Kava; music: Mel Marvin; dir: Gideon Y. Schein

PRODUCTIONS 1982-83

A History of the American Film, Christopher Durang; music: Mel Marvin; dir: Howard J. Millman
The Gin Game, D.L. Coburn; dir: Stephen Rothman
Tartuffe: Alias "The Preacher", adapt: Eberle Thomas and Robert Strane, from Molière; dir: Eberle Thomas
Mass Appeal, Bill C. Davis; dir: Gus Kaikkonen
Alms for the Middle Class, Stuart Hample; dir: WIlliam Ludel
Ah, Wilderness!, Eugene O'Neill; dir: Thomas Gruenewald

DESIGNERS

Sets: Bennet Averyt, William Barclay, Bob Barnett, Gary Baugh, Jeremy Conway, David Emmons, Susan Hilferty, Richard Hoover, Richard M. Isackes, John Jensen, John Kasarda, Rick Pike.
Costumes: Pamela Scofield, Mary-Anne Aston, Henri Ewaskio, Ellen Kozak, Karen Matthews.
Lights: William Armstrong, Bennet Averyt, Jeffrey Beecroft, Sid Bennett, Rachel Budin, John Gisondi, Phil Monat, Walter R. Uhrman, Ann Wrightson.

GeVa Theatre. Brian Coughlin, Matthew Kimbrough, Alison Fraser and Monique Morgan in A History of the American Film. *Photo: George Kamper Ltd.*

GREGORY MOSHER
Artistic Director

ROCHE SCHULFER
Managing Director

DAVID OFNER
Board Chairman

200 South Columbus Drive
Chicago, IL 60603
(312) 443-3811 (business)
(312) 443-3800 (box office)

FOUNDED 1925
The Art Institute of Chicago

SEASON
September-July

SCHEDULE
Evenings
Tuesday-Sunday

Matinees
Thursday, Sunday

FACILITIES
Mainstage
Seating capacity: 683
Stage: proscenium

Studio
Seating capacity: 135
Stage: proscenium

FINANCES
July 1, 1982-June 30, 1983
$2,932,000 operating expenses
$1,977,000 earned income
$ 955,000 grants/contributions

AUDIENCE
Annual attendance: 220,000
Subscribers: 14,800

TOURING CONTACT
Roche Schulfer

BOOKED-IN EVENTS
Theatre, music, dance, lectures, special events

AEA LORT (B) contract

Under the artistic direction of Gregory Mosher, the Goodman Theatre is dedicated to the idea that theatre is an essential means of exploring human issues and that its meaning derives from illuminating and affecting society. The Goodman's commitment is to the playwright as the theatre's primary artistic impulse, an impulse which is given life by the actors, supported by the staff and designers, and given coherence by the directors.

In both theatres at the Goodman, play selection seeks to reach all segments of the community and explore not only the world outside the theatre but also the ways in which we look at the theatrical experience itself. Among new works presented during the past few seasons have been plays by Edward Albee, John Guare, Emily Mann, Mustapha Matura, Elaine May, Richard Nelson, Shel Silverstein, Wole Soyinka, Derek Walcott and Tennessee Williams. The Goodman has also produced the premieres of David Mamet's *American Buffalo, A Life in the Theatre, Lone Canoe, Edmond* and *The Disappearance of the Jews.*

Tennessee Williams' last play, *A House Not Meant to Stand,* was developed over 20 months at the Goodman, beginning as a fully produced one-act in the Studio in 1980, and finally being produced as a full-length mainstage play in 1982.

Different theatrical forms and unusual collaborations are frequently pursued in such productions as *The Comedy of Errors,* which featured the Flying Karamazov Brothers and other new vaudevillians; and *The Beckett Project,* which brought together David Warrilow of Mabou Mines, Rick Cluchey of the San Quentin Drama Workshop and director Alan Schneider, among others, to participate in three short Beckett plays. The Goodman has also developed an ongoing collaboration with The Remains Theatre, and offered special presentations of performance artists Spalding Gray, Estelle Parsons in *Miss Margarida's Way* and *Kukla and Ollie Live!*

Programs and services

Lectures; post-play discussions; internships; summer performance workshops for high school students; professional classes; writers in performance series; volunteer program; school touring.

Goodman Theatre. Rick Cluchey and David Warrilow in Ohio Impromptu. Photo: Linda Schwartz.

PRODUCTIONS 1981-82

The Front Page, Ben Hecht and Charles MacArthur; dir: Michael Maggio

A Christmas Carol, adapt: Barbara Field, from Charles Dickens; dir: Tony Mockus

Panto, Derek Walcott; dir: Gregory Mosher

Lakeboat, David Mamet; dir: Gregory Mosher

A House Not Meant to Stand, Tennessee Williams; dir: Andre Ernotte

Sganarelle, An Evening of Molière Farces, adapt from Molière; trans: Albert Bermel; dir: Andrei Serban (American Repertory Theatre production)

The Woolgatherer, William Mastrosimone; dir: Sandra Grand

Edmond, David Mamet; dir: Gregory Mosher

PRODUCTIONS 1982-83

The Man Who Had Three Arms, Edward Albee; dir: Edward Albee

A Christmas Carol

The Comedy of Errors, William Shakespeare; dir: Robert Woodruff

The Dining Room, A.R. Gurney, Jr.; dir: Michael Maggio

Red River, Pierre Laville; trans: David Mamet; dir: Robert Woodruff

A Soldier's Play, Charles Fuller; dir: Douglas Turner Ward (Negro Ensemble Company production)

The Beckett Project:
  Ohio Impromptu, Samuel Beckett; dir: Alan Schneider
  Eh Joe, Samuel Beckett; adapt: Rick Cluchey; dir: Rick Cluchey
  A Piece of Monologue, Samuel Beckett; dir: Rocky Greenberg and David Warrilow

Jungle Coup, Richard Nelson; dir: David Chambers

Gardenia, John Guare; dir: Gregory Mosher

The Disappearance of the Jews, David Mamet; dir: Gregory Mosher

Hotline, Elaine May; dir: Art Wolff

Gorilla, Shel Silverstein; dir: Art Wolff

Mark Twain Today, Ron Falzone; dir: Stephen Scott

DESIGNERS

Sets: Bill Bartelt, Felix E. Cochren, Philip Eickhoff, David Emmons, David Gropman, John Jensen, Franne Lee, Michael Merritt, Gregory Mosher, Joseph Nieminski, Kevin Rigdon, Karen Schulz, Michael H. Yeargan.

Costumes: Barbara A. Bell, James Edmund Brady, Nan Cibula, Judy Dearing, Philip Eickhoff, David Gropman, Susan Hilferty, Marsha Kowal, Franne Lee, William Ivey Long, Dunya Ramicova, Christa Scholtz, Teresita Garcia Suro.

Lights: Rachel Budin, Robert Christen, F. Mitchell Dana, Paul Gallo, Rocky Greenberg, James F. Ingalls, Allen Lee Hughes, Rita Pietraszek, Kevin Rigdon, Jennifer Tipton.

The Great-American Children's Theatre Company

TERI SOLOMON MITZE
Producer

JEANNE NORMOYLE
Production Manager

RANDY McELRATH
Board President

Box 92123
Milwaukee, WI 53202
(414) 276-4230

FOUNDED 1976
Teri Solomon Mitze, Thomas C. Mitze

SEASON
October-May

SCHEDULE
Matinees
Monday-Friday
Selected Saturdays, Sundays

FACILITIES
Pabst Theatre
144 E. Wells St.
Seating capacity: 1,432
Stage: proscenium

Madison Civic Center
211 State St.
Seating capacity: 2,215
Stage: proscenium

Oriental Theatre
2230 N. Farwell
Seating capacity: 2,000
Stage: proscenium

FINANCES
July 1, 1981-June 30, 1982
$527,000 operating expenses
$444,000 earned income
$ 37,000 grants/contributions

AUDIENCE
Annual attendance: 180,000

BOOKED-IN EVENTS
Children's theatre

In 1976, The Great-American Children's Theatre Company was created to produce and present professional plays for young audiences; to bring these youngsters to a legitimate theatre to see the performances; and to interest parents, teachers and children in the performing arts through drama, musicals and educational programs.

The years 1981 through mid-1983 were filled with growth and progress. These seasons included newly commissioned scripts which were shaped by actors, directors and designers familiar with resident professional theatre but new to children's theatre. A variety of exciting regional theatre productions resulted.

In eight seasons, 670,000 people have attended The Great-American Children's Theatre at its various performing spaces. Another 70,000 have participated in the educational in-school program known as "A Peek Behind the Scenes." These encouraging statistics indicate that theatre for children has grown in popularity and become an important, viable branch of the performing arts.

Great-American's specialized youth audience is eager for new experiences. The challenge is to stimulate their imaginations and interest, and show that theatre can compete within the expanding spectrum of youth-oriented entertainment.

Programs and services

A Peek Behind the Scenes program-in-schools.

PRODUCTIONS 1981-82

The Last on the List, book: Bill Solly and Donald Ward; music and lyrics: Bill Solly; dir: Montgomery Davis
The Wind in the Willows, adapt: Daniel Stein, from Kenneth Grahame; dir: Patrick Tovatt

PRODUCTIONS 1982-83

A Fine-Feathered Review, book, music and lyrics: Bill Solly; dir: Montgomery Davis
Merlin, Hugh Corcoran; dir: Ewel Cornett

DESIGNERS

Sets: Allen H. Jones, D. Albert Tucci.
Costumes: Susan Tsu, D. Albert Tucci.
Lights: Spencer Mosse, Carl Schmidt.

The Great-American Children's Theatre Company. Mary Broussard and Scott Borisy in Merlin. *Photo: Ralph Pabst.*

The Great Lakes Shakespeare Festival

VINCENT DOWLING
Producing Director

MARY BILL
Managing Director

NATALIE EPSTEIN
Board President

250 Bulkley Bldg.
1501 Euclid Ave.
Cleveland, OH 44115
(216) 241-5490 (business)
(216) 523-1755 (box office)

FOUNDED 1962
Community members

SEASON
June-December

SCHEDULE
Evenings
Tuesday-Saturday

Matinees
Wednesday, Sunday

FACILITIES
The Ohio Theatre
1511 Euclid Ave.
Seating capacity: 819
Stage: proscenium

FINANCES
November 1, 1981-October 31, 1982
$1,874,000 operating expenses
$1,062,000 earned income
$ 932,000 grants/contributions

AUDIENCE
Annual attendance: 98,551
Subscribers: 6,801

TOURING CONTACT
Mary Bill

BOOKED-IN EVENTS
Theatre

AEA LORT (B) contract

The Great Lakes Shakespeare Festival has evolved into a true company, responsive to the needs of its audience as well as its actors, directors, designers and technicians. It is composed of artists who wish to develop their craft on a continuing basis through work on the classics, while at the same time experimenting with new writing and new approaches to performance, staging and production.

At Great Lakes there is an emphasis on transforming classical materials from one medium to another. Dylan Thomas' *A Child's Christmas in Wales* was adapted into a full-length musical, as was George Bernard Shaw's one-act play, *The Shewing Up of Blanco Posnet*.

The company continues to develop its own voice and body language springing from America's native rhythms and made clearer and more beautiful through continuous first-rate training. Daily voice sessions for the actors are incorporated into every

Great Lakes Shakespeare Festival. The Life and Adventures of Nicholas Nickleby.
Photo: Martha Swope.

The Guthrie Theater

rehearsal period. The player and the play, in that order, are the primary concerns of Great Lakes Shakespeare Festival in creating its style.

Programs and services

Programs-in-schools; touring; second stage productions.

PRODUCTIONS 1982

As You Like It, William Shakespeare; dir: Thomas Gruenewald
The Playboy of the Western World, John Millington Synge; dir: Vincent Dowling
Piaf: La Vie l'Amour, Gay Marshall and Lane Bateman; dir: Vincent Dowling
The Life and Adventures of Nicholas Nickleby, adapt: David Edgar, from Charles Dickens; music and lyrics: Stephen Oliver; dir: Robert Lanchester and Edward Stern
A Child's Christmas in Wales, adapt: Jeremy Brooks and Adrian Mitchell, from Dylan Thomas; dir: Clifford Williams

PRODUCTIONS 1983

The Merry Wives of Windsor, William Shakespeare; dir: Clifford Williams
Blanco!, adapt: Vincent Dowling; music: Skip Kennon; lyrics: Michael Korie; dir: Vincent Dowling
Waiting for Godot, Samuel Beckett; dir: Eamon Morrissey
Henry V, Williams Shakespeare; dir: Gregory Boyd
A Child's Christmas in Wales

DESIGNERS

Sets: John Ezell.
Costumes: Mary-Anne Aston, Paul Costelloe, Gene Lakin, Vera Polovko-Mednikov, Estelle Painter, Lewis A. Rampino, Kurt Wilhelm.
Lights: Joseph Appelt, Kirk Bookman, Toni Goldin, Robert Jared, Natasha Katz, Roger Morgan, Susan A. White.

The Guthrie Theater. Melodie Somers and Michael Butler in Candide. *Photo: Joe Giannetti.*

LIVIU CIULEI
Artistic Director

DONALD SCHOENBAUM
Managing Director

SANDRA J. HALE
Board President

725 Vineland Place
Minneapolis, MN 55403
(612) 347-1100 (business)
(612) 377-2224 (box office)

FOUNDED 1963
Tyrone Guthrie, Oliver Rea, Peter Zeisler

SEASON
June-March

SCHEDULE
Evenings
Tuesday-Sunday
Matinees
Wednesday, Saturday

FACILITIES
Seating capacity: 1,441
Stage: thrust

FINANCES
April 1, 1982-March 31, 1983
$6,762,000 operating expenses
$3,964,000 earned income
$1,724,000 grants/contributions

AUDIENCE
Annual attendance: 450,947
Subscribers: 13,266

TOURING CONTACT
Chris Tschida

BOOKED-IN EVENTS
Theatre, dance, music, comedy

AEA LORT (A) contract

In the time since Liviu Ciulei assumed the role of artistic director in 1981, an exciting change of direction has taken place at The Guthrie Theater. A new style of performance has emerged, utilizing elements of both realism and the avant-garde, and resulting in a blend of the best of what is traditional with a contemporary vision and approach. Such striking and innovative productions as Richard Foreman's *Don Juan*, Andrei Serban's *The Marriage of Figaro*, Garland Wright's *Candide* and Ciulei's own *Peer Gynt* and *The Tempest* have caught the attention of the theatre world, exploring new artistic possibilities.

Ciulei has said repeatedly that in order to be vital, the theatre must search for what is true and lasting in dramatic literature and present it to modern audiences in ways that will be stimulating and meaningful for them. Both artistic and financial risks are necessary to achieve this end, and so careful season planning — balancing plays and performance styles to appeal to a variety of audiences without sacrificing creative integrity — is crucial to the continued successful existence of the theatre.

The Guthrie's artists are always searching for new forms of expression, new visual and dramatic techniques. In Ciulei's words, "It is not possible to reconstruct yesterday, it doesn't work. This doesn't necessarily mean we do [plays] experimentally. It just means we try to discover what is in the play, what makes it art, what touches us today. Then we search for the best means to present it to today's audiences. If those 'means' reveal the enduring qualities of the play that have made it a classic, then it will remain in the consciousness of the spectator."

Programs and services

Touring; pre- and post-performance symposia; classes; signed performances for the deaf; literary, administrative and technical internships; workshops; costume fashion shows.

PRODUCTIONS 1981-82

The Tempest, William Shakespeare; dir: Liviu Ciulei
Don Juan, Molière; trans: Donald M. Frame; dir: Richard Foreman
Our Town, Thornton Wilder; dir: Alan Schneider
Foxfire, Susan Cooper and Hume Cronyn; dir: Marshall W. Mason
Eli: A Mystery Play of the Sufferings of Israel, Nelly Sachs; trans: Christopher Holme; dir: Garland Wright
Eve of Retirement, Thomas Bernhard; trans: Gitta Honegger; dir: Liviu Ciulei
A Christmas Carol, adapt: Barbara Field, from Charles Dickens; dir: Jon Cranney
As You Like It, Williams Shakespeare; dir: Liviu Ciulei
Trouble Begins at Eight, Christopher Markle; dir: Christopher Markle
The Rainmaker, N. Richard Nash; dir: David Chambers

PRODUCTIONS 1982-83

Summer Vacation Madness, Carlo Goldoni; dir: Garland Wright
Requiem for a Nun, William Faulkner; dir: Liviu Ciulei
The Marriage of Figaro, Pierre de Beaumarchais; trans: Richard Nelson; dir: Andrei Serban
Room Service, John Murray and Allen Boretz; dir: Harold Stone
Heartbreak House, George Bernard Shaw; dir: Christopher Markle
A Christmas Carol, adapt: Barbara Field, from Charles Dickens; dir: Christopher Markle
Entertaining Mr. Sloane, Joe Orton; dir: Gary Gisselman
Peer Gynt, Henrik Ibsen; trans: Rolf Fjelde; dir: Liviu Ciulei
Talley's Folly, Lanford Wilson; dir: David Feldshuh

DESIGNERS

Sets: John Arnone, Jack Barkla, John Lee Beatty, Liviu Ciulei, Karl Eigsti, Richard Foreman, James Guenther, Adrianne Lobel, Santo Loquasto, Beni Montresor, Michael Yeargan.
Costumes: Jared Aswegan, Lawrence Casey, Jack Edwards, James Guenther, Ann Hould-Ward, Santo Loquasto, Jennifer von Mayrhauser, Beni Montresor, Marjorie Slaiman, Kurt Wilhelm, Patricia Zipprodt.
Lights: William Armstrong, Craig Miller, Karlis Ozols, Dennis Parichy, Richard Riddell, Paul Scharfenberger, Duane Schuler, Patrick Shaughnessy, Jennifer Tipton.

Hartford Stage Company. Michele Shay and Alan Mixon in The Greeks. *Photo: Lanny Nagler.*

Hartford Stage Company

MARK LAMOS
Artistic Director

C. WILLIAM STEWART
Managing Director

PETER R. WILDE
Board President

50 Church St.
Hartford, CT 06103
(203) 525-5601 (business)
(203) 527-5151 (box office)

FOUNDED 1964
Jacques Cartier

SEASON
October-June

SCHEDULE
Evenings
Tuesday-Sunday

Matinees
Wednesday, Sunday

FACILITIES
John W. Huntington Theatre
Seating capacity: 489
Stage: thrust
The Old Place
65 Kinsley St.
Seating capacity: 225
Stage: thrust

FINANCES
July 1, 1982-June 30, 1983
$1,921,000 operating expenses
$1,268,000 earned income
$ 599,000 grants/contributions

AUDIENCE
Annual attendance: 130,000
Subscribers: 13,358

AEA LORT (C) contract

Innovation, theatricality, daring and visual exuberance characterize the aims of the Hartford Stage Company in its annual six-play season. Under the artistic direction of Mark Lamos, the theatre is committed to original explorations of large-scale classical works, and world premieres investigating contemporary values in unusual and entertaining ways. The company strives to serve the community by encouraging and supporting writers, actors, directors and designers in the realization of their artistic goals.

Since 1977, the theatre has been housed in a $2.5 million thrust stage theatre at the hub of a major urban renewal project. Its former home, now called The Old Place and under the direction of associate artistic director Mary B. Robinson, is developing as a training ground for new artists by undertaking alternative projects: commissioning children's theatre works; presenting a lunchtime series of one-acts; and giving staged readings of new plays. Hartford Stage Company publishes *On the Scene,* a subscriber magazine with original theatre articles, and a study guide mailed to schools participating in the student matinee series. Both are published six times a year.

Each summer the company sponsors a Youth Theatre program for inner-city teenagers which produces a full-scale musical under professional direction. In 1980, this program received national recognition on CBS television. In this way, Hartford Stage continues to contribute to the revitalization of the inner city.

The company is actively guided by a governing board of directors which sets policies, raises funds and selects the theatre's leadership. An administrative staff of 52 works year-round and seasonally, while a company of artists is hired for each production, many of whom return throughout the season.

Programs and services

Internships; study guides; *On the Scene* subscriber magazine; lectures; Sundays at Six discussion series; summer youth theatre.

PRODUCTIONS 1981-82

Antony and Cleopatra, William Shakespeare; dir: Mark Lamos

The Hartman Theatre

Kean, Jean-Paul Sartre; trans: Frank Hauser; dir: Mark Lamos
The Wake of Jamey Foster, Beth Henley; dir: Ulu Grosbard
The Greeks, adapt: John Barton and Kenneth Cavander; trans: Kenneth Cavander; dir: Mark Lamos and Mary B. Robinson
The Isle Is Full of Noises, Derek Walcott; dir: Douglas Turner Ward
Greater Tuna, Jaston Williams, Joe Sears and Ed Howard; dir: Ed Howard and Mark Lamos
Twinkle, Twinkle, Ernest Thompson; dir: Mary B. Robinson
Forbidden Copy, Percy Granger; dir: Mary B. Robinson
Am I Blue, Beth Henley; dir: R. Stuart White
Mojo, Alice Childress; dir: Clay Stevenson
The Enormous Egg, adapt: Mary B. Robinson, from Oliver Butterworth; dir: Mary B. Robinson

PRODUCTIONS 1982-83

On Borrowed Time, Paul Osborn; dir: Tony Giordano
The Great Magoo, Ben Hecht and Gene Fowler; dir: Mark Lamos
The Portage to San Cristobal of A.H., adapt: Christopher Hampton, from George Steiner; dir: Mark Lamos
Dog Eat Dog, Mary Gallagher; dir: Mary B. Robinson
The Misanthrope, Molière; trans: Richard Wilbur; dir: Mark Lamos
The Glass Menagerie, Tennessee Williams; dir: George Keathley

DESIGNERS

Sets: John Conklin, Andrew Jackness, Santo Loquasto, David Potts, Kevin Rupnik, Karen Schulz, Tony Straiges, Bob Thayer, Ruth A. Wells.
Costumes: Jeanne Button, Nan Cibula, John Conklin, Linda Fisher, Santo Loquasto, Jennifer von Mayrhauser, David Murin, Merrily Murray-Walsh, Dunya Ramicova, Anne Thaxter Watson.
Lights: Pat Collins, Arden Fingerhut, Paul Gallo, James F. Ingalls, Robert Jared, Michael Rice.

EDWIN SHERIN
Producing Artistic Director

HARRIS GOLDMAN
Executive Director

ARTHUR W. HOOPER
Board Chairman

Box 521
Stamford, CT 06904
(203) 324-6781 (business)
(203) 323-2131 (box office)
(212) 581-0177 (NY direct line)

FOUNDED 1975
Del and Margot Tenney

SEASON
September-May

SCHEDULE

Evenings
Tuesday-Sunday

Matinees
Wednesday, Saturday, Sunday

FACILITIES
Stamford Center for the Arts
307 Atlantic St.
Seating capacity: 654
Stage: proscenium

FINANCES
July 1, 1982-June 30, 1983
$1,119,000 operating expenses
$ 865,000 earned income
$ 254,000 grants/contributions

The Hartman Theatre. Michael Moriarty and John Rubinstein in The Caine Mutiny Court-Martial. *Photo: Gerry Goodstein.*

AUDIENCE
Annual attendance: 80,000
Subscribers: 7,754

TOURING CONTACT
Harris Goldman

BOOKED-IN EVENTS
Opera, ballet, concerts

AEA LORT (B) contract

Located only 45 minutes from New York City, the Hartman Theatre is in a rare position among resident professional theatres. The Hartman serves the communities of Fairfield and Westchester counties, a discerning audience with an unlimited array of readily accessible performing arts events from which to choose. In recent years, the Hartman has attracted creative artists with national reputations such as Henry Fonda, Jane Alexander, Shirley Knight, Richard Kiley, Neil Simon, Michael Learned, Jack Warden, John Rubinstein, Robin Wagner and Michael Moriarty.

The company performs in the old Stamford Theatre, a 1,000-seat theatre built in 1914, which in its earlier days hosted such luminaries as Lillian Gish and the Lunts. The ambience of the auditorium demands productions that are forceful enough to fill the large proscenium stage and project effectively to the farthest seat in the house. This auditorium will remain intact as the core of the Stamford Center for the Arts, the product of major renovation and expansion in progress around the current facility.

The Hartman's artistic course emphasizes new plays and musicals. In the 1982-83 season, the theatre distinguished itself by producing two world premieres, an American premiere and two revivals of American classics. Two Hartman productions—*Steaming* and *The Caine Mutiny Court-Martial* moved on to New York.

Programs and services
Conversations at the Hartman lunchtime discusson series; post-performance discussions; speaker's bureau; readings; signed and infra-red performances for the deaf and hearing-impaired; internships; backstage tours; *Playnotes* subscriber magazine.

PRODUCTIONS 1981-82

Hedda Gabler, Henrik Ibsen; trans: Eva Le Gallienne; dir: Edwin Sherin
Catholics, Brian Moore; dir: Tom Kerr
The Millionairess, George Bernard Shaw; dir: Jerome Kilty
Night Must Fall, Emlyn Williams; dir: Edwin Sherin
The Magistrate, Arthur Wing Pinero; dir: Edward Hastings
Mahalia, book and lyrics: Don Evans; music: John Lewis; dir: Gerald Freedman

PRODUCTIONS 1982-83

A Streetcar Named Desire, Tennessee Williams; dir: Edwin Sherin
Steaming, Nell Dunn; dir: Roger Smith
A Christmas Carol, book and lyrics adapt: Sheldon Harnick, from Charles Dickens; music: Michel Legrand; dir: Charles Abbott
The Caine Mutiny Court-Martial, Herman Wouk; dir: Arthur Sherman
Actors and Actresses, Neil Simon; dir: Glenn Jordan
The Three Musketeers, adapt: Mark Bramble, from Alexandre Dumas; music: Rudolf Friml; lyrics: P.G. Wodehouse and Clifford Grey; dir: Mark Bramble

DESIGNERS

Sets: Don Beaman, Victor Capecce, John Falabella, Robert Fletcher, Richard M. Isackes, James Leonard Joy, Marjorie Bradley Kellogg, Robin Wagner, Nancy Winters.
Costumes: Judy Dearing, Robert Fletcher, Jane Greenwood, Jennifer von Mayrhauser, Allen E. Munch, David Murin, Nancy Potts, Ann Wallace, Freddy Wittop.
Lights: Sid Bennett, Pat Collins, Marcia Madeira, John McLain, Roger Meeker, Marilyn Rennagel, Bill Williams, Andrea Wilson.

Hippodrome State Theatre

GREGORY HAUSCH
MARY HAUSCH
KERRY McKENNEY
MARSHALL NEW
Artistic Directors

CHRISTINA TANNEN
Managing Director

CHARLES I. HOLDEN, JR.
Board President

25 Southeast 2nd Place
Gainesville, FL 32601
(904) 373-5968 (business)
(904) 375-4477 (box office)

FOUNDED 1973
Bruce Cornwell, Mary Hausch, Gregory Hausch, Kerry McKenney, Marshall New

SEASON
July-June

SCHEDULE
Evenings
Tuesday-Sunday

Matinees
Saturday, Sunday

FACILITIES
Mainstage
Seating capacity: 266
Stage: thrust

Second Stage
Seating capacity: 98
Stage: proscenium

FINANCES
June 1, 1982-May 31, 1983
$621,000 operating expenses
$320,000 earned income
$301,000 grants/contributions

AUDIENCE
Annual attendance: 109,700
Subscribers: 3,333

TOURING CONTACT
Pete Theoktisto

BOOKED-IN EVENTS
Theatre, music, dance, solo performances

AEA LORT (D) contract

The artistic goal of the Hippodrome State Theatre since its inception has been to produce the best in contemporary theatre. Because Gainesville is a culturally rich university community where numerous classics and musical comedies are produced annually, the Hippodrome has chosen to offer its audiences the newer voices and styles of world theatre. An occasional classic is revived, but from a contemporary point of view and with a contemporary look.

The Hippodrome's artistic direction is determined by the collective input and individual tastes of its four founder/artistic directors. Audiences have found this eclecticism and variety of directorial style exciting. Several of the co-directors adapt material from novels, screenplays, folk tales, etc.; at least one original script is produced each year; and guest directors are invited on a regular basis as a way of revitalizing the work of the founding directors.

The Hippodrome stages its season on a three-quarter thrust stage in an intimate, 266-seat house, and scenic design stresses environmental concepts. Directorial approaches change according to material, of course, but many of the Hippodrome's productions are abstract, or borrow directly from the innovations of experimental theatre of the past 15 years. Realistic theatre is also presented, but more often the audience is asked to complete the scenic illusion with its imagination rather than by observing literal detail. Audience participation is frequently a deliberate—or sometimes an inadvertent—result of a play's confrontational presentation or the theatre's intimacy.

Hippodrome actors create in an atmosphere of artistic freedom and professional discipline. Emphasis is placed on improvisation, ensemble interaction and an approach to every play as an original production. Approximately 30 local, company performers make up the core of the Hippodrome's artistic staff; the theatre attempts to use regional and state professionals whenever additional actors are needed.

Programs and services

School touring; film series; internships; workshops for children and adults.

Hippodrome State Theatre. The Saint and the Football Players. *Photo: Gary S. Wolfson.*

PRODUCTIONS 1981-82

I Ought to Be in Pictures, Neil Simon; dir: Marshall New
Morning's at Seven, Paul Osborn; dir: Kent Stephens
Whose Life Is It Anyway?, Brian Clark; dir: Gregory Hausch
Pantomime, Derek Walcott; dir: Kenneth Korsby
Man Friday, Adrian Mitchell; dir: Marshall New
Deathtrap, Ira Levin; dir: Gregory Hausch
Terra Nova, Ted Tally; dir: Kerry McKenney
The Gin Game, D.L. Coburn; dir: Mary Hausch
The Robber Bridegroom, book and lyrics: Alfred Uhry; music: Robert Waldman; dir: Kerry McKenney

PRODUCTIONS 1982-83

New Play Festival:
  Wild Rose Branches, Phoeff Sutton; dir: Kerry McKenney
  I Am Waiting, Claudia Johnson; dir: Mary Hausch
  The Boogey Man, Edward Clinton; dir: Marshall New
Sanibel and Captiva, Megan Terry; dir: Michael Beistle
The Showdown, Shelley Mickle; dir: Mary Hausch
The Pie Rate's Off, Jeffrey Smart; dir: Phoeff Sutton

Beyond Therapy, Christopher Durang; dir: Gregory Hausch
The Dining Room, A.R. Gurney, Jr.; dir: Kerry McKenney
A Christmas Carol, adapt: Gregory Hausch, from Charles Dickens; dir: Gregory Hausch
The Saint and the Football Players, Lee Breuer; dir: Lee Breuer
Key Exchange, Kevin Wade; dir: Gregory Hausch
We Won't Pay! We Won't Pay!, Dario Fo; trans: R.G. Davis; dir: Marshall New
Children of a Lesser God, Mark Medoff; dir: Mary Hausch

DESIGNERS

Sets: Carlos Asse, Marilyn Wall-Asse, Lee Breuer, Gregory Hausch, Paul Hilton, Kerry McKenney, Jim Morgan.
Costumes: Marilyn Wall-Asse, Leslie Klein.
Lights: Sheldon Warshaw.

Honolulu Theatre for Youth

JOHN KAUFFMAN
Artistic Director

JANE CAMPBELL
Managing Director

SUZANNE CASE
Board President

Box 3257
Honolulu, HI 96801
(808) 521-3487

FOUNDED 1955
Nancy Corbett

SEASON
July-May

SCHEDULE

Evenings
Friday, Saturday

Matinees
Sunday

FINANCES
June 1, 1982-May 31, 1983
$406,000 operating expenses
$277,000 earned income
$101,000 grants/contributions

AUDIENCE
Annual attendance: 125,000

TOURING CONTACT
Jane Campbell

Honolulu Theatre for Youth is the leading theatre presence in Hawaii and the only professional theatre in the state. While its primary concern is theatre for young audiences ("young" ranging from pre-schoolers to young adults), it reaches increasingly deeper into the general community as adult theatregoers become aware of the quality of the work.

Artistic responsbility and direction are vested in the artistic and managing directors, but in recent years, the board of trustees has assumed a stronger role in setting forth philosophy while taking on increased fund-raising responsibility. The board-staff relationship is mutually supportive and artistic freedom is respected.

Board and staff together recently drew up a statement of purpose which reads, in part:

— HTY speaks to and celebrates its richly varied community.
— Theatre is a forum for ideas and an art form deserving of high professionalism.
— Quality theatre results from the work of dedicated, talented professionals who are paid for their work and who work in a realm of artistic freedom.
— HTY's target audience encompasses all young people in Hawaii; attendance by families and adults is encouraged in the belief that good theatre speaks to people of all ages.
— HTY provides a diversity of theatrical experiences: classics of dramatic literature, quality works with popular appeal, material that speaks to contemporary concerns of young people and material of Hawaiian and Pacific themes.
— New work is the lifeblood of the theatre, and developing new work for young people is a key responsibility of HTY.
— A healthy theatre needs a perceptive and supportive audience; this is developed through constant and aggressive promotion and by producing quality work.

Honlulu Theatre for Youth has no performing facility of its own. Rather, it performs at various state- and city-owned spaces on the island of Oahu.

Programs and services

Summer children's workshops; touring Hawaiian islands and Samoa; workshops-in-schools.

Honolulu Theatre for Youth. Phyllis Look, Dando Kluever, Russell Omori and Norris Shimabuku in Clowns. *Photo: P.J. O'Reilley.*

Note: During the 1981-82 and 1982-83 seasons, Kathleen Collins served as artistic director.

PRODUCTIONS 1981-82

A Midsummer Night's Dream, William Shakespeare; dir: Kathleen Collins
Dracula, adapt: Hamilton Deane and John L. Balderston, from Bram Stoker; dir: Kathleen Collins

Horse Cave Theatre

Islands—Further, Farther and Beyond,
  Kathleen Collins; dir: Kathleen Collins
The Hidden Place, George Herman; dir:
  Kathleen Collins
*Na Keiki Haku Mele O Ka Aina (The
  Children of the Land Are Poets),* adapt:
  Kathleen Collins; dir: Kathleen Collins
In a Very Special House, Phyllis Look; dir:
  Phyllis Look

PRODUCTIONS 1982-83

Ali Baba and the 40 Thieves, Gregory A.
  Falls; dir: Kathleen Collins
The Masque of Beauty and the Beast, Michael
  Brill; dir: Kathleen Collins
Chicken Skin, Ron Nakahara; dir: Ron
  Nakahara
The Diary of Anne Frank, Frances Goodrich
  and Albert Hackett; dir: Kathleen
  Collins
Clowns, Stephan Rey; dir: Kathleen Collins

DESIGNERS

Sets: Joseph D. Dodd, Mary Lewis,
  Richard G. Mason, Lloyd S. Riford III,
  Charles Walsh.
Costumes: Joseph D. Dodd, Virginia West.
Lights: Mary Lewis, Lloyd S. Riford III.

WARREN HAMMACK
Artistic Director

PAMELA WHITE
Administrative Director

EVELYN SALISBURY
Board President

Box 215
Horse Cave, KY 42749
(502) 786-1200 (business)
(502) 786-2177 (box office)

FOUNDED 1977

SEASON
June-September

SCHEDULE
Evenings
Tuesday-Sunday

Matinees
Saturday

FACILITIES
107-109 Main St.
Seating capacity: 355
Stage: thrust

FINANCES
October 1, 1981-September 30, 1982
$210,000 operating expenses
$ 76,000 earned income
$141,000 grants/contributions

AUDIENCE
Annual attendance: 16,201
Subscribers: 712

BOOKED-IN EVENTS
Theatre, music

AEA LORT (D) contract

Horse Cave Theatre is dedicated to introducing classic drama to new audiences which are far-removed from the major metropolitan centers. Created in 1977 by residents of south central Kentucky, the theatre's mission is to serve the citizens of Kentucky and Tennessee by presenting the best works from our theatrical heritage. In a predominantly rural region, the theatre has fostered and nurtured a new and enthusiastic group of theatregoers by introducing them to contemporary and American works as well as such classic dramatists as Shakespeare, Chekhov, Goldsmith and Molière.

Guiding Horse Cave from its inception has been its artistic director Warren Hammack, who has invited in talented guest directors and designers, each chosen for his or her particular contribution to a work. Horse Cave's rotating repertory schedule allows actors to confront a range of stylistic challenges.

The theatre's dedication to the classics is also evident in its programs for student audiences. The educational outreach program has been emphasized since a survey of school districts closest to the theatre revealed that few have drama courses in their curricula. Horse Cave stages a Shakespearean production shortly after school opens each fall, and in 1983, *Macbeth* played to 96 percent capacity.

Horse Cave Theatre takes its name from its tiny community, and makes its home in the historic Thomas Opera House, built in

Horse Cave Theatre. Warren Hammack, Pamela White and Lowell Williams in A Lesson from Aloes. *Photo: Gerald Matera.*

Hudson Guild Theatre

1911. World famous Mammoth Cave is nearby, each year attracting summer tourists who mingle with area residents in Horse Cave's audiences.

Programs and services

Educational outreach program; summer classes; apprenticeships; internships; residency in Nashville.

PRODUCTIONS 1981-82

She Stoops to Conquer, Oliver Goldsmith; dir: Warren Hammack
The Heiress, Ruth and Augustus Goetz; dir: Jack Wann
A Lesson from Aloes, Athol Fugard; dir: Michael Hankins
The Book of Job, Orlin Corey; dir: Orlin Corey
A Thousand Clowns, Herb Gardner; dir: Warren Hammack
Macbeth, William Shakespeare; dir: David Shookhoff

PRODUCTIONS 1982-83

Harvey, Mary Chase; dir: Jack Wann
Talley's Folly, Lanford Wilson; dir: Pamela White
The Imaginary Invalid, Molière; adapt: Miles Malleson; dir: Warren Hammack
Cat on a Hot Tin Roof, Tennessee Williams; dir: Warren Hammack
Othello, William Shakespeare; dir: Jerome Guardino
The Book of Job

DESIGNERS

Sets: Linda Blase, James Taylor.
Costumes: Vada Birkhead, Irene Corey, Thomas Leigh.
Lights: Linda Blase, Dennis Reed, James Taylor.

DAVID KERRY HEEFNER
Producing Director

DANIEL SWEE
General Manager

MARGARET VAN D. COOK
Board President

441 West 26th St.
New York, NY 10001
(212) 760-9836 (business)
(212) 760-9810 (box office)

FOUNDED 1896
John Lovejoy Elliott

SEASON
October-June

SCHEDULE

Evenings
Wednesday-Sunday

Matinees
Saturday, Sunday

FACILITIES

Arthur Strasser Auditorium
441 West 26th St.
Seating capacity: 135
Stage: proscenium

FINANCES
July 1, 1982-June 30, 1983
$217,000 operating expenses
$119,000 earned income
$ 81,000 grants/contributions

AUDIENCE
Annual attendance: 18,000
Subscribers: 1,600

AEA letter of agreement

Hudson Guild Theatre's primary interest is in finding new plays and playwrights, and introducing them to its New York City audience. The works of both American and European authors are presented each season by dedicated actors, directors and designers, many of whom return to HGT time and again, generating a familial atmosphere.

HGT began as a community theatre in 1896, a year after the founding of the Hudson Guild Neighborhood House, its parent organization. The first professional theatre was established in 1933 under the federal Works Projects Administration (WPA). In the 1940s and '50s HGT was again an amateur organization, becoming fully professional again in 1975.

As an integral part of a settlement house,

Hudson Guild Theatre. David Leary and Terry Alexander in Sus. Photo: Charles Marinaro.

Huntington Theatre Company

HGT is involved in the community and provides classes and workshops in theatre, dance and music to neighborhood residents.

Programs and services

Staged and unstaged readings; professional and non-professional classes and workshops.

PRODUCTIONS 1981-82

Sleep Beauty, Arthur Meryash, dir: Arthur Feinsod and Jordan Deitcher
Beside the Seaside, Stephen Temperley; dir: Vivian Matalon
Vamps and Rideouts, adapt: Phyllis Newman and James Pentecost; music: Jule Styne; lyrics: various; dir: James Pentecost
Wonderland, Margaret Keilstrup; dir: David Kerry Heefner
Emigres, Slawomir Mrozek; trans: Maciej Wrona, Teresa Wrona and Robert Holman; dir: Thomas Gruenewald

PRODUCTIONS 1982-83

Hooters, Ted Tally; dir: David Kerry Heefner
Breakfast with Les and Bess, Lee Kalcheim; dir: Barnet Kellman
Blood Relations, Sharon Pollock; dir: David Kerry Heefner
Sus, Barrie Keeffe; dir: Geoffrey Sherman
Accounts, Michael Wilcox; dir: Kent Paul

DESIGNERS

Sets: Jane Clark, James Leonard Joy, Paul Kelly, Lawrence Miller, Roger Mooney, Ron Placzek, William Ritman, Dean Tschetter, Paul Wonsek.
Costumes: Timothy Dunleavy, Edi Giguere, Bob Graham, Barbara Hladsky, David Loveless, Cynthia O'Neal, Mariann Verheyen, Joan E. Weiss.
Lights: Ian Calderon, Jeff Davis, Phil Monat, David Murdock, Richard Nelson, Paul Wonsek.

Huntington Theatre Company. David Purdham and Laura Gardner in The Taming of the Shrew. *Photo: Gerry Goodstein.*

PETER ALTMAN
Producing Director

MICHAEL MASO
Managing Director

GERALD GROSS
Board President

264 Huntington Ave.
Boston, MA 02115
(617) 353-3320 (business)
(617) 266-3913 (box office)

FOUNDED 1982
Trustees of Boston University

SEASON
October-June

SCHEDULE
Evenings
Tuesday-Sunday

Matinees
Wednesday, Saturday, Sunday

FACILITIES
Seating capacity: 850
Stage: proscenium

FINANCES
July 1, 1982-June 30, 1983
$1,199,000 operating expenses
$ 550,000 earned income
$ 648,000 grants/contributions

AUDIENCE
Annual attendance: 57,000
Subscribers: 4,153

BOOKED-IN EVENTS
Music, dance

AEA LORT (B) contract

The Huntington Theatre Company was founded in June 1982 as the professional resident theatre at Boston University. Its aim is to produce an annual season of classic and

Illusion Theater

superior contemporary plays acted, directed and designed at a standard of excellence comparable to that of the nation's leading professional companies.

The Huntington strives to be daring in its choice of plays, and in the artists it employs —while remaining profoundly respectful of tradition and craft. The criteria for selecting works are literacy, the presence of forceful ideas, skillful construction and, above all, dramatic situations and characters created with truth and vitality.

The growth of the Huntington's audiences over its first two seasons vivdly affirms that this policy is gaining the appreciation of a widening public. It is today more determined than ever to pursue these objectives.

Programs and services

Speaker's bureau; student matinees.

PRODUCTIONS 1982-83

Night and Day, Tom Stoppard; dir: Toby Robertson
The Dining Room, A.R. Gurney, Jr.; dir: Thomas Gruenewald
Translations, Brian Friel; dir: Jacques Cartier
Time and the Conways, J.B. Priestley; dir: Elinor Renfield
The Taming of the Shrew, William Shakespeare

DESIGNERS

Sets: Franco Colavecchia, Richard M. Isackes, Rachel Kurland, James Leonard Joy, Hugh Landwehr.
Costumes: Michaele Hite, Mariann Verheyen, Ann Wallace.
Lights: Jeff Davis, Roger Meeker, William Mintzer.

Illusion Theater. Kate Fuglei and Bruce Bohne in Becoming Memories. *Photo: Avis Mandel.*

MICHAEL ROBINS
BONNIE MORRIS
Producing Directors

JOHN MONTILINO
Managing Director

PETER HAMES
Board President

528 Hennepin Ave., #205
Minneapolis, MN 55403
(612) 339-7651

FOUNDED 1974
Michael Robins, Carole Harris Lipschultz

SEASON
September-June

SCHEDULE

Evenings
Wednesday-Sunday

Matinees
Saturday

FACILITIES

Studio
304 North Washington Ave.
Seating capacity: 50-100
Stage: flexible

Southern Theatre
1420 Washington Ave.
Seating capacity: 125-150
Stage: flexible

The Independent Eye

FINANCES
July 1, 1982-June 30, 1983
$370,000 operating expenses
$125,000 earned income
$246,000 grants/contributions

AUDIENCE
Annual attendance: 40,000

TOURING CONTACT
Nancy Riestenberg

AEA Guest Artist contract

Illusion Theater, originally a mime theatre, now retains a resident company of actors working with various playwrights and directors to create new plays that entertain, enrich and educate its audiences. The theatre creates new works through a three-phase collaborative process which includes creation/development, workshops and final productions. The resident acting company is the essential core of this process, maintaining ongoing working relationships with directors and writers to facilitate the creation of new works for the American theatre.

The process also includes special collaboration with human service professionals to create works based on specific current social issues. Choices of style and content are continually evolving and follow the needs of the company, encompassing that which has been learned in previous seasons, and the artistic vision of the producing directors.

Recently, Illusion has moved beyond its dedication to creating original works to bring its own style to classical plays as well.

Programs and services

Programs in schools; workshops; Applied Theater Program, collaboration with human service professionals.

PRODUCTIONS 1981-82

Spring Awakening, Frank Wedekind; adapt: Nancy Beckett; dir: David Feldshuh
The Short Wave Man, John Orlock; dir: Donna Breed
Fall Down Go Boom, Gary Amdahl; dir: D. Scott Glasser
Push-Ups, Lee Blessing, Michael Robins and Alfred Harrison; dir: D. Scott Glasser
Virginia Behind the Cotton Wool, company-developed; dir: Michael Robins
The Yellow Wallpaper, adapt: Marysue Moses and company, from Charlotte Perkins Gilman; dir: Sheila Reiser
Willa, Marisha Chamberlain; dir: Michael Robins
Touch, Michael Robins, Bonnie Morris, Cordelia Anderson and company; dir: Michael Robins
No Easy Answers, Michael Robins, Bonnie Morris, Cordelia Anderson and company; dir: D. Scott Glasser
Bert, Alfred Harrison; dir: Alfred Harrison

PRODUCTIONS 1982-83

Touch
No Easy Answers
Push-Ups
Sleepover, Ronnie Paris; dir: David Shookhoff
The Yellow Wallpaper
Relics, Bonnie Morris, Mary McDevitt and Steven Epp; dir: Michael Robins
Cocoanuts, book: George S. Kaufman; music and lyrics: Irving Berlin; dir: David Feldshuh
Bert
Becoming Memories, Arthur Giron and company; dir: Michael Robins

DESIGNERS

Sets: David Krchelich.
Costumes: Sue Haas, Barrie Smeeth.
Lights: David Krchelich, Jeff Bartlett.

CONRAD BISHOP
Artistic Director

LINDA BISHOP
Administrative Director

JOHN D. LeFEVER
Board Chairman

208 East King St.
Lancaster, PA 17602
(717) 393-9088

FOUNDED 1974
Conrad and Linda Bishop

SEASON
September-June

SCHEDULE
Evenings
Thursday-Sunday

FACILITIES
Eye Theatre Works
Seating capacity: 80
Stage: flexible

FINANCES
July 1, 1982-June 30, 1983
$68,000 operating expenses
$47,000 earned income
$21,000 grants/contributions

AUDIENCE
Annual attendance: 13,000
Subscribers: 124

TOURING CONTACT
Linda Bishop

BOOKED-IN EVENTS
Theatre, music, poetry readings

The Independent Eye is a national touring ensemble which uses a wide range of storytelling forms to examine deeply felt, commonly shared human experience. Since 1974, the Eye has presented more than 1,700 performances in 33 states and abroad, for theatres and festivals, colleges, churches, prisons, social agencies and community groups. Sites have ranged from Off Broadway to a South Georgia farm commune, from Phoenix to Jerusalem.

The Independent Eye. Elizabeth Fuller and Conrad Bishop in Medea/Sacrament. *Photo: F. Ackerman.*

In 1977, the Eye moved from Chicago to Lancaster, Pennsylvania, and began a variety of local programs to supplement its national touring. In its region of Pennsylvania Duth traditionalism, the Eye Theatre Works is unique in presenting a subscription season devoted to thematic and stylistic experiment. The theatre serves as a base for single-production work such as a surreal collage based on writings by children—*Calls from a Curious Planet*—and for creation of pieces designed for the long-term repertoire and touring. *Full Hookup*, presented as a staged reading jointly by the Eye and Milwaukee's Theatre X, went on to the new play festival at Actors Theatre of Louisville. *Medea/Sacrament* premiered in Lancaster, toured, and was then presented in New York, hosted by CSC Repertory.

The Eye's approach, even with serious material, is basically comic, focusing on human incongruities and including the radical shifts of mood, contradictions and anachronisms common to real experience. A broad range of styles is used to extend the resources of a small ensemble and to embody story metaphor in performance structure: suspense melodrama in *Goners;* cabaret revue-style in *Families* and *Le Cabaret de Camille;* fragmentary naturalism in *Dessie* and *Lifesaver;* and a mask/puppet dream expressionism in *Macbeth, Marvels* and the current *Medea/Sacrament*. The Eye has also created a series of plays, "Theatre for Human Values," designed to stimulate discussion on social concerns. These have been featured at national family issues conferences, used in training programs for teachers, medical students and social workers, and won a number of national broadcast awards. In all work, the performers' personal commitment to content and the shared response of the audience are primary.

Programs and services

Staged readings; touring; internships.

PRODUCTIONS 1981-82

Le Cabaret de Camille, Conrad Bishop and Camilla Schade
Medea/Sacrament, Conrad Bishop and Elizabeth Fuller
Families, Conrad Bishop and company
Dessie, Conrad Bishop and Elizabeth Fuller
Lifesaver, Conrad Bishop and company

PRODUCTIONS 1982-83

(Acts of) Kindness, John D. Schneider
Calls from a Curious Planet, Conrad Bishop
Medea/Sacrament
Le Cabaret de Camille
Dessie
Action News, Conrad Bishop and Elizabeth Fuller

All productions directed by Conrad Bishop

DESIGNERS

Sets: Conrad Bishop.
Costumes: Camilla Schade.
Lights: Conrad Bishop.

Indiana Repertory Theatre

TOM HAAS
Artistic Director

LEN ALEXANDER
Managing Director

EDGAR G. DAVIS
Board Chairman

140 West Washington St.
Indianapolis, IN 46204
(317) 635-5277 (business)
(317) 635-5252 (box office)

FOUNDED 1972
Benjamin Mordecai, Gregory Poggi, Edward Stern

SEASON
October–May

SCHEDULE

Evenings
Tuesday–Sunday

Matinees
Sunday

FACILITIES

Mainstage
Seating capacity: 583
Stage: modified thrust

Upperstage
Seating capacity: 245
Stage: proscenium

The Cabaret
Seating capacity: 140
Stage: flexible

FINANCES
July 1, 1982–June 30, 1983
$1,830,000 operating expenses
$1,176,000 earned income
$ 657,000 grants/contributions

AUDIENCE
Annual attendance: 157,000
Subscribers: 13,000

BOOKED-IN EVENTS
Theatre, music, dance, nightclub acts

AEA LORT (B) contract

The Indiana Repertory Theatre defines itself as an American populist theatre — that is, each performance is a self-defining one. Previous exposure to a particular theatrical form or cultural heritage should not be necessary to the enjoyment of a production. Texts are consistently chosen to emphasize or explore contemporary American concerns—political, social or emotional. Thus, the IRT may be seen as American in viewpoint, though not exclusively American in repertoire.

A resident company of approximately 10 actors constitutes the core of each production. By seeing the same actors transform into a number of distinct characters, audiences discover a unique property of theatre; the actors, in turn, continue to explore as a company various dramatic genres. With time, a certain artistic shorthand is developed which enables the theatre to mold its own distinctive and consistent production style. Such company work is integral, for example, to the Shakespearean cycle begun several seasons ago with *Hamlet* and continued in the 1983-84 season with *Henry IV, Parts 1 and 2* in rotating repertory.

Work on the Mainstage combines the traditional classical repertoire with American fare, both neglected and established. The Upperstage presents works of significantly smaller scale or of a more specifically contemporary viewpoint. This space is frequently referred to as the "alternative theatre," and houses a progressive dance company and traveling artists in addition to the theatre's own productions. The Cabaret, the theatre's only year-round program, was established to recognize the significance of American musical comedy in the arts. Cabaret musicals are generally satirical in tone and unabashedly entertaining in intent.

Overall, the 1983-84 season, designed to utilize all three theatres fully, shows a significant expansion in programming and reflects the community's growing acceptance of IRT's artistic aims.

Programs and services

Dance company in residence; programs-in-schools; speaker's bureau; artistic, administrative and technical internships; *Marquee* subscriber newsletter.

Indiana Repertory Theatre. Bella Jarrett and Priscilla Lindsay in You Can't Take It with You. *Photo: Terri Horvath.*

PRODUCTIONS 1981-82

Hamlet, William Shakespeare; dir: Tom Haas
A Lesson from Aloes, Athol Fugard; dir: Edward Cornell
A Christmas Carol, adapt: Tom Haas, from Charles Dickens; dir: Tom Haas
Coming Attractions, Ted Tally; dir: Tom Haas
She Stoops to Conquer, Oliver Goldsmith; dir: William Peters
Rain, adapt: John Colton and Clemence Randolph, from W. Somerset Maugham; dir: Tom Haas
Operetta, My Dear Watson, book: Tom Haas; music: W.S. Gilbert and Arthur Sullivan; dir: Tom Haas
The Siege of Frank Sinatra, Denis Whitburn; dir: Ted Weiant
Billy Bishop Goes to War, John Gray and Eric Peterson; dir: Ben Cameron
Home, Samm-Art Williams; dir: Israel Hicks

PRODUCTIONS 1982-83

A Midsummer Night's Dream, William Shakespeare; dir: Tom Haas
Billy Bishop Goes to War
A Christmas Carol, adapt: Tom Haas, from Charles Dickens; dir: Scott Wentworth
Tartuffe, Molière; trans: Richard Wilbur; dir: David Rotenberg
You Can't Take It with You, George S. Kaufman and Moss Hart; dir: Ben Cameron
Desire Under the Elms, Eugene O'Neill; dir: Tom Haas
Pal Joey, book: John O'Hara; music and lyrics: Richard Rodgers and Lorenz Hart; dir: Tom Haas

DESIGNERS

Sets: Bob Barnett, Kate Edmunds, Ming Cho Lee, Tom Lynch, Russell Metheny, Steven Rubin, Karen Schulz, Douglas Stein, Michael H. Yeargan.
Costumes: Leon I. Brauner, Susan Hilferty, Martha Kelly, Gene K. Lakin, Judianna Makovsky, Steven Rubin, Bill Walker, Michel Yeuell.
Lights: William Armstrong, Frances Aronson, Rachel Budin, Stuart Duke, Robert Jared, Craig Miller.

INTAR (INTERNATIONAL ARTS RELATIONS)

MAX FERRA
Artistic Director

DENNIS FERGUSON-ACOSTA
Managing Director

STANLEY STAIRS
Board President

Box 788
New York, NY 10108
(212) 695-6134

FOUNDED 1966
Max Ferrá, Leonor Datil, Elsa and Frank Robles

SEASON
September-June

SCHEDULE
Evenings
Wednesday-Sunday

Matinees
Saturday, Sunday

FACILITIES
420 West 42nd St.
Seating capacity: 99
Stage: proscenium

508 West 53rd St.
Seating capacity: 75
Stage: proscenium

FINANCES
July 1, 1982-June 30, 1983
$385,000 operating expenses
$ 71,000 earned income
$304,000 grants/contributions

AUDIENCE
Annual attendance: 5,189

BOOKED-IN EVENTS
Theatre, music, dance

AEA Showcase code and Mini contract

INTAR's visibility has grown rapidly over the last few years, and its efforts to develop Hispanic American plays are beginning to show results. INTAR has produced plays by emerging Latin playwrights, as well as the American premieres of works by such authors as Fernando Arrabal and Mario Vargas Llosa.

INTAR's annual three-play season is chosen from a series of 10-to-15 staged readings held late each summer. These plays are the finalists in a year-round search of a wide spectrum of international and American Hispanic works, including plays developed in INTAR's Hispanic Playwrights-in-Residence Laboratory. The readings are open to theatre professionals and producers as well.

INTAR's research and development program now includes plans for a network of domestic and international delegates working to identify outstanding Hispanic theatrical talent and further the awareness of INTAR and its work. Throughout the 1982-83 season INTAR held general auditions exclusively for English-speaking Hispanic actors, which has resulted in a file of more than 600 Latin actors and actresses.

The primary goal of INTAR has always been to make a contribution to the theatre through the encouragement and support of artists who voice the concerns and expressions of their Latin heritage. In this way, the theatre hopes to inject a rich and vibrant sensibility into the performing arts in this country.

Programs and services

Playwrights-in-Residence Laboratory; gallery exhibitions; management and production internships.

PRODUCTIONS 1981-82

Crisp!, book adapt: Max Ferrá and Dolores Prida; music: Galt MacDermot; lyrics: Dolores Prida; dir: Max Ferrá
The Extravagant Triumph of Jesus Christ, Karl Marx and William Shakespeare, Fernando Arrabal; trans: Miguel Falquez-Certain; dir: Eduardo Manet
Last Latin Lover, Ricardo Halac; adapt: Leonard Melfi and Max Ferrá; dir: Max Ferrá

PRODUCTIONS 1982-83

Exiles, Ana Maria Simo; dir: Maria Irene Fornes
Union City Thanksgiving, Manuel Martin, Jr.; dir: Andre Ernotte
The Señorita from Tacna, Mario Vargas Llosa; trans: Joanne Pottlitzer and Raoul Rizik; dir: Michael Kahn

DESIGNERS

Sets: Carlos Almada, Randy Barcelo, Larry Brodsky, Paulette Crowther, Michael Sharp, Loren Sherman, Pat Woodbridge.
Costumes: Randy Barcelo, Gabriel Berry, Karen Matthews, Sue Schmidt, Deborah Shaw, Debra Stein.
Lights: Rachel Budin, Edward M. Greenberg, Tom Hennes, Cheryl Thacker.

INTAR. Diva Osorio, Emilio Del Pozo and Miriam Cruz in Union City Thanksgiving. *Photo: Charles Marinaro.*

Interart Theatre

MARGOT LEWITIN
Artistic Director

COLETTE BROOKS
Associate Artistic Director

SAM SWEET
Managing Director

BILL PERLMAN
Board President

549 West 52nd St.
New York, NY 10019
(212) 246-1050 (business)
(212) 279-4200 (box office)

FOUNDED 1970
Marjorie De Fazio, Margot Lewitin, Alice Rubenstein, Jane Chambers

SEASON
October–June

SCHEDULE

Evenings
Tuesday–Saturday

Matinees
Friday, Saturday

FACILITIES

Interart Theatre
Seating capacity: 40–74
Stage: flexible

Interart Theatre Annex
552 West 53rd St.
Seating capacity: 40–74
Stage: flexible

FINANCES
July 1, 1982–June 30, 1983
$118,000 operating expenses
$ 41,000 earned income
$ 77,000 grants/contributions

AUDIENCE
Annual attendance: 8,400

AEA letter of agreement

Interart Theatre. William Winkler, Kenneth Ryan and Andrew Davis in Mercenaries.
Photo: Carol Halebian.

The Interart Theatre is committed to exploring all areas of theatrical expression. While emphasizing the presentation of new plays and playwrights, Interart also undertakes projects designed to encourage the development of directors and designers whose work might revolve around established texts or more experimental material. In addition, Interart attempts to foster the creation of theatre pieces by talented non-theatre artists who have expressed a strong desire to explore the medium. All mainstage productions are fully mounted with the design elements realized as completely as possible.

Interart is also committed to the longer-term development of playwrights and new scripts, and to creating a situation in which ongoing exploratory work can be conducted outside the confines of the standard rehearsal-production period. To these ends, the theatre instituted a Developmental Workshop Reading Series in 1980 that has now become an established adjunct of its mainstage season. These workshops allow playwrights the chance to expose not quite "finished" work to the helpful scrutiny of peers without the pressures of production, and also allow Interart to search out and develop work that is clearly deserving of future mainstage production.

To understand the full intent and direction of the Interart Theatre, one must view it within the context of its parent organization, the Women's Interart Center. The Center is a nonprofit, multi-arts organization which produces work by artists (primarily but not exclusively women) in varying disciplines. The center provides space and facilities for artists to explore the full gamut of the media, performing arts and visual arts through workshops, colloquia and productions. By encouraging artists and audiences to venture into various media, by stressing the interactive exchanges inherent in the concept "interart," the center aims to expand its vision and constantly enliven its ideas of what art is and can be.

Programs and services

Developmental Workshop Reading Series; Integrated Media Arts Program: training in acting, directing and writing, and artistic apprenticeships.

PRODUCTIONS 1981-82

Mercenaries, James Yoshimura; dir: Margot Lewitin
Whorl, Lee Nagrin; dir: Lee Nagrin
A Pretty Passion, Sally Ordway; dir: Kay Carney
Food, Sondra Segal and Roberta Sklar; dir: Roberta Sklar

PRODUCTIONS 1982-83

Growing Up Gothic, Clare Coss; dir: Margot Lewitin
Fish Riding Bikes, Claire Luckham; dir: Denise Gordon
Range, Joanne McEntire; dir: Jeannine Haas

DESIGNERS

Sets: Kate Edmunds, Durin Hunecki, James Meares, Christina Weppner.
Costumes: Kate Edmunds, Tom McAlister, Sally Ann Parsons, Christina Weppner.
Lights: Rachel Budin, Tony Giovannetti, Bruce Hudgens, David Weiss, Ann Wrightson.

Intiman Theatre Company

MARGARET BOOKER
Artistic Director

SIMON SIEGL
General Manager

PAMELA SCHELL
Board President

801 Pike St.
Seattle, WA 98101
(206) 624-4541 (business)
(206) 587-5766 (box office)

FOUNDED 1972
Margaret Booker

SEASON
May-October

SCHEDULE
Evenings
Tuesday-Sunday
Matinees
Saturday

FACILITIES
2nd Stage Theatre
1419 8th Ave.
Seating capacity: 388
Stage: thrust

FINANCES
January 1, 1982-December 31, 1982
$878,000 operating expenses
$799,000 earned income
$345,000 grants/contributions

AUDIENCE
Annual attendance: 50,000
Subscribers: 4,750

TOURING CONTACT
Simon Siegl

AEA LORT (C) contract

Named after Strindberg's intimate theatre in Stockholm, the Intiman Theatre Company was founded by artistic director Margaret Booker in 1972, and employs a resident company of actors and technicians. Working on a European model, the actors perform both large and small roles as assigned throughout the season.

The six-play subscription series emphasizes classics and modern masterpieces of dramatic literature. Each season is focused on a major international project, which includes production of a mainstage classic and a related series of staged readings of new works by representative foreign authors. Intiman also engages foreign artists, including guest directors and designers, to work with the company on the project, to broaden and challenge its knowledge of theatre, and to lend varying artistic perspectives and impact. Intiman offers specialized training to its professional actors in areas such as period style, dialects and stage combat.

The company's production style supports both the text and the performing artist. Intiman believes that an optimum actor-audience relationship is vital to the theatre experience, and for the past eight years it

Intiman Theatre Company. Will Huddleston, Michael Santo and Catherine O'Connell in School for Wives. *Photo: Chris Bennion.*

Jewish Repertory Theatre

plays have been performed in an intimate 342-seat facility that places actors in close proximity to the audience.

During 1984, the company will move to new facilities in a renovated downtown building, continuing its presence as a major Seattle performing arts organization.

Programs and services

New Plays Onstage Festival; symposia; school tours; internships; post-play discussions; volunteers.

PRODUCTIONS 1982

Hay Fever, Noel Coward; dir: Margaret Booker
A Delicate Balance, Edward Albee; dir: Nagle Jackson
She Stoops to Conquer, Oliver Goldsmith; dir: Margaret Booker
The Wild Duck, Henrik Ibsen; trans: Christopher Hampton; dir: Margaret Booker
A Dreamplay, August Strindberg; trans: Harry G. Carlson; dir: Peter Oskarson

PRODUCTIONS 1983

Misalliance, George Bernard Shaw; dir: Margaret Booker
Dear Liar, Jerome Kilty; dir: Robert Brink
The Crucifer of Blood, Paul Giovanni; dir: Margaret Booker
In the Jungle of Cities, Bertolt Brecht; dir: Christof Nel
The Ribadier System, Georges Feydeau; dir: Nagle Jackson
The Seagull, Anton Chekhov; dir: Margaret Booker

DESIGNERS

Sets: William Bloodgood, Dennis Bradford, Andreas Braito, Robert A. Dahlstrom, Karen Gjelsteen, Peter Holm, Michael Miller.
Costumes: Carol H. Beule, Peter Holm, Veronica Leo, John Sullivan, Susan Tsu, Kurt Wilhelm, Andrew Yellusich.
Lights: Robert Peterson, James Sale, Robert Scales, Greg Sullivan.

Jewish Repertory Theatre. Harvey Pierce, Herman O. Arbeit and Frank Nastasi in Taking Steam. *Photo: Adam Newman.*

RAN AVNI
Artistic Director

DONALD GELLER
Executive Director

ALFRED L. PLANT
Board Chairman

344 East 14th St.
New York, NY 10003
(212) 674-7200

FOUNDED 1974
Ran Avni

SEASON
October-June

SCHEDULE
Evenings
Tuesday-Thursday, Saturday, Sunday

Matinees
Sunday

FACILITIES
Milton Weill Auditorium
Seating capacity: 99
Stage: proscenium

FINANCES
July 1, 1982-June 30, 1983
$158,000 operating expenses
$105,000 earned income
$ 44,000 grants/contributions

AUDIENCES
Annual attendance: 20,000
Subscribers: 900

AEA Funded Nonprofit Theatre code and Mini contract

The Jewish Repertory Theatre was founded in 1974 to present plays in English that related to the Jewish experience. Nine seasons and 45 productions later, this naive goal has become a complex, challenging and, at times, frustrating concept. Unlike other cultural or ethnic groups, JRT had to (and still must) live down the old stigma attached to the genre of Yiddish theatre. While it was that very heritage that produced many of JRT's plays and ideas, the need to move in more creative directions became clear.

JRT began producing new plays and is now committed almost exclusively to them. The theatre challenges playwrights to confront elements in their lives that they might otherwise choose to avoid. It strives toward artistic excellence in order to compete for scripts as a specialty theatre in the general marketplace.

JRT has proven by its exceptional attendance figures that audiences can feel comfortable in "that kind" of theatre without being isolated; an encouraging sign that JRT is filling an important void. It has also proven an example to other ethnic theatres that, in these times when artists struggle with their

The Julian Theatre

reasons for creating, searching for one's roots and uniqueness is all right. In the age of technology and commercial generalization, JRT is attempting to enrich the cultural experience as a whole by looking into the ingredients: and a prime ingredient is a good play which makes a universal statement by dealing honestly and directly with its environment.

Programs and services

Writers Lab staged readings.

PRODUCTIONS 1981-82

Awake and Sing!, Clifford Odets; dir: Lynn Polan
Elephants, David Rush; dir: Edward M. Cohen
Delmore, Delmore Schwartz and Donald Margulies; dir: Florence Stanley
Pantagleize, Michel de Ghelderode; dir: Anthony McKay
Vagabond Stars, book: Nahma Sandrow; music: Raphael Crystal; lyrics: Alan Poul; dir: Ran Avni

PRODUCTIONS 1982-83

After the Fall, Arthur Miller; dir: William Shroder
Friends Too Numerous to Mention, Neil Cohen and Joel Cohen; dir: Alan Coulter
Ivanov, Anton Chekhov; dir: Anthony McKay
Taking Steam, Kenneth Klonsky and Brian Shein; dir: Edward M. Cohen
My Heart Is in the East, book: Linda Kline; music: Raphael Crystal; lyrics: Richard Engquist; dir: Ran Avni

DESIGNERS

Sets: Jeffrey Schneider, Geoffry Hall, Michael Smith, Mike Boyer, Ken Rothchild.
Costumes: Karen Hummel, Laura Drawbaugh, Linda Vigdor, Jessica Fassman, Gayle Goldberg.
Lights: Phil Monat, Dan Kinsley, Naomi Berger.

The Julian Theatre. Raynard Green, Bobby Joe Woodward, Hansford Prince and Adilah in Daddy. *Photo: Allen Nomura.*

RICHARD REINECCIUS
Artistic/General Director

SYLVIA TUCKER
Associate Administrator

GEORGE CROWE
Board Chairman

953 De Haro St.
San Francisco, CA 94107
(415) 647-5525 (business)
(415) 647-8098 (box office)

FOUNDED 1965
Richard Reineccius, Douglas Giebel, Brenda Berlin

SEASON
October-July

SCHEDULE

Evenings
Wednesday-Sunday

Matinees
Sunday

FACILITIES

Potrero Hill Neighborhood House
Seating capacity: 175
Stage: flexible

FINANCES
July 1, 1982-June 30, 1983
$153,000 operating expenses
$ 57,000 earned income
$ 97,000 grants/contributions

AUDIENCE
Annual attendance: 16,800
Subscribers: 294

TOURING CONTACT
Staff

BOOKED-IN EVENTS
Ethnic and experimental theatre, dance

AEA letter of agreement

The Julian Theatre's purpose is to produce new plays and adaptations or revivals that are gutsy and socially relevant, resonating with the historical and contemporary concerns of the cosmopolitan San Francisco area. While its emphasis is on American writers—particularly those from the West Coast—the company also seeks important works from other countries, commissioning translations when possible.

In addition to a full producing season, the company works with area writers of all ethnic groups in developing their plays for public readings or future production at the Julian and other theatres.

Directors, performers and staff are generally chosen from the pool of San Francisco Bay Area talent, with current union agree-

L.A. Public Theatre

ments allowing for a combination of professional and non-professional artists.

The company performs in a landmark neighborhood center overlooking San Francisco Bay, and tours throughout the area and state as much as funds permit.

Programs and services

Staged readings; internships; touring; post-performance discussions.

PRODUCTIONS 1981-82

The Boys Own Story, Peter Flannery; dir: Richard Seyd
The Island and *Sizwe Bansi Is Dead,* Athol Fugard; dir: Luther James (Oregon Shakespearean Festival production)
A Full Length Portrait of America, Paul D'Andrea; dir: John H. Doyle
Back to Back, Al Brown; dir: Al Brown
The Two Tigers, Brian McNeill; dir: Brenda Berlin
The Accident, Friedrich Düerrenmatt; trans: Robert Goss; dir: Cab Covay

PRODUCTIONS 1982-83

In the Matter of J. Robert Oppenheimer, Heinar Kipphardt; dir: Mohammad Kowsar
Back to Back
The Heist, Samy Fayad; trans and adapt: David Lifson; dir: Chris Pagano
Bloodlines to Oblivion, Jamal; dir: John H. Doyle
Daddy, Ed Bullins; dir: John H. Doyle
Igugu Lethu, company-developed (U-Zulu Dance Theatre co-production)

DESIGNERS

Sets: Donald Cate, Cab Covay, Alan Curreri, Michael Dingle, Joel Eis, Steven Rehn.
Costumes: Regina Cate, Jim Piddock, Irene Rosen, Gael Russell.
Lights: Donald Cate, Michael Dingle, Joel Eis, Peter Garrison, Laurie Manarik, Susan Paigen.

L.A. Public Theatre. Julie Payne, Adam Arkin and Charles Levin in Rich and Famous. *Photo: David Hiller.*

PEG YORKIN
Producer/Board President

JUDY DONOGHUE
General Manager

8105 West 3rd St.
Los Angeles, CA 90048
(213) 651-0491 (business)
(213) 659-6415 (box office)

FOUNDED 1973
Community members

SEASON
October-August

SCHEDULE
Evenings
Tuesday-Sunday

Matinees
Sunday

FACILITIES
Coronet Theatre
366 North La Cienega Blvd.
Seating capacity: 272
Stage: proscenium

FINANCES
November 1, 1981-October 31, 1982
$963,000 operating expenses
$519,000 earned income
$409,000 grants/contributions

AUDIENCE
Annual attendance: 40,000
Subscribers: 4,339

TOURING CONTACT
Jan Steadman

AEA LORT (C) contract

The L.A. Public Theatre started in 1973 as the L.A. Shakespeare Festival, a professional

L.A. Stage Co.

company which toured the parks and played in an outdoor amphitheatre, free to the public. It became apparent that free theatre was no longer viable, particularly with cuts in government funding; so in 1980, the newly christened L.A. Public Theatre began doing contemporary plays, and in 1981 it was able to start a subscription season at the 272-seat Coronet Theatre.

The theatre's emphasis is on plays which are new — or new to Los Angeles — and which address universal concerns. L.A. Public is one of three mid-size houses in Los Angeles working under a LORT (C) contract.

The Public's children's theatre component, which has been in existence since 1977, tours area schools, and presents weekend matinee and holiday performances at the Coronet. The theatre's emphasis is on original work, though it also produces plays from the standard children's repertoire.

The L.A. Public's funding is derived from a combination of ticket revenue, contributions and a unique bingo game, and the theatre has had one of its plays taped for cable television. Los Angeles is fast becoming a vital theatre city — and the L.A. Public Theatre is an integral part of this growth.

Programs and services

School touring; programs-in-schools.

PRODUCTIONS 1981-82

Home, Samm-Art Williams; dir: LeRoy McDonald
Close Ties, Elizabeth Diggs; dir: Arvin Brown
Put Them All Together, Anne Commire; dir: Norman Cohen
Rich and Famous, John Guare; dir: Kim Friedman
On Trial, Brian Way; dir: Barry Moore
The Code Breaker, Pauline C. Conley; dir: Rita Giomi

PRODUCTIONS 1982-83

The Basement Tapes, Erik Brogger; dir: Robert Engels
How I Got That Story, Amlin Gray; dir: Eve Brandstein
Desert Fire, Roger Holzberg and Martin Casella; dir: Norman Cohen
Shay, Anne Commire; dir: Anne Commire
The Millionaire y el Pobrecito, adapt: Ruben Sierra, from Mark Twain; dir: Ruben Sierra

DESIGNERS

Sets: D. Martyn Bookwalter, Michael Devine, Christopher M. Idoine, Steve Jezewski, John Kavelin, Jeanine Lambeth, Jack Pelton, John Hieronymus Stone, Robert Yodice.
Costumes: Carol Brolaski, Marianna Elliott, Anna Belle Kaufman, Susan Nininger, Douglas Spesert, Sherry Thompson.
Lights: Orville Ballard, Jr., Brian Gale, Karen M. Katz, Ed Layton, Barbara Ling, Greg Sullivan, Paulie Jenkins.

SUSAN DIETZ
Artistic Director

JOSH SCHIOWITZ
Producing Director

LENNY BEER
Board President

1642 North Las Palmas Blvd.
Hollywood, CA 90028
(213) 461-4919 (business)
(213) 461-2755 (box office)

FOUNDED 1980
Susan Dietz, Lenny Beer, Jason Wallach

SEASON
Year-round

SCHEDULE

Evenings
Tuesday-Sunday

Matinees
Sunday

FACILITIES

L.A. Stage Co.
Seating capacity: 377
Stage: proscenium

L.A. Stage Co. West
205 North Canon Drive, Beverly Hills
Seating capacity: 348
Stage: proscenium

FINANCES
July 1, 1982-June 30, 1983
$1,761,000 operating expenses
$1,847,000 earned income

AUDIENCE
Annual attendance: 125,000

BOOKED-IN EVENTS
Comedy, music

AEA LORT (B) and Theatre for Young Audiences contracts

The L.A. Stage Co. is a resident, nonprofit theatre which, in its second year, is producing plays in two mid-size theatres. Caryl Churchill's *Cloud 9* marked the opening of L.A. Stage Co. West in Beverly Hills, and

L.A. Stage Co. Christina Pickles and Jack Bannon in Cloud 9. *Photo: Ed Krieger.*

Sister Mary Ignatius . . . continues its controversial and successful run at the L.A. Stage Co. in the heart of Hollywood.

The theatre's founders began with several goals: to create a theatre where plays which had had successful non-professional productions could find larger audiences via a professional mounting; and to produce plays which were new to L.A., encompassing the sexual, political, philosophical and racial plurality of American society. The first goal was clearly reflected in the company's first three productions, all of which began in smaller theatres: Wendy Wasserstein's *Uncommon Women and Others*, *The Fox* adapted from D.H. Lawrence, and *Nuts*, the courtroom drama by Tom Topor which ran for a record-breaking 49 weeks.

The second goal has been fulfilled not only by *Sister Mary* and *Cloud 9*, but by co-productions with L.A. Theatre Works of the thoughtful and unusual family entertainments *Did You Ever See A Unicorn?* based on the works of Shel Silverstein, and *Daniel in Babylon* by Doris Baizley.

L.A. Stage Co.'s next major effort will be to produce a four-play subscription season which will include a combination of L.A. premieres, the best of recent non-professional productions and new plays selected from the hundreds submitted to the theatre from around the country. The season will attempt to speak to a changing society and a changing theatrical community.

Programs and services

Sid 'n Ernie Show children's theatre workshop; Nu Moovez short experimental films; Ada Brown Mather Tackling Shakespeare Workshop.

PRODUCTIONS 1981-82

Uncommon Women and Others, Wendy Wasserstein; dir: Susan Dietz
The Fox, adapt: Allan Miller, from D.H. Lawrence; dir: Allan Miller
Nuts, Tom Topor; dir: Lewis Palter
Did You Ever See a Unicorn?, adapt: Dianne Haak, from Shel Silverstein; dir: Dianne Haak

PRODUCTIONS 1982-83

Nuts
Sister Mary Ignatius Explains It All for You and *The Actor's Nightmare*, Christopher Durang; dir: Warner Shook
Daniel in Babylon, Doris Baizley; dir: Matt Casella
Cloud 9, Caryl Churchill; dir: Don Amendolia

DESIGNERS

Sets: Vicki Baral, Gerry Hariton, Jay Morley, David L. D'Ovidio.
Costumes: Sylvia Moss, Rachel Perkoff, Elaine Saussotte, Hilary Sloane.
Lights: Vicki Baral, Cynthia Bishop, Gerry Hariton, Christopher Milliken, Steven Pliska.

L.A. Theatre Works

SUSAN ALBERT LOEWENBERG
Producing Director

SARA MAULTSBY
Associate Producing Director

ROBERT GREENWALD
Board President

681 Venice Blvd.
Venice, CA 90261
(213) 827-0808

FOUNDED 1974
Jeremy Blahnik, Robert Greenwald

SEASON
October–August

SCHEDULE
Evenings
Tuesday–Sunday

Matinees
Sunday

FINANCES
October 1, 1981–September 30, 1982
$258,000 operating expenses
$108,000 earned income
$168,000 grants/contributions

AUDIENCE
Annual attendance: 15,111
Subscribers: 100

TOURING CONTACT
Sara Maultsby

BOOKED-IN EVENTS
Theatre, dance, music

AEA LORT (D) amd Guest Artist contracts, and 99-seat waiver

Since 1974 L.A. Theatre Works has grown from a small group of artists exploring ways to make theatre in unorthodox settings — prisons, hospitals, community workshops — to a formal producing organization which develops and presents the new and innovative work of emerging and established playwrights from the United States and abroad. Plays are developed from experiments with new forms; from workshops with culturally diverse groups; and from the work of specially commissioned playwrights. Its 1982-83 production of *Greek* brought the artistry of English playwright/actor/director Steven Berkoff to this country.

In the 1983-84 season, Berkoff and Yugoslavian director Ljubisa Ristic will work with L.A. Theatre Works to develop two new plays for production by the company. Through collaboration with these internationally known artists, L.A. Theatre Works seeks to contribute to the growing practice of national and international exchange among theatre groups with similar aesthetics and shared notions about the role of theatre in society; to examine the common concerns of theatre artists in the world today; and to introduce Los Angeles and other American audiences to new forms and experiences in the theatre.

In the past nine years L.A. Theatre Works has produced 20 theatre pieces and a one-hour documentary film, *Jump Street;* has conducted more than 70 theatre, writing, dance, music and visual arts workshops in social institutions and in the community; and has initiated a weekly New Play Reading Series.

Plans for the future include occupancy in a newly renovated performance space in Venice, California, and continued participation with two other arts organizations in the development of a shared cultural complex in Venice: a place where audiences and artists may go to provocative journeys into the visual, literary and performing arts.

Ken Danziger, John Francis, Gillian Eaton and Paddi Edwards in Greek. *Photo: Hariton-Baral.*

Programs and services

Play reading series; workshops; touring.

PRODUCTIONS 1981-82

Did You Ever See a Unicorn?, adapt: Dianne Haak, from Shel Silverstein; dir: Dianne Haak
Greek, Steven Berkoff; dir: Steven Berkoff
Extended Attack, Patrick Bennett; dir: John-Frederick Jones
Potato-Faced Blindman and Other Stories, Dianne Haak; dir: Dianne Haak

PRODUCTIONS 1982-83

Greek
Daniel in Babylon, Doris Baizley; dir: Matt Cassella
The Whale Concerts, Liebe Grey; dir: Liebe Grey
The Limited Edition Ronald Firbank, Crispin Thomas; dir: Crispin Thomas

DESIGNERS

Sets: Vicki Baral, David Brewer, Phil Brisler, Gerry Hariton, Lance Parker, Crispin Thomas.
Costumes: David Brewer, Liebe Grey, John-Frederick Jones, Peter Mitchell, Crispin Thomas.
Lights: Vicki Baral, Gerry Hariton, Gayle Marks, Crispin Thomas.

Living Stage Theatre Company

ROBERT ALEXANDER
Director

CATHERINE IRWIN
Managing Director

LINDA FINKELSTEIN and DAVID R. ANDERSON
Board Co-chairs

6th & Maine Aves., SW
Washington, DC 20024
(202) 554-9066

FOUNDED 1966
Robert Alexander

SEASON
October-May

SCHEDULE
Evenings
Monday-Saturday

FINANCES
July 1, 1982-June 30, 1983
$261,000 operating expenses
$ 20,000 earned income
$241,000 grants/contributions

AUDIENCE
Annual attendance: 10,000

TOURING CONTACT
Katha Kissman, Robert Alexander

AEA LORT (B) contract

Since its inception 17 years ago, the Living Stage Theatre Company has been the community venture of Arena Stage. Its thrust is actively to encourage the artistry of its audiences by creating works whose content arises from the terrors, anguishes, ecstasies, loves and dreams of its audiences—the community. The company believes in the perfectability of the human being and reveres the creative genius of the young.

Living Stage's audiences consist of children, teens, adults, senior citizens, children and adults in prison, and children and adults who have physical and mental disabilities. Although the company improvises on the themes of its audiences, it has also created more than 40 pieces for various age groups that express the concerns of humankind. The Living Stage script consists of more than 900 poems and quotes by children and adults, and more than 800 songs that are used improvisationally to make social comments on the emotional lives of the characters.

The company has created a new piece on nuclear terror called *Basta! Basta!*, as well as *Think about the Children*, a full-length piece dealing with the brutalization of children at the hands of uncaring adults. Performances are provided free of charge to all community groups throughout the season.

In the words of Federico Garcia Lorca, "Art is not a mirror, but a hammer. It does not reflect, it shapes! The poem, the song, the picture is only water drawn from the well of the people and it should be given back to them in a cup of beauty so that they may drink and in drinking understand themselves."

Programs and services

Professional and non-professional training; student and prison workshops; programs-in-schools; improvisation workshops; national touring; support groups; newsletter.

PRODUCTIONS 1981-83

All productions are developed by The Living Stage Theatre Company.

Rebecca Rice, Oran Sandel and Jennifer Nelson in Basta! Basta! *Photo: Joan Marcus.*

Long Wharf Theatre

ARVIN BROWN
Artistic Director

M. EDGAR ROSENBLUM
Executive Director

C. NEWTON SCHENCK
Board Chairman

222 Sargent Dr.
New Haven, CT 06511
(203) 787-4284 (business)
(203) 787-4282 (box office)

FOUNDED 1965
Jon Jory, Harlan Kleiman

SEASON
October-June

SCHEDULE
Evenings
Tuesday-Sunday

Matinees
Wednesday, Saturday, Sunday

FACILITIES
Main Stage
Seating capacity: 484
Stage: thrust

Stage II
Seating capacity: 199
Stage: flexible

FINANCES
July 1, 1981-June 30, 1982
$2,362,000 operating expenses
$1,655,000 earned income
$ 691,000 grants/contributions

AUDIENCE
Annual attendance: 140,033
Subscribers: 13,688

AEA LORT (B) and (D) contracts

Now in its 19th season, Long Wharf Theatre continues to emphasize new and established, home-grown and foreign works that explore human relationships and suit the company's long-standing reputation as an actor's theatre. The intimacy of LWT's two performance spaces — the Main Stage and the five-year-old Stage II, which was created to

Long Wharf Theatre. Peter MacNicol and Peter Gallagher in Another Country. *Photo: William B. Carter.*

highlight new plays—has greatly enhanced audience involvement.

Many of the world's leading theatrical craftsmen have brought their skills to the unique environment of New Haven, with its simultaneous proximity to New York and total independence of big-city commercial pressures. For all its success at home, much of Long Wharf's renown comes from the extended life its productions have experienced on Broadway, Off Broadway and on television. Moving to New York stages, virtually intact, such productions as *Quartermaine's Terms* and *A View from the Bridge* have quite naturally shed luster on their source. Millions of television viewers nationwide have seen the PBS *Theater in America* presentations of *The Widowing of Mrs. Holroyd*, *Forget-Me-Not Lane* and *Ah, Wilderness!* The awards and acclaim arising from such transfers are rewarding, but, to the exasperation of many an ardent young playwright or actor, a Broadway run is far from being LWT's first priority: the potential for transfer does not enter into script selection or casting.

Long Wharf could support a facility twice its current size, perhaps a season twice as full as it now presents. But the LWT philosophy demands the best possible presentation of the single play in progress. A continuity of leadership underlies and reinforces that guideline: an artistic director and board chairman who have been part of LWT since its inception, and an executive director of only slightly shorter tenure. For Long Wharf, internal growth comes before external expansion.

Programs and services

Signed performances for the hearing impaired; backstage tours; seminars.

PRODUCTIONS 1981-82

This Story of Yours, John Hopkins; dir: John Tillinger
A Day in the Death of Joe Egg, Peter Nichols; dir: Arvin Brown
A View from the Bridge, Arthur Miller; dir: Arvin Brown
The Workroom, Jean-Claude Grumberg; trans: Tom Kempinski; dir: Kenneth Frankel
Lakeboat, David Mamet; dir: John Dillon
The Doctor's Dilemma, George Bernard Shaw; dir: Kenneth Frankel
The Carmone Brothers' Italian Food Products Corp's Annual Pasta Pageant, Tom Griffin; dir: William Ludel
Ethan Frome, adapt: Owen Davis and Donald Davis, from Edith Wharton; dir: Kenneth Frankel
The Front Page, Ben Hecht and Charles MacArthur; dir: Harris Yulin
Molly, Simon Gray; dir: Stephen Hollis

PRODUCTIONS 1982-83

Open Admissions, Shirley Lauro; dir: Arvin Brown
Two by A.M., Arthur Miller; dir: Arthur Miller
Holiday, Philip Barry; dir: John Pasquin
Quartermaine's Terms, Simon Gray; dir: Kenneth Frankel
Another Country, Julian Mitchell; dir: John Tillinger
The Lady and the Clarinet, Michael Cristofer; dir: Gordon Davidson
The Guardsman, Ferenc Molnar; trans: Grace I. Colbron and Hans Bartsch; dir: Harris Yulin
Free and Clear, Robert Anderson; dir: Arvin Brown
Pal Joey, book: John O'Hara; music: Richard Rodgers; lyrics: Lorenz Hart; dir: Kenneth Frankel
The Cherry Orchard, Anton Chekhov; adapt: Jean-Claude van Itallie; dir: Arvin Brown

DESIGNERS

Sets: John Conklin, Karl Eigsti, Andrew Jackness, David Jenkins, John Jensen, Marjorie Bradley Kellogg, Hugh Landwehr, Laura Maurer, Steven Rubin, Michael H. Yeargan.
Costumes: Linda Fisher, Jane Greenwood, Gary Jones, Rachel Kurland, Carol Oditz, Ann Roth, Bill Walker, Robert Wojewodski.
Lights: Pat Collins, Geoffrey T. Cunningham, Jamie Gallagher, Paul Gallo, Judy Rasmuson, Ronald Wallace.

Looking Glass Theatre

PAMELA MESSORE
Producing Director

SIMONE JOYAUX
Board President

175 Mathewson St.
Providence, RI 02903
(401) 331-9080

FOUNDED 1965
Elaine Ostroff, Arthur Torg

SEASON
October-June

FINANCES
July 1, 1982-June 30, 1983
$56,000 operating expenses
$29,000 earned income
$27,000 grants/contributions

AUDIENCE
Annual attendance: 55,000
Subscribers: 150

TOURING CONTACT
Ruby Shalansky

Children's theatre should move young people to investigate their social, intellectual, emotional and imaginative environment. The challenge is to present plays that speak to children about issues at their level of understanding, without sacrificing quality because they are "children's plays." Children deserve a cultural environment that inspires, motivates, as well as challenges the status quo.

As a professional touring company, Looking Glass Theatre has served New England's young people for 18 years. Experimenting with many theatrical modes, LGT has successfully developed a participatory style for in-school audiences that both educates and entertains. In recent years, LGT has produced plays that deal with such varied subjects as the metric system, handicapped siblings, folklore in America, Shakespeare, communication between children and the elderly, and the participation of children in historical events.

For too long children's theatre consisted of rehashing fairy tales. Looking Glass is developing and producing new works that

Los Angeles Actors' Theatre

Looking Glass Theatre. Eileen Boarman, Mark O'Banks and James McGrath in Stone Soup. *Photo: Susanne Spencer.*

speak directly to children about their lives and nudge their social consciences. In addition to its regular touring season, LGT offers a six-week subscription series open to the general public. Parents and their children willingly participate in the creative process while having a good time. As part of an effort for greater outreach, LGT has entertained special audiences: the mentally retarded, the physically disabled, the deaf and — as one special play required — children with their grandparents in nursing homes.

Additionally, LGT conducts weekly creative drama workshops and a summer acting apprentice program whereby local youngsters can be entertained free of charge by their own peers.

Programs and services

Creative drama workshops; acting apprenticeships; internships.

PRODUCTIONS 1981-82

Eloise at Christmastime, Kay Thompson; dir: Pamela Messore
Ghost Tales of the South, David Leong; dir: Pamela Messore
Tuesday's Child, Paula Ewin and company; dir: Paula Ewin

PRODUCTIONS 1982-83

Stone Soup, company-adapt; dir: Pamela Messore
Sam Patch & Company, Amy Leonard; dir: Pamela Messore
Sharing, Mark Eichman; dir: Pamela Messore
The Stars in the Sky, company-adapt; dir: Clare Vadeboncoeur

DESIGNERS

Sets: Jan Infante, Leah Reynolds.
Costumes: Jeffrey Burrows, Clare Vadeboncoeur.

BILL BUSHNELL
Producing/Artistic Director

DIANE WHITE
Producer

ALAN MANDELL
Consulting Director

ALAN BLOCH
Board President

1089 North Oxford Ave.
Los Angeles, CA 90029
(213) 464-5603 (business)
(213) 464-5500 (box office)

FOUNDED 1975
Ralph Waite

SEASON
Year-round

SCHEDULE
Evenings
Tuesday-Sunday

Matinees
Sunday

FACILITIES
Mainstage
Seating capacity: 174
Stage: thrust

Half-Stage
Seating capacity: 40
Stage: flexible

Caminito Theatre
855 North Vermont Ave.
Seating capacity: 99
Stage: thrust

FINANCES
May 1, 1982-April 30, 1983
$624,000 operating expenses
$374,000 earned income
$391,000 grants/contributions

AUDIENCE
Annual attendance: 48,066
Subscribers: 4,500

TOURING CONTACT
Reuben Mack

Los Angeles Actors' Theatre. Robin Ginsburg, Martin Ferrero and Roger Kern in Houseguest.

BOOKED-IN EVENTS
Theatre, music, dance, performance art

AEA Hollywood Area Theatre contract, letter of agreement and 99-seat waiver.

The Los Angeles Actors' Theatre is a multicultural professional theatre and performance laboratory dedicated to developing and producing new American plays in new interpretations.

At the heart of LAAT's artistic philosophy is the belief that theatre is a synthesizer of all the arts, that all theatre is political in the universal sense, that the role of artists is to agitate, to propagate and to disseminate their perception of the truth. The company aims to produce theatre that is joyful, beautiful and passionate as it reflects the toughness of life and the vitality of living.

Much of LAAT's work is dedicated to the development of new playwrights and theatre artists who speak to and work within the diverse communities comprising Los Angeles, and — through this microcosm — the world at large. From this diverse base derives the theatre's continuing professional training projects, artistic and casting policies which reflect a Third World consciousness, and an emphasis on the production of new work. In its first eight years, the LAAT has developed and presented more than 175 world or West Coast premieres.

The theatre is in the process of a move, and its transition season (August 1983-December 1984) features 11 premiere productions in addition to the 6th Festival of Premieres. In March 1985, LAAT opens its Performing Arts Center in downtown Los Angeles. The Center will house four theatres seating 499, 348, 320 and 99; a 6,000-square-foot art gallery/lobby; an arts bookstore; *Cafe Godot,* a streetside cafe; *514 South,* a 140-seat restaurant/cabaret; and complete rehearsal, production and administrative facilities. In the Performing Arts Center, LAAT will continue to produce new work, will add productions drawn from the established American repertoire, and will host individual artists; music, theatre and dance companies; and performance and visual artists.

Programs and services

Playwrights' Project; Directors' Project; Actors' Project; Latino Actors' Project; Silence Aloud deaf/hearing-impaired project; Sneak Previews free productions; production and administrative internships; apprenticeships.

PRODUCTIONS 1981-82

We Won't Pay! We Won't Pay!, Dario Fo; adapt: R.G. Davis; dir: R.G. Davis
Martha Rose and the Miners, book, music and lyrics: Greg Ellis and Sheila Ellis; dir: Al Rossi
The Last Yiddish Poet and *Coming from a Great Distance,* adapt: Correy Fischer, Albert Greenberg and Naomi Newman; dir: Naomi Newman

Mabou Mines

Faces of Love, adapt: Carol Teitel; dir: Bruce Franchini
Nevis Mountain Dew, Steve Carter; dir: Edmund J. Cambridge
3 by Beckett, Samuel Beckett; dir: Alan Mandell:
  Rockaby
  Ohio Impromptu
  Footfalls
Park Your Car in the Harvard Yard, Israel Horovitz; dir: Bill Bushnell
These Men, Mayo Simon; dir: Bill Bushnell
Houseguest, Mario Diament; dir: Jaime Jaimes
The Sun Always Shines for the Cool, Miguel Piñero; dir: Jaime Sanchez
6th Playwrights' Workshop of One Acts

PRODUCTIONS 1982-83

I Am a Woman, adapt: Paul Austin and Viveca Lindfors; dir: Paul Austin
Familiar Faces/Mixed Feelings, Botho Strauss; trans: Fred Haines; dir: Fred Haines
Gandhiji, Rose Leiman Goldemberg; dir: Marilyn Coleman
Artaud at Rodez, Charles Marowitz; dir: Charles Marowitz
Female Parts, Dario Fo and Franca Rame; dir: Adam Leipzig and Lee Rose
Dame Lorraine, Steve Carter; dir: Edmund J. Cambridge
The Quannapowitt Quartet, Israel Horovitz; dir: Alan Mandell
The Primary English Class, Israel Horovitz; dir: Ray Whelan
Native Speech, Eric Overmyer; dir: John Olon
Last Tape (and Testament) of Richard M. Nixon, Donald Freed and Arnold M. Stone; dir: Robert Harders
7th Louis B. Mayer Playwrights' Workshop Festival

DESIGNERS

Sets: Fred Chuang, David De Voss, A. Clark Duncan, Ray Elmendorf, Steve Lavino, Barbara Ling, Russell Pyle, Steve Ralph, John York.
Costumes: Naila Aladdin, Michele Jo Blanche, Fred Chuang, Marianna Elliott, Katja Watkins.
Lights: Fred Chuang, Magda Gonzalez, Steve Lavino, Barbara Ling, Mary Martin, Russell Pyle, Don Reck.

JoANNE AKALAITIS, LEE BREUER, L.B. DALLAS, RUTH MALECZECH, GREG MEHRTEN, B-ST. JOHN SCHOFIELD, FREDERICK NEUMANN, TERRY O'REILLY, WILLIAM RAYMOND
Company Members

c/o Performing Artservices
325 Spring St.
New York, NY 10013
(212) 243-6153

FOUNDED 1970
JoAnne Akalaitis, Lee Breuer, Philip Glass, Ruth Maleczech, David Warrilow

SEASON
Year-round

SCHEDULE
Evenings
Tuesday-Sunday

Mabou Mines. Ellen McElduff in Dead End Kids. *Photo: Carol Rosegg.*

FINANCES
July 1, 1980–June 30, 1981
$333,000 operating expenses
$145,000 earned income
$200,000 grants/contributions

AUDIENCE
Annual attendance: 150,000

TOURING CONTACT
Cynthia Hedstrom

Mabou Mines is a collaborative theatre company formally founded in 1970, following years of shared work by its founding members JoAnne Akalaitis, Lee Breuer and Ruth Maleczech in San Francisco, and later in Europe with Philip Glass and David Warrilow. The company spent three early years in residence at LaMama E.T.C., and has performed at the New York Shakespeare Festival's Public Theater since 1975.

The company's work is directed primarily toward the creation of original theatre pieces — from the "Animations" (*Red Horse, B. Beaver* and *Shaggy Dog*) through *A Prelude to Death in Venice, Dead End Kids, Wrong Guys* and *Cold Harbor*. Mabou Mines is also considered among the theatre's foremost interpreters of Samuel Beckett.

The company has developed a formal yet accessible performance style, synthesizing motivational acting, narrative acting and mixed media performance. Mabou Mines has continually sought collaborations with artists from other disciplines: painters, sculptors, filmmakers and video artists have effected a unique form of theatre design. Musicians with whom the company has developed a rich relationship include Philip Glass and Bob Telson.

Concerns with acting style and space have not diminished a commitment to language as the basic ingredient of theatre, language which varies from the American colloquialism of the "Animations" to the arch and romantic style of Collette to the terse prose of Beckett.

Mabou Mines has most recently extended its explorations to other media: a radio drama program has yielded two series, *Keeper* and *The Joey Schmerda Story;* and company members have begun to create new works for film, video and opera. The company also continues its extensive program of residencies and touring both in the United States and internationally.

Programs and services

Residencies; touring.

PRODUCTIONS 1982

The Tempest, William Shakespeare; dir: Lee Breuer
Wrong Guys, company-adapt, from James Strahs; dir: Ruth Maleczech
A Prelude to Death in Venice, Lee Breuer; dir: Lee Breuer
The Lost Ones, Samuel Beckett; adapt: Lee Breuer; dir: Lee Breuer
Come and Go, Samuel Beckett; dir: Lee Breuer
Dead End Kids, JoAnne Akalaitis; dir: JoAnne Akalaitis
Cold Harbor, Bill Raymond and Dale Worsley; dir: Bill Raymond and Dale Worsley

PRODUCTIONS 1983

Hajj, Lee Breuer and Ruth Maleczech; dir: Lee Breuer
Dead End Kids
Company, Samuel Beckett; company-adapt; dir: Frederick Neumann and Honora Fergusson
Keeper, company-adapt

DESIGNERS

Sets: JoAnne Akalaitis, Julie Archer, Thom Cathcart, L.B. Dallas, David Hardy, Robert Israel, Michael Kuhling, Ruth Maleczech, Alison Yerxa.
Costumes: Dru-ann Chukram, Ann Farrington, Greg Mehrten, Sally Rosen.
Lights: Julie Archer, Beverly Emmons, Michael Kugling, Craig Miller, Stephanie Rudolph, B-St. John Schofield, Ken Tabachnick, Robin Thomas.

Magic Theatre

JOHN LION
General Director

MARCIA O'DEA
General Manager

FRED CARROLL
Board President

Fort Mason Center, Bldg. D
San Francisco, CA 04123
(415) 441-8001 (business)
(415) 441-8822 (box office)

FOUNDED 1967
John Lion

SEASON
October–August

SCHEDULE
Evenings
Wednesday–Sunday

Matinees
Sunday

FACILITIES
Magic Theatre Southside
Seating capacity: 130
Stage: proscenium

Magic Theatre Northside
Seating capacity: 130
Stage: thrust

FINANCES
July 1, 1982–June 30, 1983
$454,000 operating expenses
$215,000 earned income
$249,000 grants/contributions

AUDIENCE
Annual attendance: 32,000
Subscribers: 2,600

BOOKED-IN EVENTS
Theatre, performance art

AEA letter of agreement

For 17 years the Magic Theatre has been one of the most influential forces in contemporary theatre. Through its focus on and commitment to the playwright, the Magic has an outstanding record in the development of

Magic Theatre. Ed Harris and Kathy Baker in Fool for Love. *Photo: Valentine Atkinson.*

new works by established and emerging authors. The theatre has premiered more than 125 productions including works by Sam Shepard, Adele Edling Shank, Michael McLure, John O'Keefe, Martin Epstein and Wolfgang Bauer, while they were in residence at the theatre.

Recently, the Magic has sought to expand the concept of "playwright" to include performance artists, and has helped to foster San Francisco's unique status as the home of such pioneering artists as the SOON 3 and Nightfire companies, and performance artist Winston Tong.

It is the theatre's policy to make a residency commitment of several years' duration to its playwrights, thereby allowing them to develop their work in active collaboration with directors, actors and designers. The success of this approach is best evidenced in such productions as Shepard's *Buried Child* (which later won a Pulitzer Prize), and works by other authors which have gone on to be produced at theatres across the country. These include Adele Edling Shank's *Sand Castles* and Nancy Fales Garrett's *Playing in Local Bands*.

Under the guidance of dramaturg Martin Esslin, who has brought international authors to the attention of the Magic, the theatre has achieved worldwide recognition and its playwrights have received honors including Obie Awards, L.A. Dramalogue Awards and Bay Area Critics Awards, in addition to the Pulitzer Prize.

In its continuing commitment to the search for promising playwrights, the theatre reads more than 1,000 new scripts each year and actively participates in national playwrights conferences. Plays produced at the Magic have been featured in many anthologies and critical works published on contemporary theatre.

Operating at over 90 percent capacity, the theatre has struck a comfortable balance between the demands of its audience and its own aesthetic. A challenge grant from the National Endowment for the Arts, and funding from major corporations and foundations have allowed expansion of the season and operation in order that the company might more fully realize its goals.

Programs and services

Free public forums; newsletter.

PRODUCTIONS 1981-82

Stuck, Adele Edling Shank; dir: Theodore Shank
Passing Shots, Stephen Yafa; dir: Albert Takazauckas
Renaissance Radar, company-developed; dir: Alan Finneran (SOON 3 production)
The Debt, John Robinson, dir: Ken Grantham
Off Center, Martin Epstein; dir: Martin Epstein
Possum Song, Martin Epstein; dir: Martin Epstein
Ghosts, John O'Keefe; dir: John O'Keefe
Fire at Luna Park, Theodore Faro Gross; dir: Robert Robinson
Curse of the Starving Class, Sam Shepard; dir: John Lion

PRODUCTIONS 1982-83

Sand Castles, Adele Edling Shank; dir: Theodore Shank
Chucky's Hunch, Rochelle Owens; dir: Elinor Renfield
Secret Numbers, John Lion; dir: Albert Takazauckas
Fool for Love, Sam Shepard; dir: Sam Shepard
Voodoo Automatic and *Red Rain,* company-developed; dir: Alan and Bean Finneran (SOON 3 production)
Sin, Sex and Cinema, Roger Nieboer; dir: Theodore Shank
Singapore Sling, Wolfgang Bauer; trans: Martin Esslin and Renata Esslin; adapt: John Lion; dir: Geoffrey Reeves
Playing in Local Bands, Nancy Fales Garrett; dir: Nancy Gabor

DESIGNERS

Sets: John Ammirati, Larry Beard, Alan Finneran, Bean Finneran, Bernie Lubell, Abe Lubelski, Michael Lynch, Ferdinand Penker, Theodore Shank, Andrew Stacklin.
Costumes: Barbara Bush, Nancy Castle, Deborah Capen D'Orazi, Karin Epperlein, Ardyss Golden, Carla Kramer, Deborah Brothers Lowry, Elaine McKeen, Gael Russell, Robert Yuen.
Lights: John Chapot, Joe Dignan, Margaret Anne Dunn, Patty Ann Farrell, Kurt Landisman, Peter Kaczorowski, John Rathman.

Manhattan Punch Line

STEVE KAPLAN
Artistic Director

MITCH McGUIRE
Executive Director/Board President

410 West 42nd St., 3rd Floor
New York, NY 10036
(212) 239-0827

FOUNDED 1979
Mitch McGuire, Steve Kaplan

SEASON
October-June

SCHEDULE
Evenings
Thursday-Sunday

Matinees
Sunday

FACILITIES
Lion Theatre
Seating capacity: 99
Stage: proscenium

FINANCES
July 1, 1982-June 30, 1983
$155,000 operating expenses
$ 76,000 earned income
$ 79,000 grants/contributions

AUDIENCE
Annual attendance: 7,500
Subscribers: 100

BOOKED-IN EVENTS
Stand-up comics

AEA Funded Nonprofit Theatre code

Manhattan Punch Line is dedicated to the spirit of the comic, the gadfly, the satirist, the clown. It sees laughter as both a curative and cauterizing agent—and in a world that appears to be heading toward an irrational end, comedy may be the only rational stance.

The Punch Line presents new comic plays and revives lost plays, forgotten plays, underproduced plays—and sometimes plays that just feel left out of things. It also serves as a venue for stand-up comics, revue performers, composers, singers and improvisers. (They'll present comic sculptors, if they can get hold of some.)

This unusual theatre's concept of comedy is Aristotelian: in other words, if it ain't tragedy, maybe it's comedy. And even then, who knows?

Manhattan Punch Line has worked to create a space for actors, directors, designers, comics and playwrights in which they can all share and grow. Its vision is one of excellence, innovation and artistic integrity. Oh yes, and World Domination, let's not forget about that!

Programs and services

Staged readings of new comedies; management internships; Comedy Corp one-year performance training program.

Manhattan Punch Line Theatre. Terry Lehman, Brian Rose, John Monteith, Harry Goz and Baxter Harris in Ferocious Kisses. *Photo: Jack Konohoe.*

PRODUCTIONS 1981-82

Badgers, Donald Wollner; dir: Ellen Sandler
The Coarse Acting Show, Michael Green; dir: Jerry Heymann
The Italian Strawhat, Eugene Labiche and Marc Michel; trans: Jerry Heymann; dir: Steve Kaplan
Ferocious Kisses, Gil Schwartz; dir: Josh Mostel
The Roads to Home, Horton Foote; dir: Calvin Skaggs
What a Life, Clifford Goldsmith; dir: Jerry Heymann

PRODUCTIONS 1982-83

It's Only a Play, Terence McNally; dir: Paul Benedict
The Butter and Egg Man, George S. Kaufman; dir: Steve Kaplan
Without Willie, Barrie Cockburn; dir: Jerry Heymann
Comedians, Trevor Griffith; dir: Munson Hicks
A Kiss Is Just a Kiss, Paul Foster; dir: Don Scardino

DESIGNERS

Sets: William Barclay, Reagan Cook, Oliver D'Arcy, Jeffrey Hall, Rob Hamilton, Charles McCarry, Johniene Papandreas, John Wright Stevens, Nancy Tobias, Joseph Vargas.
Costumes: Amanda Aldrich, Lorraine Calvert, Gail Everhart, E.D. Gigere, Anne Hould-Ward, Karen Hummel, Judianna Makovsky, Oleska, Michele Reisch, David Robinson, Julie Schwolow.
Lights: Betsy Adams, Gregory Chabay, Josh Dachs, Richard Dorfman, John Hickey, Gregory MacPherson, Ruth Roberts, Dennis Size.

Manhattan Theatre Club

LYNNE MEADOW
Artistic Director

BARRY GROVE
Managing Director

PAUL B. KOPPERL
Board President

321 East 73rd St.
New York, NY 10021
(212) 288-2500 business
(212) 472-0600 box office

FOUNDED 1970
A.E. Jeffcoat, Peregrine Whittlesey, Margaret Kennedy, Victor Germack, Joseph Tandet

SEASON
September-June

SCHEDULE
Evenings
Tuesday-Sunday

Matinees
Saturday, Sunday

FACILITIES
DownStage
Seating capacity: 158
Stage: proscenium

UpStage
Seating capacity: 100
Stage: thrust

Cabaret
Seating capacity: 55
Stage: cabaret

FINANCES
July 1, 1982-June 30, 1983
$1,706,000 operating expenses
$ 881,000 earned income
$ 737,000 grants/contributions

AUDIENCE
Annual attendance: 60,000
Subscribers: 6,927

AEA Off Broadway contract

Under the guidance of Lynne Meadow and Barry Grove, the Manhattan Theatre Club has grown from a showcase theatre to one of this country's most dynamic and productive cultural centers.

A theatre of national and international scope, MTC has four primary goals: 1) To present challenging, well-crafted plays and musicals by major writers from America and around the world; 2) to bring to the stage the finest performers, directors and designers; 3) to support and enrich the art of American playwriting, especially through the discovery and development of new American writers; and 4) to develop a committed, discriminating audience for the theatre.

The Theatre Club has been committed to

Manhattan Theatre Club. Sam Waterston, James Woods and Jobeth Williams in Gardenia. *Photo: Gerry Goodstein.*

Mark Taper Forum

presenting the provocative work of the world's best writers—and to demonstrating the infinite variety of their theatrical expression. MTC produces plays, musicals and literary events for an annual audience of approximately 60,000. The DownStage Theatre season features five full productions, while, in the slightly smaller UpStage Theatre, the focus is on the development of plays and musicals by newer writers. Writers-In-Performance is a series of readings by well known authors of prose and poetry, which emphasizes the range, diversity and excitement of contemporary writing.

Many plays originating at MTC have become staples of the resident professional theatre repertoire or have moved on to extended runs on or Off Broadway. They have been seen on television, adapted for the movies and seen on tour around the world. However, the theatre's goal remains constant: to provide a professional forum for new plays and musicals regardless of their commercial potential.

The theatre's programs are supported by a subscription audience of close to 7,000. MTC keeps its theatre accessible to the broadest possible community through student, senior citizen and group discounts, free ticket distribution and frequent post-performance discussions.

Programs and services

In-the-Works staged reading series; Playwrights Unit; After Hours cabaret performances; Friends of MTC volunteer program; internships; Arts Connection student training program; newsletter.

PRODUCTIONS 1981-82

Crossing Niagara, Alonso Alegria, dir: Andre Ernotte
No End of Blame, Howard Barker; dir: Walton Jones
Sally and Marsha, Sybille Pearson; dir: Lynne Meadow
Gardenia, John Guare; dir: Karel Reisz
The Singular Life of Albert Nobbs, Simone Benmussa; trans: Barbara Wright; dir: Simone Benmussa
The Resurrection of Lady Lester, OyamO; dir: Andre Mtumi
And I Ain't Finished Yet, Eve Merriam; dir: Sheldon Epps
Strange Snow, Stephen Metcalfe; dir: Thomas Bullard
Livin' Dolls, Scott Wittman and Marc Shaiman; dir: Richard Maltby, Jr.
Scenes from La Vie de Boheme, Anthony Giardina; dir: Douglas Hughes

PRODUCTIONS 1982-83

Talking With, Jane Martin; dir: Jon Jory
The Three Sisters, Anton Chekhov; trans: Jean-Claude van Itallie; dir: Lynne Meadow
Summer, Edward Bond; dir: Douglas Hughes
Elba, Vaughn McBride; dir: Tom Bullard
On the Swing Shift, music: Michael Dansicker; lyrics: Sarah Schlesinger; dir: Martin Charnin
Standing on My Knees, John Olive; dir: Robert Falls
Skirmishes, Catherine Hayes; dir: Sharon Ott
Triple Feature:
  Slacks and Tops, Harry Kondoleon; dir: Douglas Hughes
  Half a Lifetime, Stephen Metcalfe; dir: Dann Florek
  The Groves of Academe, Mark Stein; dir: Steven Schachter
Early Warnings, Jean-Claude van Itallie; dir: Steven Kent

DESIGNERS

Sets: John Lee Beatty, Kate Edmunds, David Emmons, Adrianne Lobel, Santo Loquasto, Atkin Pace, David Potts, Tony Straiges, Pat Woodbridge, Stuart Wurtzel.
Costumes: Nan Cibula, Judy Dearing, Timothy Dunleavy, Gwen Fabricant, Linda Fisher, Jess Goldstein, Susan Hilferty, Santo Loquasto, Patricia McGourty, Dunya Ramicova, Ann Roth, Rita Ryack, Christa Scholtz.
Lights: William Armstrong, Pat Collins, Arden Fingerhut, Craig Miller, William Mintzer, Robby Monk, Dennis Parichy, Cheryl Thacker, Donald Edmund Thomas, Jennifer Tipton, Marc B. Weiss, Ann Wrightson.

GORDON DAVIDSON
Artistic Director

WILLIAM P. WINGATE
Managing Director

RICHARD E. SHERWOOD
Board President

135 North Grand Ave.
Los Angeles, CA 90012
(213) 972-7353 business
(213) 972-7654 box office

FOUNDED 1967
Gordon Davidson

SEASON
Year-round

SCHEDULE
Evenings
Tuesday-Sunday

Matinees
Saturday, Sunday

FACILITIES
Main Stage
205 North Grand Ave.
Seating capacity: 742
Stage: thrust

Forum Laboratory
2580 Cahuenga Blvd.
Seating capacity: 99
Stage: flexible

Itchey Foot
801 West Temple St.
Seating capacity: 99
Stage: cabaret

FINANCES
July 1, 1982-June 30, 1983
$5,999,000 operating expenses
$3,287,000 earned income
$2,639,000 grants/contributions

AUDIENCE
Annual attendance: 282,828
Subscribers: 29,000

TOURING CONTACT
Jemi Reis

BOOKED-IN EVENTS
Theatre

Mark Taper Forum. Michael Learned and Thomas Harrison in A Month in the Country. *Photo: Jay Thompson.*

AEA LORT (A) and (B) contracts

The Mark Taper Forum, under the artistic direction of Gordon Davidson, has in its 17 seasons built a reputation for excellence in the development of new plays and voices for the theatre, and for its continuing commitment to serving the broadest possible audience in its extended community. Since 1967, the Taper has presented well over 200 European and American plays ranging from classic to contemporary. Of these, more than 115 have been world premieres, including Michael Cristofer's Pulitzer Prize-winning *The Shadow Box,* Mark Medoff's *Children of a Lesser God,* Daniel Berrigan's *The Trial of the Catonsville Nine* and Luis Valdez' *Zoot Suit.*

While remaining a pioneer in the development and presentation of new material, the Taper is now also strengthening its commitment to the effective presentation of classical material through the establishment of a repertory company. Currently, a core company appears in an extended repertory slot of several plays at the end of each season. Long-term plans for the company call for a year-round repertory season in a proscenium house.

The majority of the Taper's other work continues to focus on new plays and playwrights. World, American and West Coast premieres dominate the mainstage subscription season. The New Theatre for Now program serves as a mid-sized outlet for unusual dramatic works and innovative staging concepts, and the Forum Laboratory offers a smaller, sheltered working space for this same exploration, free from critical and box office pressures. Sundays at the Itchey Foot, one of the Taper's newer programs, offers informal readings from non-dramatic sources (memoirs, short fiction, poetry, first-person narratives) at a local restaurant in a cabaret-style setting.

Programs and services

Improvisational Theatre Project for young audiences; Operation Discovery ticket discount program; Project D.A.T.E. deaf access program; workshops and staged readings; post-performance discussions.

PRODUCTIONS 1981-82

A Lesson from Aloes, Athol Fugard; dir: Daniel Petrie
A Tale Told, Lanford Wilson; dir: Marshall W. Mason
Number Our Days, Suzanne Grossmann; dir: John Hirsch
Tales from Hollywood, Christopher Hampton; dir: Gordon Davidson
A Flea in Her Ear, Georges Feydeau; adapt: Suzanne Grossmann and Paxton Whitehead; dir: Tom Moore

McCarter Theatre Company

The Misanthrope, Molière; trans: Richard Wilbur; dir: Diana Maddox

PRODUCTIONS 1982-83

A Soldier's Play, Charles Fuller; dir: Douglas Turner Ward (Negro Ensemble Company production)
Metamorphosis, adapt: Steven Berkoff, from Franz Kafka; dir: Steven Berkoff
Accidental Death of an Anarchist, Dario Fo; adapt: John Lahr; dir: Mel Shapiro
Grown Ups, Jules Feiffer; dir: John Madden
A Month in the Country, Ivan Turgenev; dir: Tom Moore
Richard III, William Shakespeare; dir: Diana Maddox

DESIGNERS

Sets: John Lee Beatty, Edward Burbridge, Michael Devine, Ralph Funicello, David Jenkins, Tom Lynch, Thomas A. Walsh, Peter Wexler.
Costumes: Robert Blackman, Laura Crow, Judy Dearing, Marianna Elliott, Peter J. Hall, Anna Belle Kaufman, Sam Kirkpatrick, Csilla Marki, Dunya Ramicova, Carrie Robbins, Terrence Tam Soon, Julie Weiss.
Lights: Martin Aronstein, Arden Fingerhut, Paul Gallo, John Gleason, Tharon Musser, Dennis Parichy, Marilyn Rennagel.

NAGLE JACKSON
Artistic Director

ALISON HARRIS
Managing Director

EDWARD E. MATTHEWS
Board President

91 University Place
Princeton, NJ 08540
(609) 452-3616 business
(609) 452-5200 box office

FOUNDED 1972
Daniel Seltzer

SEASON
October–April

SCHEDULE
Evenings
Thursday–Sunday

Matinees
Sunday

FACILITIES
Seating capacity: 1,077
Stage: proscenium

Stage II
185 Nassau St.
Seating capacity: 125
Stage: thrust

Princeton Inn College Theatre
Seating capacity: 100
Stage: flexible

McCarter Theatre Company. Thomas Lee Sinclair, Randy Graff and Tommy Breslin in Keystone. Photo: Robert I. Faulkner.

FINANCES
July 1, 1982–June 30, 1983
$2,703,000 operating expenses
$1,828,000 earned income
$ 900,000 grants/contributions

AUDIENCE
Annual attendance: 200,000
Subscribers: 15,000

TOURING CONTACT
James Olson

BOOKED-IN EVENTS
Theatre, music, dance

AEA LORT (B) contract

The McCarter Theatre is a performing arts center housing drama, dance, music and film subscription series in addition to several specially booked-in events. The drama series, consisting of five new productions and one revival annually, is presented by a resident acting ensemble, frequently augmented by guest artists. The continuity and tradition of quality sustained by the McCarter's acting company have engendered a loyal and sizable subscription audience from throughout New Jersey and northern Pennsylvania. The company prides itself on its attention to world classics produced in full-scale productions.

The McCarter has generated several new scripts which have gone on to be produced on Broadway and at theatres throughout the country. The Playwrights-at-McCarter series of readings and the annual Stage II productions are the usual stepping stones for script development, culminating, if successful, in mainstage production.

Despite its proximity to New York and its history as a "tryout house," McCarter has striven, since the inception of the resident company in 1979, to change that image and to form a strong theatrical ensemble dedicated to the demanding and sophisticated audience which surrounds it. In the McCarter Theatre Company, *company* is the dominant word.

Programs and services

Workshops: summer Shakespeare classes and Cadet Program; Playwrights-at-McCarter staged readings; lectures and seminars; film series; internships.

PRODUCTIONS 1981-82

Just Between Ourselves, Alan Ayckbourn; dir: Nagle Jackson
The Night of the Iguana, Tennessee Williams; dir: William Ludel
Keystone, book: John McKellar; music: Lance Mulcahy; lyrics: John McKellar and Dion McGregor; dir: Nagle Jackson
Iphigenia in Aulis, Euripides; trans: W.S. Merwin and George E. Dimock, Jr.; dir: Spyros Evangelatos
Arms and the Man, George Bernard Shaw; dir: Nagle Jackson
A Christmas Carol, adapt: Nagle Jackson, from Charles Dickens; dir: Nagle Jackson
The Overland Rooms, Richard Hobson; dir: Robert Lanchester

PRODUCTIONS 1982-83

Blithe Spirit, Noel Coward; dir: William Woodman
Hamlet, William Shakespeare; dir: Nagle Jackson
The Day They Shot John Lennon, James McLure; dir: Robert Lanchester
The Three Sisters, Anton Chekhov; trans: Randall Jarrell; dir: Nagle Jackson
A Delicate Balance, Edward Albee; dir: Paul Weidner
A Christmas Carol
At This Evening's Performance, Nagle Jackson; dir: Nagle Jackson

DESIGNERS

Sets: Daniel Boylen, Lisa Martin Cameron, Elizabeth Fisher, Desmond Heeley, John Jensen, Brian Martin, Giorgos Patsas.
Costumes: Nanzi Adzima, Elizabeth Covey, Desmond Heeley, M.L. Holmes, John Jensen, Giorgos Patsas, Susan Rheaume.
Lights: Lowell Achziger, Frances Aronson, F. Mitchell Dana, Don Ehman, Richard Moore, Sean Murphy, Marc B. Weiss.

Medicine Show Theatre Ensemble

BARBARA VANN
JAMES BARBOSA
Artistic Directors

6 West 18th St.
New York, NY 10011
(212) 255-4991

FOUNDED 1970
Barbara Vann, James Barbosa

SEASON
September–July

SCHEDULE
Evenings
Wednesday–Saturday

FACILITIES
Newfoundland Theatre
Seating capacity: 74
Stage: arena

FINANCES
August 1, 1981–July 31, 1982
$74,000 operating expenses
$30,000 earned income
$25,000 grants/contributions

AUDIENCE
Annual attendance: 10,000

TOURING CONTACT
James Barbosa

BOOKED-IN EVENTS
Theatre, dance, poetry, music

Medicine Show Theatre Ensemble is a conglomerate of highly individual artists who value their art more than their careers. They call what they do comedy — for lack of a better word — because they view life as a comedy. So the works aren't always funny, but even the darkest works are imbued with light, and all are performed with an energy and joy that defies circumstance. The performers are dedicated, skilled and stylistically adroit.

Like Molière's friend who discovered he was speaking prose, the company has been accused of opera, absurdity, performance art, existentialism, imagination and other postmodern inventions. It stands accused. It has never been indicted on counts of soap

Medicine Show Theatre Ensemble. Chris Brandt and Barbara Vann in Extraordinary Histories. *Photo: Michael Hunold.*

opera, conservatism, *Kultur* or sensitive portrayals of family life.

The Medicine Show produces a very full season which includes a holiday musical, performance, art, and poetry and dance events. The company is concerned with making theatre-going an exciting community event for those lively citizens who do not choose numbness as their favorite kind of relaxation.

The artists like going to Europe, which they do every few years, because there they are treated with kindness, and given awards and good things to eat. They also go to universities in the U.S., where the food isn't as good, but where they meet clever young people, some of whom eventually join the company.

Their theatre space, called the Newfoundland, is small, architecturally interesting and rented. The company is seeking a permanent home.

Currently the Medicine Show is creating a music-theatre work suited to its willful naiveté. Derived from Horatio Alger's *Songs of Innocents*, it celebrates those Golden Spikes that united childhood with materialism. Medicine Show is never at a loss for ideas— only for time and money.

Despite occasional bouts of irony, perversity or despair, Medicine Show is passionately devoted to its work — for as David Garrick was heard to remark, "You can always humbug the town with tragedy but comedy is a serious business."

PRODUCTIONS 1981-82

Don Juan in Hell, George Bernard Shaw; dir: Robert Pucci
Classy Comics, company-adapt, from Ring Lardner, George S. Kaufman and Gertrude Stein; dir: Barbara Vann
City Games, William Hellermann; dir: William Hellermann
The Mummers' Play, Stephen P. Policoff; dir: Barbara Vann
Extraordinary Histories, company-adapt, from Edgar Allan Poe; dir: James Barbosa
Red, Hot & Blue, book: Howard Lindsay and Russell Crouse; music and lyrics: Cole Porter; dir: Barbara Vann.

PRODUCTIONS 1982-83

Extraordinary Histories
Fifty Million Frenchmen, book: Herbert Fields; music and lyrics: Cole Porter; dir: Barbara Vann.
Don Juan in Hell
As You Like It, William Shakespeare; dir: Barbara Vann.
The Ubu Revue, adapt: Stephen P. Policoff and Adam Beckerman, from Alfred Jarry; dir: Barbara Vann.
Complex Pleasures, Michael Rice and William Hellermann; dir: Barbara Vann, Michael Rice and William Hellermann
The Age of Invention, Theodora Skipitares; dir: Theodora Skipitares
Two American Families, two one-act plays; dir: James Barbosa:
  Oh, My Irish Ancestors, Patrick Sullivan
  Three Sisters Who Are Not Sisters, Gertrude Stein
Paris, book: Martin Brown; music and lyrics: Cole Porter; dir: Barbara Vann

DESIGNERS

Sets: Antoni Miralda, Robert Pucci, Lee Brozgold, Patrick Sullivan, Jeff Way, Theodora Skipitares, William Hellermann.
Costumes: Martha Bard, Lee Brozgold, Jeff Way.
Lights: Robert Seder, Robert Pucci.

Merrimack Regional Theatre

DANIEL L. SCHAY
Producing Director

RICHARD D. BOURNIVAL
Board President

Box 228
Lowell, MA 01853
(617) 454-6324 business
(617) 454-3926 box office

FOUNDED 1979
John R. Briggs, Mark Kaufman

SEASON
October-May

SCHEDULE

Evenings
Tuesday-Sunday

Matinees
Wednesday, Sunday

FACILITIES

Mahoney Hall
Broadway & Wilder Sts.
Seating capacity: 420
Stage: proscenium

Liberty Hall
East Merrimack St.
Seating capacity: 450
Stage: thrust

FINANCES
July 1, 1982-June 30, 1983
$300,000 operating expenses
$161,000 earned income
$139,000 grants/contributions

AUDIENCE
Annual attendance: 20,000
Subscribers: 3,100

AEA LORT (D) contract

The Merrimack Regional Theatre brings the particular joys and challenges of live theatre to a developing audience in a unique area of New England. The theatre's repertoire reflects an awareness of its singular home: a community with a multi-ethnic, working class past and a high-tech, white collar future. Works of proven merit and more universal appeal are also produced, bringing the wealth of dramatic literature to a new audience.

The Merrimack keenly feels its social roles as a primary source of shared emotion and experience. Any number of literary, stylistic or political viewpoints may be expressed onstage; what is always present is a concern for the essence of theatre: the reaching, touching, transforming of the audience. The very process of theatre — the magic that takes place in a given room, in real time, among those onstage and those in the house—is the core of the work. Theatre itself is seen as both a refuge from and a response to the alienation that is increasingly felt in contemporary society.

Merrimack's company consists of the accomplished actors, directors and designers who have enjoyed working together in various combinations, in an atmosphere of professional collaboration, to produce theatre in Lowell season after season. While much of the company comes from the large talent pool of New York, the theatre does make a special effort to employ and encourage New England artists.

In October 1984, the theatre will move

Merrimack Regional Theatre. Maryann Plunkett and Emily Hacker in The Miracle Worker. *Photo: Jo Anne B. Weisman.*

Milwaukee Repertory Theater

into a newly renovated 475-seat performance space in downtown Lowell. This new facility will provide far more flexible production capabilities, as well as space for training/conservatory programs. This new home, combined with increasing financial stability and a growing audience, will contribute to the theatre's continued artistic growth.

Programs and services

Cultural Resources Program; internships.

Note: During the 1981-82 and 1982-83 seasons, Mark Kaufman served as artistic director.

PRODUCTIONS 1981-82

The Miracle Worker, William Gibson; dir: Mark Kaufman
The Lion in Winter, James Goldman; dir: Nora Hussey
Two for the Seesaw, William Gibson; dir: Ted Davis
The Price, Arthur Miller; dir: Mark Kaufman
The Gin Game, D.L. Coburn; dir: Arif Hasnain
The Mousetrap, Agatha Christie; dir: Mark Kaufman

PRODUCTIONS 1982-83

Da, Hugh Leonard; dir: Terence Lamude
The Seven Year Itch, George Axelrod; dir: Larry Carpenter
Talley's Folly, Lanford Wilson; dir: Josephine R. Abady
Veronica's Room, Ira Levin; dir: Robert W. Tolan
Tintypes, music and lyrics: various; adapt: Mary Kyte, Mel Marvin and Gary Pearle; dir: James Peskin

DESIGNERS

Sets: Michael Anania, Matthew Bliss, Dennis Bradford, Edward Cesaitis, Duke Durfee, David Lockner, David Potts, Jim Steere, Pat Woodbridge.
Costumes: Amanda Aldridge, Joellen Bendall, Barbara Forbes, Carol Kunz, Karl Wendelin.
Lights: John Gisondi, David Lockner.

JOHN DILLON
Artistic Director

SARA O'CONNOR
Managing Director

T. MICHAEL BOLGER
Board President

929 North Water St.
Milwaukee, WI 53202
(414) 273-7121 (business)
(414) 273-7206 (box office)

FOUNDED 1954
Mary John

SEASON
September-May

SCHEDULE
Evenings
Tuesday-Sunday

Matinees
Wednesday, Sunday

FACILITIES
Seating capacity: 504
Stage: thrust

Pabst Theater
144 East Wells St.
Seating capacity: 1,398
Stage: proscenium

Court Street Theater
315 West Court St.
Seating capacity: 99
Stage: flexible

FINANCES
July 1, 1982-June 30, 1983
$2,110,000 operating expenses
$1,432,000 earned income
$ 678,000 grants/contributions

AUDIENCE
Annual attendance: 190,000
Subscribers: 19,700

TOURING CONTACT
Fran Serlin-Cobb

AEA LORT (C) contract

The Milwaukee Repertory Theater is a resident company with an interest in enlarging the body of work available to the American theatre through new plays, the revitalization of neglected classics and the translation of contemporary works from abroad. The MRT's artistic life centers on a core of resident actors, directors, playwrights and designers, augmented by artists from other areas who have formed strong attachments to the company.

Conscious of its Milwaukee identity, the MRT maintains strong creative ties to its region, commissioning works based on the social and political experience of the upper Midwest or reviving plays with Wisconsin origins. The company tours the region on a regular basis.

The theatre also pursues a vigorous program of exchange. In the U.S., a cooperative relationship has developed with the Berkeley Repertory Theatre. Overseas, liaisons with the Royal Exchange Theatre in Manchester, England, and the Institute of Dramatic Arts and Waseda Sho-gekijo in Tokyo have led to the exchange of English and American actors and directors, the production of an MRT playwright's work in England, presentation of a contemporary Japanese play in Milwaukee, the introduction of Japanese director Tadashi Suzuki's work to the U.S., and two major performance tours by the MRT to Japan. Translations of contemporary works from Mexico and France have also been introduced to Milwaukee audiences.

The Lab is a company of students from academic training programs, and provides a bridge for young actors to the professional experience while meeting the MRT's need for an exploratory laboratory. The MRT sees itself as a link between its community and the larger human experience.

Programs and services

Administrative, technical and artistic internships and apprenticeships; programs-in-schools; study materials; student and senior citizen ticket discounts; services for the deaf, blind and handicapped; regional touring; post-play discussions; workshops and staged readings; newsletter; script publication; speaker's bureau; voluntary auxiliary.

Milwaukee Repertory Theater. Eric Hill and James Pickering in Secret Injury, Secret Revenge. *Photo: Mark Avery.*

PRODUCTIONS 1981-82

Fridays, Andrew Johns; dir: John Dillon
Have You Anything to Declare?, M.A. Hennequin and E.P. Veber; trans: Robert Cogo-Fawcett and Braham Murray; dir: Braham Murray
Boesman and Lena, Athol Fugard; dir: Sharon Ott
Kingdom Come, Amlin Gray; dir: John Dillon and Sharon Ott
Born Yesterday, Garson Kanin; dir: Robert Goodman
Secret Injury, Secret Revenge, Pedro Calderon de la Barca; trans: Linda E. Haughton; adapt: Amlin Gray; dir: Rene Buch
A Christmas Carol, adapt: Nagle Jackson, from Charles Dickens; dir: Nick Faust
The Fall Guy, Linda Aronson; dir: Eric Hill and Nick Faust
Countertalk, Andrew Johns; dir: Eric Hill
Today's Special, Andrew Johns; dir: Eric Hill
At Fifty, She Discovered the Sea, Denise Chalem; trans: Sara O'Connor; dir: Sharon Ott and Arden Fingerhut
Dinah Washington Is Dead, Kermit Frazier; dir: Sharon Ott
The Oedipus Project, Sophocles; trans: Stephen Berg and Diskin Clay; dir: Sharon Ott and Daniel Stein

PRODUCTIONS 1982-83

Miss Lulu Bett, Zona Gale; dir: John Dillon
Buried Child, Sam Shepard; dir: Sharon Ott
The Glass Menagerie, Tennessee Williams; dir: John Dillon
The Foreigner, Larry Shue; dir: Nick Faust
Uncle Vanya, Anton Chekhov; trans: Richard Cottrell; dir: Richard Cottrell
The Government Man, Felipe Santander; trans: Joe Rosenberg; dir: John Dillon
A Christmas Carol
The Pentecost, William Stancil; dir: Rob Goodman
The Eighties, or Last Love, Tom Cole; dir: Sharon Ott
The Fuhrer Is Still Alive, Tsuneari Fukuda; trans: Thomas Rimer; dir: Tetsuo Arakawa

DESIGNERS

Sets: Virginia Dancy, Christopher M. Idoine, David Jenkins, Hugh Landwehr, Laura Maurer, Bil Mikulewicz, Tim Thomas, Elmon Webb.
Costumes: Elizabeth Covey, Joy Barrett Densmore, Katherine E. Duckert, Linda Fisher, Sam Fleming, Ellen M. Kozak, Colleen Muscha, Carol Oditz, Mary Piering, Patricia M. Risser, Gayle M. Strege, Kurt Wilhelm.
Lights: Rachel Budin, Dawn Chiang, Arden Fingerhut, Dan J. Kotlowitz, Spencer Mosse, Dan Broverney, Ben White.

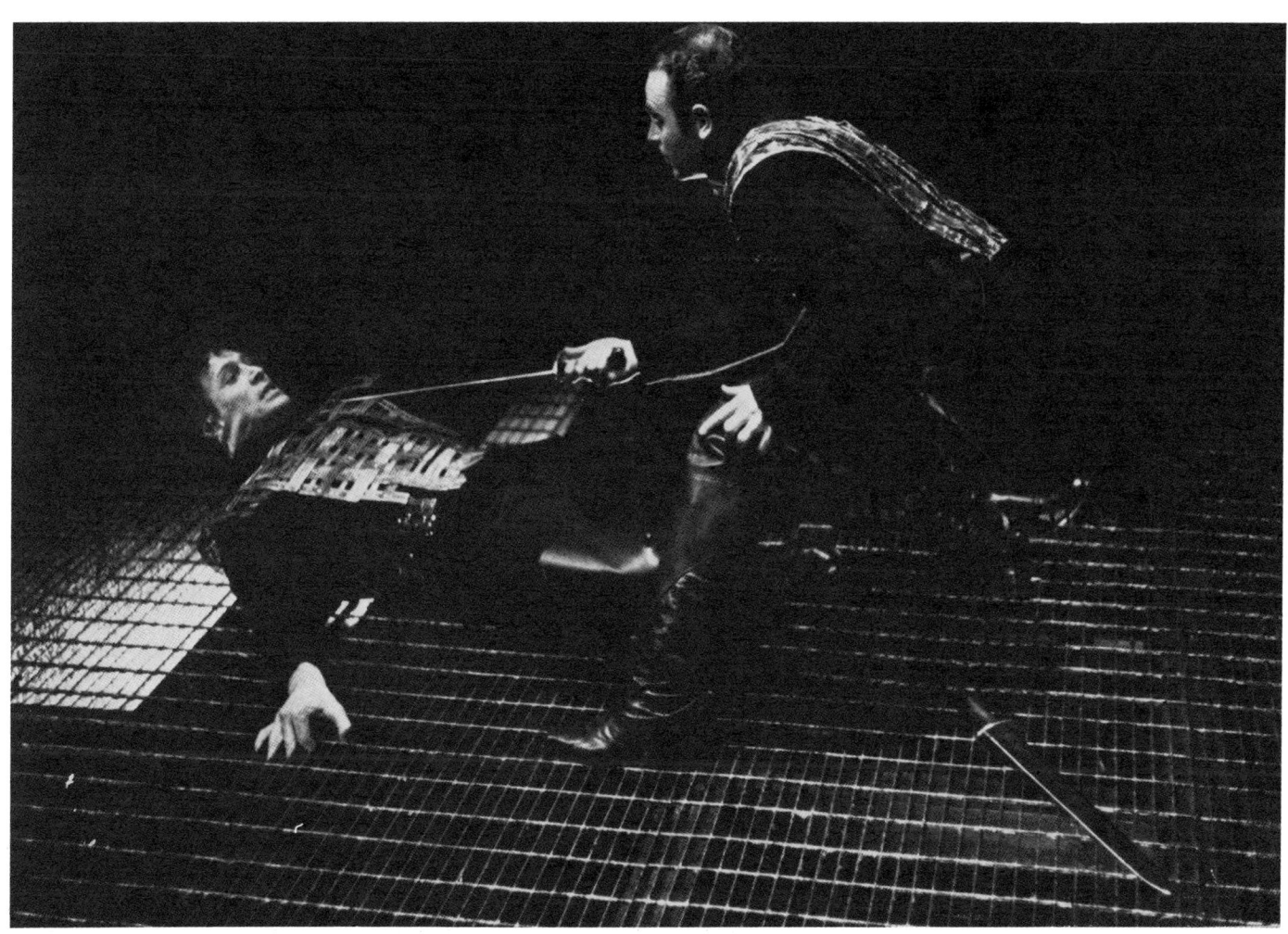

Missouri Repertory Theatre

PATRICIA McILRATH
Artistic Director

JAMES COSTIN
Executive Director

JOHN A. MORGAN
Board Chairman

Performing Arts Center, #404
4949 Cherry St.
Kansas City, MO 64110
(816) 363-4300, ext. 226 (business)
(816) 276-2704 (box office)

FOUNDED 1964
Patricia McIlrath

SEASON
July-December, February-April

SCHEDULE

Evenings
Tuesday-Sunday

Matinees
Sunday

FACILITIES

Helen F. Spencer Theatre
Seating capacity: 595-733
Stage: flexible

J.C. Nichols Theatre I
69th and Oak Sts.
Seating capacity: 450
Stage: thrust

J.C. Nichols Studio Theatre
Seating capacity: 75
Stage: arena

FINANCES
May 1, 1982-April 30, 1983
$1,995,000 operating expenses
$1,107,000 earned income
$1,200,000 grants/contributions

AUDIENCE
Annual attendance: 97,000
Subscribers: 4,900

TOURING CONTACT
Robert Thatch

AEA LORT (B) contract

Missouri Repertory Theatre. Cynthia M. Rendlen, Kevin Paul Hofeditz and Peg Small in Hay Fever. Photo: Jon Dunn.

Missouri Repertory Theatre, now well-established in the new Helen F. Spencer Theatre of the Center for the Performing Arts on the University of Missouri-Kansas City campus, is in its 20th season. A result of extraordinary interaction among the university, the metropolitan community and the nonprofit theatre, Missouri Rep maintains a strong connection to the separate but related professional theatre training program of the university.

The theatre maintains these hallmarks: a resident company; a rotating repertory of classic and new plays executed with relevance to modern times; at least one new play per season; the appointment of nationally and internationally recognized directors, designers and artists; and the use, as appropriate, of interns and residents of the UMKC three-year Master of Fine Arts programs. The Rep format consists of three series — summer, winter and the *Christmas Carol* holiday special. The Rep tour, inaugurated in 1968, follows the summer series and now serves six states.

Since its 1979 incorporation as an independent professional company, the Rep has made vast strides both fiscally and aesthetically. Last season's production of *The Life and Adventures of Nicholas Nickleby,* which played to full houses, greatly expanded the Rep's audience and enhanced its national image.

Missouri Rep is dedicated to the philosophy that theatre art is central, not peripheral. It aims to provide year-round theatre experiences full of stimulation, revelation, excitement and celebration for its expanding regional audiences and company. In so doing, the Rep also bridges the gap between academic and professional theatre for those committed to acquiring the exacting professional training needed for a career in the theatre.

The Missouri Rep Second Stage, devoted to new plays, is another performance opportunity for students at all levels, as are understudy performances of all Rep plays. Major civic support has enabled the Rep to more than double its operating budget since incorporation, affording metropolitan Kansas City a major cultural institution deeply affecting cultural life in the American Midwest.

Programs and services

Touring; programs-in-schools; internships and apprenticeships.

Music-Theatre Group/ Lenox Arts Center

PRODUCTIONS 1981-82

The Three Sisters, Anton Chekhov; trans: Elisaveta Fen; dir: Cedric Messina

Talley's Folly, Lanford Wilson; dir: James Assad

Picnic, William Inge; dir: Patricia McIlrath

The Good Person of Szechwan, Bertolt Brecht; trans: Ralph Manheim; dir: John Reich

The Royal Family, George S. Kaufman and Edna Ferber; dir: Albert Pertalion

Loose Ends, Michael Weller; dir: Francis J. Cullinan

Crown of Thorn, Wendy MacLaughlin; dir: James Assad

Macbeth, William Shakespeare; dir: Norris Houghton

A Christmas Carol, adapt: Barbara Field, from Charles Dickens; dir: James Assad

PRODUCTIONS 1982-83

Antony and Cleopatra, William Shakespeare; dir: Erik Vos

Hay Fever, Noel Coward; dir: Francis J. Cullinan

The Magnificent Yankee, Emmet Lavery; dir: Albert Pertalion

Terra Nova, Ted Tally; dir: James Assad

The Innocents, adapt: William Archibald, from Henry James; dir: Cedric Messina

Translations, Brian Friel; dir: Vincent Dowling

The Life and Adventures of Nicholas Nickelby, adapt: David Edgar, from Charles Dickens; dir: Leon Rubin and James Assad

A Christmas Carol

DESIGNERS

Sets: John Ezell, W. Steven Graham, Harry Feiner, Howard Jones, David Potts, Carolyn Ross, Tom Shenk.

Costumes: Michelle Bechtold, Douglas Enderle, Victoria Marshall, Vincent Scassellati, Baker S. Smith, John Carver Sullivan, Mariann Verheyen, Tom Shenk, Judith Dolan.

Lights: Joseph Appelt, Robert Jared, Ruth Ludwick, Keri Muir, Susan A. White.

Music Theatre Group/Lenox Arts Center. James Javore, Kate Hurney, Carmen Pelton and Avery Tracht in The Mother of Us All. *Photo: Frank Fournier.*

LYN AUSTIN
Producing Director

DIANE WONDISFORD
Managing Director

EDWARD MILLER
Board Chairman

735 Washington St.
New York, NY 10014
(212) 924-3108 (business)
(212) 582-1978 (box office)

Lenox Arts Center
Box 858
Stockbridge, MA 01262
(413) 298-9463

FOUNDED 1970
Lyn Austin

SEASON
New York
September-May

Stockbridge
June-August

SCHEDULE
New York evenings
Tuesday-Saturday

New York matinees
Saturday

Stockbridge evenings
Wednesday-Saturday

FACILITIES

The Theatre at St. Clement's Church
423 West 46th St., NY
Seating capacity: 99
Stage: flexible

Citizen's Hall
Stockbridge, MA
Seating capacity: 99
Stage: flexible

FINANCES
July 1, 1982-June 30, 1983
$277,000 operating expenses
$ 59,000 earned income
$218,000 grants/contributions

AUDIENCE
Annual attendance: 18,000
Subscribers: 230 (NY only)

TOURING CONTACT
Lyn Austin

AEA Mini contract and letter of agreement

Music-Theatre Group/Lenox Arts Center, pioneering in the development of new musical theatre, has nurtured the talents of newly discovered and established artists. Its distinctive work stems from the unique combination of theatre, music and dance.

Distinguished productions of the Group include *Poppie Nongena, A Metamorphosis in Miniature, The Columbine String Quartet Tonight!, The Tennis Game, The Club, Nightclub Cantata, Hotel for Criminals* and *Doctor Selavy's Magic Theater*. Notable artists with whom MTG/LAC has worked include Stanley Silverman, Richard Foreman, Richard Peaslee, Elizabeth Swados, Tommy Tune, George Trwo, Noa Ain, Martha Clarke and Andre Gregory. For eight years the group has made its home in New York City from September to May, having recently moved to a new playing space at St. Clement's, and for 11 years the group has made its summer home in Stockbridge, Mass.

In all of its work, MTG/LAC endeavors to create fresh, dynamic collaborations by bringing together just the right writer (who up to that point might have been working solely as a poet or novelist), or just the right composer with just the right director (who formerly might have been solely a choreographer). The focus is on in-depth work with each artist in the hope of developing major writers, composers and directors.

Among its awards, MTG/LAC has received 17 Obie Awards, the most recent of which includes a special citation to the group for its production of Virgil Thomson and Gertrude Stein's opera *The Mother of Us All*.

PRODUCTIONS 1981-82

A Metamorphosis in Miniature, adapt: Jeff Wanshel, from Franz Kafka; dir: Martha Clarke
The Long Journey of Poppie Nongena, adapt: Sandra Kotze and Elsa Joubert; music: Sophie Mgcina; dir: Hilary Blecher
Bonesongs, Andre Gregory; dir: Twyla Tharp
Trio, Noa Ain; dir: Bill Goeller
The Juniper Tree, A Tragic Household Tale, Wendy Kesselman; dir: Larry Pine
The Wild Gardens of Loup Garou, adapt: Carman Moore, from Ishmael Reed and Colleen McElroy; dir: Marilyn Worrell

PRODUCTIONS 1982-83

Poppie Nongena
The Mother of Us All, book: Gertrude Stein; music: Virgil Thomson; dir: Stanley Silverman
The Juniper Tree, A Tragic Household Tale
The Day, the Night, Welcome Msomi; dir: Welcome Msomi

DESIGNERS

Sets: Power Boothe, Lawrence Casey, Andrew Jackness, Eugene Lee, Rosaria Sinisi.
Costumes: Lawrence Casey, Shura Cohen, Ann Emonts, Karen Matthews.
Lights: William Armstrong, Jim Bay, William Beautyman, Jim Ingalls, Jackie Manasee, Marilyn Rennagel, Penny Stegenga.

Nassau Repertory Theatre

CLINTON J. ATKINSON
Artistic Director

Kenneth E. Hahn
Managing Director

GEORGE GIMPEL
Board Chairman

Box 190
62 Nichols Ct.
Hempstead, NY 11550
(516) 292-9340 (business)
(516) 486-0222 (box office)

FOUNDED 1975
Susan E. Barclay

SEASON
October-June

SCHEDULE
Evenings
Thursday-Sunday

Matinees
Wednesday, Sunday

FACILITIES
Hays Theatre
1000 Hempstead Ave., Rockville Centre
Seating capacity: 498
Stage: proscenium

FINANCES
September 1, 1982-August 31, 1983
$324,000 operating expenses
$201,000 earned income
$115,000 grants/contributions

AUDIENCE
Annual attendance: 21,900
Subscribers: 3,250

AEA letter of agreement

The Nassau Repertory Theatre, presently Long Island's only full-time resident professional theatre, is committed to creating a permanent theatre that is a lively, integral part of the Long Island community. Striving always for production excellence, the NRT recognizes its special geographic position and offers its suburban audience a viable alternative to the costly and time-consuming experience of New York theatregoing.

The theatre's artistic philosophy focuses on producing works from four areas of dramatic literature: masterworks of world theatre from the last century; rarely seen works of master playwrights; revivals of works with new relevance; and examples of specialized theatrical genres which expand the artistic awareness of both audience and performer. At present, the NRT does not recreate works recently produced on or Off Broadway, and presents no new works, although many of its rarely seen plays are virtually new to the audience.

Growth is a key word in the development of the NRT. When it was founded in 1975 by Susan E. Barclay, it functioned as a small non-Equity company performing first in a government building auditorium and then at the Herricks Center Theatre in a recycled junior high school. With the 1983-84 season, the NRT will settle into the Hays Auditorium of Molloy College in Rockville Centre, where for the first time it will enjoy the blessings of a fully equipped stage, auditorium and lobby.

Under the direction of Clinton J. Atkinson and Kenneth Hahn, an active board of directors has been developed and subscriptions have risen 33 percent over the past few seasons. Production standards benefit from the theatre's proximity to New York City: while many actors and designers return to NRT, each production is approached individually to take advantage of the fluid talent pool of the area.

Long-range plans include a permanent home in a centrally located theatre, an ancillary conservatory program, expansion of the season to a year-round schedule and a new play program which commissions and produces new works and translations.

Programs and services

Student and senior citizen ticket discounts; newsletter; theatre guild; post-play discussions; administrative internships; signed performances.

PRODUCTIONS 1981-82

Private Lives, Noel Coward
The Eccentricities of a Nightingale, Tennessee Williams

Nassau Repertory Theatre. Donald Reeves, Matt McCoy, Jill Hill and Kathleen Kellaigh in Bus Stop. *Photo: Cathy Blaivas.*

The Fantasticks, book and lyrics: Tom Jones; music: Harvey Schmidt
Flirtations, Arthur Schnitzler; trans: A.S. Wensinger and Susanne Mrozik; adapt: Clinton J. Atkinson and S.S. Wensinger
Overruled and *Village Wooing,* George Bernard Shaw
Spider's Web, Agatha Christie

PRODUCTIONS 1982-83

Gigi, Anita Loos
Rocket to the Moon, Clifford Odets
Charley's Aunt, Brandon Thomas
Ghosts, Henrik Ibsen; trans: William Archer
Bus Stop, William Inge

All productions directed by Clinton J. Atkinson

DESIGNERS

Sets: Gerard P. Bourcier, Daniel H. Ettinger, Joseph Forbes, Andrew Earl Jones, Ron Placzek, James Singelis, Jack Stewart.
Costumes: Otis Gustafson, Fran Rosenthal, Margie Peterson, Deborah Stein, Muriel Stockdale, Barbara Weiss, Joan E. Weiss, Heidi Hollman.
Lights: John Hickey.

National Black Theatre

BARBARA ANN TEER
Executive Producer

KEIBU FAISON
Administrative Director

EUGENE CALLENDER
Board President

9 East 125th St.
Harlem, NY 10035
(212) 427-5615

FOUNDED 1968
Barbara Ann Teer

SEASON
April-November

SCHEDULE
Evenings
Thursday-Sunday

Matinees
Sunday

FACILITIES
Seating capacity: 125
Stage: arena

FINANCES
November 1, 1981-October 31, 1982
$163,000 operating expenses
$ 45,000 earned income
$137,000 grants/contributions

AUDIENCE
Annual attendance: 24,000

TOURING CONTACT
Keibu Faison

BOOKED-IN EVENTS
Theatre, dance, music

National Black Theatre. Jon Beale, Barbara Jones and Tunde Samuel in Soul Fusion. *Photo: Con Edison.*

The National Black Theatre strives to be:
—An institution of culture that is vibrant, active, alive—the place to go when a person wants to be regenerated, turned on, re-energized, strengthened and inspired;
—A place that draws people from Harlem and beyond, providing an environment where the humanity of all people is acknowledged, recognized and affirmed;
—A place where all people regardless of their cultural origins can experience and heighten their understanding of the spiritual and cultural heritage of African Americans, and where African Americans can increase their understanding and appreciation of the connection they have to their African lineage and tradition.

NBT's purpose is to institutionalize a culture which flows from a spiritual tradition rooted in an African American perception of thinking and being. It produces theatrical expressions which flow from a cultural sound called "soul." This "soul force" is used to fill NBT's audiences with light, creating inspiration, participation and self-realization.

NBT is a theatre of celebraton and its goal is to transform the experience of theatre into a celebration of life.

Programs and services

Artistic and management workshops; international touring; children's classes.

PRODUCTIONS 1981-82

Soul Fusion II, Nabii Faison and Barbara Ann Teer; dir: Nabii Faison and Barbara Ann Teer
Face It Baby, It's Really Your Show!, company-developed; dir: Keibu Faison

Note: Due to fire, no plays were produced in the 1982-83 season.

DESIGNERS

Sets: Nabii Faison.
Costumes: Barbara Jones.
Lights: Nabii Faison, Isyla Haynes.

Nebraska Theatre Caravan

CHARLES JONES
Executive Director

CAROLYN RUTHERFORD
Manager

BARBARA FORD
Board President

6915 Cass St.
Omaha, NE 68132
(402) 553-4890

FOUNDED 1976
Charles Jones, Omaha Community Playhouse

SEASON
September-May

FACILITIES
Omaha Playhouse
Seating capacity: 500
Stage: proscenium

FINANCES
June 30, 1982-July 1, 1983
$466,000 operating expenses
$434,000 earned income
$ 34,000 grants/contributions

AUDIENCE
Annual attendance: 224,000

TOURING CONTACT
Carolyn Rutherford

Nebraska Theatre Caravan is dedicated to the actor and his audience, a one-on-one direct confrontation, celebration and sharing. It offers audiences living hundreds of miles from major theatre centers an opportunity to share the abundant talents and volatile energy of live theatre craftsmen.

Since 1976 the Caravan has been serving thousands of people through its unique touring program. Established through direct dialogue with Nebraska citizens, the original company of eight actors boldly trekked across the state creating productions that were ebullient and highly personal. The company's traditional emphasis on the actor-audience relationship has endured although productions now travel with complete scenery, costumes and production elements, utilizing more than 60 performers and 26 technicians each season.

Nebraska Theatre Caravan. John Foley and Jerry Longe in A Christmas Carol. *Photo: John McIntyre.*

Play selection has been greatly influenced by the audiences the Caravan serves. In touring to small communities, it must provide for a wide range of ages and tastes; therefore, each season the company mounts one major production for adults, one specifically designed for college and high school audiences and one for young audiences. The Caravan also tours two separate productions of *A Christmas Carol* to the upper Midwest and New England each year.

The impact of the company has been significant. A new theatre complex, the Henry Fonda Theatre Center, is being built on the site of the Omaha Community Playhouse, and will serve as a home for the Caravan when it is not touring. The new building has been designed to accommodate the flexible and highly adaptable style developed by the Caravan performers over the past seasons.

Programs and services

Workshops; study guides and sponsor handbook.

PRODUCTIONS 1981-82

Tintypes, music and lyrics: various; adapt: Mary Kyte, Mel Marvin and Gary Pearle; dir: Carl Beck

As You Like It, William Shakespeare; dir: Charles Jones
Monkey, Monkey, Charles Jones; dir: Charles Jones
A Christmas Carol, adapt: Charles Jones, from Charles Dickens; dir: Eleanor and Charles Jones

PRODUCTIONS 1982-83

Strider, book: Mark Rozovsky; lyrics: Uri Riashentsev and Steve Brown; adapt: Robert Kalfin and Steve Brown; music: S. Vetkin and Mark Rozovsky; dir: Carl Beck
The Night Thoreau Spent in Jail, Jerome Lawrence and Robert E. Lee; dir: Carl Beck
Treasure Island, adapt: Aurand Harris, from Robert Louis Stevenson; dir: Aurand Harris
A Christmas Carol

DESIGNERS

Sets: James Othuse, Steven Wheeldon.
Costumes: Karen Brewster, Denise Ervin.
Lights: James Othuse, Steven Wheeldon.

New American Theater

J.R. SULLIVAN
Producing Director

KATHRYN HILBERT
Board President

117 South Wyman St.
Rockford, IL 61101
(815) 963-9454 business
(815) 964-8023 box office

FOUNDED 1972
J.R. Sullivan

SEASON
September-July

SCHEDULE
Evenings
Wednesday-Sunday

Matinees
Wednesday, Saturday

FACILITIES
118 South Main St.
Seating capacity: 270
Stage: thrust

FINANCES
July 1, 1982-June 30, 1983
$316,000 operating expenses
$231,000 earned income
$ 88,000 grants/contributions

AUDIENCE
Annual attendance: 35,000
Subscribers: 3,037

TOURING CONTACT
Judith Barnard

BOOKED-IN EVENTS
Theatre

AEA Guest Artist contract

New American Theater was founded in 1972 as a resident professional company in downtown Rockford—a working class city of slightly less than 150,000—to serve the Illinois-Wisconsin state line area. Its goal was simple: to produce a variety of works each season, awakening new audiences to the vitality and substance of theatre. NAT set out to focus on contemporary works balanced by selections from the rich heritage of the American and international theatre.

First taking up residence in a converted synagogue shared by a folk music club, and later performing in a rented space, the company finally took up permanent residence in 1975, in Rockford's downtown mall, retaining its original goals. The "New" in New American Theater stands not only for its production of new plays but for its vitality and its style of presenting them. Its resident company members, responsive to one another and to the audience, intensify not only the theatre's immediacy but its purpose. They feel that although theatre artists are fond of saying that art is the most palpable, immediate means of celebrating the human condition, they far too often seem to be talking only to one another. New American Theater wants to intensify for its audience the *act* of theatre—the act of community—which is central to NAT's view of itself.

New American Theater attempts to be more than a cultural institution, a term suggesting status but also stagnation. It wishes to be seen as *theatre:* entertaining, enlightening, disturbing and stimulating, as well as responsive to its community, taking its place in a society that wrestles with problems while celebrating life's joys.

Programs and services

Black Theater Ensemble; Young American Theater high school troupe; student and adult classes; Noontime Play Series; touring; children's theatre.

PRODUCTIONS 1981-82

On Golden Pond, Ernest Thompson; dir: J.R. Sullivan
Wild Oats, John O'Keeffe; dir: J.R. Sullivan
Room Service, John Murray and Allen Boretz; dir: J.R. Sullivan

New Dramatists

A Man for All Seasons, Robert Bolt; dir: J.R. Sullivan
Whose Life Is It, Anyway?, Brian Clark; dir: Ginny MacDonald
Talley's Folly, Lanford Wilson; dir: J.R. Sullivan
A Midwinter Night's Dream: "Lester and the Winter Visitors", adapt: Matt Swan; dir: Matt Swan
Private Lives, Noel Coward; dir: J.R. Sullivan
Romantic Comedy, Bernard Slade; dir: Carl Balson
The Gin Game, D.L. Coburn; dir: J.R. Sullivan

PRODUCTIONS 1982-83

Morning's at Seven, Paul Osborn; dir: J.R. Sullivan
Bedroom Farce, Alan Ayckbourn; dir: J.R. Sullivan
The Gift of the Magi, adapt: Peter Ekstrom, from O. Henry; dir: J.R. Sullivan
Ludlow Ladd, book: Michael Colby; music: Jerry Markow; dir: J.R. Sullivan
The Miser, Molière; trans: Miles Malleson; dir: J.R. Sullivan
Clara's Play, John Olive; dir: J.R. Sullivan
Home, Samm-Art Williams; dir: J.R. Sullivan
5th of July, Lanford Wilson; dir: J.R. Sullivan
A Life, Hugh Leonard; dir: J.R. Sullivan
The Dining Room, A.R. Gurney, Jr.; dir: B.J. Jones
A Thousand Clowns, Herb Gardner; dir: Ricki G. Ravitts
The Bunkhouse, Terrence Ortwein; dir: J.R. Sullivan
Candide, book: Hugh Wheeler; music: Leonard Bernstein; lyrics: Richard Wilbur and Stephen Sondheim; dir: J.R. Sullivan

DESIGNERS

Sets: Michael S. Philippi, James Wolk.
Costumes: Jon R. Accardo, Deborah Atkins Archer.
Lights: Joseph Gilg, Michael S. Philippi, James Wolk.

New American Theater. Lynda DeLaforgue, Stephen Vrtol III, Matt Swan, Paul Logli and Norman Nuber II in Room Service. *Photo: David Bishop.*

THOMAS G. DUNN
Executive Director

CASEY CHILDS
Program Director

ZILLA LIPPMANN
Board President

424 West 44th St.
New York, NY 10036
(212) 757-6960

FOUNDED 1949
Michaela O'Harra, John Golden, Moss Hart, Oscar Hammerstein II, Richard Rodgers, John Wharton, Howard Lindsay

SEASON
September-June

SCHEDULE
Evenings
Wednesday-Friday, alternate weeks

FACILITIES
Mainstage
Seating capacity: 100
Stage: flexible

Lindsay/Crouse Studio
Seating capacity: 40
Stage: flexible

FINANCES
July 1, 1981-June 30, 1982
$390,000 operating expenses
$ 10,000 earned income
$380,000 grants/contributions

AUDIENCE
Annual attendance: 8,300

New Dramatists was founded in 1949 to encourage and develop playwriting in America. To participate in its programs, a playwright applies for membership, submitting two full-length original scripts to an admissions committee composed of active members, alumni and theatre professionals. Once admitted, a playwright is a full participating member for a minimum of three and a maximum of seven years. New Dramatists charges its members neither fees nor dues, and seeks no rights, royalties or profits from its members' work.

New Dramatists offers a range of programs for members centering on the idea that playwriting is a craft as well as an art, and that knowing the basics of this craft is an essential complement to talent. Most members have achieved a certain level of accomplishment before joining New Dramatists, and all have demonstrated professional intent and exceptional promise. In the end, however, education, ambition, talent and dreams are only part of the prerequisite for becoming a successful playwright: New Dramatists can provide the other part by giving writers an opportunity to explore the "how" of their craft.

Programs include multi-tiered readings of works-in-progress, a national script distribution service to resident theatres, script analysis panels, domestic and international playwright exchanges, a members' bulletin, library and loan fund. The intangible services are more difficult to list but include encouragement, support, membership in a community of writers and—perhaps most important—a belief in the process.

New Dramatists alumni in its 34 years of existence include Robert Anderson, Ed Bullins, Richard Foreman, Paddy Chayefsky, Israel Horovitz, Michael Stewart, William Inge, William Gibson, John Guare and Lanford Wilson. Current members and alumni have contributed more than 200 plays to the American theatre.

While commercial success for any member is gratifying and welcome, it is not the primary goal of New Dramatists. Focused always on producing *playwrights* rather than plays, it is a workshop in the purest sense of the word: a place where work can be done, a climate and opportunity for inspiration and the means to realize aspiration.

Programs and services

Internships; script copying; ScriptShare distribution service; writers' studios; dramaturgical panels; loan fund; low-cost rehearsal space; readings; newsletter; library.

PRODUCTIONS 1981-82

Americana, John Patrick Shanley; dir: Gordon Edelstein
The Bathers, Victor Steinbach; dir: Tom Bullard

New Federal Theatre

New Dramatists. Dierdre O'Connell, Todd Stockman and "Shawn" in His Master's Voice.

The Saddest Summer of Val, Dennis McIntyre; dir: Tom Bullard
Three One Acts, Stanley Taikeff; dir: Tom Gruenewald
Sky Blue Pink, David Hill; dir: Scott Rubsam
Gardens of Eden, Romulus Linney; dir: M. Elizabeth Osborn
The Great Gorilla Musical, John Patrick Shanley; dir: Susan Gregg
Kids and Dogs, Phil Bosakowski; dir: Casey Childs
Dolorosa Sanchez, Stanley Taikeff; dir: Lew Shena
Outpost, Gus Edwards; dir: Roger Hendricks Simon
The Release of a Live Performance, Sherry Kramer; dir: Pat Carmichael
The Name of the Game is 'Ben', Dennis McIntryre; dir: Allen R. Belknap
America Was, Jack Heifner; dir: Will MacAdam
Winterfire, Jack Gilhooley; dir: Susan Gregg

PRODUCTIONS 1982-83

Signs of Life, Joan Schenkar; dir: Susan Gregg
Maggie Magalita, Wendy Kesselman; dir: Carole Rothman
April Snow, Romulus Linney; dir: M. Elizabeth Osborn
The Full Circle of the Traveling Squirrel, Robert Lord; dir: Jack Hofsiss
His Master's Voice, Dick Zigun; dir: Susan Gregg
Civilization and Its Malcontents and *Aristotle Said*, Stanley Taikeff; dir: Thomas Gruenewald
The Bathers, Victor Steinbach; dir: Steven Robman
Kid Purple, Don Wollner; dir: Dallas Murphy, Jr.
Hidden Parts, Lynne Alvarez; dir: Harvey Seifter
Partial Objects, Sherry Kramer; dir: Jim Milton
Tenement, Gus Edwards; dir: Bob Engels
Ohio Tip-Off, James Yoshimura; dir: Charles Edward Shain
Chopin in Space, Phil Bosakowski; dir: Robert Hall
Inferno, John Patrick Shanley; dir: Susan Gregg
Flies in the Buttermilk, Stephen Levi; dir: Thomas Gruenewald
Beyond Here Are Monsters, James Nicholson; dir: Gideon Y. Schein
Jacinta, Peter Dee; dir: Susan Gregg
Bully, Paul D'Andrea; dir: David Feldshuh

WOODIE KING, JR.
Producer

IRWIN ROBINSON
Board Chairman

466 Grand St.
New York, NY 10002
(212) 598-0400

FOUNDED 1970
Woodie King, Jr.

SEASON
September-July

SCHEDULE

Evenings
Thursday-Sunday

Matinees
Sunday

FACILITIES

Playhouse
Seating capacity: 350
Stage: proscenium

Experimental Theatre
Seating capacity: 150
Stage: thrust

Recital Hall
Seating capacity: 100
Stage: flexible

FINANCES
July 1, 1981-June 30, 1982
$375,000 operating expenses
$100,000 earned income
$200,000 grants/contributions

AUDIENCE
Annual attendance: 45,000

TOURING CONTACT
Woodie King, Jr.

BOOKED-IN EVENTS
Theatre

AEA Showcase code

Where can the minority writer or theatre artist find a place in which to work at his craft? The New Federal Theatre believes it is in the nonprofit professional theatre and has

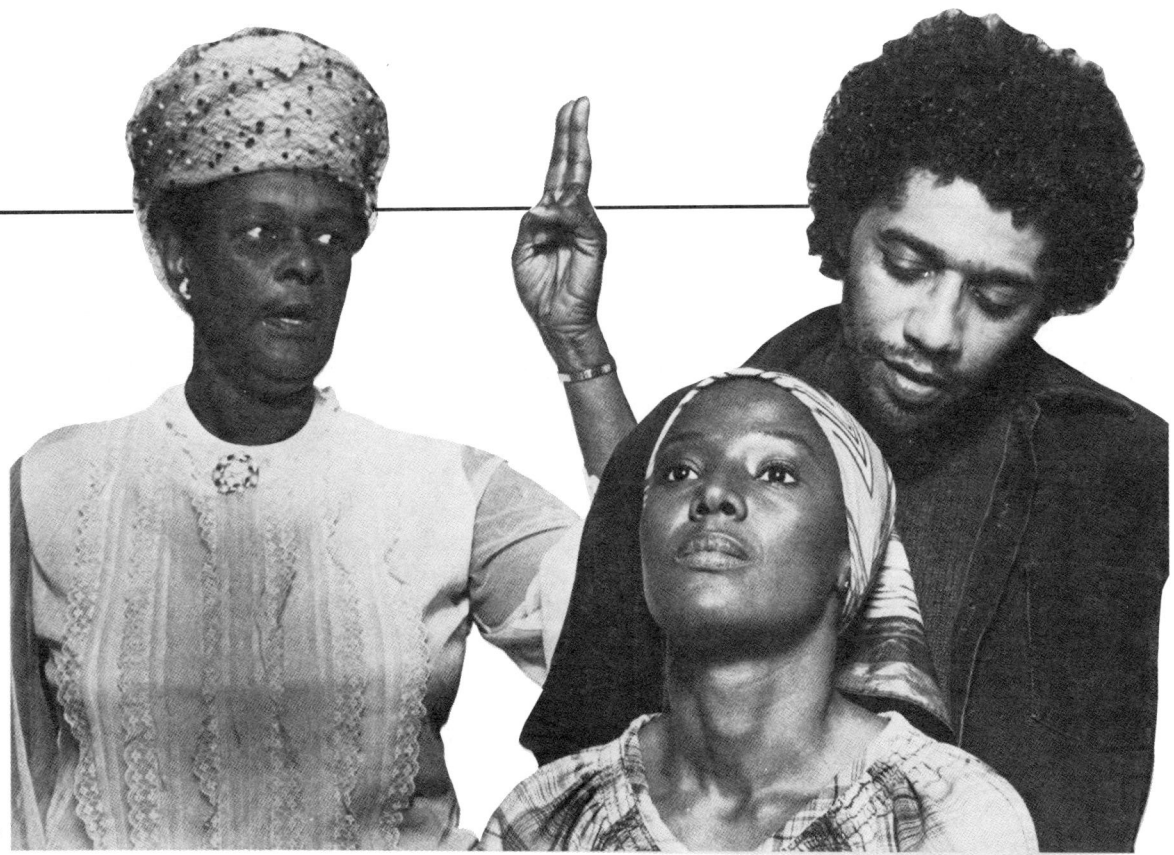

New Federal Theatre. Minnie Gentry, Barbara Smith and Otis Young-Smith in Trio. *Photo: Bert Andrews.*

set out to provide just such an outlet.

Henry Street Settlement's New Federal Theatre has just entered its 14th season, having begun operation in 1970 as an offshoot of the New York State Council on the Arts' Ghetto Arts Program. It is now almost impossible to turn on the television and not see a New Federal alumnus; and writers first presented at NFT are now part of the American literary mainstream. New Federal audiences represent a cross-section of New York City's black, Hispanic, Asian American and more traditional American theatregoers.

Plays that have gone on to garner national recognition after appearing at the New Federal include *The Taking of Miss Janie* by Ed Bullins, which received three Obie Awards and The Drama Critics Circle Award for best new American play; *Showdown* by Don Evans and *Prodigal Sister* by J.E. Franklin and Mikki Grant, both of which toured extensively; *For Colored Girls who have Considered Suicide/ When the Rainbow is Enuf* by Ntozake Shange, which journeyed to Broadway; and David Henry Hwang's *The Dance and the Railroad*, which played at the New York Shakespeare Festival for six months, won three Obie Awards and was taped for cable television.

For the last two years, New Federal Theatre was selected by the American Academy and Institute of Arts and Letters to produce the award-winning Richard Rodgers Musicals, *Child of the Sun* (1981) and *Portrait of Jennie* (1982).

Programs and services

Workshops for black theatre, Hispanic theatre, black women playwrights, technical theatre and theatre management; acting and dance classes.

PRODUCTIONS 1981-82

Child of the Sun, book, music and lyrics: Damien Leake; dir: Harold Scott
The World of Ben Caldwell, Ben Caldwell; dir: Richard Gant
Boy and Tarzan Appear in a Clearing, Amiri Baraka; dir: George Ferenz
Who Loves the Dancer, Rob Penny; dir: Shauneille Perry
Keyboard, Matt Robinson; dir: Shauneille Perry
Love, Carolyn M. Rodger; dir: Shauneille Perry
Black Peoples Party, Earl Anthony; dir: Norman Riley
A Day Out of Time, Alan Foster Friedman; dir: Harold Guskin
Paper Angel, Ginny Lim; dir: John Lone
La Chafa, Tato Laveria; dir: Raul Davila

PRODUCTIONS 1982-83

Portrait of Jennie, book: Dennis Rosa and Enid Futterman; music: Howard Marren; lyrics: Enid Futterman; dir: Dennis Rosa
The Upper Depths, David Rappaport; dir: Robert Kalfin
Jazz Set, Ron Milner; dir: Norman Riley and Ron Milner
Adam, book: June Tansy; music and lyrics: Richard Ahlert; dir: Don Evans
Liberty Call, Burial Clay I; dir: Samm-Art Williams
Champeeen, book, music and lyrics: Melvin Van Peebles; dir: Melvin Van Peebles
Trio, Bill Harris; dir: Nathan George
Wilderness of Shur, Nicholas Biel; dir: Gordon Edelstein
Home, Samm-Art Williams; dir: Woodie King, Jr.

DESIGNERS

Sets: Robert Edmonds, Dale Gordon, Lew Harrison, John Scheffler, Chris Thomas, Michael Yeargan.
Costumes: Judy Dearing, Penny Howell, Myrna Colly Lee, Sally Lesser, Karen Perry, Charles Schoonmaker, Quay Truitt.
Lights: Jeff Davis, Dale Gordon, Shirley Prendergast, Lynne Reed, Sandra Ross, Marshall Williams.

New Jersey Shakespeare Festival

PAUL BARRY
Artistic Director

ELLEN BARRY
Producing Director

DOUGLAS S. EAKELEY
Board President

Drew University
Route 24
Madison, NJ 07940
(201) 377-5330 (business)
(201) 377-4487 (box office)

FOUNDED 1963
Paul Barry

SEASON
June-December

SCHEDULE

Evenings
Tuesday-Sunday

Matinees
Wednesday

FACILITIES

Bowne Theatre
Seating capacity: 238
Stage: thrust

FINANCES
January 1, 1982-December 31, 1982
$483,000 operating expenses
$303,000 earned income
$170,000 grants/contributions

AUDIENCE
Annual attendance: 40,000
Subscribers: 3,200

BOOKED-IN EVENTS
Dance, theatre, mime, music, children's theatre

AEA LORT (D) contract

The New Jersey Shakespeare Festival annually presents three classics — including two or three plays of Shakespeare — in rotating repertory, followed by three to four other plays, usually contemporary, for four weeks each. Twelve Monday Night guest attractions showcase various other art forms, further diversifying the season.

New Jersey Shakespeare Festival. Gary Sloan and Robin Leary in Twelfth Night. *Photo: Jerry Dalia.*

The Festival, founded in 1963 in Cape May, began anew when it moved to Drew University in 1982. To date, it has mounted 145 productions including 43 by Shakespeare, and the works of some 80 other authors. Recent notable productions include a *Timon of Athens* set during the 1929 stock market crash; repertory pairings of *Hamlet* with *Rosencrantz and Guildenstern Are Dead,* and *Travesties* with *The Importance of Being Earnest;* and the rarely seen *Cymbeline.*

The Festival is committed to the preservation of the American classic theatre and to the development of artists for it. Eventually, the entire Shakespeare canon will be offered (only seven of the plays remain unproduced by the company at this time). The Festival continues to schedule large-cast classics, despite the financial and artistic constraints which discourage so many theatres from undertaking them, because it believes that Americans are best equipped to play the classics in their own country, and that the challenge of great roles alone develops great actors.

The Festival is also committed to providing the increasingly rare challenge of rotating repertory: not only to professionals, but to some 80 interns from across the country each year, chosen from around 1,000 applicants.

New Jersey Shakespeare Festival takes

New Playwrights' Theatre

pride in building new audiences for the classics: its subscription renewal rate is 70 percent; audiences in 11 years have averaged 80 percent of capacity; and seven of those seasons have ended "in the black," with an average of 67 percent of its budget covered by earned income. In 1982, the theatre was supported by grants from 62 corporations, 800 individuals, and 8 foundations and government agencies.

Programs and services

Internships; Monday Night Special guest attractions; workshop productions; understudy matinees; programs-in-schools.

PRODUCTIONS 1982

Twelfth Night, William Shakespeare; dir: Paul Barry
Timon of Athens, William Shakespeare; dir: Paul Barry
Wild Oats, John O'Keeffe; dir: Christopher Martin
Our Town, Thornton Wilder; dir: Paul Barry
Cat on a Hot Tin Roof, Tennessee Williams; dir: Paul Barry
5th of July, Lanford Wilson; dir: Paul Barry

PRODUCTIONS 1983

War of the Roses, adapt: Paul Barry; dir: Paul Barry:
   Henry VI, William Shakespeare
   Edward IV, William Shakespeare
   Richard III, William Shakespeare
Let's Get a Divorce, Victorien Sardou; dir: Dan Held
Born Yesterday, Garson Kanin; dir: Paul Barry
Beyond the Fringe, Jonathan Miller, Dudley Moore, Peter Cook and Allan Bennett; dir: Paul Barry

DESIGNERS

Sets: Ann E. Gumpper, Michael Sharp.
Costumes: Kathleen Blake, Heidi Hollmann, Alice S. Hughes.
Lights: Richard Dorfman.

HARRY M. BAGDASIAN
Artistic Director

TODD BETHEL
Managing Director

FRANZ JAGGAR
Board Chairman

1742 Church St., NW
Washington, DC 20036
(202) 232-4527 (business)
(202) 232-1122 (box office)

FOUNDED 1972
Harry M. Bagdasian

SEASON
July-June

SCHEDULE
Evenings
Tuesday-Sunday

Matinees
Saturday

FACILITIES
Seating capacity: 125
Stage: flexible

FINANCES
July 1, 1981-June 30, 1982
$290,000 operating expenses
$113,000 earned income
$198,000 grants/contributions

AUDIENCE
Annual attendance: 16,000
Subscribers: 1,000

AEA Guest Artist contract

New Playwrights' Theatre is dedicated to the support and development of American playwriting talent through extensive personal dramaturgical assistance, workshops, readings and full productions. Its board of trustees, staff and volunteers believe that playwrights and composers need a stage — their own stage — a safe environment in which they can develop both their material and their skills.

The center of NPT's work is the developmental process. Unsolicited manuscripts are accepted from October through June; scripts may be new, or those which have had productions elsewhere but which need further development.

After manuscripts are evaluated, selected authors are brought to Washington for a series of staged and unstaged readings which may continue for up to several years and may, if appropriate, culminate in full productions. This reading series involves 15 to 20 authors each year, some for multiple readings during a season, with rehearsal periods varying from several days to several weeks. Readings are complemented, as necessary, by personal dramaturgical assistance from a staff member or resident playwright.

NPT's subscription season consists of five

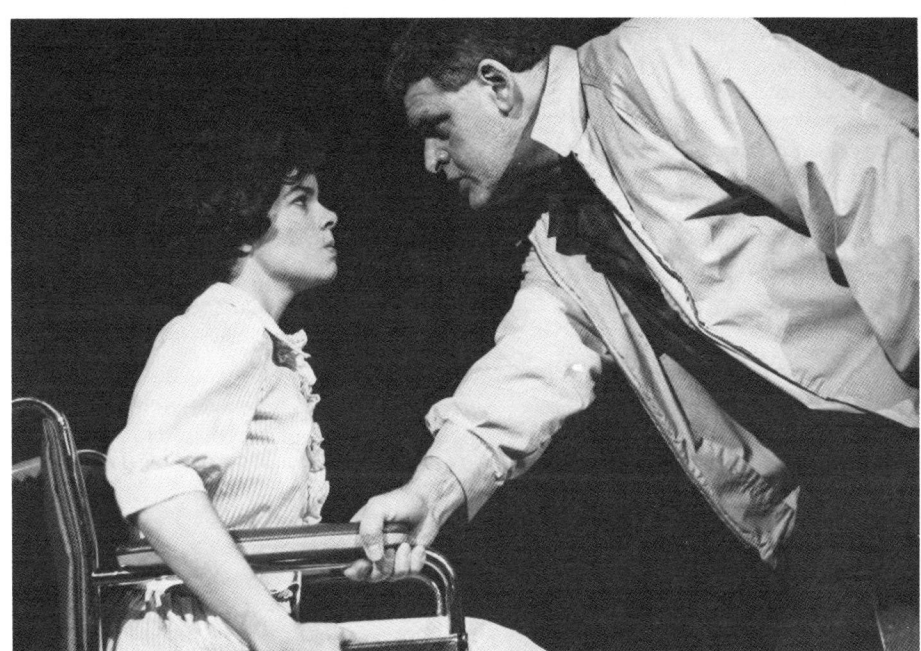

New Playwrights' Theatre. Marcia Gay Harden and Dion Anderson in And They Dance Real Slow in Jackson. *Photo: Doc Dougherty.*

New York Shakespeare Festival

to seven full productions selected from the scripts in development. Since the needs of each play and playwright vary considerably, artists are jobbed in, and auditions are held several times a year as needed.

Programs and services

Readings; internships; professional and non-professional training.

PRODUCTIONS 1981-82

Nightmare!!, book, music and lyrics: Tim Grundmann; dir: Ken Bloom
Eulogy, Diane Ney; dir: Harry M. Bagdasian
Phallacies, John Nassivera; dir: Fred Zirm
One-Act Festival:
   The Tangled Snarl, John Rustan and Frank Semerano; dir: John E. Jacobsen
   Never Say Never, Tobey Chappell; dir: John E. Jacobsen
   The Finer Points of the Situation, Peter Perhonis; dir: Jay Beckner
   The Lives of the Great Composers, Tim Grundmann; dir: Ken Bloom
Jessie's Land, Ernest Joselovitz; dir: Jim Nicola

PRODUCTIONS 1982-83

The New, Improved Bride of Sirocco, Tim Grundmann; dir: Harry M. Bagdasian and Robbie McEwen
Blood Relations, Michael Wright; dir: Jim Nicola
Out of the Reach of Children, Cornelia Ravenal; dir: Fred Lee
And They Dance Real Slow in Jackson, Jim Leonard, Jr.; dir: Tom Evans
Stopover on Whitney Street, Peter Perhonis; dir: Harry M. Bagdasian
Burrhead, Deborah Pryor; dir: Jim Nicola and Lloyd Rose

DESIGNERS

Sets: Wally Coberg, Lewis Folden, James Albert Hobbs, Russell Metheny.
Costumes: Elizabeth Bass, Maryclare Gromet, Jane Schloss Phalen, Mary Ann Powell, Henry Shaffer.
Lights: Lewis Folden, James Albert Hobbs, James Katen, Richard Moore.

JOSEPH PAPP
Producer

ROBERT KAMLOT
General Manager

LuESTHER T. MERTZ
Board Chairman

Public Theater
425 Lafayette St.
New York, NY 10003
(212) 598-7100 (business)
(212) 598-7150 (box office)
(212) 861-7277 (Delacorte box office)

FOUNDED 1954
Joseph Papp

SEASON
Year-round

SCHEDULE
Evenings
Tuesday-Sunday

Matinees
Saturday, Sunday

FACILITIES
Public Theater:
Newman Theater
Seating capacity: 299
Stage: proscenium

Martinson Hall
Seating capacity: 190
Stage: flexible

LuEsther Hall
Seating capacity: 150
Stage: flexible

The Other Stage
Seating capacity: 100
Stage: flexible

Anspacher Theater
Seating capacity: 188
Stage: 3/4 arena

Central Park:
Delacorte Theater
Seating capacity: 1,932
Stage: thrust

FINANCES
July 1, 1982-June 30, 1983
$9,203,000 operating expenses
$6,559,000 earned income
$2,644,000 grants/contributions

AUDIENCE
Annual attendance: 2,810,447
Subscribers: 5,539

BOOKED-IN EVENTS
Theatre, dance, special events

AEA Production, LORT (B), Off Broadway contracts and AEA Showcase code

Since 1956, under the continuous leadership of Joseph Papp, the New York Shakespeare Festival has operated in the belief that a theatre with the highest professional standards can and should reach a broadly based public. From this guiding principle has emerged a contemporary theatre of range and quality, rooted in the classics, with new American plays as its primary focus.

Each summer for the past 27 years, the Festival has presented classic productions, usually by Shakespeare, in Central Park's Delacorte Theater and on tour throughout the parks and neighborhoods of the five boroughs. More than 100,000 people annually attend park performances at no charge. The Festival's permanent home is the landmark Public Theater, formerly the Astor Library, which contains six performing spaces ranging from 99 to 299 seats. There, a repertoire of new American plays which cut deeply into the nature of contemporary society has been developed by an emerging generation of actors, directors and designers.

The multiple stages of the Public have also served as home for a number of theatre companies and guest artists, including Mabou Mines (listed separately in this book), Meredith Monk's The House, the Dodger Theater Company, Richard Foreman and Joseph Chaikin. Most recently, NYSF has hosted productions by Britain's Joint Stock, and Hesitate and Demonstrate companies, and has participated in an exchange with the Royal Court Theatre, as part of the "Britain Salutes New York" celebration.

In addition, the Public Theater is a center for various other performing arts with two

New York Shakespeare Festival. The Death of Von Richthofen As Witnessed from Earth. Photo: Martha Swope.

year-round series, "New Jazz at the Public" and "Films at the Public," which features rarely seen films. Film at the Public's ancillary program, Public Service Series, offers free weekend screenings of socially relevant films.

The Festival adheres to a policy of free and low-cost tickets to attract a wide audience; a variety of discount programs provides up to 50 percent reductions, developing new and vibrant audiences.

In order to make Public Theater and Central Park productions even more widely available, the lives of a number of productions have been extended on Broadway, Off Broadway, on network and cable television, on film and on national tours. These include the still-running *A Chorus Line,* as well as *I'm Getting My Act Together and Taking It on the Road, Sticks and Bones, Runaways, That Championship Season, The Dance and the Railroad, The Pirates of Penzance* and *Plenty.*

Programs and services

Film at the Public; New Jazz at the Public; Music/Theater Program readings and workshops; free and discounted tickets.

PRODUCTIONS 1981-82

The Tempest, William Shakespeare; dir: Lee Breuer
Henry IV, Part I, William Shakespeare; dir: Des McAnuff
The Laundry Hour, Mark Linn-Baker, Lewis Black and William Peters; dir: William Peters
The Dance and the Railroad, David Henry Hwang; dir: John Lone
The Ballad of Dexter Creed, Michael Moriarty; dir: James Milton
Family Devotions, David Henry Hwang; dir: Robert Allan Ackerman
Twelve Dreams, James Lapine; dir: James Lapine
Specimen Days, Meredith Monk; dir: Meredith Monk
Zastrozzi, George Walker; dir: Andrei Serban
Lullabye and Goodnight, Elizabeth Swados; dir: Elizabeth Swados
Three Acts of Recognition, Botho Strauss; trans: Sophie Wilkins; dir: Richard Foreman
Goose and Tomtom, David Rabe; dir: John Pynchon Holms
The Haggadah, adapt: Elizabeth Swados, from Elie Wiesel; dir: Elizabeth Swados
Antigone, Sophocles; trans: John Chioles; dir: Joseph Chaikin
Red and Blue, Michael Hurson; dir: JoAnne Akalaitis
A Chorus Line, book: James Kirkwood and Nicholas Dante; music: Marvin Hamlisch; lyrics: Edward Kleban; dir: Michael Bennett
The Pirates of Penzance, book: W.S. Gilbert; music: Arthur Sullivan; music adapt: William Elliott; dir: Wilford Leach

PRODUCTIONS 1982-83

Don Juan, Molière; trans: Donald M. Frame: dir: Richard Foreman
A Midsummer Night's Dream, William Shakespeare; dir: James Lapine

North Carolina Shakespeare Festival

The Death of Von Richthofen as Witnessed from Earth, Des McAnuff; dir: Des McAnuff
Plenty, David Hare; dir: David Hare
Hamlet, William Shakespeare; dir: Joseph Papp
Necessary Ends, Marvin Cohen; dir: James Milton
Top Girls, Caryl Churchill; dir: Max Stafford-Clark
Buried Inside Extra, Thomas Babe; dir: Joseph Papp
Egyptology, Richard Foreman: dir: Richard Foreman
Fen, Caryl Churchill; dir: Les Waters (Joint Stock Company production)
Goodnight, Ladies, Hesitate and Demonstrate Company; dir: Geraldine Pilgram (Hesitate and Demonstrate Company production)
A Chorus Line
The Pirates Penzance

DESIGNERS

Sets: JoAnne Akalaitis, Julie Archer, John Arnone, Mike Boak, Jim Clayburgh, Richard Foreman, John Gisondi, David Gropman, John Gunter, Linda Hartinian, Peter Hartwell, Robert Israel, Sally Jacobs, David Jenkins, Michael Kuhling, Heidi Landesman, Manuel Lutgenhorst, Gerald Marks, David Mitchell, Douglas Schmidt, Karen Schultz, Julie Taymor, Dean Tschetter, Stuart Wurtzel, Yoshio Yabara, Robert Yodice.
Costumes: Theoni Aldredge, Randy Barcelo, Leslie Calumet, Judy Dearing, Jane Greenwood, Sally Jacobs, Willa Kim, Amanda J. Klein, Franne Lee, William Ivey Long, Manuel Lutgenhorst, Patricia McGourty, Greg Mehrten, Carol Oditz, Sally Rosen, Hilary Rosenfeld, Pam Tait, Julie Taymor, Dean Tschetter, Yoshio Yabara, Patricia Zipprodt.
Lights: Julie Archer, John Arnone, Frances Aronson, Fred Buchholz, F. Mitchell Dana, Beverly Emmons, Arden Fingerhut, John Gisondi, Ralph Holmes, Marcia Madeira, Craig Miller, Spencer Mosse, Richard Nelson, B-St. John Schofield, Tom Skelton, Victor En Yu Tan, Jennifer Tipton, Robin Myerscough-Walker.

MALCOLM MORRISON
Artistic Director

MARK WOODS
Managing Director

E.J. PAISLEY
Board Chairman

Box 6066
High Point, NC 27262
(919) 889-1544 (business)
(919) 887-3001 (box office)

FOUNDED 1977
Mark Woods, Stuart Brooks

SEASON
July-October, December

SCHEDULE
Evenings
Tuesday-Sunday

Matinees
Sunday

FACILITIES
High Point Theatre
220 East Commerce St.
Seating capacity: 640
Stage: proscenium

FINANCES
January 1, 1982-December 31, 1982
$439,000 operating expenses
$143,000 earned income
$244,000 grants/contributions

AUDIENCE
Annual attendance: 125,000
Subscribers: 2,686

TOURING CONTACT
Pedro Silva

AEA letter of agreement

As an actor-oriented theatre, the North Carolina Shakespeare Festival is committed to creating an environment in which artists are given every opportunity to develop and express their versatility.

North Carolina Shakespeare Festival. Kim Shipley, David Lenthall and Jay Freer in King John. *Photo: Jerry Samet.*

NCSF explores plays of all types that demonstrate breadth of vision, depth of perception and enduring treatment. The belief that the actor is at the heart of all major theatrical experiences is paramount. Productions are chosen on the basis of the opportunities they afford the artists through stylistic and thematic diversity. The concept of any given production is executed with a profound concern for excellence and definition.

NCSF recognizes the need of theatre artists to develop and establish new modes of expression, as well as communicating the contemporary human experience. Consequently, the firm intention of the company (while mounting the major dramatic works of previous generations and cultures) is to develop as yet unrecognized American works, and nurture and challenge the artists who present that work.

NCSF also recognizes its responsibility to engage in activities other than performance. An Actor-in-the-Schools program exists to promote a heightened awareness of the creative process and an excitement about attend-

North Light Repertory

ing live theatre. Recently, NCSF launched an outreach program which, through extensive touring, has played to tens of thousands of adults and young people in North Carolina, most of whom have never seen a live theatre performance. This project will now be integrated into the Festival's ongoing programs, as part of its artistic mission.

Programs and services

Programs-in-schools; outreach touring.

PRODUCTIONS 1982

King John, William Shakespeare; dir: Malcolm Morrison
Romeo and Juliet, William Shakespeare; dir: Peter Bennett
A Flea in Her Ear, Georges Feydeau; trans: John Mortimer; dir: Robert Murray
A Christmas Carol, adapt: Malcolm Morrison, from Charles Dickens; dir: Malcolm Morrison

PRODUCTIONS 1983

Two Gentlemen of Verona, William Shakespeare; dir: Malcolm Morrison
Light Up the Sky, Moss Hart; dir: Pedro Silva
Of Mice and Men, John Steinbeck; dir: Mark Woods
Long Day's Journey into Night, Eugene O'Neill; dir: Malcolm Morrison
This Wooden 'O', adapt: Randell Haynes; dir: Randell Haynes
The Hollow Crown, adapt: John Barton; dir: Malcolm Morrison
Othello, William Shakespeare; dir: Malcolm Morrison

DESIGNERS

Sets: Neil Bierbower, Deborah Jasien, Mark Pirolo.
Costumes: Janet Bobceam, Mark Pirolo, Christine Turbitt.
Lights: Philip Gibson, Tracey Peck, Paul Valoris, Michael Orris Watson.

MICHAEL MAGGIO
Artistic Director

JEFFREY BENTLEY
Managing Director

EVELYN SALK
Board President

2300 Green Bay Road
Evanston, IL 60201
(312) 869-7732 (business)
(312) 869-7278 (box office)

FOUNDED 1974
Gregory Kandel

SEASON
October-June

SCHEDULE
Evenings
Tuesday-Sunday

Matinees
Saturday, Sunday

FACILITIES
Kingsley Theatre
Seating capacity: 298
Stage: proscenium

North Light Repertory Company. Laurel Cronin and Diane D'Aquila in The Impromptu of Outremont. *Photo: Lisa Ebright.*

FINANCES
July 1, 1982-June 30, 1983
$729,000 operating expenses
$499,000 earned income
$200,000 grants/contributions

AUDIENCE
Annual attendance: 56,000
Subscribers: 7,100

BOOKED-IN EVENTS
One-man shows, cabaret

AEA LORT (D) contract

North Light Repertory believes in theatre as the intersection point of all the arts, literary, visual and performing. The company remains committed to the task of providing an arena in which text, stage and actor can interact with an ever-widening audience.

Since the company was founded by Gregory Kandel in 1974, North Light has sought to serve a dual constituency. For theatre artists, it provides a supportive and stimulating environment in which playwrights, actors, designers and directors can pursue the development of their crafts. These artists are primarily drawn from Chicago's considerable talent pool, but on occasion, guest artists from outside the community are employed.

North Light serves its audiences by striving to produce plays that enlighten, enrich and entertain. The five-play Main Season includes regional premieres of American and international works, re-examinations of established or classic plays, and new American works. Recent seasons have included successful productions of Edward Albee's *Who's Afraid of Virginia Woolf?*, Simon Gray's *The Rear Column* and the American professional premiere of *Les Belles Soeurs* by Michel Tremblay.

The theatre's Satellite Season addresses itself to the development of new scripts and allows playwrights to view their efforts in staged readings before a subscription audience.

Programs and services

Artistic, technical and administrative internships; classes and workshops; ticket discounts; creative drama for the elderly, veterans and the handicapped.

Note: During the 1981-82 and 1982-83 seasons, Eric Steiner served as artistic director.

PRODUCTIONS 1981-82

Plymouth Rock Isn't Pink, William Hamilton; dir: Eric Steiner
The Glass Menagerie, Tennessee Williams; dir: Eric Steiner
The Rear Column, Simon Gray; dir: John Malkovich
Les Belles Soeurs, Michel Tremblay; trans: John Van Burek and Bill Glassco; dir: Eric Steiner
The Promise, Aleksei Arbuzov; trans: Ariadne Nicolaeff; dir: Gus Kaikkonen

PRODUCTIONS 1982-83

Who's Afraid of Virginia Woolf?, Edward Albee; dir: Eric Steiner
Filthy Rich, George F. Walker; dir: Robert Woodruff
Duet for One, Tom Kempinski; dir: Jeffrey Hayden
Children, A.R. Gurney, Jr.; dir: Mary F. Monroe
The Impromptu of Outremont, Michel Tremblay; trans: John Van Burek; dir: Eric Steiner

DESIGNERS

Sets: Nels Anderson, Robert Barnett, Gary Baugh, Jeremy Conway, David Emmons, Shawn Kerwin, Michael Merritt.
Costumes: Kate Bergh, Jessica Hahn, Jordan Ross, Nan Zabriskie.
Lights: Stuart Duke, Dawn Hollingsworth, Robert Shook.

Odyssey Theatre Ensemble

RON SOSSI
Artistic Director

LUCY POLLAK
General Manager

PHILIP BARRY
Board President

12111 Ohio Ave.
Los Angeles, CA 90025
(213) 879-5221 (business)
(213) 826-1626 (box office)

FOUNDED 1968
Ron Sossi

SEASON
July-June

SCHEDULE
Evenings
Wednesday-Sunday

FACILITIES
Odyssey 1
Seating capacity: 99
Stage: flexible

Odyssey 2
Seating capacity: 95
Stage: thrust

Odyssey 3
Seating capacity: 90
Stage: arena

FINANCES
July 1, 1982-June 30, 1983
$325,000 operating expenses
$327,000 earned income
$ 81,000 grants/contributions

AUDIENCE
Annual attendance: 30,000
Subscribers: 2,100

TOURING CONTACT
Lucy Pollak

BOOKED-IN EVENTS
Dance, music, children's and experimental theatre

AEA 99-seat waiver

Odyssey Theatre Ensemble. Garret Pearson, Franklyn Seales and Hy Pyke in The Frogs.

The 1982–83 season at Odyssey Theatre Ensemble included more production activity than any year to date: a six-play season including plays from England, Germany, Italy, Canada and America; nine non-season original works; a California tour and a full series of staged readings. In addition, the Odyssey has launched the L.A. premiere of David Edgar's *Mary Barnes* and an ambitious production of Aristophanes' *The Frogs* utilizing a full orchestra and chorus on a stage entirely flooded with water.

The vision of the Odyssey continues to be international in scope; innovative in approach; eclectic in performance and directorial styles; provocative and "dangerous" in content; and popular rather than elitist in audience appeal.

Well on its way toward the creation of America's first international experimental theatre complex and research center—a five-theatre facility to be located in Santa Monica, Calif.—the Odyssey maintains its position on the cutting edge of Southern California theatre, and was cited for this position last year by the Los Angeles Drama Critics when they bestowed the annual Margaret Harford Award on the company.

OTE is keenly devoted to the idea that truly important American playwriting, acting and directing cannot ferment solely within the confining bonds of traditional American naturalism; and that a theatre interested in advancing the art form must expose its artists as well as its audience to the most important current world ideas. Toward that end, the theatre continues its policy of devoting half of its production activity to material from other countries, cultures and styles, and the other half to new works by local writers, particularly those works which expand the possibilities of the medium.

The Odyssey's direction and dream remain consistent, as its scope and the sheer quantity of activity increase geometrically from year to year. Still a maverick in an "industry"-dominated town, OTE stubbornly adheres to its philosophy that theatre must exist on its own terms and not as an extension of, or "bush league" for film and television. Theatre's survival absolutely depends upon its passionate, never-ceasing search for its own voice, its own style, its own unique possibilities.

Programs and services

Touring; workshops; staged readings.

PRODUCTIONS 1981-82

No Scratch, Frederick Bailey; dir: Frederick Bailey
The Mandrake, Niccolo Machiavelli; adapt: Igor Dimont and Karl Maurer; dir: Igor Dimont
Yerma, Federico Garcia Lorca; trans: James Graham-Lujan and Richard L. O'Connel; dir: Stephen Fischer
Fantod: A Victorian Reverie, Amlin Gray; dir: Ron Sossi
Skin, David Scott Milton; dir: Jonathon Estrin
Something's Rockin' in Denmark, Cliff Jones; dir: Bill Castellino
Don Juan Comes Back from the War, Odon Von Horvath; dir: Deborah LaVine

Brechtfest I:
  The Exception and the Rule, book and lyrics: Bertolt Brecht; music: Randolph Dreyfuss; trans: Eric Bentley; dir: Frank Condon
  The Little Mahagonny, book and lyrics: Bertolt Brecht; music: Kurt Weill; trans: Michael Feingold; dir: Ina Wittich and Ron Sossi
Brechtfest II:
  The Baden Teaching Play, Bertolt Brecht; trans: Lee Baxandall; dir: Ron Sossi
  Brecht Meets the House Un-American Activities Committee, adapt: Cyndy Turnage and Ron Sossi; dir: Cyndy Turnage and Ron Sossi

Nightclub Cantata, Elizabeth Swados; dir: Bill Castellino
Power Lines, Joel Schwartz; dir: George Boyd

PRODUCTIONS 1982-83

Ionescopade, adapt: Robert Allan Ackerman; music and lyrics: Mildred Kayden; dir: Bill Castellino
End of Summer, S.N. Behrman; dir: John Allison
Confessions of an Irish Rebel, adapt: Shay Duffin, from Brendan Behan; dir: Denis Hayes
Einstein: The Man Behind the Genius, Willard Simms; dir: Willard Simms
Nabakov, adapt: Albert Paulsen; dir: Albert Paulsen
Mary Barnes, David Edgar; dir: Ron Sossi
A Not So Silent Night, Paul Vanase; dir: Paul Vanase
Chucky's Hunch, Rochelle Owens; dir: Elinor Renfield
The Frogs, Aristophanes; book adapt: Burt Shevelove; music and lyrics: Stephen Sondheim; dir: Ron Sossi
In the Matter of J. Robert Oppenheimer, Heinar Kipphardt; dir: Frank Condon

DESIGNERS

Sets: Donald Cate, Clark Duncan, Nancy Dunn Eisenman, Dan Fendel, Christopher M. Idoine, Anatol Krashyasky, Steve Lavino, Dan McCleary, Russell Pyle.
Costumes: Camille Argus, Elizabeth Olsen Castro, Delores Deluxe, Jerry Frankel, Dagmar Grossman, Betsy Heiman, Esther Kashkin, Kate Lindsay, Susan Nininger, Brenda Waugh.
Lights: Paulie Jenkins, Karen M. Katz, Christine Lomaka, Ilya Midlin, Russell Pyle, David Taylor, Larry Weber.

The Old Creamery Theatre Company

THOMAS PETER JOHNSON
Artistic Director

ROBERT A. ROSENBAUM
Executive Director

TOM ANDERSON
Board President

Box 160
Garrison, IA 52229
(319) 477-3925 (business)
(319) 477-3165 (box office)

FOUNDED 1971
Thomas Peter Johnson

SEASON
April-December

SCHEDULE
Evenings
Thursday-Sunday

Matinees
Sunday

FACILITIES
Main Stage
Seating capacity: 262
Stage: thrust

Brenton Stage
Seating capacity: 110
Stage: flexible

FINANCES
January 1, 1982-December 31, 1982
$325,000 operating expenses
$211,000 earned income
$ 90,000 grants/contributions

AUDIENCE
Annual attendance: 60,000

TOURING CONTACT
Lauren Green-Caldwell, Meg Merckens

AEA letter of agreement

In 1971 The Old Creamery Theatre Company was created with the dream of taking theatre to as many people in the Midwest as possible. This idea was expanded to include the establishment of a full repertory company which is now in its 13th year of production.

During its repertory season, the company performs for an audience of approximately 30,000, followed by a tour throughout Iowa and the six surrounding states with a wide variety of productions for children and adults.

In addition to its Main Stage, The Old Creamery's facilities now include the Brenton Stage, a smaller flexible theatre. This allows performance of significant plays that might not be economically feasible on the Main Stage. The Old Creamery is committed to the introduction and development of new talent through such activities as the Iowa Playwriting Contest and the New Director's Workshop series.

Education and community outreach are basic to the Old Creamery philosophy: workshops are offered both on tour and at the Garrison facilities. Artistic, administrative and technical/production internships are available each year, in addition to an Equity candidacy program.

While Iowa is far from New York, it is not by any means an uneducated or backward state, and Old Creamery's audiences demand quality and variety. The Old Creamery attempts to serve them because it believes that, in a sense, they *are* the theatre.

In 1980, Governor Robert D. Ray awarded the theatre the Distinguished Service Award in recognition of its significant artistic contribution to the state of Iowa.

Programs and services

Touring; workshops; internships.

PRODUCTIONS 1982

Talley's Folly, Lanford Wilson, dir: Thomas Peter Johnson
A Gentleman and a Scoundrel, Jack Sharkey; dir: Thomas Peter Johnson
The Last Monthly Meeting of the Brothers Westmoreland, Gregory Lindeman; dir: Mick Denniston
Joseph and the Amazing Technicolor Dreamcoat, book and lyrics: Tim Rice; music: Andrew Lloyd Webber; dir: Thomas Peter Johnson
Midnight Cabaret, company-developed; dir: Thomas Peter Johnson

Old Globe Theatre

JACK O'BRIEN
Artistic Director

THOMAS HALL
Managing Director

J. STACEY SULLIVAN
Board Chairman

Box 2171
San Diego, CA 92112
(619) 231-1941 (business)
(619) 239-2255 (box office)

FOUNDED 1937
Community members

SEASON
January-October

SCHEDULE
Evenings
Tuesday-Sunday

Matinees
Saturday, Sunday

FACILITIES
El Prado, Balboa Park

Old Globe Theatre
Seating capacity: 581
Stage: proscenium

Festival Stage
Seating capacity: 617
Stage: thrust

Cassius Carter Centre Stage
Seating capacity: 225
Stage: arena

FINANCES
November 1, 1981-October 31, 1982
$3,927,000 operating expenses
$2,346,000 earned income
$1,346,000 grants/contributions

AUDIENCE
Annual attendance: 275,000
Subscribers: 35,000

TOURING CONTACT
Tom Corcoran, Jim Bush

BOOKED-IN EVENTS
Theatre, music, dance, film, lectures

AEA LORT (B) contract

The Old Globe Theatre, having bounced back from the fire that levelled the original landmark in 1978, is in a tremendously exciting period of growth and expansion. Within its three-theatre complex (including the new $6.5 million Old Globe), the Globe has begun to produce a remarkable range of plays in a nine-month season that stretches from January through September, and includes a month-and-a-half of rotating repertory during its summer festival.

Selection of plays includes new and original scripts and at least three Shakespearean productions in any given season; the flavor of the work is distinctly American, reflecting the philosophy that American actors need and deserve exposure to the great classical roles to fully realize their potential. As a result, the audiences in Balboa Park witness a season that offers skilled actors from both local and regional talent pools, as well as many actors now working primarily in film and television. This blending of personalities and talent makes for a vigorous company that is challenged and stretched by working in two or three different theatre spaces within the period of a few months.

Executive producer and founder Craig Noel's original vision of "human playing spaces" has been enriched immeasurably by the appetites of important American actors eager to assay the great roles. The Globe continues to break ground in new directions, revitalizing the regional spirit in a range of work spanning the classics to world premieres, while continuing a 40-year-old theatrical tradition.

Programs and services

Educational tours; Page-to-Stage training program; Plays-in-Progress readings; artistic and administrative internships; non-professional classes.

PRODUCTIONS 1981-82

As You Like It, William Shakespeare; dir: Craig Noel
Sorrows of Stephen, Peter Parnell; dir: Andrew J. Traister
Yankee Wives, David Rimmer; dir: Jack O'Brien
Oh, Coward!, music and lyrics: Noel Coward; adapt: Roderick Cook; dir: G. Wood

Wait Until Dark, Frederick Knott; dir: Thomas Peter Johnson
The Gin Game, D.L. Coburn; dir: Thomas Peter Johnson
Once Upon a Mattress, book: Jay Thompson, Marshall Barer and Dean Fuller; music: Mary Rodgers; lyrics: Marshall Barer; dir: Thomas Peter Johnson
Short Stuff, company-developed; dir: David Berendes
The Sunshine Boys, Neil Simon; dir: Thomas Peter Johnson

PRODUCTIONS 1983

Slow Dance on the Killing Ground, William Hanley; dir: Steve Shaffer
Murder at the Howard Johnson's, Ron Clark and Sam Bobrick; dir: Thomas Peter Johnson
September Song, Alex Gottlieb; dir: Richard D. Burk
Lone Star, James McLure; dir: Richard D. Burk
Tintypes, music and lyrics: various; adapt: Mary Kyte, Mel Marvin and Gary Pearle; dir: Thomas Peter Johnson
Midnight Cabaret
Tribute, Bernard Slade; dir: Thomas Peter Johnson
The Belle of Amherst, William Luce; dir: Steve Shaffer
Something's Afoot, James McDonald, David Vos and Robert Gerlach; dir: Thomas Peter Johnson
Ladyhouse Blues, Kevin O'Morrison; dir: Thomas Peter Johnson
Godspell, book: John-Michael Tebelak; music and lyrics: Stephen Schwartz; dir: Thomas Peter Johnson

DESIGNERS

Sets: David Berendes, Herb Caldwell, Jeff Finger, Beth Johns, Thomas Peter Johnson, Julie McVay, Charles E. Whisenand.
Costumes: Herb Caldwell, Marquetta Senters, Mary Woolever.
Lights: David Berendes, Richard D. Burk, Herb Caldwell, Beth Johns, Gene Larche, Julie McVay, Grover Smittle, Charles E. Whisenand.

The Old Creamery Theatre Company. Short Stuff.
Photo: Meg Merckens.

Misalliance, George Bernard Shaw; dir: Paxton Whitehead
Moby Dick Rehearsed, Orson Welles; dir: David McClendon
The Miser, Molière; adapt: Miles Malleson; dir: Joseph Hardy
The Tempest, William Shakespeare; dir: Jack O'Brien
Billy Bishop Goes to War, John Gray and Eric Peterson; dir: Craig Noel
The Taming of the Shrew, William Shakespeare; dir: Joseph Hardy
The Importance of Being Earnest, Oscar Wilde; dir: Tom Moore
The Gin Game, D.L. Coburn; dir: Jack O'Brien

PRODUCTIONS 1983

The Skin of Our Teeth, Thornton Wilder; dir: Jack O'Brien
Terra Nova, Ted Tally; dir: Gerald Gutierrez
Clap Your Hands, Ellis Rabb; dir: Ellis Rabb
Mass Appeal, Bill C. Davis; dir: David McClendon
Wings, Arthur Kopit; dir: Eve Roberts
The Dining Room, A.R. Gurney, Jr.; dir: Craig Noel
Twelfth Night, William Shakespeare; dir: Jack O'Brien
Henry IV, Part I, William Shakespeare; dir: James Dunn
Talley's Folly, Lanford Wilson; dir: Andrew J. Traister
Arsenic and Old Lace, Joseph Kesselring; dir: Craig Noel
The Rivals, Richard Brinsley Sheridan; dir: Joseph Hardy
Macbeth, William Shakespeare; dir: Jack O'Brien

DESIGNERS

Sets: Marc Donnelly, Kent Dorsey, Richard Hay, Robert Morgan, Alan K. Okazaki, Steven Rubin, Douglas W. Schmidt, Richard Seger, Douglas Stein.
Costumes: Alan Armstrong, Sally Cleveland, Deborah Dryden, Ann Emonts, Mary Gibson, Dianne Holly, Sam Kirkpatrick, Robert Morgan, Ann Roth, Steven Rubin.
Lights: Kent Dorsey, John B. Forbes, Gilbert V. Helmsley, John McLain, Craig Miller, Robert Peterson, David G. Segal.

Old Globe Theatre. Monique Fowler, Sada Thompson, Jeffrey Combs, Harold Gould and friend in The Skin of Our Teeth.

Omaha Magic Theatre

JO ANN SCHMIDMAN
Producing Director/Board President

2309 Hanscom Blvd.
Omaha, NB 68105
(402) 346-1227

FOUNDED 1969
Jo Ann Schmidman

SEASON
September-August

SCHEDULE
Evenings
Friday-Monday

FACILITIES
1417 Farnam St.
Seating capacity: 100
Stage: flexible

FINANCES
September 1, 1982-August 31, 1983
$264,000 operating expenses
$ 29,000 earned income
$236,000 grants/contributions

AUDIENCE
Annual attendance: 165,000

TOURING CONTACT
Eve Felder

BOOKED-IN EVENTS
Theatre, film, music

Omaha Magic Theatre. Kegger. Photo: Megan Terry.

The Omaha Magic Theatre, in its 14th year under the artistic direction of Jo Ann Schmidman, continues to develop and produce new American musical theatre. As a vital, highly professional and disciplined company of artists, OMT produces from four to eight new pieces each season; more than 60 new works have been created to date, all developed with playwright, director, designer and composer (working independently) in residence. Thus, a final production is the synthesis of many artistic visions.

OMT is dedicated to the investigation of innovative theatrical techniques and modes of presentation, with a goal of redefining and transforming traditional forms, giving new scope to the work of American theatre artists. Each piece evolves and is fine-tuned through successive 'long run' performances. Multiple art forms are combined to expand and explore the limits of theatrical consciousness. Soft-sculpture set and prop pieces and an innovative mix of musical and performance art styles enhance the audience experience, and productions are written to present objective, well-rounded views of contemporary human concerns.

After premiering in Omaha, many pieces tour extensively as part of a complete theatre residency package. Residencies include performance, theatre history and writing workshops, a fine arts and social issue curriculum for secondary schools, and an extensive "how to produce a fine arts event" guide for local sponsor/producers. Seven pieces are kept in the touring repertoire at all times.

OMT's 1982-83 *Kegger* tour included the Secretarial Conference for Youth on Drinking and Driving, in Washington, D.C.; performances in juvenile and adult prisons, junior and senior high schools, and on Indian Reservations; and much work with special audiences who might not ordinarily attend theatre. In 1980, OMT accepted a commission to perform at the Winter Olympics in Lake Placid, N.Y.

To meet the constant demand for topical new scripts, the theatre distributes final acting editions of OMT-developed plays, which include detailed stage directions, workshop procedures, photos, soft-sculpture instructions and sound environment directives.

Programs and services

Workshops and residencies; ticket discounts and distribution; post-play discussions; staged readings; newsletter; fine arts displays.

One Act Theatre Company of San Francisco

PRODUCTIONS 1981-82

Goona Goona, book and lyrics: Megan Terry; music: Lynn Herrick

Running Gag, book: Jo Ann Schmidman; music: Lynn Herrick and Marianne de Pury; lyrics: Megan Terry

Aliens under Glass, book: Jo Ann Schmidman, Megan Terry and Sora Kim; music: John Sheehan; lyrics: John Sheehan, Jo Ann Schmidman and Janet Kripal

Velveeta Meltdown, Jo Ann Schmidman

All productions directed by Jo Ann Schmidman

PRODUCTIONS 1982-83

Kegger, book and lyrics: Megan Terry; music: Marianne de Pury and Joe Budenholzer; dir: Jo Ann Schmidman

I'm Happier Than You, book and lyrics: Megan Terry; music: Marianne de Pury and Lynn Herrick; dir: Jo Ann Schmidman

Advance, Megan Terry; dir: Jo Ann Schmidman

Fifteen Million Fifteen Year-Olds, book and lyrics: Megan Terry; music: Joe Budenholzer; dir: Jo Ann Schmidman

Dingaling, James Larson; dir: Jo Ann Schmidman

Katmandu, Megan Terry; dir: Megan Terry

Molly Bailey's Traveling Family Circus—Featuring Scenes from the Life of Mother Jones, book and lyrics: Megan Terry; music: Jo Anne Metcalf; dir: Jo Ann Schmidman

Room 17C, book and lyrics: Rosalyn Drexler; music: Joe Budenholzer; dir: Jo Ann Schmidman

DESIGNERS

Sets: Joe Budenholzer, Diane Degan, Greg Gibson, Sora Kim, Jo Ann Schmidman, Megan Terry.

Costumes: Juli Birney, Meg Flamer, Dot Oleson, Elizabeth Scheuerlein, Jo Ann Schmidman, Megan Terry.

Lights: Colbert McClellan.

RIC PRINDLE
Artistic Director

STEVE SIGEL
General Manager

DONALD KINNAIRD
Board President

430 Mason St.
San Francisco, CA 94102
(415) 421-5355 (business)
(415) 421-6162 (box office)

FOUNDED 1976
Peter Tripp, Jean Schiffman, Laurellee Westaway

SEASON
October–September

SCHEDULE

Evenings
Thursday-Sunday

Matinees
Wednesday, Sunday

FACILITIES

One Act Theatre
Seating capacity: 100
Stage: thrust

One Act II
Seating capacity: 80
Stage: thrust

FINANCES
August 1, 1982-July 31, 1983
$254,000 operating expenses
$128,000 earned income
$125,000 grants/contributions

AUDIENCE
Annual attendance: 22,000
Subscribers: 740

TOURING CONTACT
Steve Sigel

AEA 99-seat waiver

The artistic mission of the One Act Theatre Company is to develop and produce new and rarely produced one-act plays, using a professional repertory company of actors, directors, designers and playwrights. The following principles guide the company:

— Theatre is unique in its power to involve us in an immediate experience of our common humanity.

— The audience is a key component of the theatrical process, so theatre must be aware of and receptive to all segments of the community, with a particular commitment to developing future audiences among young people.

— The concept of a resident ensemble of outstanding theatre practitioners working collaboratively is essential to achieving the highest standards of artistry. The continuity inherent in this process develops trust, a common language and a willingness to take risks — a collective condition which fosters the growth of the individual. To maintain such a company, members must be artistically and financially rewarded for their skills and commitment.

— The one-act play is a major theatrical genre which deserves greater recognition because of its unique advantages. One-acts expose audiences to a variety of entertainment in a single evening; they create an intense and heightened focus on a single event; they provide an effective developmental form for emerging playwrights; they enable a theatre to maintain a repertoire of considerable depth and variety as well as quantity (suitable for touring and for quick, efficient mounting for special community projects); they are often neglected by commercial theatres; and they are highly adaptable to other media.

— The development and production of new works is of crucial importance to the continued promise and vitality of theatre.

Programs and services

Lunchtime Theatre; student matinees; Playwrights Theatre developmental unit; staged readings; touring; radio drama series; One Act Television Theatre pilot program with local public broadcasting system; internships; workshops.

One Act Theatre Company of San Francisco. Ed Markmann and Q Lewis in Swan Song. *Photo: Pamela Clarke.*

O'Neill Theater Center

Note: During the 1981-82 season, Peter Tripp served as artistic director.

PRODUCTIONS 1981-82

Decrescendo, Irene Oppenheim; dir: Eileen Kane
Fits and Starts, Grace McKeaney; dir: Carla Sarvis
Autumn Ladies, Susan Nanus; dir: Simon Levy
Emma Rothstein, Leslie Brody; dir: Peter Tripp
A Night in Bulgaria, Deborah Rogin; dir: Anita Merzel
Schubert's Last Serenade, Julie Bovasso; dir: David Sanford
San Joaquin Blues, Michael Lynch; dir: Simon Levy
Desert Weather, Michael Lynch; dir: Roxanne Rogers
Something Unspoken, Tennessee Williams; dir: Carla Sarvis
Bea, Frank, Richie and Joan, Renee Taylor and Joseph Bologna; dir: Peter Tripp
Hoss Drawin', Leon Martell; dir: Leon Martell and Beth Ruscio

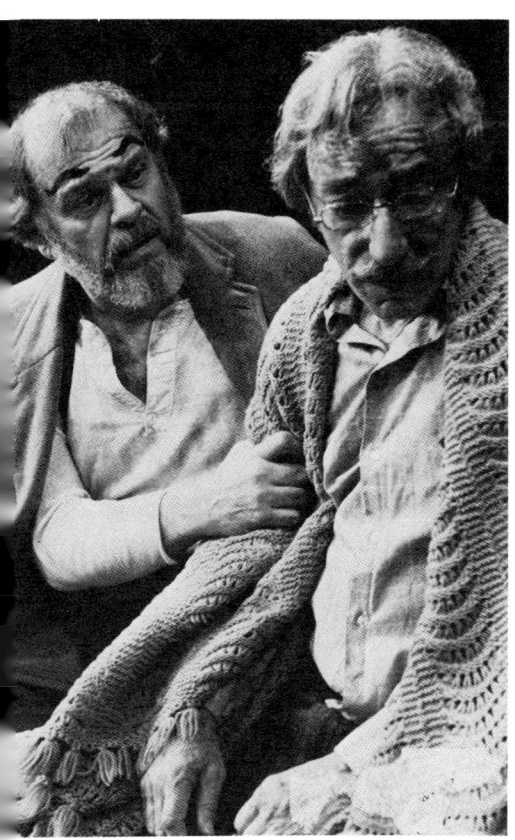

Last Call, Daniel Curzon; dir: Ed Decker
A Good Time, Ernest Thompson; dir: Peter Tripp
Yanks 3, Detroit 0, Top of the Seventh, Jonathan Reynolds; dir: Peter Tripp
Augustus Does His Bit, George Bernard Shaw; dir: Terry O'Brien
The Farewell Supper, Arthur Schnitzler; dir: Ed Decker
Bedtime Story, Sean O'Casey; dir: William Oliver
A Sunny Morning, Serafin and Joaquin Alvarez Quintero; dir: Peter Tripp

PRODUCTIONS 1982-83

Pvt. Wars, James McLure; dir: Peter Tripp
God, Woody Allen; dir: Peter Tripp
The Hundred Years' War, Holly Kern; dir: Peter Tripp
Romantic Comedy, Bernard Slade; dir: Ed Decker
Adaptation, Elaine May; dir: Ed Decker
Rosa, Peter Barnes; dir: JD Trow
Mrs. Dally Has a Lover, William Hanley; dir: Thom Elkjer
Swan Song, Anton Chekhov; trans: George House; dir: Ric Prindle
The Forced Marriage, Molière; trans: William Oliver; dir: William Oliver
Village Wooing, George Bernard Shaw; dir: Simon Levy
The Long Goodbye, Tennessee Williams; dir: Ric Prindle
Mandate, Craig Pettigrew; dir: Simon Levy
Taps at 8:23, Holly Kern; dir: Tom McDermott
An American Dream, Edward Albee; dir: Marc Rosenblatt
After Magritte, Tom Stoppard; dir: JD Trow

DESIGNERS

Sets: Michael Allen, Bruce Brisson, Deborah Capen, Stephen Elspas, Valentine Hooven, Peggy McDonald, Jon Riggs, Cheryl Stewart, Joanna Willis.
Costumes: Michael Allen, Judith Boraas, Deborah Capen, Ardyss Golden, Suzanne Raftery, Gael Russell.
Lights: Rhonda Birnbaum, Derek Duarte, Kurt Graffy, Kurt Landisman, Brian Russell, Will Simonds, Whitney Watson.

GEORGE C. WHITE
President

LLOYD RICHARDS
Artistic Director, National Playwrights Conference

234 West 44th St., Suite 901
New York, NY 10036
(212) 382-2790

305 Great Neck Road
Waterford, CT 06385
(203) 443-5378

FOUNDED 1964
George C. White

SEASON
July-August

SCHEDULE
Evenings
Monday-Saturday

Matinees
Saturday

FACILITIES
Barn Theater
Seating capacity: 200
Stage: flexible

Amphitheater
Seating capacity: 300
Stage: thrust

Instant Theater
Seating capacity: 200
Stage: arena

FINANCES
July 1, 1981-June 30, 1982
$2,493,000 operating expenses
$1,673,000 earned income
$ 907,000 grants/contributions

AUDIENCE
Annual attendance: 5,000

BOOKED-IN EVENTS
Theatre, music

AEA LORT (C) contract

The National Playwrights Conference of the O'Neill Theater Center began in 1964, significantly more than a generation ago. There are people now working in the theatre who are unacquainted with the conditions out of which the Playwrights Conference became a necessity: the unfilled need of writers for a place to work with other theatre professionals on the development of new scripts, with the freedom to fail, far from the reach of criticism and the demands of an audience.

Each year, the artists involved in the Conference ask themselves two ritual questions, hoping that their responses will be real and not ritual: Does the necessity for identifying and supporting the work of new playwrights still exist? Should we continue in the development of new work and new writers? So far, the conclusion has been that not enough play development is taking place in America, and more importantly, that it is not being done well enough.

In a world that daily takes itself to the verge of self-destruction, audiences can stand the diversion that is entertainment, but they also absolutely need the civilizing influence of thoughtful, provocative theatre. To have that, America needs playwrights with a command of their craft and the imagination and intelligence to constructively provoke our thinking—playwrights who will lead us to the questions and demand the answers that may avert destruction and make of life an art that is productive and joyous.

America is a country wealthy in natural resources. Its most important resource is its people, with their ingenuity and intelligence. The National Playwrights Conference strives to cultivate those with a talent for playwriting so that they in turn might move and affect us all.

Programs and services

National Critics Institute; National Theater Institute; Creative Arts in Education; National Opera-Music Theater Conference; National Playwrights Directory; Media Arts Program; Monte Cristo Cottage theatre collection and library.

O'Neill Theater Center. Leonard Jackson, Joe Seneca and Robert Judd in *Ma Rainey's Black Bottom*. Photo: A. Vincent Scarano.

PRODUCTIONS 1982

A Knife in the Heart, Susan Yankowitz; dir: Dennis Scott
Stitchers and Starlight Talkers, Kathleen Betsko; dir: Amy Saltz
The Further Adventures of Sally, Russell Davis; dir: Tony Giordano
Poppa, Dorothy Fields; dir: John Pasquin
Playing in Local Bands, Nancy Fales Garrett; dir: William Ludel
Clara Toil, Harry Kondoleon; dir: Barnet Kellman
Some Rain, Edward Luczak; dir: William Partlan
Proud Flesh, James Nicholson; dir: William Ludel
The Bunkhouse, Terrence Ortwein; dir: John Pasquin
Ghost Dancing, Phillip Penningroth; dir: John Pasquin
The Conquest, Betsy Julia Robinson; dir: Barnet Kellman
Coyote Ugly, Lynn Seifert; dir: Tony Giordano
First Draft, Yale Udoff; dir: Dennis Scott
AWOL, Carol Williams, dir: Amy Saltz
Ma Rainey's Black Bottom, August Wilson; dir: William Partlan

PRODUCTIONS 1983

Danny and the Deep Blue Sea, John Patrick Shanley; dir: Amy Saltz
Strega or the Witch, Anna Theresa Cascio; dir: Dennis Scott
The Day of the Picnic (The Witch Doctor's Revenge), Russell Davis; dir: Tony Giordano
Independence, Lee Blessing; dir: Barnet Kellman
Ohio Tip-Off, James Yoshimura; dir: Walton Jones
The Limb King, Keith Reddin; dir: John Pasquin
The Able-Bodied Seaman, Alan Bowne; dir: Dennis Scott
Melody Sisters, Anne Commire; dir: Walton Jones
Fences, August Wilson; dir: William Partlan
Open Heart, William di Canzio; dir: Amy Saltz
Great Divide, Robert Litz; dir: Dennis Scott

DESIGNERS

Sets: Bill Burner, C. Russell Christian, Kate Edmunds, Fred Voelpel, Michael Yeargan.
Lights: Jeff Goodman, Ann Wrightson.

Ontological-Hysteric Theatre

RICHARD FOREMAN
Director/Board President

GEORGE ASHLEY
Administrative Director

c/o Performing Artservices
325 Spring St.
New York, NY 10013
(212) 243-6153

FOUNDED 1968
Richard Foreman

FINANCES
July 1, 1980-June 30, 1981
$90,000 operating expenses
$48,000 earned income
$43,000 grants/contributions

Richard Foreman's Ontological-Hysteric Theatre is known in Europe as well as in America as one of the world's seminal avant-garde theatres. Foreman has written, designed and directed plays, operas and musicals for his own company and has also staged classical works here and abroad, including Brecht's *Threepenny Opera,* Molière's *Don Juan* and *Die Fledermaus* by Johann Strauss. The artistic philosophy of OHT is best reflected in Foreman's own words:

"I belong to that critical school which is upsetting a lot of people these days, which goes under the name of Decontructionist and believes that there is no 'proper' interpretation of a text; that a text is essentially saying more than the author knows it is saying; and that therefore, one interpretation is possible, and its opposite is also possible.

"Art is an essentially spiritual activity, having therapeutic aims. The lesson of art, the therapy of art, the spiritual gift of art, is to teach us and to help our audiences discover with us that one can live with compassion, with lucidity, with energy in a sea of conflicting impulses and interpretations. . . .

"There is an inevitable, unavoidable drift into meaning and significance in life. The exciting task of the artists is to try and stretch that rubber band so the drift into coherence covers the most ground. I'm not trying to bring chaos out of order. Rather, I'm trying to say that life *is* chaotic, that we inherit a grid that makes us think its more orderly than it is, and that the task is to rise above the chaos so it doesn't trip us up and infect us any more than it has to. But the task is to accomplish this without projecting a non-existent order back upon that choas."

PRODUCTIONS 1981-82

Don Juan, Molière; trans: Donald M. Frame
Cafe Amerique, Richard Foreman
Madame Adare, Richard Foreman and Stanley Silverman
Three Acts of Recognition, Botho Strauss

PRODUCTIONS 1982-83

Egyptology (My Head Was a Sledgehammer), Richard Foreman
Die Fledermaus, Johann Strauss
Dr. Faustus Lights the Lights, Gertrude Stein; French trans: Marie-Claire Pasquier

All productions directed and designed by Richard Foreman

Ontological-Hysteric Theatre. Roy Brocksmith, Pamela Payton-Wright and John Seitz in Don Juan. *Photo: Martha Swope.*

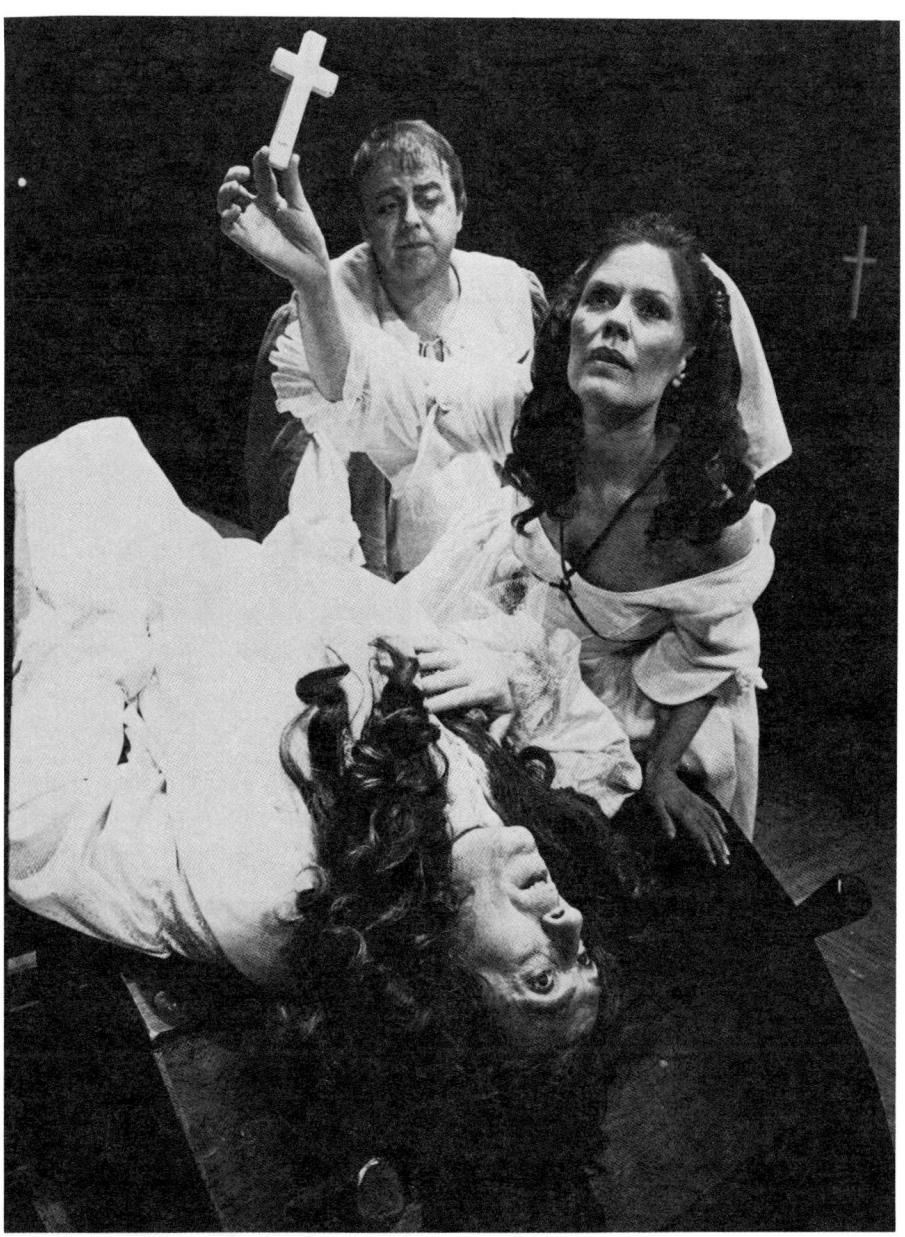

Oregon Shakespearean Festival

JERRY TURNER
Artistic Director

WILLIAM W. PATTON
Executive Director

WILLIAM PURDY
Board President

Box 158
Ashland, OR 97520
(503) 482-2111 (business)
(503) 482-4331 (box office)

FOUNDED 1935
Angus L. Bowmer

SEASON
February-October

SCHEDULE

Evenings
Tuesday-Sunday

Matinees
Saturday, Sunday (spring, fall)
Tuesday-Sunday (summer)

FACILITIES
15 South Pioneer St.

Elizabethan Stage
Seating capacity: 1,194
Stage: thrust

Angus Bowmer Theatre
Seating capacity: 601
Stage: thrust

Black Swan Theatre
Seating capacity: 140
Stage: arena

FINANCES
November 1, 1981-October 31, 1982
$4,000,000 operating expenses
$3,116,000 earned income
$1,140,000 grants/contributions

AUDIENCE
Annual attendance: 313,817

TOURING CONTACT
Paul Nicholson

BOOKED-IN EVENTS
Music

AEA Guest Artist contract

The Oregon Shakespearean Festival was founded in 1935 to present Shakespeare's works on a stage roughly equivalent to those of Elizabethan playhouses. Today, the Festival operates a large outdoor playhouse modeled after the historic Fortune Theatre; a modern indoor theatre known as the Angus Bowmer; and the Black Swan, an intimate "black box" space.

The professional company is dedicated to producing important works of dramatic literature. Production style is dictated first and foremost by the demands of the text and vision of the author; secondly, by the talent and sensibilities of the company; and finally, by contemporary taste and the experience of the audience.

The Festival intends to provide a theatrical bridge between our cultural heritage and modern experience. Its task is to select and perform plays of dramatic stature—ancient and contemporary, classical and modern—which speak to the human condition; and to present them as vividly, clearly and boldly as resources permit, making demands on the audience as well as the company in pursuit of an impossible vision: the definitive production.

Almost as important as the repertoire is the selection, nurturing and care of the company. Both continuity and freshness are assured by the systematic welcoming and training of new talent. The Festival accepts new members in order to fulfill its obligation to train artists for classical work, and as a necessary protection against staleness and complacency.

Programs and services

Programs-in-schools; Monday Medley concert series; film series; lectures; Festival Institute discussion and seminar series; backstage tours; *Prologue* newsletter; production and administrative internships; workshops.

PRODUCTIONS 1981-82

Othello, William Shakespeare; dir: Sanford Robbins
Julius Caesar, William Shakespeare; dir: Jerry Turner

Oregon Shakespearean Festival. Henry V. Photo: Hank Kranzler.

Organic Theater Company

The Comedy of Errors, William Shakespeare; dir: Julian Lopez-Morillas
Romeo and Juliet, William Shakespeare; dir: Dennis Bigelow
Henry V, William Shakespeare; dir: Pat Patton
Inherit the Wind, Jerome Lawrence and Robert E. Lee; dir: Dennis Bigelow
Blithe Spirit, Noel Coward; dir: Pat Patton
Spokespong, book and lyrics: Stewart Parker; music: Jimmy Kennedy; dir: Denis Arndt
The Matchmaker, Thornton Wilder; dir: Rod Alexander
Wings, Arthur Kopit; dir: James Moll
Hold Me!, Jules Feiffer; dir: Paul Barnes
The Father, August Strindberg; trans: Jerry Turner; dir: Jerry Turner

PRODUCTIONS 1982-83

Hamlet, William Shakespeare; dir: Robert Benedetti
Cymbeline, William Shakespeare; dir: J.H. Crouch
Much Ado About Nothing, William Shakespeare; dir: Dennis Bigelow
Richard III, William Shakespeare; dir: Denis Arndt
Man and Superman, George Bernard Shaw; dir: James Moll
Ah, Wilderness!, Eugene O'Neill; dir: Jerry Turner
The Matchmaker
What the Butler Saw, Joe Orton; dir: Pat Patton
Dracula, Richard Sharp; dir: Richard Geer
Don Juan in Hell, George Bernard Shaw; dir: James Moll
The Entertainer, John Osborne; dir: Dennis Bigelow
Dreamhouse, Stuart Duckworth; dir: Jerry Turner

DESIGNERS

Sets: William Bloodgood, Karen Gjelsteen, Richard L. Hay.
Costumes: Martha Burke, Candice Cain, Jeannie Davidson, Deborah M. Dryden, Claudia Everett, Michael Olich, Warren Travis, Mariann Verheyen, Carole Wheeldon.
Lights: Peter W. Allen, Robert Peterson, James Sale.

STUART GORDON
Producing Director

NICK RABKIN
General Manager

DAN LIEBENTRITT
Board Chairman

3319 North Clark St.
Chicago, IL 60657
(312) 327-5507 (business)
(312) 327-5588 (box office)

FOUNDED 1969
Stuart Gordon, Carolyn Purdy-Gordon

SEASON
Year-round

SCHEDULE
Evenings
Wednesday-Sunday

Matinees
Sunday

Organic Theater Company. Jackie Taylor and Christopher Michael Moore in E/R Emergency Room. Photo: Stuart Gordon.

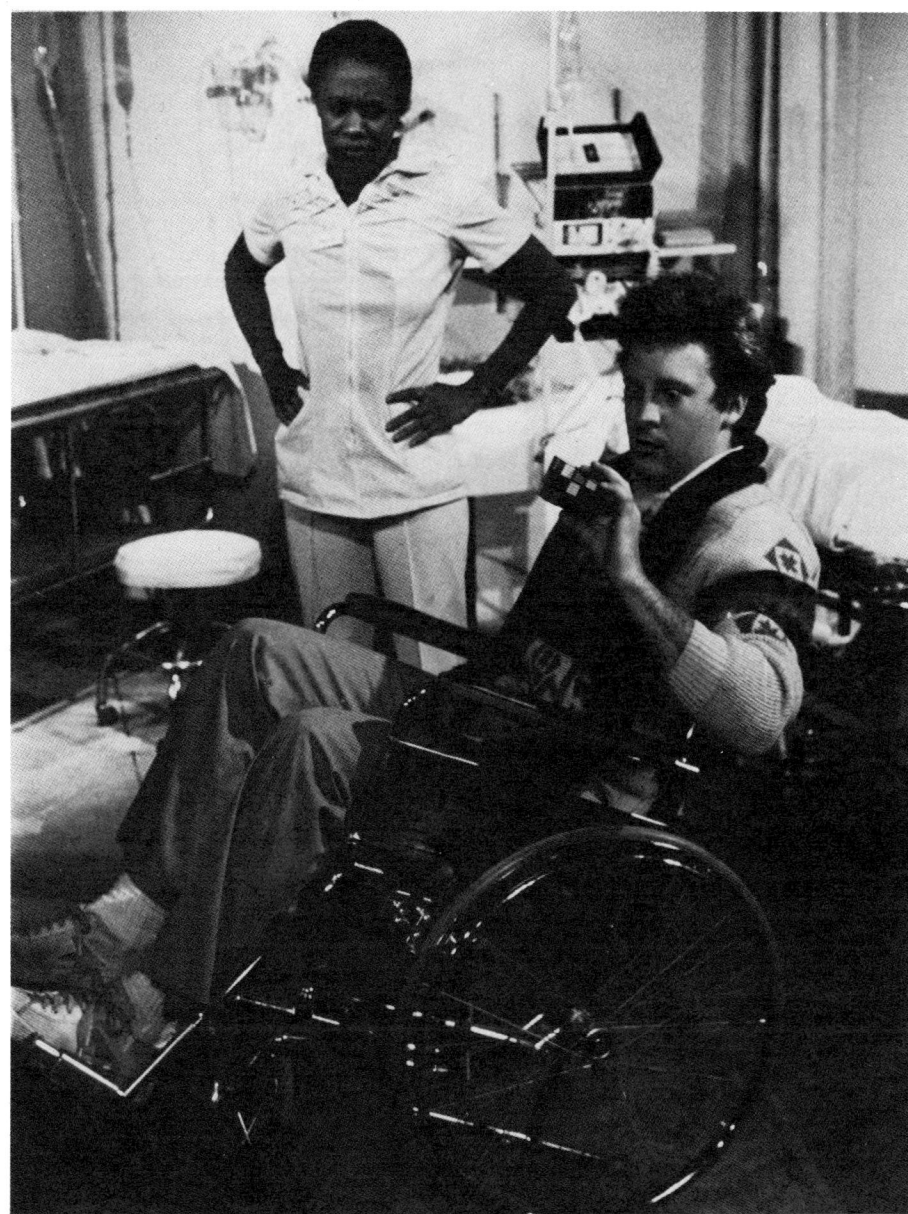

FACILITIES
Seating capacity: 270
Stage: flexible

FINANCES
January 1, 1982–December 31, 1982
$600,000 operating expenses
$339,000 earned income
$261,000 grants/contributions

AUDIENCE
Annual attendance: 60,000
Subscribers: 400

TOURING CONTACT
Don Gunn

AEA LORT (D) contract, letter of agreement

The Organic Theater Company is a theatre of the unexpected; it is a theatre that always attempts to astound and amaze by being totally unpredictable, with each play quite different from the last. Over the last 11 years, the Organic has produced a variety of original, company-developed works and world premiere adaptations.

Besides insuring the future of the theatre by offering a showcase for new playwrights, actors, musicians and designers, this approach encourages the development of plays using a method which has proven most artistically productive: with a playwright-in-residence. It is commonly acknowledged (although conveniently forgotten) that ancient Greek theatre — as well as all of Shakespeare and Chekhov — were created by bringing together a playwright and a theatre company, allowing them to shape and reshape a work together. The Organic is devoted to the company ideal and it knows that good theatre companies, like good marriages, are rare.

The Organic is engaged in finding new ways of expressing an emotion or an idea, and believes that theatre must be immediate. It must find new ways to break through the walls we all build, composed of the boring cliches of everyday existence. It must delight us, shock us, make us weep and generally reaffirm us as living human beings.

The Organic's space provides an intimate environment for both actor and audience, and audiences are always asked to participate, if only with their imaginations.

The company's production of *E/R Emergency Room*, like its earlier work *Bleacher Bums*, was created improvisationally by the company, and its great success (it has become the longest running play in Chicago history) reflects the excitement that can be generated when audiences see themselves onstage — their lives transformed into art.

Upcoming projects along these lines include a play about commodities dealers, the wild adventures of Ben Hecht and Charles MacArthur as cub reporters in turn-of-the-century Chicago, and a play depicting an evening in a Chicago massage parlor. Currently in the works is a piece composed of the company's version of the 1984 Democratic convention, with the audience playing the delegates and choosing the presidential nominee.

Programs and services

Classes; staged readings.

PRODUCTIONS 1981

The King Must Die, adapt: Stuart Gordon and William J. Norris, from Mary Renault
The Adventures of Huckleberry Finn, company-adapt, from Mark Twain
Dr. Rat, adapt: Richard Fire, from William Kotzwinkle; music and lyrics: June Shellene-Jans and Richard Fire

PRODUCTIONS 1982

E/R Emergency Room, company-adapt

All productions directed by Stuart Gordon

DESIGNERS

Sets: Rick Paul.
Costumes: Cookie Gluck, Mary Griswold, Marsha deBoeuf, Kaye Nottbusch, John Paoletti, Rick Paul.
Lights: Geoffrey Bushor, Mark S. Mongold, Jeff Ravitz.

Paper Mill Playhouse

ANGELO DEL ROSSI
Executive Producer

WADE MILLER
General Manager

FLOYD H. BRAGG
Board President

Brookside Drive
Millburn, NJ 07041
(201) 379-3636 (business)
(201) 376-4343 (box office)

FOUNDED 1934
Frank Carrington, Antoinette Scudder

SEASON
September–July

SCHEDULE
Evenings
Tuesday–Sunday

Matinees
Thursday, Sunday

FACILITIES
Seating capacity: 1,192
Stage: proscenium

FINANCES
July 1, 1982–June 30, 1983
$4,052,000 operating expenses
$3,590,000 earned income
$ 388,000 grants/contributions

AUDIENCE
Annual attendance: 308,656
Subscribers: 26,627

BOOKED-IN EVENTS
Children's theatre, music, dance

AEA Council on Stock Theatre and Theatre for Young Audiences contracts

As New Jersey's official State Theatre, the Paper Mill Playhouse stresses diversity in its programming. The core of its season is a six-event subscription series featuring plays, musicals and operettas. The Playhouse is especially committed to presenting the wide spectrum of American musical theatre, from

Paper Mill Playhouse. The New Moon. *Photo: Terence A. Gili.*

Pennsylvania Stage Company

the rarely produced works of Sigmund Romberg and Victor Herbert, through the large scale musical comedy favorites, to the development of original musical theatre works. Each production is cast individually, drawing upon the pool of acting and directing talent available in the area.

From its founding in 1934, the Playhouse occupied a renovated 19th century mill, until most of the facility was destroyed by arson in 1980. After the fire, a major fundraising campaign was launched and the rebuilt $5 million Playhouse opened in the fall of 1982. The new facility was designed to incorporate the best elements of the traditional proscenium theatre.

In attempting to serve a wide range of tastes and interests, the Playhouse also presents an extensive program of children's theatre, a dance series, a concert series, play readings and a summer festival. Paper Mill is New Jersey's largest performing arts organization and promotes co-production arrangements with the state's major symphony orchestra, opera and dance companies.

Programs and services

New play series; newsletter; children's theatre; summer festival; dance series; concert series; sign language performances; speaker's bureau; senior citizen series.

Note: Due to renovation, no plays were produced during the 1981-82 season.

PRODUCTIONS 1982-83

Robert & Elizabeth, book and lyrics: Ronald Millar; music: Ron Grainer; dir: Robert Johanson.
You Can't Take It with You, Moss Hart and George S. Kaufman; dir: Ellis Rabb
Mass Appeal, Bill C. Davis; dir: Geraldine Fitzgerald
Suite in Two Keys, Noel Coward, dir: Richard Barr
New Moon, book and lyrics: Oscar Hammerstein II, Frank Mandel and Lawrence Schwab; music: Sigmund Romberg; dir: Robert Johanson
Man of La Mancha, book: Dale Wasserman; music: Mitch Leigh; lyrics: Joe Darion; dir: Rudy Tronto

DESIGNERS

Sets: Daniel Ettinger, David Gropman, James Morgan, Helen Pond, Herbert Senn, James Tilton, Paul Wonsek.
Costumes: Guy Geoly, William Ivey Long, Neil Spisak, Vida Thomas.
Lights: Steve Cochrane, F. Mitchell Dana, David Kissel, Nananne Porcher, Dierdre A. Taylor, James Tilton.

GREGORY S. HURST
Producing Director

GARY C. PORTO
General Manager

DAVID H. KELLY
Board President

837 Linden St.
Allentown, PA 18101
(215) 434-6110

FOUNDED 1977
Anna Rodale

SEASON
September-May

SCHEDULE
Evenings
Tuesday-Sunday

Matinees
Thursday, Sunday

FACILITIES
J.I. Rodale Theatre
Seating capacity: 274
Stage: proscenium

FINANCES
July 1, 1982-June 30, 1983
$884,000 operating expenses
$528,000 earned income
$364,000 grants/contributions

AUDIENCES
Annual attendance: 75,000
Subscribers: 6,000

BOOKED-IN EVENTS
Solo artists, theatre, dance, music

AEA LORT (C) contract

The Pennsylvania Stage Company discovers, develops and stages new American musicals and dramatic works, and rediscovers neglected 20th century American plays, staging them in new ways. Plays are selected because they speak to the PSC audience, and because they have a passion and immediacy that calls for them to be done now.

Since 1978, PSC has presented nine world premieres, five of which were musicals. The works have had impact beyond the Lehigh

Valley, garnering New York runs and subsequent productions. PSC emphasizes those plays that explore the mythic and realistic history of America, believing in particular that the American musical is a unique art form. The creative structure of the company has progressed to the point where it can give birth to original musical plays. In the case of *Song of Myself,* PSC developed an idea into a musical play, allowing a team of collaborators to devote 11 months to dramatically interpreting a specific view of Walt Whitman's life. The narrative, with its synthesis of music, language and action served as an ideal means to present the rich fabric of America.

The crux of PSC's artistic philosophy is that the play—whether new or a revival—should help us rediscover the glory and optimism in our lives while allowing us to embrace the human spirit. PSC wants its audience to be in touch with the best, most humane part of themselves, and so produces plays that in some way portray the essence of what it means to be human, plays which examine what man needs to believe in, so that he may better understand contemporary America.

PSC intends to continue to present theatre that magnifiies the life of its community, enabling its audience to explore ideas, images and issues vital to its community, through the larger-than-life miracle of theatre.

Programs and services

Student and senior citizen matinees; study guides; post-play discussion; artists-in-schools; staged readings; newsletter; associate/intern program.

PRODUCTIONS 1981-82

Deathtrap, Ira Levin; dir: Susan Kerner
The Gin Game, D.L. Coburn; dir: Stephen Rothman
Song of Myself, book: Gayle Stahlhuth and Gregory S. Hurst; music: Arthur Harris; lyrics: Gayle Stahlhuth; dir: Gregory S. Hurst
The Price, Arthur Miller; dir: Thomas Gruenewald
Nurse Jane Goes to Hawaii, Allan Stratton; dir: Sue Lawless
Two Gentlemen of Verona, William Shakespeare; dir: Gregory S. Hurst

PRODUCTIONS 1982-83

Ain't Misbehavin', music and lyrics: Fats Waller, et al.; adapt: Murray Horwitz and Richard Maltby, Jr.; dir: Bick Goss
Born Yesterday, Garson Kanin; dir: Stephen Rothman
Shim Sham, book: Eric Blau; lyrics and music: Johnny Brandon; dir: Gregory S. Hurst
Ready or Not, Casey Kelly: dir: Susan Kerner
Blithe Spirit, Noel Coward; dir: Ken Jenkins
Desire under the Elms, Eugene O'Neill; dir: Gregory S. Hurst
Mass Appeal, Bill C. Davis; dir: Pamela K. Pepper

DESIGNERS

Sets: Dagmar Bardo, Ursula Belden, Curtis Dretsch, David Potts, Raymond C. Recht, William Schroder, Robert Thayer, Kevin Wiley, Paul Wonsek.
Costumes: Mary-Anne Aston, Bernard Johnson, Thomas Keller, Colleen Muscha, Elizabeth P. Palmer, David Toser, Kenneth M. Yount.
Lights: Betsy Adams, Dagmar Bardo, Sid Bennett, Curtis Dretsch, Mark Hendren, Todd Lichtenstein.

Pennsylvania Stage Company. Shelley Hack and Fritz Sperberg in Born Yesterday. *Photo: Gregory M. Fota.*

The People's Light and Theatre Company

DANNY S. FRUCHTER
Producing Director

SUSAN MEDAK
Managing Director

MARY E. VAN RODEN
Board President

39 Conestoga Road
Malvern, PA 19355
(215) 647-1900 (business)
(215) 644-3500 (box office)

FOUNDED 1974
Danny S. Fruchter, Margaret E. Fruchter, Richard L. Keeler, Ken Marini

SEASON
March-January

SCHEDULE

Evenings
Tuesday-Sunday

Matinees
Sunday, Wednesday

FACILITIES

Mainstage
Seating capacity: 400
Stage: flexible

Second Stage
Seating capacity: 80
Stage: modified thrust

FINANCES
February 1, 1982-January 31, 1983
$669,000 operating expenses
$442,000 earned income
$239,000 grants/contributions

AUDIENCE
Annual attendance: 90,000
Subscribers: 6,800

TOURING CONTACT
Susan Medak

AEA letter of agreement

The central idea governing all activities at The People's Light and Theatre Company, and anchoring the spirit of its endeavors, is not new. Simply put—it is the hope that the world will have been enriched by the theatre's presence. Through theatre art, the company attempts to serve.

People's Light is dedicated to encouraging theatre craftsmen and audiences to think and care deeply about the process of art and its service to society. It produces plays to engage and entertain audiences by stimulating laughter from the heart and soul and by exploring feelings previously untapped. Most important, it hopes to encourage imaginative thought leading to positive actions which will change its community for the better.

As theatre workers, People's Light company members understand that good theatre is essentially an heroic act, and that they must be prepared to fly in the face of public acceptance; the "every man for himself" syndrome which afflicts American life cannot apply. The aim is to examine — not escape from—reality: to "hold the mirror up to nature."

In addition to serving its audience, its community and the company itself, People's Light hopes to serve future generations by acting as a repository for a wide range of individual visions sustained within a nurturing and protective environment. In order to achieve its artistic goals, a company of artists and support staff committed to those goals is maintained and provided with the security that comes from continuous employment and positive working conditions.

Additionally, People's Light attempts to reach out to non-traditional audiences and support new work, as well as aspiring to present a classical and contemporary repertoire at the highest professional level.

Programs and services

Summerstage acting and improvisation workshops; prison tour; professional and non-professional acting classes; programs-in-schools; children's theatre; internships; newsletter.

PRODUCTIONS 1981-82

Arms and the Man, George Bernard Shaw; dir: Louis Lippa
Rear Column, Simon Gray; dir: John Loven
The Sea Horse, Edward Moore; dir: John Loven
Julius Caesar, William Shakespeare; dir: Danny S. Fruchter
Tartuffe, Molière; trans: Richard Wilbur; dir: Joseph Leonardo
A Lesson from Aloes, Athol Fugard; dir: Charles Conwell
2nd Annual New Play Festival:
   The Subject Animal, Larry Atlas; dir: Pamela Berlin
   In the Garden of Eden, Shirley Lauro; dir: Louis Lippa
   Cemetary Man and *Rupert's Birthday*, Ken Jenkins; dir: Ken Jenkins
   Tallahassee, Michael Morin; dir: Susan Gregg
   American Garage, Peter Maloney; dir: Ernie Schier
   Romance, Charles Leipart; dir: Michael Nash
   Delusions of a Government Witness, Louis Lippa; dir: Louis Lippa
   The Interrogation, Murphy Guyer; dir: Michael Nash
   Lunchbreak, Robert Schenkkan; dir: Steven D. Albrezzi
   The Groves of Academe, Mark Stein; dir: Robert Hall
   Precious Blood, Frank South; dir: Murphy Guyer

PRODUCTIONS 1982-83

Talking With, Jane Martin, dir: Steven D. Albrezzi
The Proprietor, Louis Lippa; dir: John Loven
The Marriage Proposal, Anton Chekhov; dir: Louis Lippa
The Interlude, George Bernard Shaw; dir: Mary Brion
The Wind in the Willows, Kenneth Grahame; adapt: Abigail Adams; dir: Abigail Adams
The Importance of Being Earnest, Oscar Wilde; dir: Abigail Adams
3rd Annual New Play Festival:
   The Southgate Porter, Louis Lippa; dir: Michael Nash
   The Survivalist, Robert Schenkkan; dir: Peter DeLaurier
   The Value of Names, Jeffrey Sweet; dir: Danny S. Fruchter
   Closing Notice, Judy Engles; dir: Louis Lippa

Periwinkle Productions

Welfare Lady, Louis Lippa; dir: Pamela Berlin
Elmo and June Confront Concepts Much Larger Than Themselves, Paul A. Barrosse; dir: Paul Hastings
Powder, Judy Engles; dir: Murphy Guyer
The Dream Home, Mark Stein; dir: Thomas Gruenewald
The Habitual Acceptance of the Near Enough, Kent Broadhurst; dir: John Loven
Stories, Murphy Guyer; dir: Thomas Gruenewald
Malvey, Michael Jerrold; dir: Eric Forsythe

DESIGNERS
Sets: Norman B. Dodge, Jr., Elizabeth Fisher, James F. Pyne, Jr., Eric Schaeffer, Robert Smythe, Michael Zajchowski.
Costumes: Susan Dimsmore, Megan Fruchter, Lisa Hemphill-Burns, Colleen Muscha, Susan Pratt.
Lights: Norman B. Dodge, Jr., Richard Keeler, James F. Pyne, Jr., Joseph Ragey, Adrienne Reimer, Robert Smythe.

SUNNA RASCH
Artistic Director/Producer/Board President

CATHY FARRIS
Business Manager

19 Clinton Ave.
Monticello, NY 12701
(914) 794-1666 (business)
(914) 794-4992 (box office)

FOUNDED 1963
Sunna Rasch

SEASON
Year-round

FINANCES
August 1, 1982–July 31, 1983
$100,000 operating expenses
$ 77,000 earned income
$ 20,000 grants/contributions

AUDIENCE
Annual attendance: 115,800

TOURING CONTACT
Sunna Rasch

The People's Light and Theatre Company. Douglas Wing, Karen McLaughlin and Peter Johnson in The Importance of Being Earnest. *Photo: Alan Tepper.*

Periwinkle Productions is committed to presenting theatre to young audiences which simultaneously opens up feelings, expands understanding and motivates imagination and creativity. The tangible effects of this are multitudinous, and are expressed in the many letters from young people who have been moved to write a poem or express an idea after having had a Periwinkle experience.

Hallmarks of a Periwinkle production are its original script, simplified sets and the freshness and spontaneity of its actors. In 1978, Periwinkle received the American Theatre Association's Jennie Heiden Award for Excellence.

Periwinkle programs are created for various age levels, from primary through senior high. A common theme is self-discovery, as in *The Magic Word,* where two children explore their own creativity in trying to make a somber father smile; or *Halfway There,* concerning teenage drug and alcohol addiction. Other scripts deal with fear of failure, the basic nature of people, appreciation of our

Periwinkle Productions: Halfway There. *Photo: Diana Mara Henry.*

heritage and liberties, and the feeling of alienation.

In production, emphasis is placed both on artistic and entertainment values — this is foremost. Simultaneously, however, Periwinkle believes its plays must convey an underlying thread of values.

Periwinkle does extensive in-school touring, accompanied by study guides and follow-up workshops. It also presents some public and weekend performances, hoping that adults in the audience will enjoy the shows as much as the children.

The theatre also strives to develop new playwrights: in 1983, a teenager, Lynnette Serrano (a winner of the 1982 Young Playwrights Festival in New York) collaborated with the Periwinkle team to write *Halfway There.*

Periwinkle seeks continually to build new audiences—among youth—for the arts. To this end, it now performs before youth groups, drug rehabilitation centers and reform schools in addition to its regular school, park and community audiences.

Programs and services

Programs-in-schools; workshops; management internships; study guides.

PRODUCTIONS 1981-82

America, Yes!, Sunna Rasch; dir: Dennis McGovern
The Magic Word, Sunna Rasch; music: Scott Laughead; dir: Bill Wesbrooks
Woolen Sox, Wil Robertson; dir: Wil Robertson
Elastic, James Greenberg and Peter Ford; dir: Sunna Rasch

PRODUCTIONS 1982-83

Halfway There, Lynnette Serrano; music: Ken Laufer and Ed Kershen; dir: Jack Sims
America, Yes!
The Storytellers, Everett Hoag and Sunna Rasch; dir: Everett Hoag
Extravaganza, Everett Hoag; dir: Everett Hoag
The Magic Word

DESIGNERS

Costumes: Everett Hoag, Marcie Miller, Susan Scherer.

Philadelphia Drama Guild

GREGORY POGGI
Artistic/Managing Director

DANIEL PROMISLO
Board Chairman

220 South 16th St.
Philadelphia, PA 19102
(215) 546-6789 (business)
(215) 898-6791 (box office)

FOUNDED 1956
Sidney S. Bloom

SEASON
October-May

SCHEDULE

Evenings
Tuesday-Sunday

Matinees
Wednesday, Saturday

FACILITIES
3680 Walnut St.

Zellerbach Theatre
Seating capacity: 944
Stage: thrust

Studio Theatre
Seating capacity: 120
Stage: proscenium

FINANCES
June 1, 1982-May 30, 1983
$1,363,000 operating expenses
$ 909,000 earned income
$ 514,000 grants/contributions

AUDIENCE
Annual attendance: 96,017
Subscribers: 14,467

AEA LORT (B) contract

The Philadelphia Drama Guild, the major resident company in a tri-state area, is dedicated to being a theatre of involvement. It consistently challenges, stimulates and involves its audiences in both the process and the end results of theatre.

Since his arrival in 1979, artistic/managing director Gregory Poggi has led the Guild in this new direction. (Founded in 1956 as an amateur group, the Drama Guild evolved

Philadelphia Drama Guild. Patricia Elliott, Dwight Schultz and Valerie Mahaffey in The Keeper. *Photo: Kenneth Kauffman.*

by 1971 into a professional company, emphasizing a traditional repertoire of British and modern European theatre.)

Plays are selected based on their authors' authentic and immediate voices. They center on powerful emotional, social and personal concerns. Relationships, family conflicts, the individual's responses to alienation in his society — urgent issues in today's world dominated by technology and mass media—are reflected in the Guild's five-play mainstage season.

Striving to include works by playwrights who might not otherwise be professionally produced in the area, the Guild challenges audiences and encourages an understanding of their own roles in the larger social framework. Under Poggi's leadership, the Guild accomplishes its goals by focusing on classic American plays, new plays, playwrights new to the area and "rediscovered" works.

Recognizing its responsibility to offer an environment that nurtures the collaborative process, the Drama Guild is steadily building its own group of artists who work there on a continuing basis, regarding it as their creative home.

Programs and services

Playwrights' Project staged readings and discussions; educational and community outreach; publications.

PRODUCTIONS 1981-82

Of Mice and Men, John Steinbeck; dir: Kurt Reis
Gemini, Albert Innaurato; dir: Jerry Zaks
Dear Daddy, Denis Cannan; dir: William Woodman
Servant of Two Masters, Carlo Goldoni; adapt: Tom Cone; dir: Andre Ernotte
The Contest, Shirley Lauro; dir: Jerry Zaks

PRODUCTIONS 1982-83

The Keeper, Karolyn Nelke; dir: Steven Schachter
The Diary of Anne Frank, Frances Goodrich and Albert Hackett; dir: William Woodman
Talley's Folly, Lanford Wilson; dir: Charles I. Karchmer
Daughters, John Morgan Evans; dir: Tony Giordano
All My Sons, Arthur Miller; dir: William Woodman

DESIGNERS

Sets: John Conklin, Eldon Elder, John Falabella, John Jensen, Roger Mooney, Christopher Nowak, Karen Schulz, Patricia Woodbridge.
Costumes: Patricia Adshead, Frankie Fehr, Linda Fisher, Jess Goldstein, David Murin, John David Ridge, Ernest Allen Smith, Susan Tsu, Jennifer von Mayrhauser.
Lights: William Armstrong, Pat Collins, F. Mitchell Dana, Dennis Parichy, Jane Reisman, Ann Wrightson.

Pittsburgh Public Theater

LARRY ARRICK
Artistic Director

DENNIS A. BABCOCK
Managing Director

RICHARD K. MEANS
Board President

Suite G-100
One Allegheny Sq.
Pittsburgh, PA 15212
(412) 323-8200 (business)
(412) 321-9800 (box office)

FOUNDED 1975
Joan Apt, Margaret Rieck, Ben Shaktman

SEASON
Mainstage
September-June

Summer program
July-August

SCHEDULE
Evenings
Tuesday-Sunday

Matinees
Saturday, Sunday, alternate Thursday

FACILITIES
One Allegheny Sq.
Seating capacity: 428
Stage: arena

FINANCES
September 1, 1982-August 31, 1983
$2,332,000 operating expenses
$1,423,000 earned income
$ 910,000 grants/contributions

AUDIENCE
Annual attendance: 127,758
Subscribers: 13,568

BOOKED-IN EVENTS
Theatre, special events

AEA LORT (C) contract

The 1982-83 season was one of change, innovation and continued growth for the Pittsburgh Public Theater. Critical and audience response to the first season under the joint leadership of Larry Arrick and Dennis A. Babcock was enthusiastic; subscriptions reflected a 5.8 percent increase and single ticket sales were up by 6.9 percent.

Arrick's concept of "exploding the space" was implemented by turning the Public's entire three-tiered arena theatre into a barn for *Tom Jones,* which opened the eighth season. That production also marked the introduction of a flexible seating design that made 2,500 additional seats available during each show's run. Later in the season, *Quilters* became the second-most highly attended play in PPT history, and the first mainstage production to be revived by popular demand. Another recent innovation was a series of original lobby displays created to complement the on-stage designs.

The 1982-83 season also saw the expansion of special-event and summer programming, as The Flying Karamazov Brothers presented their Broadway-bound show for a two-week run. Other summer special events included William Windom as *Thurber,* the comedy team Monteith and Rand and Avner the Eccentric.

Since its inception in 1975, Pittsburgh Public Theater has developed from a three-play, three-month season to a six-play, year-round operation. Subscriptions have doubled and the budget has grown from $390,000 to more than $2 million. The Public recieves support from 104 corporations and foundations, 2,800 individual contributors and all major national, state, county and city agencies.

Programs and services

Internships; training; technical assistance; student, handicapped and senior citizen performances; programs-in-schools.

Note: During the 1981-82 season, Ben Shaktman served as general director/ artistic director.

PRODUCTIONS 1981-82

Betrayal, Harold Pinter; dir: Larry Arrick
Juno and the Paycock, Sean O'Casey; dir: Larry Arrick
Tintypes, music and lyrics: various; adapt: Mary Kyte, Mel Marvin and Gary Pearle; dir: Judith Haskell
Home, Samm-Art Williams; dir: Woodie King, Jr.
Tartuffe, Molière; trans: Richard Wilbur; dir: Larry Arrick
A Midsummer Night's Dream, William Shakespeare; dir: Stephen Kanee

PRODUCTIONS 1982-83

Tom Jones, adapt: Larry Arrick, from Henry Fielding; music and lyrics: Barbara Damashek; dir: Larry Arrick
A Streetcar Named Desire, Tennessee Williams; dir: Larry Arrick
Quilters, Molly Newman and Barbara Damashek; music and lyrics: Barbara Damashek; dir: Barbara Damashek
Alms for the Middle Class, Stuart Hample: dir: Larry Arrick
Who's Afraid of Virginia Woolf?, Edward Albee; dir: Larry Arrick
The Price, Arthur Miller; dir: Gene Lesser

DESIGNERS

Sets: Jonathan Arkin, Ursula Belden, John Jensen, Thomas A. Walsh.
Costumes: Jess Goldstein, Flozanne A. John, Elizabeth P. Palmer, William Schroder, Rebecca Senske, David Toser.
Lights: Kristine Bick, Allen Lee Hughes, Robert Jared, Dennis Parichy, Ron Wallace.

Pittsburgh Public Theater. Derek Meader, Cynthia Strickland, Myrna Paris, Don Howard and Anne Kerry in Tom Jones. *Photo: Chuck Fuhrer.*

Playhouse on the Square

JACKIE NICHOLS
Executive Director

SAN STARK
Administrative Director

GENE KATZ
Board President

2121 Madison Ave.
Memphis, TN 38104
(901) 725-0776 (business)
(901) 726-4656 (box office)

FOUNDED 1968
Jackie Nichols

SEASON
Year-round

SCHEDULE

Evenings
Wednesday-Friday

Matinees
Wednesday

FACILITIES

Playhouse on the Square
Seating capacity: 200
Stage: thrust

Circuit Playhouse
1705 Poplar Ave.
Seating capacity: 150
Stage: proscenium

FINANCES
July 1, 1981-June 30, 1982
$257,000 operating expenses
$179,000 earned income
$ 72,000 grants/contributions

AUDIENCE
Annual attendance: 45,000
Subscribers: 1,600

Playhouse on the Square is committed to providing a training ground for developing actors and technicians in a resident company environment. Company members and interns have an opportunity to work in a permanent situation over a year or more, assuming a range of acting assignments which vary widely in style and role size. A pragmatic view of the theatre as a business is presented while providing the artist flexibility within a realistic budget.

The development of new work or new approaches to traditional material is encouraged, and directors and designers are provided as much artistic freedom as is possible. Playhouse on the Square — along with its umbrella organization Circuit Playhouse, Inc. — maintains a deaf theatre company known as A Show of Hands, which tours the Southeast. A Show of Hands also works with Playhouse staff and company members to develop sign communication as a means of artistic expression.

Several environmental theatre events staged by the Playhouse have helped it reach out to its community. These include a production of Lanford Wilson's *Hot l Baltimore* staged in a local hotel lobby; Aristophanes' *The Frogs* presented in an outdoor swimming pool atop a motor inn; *The Rocky Horror Show* at an old movie house; and *Joseph and the Amazing Technicolor Dreamcoat* in a downtown church.

Programs and services

Internships; deaf theatre workshops and performances.

PRODUCTIONS 1981-82

Tribute, Bernard Slade; dir: Breton Frazier
Arsenic and Old Lace, Joseph Kesselring; dir: Brad Ford
God Bless You, Mr. Rosewater, book adapt and lyrics: Howard Ashman, from Kurt Vonnegut; music: Alan Menken; dir: Ron Wachholtz

PlayMakers Repertory Company

Frankenstein, adapt: Tim Kelly, from Mary Shelley; dir: Ron Wachholtz
Comedy of Errors, William Shakespeare; dir: Brad Ford
Little Foxes, Lillian Hellman; dir: Ron Wachholtz
Fiddler on the Roof, book: Joseph Stein; music: Jerry Bock; lyrics: Sheldon Harnick; dir: Ron Wachholtz
The Fantasticks, book and lyrics: Tom Jones; music: Harvey Schmidt; dir: Ron Wachholtz
Jacques Brel Is Alive and Well and Living in Paris, adapt: Eric Blau and Mort Suman; music and lyrics: Jacques Brel; dir: Mel Shrawder

PRODUCTIONS 1982-83

Arts & Leisure, Randy Hall; dir: Ron Wachholtz
Chicago, book: Fred Ebb and Bob Fosse; music: John Kander; lyrics: Fred Ebb; dir: Barry Fuller
To Kill a Mockingbird, adapt: Cathey Sawyer, from Harper Lee; dir: Cathey Sawyer
Cabaret, book: Joe Masteroff; music: John Kander; lyrics: Fred Ebb; dir: Marc Martinez
The Lion in Winter, James Goldman; dir: Ron Wachholtz
The Elephant Man, Bernard Pomerance; dir: Cathey Sawyer
Mister Roberts, Thomas Heggen and Joshua Logan; dir: Cathey Sawyer
1776, book: Peter Stone; music and lyrics: Sherman Edwards; dir: Ron Wachholtz

DESIGNERS

Sets: Brad Ford, Jeff Robin Modereger, Jackie Nichols, Steve Pair, Noel Rennerfeldt, Russell Smith, Craig Spain, Ron Wachholtz.
Costumes: David Jilg, Becky Wachholtz.
Lights: David Brewer, Richard Crowell, Brad Ford, Stephen Forsyth.

Playhouse on the Square. Jean Jackson and Betty May Collins in Arsenic and Old Lace. *Photo: Saul Brown.*

MILLY S. BARRANGER
Executive Producer

GREGORY BOYD
Artistic Director

ROBERT W. TOLAN
Producing Director

203 Graham Memorial 052-A
University of North Carolina
Chapel Hill, NC 27514
(919) 962-1122 (business)
(919) 962-1121 (box office)

FOUNDED 1976
Arthur L. Houseman

SEASON
September-April

SCHEDULE
Evenings
Tuesday-Sunday

Matinees
Sunday

FACILITIES
PlayMakers Theatre
Seating capacity: 285
Stage: proscenium

Paul Green Theatre
Seating capacity: 505
Stage: thrust

PlayMakers Repertory Company. Sharon Lawrence, Henry Hoffman and Michael Cumpsty in The Greeks. *Photo: Michal Louden.*

FINANCES
July 1, 1982-June 30, 1983
$514,000 operating expenses
$165,000 earned income
$351,000 grants/contributions

AUDIENCE
Annual attendance: 39,300
Subscribers: 3,902

AEA LORT (D) contract

PlayMakers Repertory Company is a permanent company of artists and administrators committed to bringing the highest level of artistic achievement to its state and region. To accomplish this, the company of professional directors, actors, designers and playwrights is brought together with journeyman actors, costumers and technicians to produce a season with a distinctive production style.

The resident company is also augmented by a distinguished group of associates in directing and design. These associates have a long-term commitment to the company, although they fulfill other professional commitments elsewhere, and are the company's link to the rest of the theatre community, both conveying the ideas of PlayMakers to other theatres and bringing the influence of their work in other places to PlayMakers.

The season is selected by a directorate composed of the executive producer, artistic director and producing director, in consultation with the associate artists. The repertoire is informed by the company's desire to bring before audiences: a) significant re-interpretations of classic and modern plays; b) new plays by resident playwrights; and c) new materials created for the stage — especially the adaptation of regional non-dramatic literature.

PlayMakers' goal of maintaining a professional company is aided by the highly selective Professional Theatre Training Program of the University of North Carolina at Chapel Hill, which offers unparalleled opportunities for interaction between professionals and students preparing for Master of Fine Arts degrees.

The 1983-84 season marks a new era in PlayMakers' development as North Carolina's only full-time resident professional company. Under new leadership, the theatre will launch PlayFest '84, a spring festival of "comedy with a British accent," featuring the premiere of a new musical.

Programs and services

Professional training program; internships; student matinee series; student and senior citizen discounts; post-performance discussions; PlayMaking newsletter; volunteer auxiliary; staged readings; playwright-in-residence; new play development program.

Note: During the 1981-82 and 1982-83 season, David Rotenberg served as artistic director.

PRODUCTIONS 1981-82

The Front Page, Ben Hecht and Charles MacArthur; dir: David Rotenberg
Betrayal, Harold Pinter; dir: David Rotenberg
The Glass Menagerie, Tennessee Williams; dir: Gregory Boyd
Angel Street, Patrick Hamilton; dir: Gregory Boyd
Mobile Hymn, Robert Litz; dir: David Rotenberg
Twelfth Night, William Shakespeare; dir: David Rotenberg

PRODUCTIONS 1982-83

Life on the Mississippi, book, music and lyrics: Bland Simpson and Tommy Thompson; dir: David Rotenberg
A Moon for the Misbegotten, Eugene O'Neill; dir: Gregory Boyd
The Greeks, adapt: Kenneth Cavander and John Barton; dir: Gregory Boyd and David Rotenberg
Pygmalion, George Bernard Shaw; dir: Gregory Boyd

DESIGNERS

Sets: Norman Coates, David M. Glenn, Peter David Gould, Linwood Taylor.
Costumes: Laurel Clayson, Bobbi Owen, Suzanne Y. Wilkins.
Lights: Norman Coates.

The Playwrights' Center

LEE BLESSING, CINDY COOPER, BARBARA FIELD, JOHN OLIVE
Artistic Directorate

JOHN H. POTTER
Business Manager

ARCHIBALD I. LEYASMEYER
Board President

2301 Franklin Ave. East
Minneapolis, MN 55406
(612) 332-7481

FOUNDED 1971
Gregg Almquist, Erik Brogger, Barbara Field, Charles Nolte

SEASON
Year-round

SCHEDULE
Evenings
Monday

FACILITIES
Seating capacity: 150
Stage: flexible

FINANCES
July 1, 1982-June 30, 1983
$392,000 operating expenses
$ 88,000 earned income
$268,000 grants/contributions

AUDIENCE
Annual attendance: 80,000

TOURING CONTACT
John H. Potter

BOOKED-IN EVENTS
Theatre, music, dance

AEA letter of agreement

Starting with a $2,000 annual budget in 1971, The Minnesota Playwriting Laboratory began by presenting readings and productions in a variety of local theatres and coffeehouses. In 1975, the organization was renamed The Playwrights' Lab and was awarded a major grant from the Jerome Foundation which was designed to provide direct and much needed financial aid to playwrights. This playwrights-in-residence program has become the cornerstone of the Lab's activities.

In 1978, because the demands of play production badly strained the resources of the small staff — and because the smaller local theatres (inspired by the Lab) had begun producing new plays — the decision was made to stop producing and focus on intensive developmental readings and workshops. The Lab would function as a liaison between playwrights and theatres, but would not itself produce new plays. Soon after this decision was made, plays developed at the Lab began to attract the attention of professionals both in the U.S. and abroad. In 1980 another change occurred: The Playwrights' Center was formed, providing an umbrella structure for the organization's component programs: The Playwrights' Lab, The Midwest Playwrights' Program and Storytalers touring company.

The Playwrights' Lab awards stipends ranging from $3,000 to $10,000 to nine playwrights annually as well as supporting intern, apprentice and associate playwright-in-residence programs. The Lab offers cold readings, workshops, staged readings, discussions and critiques with a company of professional actors, directors, dramaturgs and playwrights. Exchange programs, script referrals, script critiques, job and contest listings and grant information are available. The Lab also maintains working relationships with theatres across the country: several hundred theatres periodically request script information.

The Midwest Playwrights' Program was established in 1976 by noted playwright Dale Wasserman, and exists to provide a creative atmosphere and a pragmatic approach to playwriting. Ten playwrights from the upper midwest are selected annually to participate in this two-week intensive workshop.

The oldest touring theatre company in Minnesota, Storytalers specializes in audience participation plays and workshops for children and families, particularly original works and adaptations.

Programs and services

The Playwrights' Lab; Midwest Playwrights' Program; Storytalers touring company; nonprofessional classes; internships; student performances; programs-in-schools; study materials; free ticket distribution; post-performance discussions; cold and staged readings; workshops; children's theatre; newsletter; speaker's bureau; theatre rental; script critiques; script library.

Note: During the 1981-82 season Christopher D. Kirkland served as artistic director.

PRODUCTIONS 1981-83

Seasons strictly devoted to staged readings, non-performance workshops and touring.

The Playwrights' Center. Robert Falls, Henry Strozier and Susan Petri in rehearsal for Phillip and Felicity.

Playwrights Horizons

ANDRE BISHOP
Artistic Director

PAUL S. DANIELS
Managing Director

ANN G. WILDER
Board Chairman

416 West 42nd St.
New York, NY 10036
(212) 564-1235 (business)
(212) 279-4200 (box office)

FOUNDED 1971
Robert Moss

SEASON
Year-round

SCHEDULE
Evenings
Tuesday-Sunday

Matinees
Sunday

FACILITIES
Mainstage
Seating capacity: 150
Stage: proscenium

Studio
Seating capacity: 74
Stage: flexible

FINANCES
September 1, 1982-August 31, 1983
$3,500,000 operating expenses
$2,500,000 earned income
$1,000,000 grants/contributions

AUDIENCE
Annual attendance: 170,000
Subscribers: 2,900

AEA Off Broadway and Mini contracts

Playwrights Horizons, celebrating its second decade, continues to be dedicated to the support and development of American playwrights, composers and lyricists, and to the production of their work. Through readings, concerts, workshops and full-scale productions, the theatre offers its writers a professional facility in which to grow. A young and energetic staff provides them with an atmosphere of warmth, enthusiasm and personal attention.

Playwrights Horizons is a *writer's* theatre, and in that sense is very different from just a theatre that produces a season of new plays. It has nine resident playwrights who occupy, though not exclusively, the focus of its attention. These writers — Christopher Durang, William Finn, A.R. Gurney, Jr., Albert Innaurato, James Lapine, Peter Parnell, Jonathan Reynolds, Ted Tally, Wendy Wasserstein — serve as the theatre's artistic board, define its sensibility and style, and participate in an extensive commissioning program.

In its two performance spaces on West 42nd Street, Playwrights has been a pioneer in the redevelopment that has transformed a block of "porno parlors" into a thriving string of Off Broadway theatres known as Theatre Row. It has produced more than 200 new plays and musicals, and its notable successes include *Kennedy's Children, Vanities, Gemini, Say Goodnight Gracie, Table Settings, Coming Attractions, March of the Falsettos, Sister Mary Ignatius Explains It All for You, The Dining Room, Geniuses* and the recent criti-

cally acclaimed revival of *The Transfiguration of Benno Blimpie*. Playwrights Horizons has won the Obie, Drama Desk and Outer Critics Circle Awards, and was the recipient of the 1983 Margo Jones Award.

Programs and services

Readings; internships; musical theatre cabaret series.

Playwrights Horizons. Kurt Knudson, Christine Ebersole, David Rasche and Peter Evans in Geniuses.

PRODUCTIONS 1981-82

Sister Mary Ignatius Explains It All for You, and *The Actor's Nightmare,* Christopher Durang; dir: Jerry Zaks
Kudzu, Jane Chambers; dir: Sloane Shelton
The Dining Room, A.R. Gurney, Jr.; dir: David Trainer
Sleeparound Town, Sarah Kernochan; dir: Thomas Hulce
Geniuses, Jonathan Reynolds; dir: Gerald Gutierrez
Herself As Lust, Albert Innaurato; dir: Albert Innaurato
Herringbone, book: Tom Cone; music: Skip Kennon; lyrics: Ellen Fitzhugh; dir: Ben Levit

PRODUCTIONS 1982-83

The Rise and Rise of Daniel Rocket, Peter Parnell; dir: Gerald Gutierrez
Buck, Ronald Ribman; dir: Elinor Renfield
America Kicks Up Its Heels, book: Charles Rubin; music and lyrics: William Finn; dir: Mary Kyte and Ben Levit
The Transfiguration of Benno Blimpie, Albert Innaurato; dir: Albert Innaurato
Christmas on Mars, Harry Kondoleon; dir: Andre Ernotte
That's All, Folks!, Mark O'Donnell; dir: Douglas Hughes
Sunday in the Park with George, book: James Lapine; music and lyrics: Stephen Sondheim; dir: James Lapine

DESIGNERS

Sets: John Arnone, Jeffrey Beecroft, Andrew Jackness, Santo Loquasto, Thomas Lynch, Leon Munier, Christopher Nowak, Loren Sherman, Karen Schulz, Douglas Stein, Tony Straiges.
Costumes: Ann Emonts, Ann Hould-Ward, William Ivey Long, Karen Matthews, Rita Ryack, Santo Loquasto, Darrell Thompson, Debra Shaw, David Woolard, Patricia Ziprodt.
Lights: Frances Aronson, Rachel Budin, Paul Gallo, John Gisondi, James F. Ingalls, Richard Nelson, Loren Sherman, David N. Weiss, Anne Wrightson.

Portland Stage Company

BARBARA ROSOFF
Artistic Director

PATRICIA EGAN
Managing Director

JOSIAH H. DRUMMOND, JR.
Board President

Box 1458
Portland, ME 04104
(207) 774-1043 (business)
(207) 774-0465 (box office)

FOUNDED 1974
Ted Davis

SEASON
October-April

SCHEDULE
Evenings
Tuesday-Sunday

Matinees
Thursday, Saturday, Sunday

FACILITIES
Portland Performing Arts Center
25A Forest Ave.
Seating capacity: 289
Stage: proscenium

FINANCES
June 1, 1982-May 31, 1983
$353,000 operating expenses
$221,000 earned income
$125,000 grants/contributions

AUDIENCE
Annual attendance: 25,000
Subscribers: 2,340

BOOKED-IN EVENTS
Theatre, music, dance

AEA letter of agreement

Portland Stage Company entered its 10th anniversary season with a move to a new 289-seat facility at the Portland Performing Arts Center, reflecting the company's growth and Portland's commitment to a wide range of professional performing arts.

Under Barbara Rosoff's artistic leadership since August 1981, the company has solidi-

Paul Walker, Robert Burns and Etain O'Malley in Ecco! *Photo: Dean Abramson.*

fied its commitment to the development and production of new American plays as the focus of a balanced program which also includes classic and contemporary work of relevance and merit. Two world premieres were produced in the 1981-82 season: *Alterations* by Leigh Curran and *The Death of A Miner* by Paula Cizmar (co-produced with the Women's Project of the American Place Theatre in New York), affirming this commitment to American writers. In recognition, the company was selected as one of the five theatres to participate in the first annual FDG/CBS New Plays Program. *Ecco!* by Gerry Bamman was selected for production as part of this program, and was further recognized as the recipient of the FDG/CBS National Residency Award which commends the collaboration of a playwright and a theatre.

In addition to offering playwrights, actors, directors and designers an environment in which to explore the best of themselves, Portland Stage Company is deeply committed to the growth of its audience through challenging programming and an increasing number of educational outreach projects. The move to a new home will allow for the company's economic growth, will provide improved facilities for administrators, artists and technicians, and will be the springboard for its further evolution in scope and in its impact on the lives of the people of Maine.

Programs and services

Artists-in-residence; Lunchtime Lecture Previews; Curtain Call Discussions; school matinees; internships; new play readings.

PRODUCTIONS 1981-82

The Glass Menagerie, Tennessee Williams; dir: Patricia Carmichael
Alterations, Leigh Curran; dir: Barbara Rosoff
Private Lives, Noel Coward; dir: Edward Herrmann
The Sea Horse, Edward J. Moore; dir: Gordon Edelstein
The Death of a Miner, Paula Cizmar; dir: Barbara Rosoff

PRODUCTIONS 1982-83

Getting Out, Marsha Norman; dir: Barbara Rosoff
The Dining Room, A.R. Gurney, Jr.; dir: Lynn Polan
Gardenia, John Guare; dir: Barbara Rosoff
A Lesson from Aloes, Athol Fugard; dir: Arden Fingerhut
How I Got That Story, Amlin Gray; dir: Louis Rackoff
Ecco!, Gerry Bamman; dir: Barbara Rosoff

DESIGNERS

Sets: John Doepp, Marjorie Bradley Kellogg, Leslie Taylor, Patricia Woodbridge.
Costumes: Marie Anne Chiment, Heidi Hollman, Rachel Kurland, Ellen McCartney, Eren Ozker, Leslie Taylor, Robert Wojewodski.
Lights: John Doepp, Arden Fingerhut, Dale Jordan, Greg Marriner, Ann Wrightson.

Puerto Rican Traveling Theatre Company

MIRIAM COLON EDGAR
Executive Director

ALBERTO CABALLERO
Board Chairman

141 West 94th St.
New York, NY 10025
(212) 354-1293

FOUNDED 1967
Miriam Colon Edgar, George Edgar

SEASON
January-June

SCHEDULE

Evenings
Wednesday-Sunday

Matinees
Saturday, Sunday

FACILITIES
304 West 47th St.
Seating capacity: 196
Stage: proscenium

FINANCES
October 1, 1981-September 30, 1982
$455,000 operating expenses
$ 75,000 earned income
$311,000 grants/contributions

AUDIENCE
Annual attendance: 18,449
Subscribers: 614

TOURING CONTACT
Sonia Pomales

BOOKED-IN EVENTS
Music, dance, poetry

AEA letter of agreement

Since the Puerto Rican Traveling Theatre was inaugurated 16 years ago, its guiding philosophy has been that it be a vehicle for bringing artistic ventures to the financially depressed areas where millions of taxpayers are deprived of the benefit of the cultural dollar. This is consistent with the company's efforts to train youths who, because of financial difficulties, have no access to professional commercial schools. These ideals will continue to inform the theatre's endeavors.

The free-of-charge Playwrights Unit, founded in 1977, consists of both a beginning and an advanced division; its purpose is to guide a play from early drafts to a final version, within a constructive, supportive atmosphere. While people of all backgrounds are welcome and enrolled, the Unit's main purpose has been the development of Hispanic playwrights.

The 1983 Training Unit for Youngsters consisted of more than 250 students who took classes in speech and acting (offered in both English and Spanish), music theory, chorus, afro-caribbean jazz, modern dance, movement and collective writing, in addition to participating in workshops on auditioning. The purpose of these free classes is to offer the theatre as a career alternative.

PRTT's mainstage season strives to present the best professional design and direction at work to serve outstanding examples of Hispanic literature, using the finest His-

Puerto Rican Traveling Theatre Company. Ilka Tanya Payan, Hugo Halbrich and George Bass in Inquisition. *Photo: Peter Krupenye.*

Repertorio Español

panic actors. This season marks the 17th year of the Touring Unit, whose annual tour reaffirms the theatre's commitment to its constituency and its original purpose: to bring the best of Hispanic culture to the people, wherever they live.

Programs and services

Training Unit for young people and playwrights; touring; staged readings; internships.

PRODUCTIONS 1982

The Man and the Fly, Jose Ruibal; trans: Gregory Rabassa; dir: Jack Gelber
She, That One, He and the Other, Jacobo Morales; trans: Manuel Power Viscasillas; dir: Alba Oms
Paper Flowers, Egon Wolff; trans: Margaret Peden; dir: Victoria Espinosa
The Love of Don Perlimplin and Belisa in the Garden, Federico Garcia Lorca; trans: James Graham Lujan and Richard L. O'Connell; dir: Victoria Espinosa
The Story of Don Cristobal, Federico Garcia Lorca; trans: William I. Oliver; dir: Victoria Espinosa

PRODUCTIONS 1983

Inquisition, Fernando Arrabal; trans: Gregory Rabassa; dir: Angel Berenguer
The Great Confession, Sergio de Cecco and Armando Chulak; trans: Pilar Zalamea; dir: Max Ferrá
The Oxcart, Rene Marques; trans: Charles Pilditch; dir: Roberto Rodriquez Suarez
Marine Tiger, Estrella Artau; dir: Alba Oms

DESIGNERS

Sets: John Berger, Reagan Cook, Gary English, Andrew Jackness, Loren Sherman, Christopher Stapleton, Christina Weppner.
Costumes: Carmen Chirino, Maria Contessa, Efraim Malave, Deborah Shaw, Nancy Thun.
Lights: Gary D. Cooper, Jeffrey Schissler, John Tissot.

RENE BUCH
Artistic Director

GILBERTO ZALDIVAR
Producer/Board President

138 East 27th St.
New York, NY 10016
(212) 889-2850

FOUNDED 1968
Gilberto Zaldivar, Rene Buch

SEASON
Year-round

SCHEDULE
Evenings
Tuesday, Thursday-Sunday

Matinees
Saturday, Sunday

FACILITIES
Gramercy Arts Theatre
Seating capacity: 154
Stage: proscenium

FINANCES
September 1, 1981-August 31, 1982
$580,000 operating expenses
$280,000 earned income
$300,000 grants/contributions

AUDIENCE
Annual attendance: 60,000

TOURING CONTACT
Gilberto Zaldivar

Fired from the beginning with a desire to present in Spanish the repertoire of Spain's Golden Age of theatre, along with the best contemporary Latin American plays — all virtually unknown in the United States — Repertorio Español has become, in 15 years, a full-fledged company of devoted professional actors, directors and designers; the presenter of a yearly season of some nine plays running in repertory; a touring company that has travelled around the U.S. and to 14 foreign countries; the host of visiting theatre artists from abroad and — since last year — a musical as well as a dramatic theatre.

What has distinguished the company is a strict adherence to the highest standard of performance. Care has taken precedence over growth. Care has also led to choices of all kinds: of actors, of plays, of visual styles. Each production, when properly unified, expresses the theatre's conviction that the actor, stripped of all unnecessary embellishment and distraction, can create a dramatic universe. Some of Repertorio's actors have worked together for seven or eight years, achieving a unity of style not possible under any other circumstances.

But the company is restless in the face of new goals. Chief among these is the commissioning of works expressly for the company, a possibility which has attracted the interest of a number of contemporary Hispanic writers.

Repertorio Español, being a New York-based company, can develop in ways not possible for other American or Latin American companies: it has both the artistic allure and the bi-cultural status that can clarify and broaden the Hispanic experience in the United States.

Programs and services

Touring.

PRODUCTIONS 1981-82

Doña Rosita, La Soltera, Federico Garcia Lorca
Te Juro Juana Que Tengo Ganas, Emilio Carballido
La Corte de Faraon, Perrin and Palacios; music: Vicente Lleo
El Dia Que Me Quieras, Jose Ignacio Cabrujas
La Vida Es Sueño, Pedro Calderon de la Barca
Toda Desnudez Sera Castigada, Nelson Rodriguez
All productions directed by Rene Buch.

PRODUCTIONS 1982-83

A Secreto Agravio, Secreta Venganza, Pedro Calderon de la Barca; dir: Rene Buch
El Dia Que Me Quieras
Te Juro Juana Que Tengo Ganas

Doña Rosita La Soltera
La Corte de Faraon
La Zapatera Prodigiosa, Federico Garcia Lorca; dir: Peter Wallace
Teoria y Juego del Duende, adapt: Pilar Rioja; dir: Pilar Rioja
Como Ser Una Buena Madre, Ricardo Talesnik; dir: Ricardo Talesnik
Las Quiero a Las Dos, Ricardo Talesnik; dir: Ricardo Talesnik

Doña Francisquita, book: Federico Romero and Guillermo Fernandez Shaw; music: Amadeo Vives; dir: Rene Buch

DESIGNERS

Sets: Robert Weber Federico.
Costumes: Maria Ferreira Contessa, Robert Weber Federico.
Lights: Robert Weber Federico.

Repertorio Español. A Secreto Agravio, Secreta Venganza. Photo: Gerry Goodstein.

The Repertory Theatre of St. Louis

STEVEN WOOLF
Acting Artistic Director/Managing Director

ROBERT C. MANION
Board Chairman

Box 28030
St. Louis, MO 63119
(314) 968-7340 (business)
(314) 968-4925 (box office)

FOUNDED 1966
Webster College

SEASON
September-April

SCHEDULE

Evenings
Tuesday-Sunday

Matinees
Wednesday, Saturday, Sunday

FACILITIES
130 Edgar Road

Mainstage
Seating capacity: 734
Stage: thrust

Studio Theatre
Seating capacity: 125
Stage: flexible

FINANCES
June 1, 1981-May 31, 1982
$1,700,000 operating expenses
$1,000,000 earned income
$ 700,000 grants/contributions

AUDIENCE
Annual attendance: 180,219
Subscribers: 15,815

TOURING CONTACT
Kim Bozark

BOOKED-IN EVENTS
Theatre

AEA LORT (B) and Theatre for Young Audiences contracts

The Repertory Theatre of St. Louis. Joneal Joplin, Holly Hunter and Constance Barry in Buried Child. *Photo: Scott Dine.*

The Repertory Theatre of St. Louis is constantly looking for actors, directors, designers, technicians and administrators who are committed to doing their best professional work as a part of the St. Louis community. The theatre wants its audience members to enjoy that sense of participation that will confirm that they are humans with emotions and ideas that need to be identified, addressed—or at least questioned.

The entire range of classic and contemporary drama continues to be performed in the 700-seat thrust theatre, with particular attention paid to works that challenge, provoke and entertain. Here, the Rep's technical production team can expand and develop its contribution to the art form.

The 125-seat flexible Studio Theatre is a forum in which to present ambitious work artistically. It is here that the theatre has the freedom to present finished and unfinished work, readings or happenings. Here, young designers and technicians gain experience and exposure in preparation for the responsibility of a Mainstage show.

The theatre's outreach programs include a speaker's bureau and the popular Imaginary Theatre Company, a touring troupe which plays throughout the midwest, bringing its distinctive story-theatre style to indigenous folk tales and literary classics. Yearly, the Imaginary travels to schools, fairs and community centers.

The Repertory Theatre of St. Louis seeks to lead its audience, not follow them, never forgetting its regional theatre mandate: to serve as a catalyst in the cultural life of the community, to excite, to stretch and to entertain.

Programs and services

The Imaginary Theatre touring company.

The Road Company

Note: During the 1981-82 and 1982-83 seasons, Wallace Chappell served as artistic director.

PRODUCTIONS 1981-82

The Threepenny Opera, book and lyrics: Bertolt Brecht; music: Kurt Weill; adapt: Mark Blitzstein; dir: Wallace Chappell
Buried Child, Sam Shepard; dir: Timothy Near
A Christmas Carol, adapt: Addie Walsh, from Charles Dickens; dir: Wallace Chappell
One for the Road, Max Morath; dir: Neal Kenyon
Romeo and Juliet, William Shakespeare; dir: Philip Kerr
Charley's Aunt, Brandon Thomas; dir: Ian Trigger
Brecht on Brecht, adapt and trans: George Tabori; dir: Jan Eliasberg
A Lesson from Aloes, Athol Fugard; dir: Jan Eliasberg

PRODUCTIONS 1982-83

Tartuffe, Molière; adapt: Miles Malleson; dir: Philip Kerr
A Tale of Two Cities, adapt: Wallace Chappell, from Charles Dickens; dir: Wallace Chappell
A Christmas Tapestry, adapt: Jan Eliasberg, from Anton Chekhov; dir: Jan Eliasberg
Present Laughter, Noel Coward; dir: Philip Kerr
Hedda Gabler, Henrik Ibsen; trans: Rolf Fjelde; dir: Jan Eliasberg
Under the Ilex, Clyde Talmadge; dir: Charles Nelson Reilly
Sore Throats, Howard Brenton; dir: Jan Eliasberg

DESIGNERS

Sets: Karen Connolly, Tom H. John, Tim Jozwick, Marjorie Bradley Kellogg, John Roslevich, Jr., Carolyn L. Ross, John Carver Sullivan.
Costumes: Dorothy L. Marshall, Carolyn L. Ross, Jan Alois Stein, John Carver Sullivan, Noel Taylor.
Lights: Max De Volder, Glenn Dunn, Gilbert V. Hemsley, Jr., Peter E. Sargent.

ROBERT H. LEONARD
Artistic Director

R. RAYMOND MOORE
Managing Director

JUNE TROXLER
Board President

Box 5278
Johnson City, TN 37603
(615) 926-0781 (business)
(615) 926-7726 (box office)

FOUNDED 1975
Robert H. Leonard

SEASON
November, February, May (resident)
September-October, March-April (touring)

SCHEDULE
Evenings
Thursday-Saturday

Matinees
Sunday

FACILITIES
Mountain Home Memorial Theatre
Seating capacity: 672
Stage: proscenium

The Road Company. Kelly R. Hill, Jr., Emily Green and Dennis Frederick in Horsepower—An Electric Fable. *Photo: Peter Montanti.*

FINANCES
July 1, 1982-June 30, 1983
$170,000 operating expenses
$ 70,000 earned income
$100,000 grants/contributions

AUDIENCE
Annual attendance: 27,000
Subscribers: 300

TOURING CONTACT
Bill Dunham

end galley 421

The Road Company is an ensemble-oriented, community-based theatre striving to serve the upper Tennessee Valley by creating, producing and touring plays which reflect the interests, concerns and experiences of the people in its community. The principal motivation of the company is to create new works through ensemble improvisational techniques; however, other creative avenues — such as collaboration with a writer-in-residence — are also applied.

As the name implies, The Road Company began strictly as a touring ensemble, but has since added a resident season in its hometown of Johnson City. Working in the Tennessee Valley has provided the company with a strong sense of ensemble and clarified the requirements for artistic nourishment of that ensemble and its members. The isolation of six actors working in a community removed from the usual theatre traditions might potentially be as detrimental as the artist/community relationship is potentially fertile. In response, the company has modeled itself as an extended family, wherein actors may move in and out as is mutually beneficial to the individual and the group. Also, guest artists are brought into the company to answer the needs of its ambitious schedule.

Steven Kent (former Provisional Theatre artistic director), choreographer Susan Spaulding, musical director and arranger Doug Dorschug and playwrights Jo Carson, Rebecca Ranson and Russell Davis have all been in residence in Johnson City for workshops, productions and other activities.

The Road Company's mission to produce new work reflective of its community is more a direction than a goal, with the goal being to reach a standard of excellence established by the general public in the Valley and the professional theatre community throughout the nation. The circular relationship in which the artistic source is found by the artist within the audience, shaped by the artist, then given back to the audience in performance, is strenuously pursued in as conscious a manner as possible. Having chosen and defined this community, The Road Company seeks to serve it as a vehicle for cultural, social and historic expression.

Programs and services

Improvisation workshops; touring.

PRODUCTIONS 1981-82

Horsepower—An Electric Fable, Jo Carson and company
The Flying Lemon Circus, company-developed
Little Chicago, book: Jo Carson and company; music and lyrics: Richard Blaustein
One Potato, Two, Rebecca Ranson
Gold Dust, book: Jon Jory; music and lyrics: Jim Wann

All productions directed by Robert H. Leonard

PRODUCTIONS 1982-83

Little Chicago
The Flying Lemon Circus
Vanities, Jack Heifner; dir: Emily Green
The Further Adventures of Sally, Russell Davis; dir: Robert H. Leonard
One Potato, Two
Blind Desire, company-developed; dir: Robert H. Leonard

DESIGNERS

Sets: Margaret Baker, Richard E. Cannon, John Fitzpatrick, Lucinda Flodin, Dennis K. Frederick, Kelly R. Hill, Jr., Mike Russell, Parris Zirkenbach.
Costumes: Margaret Baker, John Fitzpatrick, Lucinda Flodin, Christine Murdock, Sally Carlson Stipe.
Lights: Dennis K. Frederick, Robert H. Leonard.

Roadside Theater

DUDLEY COCKE
Director

DONNA PORTERFIELD
Managing Director/Board Chairman

Box 743
Whitesburg, KY 41858
(606) 633-0108

FOUNDED 1974
Don Baker

SEASON
Year-round

FACILITIES
Appalshop Theater
306 Madison St.
Seating capacity: 160
Stage: thrust

FINANCES
January 1, 1981-December 31, 1981
$130,000 operating expenses
$ 71,000 earned income
$ 68,000 grants/contributions

AUDIENCE
Annual attendance: 36,400

TOURING CONTACT
Donna Porterfield

BOOKED-IN EVENTS
Music, theatre

From its beginning in 1974, Roadside Theater's purpose has been to make quality popular theatre in the southern Appalachian mountains, where none existed before. To make this theatre which speaks intimately to a particular place and people, Roadside's members (nearly all of whom were born and raised there), have immersed themselves in their indigenous rural culture. The company has created its theatrical form and content from Appalachian storytelling, music and oral history.

Roadside was founded as a touring theatre so that it might reach the entire region. Productions are streamlined by design, using no sets and minimal props, costumes and lighting. This enables the company to perform in schools, churches, tents, community cen-

Roadside Theater. Frankie Taylor and Don Baker in Red Fox/Second Hangin'. *Photo: Dan Carraco.*

ters, prisons, old-age homes and other non-traditional theatre spaces. Roadside has always maintained a commitment to these non-traditional audiences and that commitment has influenced its aesthetic. Roadside also performs in theatres, and recently moved into its own 160-seat space, where its repertoire is presented regularly. (The company continues to be available for touring year-round.)

In 1983-84, Roadside is producing two new shows, continuing to experiment with radio and television and stepping up its development of Appalachian playwriting and acting talent. Plans call for more artistic exchanges — such as a four-way tour with A Traveling Jewish Theatre, the Free Southern Theatre and El Teatro Campesino. Roadside will also perform for extended periods in San Francisco, New York and New Orleans.

Roadside sees itself as a means to an end. Its work provides audiences with the opportunity to focus on human drama and see that the conflicts, defeats and yearnings of Appalachian people are as important as those of others in other places. It also prompts self-recognition and pride in its audience members and serves to strengthen community, cultural and historical bonds. The company has chosen to make its theatre from within the confines of its place and culture, but this confinement has resulted in a feeling of artistic freedom and an ability to reach widespread audiences.

Programs and services

Productions available on radio, record and videotape; workshops in oral history, storytelling, rural theatre organization.

PRODUCTIONS 1981-82

Mountain Tales and Music, company-developed
Red Fox/Second Hangin', Dudley Cocke and Don Baker; dir: Dudley Cocke
Brother Jack, Ron Short and Don Baker; dir: Don Baker
South of the Mountain, Ron Short; dir: Dudley Cocke

PRODUCTIONS 1982-83

Mountain Tales and Music
Red Fox/Second Hangin'
Brother Jack
South of the Mountain

DESIGNERS

Lights: Don Baker, Ron Short.

Roundabout Theatre Company

GENE FEIST
Producing Director

TODD HAIMES
Managing Director

CHRISTIAN C. YEGEN
Board Chairman

333 West 23rd St.
New York, NY 10011
(212) 924-7160 (business)
(212) 242-7800 (box office)

FOUNDED 1965
Gene Feist, Michael Fried

SEASON
September-August

SCHEDULE
Evenings
Tuesday-Saturday

Matinees
Wednesday, Saturday, Sunday

FACILITIES
Stage One
Seating capacity: 300
Stage: proscenium

Susan Bloch Theatre
307 West 26th St.
Seating capacity: 150
Stage: thrust

FINANCES
July 1, 1982-June 30, 1983
$2,100,000 operating expenses
$1,700,000 earned income
$ 400,000 grants/contributions

AUDIENCE
Annual attendance: 270,000
Subscribers: 22,000

TOURING CONTACT
Ralph Roseman

AEA LORT (C) and (D) contracts

The Roundabout Theatre Company's repertoire is eclectic, spanning the literature of the past 500 years. It is dedicated to its role as a conservator of the world's dramatic heri-

Roundabout Theatre Company. Robert Stattel, Carol Teitel and Philip Bosco in The Learned Ladies. *Photo: Martha Swope.*

tage, mounting productions of the great plays for audiences who may have read or studied them, but have never seen these works performed.

Most recently, Roundabout's emphasis has been on rediscovering for its New York audiences the plays of Britain's dramatic renaissance, which began in the late 1940s. The company is now turning its focus toward the Irish theatre: in coming seasons it will be presenting plays by Brian Friel, Sean O'Casey and John Millington Synge. Plans also include productions of great American works by Tennessee Williams, William Inge, Eugene O'Neill and Arthur Miller.

Roundabout rejects the term "revival," since each of its plays is approached as if it were a new work requiring a fresh approach and concept. It is interested in working with actors whose training allows them to play contemporary as well as classical roles. Directors are sought who have—in addition to a strong theatrical background—heightened psychological insight into plot development and characterization.

As it has for its entire 18-year history, Roundabout's philosophy remains centered on presenting quality theatre at affordable prices for audiences of all ages and incomes.

Programs and services

Community outreach; Union Ticket Program; Corporate Ticket Program; internships.

PRODUCTIONS 1981-82

Misalliance, George Bernard Shaw; dir: Stephen Porter
Miss Julie and *Playing with Fire,* August Strindberg; trans: Michael Meyer; dir: Gene Feist
A Kurt Weill Cabaret, adapt: Martha Schlamme; dir: Alvin Epstein
Dear Liar, Jerome Kilty; dir: Jerome Kilty
The Caretaker, Harold Pinter; dir: Anthony Page
The Chalk Garden, Enid Bagnold; dir: John Stix
The Learned Ladies, Molière; trans: Richard Wilbur; dir: Norman Ayrton
The Fox, adapt: Allan Miller, from D.H. Lawrence; dir: Allan Miller
The Browning Version, Terence Rattigan; dir: Stephen Porter
The Twelve-Pound Look, J.M. Barrie; dir: Stephen Porter

PRODUCTIONS 1982-83

The Holly and the Ivy, Wynyard Browne; dir: Lindsay Anderson
The Entertainer, John Osborne; dir: William Gaskill
Winners, Brian Friel; dir: Nye Heron
How He Lied to Her Husband, George Bernard Shaw; dir: Nye Heron
Duet for One, Tom Kempinski; dir: Jeffrey Hayden
The Knack, Ann Jellicoe; dir: Geoffrey Sherman
Ah, Wilderness!, Eugene O'Neill; dir: John Stix

DESIGNERS

Sets: Kenneth Foy, Roger Mooney, Michael Sharp, Douglas Stein.
Costumes: Judith Dolan, Sarah G. Conly, Deborah Dryden, A. Christina Giannini, Jane Greenwood, Jessica Hahn, Richard Hieronymus, Gene Lakin, John David Ridge.
Lights: Martin Aronstein, Barry Arnold, Patrick Kelly, David F. Segal, Marshall Spiller, Judy Rasmuson, Walter Uhrman, Ronald Wallace.

Round House Theatre

JEFFREY B. DAVIS
Artistic Director

LINDA A. YOST
Arts Coordinator

12210 Bushey Drive
Silver Spring, MD 20902
(301) 468-4172 (business)
(301) 468-4234 (box office)

FOUNDED 1978
Montgomery County Government

SEASON
September-August

SCHEDULE
Evenings
Wednesday-Saturday

Matinees
Sunday

FACILITIES
Seating capacity: 216
Stage: thrust

FINANCES
July 1, 1982-June 30, 1983
$374,000 operating expenses
$194,000 earned income
$ 1,500 grants/contributions

AUDIENCE
Annual attendance: 61,500
Subscribers: 2,240

TOURING CONTACT
Vickie Arnold

BOOKED-IN EVENTS
Theatre, children's theatre

AEA Guest Artist contract

The Round House Theatre is a professional resident company founded and operated by Maryland's Montgomery County Department of Recreation. Located in the suburbs of Washington, D.C., it is a pioneer in the modern concept of encouraging actors, directors, designers and staff to live and work in a community setting. Staff members share their talents with citizens through tours, workshops and a carefully designed program of multidisciplinary classes for all ages; technical support for local arts groups and coordinated programming with the school system and local municipalities are also offered.

The Round House is committed to the artistic growth of its resident company, with plays chosen to enhance that growth. In this way, it treats its 2,240 subscribers to a wide spectrum of theatre. Since 1978 the company has produced classics, new plays, adaptations, musicals and original, full-length mime plays. Through it all, a true ensemble has developed, dedicated to the pursuit of an intelligent, honest and spontaneous performance style.

The most significant growth of Round House artists results from their constant interaction with the community. Company members are deeply involved in RHT's integrated program of theatre studies, which maintains two objectives: to discover, nurture and develop the inner resources of each student; and to introduce, teach and develop basic theatrical skills. The company also creates original theatre for children and teens which tours area schools, making the sometimes mysterious process of theatre accessible to the community and deepening the relationship between artists and audience.

By bringing artists, community and government together, the Round House has emerged as a new model for arts development in a contemporary American community.

Programs and services

Classes, workshops and labs; touring; programs-in-schools; internships; arts day camp; resident theatre camp; children's chorus; community musical production; children's theatre; Actors Associates volunteer program.

PRODUCTIONS 1981-82

Deathtrap, Ira Levin; dir: Jeffrey B. Davis
The Butterfingers Angel, William Gibson; dir: Jerry Whiddon
The Three Sisters, Anton Chekhov; trans: Constance Garnett; dir: David Cromwell
The Man of Destiny and *Augustus Does His Bit,* George Bernard Shaw; dir: Jeffrey B. Davis
Scapino!, Frank Dunlop and Jim Dale; dir: Jeffrey B. Davis

PRODUCTIONS 1982-83

Cat on a Hot Tin Roof, Tennessee Williams; dir: David Cromwell
How the Other Half Loves, Alan Ayckbourn; dir: Jeffrey B. Davis
The Sign of Four, adapt: John Edwards, from Sir Arthur Conan Doyle; dir: Douglas A. Cumming
A Life in the Theatre, David Mamet; dir: Jerry Whiddon
Tristan and Isolt, Mark Jaster; dir: Mark Jaster
In Circles, book: Gertrude Stein; music: Al Carmines; dir: Jeffrey B. Davis

DESIGNERS

Sets: Douglas A. Cumming, Craig Talbot, Richard H. Young.
Costumes: Leslie Marie-Cocuzzo, Kate Cowart, Rosemary Pardee-Holz, Pamela MacFarlane, Lilian Mikiver.
Lights: Douglas A. Cumming, John Gabbert, Geoffrey B. Grob, James J. Taylor, Richard H. Young.

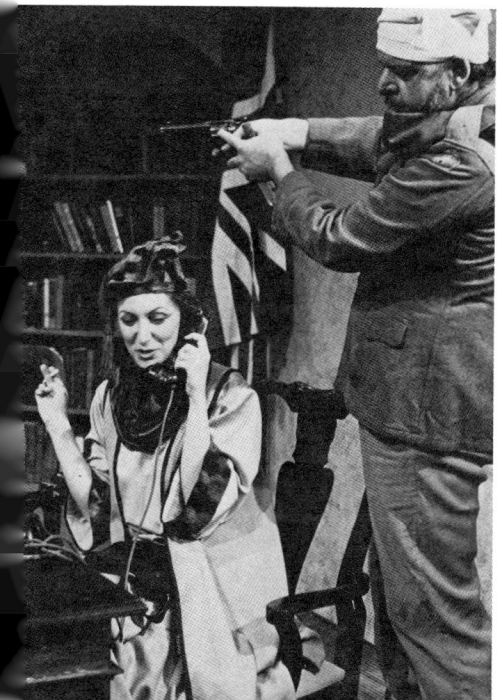

Round House Theatre. Greta Lambert and Dion Anderson in Augustus Does His Bit. *Photo: Brian Eggleston.*

San Diego Repertory Theatre

SAM WOODHOUSE
Producing Director

DOUGLAS JACOBS
Artistic Director

TRINA KAPLAN
Business Manager

JOHN MESSNER
Board President

1620 Sixth Ave.
San Diego, CA 92101
(619) 231-3586 (business)
(619) 235-8025 (box office)

FOUNDED 1976
Sam Woodhouse, Douglas Jacobs

San Diego Repertory Theatre. Tavis Ross and David J. Partington in True West. *Photo: Kevin Hogan.*

SEASON
January-November

SCHEDULE
Evenings
Tuesday-Sunday

Matinees
Sunday

FACILITIES
Seating capacity: 212
Stage: proscenium

FINANCES
July 1, 1982-June 30, 1983
$425,000 operating expenses
$305,000 earned income
$ 99,000 grants/contributions

AUDIENCE
Annual attendance: 59,684
Subscribers: 2,750

BOOKED-IN EVENTS
Theatre, music, playreadings

AEA Guest Artist contract

San Diego Repertory Theatre is dedicated to bringing enlightening, thought-provoking, compelling theatre experiences to the people of its home city. The emphasis is on San Diego, West Coast and world premieres of new plays, seldom-seen classics and unique revivals of well-known classics. The Rep is committed to nurturing and showcasing the talents of local playwrights, directors, designers and actors.

Begun in 1975-76 as a contemporary commedia dell'arte ensemble performing in the parks of San Diego, in 1977 the Rep opened the city's first resident playhouse in over a decade at the former St. Cecilia's Chapel in downtown San Diego.

The Rep has become known for its productions of innovative, unique, often controversial works, including Sam Shepard's *True West* and Samm-Art Williams' *Home* (both San Diego premieres), Alonso Alegria's *Crossing Niagara* and Paula Cizmar's *Death of a Miner* (both West Coast premieres). Shakespeare's rarely produced *Titus Andronicus* was staged at the Rep in 1982, and its 1983 production of *Children of a Lesser God* was a sell-out.

In addition to mainstage productions, in 1982 the theatre instituted a Satellite Season which includes staged readings, live music and productions by touring groups and local artists. That same year saw the inception of "Go Like 60," a theatre project whose purpose is to develop and present plays performed by seniors which explore life as a senior citizen in the 1980s. These plays are designed for easy and economical touring to local organizations.

Future plans include increased emphasis on new play development and production, the creation of a comprehensive conservatory training program and a continuing dedication to providing San Diego with exciting, high-quality theatre.

Programs and services

Go Like 60 touring program for senior citizens; touring; staged readings.

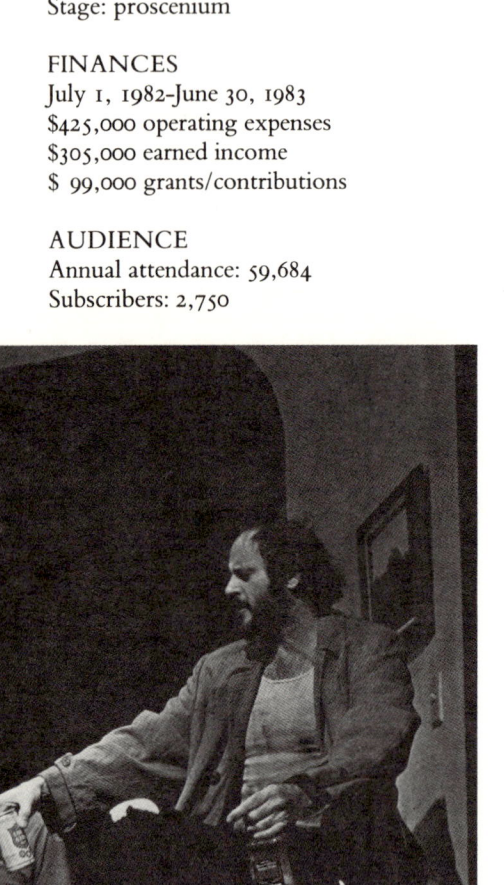

San Jose Repertory Company

PRODUCTIONS 1982

Tintypes, music and lyrics: various; adapt: Mary Kyte, Mel Marvin and Gary Pearle; dir: James Manley
True West, Sam Shepard; dir: Sam Woodhouse
Death of a Salesman, Arthur Miller; dir: Douglas Jacobs
Home, Samm-Art Williams; dir: Floyd Gaffney
Division Street, Steve Tesich; dir: Sam Woodhouse
Titus Andronicus, William Shakespeare; dir: Douglas Jacobs
The Club, Eve Merriam; dir: Frolic Taylor
A Christmas Carol, adapt: Douglas Jacobs, from Charles Dickens; dir: Sam Woodhouse
Just a Song at Twilight, Marcia Savin; dir: Tavis Ross

PRODUCTIONS 1983

Crossing Niagara, Alonso Alegria; dir: Douglas Jacobs
The Death of a Miner, Paula Cizmar; dir: Douglas Jacobs
Children of a Lesser God, Mark Medoff; dir: Sam Woodhouse
Mrs. Warren's Profession, George Bernard Shaw; dir: Douglas Jacobs
A Funny Thing Happened on the Way to the Forum, book: Burt Shevelove and Larry Gelbart; music and lyrics: Stephen Sondheim; dir: Sam Woodhouse
In the Matter of J. Robert Oppenheimer, Heinar Kipphardt; dir: Douglas Jacobs
A Christmas Carol
Admit One, Elyse Nass; dir: Mark Hardiman
Second Chance, Elyse Nass; dir: Tavis Ross
Salad Days, Jan Kubicki; dir: Tavis Ross

DESIGNERS

Sets: Mark Donnelly, Fred Duer, Steve Lavino, Charles McCall, Ron Ranson, Stephen Storer.
Costumes: Mary Gibson, Ingrid Helton, Sally Rosen-Thomas, Carolyn Satter.
Lights: John Curcio, Willa Mann-Day, Mark Donnelly, Fred Duer, L.B. Gunn, Nell Martin, Joseph D. Naftel.

JAMES P. REBER
Executive Producer

DAVID LEMOS
Producing Director

PHILIP HAMMER
Board President

Box 9584
San Jose, CA 95157
(408) 294-7572

FOUNDED 1980
James P. Reber

SEASON
November-May

SCHEDULE
Evenings
Tuesday-Sunday

Matinees
Wednesday, Sunday

FACILITIES
Montgomery Theatre
291 South Market St.
Seating capacity: 500
Stage: proscenium

FINANCES
July 1, 1982-June 30, 1983
$401,000 operating expenses
$250,000 earned income
$134,000 grants/contributions

San Jose Repertory Company. James J. Houghton, Kathleen Amorose and Kevin Schwartz in The Lion in Winter. *Photo: Sharon Hall.*

AUDIENCE
Annual attendance: 34,500
Subscribers: 6,000

AEA LORT (D) contract

In 1980, San Jose became the nation's fastest growing and 17th-largest city. It was, however, one of only three of the cities in the top 20 without a major professional theatre company. San Jose Repertory Company was formed the following year to meet this need.

Founded by James P. Reber, San Jose Rep is dedicated to providing its community and the Santa Clara Valley with theatre that represents the interests, tastes and values unique to the "Silicon Valley," the nation's center for computer technology. The Rep recognizes the dual need to provide theatre that can entertain at the same time it compels its audiences to examine the quality of their lives and world they live in. It presents a five-play season in its 500-seat Montgomery Theatre which ranges from fresh adaptations of the classics to newer, more challenging works. Plans to open a second, 70-seat performance space are in the final stages.

San Jose Rep serves a large subscription audience which has, since its inception, grown almost 300 percent each year, making the Rep a major component in the city's downtown redevelopment project. An administrative and production staff of 25 is employed, and a seven-member resident acting company is augmented by visiting artists.

Unique to San Jose Rep is its three-department structure: Administration, Development and Production departments are each headed by a full-time, year-round director working closely with the executive producer. The careful balancing of the needs of the three departments creates a strong organization capable of supporting and fostering fine artistry. The company is actively guided by a 28-member board of directors which sets policies, raises funds and helps establish long-range goals. The Rep's strong commitment to the survival of the theatre—even in hard economic times—is evidenced by its fresh approach to the "business" of nonprofit theatre management.

Programs and services

Phantasy Company touring children's theatre; Studio Stage reader's theatre series; Abraham Lincoln High School Residency Program; Behind the Scenes post-play discussions.

PRODUCTIONS 1981-82

The Taming of the Shrew, William Shakespeare; dir: Anne McNaughton
The Glass Menagerie, Tennessee Williams; dir: JD Trow
Dear Liar, Jerome Kilty; dir: Anne McNaughton
Jesse and the Bandit Queen, David Freeman; dir: Anthony Taccone
Tartuffe, Molière; trans: Richard Wilbur; dir: David Lemos
Candida, George Bernard Shaw: dir: Will Huddleston
The Trial of the Catonsville 9, Daniel Berrigan; dir: Peter Buckley
Born Yesterday, Garson Kanin; dir: Bobby Pellerin

PRODUCTIONS 1982-83

A Flea in Her Ear, Georges Feydeau; adapt: Suzanne Grossmann and Paxton Whitehead; dir: J. Steven White
The Lion in Winter, James Goldman; dir: Peter Nyberg
The Philadelphia Story, Philip Barry; dir: Will Huddleston
The Shadow Box, Michael Cristofer; dir: David Lemos and Peter Buckley
The Importance of Being Earnest, Oscar Wilde; dir: Anne McNaughton

DESIGNERS

Sets: Gene Angell, Michael Cook, Gary Daines, William Eddelman, J'te, John T. Murphy, Ron Pratt, Ralph Ryan, Roger Sherman.
Costumes: Wendy Amorose, Barbara Bush, Marcia Frederick.
Lights: J.C. Bennett, Leo J. Clarke, Kurt Landisman.

Seattle Repertory Theatre

DANIEL SULLIVAN
Artistic Director

PETER DONNELLY
Producing Director

DOROTHY L. SIMPSON
Board Chairman

155 Mercer St.
Seattle, WA 98109
(206) 447-2210 (business)
(206) 447-2222 (box office)

FOUNDED 1963
Bagley Wright

SEASON
October-May

SCHEDULE
Evenings
Tuesday-Sunday

Matinees
Wednesday, Saturday, Sunday

FACILITIES
Bagley Wright Theatre
Seating capacity: 850
Stage: proscenium

PONCHO Forum
Seating capacity: 180
Stage: flexible

FINANCES
July 1, 1982-June 30, 1983
$2,424,000 operating expenses
$1,697,000 earned income
$ 752,000 grants/contributions

AUDIENCE
Annual attendance: 198,548
Subscribers: 19,760

TOURING CONTACT
Vito Zingarelli

BOOKED-IN EVENTS
Theatre, music

AEA LORT (B) contract

The Seattle Repertory Theatre was established in 1963 at the conclusion of the Seattle World's Fair, which left the city a healthy legacy of civic pride and a cluster of handsome new buildings including the Seattle Center Playhouse, which became the Rep's home for the next 20 years.

During that time, the theatre has traveled steadily upward in terms of both audience support and national recognition and, as the largest professional theatre in the region, it has become an integral part of the Northwest cultural scene. Throughout its history, the Rep's leadership has been dedicated to the premise that dramatic literature deserves the highest possible production standards and, to that end, has attempted to attract the best artists and technicians in the profession. Emphasis is placed on the use of Seattle-based actors, reflecting the theatre's increasing commitment to the support of resident actors and the development of a local talent pool. The theatre's six-play season consists of classics, contemporary works and premieres of new plays.

October 26, 1983 marked the beginning of a new era of the Rep as its 21st season opened in the new Bagley Wright Theatre at Seattle Center. Named to honor the Rep's principal founder, this $9.5 million facility consolidates all of the theatre's operations under one roof. Most important, the 850-seat main theatre has seating on two levels, both of which are close to its proscenium stage, thus creating a sense of intimacy and interaction between audience and actors. This will allow the Rep an even wider scope in its choice of dramatic material.

The new facility also includes a large rehearsal space which doubles as a 250-seat second stage called the PONCHO Forum. This will be used to present new works.

The Seattle Rep is committed to encouraging new playwrights and reviews some 2,000 scripts annually. For the past three years this commitment has been fulfilled through the New Plays in Process series consisting of an intensive workshop/rehearsal period with the playwright in residence, culminating in a limited-run production. In the new theatre, the Rep is able to offer both the new play series and the mainstage season in close proximity, with all the necessary support facilities at hand.

Seattle Repertory Theatre. Translations. *Photo: Greg Gilbert.*

The Second Stage

Programs and services

Preview lectures; sign language performances; Theatre Praxis workshops and seminars; Sundays at 3 literary cabaret series; Students Backstage; post-play discussions; Mobile Outreach Bunch touring company; New Plays in Process Project; Northwest Stage Directors' Conference.

PRODUCTIONS 1981-82

Another Part of the Forest, Lillian Hellman; dir: Edward Hastings
Two Gentlemen of Verona, William Shakespeare; dir: Daniel Sullivan
Awake and Sing!, Clifford Odets; dir: Robert Loper
Bedroom Farce, Alan Ayckbourn; dir: Daniel Sullivan
Savages, Christopher Hampton; dir: Robert Egan
Major Barbara, George Bernard Shaw; dir: Daniel Sullivan

PRODUCTIONS 1982-83

Romeo and Juliet, William Shakespeare; dir: Daniel Sullivan
The Front Page, Ben Hecht and Charles MacArthur; dir: Daniel Sullivan
Death of a Salesman, Arthur Miller; dir: Allen Fletcher
Taking Steps, Alan Ayckbourn; dir: Daniel Sullivan
Translations, Brian Friel; dir: Robert Egan
The Vinegar Tree, Paul Osborn; dir: Daniel Sullivan

DESIGNERS

Sets: Robert Blackman, Robert Dahlstrom, Kate Edmunds, Ralph Funicello, John Kasarda, Hugh Landwehr, Scott Weldin.
Costumes: Robert Blackman, Laura Crow, Sally Richardson, Kurt Wilhelm, Robert Wojewodski.
Lights: Robert A. Dahlstrom, James F. Ingalls, Spencer Mosse, Richard Nelson, James Sale.

ROBYN GOODMAN
CAROLE ROTHMAN
Artistic Directors

ROSA VEGA
Managing Director

BARBARA HAUPTMAN
Board President

Box 1807 Ansonia Station
New York, NY 10023
(212) 564-2150

FOUNDED 1979
Robyn Goodman, Carole Rothman

SCHEDULE
Evenings
Tuesday-Sunday

FACILITIES
The McGinn/Cazale Theatre
2162 Broadway
Seating capacity: 110
Stage: proscenium

FINANCES
July 1, 1982-June 30, 1983
$180,000 operating expenses
$101,000 earned income
$ 71,000 grants/contributions

AUDIENCE
Annual attendance: 6,225
Subscribers: 750

AEA letter of agreement

With the proliferation of new plays, many significant works have been produced and then quickly forgotten. Both the artistic community and the general public are being cheated by this "fast-food" theatre trend.

The Second Stage seeks to ameliorate this situation by producing plays of the past decade. This includes plays that were ahead of their time, not accessible to a wide audience, poorly publicized or obscured by inferior productions. Whether formerly done on Broadway, in resident professional theatres or Off-Off Broadway, these plays

Christine Estabrook, Judith Ivey and Jeffrey Fahey in Pastorale.
Photo: Stephanie Saia.

Soho Repertory Theatre

need greater exposure. Often fresh creative input—as well as the perspective of time—enable a playwright to refine a work. The Second Stage feels that this process of development is essential to the work. It does not consider itself a revival house: rather, it is interested in keeping contemporary literature alive.

During the 1981-82 season, these goals were expanded to include the production of a new and unproduced play: Deborah Eisenberg's *Pastorale*. The theatre hopes from now on to produce one new play per season.

The 1983-84 season began with the opening of a permanent home for the Second Stage on Manhattan's upper west side: The McGinn/Cazale Theatre.

Programs and services

First Stage play readings; Second Stage Hands; production and administrative internships.

PRODUCTIONS 1981-82

My Sister in This House, Wendy Kesselman; dir: Carole Rothman and Inverna Lockpez
Flux, Susan Miller; dir: Michael Kahn
Pastorale, Deborah Eisenberg; dir: Carole Rothman
The Woods, David Mamet; dir: David Mamet

PRODUCTIONS 1982-83

Painting Churches, Tina Howe; dir: Carole Rothman
Something Different, Carl Reiner; dir: Michael Kahn
Winterplay, Adele Edling Shank; dir: Harris Yulin

DESIGNERS

Sets: Jim Clayburgh, Heidi Landesman, Marjorie Bradley Kellogg, Ernest Allen Smith, Douglas Stein.
Costumes: Nan Cibula, Clifford Capone, Ann Emonts, Susan Hilferty, Ernest Allen Smith, Mariann Verheyen.
Lights: William Armstrong, Frances Aronson, Pat Collins, Victor En Yu Tan, Arden Fingerhut.

JERRY ENGELBACH
MARLENE SWARTZ
Artistic Directors

MARLENE SWARTZ
Board President

19 Mercer St.
New York, NY 10013
(212) 334-9303 (business)
(212) 925-2588 (box office)

FOUNDED 1975
Jerry Engelbach, Marlene Swartz

SEASON
September-June

SCHEDULE
Evenings
Thursday-Sunday, some Mondays

Matinees
Sunday

FACILITIES
Seating capacity: 100
Stage: thrust

FINANCES
July 1, 1982-June 30, 1983
$101,000 operating expenses
$ 48,000 earned income
$ 47,000 grants/contributions

AUDIENCE
Annual attendance: 8,000
Subscribers: 800

BOOKED-IN EVENTS
Dance, music, performance artists

AEA Nonprofit Theatre code

Soho Repertory Theatre produces neglected classics and highly theatrical modern plays, including musicals and mixed-media works. It chooses plays which are active; are "discoveries"; and make one think. For years, Soho alternated adventurous work with conventional plays because the latter paid the bills: economics dictated programming. Ninety plays later, in its ninth season, the theatre hopes its compromising days are long over.

While hardly pompous enough to believe it can rescue Off-Off Broadway from the clutches of commercialism, Soho feels that it and other nonprofit theatres can help to stem the tide by taking unambiguous positions on artistic intent. Naturally, theatre should be dramatic, emotionally involving, entertaining and so on. But much of today's theatre emphasizes product over process, and in so doing, fails to explore the actual aesthetics of the medium: what differentiates it from other media and makes it an art form, rather than just a branch of show business.

Theatre is kinetic. Like dance, baseball and circus, theatre is concerned with people in three-dimensional space, acting with immediacy and a sense of danger.

Theatre is participatory. For centuries, the audience has used its imagination to "fill in" suggestions of character, time and place. The more imaginatively actors, costumes, sets and lighting are presented, the more complex and multi-layered the audience's contribution can be. As for "realism," Soho Rep believes that art must be larger than—not a representation of—life.

Theatre is intelligent. Soho looks mainly (but not exclusively) to the past as a source of rich material, because the plays challenge with creative use of language and presentation of mature ideas. A vital theatre requires the encouragement of playwrights whose work looks deeply and takes risks—work which is almost *a priori* noncommercial. Therefore, this encouragement must take the form of support from funding sources and ticket buyers who believe in process over product.

The art of theatre does not float around in space waiting to be plucked down. It can only be kept alive if theatres commit themselves to it in their work. Soho Rep hopes that its work demonstrates its commitment to theatre to the extent that its supporters gain a clearer idea about what theatre is, and demand to see *theatre* when they go to the theatre.

Programs and services

First Look staged readings; One Night Stand booked-in events.

Soho Repertory Theatre. Fanshen. *Photo: Joseph Schuyler.*

PRODUCTIONS 1981-82

Dark Ride, Len Jenkin; dir: Len Jenkin
Nathan the Wise, Gotthold Ephraim Lessing; trans: Bayard Quincy Morgan; dir: Jerry Engelbach
Subject to Fits, Robert Montgomery; dir: Barry Koron
The Girl Who Ate Chicken Bones, book and lyrics: Stan Kaplan; music: David Hollister; dir: Marlene Swartz
The Audience, libretto: Glenn Miller; music: Royce Dembo; dir: Scott Clugstone
Mr. Lion, libretto and music: Linder Chlarson; dir: Lou Rodgers
Miyako, libretto and music: Lou Rodgers; dir: Lou Rodgers
Barbarians, Barrie Keeffe; dir: Peter Byrne

PRODUCTIONS 1982-83

The Silver Tassie, Sean O'Casey; dir: Carey Perloff
Fanshen, David Hare; dir: Michael Bloom
Kid Twist, Len Jenkin; dir: Tony Barsha
Rape upon Rape, Henry Fielding; dir: Anthony Bowles

DESIGNERS

Sets: John Arnone, Barry Axtell, Steven L. Birnbaum, Duke Durfee, Louanne Gilleland, Raymond Kluga, Fred Marchese, Gerald Marks, Tarant Smith, Dorian Vernacchio.
Costumes: Steven L. Birnbaum, Mary L. Hayes, Kalina Ivanov, Gene K. Lakin, Fred Marchese, Elena Pellicciaro, David C. Woolard.
Lights: Mary Jo Dondlinger, Chaim Gitter, Rick Gray, David Noling, Bruce Porter, David M. Shepherd, David N. Weiss, Susan A. White.

South Coast Repertory

DAVID EMMES
Producing Artistic Director

MARTIN BENSON
Artistic Director

TIMOTHY BRENNAN
General Manager

ERIC WITTENBERG
Board President

Box 2197
Costa Mesa, CA 92626
(714) 957-2602 (business)
(714) 957-4033 (box office)

FOUNDED 1964
David Emmes, Martin Benson

SEASON
September-July

SCHEDULE
Evenings
Tuesday-Sunday

Matinees
Saturday, Sunday

South Coast Repertory. Ah, Wilderness! *Photo: Jay Thompson.*

FACILITIES
655 Town Center Drive

Mainstage
Seating capacity: 507
Stage: modified thrust

Second Stage
Seating capacity: 161
Stage: modified thrust

SCR Amphitheatre
Seating: variable
Stage: outdoor amphitheatre

FINANCES
September 1, 1982-August 31, 1983
$2,648,000 operating expenses
$1,938,000 earned income
$ 710,000 grants/contributions

AUDIENCE
Annual attendance: 250,000
Subscribers: 19,000

TOURING CONTACT
Kris Hagen

AEA LORT (B) and (D) contracts

South Coast Repertory is concluding its second decade of operation under its founders, David Emmes and Martin Benson. Since moving to the 4th Step Theatre complex in 1978, SCR has increased its commitment to the production of new work with each passing season. In 1982-83, seven of SCR's dozen subscription productions were new plays; five of the seven were world premieres. The Mainstage continues to offer seasons which blend classic, modern and contemporary works; in 1982-83, the Second Stage was home to a season of premieres. Additionally, SCR commissioned and produced two new plays for children.

SCR utilizes a three-faceted approach to its artistic staffing; a core company of resident designers, directors and actors who provide artistic continuity are complemented by an "extended company" of actors who have worked at SCR previously and who reside in southern California. Increasingly, these artists are augmented by a number of individuals recruited from across the country to provide the specific talents needed to realize SCR's productions.

Over the past several years, SCR has sought to form and nurture relationships with playwrights seeking to develop new work. Its support begins with a program of commissions and staged readings, ideally leading to production on one of SCR's stages. Writers affiliated with SCR come from southern California and across the country, and are in residence during critical stages of development.

Located in Costa Mesa, 35 miles south of Los Angeles, SCR is Orange County's only professional resident theatre. It serves its community with a variety of educational services, including the annual tour of an original commissioned play to area grammar schools, which plays each year to audiences of more than 60,000. High school students combine classroom study of a play with a visit to the theatre to see it in production and participate in post-performance discussions with the artists. SCR's Acting Conservatory offers year-round instruction to more than 500 children, teens and adults and its Young Conservatory Players presents three plays for children annually, in addition to touring.

Programs and services

Acting Conservatory; Educational Touring Program; Living Theatre Project; SCR on Campus; speaker's bureau; seminar series; subscriber newsletter.

PRODUCTIONS 1981-82

Ah, Wilderness!, Eugene O'Neill; dir: Martin Benson
Loose Ends, Michael Weller; dir: David Emmes
True West, Sam Shepard; dir: Lee Shallat
A Christmas Carol, adapt: Jerry Patch, from Charles Dickens; dir: John-David Keller
The Play's the Thing, Ferenc Molnar; adapt: P.G. Wodehouse; dir: Lee Shallat
Bodies, James Saunders; dir: Richard Gershman
Henry IV, Part I, William Shakespeare; dir: John Allison
The Blood Knot, Athol Fugard; dir: Martin Benson
Da, Hugh Leonard; dir: David Emmes
Coming Attractions, Ted Tally; dir: Paul Rudd
Tintypes, music and lyrics: various; adapt: Mary Kyte, Mel Marvin and Gary Pearle; dir: John-David Keller
The Man Who Could See Through Time, Terri Wagener; dir: Martin Benson
The Fitness Game!, Jerry Patch and Michael Bigelow Dixon; music: Joel Kabakov; dir: John-David Keller

PRODUCTIONS 1982-83

All in Favour Said No!, Bernard Farrell; dir: David Emmes
The Diviners, Jim Leonard, Jr.; dir: Martin Benson
Brothers, George Sibbald; dir: Lee Sankowich
A Christmas Carol
Boy Meets Girl, Bella and Sam Spewak; dir: Lee Shallat
She Also Dances, Kenneth Arnold; dir: Jules Aaron
Betrayal, Harold Pinter; dir: David Emmes
Closely Related, Bruce MacDonald; dir: Lee Shallat
The Imaginary Invalid, Molière; adapt: Donald Frame; dir: Richard Russell Ramos
Goodbye Freddy, Elizabeth Diggs; dir: Jules Aaron
Major Barbara, George Bernard Shaw; dir: Martin Benson
April Snow, Romulus Linney; dir: David Emmes
Bits & Bytes, Michael Bigelow Dixon and Jerry Patch; music: Diane King; dir: John-David Keller

DESIGNERS

Sets: Michael Devine, Mark Donnelly, Cliff Faulkner, Ralph Funicello, Keith Hein, Steve Lavino, Dwight Richard Odle, Lisette Thomas, Thomas A. Walsh.
Costumes: Carol Brolaski, Nanrose Buchman, Barbara Cox, Cliff Faulkner, Merrily Murray-Walsh, Dwight Richard Odle, Tom Rasmussen, Kim Simons, Skipper Skeoch, Charles Tomlinson.
Lights: Kent Dorsey, John Ivo Gilles, Cameron Harvey, Paulie Jenkins, Donna Ruzika, Tom Ruzika, Greg Sullivan, Susan Tuohy.

Stage One:

MOSES GOLDBERG
Producing Director

MICHELLE M. GARDNER
General Manager

HARRIETTE SEILER
Board President

721 West Main St.
Louisville, KY 40202
(502) 589-5946 (business)
(502) 584-7777 (box office)

FOUNDED 1946
Sara Spencer, Ming Dick

SEASON
September-June

SCHEDULE
Matinees
Monday-Saturday

FACILITIES
Kentucky Center for the Arts
500 West Main St.
Whitney Hall
Seating capacity: 2,400
Stage: proscenium

Moritz Von Bomhard Theatre
Seating capacity: 610
Stage: thrust

FINANCES
June 1, 1982-May 31, 1983
$309,000 operating expenses
$168,000 earned income
$141,000 grants/contributions

AUDIENCE
Annual attendance: 62,000
Subscribers: 980

TOURING CONTACT
Viven M. Niwes

BOOKED-IN EVENTS
Family theatre

AEA Theatre for Young Audiences contract

Bringing the joy of living theatre to each young person has been the goal of Stage One: The Louisville Children's Theatre since its inception in 1946. Its 38-year develop-

The Louisville Children's Theatre

ment began with a program "by children for children" and has culminated in Stage One's current status as a leading professional theatre for young audiences.

In fulfilling its commitment to the development of the creativity, awareness and social responsibility of the upcoming generation, Stage One provides productions for families to share at the various stages of their children's development. The productions are designed to appeal to specific age groups by addressing their particular problems and concerns, and by stimulating young imaginations.

The youngest audience members are introduced to theatre through participation plays which encourage them to contribute to the dramatic action. As they mature, the productions become progressively more sophisticated until they are presented with period or contemporary classics, preparing them for adult theatre experiences.

Stage One is actively involved in the development of new scripts for young audiences. It includes several new plays in each season which are written by Stage One's staff or commissioned from playwrights distinguished in theatre for young audiences.

Stage One is included in the National Endowment for the Arts Director of Artists; is a recipient of the Southeast Theatre Conference's Sara Spencer Award as the outstanding children's theatre in the Southeast; and its national tours have been endorsed by the Southern Arts Federation. The theatre was also selected to appear at the Kennedy Center's "Imagination Celebration" in Washington, D.C.

The 1983-84 season has begun Stage One's residency in the Kentucky Center for the Arts, a new multi-million dollar complex serving all of Kentucky and the surrounding states. The Center's Moritz Von Bomhard Theatre has been designed for Stage One to best accommodate young audiences, and the Whitney Theatre will house its occasional larger productions.

Stage One also presents a series of guest artists from the United States and abroad, which includes programs for family audiences complementing Stage One's own productions and helping to fulfill its mission.

Programs and services

Touring; programs-in-schools; classes for adults and children.

PRODUCTIONS 1981-82

Beauty and the Beast, Moses Goldberg; dir: Curt L. Tofteland
Diary of Anne Frank, Frances Goodrich and Albert Hackett; dir: Moses Goldberg
Christmas Firebird, Jackson Lacey; dir: Moses Goldberg
Rumpelstiltskin, company-developed; dir: Moses Goldberg
The Adventures of Hercules, Moses Goldberg; dir: Moses Goldberg
Boy Meets Girl Meets Shakespeare, adapt: Moses Goldberg; dir: Moses Goldberg

PRODUCTIONS 1982-83

Vasilisa, Moses Goldberg; dir: Moses Goldberg
Flowers for Algernon, adapt: David Rogers, from Daniel Keyes; dir: Moses Goldberg
Ozma of Oz, Suzan Zeder; dir: Suzan Zeder
Mother Goose, book adapt: Moses Goldberg; music: Lisa Palas; dir: Moses Goldberg
Jemima Boone, Moses Goldberg; dir: Moses Goldberg
Boy Meets Girl Meets Shakespeare, adapt: Curt L. Tofteland: dir: Curt L. Tofteland
Mark and Samuel and the Frog, adapt: Catherine Dezseran, from Mark Twain; dir: Catherine Dezseran

DESIGNERS

Sets: Randal R. Cochran.
Costumes: Deborah Brothers-Lowry, Lindsay W. Davis, Judy Hallberg, Donna Parrish, Ken Terrill.
Lights: Randal R. Cochran.

Stage One: The Louisville Children's Theatre. Terry Weber, Linda Parsons and Pamela Sterling in Jemima Boone. Photo: David Talbott.

StageWest

STEPHEN E. HAYS
Producing Director

JOHN SOUTHWORTH
Board President

Columbus Center
Springfield, MA 01103
(413) 781-4470 (business)
(413) 781-2340 (box office)

FOUNDED 1967
Stephen E. Hays

SEASON
October–May

SCHEDULE

Evenings
Tuesday–Sunday

Matinees
Wednesday, Sunday

FACILITIES

Blake Auditorium
Seating capacity: 480
Stage: thrust

Arms Studio Theatre
Seating capacity: 150
Stage: flexible

FINANCES
July 1, 1982–June 30, 1983
$826,000 operating expenses
$578,000 earned income
$249,000 grants/contributions

AUDIENCE
Annual attendance: 68,405
Subscribers: 704

TOURING CONTACT
Sheldon Wolf

BOOKED-IN EVENTS
Children's theatre festival, mime, magic, theatre, dance, music

AEA LORT (C) contract

Under the artistic leadership of Stephen Hays, StageWest has developed into a major Massachusetts arts institution dedicated to artistic excellence. Its repertoire and operating style assert the dignity and worth of human beings and their capacity for self-realization through the dramatic experience.

StageWest operates in the new Columbus Center complex in downtown Springfield which opened in November 1983. The complex includes the 480-seat Blake Auditorium and the 150-seat Arms Studio Theatre, as well as shops, offices, a rehearsal hall and storage space under one roof. With a population of 165,000, Springfield is a cultural melting pot; its massive downtown restoration project—of which the Columbus Center is a part—is fast nearing completion.

Although it has produced a wide variety of plays in the past 16 years, StageWest emphasizes new American works, particularly those which explore human relationships. The theatre has premiered many new works including *Marcus Brutus* by Paul Foster, *Count Dracula* by Ted Tiller, Michael Feingold's translation of *When We Dead Awaken* and Tennessee Williams' revised *Cat on a Hot Tin Roof*. StageWest does not maintain a permanent company in residence, but a small group of directors, designers and actors maintain an informal affiliation with the theatre and provide artistic continuity from season to season.

StageWest has also established itself as an educational resource. Among its many programs is its Heritage Matinee Series which has exposed thousands of students to professional theatre for the first time; its annual Children's Theatre Festival, internship program, post-performance discussions, workshops and readings.

StageWest. Holly Hunter and Bernard Frawley in Artichoke. *Photo: Bob Welsh, Jr.*

Steppenwolf Theatre Company

Programs and services

Children's Theatre Festival; internships; guest director/speaker series; workshops; readings; student matinees.

PRODUCTIONS 1981-82

Terra Nova, Ted Tally; dir: Hal Scott
Talley's Folly, Lanford Wilson; dir: Stephen E. Hays
Tintypes, music and lyrics: various; adapt: Mary Kyte, Mel Marvin and Gary Pearle; dir: Wayne Bryan
Hello and Goodbye, Athol Fugard; dir: Donald Hicken
Dead Wrong, Nick Hall; dir: Richard Gershman
Artichoke, Joanna M. Glass; dir: Timothy Near
You Never Can Tell, George Bernard Shaw; dir: Stephen E. Hays

PRODUCTIONS 1982-83

The Crucifer of Blood, Paul Giovanni; dir: Ted Weiant
Mass Appeal, Bill C. Davis; dir: Gregory Abels
Side by Side by Sondheim, music and lyrics: Stephen Sondheim, et al.; adapt: Ned Sherrin; dir: Wayne Bryan
The Belle of Amherst, William Luce; dir: Donald Hicken
Home, Samm-Art Williams; dir: Woodie King, Jr.
A Streetcar Named Desire, Tennessee Williams; dir: Timothy Near
Chapter Two, Neil Simon; dir: Stephen E. Hays

DESIGNERS

Sets: Frank J. Boros, Thomas Michael Cariello, Wally Coberg, Jeffrey A. Fiala, Joseph W. Long, Jeffrey Struckman, Paul Wonsek, Patricia Woodbridge.
Costumes: Georgia Carney, Elizabeth Covey, Leslie Miller, Jan Morrison, Rebecca Senske, Deborah Shaw, Jeffrey Struckman, John Carver Sullivan, Anne Thaxter Watson.
Lights: Barry Arnold, Bonnie Ann Brown, Ned Hallick, Paul J. Horton, Margaret Lee, Paul Wonsek.

JEFF PERRY
Artistic Director

STEPHEN B. EICH
Managing Director

DONNA VOS
Board President

2851 North Halsted
Chicago, IL 60657
(312) 472-4515 (business)
(312) 472-4141 (box office)

FOUNDED 1976
Terry Kinney, Jeff Perry, Gary Sinise

SEASON
Year-round

SCHEDULE
Evenings
Tuesday-Sunday

Matinees
Sunday

FACILITIES
Seating capacity: 221
Stage: thrust

FINANCES
October 1, 1982-September 30, 1983
$631,000 operating expenses
$320,000 earned income
$195,000 grants/contributions

AUDIENCE
Annual attendance: 49,000
Subscribers: 2,500

TOURING CONTACT
Jeff Perry

AEA Chicago Off Loop Theatre contract and letter of agreement

---

Steppenwolf Theatre Company's approach to theatre is as an ensemble, based on the tenets of other great ensembles such as the Royal Shakespeare Company and the Moscow Art Theatre. With a resident company of actors producing a wide-ranging repertoire (including established classics, neglected but important works and new plays), Steppenwolf's aim is to provide great theatre through a collective approach to dramatic art; theatre created in an atmosphere conducive to artistic growth and appreciation by audience and ensemble alike.

The individual artist's commitment to the ensemble approach is testament to its worth: seven of nine original members are still with the group after seven years. Steppenwolf strives to achieve that rare combination: talented individuals who put the group effort first, while simultaneously developing their own individual potential.

The company has sustained a shared vision of genuine, vibrant and dynamic theatre through the years. No thematic unity has been imposed on the selection of plays; yet from the company's early productions of *The Indian Wants the Bronx* and *The Dumbwaiter* to the most recent productions of *Cloud 9* and *The Miss Firecracker Contest*, an important unity emerges. Together, these productions express both an acknowledgement of the serious effects of alienation of our culture as well as an appreciation of the positive links of communication that remain open. When the ensemble performs, it takes full advantage of the dynamics of the dramatic situation to reveal to the audience the crucial and sometimes magical points of contact that remain among us.

Steppenwolf's objective is to create in Chicago a permanent resident company of national prominence, a theatre whose ongoing artistic vision includes the production of new plays, neglected plays and classics in facilities with the financial resources to attract renowned theatre artists from both the U.S. and abroad.

Programs and services

Training ensemble; programs-in-schools; professional and non-professional classes; internships; post-performance discussions; speakers.

PRODUCTIONS 1981-82

Savages, Christopher Hampton; dir: John Malkovich
Arms and the Man, George Bernard Shaw; dir: Sheldon Patinkin
No Man's Land, Harold Pinter; dir: John Malkovich

The Street Theater

Balm in Gilead, Lanford Wilson; dir: John Malkovich
Of Mice and Men, John Steinbeck; dir: Terry Kinney
Waiting for the Parade, John Murrell; dir: Gary Sinise

PRODUCTIONS 1982-83

Loose Ends, Michael Weller; dir: Austin Pendleton
True West, Sam Shepard; dir: Gary Sinise
The House, David Halliwell; dir: John Malkovich
A Prayer for My Daughter, Thomas Babe; dir: John Malkovich
And a Nightingale Sang, C.P. Taylor; dir: Terry Kinney
Cloud 9, Caryl Churchill; dir: Don Amendolia
A Moon for the Misbegotten, Eugene O'Neill; dir: Jeff Perry
The Miss Firecracker Contest, Beth Henley; dir: Gary Sinise

DESIGNERS

Sets: Louis DiCrescenzo, Deb Gohr, John Malkovich, Kevin Rigdon, John Sanchez.
Costumes: Mary Copple, Louis DiCrescenzo, Jane McIntyre, John Malkovich, Patti Minter, Wendy Oldenburg.
Lights: Louis DiCrescenzo, Terry Kinney, Kevin Rigdon, John Sanchez.

Steppenwolf Theatre Company. William Petersen and Jeff Perry in Balm in Gilead. *Photo: Lisa Ebright.*

GRAY SMITH
Executive Director

LAURENCE S. BAKER
Board Chairman

228 Fisher Ave., Room 226
White Plains, NY 10606
(914) 761-3307

FOUNDED 1970
Gray Smith

SEASON
Year-round touring

FINANCES
June 1, 1981-May 31, 1982
$172,000 operating expenses
$ 17,000 earned income
$162,000 grants/contributions

AUDIENCE
Annual attendance: 15,000

TOURING CONTACT
Gray Smith

Founded in 1970, The Street Theater reaches its audiences through year-round touring (carrying a portable stage in summer), performing plays which reflect and transform its audience's experience. Whether in the street, in prisons or in schools, audiences are not treated as spectators but as participants in a shared experience. They are approached as potential actors, given the training and opportunity to be on stage themselves. Central to the theatre's programs, therefore, are its workshop programs, which draw many of their participants from performance audiences. These workshops follow 16- to 20-week cycles at 50 to 150 hours per cycle. All are conducted by professionals with a strong commitment to developmental theatre, and many conclude with performances.

From 1971-76, The Street Theater worked in 10 state prisons and developed 30 productions through this process, all the while encouraging new playwrights — including Miguel Pinero, who has gone on to national recognition. Recent workshop programs have been either community-based or school-based, and have concentrated on a younger population ages 16-21 throughout

Studio Arena Theatre

The Street Theater. Fran Marcianio and Lonnie James in Distilled Spirits. *Photo: Ron Gabel.*

DAVID FRANK
Artistic Director

MICHAEL P. PITEK, III
Managing Director

WILLIAM E. GODIN
Board President

710 Main St.
Buffalo, NY 14202
(716) 856-8025 (business)
(716) 856-5650 (box office)

FOUNDED 1965
Neal DuBrock

SEASON
September-June

SCHEDULE

Evenings
Tuesday-Sunday

Matinees
Sunday

FACILITIES
Seating capacity: 637
Stage: thrust

FINANCES
July 1, 1982-June 30, 1983
$2,130,000 operating expenses
$1,458,000 earned income
$ 549,000 grants/contributions

AUDIENCE
Annual attendance: 129,717
Subscribers: 11,882

BOOKED-IN EVENTS
Theatre

AEA LORT (B) contract

Westchester County. Though known for its high per capita income, Westchester's increasing ethnic and cultural diversity provide a growing audience for The Street Theater's productions, and an increasing number of participants for its training program.

Since 1979, a Youth Company whose actors come from a variety of communities has been given an opportunity to work with professionals, developing their own material through collaboration or performing commissioned plays.

In street, school and community settings, The Street Theater performs for an annual audience of 12,000 to 15,000.

Programs and services

Professional training; programs-in-schools; touring; Youth Company; workshops.

PRODUCTIONS 1981—82

Distilled Spirits, Donald Nathanson and company; dir: Donald Nathanson
Crime Don't Pay No Wages, Martin Henderson, Patricia Smith and Lonnie James; dir: Lester Franklin
Flame Keepers, Donald Nathanson and Lonnie James; dir: Donald Nathanson
'Chines, Donald Nathanson; dir: Donald Nathanson
Growing Up, Donald Nathanson and company; dir: Donald Nathanson

PRODUCTIONS 1982-83

Distilled Spirits, Donald Nathanson and company; adapt: Martin Henderson; dir: Martin Henderson
Yeast Beast, Martin Henderson and company; dir: Martin Henderson
Playground, Patricia Smith and company; dir: Patricia Smith

Buffalo's Studio Arena Theatre was founded in 1965 by Neal DuBrock, and has since presented 148 productions, 27 of which were world or American premieres. Since 1980, when David Frank took the reins, it has continued primarily to present contemporary American works, including a substantial number of new plays, while extending its range by adding selected classics and unusual European works.

Studio Arena Theatre. Kathryn Grody, Donna Davis, Stephen Tobolowsky, K.T. Baumann and Robert Darnell in The Miss Firecracker Contest. *Photo: Irene Haupt.*

Simply stated, Studio Arena seeks to serve the Buffalo community in two ways: as the only continuous source of professional theatre in the area, it provides a wide range of established and accessible works that appeal to a widely varied audience; as a nonprofit organization dedicated to its art, it is committed to aesthetic goals as ends in themselves. It is Studio Arena's belief that if its heart remains devoted to an artistic mission, even its less ambitious productions will be enlivened by imagination and craft, while their popularity will help widen the audience for more demanding and unusual work (and also help pay for it). The theatre seeks to present popular productions distinguished by integrity and skill, as well as more demanding productions distinguished by lucidity and relevance—and a great variety of work that contains all of these elements.

Studio Arena has a particular affection for texts that expand beyond the dominant naturalistic conventions and scope of contemporary theatre. It takes pride in its ability to give standard works unusual but responsible treatments and to take full advantage of more theatrical scripts.

Studio Arena also strives to create an environment that is comfortable and rewarding for its visiting artists. Currently, artists are selected specifically for each production. However, relationships with visiting artists are becoming more permanent, and the theatre aims to build a core resident company over the next few years.

Programs and services

Studio Arena Theatre School; Behind-the-Scenes post-performance discussions; speaker's bureau; internships; newsletter; ticket discounts; workshops; volunteers; voucher program.

PRODUCTIONS 1981-82

Whose Life Is It, Anyway?, Brian Clark; dir: David Frank
The Miss Firecracker Contest, Beth Henley; dir: Davey Marlin-Jones
Deathtrap, Ira Levin; dir: David Frank
Tartuffe, Molière; trans: Richard Wilbur; dir: David Frank
Derelict, Robert Schenkkan; dir: A.J. Antoon
Of Mice and Men, John Steinbeck; dir: Geoffrey Sherman
Rhino Fat from Red Dog Notes, Patrick Desmond, Davey Marlin-Jones and company; dir: Davey Marlin-Jones

PRODUCTIONS 1982-83

She Stoops to Conquer, Oliver Goldsmith; dir: David Frank
True West, Sam Shepard; dir: Kathryn Long
Witness for the Prosecution, Agatha Christie; dir: David Frank
A Raisin in the Sun, Lorraine Hansberry; dir: Harold Scott
Weapons of Happiness, Howard Brenton; dir: Geoffrey Sherman
In the Sweet Bye and Bye, Donald Driver; dir: John Henry Davis
Absurd Person Singular, Alan Ayckbourn; dir: David Frank

DESIGNERS

Sets: John Arnone, Thomas Michael Cariello, Wally Coberg, Gary C. Eckhart, Grady Larkins, J. Robin Modereger, Robert Morgan, Quentin Thomas, Paul Wonsek, David Woolard.
Costumes: Judy Dearing, Andrew Blackwood Marlay, Robert Morgan, Lewis D. Rampino, Catherine B. Reich, Donna Langman, Janice I. Lines, Bill Walker.
Lights: Robert Jared, Robby Monk, Shirley Prendergast, Brett Thomas, Quentin Thomas, Michael Orris Watson, Paul Wonsek.

Syracuse Stage

ARTHUR STORCH
Producing Director

JAMES A. CLARK
Managing Director

JED DIETZ
Board President

820 East Genesee St.
Syracuse, NY 13210
(315) 423-4008 (business)
(315) 423-3275 (box office)

FOUNDED 1974
Arthur Storch

SEASON
October-May

SCHEDULE
Evenings
Tuesday-Sunday

Matinees
Wednesday, Saturday, Sunday

FACILITIES
John D. Archbold Theatre
Seating capacity: 510
Stage: proscenium

Experimental Theatre
Seating capacity: 202
Stage: proscenium

Daniel C. Sutton Pavilion
Seating capacity: 100
Stage: flexible

FINANCES
July 1, 1982-June 30, 1983
$1,429,000 operating expenses
$ 683,000 earned income
$ 745,000 grants/contributions

AUDIENCE
Annual attendance: 110,705
Subscribers: 9,206

TOURING CONTACT
Barbara Beckos

AEA LORT (C) contract

Syracuse Stage is the only professional theatre in central New York, and is committed to presenting a wide spectrum of theatrical imagery. Its seasons are planned with various purposes in mind: to encourage thought, provoke emotion, advocate change — and simply to entertain. Productions are planned through a systematic process designed to balance artistic and institutional needs, and success is measured in terms of a production's ability to engage its audience.

Syracuse Stage is also committed to the production of new plays, and generally produces two each season. Several Syracuse Stage productions have generated interest beyond Syracuse, including *Twice Around the Park* with Anne Jackson and Eli Wallach, which had a commercial run in New York; and Sam Shepard's *The Tooth of Crime*, which was co-produced with New York's La Mama ETC and played there after its Syracuse run.

The new Archbold Theatre, Syracuse Stage's primary space, features a proscenium stage with an expandable thrust; other facilities include a 125-seat cabaret theatre and a 199-seat space used primarily by the Syracuse University drama department and for special events.

Syracuse Stage enjoys a unique relationship with the University, whose active drama department exists side-by-side with the professional company. The theatre enjoys support from the Syracuse community and is recognized as a leading force in the cultural life of the region.

Syracuse Stage. Raul Aranas, Richard Allen, Peter Jay Fernandez, Stephen Mellor and Ray Wise in The Tooth of Crime. *Photo: Susan Piper Kublick.*

Tacoma Actors Guild

Programs and services

Elementary school touring; After Ours late-night entertainment; staged readings of new plays; programs-in-schools; costume collection.

PRODUCTIONS 1981-82

Betrayal, Harold Pinter; dir: Terry Schreiber
A Christmas Carol, adapt: Stephen Willems, from Charles Dickens; dir: Stephen Willems
The Merchant of Venice, William Shakespeare; dir: Ken Jenkins
Twice Around the Park, Murray Schisgal; dir: Arthur Storch
Talley's Folly, Lanford Wilson; dir: John Ulmer
K2, Patrick Meyers; dir: Terry Schreiber

PRODUCTIONS 1982-83

Cat on a Hot Tin Roof, Tennessee Williams; dir: John Going
We Won't Pay! We Won't Pay!, Dario Fo; adapt: R.G. Davis; dir: Jerome Guardino
A Christmas Carol
The Tooth of Crime, Sam Shepard; dir: George Ferencz
The Impromptu of Outremont, Michel Tremblay; trans: John Van Burek; dir: Arthur Storch
Deathtrap, Ira Levin; dir: Edward Stern
Death of a Salesman, Arthur Miller; dir: Steven Schachter

DESIGNERS

Sets: Charles Cosler, Bob Davidson, John Doepp, Kristine Haugan, William Schroder, Bill Stabile, Quentin Thomas, James Tilton, Hal Tiné, Patricia Woodbridge.
Costumes: Nanzi Adzima, James Berton Harris, Kristine Haugan, Sally Lesser, Maria Marrero, John David Ridge, William Schroder, Anne Shanto, David Toser.
Lights: Charles Cosler, Paul Mathiesen, Spencer Mosse, Michael Newton-Brown, William T. Paton, Judy Rasmuson, Robert F. Strohmeier, Marc B. Weiss.

RICK TUTOR
Artistic Director

SQUEAK ALLAN
Board President

1323 South Yakima
Tacoma, WA 98405
(206) 272-3107 (business)
(206) 272-2145 (box office)

FOUNDED 1979
Rick Tutor, William Becvar

SEASON
October-April

SCHEDULE
Evenings
Tuesday-Sunday

Matinees
Wednesday, Sunday

FACILITIES
Seating capacity: 298
Stage: flexible

FINANCES
July 1, 1982-June 30, 1983
$542,000 operating expenses
$327,000 earned income
$369,000 grants/contributions

AUDIENCE
Annual attendance: 6,000
Subscribers: 4,885

AEA LORT (D) contract

Tacoma Actors Guild was founded in 1978 as the first professional theatre in that city. Its establishment—in an abandoned school in the fading downtown area—lit a spark that ignited a fire of enthusiasm and pride in what had been a dormant community.

TAG showcases the talents of many fine actors from the Tacoma/Seattle area in a balance of traditional and contemporary drama which serves the varied tastes of the community. Company members feel strongly the obligation to themselves as artists, and are committed to the encouragement and development of new plays and promising young artists.

TAG is especially interested in introducing new directors to the Northwest, who bring with them interesting new techniques and concepts, as well as discovering new artists for the area acting pool.

TAG is a theatre organization with great spirit and drive for excellence, committed to professionalism while continuing to demand more of itself each season.

Programs and services

Newsletter; staged readings; technical internships; park shows and summer touring; post-performance discussions.

PRODUCTIONS 1981-82

That Championship Season, Jason Miller; dir: Rick Tutor
Vanities, Jack Heifner; dir: Roberta Levitow
Deathtrap, Ira Levin; dir: Sean Austin-Olson
Who's Happy Now?, Oliver Hailey; dir: David Booth
Desire under the Elms, Eugene O'Neill; dir: William Becvar
Diamond Studs: The Life of Jesse James, book: Jim Wann; music and lyrics: Bland Simpson and Jim Wann; dir: Rick Tutor

Theatre by the Sea

Tacoma Actors Guild. David Mong, C.R. Gardner and Peggy Schoditsch in Betrayal. *Photo: Fred Andrews.*

PRODUCTIONS 1982-83

Of Mice and Men, John Steinbeck; dir: Rick Tutor
The Rivals, Richard Brinsley Sheridan; dir: William Becvar
Standing on My Knees, John Olive; dir: Claudia Weill
Filumena, Eduardo De Filippo; dir: Richard Edwards
Betrayal, Harold Pinter; dir: Charles Towers
Billy Bishop Goes to War, John Gray and Eric Peterson; dir: Rick Tutor

DESIGNERS

Sets: David Butler, Karen Gjeltsteen, Phil Holte, Bruce Jackson, Kat Leighton, Stephen Packard, Scott Weldin, J.C. Wills.
Costumes: Marion Hill Cottrell, Ron Erickson, Julie James, Dan McWest, Susan Min, Michael Murphy, Sally Richardson, Leslie Simpson.
Lights: J. Patrick Elmer, Robert Peterson, Carmine Simone, William C. Strock, Charles Towers.

JEFFREY ROSENSTOCK
Producing Director

NANCY BECK
Board President

Box 927
Portsmouth, NH 03801
(603) 431-5846 (business)
(603) 431-6660 (box office)

FOUNDED 1964
Pat and C. Stanley Flower

SEASON
September-May, July-August

SCHEDULE
Evenings
Tuesday-Sunday

Matinees
Saturday, Sunday

FACILITIES
125 Bow St.
Seating capacity: 263
Stage: thrust

FINANCES
September 1, 1982-August 31, 1983
$899,000 operating expenses
$730,000 earned income
$149,000 grants/contributions

AUDIENCE
Annual attendance: 310,000
Subscribers: 4,500

TOURING CONTACT
Jeffrey Rosenstock

BOOKED-IN EVENTS
Music, dance, puppetry

AEA LORT (C) contract

Theatre by the Sea has a 20-year track record that includes the production of more than 200 plays at its original home on Ceres Street, at the Bow Street Theatre, at Prescott Park Summer Arts Festival, in institutions and on stages across the New England coast. In addition, it has brought two new works to national attention: Patrick Meyers' *K2,* which received several subsequent productions including one on Broadway; and *On the Swingshift,* a musical which later garnered a production at the Manhattan Theatre Club. Theatre by the Sea is committed to continuously exploring and redefining its role in the community, to better serve the area's needs as it grows and changes.

TBS is concerned with what Joseph Papp describes as "the essence of theatre; the process of making it," a process that depends on the commitment of talented artists, a community of theatregoers and a theatrical institution all strong and supple enough to support the process and share in its development and growth.

Collectively, the company is interested in exploring the full scope of the theatregoing experience; from a shared leisure activity to the communal search for better recognition and understanding among individuals.

To gain a position in the community that is recognized as being as vital as the post office, the supermarket, the physician and the barber, TBS artists feel they must approach their work with integrity, professional pride and artistic joy.

Programs and services

Touring; lecture and discussion series; bookshop; internships; children's workshops and performances; new play reading series; school tour; spring community show.

PRODUCTIONS 1981-82

The Mousetrap, Agatha Christie; dir: Jon Kimbell
The Rainmaker, N. Richard Nash; dir: Jon Kimbell
Charley's Aunt, Brandon Thomas; dir: Jon Kimbell
Absurd Person Singular, Alan Ayckbourn; dir: Peter Bennett
A Streetcar Named Desire, Tennessee Williams; dir: Kent Paul
K2, Patrick Meyers; dir: B. Rodney Marriott
The Man of La Mancha, book: Dale Wasserman; music: Mitch Leigh; lyrics: Joe Darion; dir: Jon Kimbell

Theater for the New City

PRODUCTIONS 1982-83

Swing Shift, music: Michael Dansicker; lyrics: Sarah Schlesinger; dir: Jack Allison

Arms and the Man, George Bernard Shaw; dir: Larry Carpenter

The Butterfingers Angel, William Gibson; dir: Tom Celli

Deathtrap, Ira Levin; dir: Peter Bennett

Children of a Lesser God, Mark Medoff; dir: Edmund Waterstreet

Mass Appeal, Bill C. Davis; dir: Tom Celli

Pippin, book: Roger O. Hirson; music and lyrics: Stephen Schwartz; dir: Loyd Sannes

DESIGNERS

Sets: Joan Brancale, Ed Cesaitis, Richard Chambers, John Doepp, Larry Fulton, Kathie Iannicelli, Mark Pirolo, Fred Voelpel.

Costumes: Eliza Dietsch Chugg, Kathie Iannicelli.

Lights: Sid Bennett, Bruce K. Morriss.

Theatre by the Sea. Pippin. Photo: Andy Edgar.

GEORGE BARTENIEFF
CRYSTAL FIELD
Artistic Directors

HARVEY SEIFTER
Managing Director

GEORGE BARTENIEFF
Board President

162 Second Ave.
New York, NY 10003
(212) 254-1109

FOUNDED 1970
George Bartenieff, Crystal Field, Lawrence Kornfeld, Theo Barnes

SEASON
Year-round

SCHEDULE
Evenings
Thursday-Sunday

FACILITIES
Cino Theater
Seating capacity: 150
Stage: proscenium

Waring Theater
Seating capacity: 200
Stage: flexible

Stanley Theater
Seating capacity: 50
Stage: flexible

FINANCES
July 1, 1982-June 30, 1983
$249,000 operating expenses
$ 48,000 earned income
$201,000 grants/contributions

AUDIENCE
Annual attendance: 55,000

TOURING CONTACT
Otis Gustavson

AEA Showcase code

Theater for the New City, now entering its 14th season, is a community-based center for the creation and performance of new American theatre, dedicated to the discov-

Theater for the New City. George Bartenieff in The Restaurant, or Your Goose is Cooked. Photo: Charles Marinaro.

ery and development of new playwrights and the nurturing of relevant writing. TNC particularly strives to amalgamate song and dance, live music and poetry into serious drama.

TNC functions as a writer's theatre—offering playwrights the opportunity to grow and develop free from commercial pressures; allowing them to work with their choice of directors, designers, composers and choreographers; commissioning new work (TNC's commissioning program is now in its sixth year of sponsoring the creation of five to eight full-length dramas and comedies each year); and providing each play selected with a fully realized mainstage production.

TNC also serves as a training ground for hundreds of young performers, directors and designers, and as a laboratory for important and emerging experimental theatre artists and companies. Since its early work with the companies of Richard Foreman, Charles Ludlam and Mabou Mines, TNC has strived to help foster the work of these and other artists — including the Bread and Puppet Theater and Spiderwoman Theater — premiering new work, commissioning new pieces and providing performance facilities.

TNC's Resident Theater Program also premieres at least 10 new full-length American plays each season, while its New Writer's Workshop (begun in 1982) provides training, workshops and play readings for its newest writers.

Theater for the New City combines its experimental/developmental ventures with a very active community outreach program. Its Summer Street Theater Program each year creates a new street opera for a company of 50 people trained in its Street Theater Workshops, involving dance, mask-making, clowning, tumbling and stiltwalking, as well as music. The production tours New York—from Central Park to the South Bronx—and is seen free of charge by 25,000 New Yorkers.

Programs and services

Resident Theater Program; New Writer's Workshop; Street Theater Program; presentation of guest companies.

PRODUCTIONS 1981-82

The Restaurant, or Your Goose is Cooked, book and lyrics: Crystal Field; music: Mark Hardwick; dir: Crystal Field
Ragged Dick, Paul Foster; dir: Lester Malizia
Miracle Man, Robert Dahdah; dir: Robert Dahdah
My Heart Is in Your Shoes, Yuri Belov; dir: Yuri Belov
Black and Blues, Ray Povod; dir: Patricia Contaxis
Selma, Shami Chaikin; dir: Karen Ludwig
Zaloominations, Paul Zaloom; dir: Paul Zaloom
Autumn Portraits, Eric Bass; dir: Eric Bass
Rent, Walter Corwin; dir: Carol Ilson
Endings, Joe Renard; dir: Joe Renard
La Bodega Sold Dreams, Miguel Pinero; dir: Tito Goya
Zeks, Maria Rasa; dir: Jonas Jurasas
A Visit, Maria Irene Fornes; dir: Maria Irene Fornes
Aboriginal Sin, Daryl Chin; dir: Daryl Chin
Lady of the Castle, Mira Specktor; dir: Andrea Balis
The Tenants, Marshall Williams; dir: Anthony Major
The Blonde Leading the Blonde, Stephen Holt; dir: John Albano
Falsies, Betsy Newman; dir: Betsy Newman
Horizontal White II, Barry Marshall; dir: Barry Marshall
A Crock of Gold, Rina Elisha; dir: Rina Elisha
Letters to Ben, Chuck Choset; dir: Lisa Simon

PRODUCTIONS 1982-83

Keep Truckin', book and lyrics: Crystal Field; music: Mark Hardwick; dir: Crystal Field
The Little Black Fish, Samad Behrangi; dir: Manuchehr Harsini
Before She Is Even Born, Leah Friedman; dir: Susan Einhorn
Umbrellas, Bicuspids and Angels, Tom LeBar; dir: Ken Buckshi
24 Inches, Robert Patrick; dir: Robert Patrick
Golden Girl, Peter Occhiogrosso; dir: Ron Link
The Owl Was a Baker's Daughter, Alice Eve Cohen; dir: Alice Eve Cohen
Lady Speaks Her Mind, Amelia Cobb Gray; dir: Amelia Cobb Gray
The Dialectic of Enlightenment, Daryl Chin; dir: Daryl Chin
Sheen's Outside, Ray Dobbins; dir: Jon Stolzberg
Commercial Theater, Ross MacLean; dir: Ellen Nichols

Theater of the Open Eye

Theater of the Open Eye. Leslie Dillingham, Keith Druhl, Kathleen McKiernan, Leigh Podgorski and John Wallace-Wilson in The Coach with the Six Insides. *Photo: Ken Howard.*

When Hell Freezes Over, Joelle Ballouzole; dir: Joelle Ballouzole
Growing Up Gothic, Clare Coss; dir: Margot Lewitin
The Beaux Arts Ball, Robert Patrick; dir: Robert Patrick
Feelers, Betsy Newmann; dir: Betsy Newmann
The Man Who Became a Woman, Martin Worman; dir: Martin Worman
Messiah, Chuck Choset; dir: Chuck Choset
The Danube, Maria Irene Fornes; dir: Maria Irene Fornes

DESIGNERS

Sets: D.E. Abraham, Luis Alonso, Anthony Angel, Eugenie Bafalous, Donald Brooks, Tim Brooks, Bobjack Callego, Reagan Cook, L.B. Dallas, Donald Eastman, Lisa Engel, Audrey Hemenway, Dolly Holmes, Sally Jacobs, Ron Kajiwara, Libby Kendall, Steve Lepre, Monica Lorca, Terri Lucas, Loette McCoy, Alex Okun, Bob Phillips, Jorge Pissarro, Douglas Pleyer, Seth Price, Joe Ray, John Sabato, Tracy Sherman, Larry Steckman, Hank Stevens, Mike Sullivan, Danny Talpers, Leslie Taylor, Elwin Charles Terrel II, Howard Thies, Christina Weppner, Marshall Williams, Joni Wong.
Costumes: Jill Anderson, Eugenie Bafaloukos, Martha Bard, Gabriel Berry, Mary Brecht, Scott Brooks, Brenda Colling, Shay Cunliffe, Jessica Fassman, Edmund Felix, Angel Jack, Lisa Keim, John Lakesmith, Cathy Lazar, Paul-Felix Montez, Monica Morrison, Susan Murton, Alex Okun, Jorge Pissaro, Soretta Rodack, Bernard Roth, Don Sheffield, Muriel Stockdale, Jeffrey Wallach, Christina Weppner.
Lights: Faith Baum, Donald Brooks, Rachel Budin, Rick Butler, Heather Carson, Manny Cavaco, Jr., Richard Currie, Harry Darrow, Ghasem Ebrahimian, Bonnie Edgecomb, Beverly Emmons, Victor En Yu Tan, Chaim Gitter, Lisa Grossman, Alvin Ho, Christopher Holt, Dale Nordan, Craig Kennedy, Curtis La Bon, Brett Landow, Ann Militello, Tim Phillips, William Plachy, Joe Ray, Rich Rogers, Joanna Schielke, Howard Thies, Joni Wong.

JEAN ERDMAN
Producing Artistic Director

AMIE BROCKWAY
Associate Artistic Director

JOSEPH CAMPBELL
Board President

316 East 88th St.
New York, NY 10028
(212) 534-6363 (business)
(212) 534-6909 (box office)

FOUNDED 1972
Jean Erdman,
Joseph Campbell

SEASON
December–June

SCHEDULE
Evenings
Thursday–Monday

Matinees
Saturday, Sunday

FACILITIES
Seating capacity: 99
Stage: flexible

FINANCES
July 1, 1982–June 30, 1983
$158,000 operating expenses
$ 67,000 earned income
$ 91,000 grants/contributions

AUDIENCE
Annual attendance: 10,000
Subscribers: 100

TOURING CONTACT
Lee TenEyck

BOOKED-IN EVENTS
Theatre, dance

AEA letter of agreement

The Foundation for the Open Eye was founded in 1972 by dancer/choreographer/director Jean Erdman and internationally renowned author/lecturer Joseph Campbell as an expression of their interest in the roots of human thought and feeling as revealed in mythic and poetic images. Through its professional theatre company, Theater of the Open Eye, the foundation presents live theatre and dance works to the public as well as an annual Holiday Dance Festival, a New Stagings Lab and a Mainstage Drama Series.

For its mainstage series, the Open Eye prefers new plays, adaptations or translations which deal with mythic heroes and/or have a poetic quality. Many of these works are staged in a style which fuses music, dance and drama, which has been dubbed "total theatre."

Among the recent total theatre productions directed and choreographed by artistic director Jean Erdman are *Moon Mysteries,* an evening of one-act plays by W.B. Yeats; *The Shining House,* a work based on Hawaiian mythology; and a revival of her award-winning 1962 production, *The Coach with the Six Insides,* based on James Joyce's *Finnegans Wake.* Erdman's productions have

Theatre Project Company

toured extensively throughout the U.S. and in Canada, Europe and Japan.

Each season, the Open Eye provides creative opportunities for approximately 100 talented professionals — playwrights, directors, choreographers, designers, composers and performers — and has always afforded unusual opportunities to women and ethnic minorities. The theatre strives for artistic excellence within a supportive atmosphere of artistic risk-taking.

Programs and services

New Stagings Lab; Joseph Campbell Seminar Series; Dance Film Series; internships; classes.

PRODUCTIONS 1981-82

Holiday Dance Festival, Jean Erdman
The Coach with the Six Insides, adapt: Jean Erdman; music: Teiji Ito; dir: Jean Erdman
Punch with Judy, Rosemary Foley; music: John Yanelli; dir: Dana Coen
The Sun Gets Blue, William "Electric" Black; music: Paul Shapiro; dir: Amie Brockway
The Ditch, adapt: Ann Scofield; music: David Simons; dir: Ann Scofield

PRODUCTIONS 1982-83

Holiday Dance Festival
Behind a Mask, adapt: Karen L. Lewis, from Louisa May Alcott; dir: Amie Brockway
Phantom Limbs, Charles Borkhuis; dir: Gitta Honnegger
La Belle Au Bois, Jules Supervielle; trans: Irma Brandeis; music: Elliot Sokolov; dir: Jean Erdman and Amie Brockway

DESIGNERS

Sets: Power Boothe, Adrienne J. Brockway, Dan Butt, Clayton Campbell, Rob Hamilton.
Costumes: Adrienne J. Brockway, Jane Clark, Sue Ellen Rohrer, Gail Ryan, Karen Selby, Esther K. Smith.
Lights: Scott Breindel, Adrienne J. Brockway, Clayton Campbell, Stoney Cook, Phil Monat, Kathryn Reid.

FONTAINE SYER
Artistic Director

CHRISTINE E. SMITH
General Manager

TALMAGE NEWTON
MICHAEL CURTH
Board Co-Chairmen

4219 Laclede
St. Louis, MO 63108
(314) 531-1301

FOUNDED 1975
Fontaine Syer, Christine E. Smith

SEASON
September-April

SCHEDULE
Evenings
Thursday-Sunday

Matinees
Sunday

FACILITIES
5209 Waterman St.
Seating capacity: 300
Stage: thrust

Theatre Project Company. Gray Stephens and Mary Ellen Falk in The Sea Horse. *Photo: Susan M. Greenburg.*

FINANCES
July 1, 1982-June 30, 1983
$237,000 operating expenses
$137,000 earned income
$101,000 grants/contributions

AUDIENCE
Annual attendance: 67,500
Subscribers: 743

TOURING CONTACT
Debra Wicks

BOOKED-IN EVENTS
Mime, dance, theatre

AEA Chicago Off Loop Theatre contract

Theatre Project Company, identified as "St. Louis' Off Broadway theatre" has, since its founding in 1975, focused its energy on developing local theatre artists and offering the metropolitan community a unique experience through both its choice of plays and its methods of production. The Project emphasizes intimacy and immediacy — and the maximum emotional connection between actors and audience. While the majority of the Project's plays are contemporary works — frequently St. Louis premieres — it also produces revivals of American and European plays and unconventional productions of classics.

The artistic core of the theatre is a group of actor-directors whose mutual exchange and

Theatre Three

support stimulate constant creative growth and challenge. While not a collective, many staff members have both artistic and management responsibilities. The benefits of this collaboration are evident in the work itself as well as in the day-to-day operation of the theatre.

The student program of the Theatre Project Company, The Muny/Student Theatre Project, is produced in cooperation with the Muny Opera, and offers touring shows and workshops for kindergarten through high school, story-telling shows, classes, apprenticeships and residencies.

Theatre Project Company is the designated theatre-in-residence at the University of Missouri/St. Louis. Project staff members teach and direct in the undergraduate theatre department; some performances are offered on campus; and the company is active in stimulating high school awareness of the university's theatre program.

The Lyn Theatre, built in 1912 and in need of complete renovation, has been donated to the Theatre Project Company. It is located in midtown St. Louis quite near Powell Hall, home of the St. Louis Symphony, and the newly restored Fox Theatre. Preliminary architectural drawings for the renovation are complete and fund-raising has begun with an eye on opening the new theatre in 1985. The Lyn will house both a proscenium theatre and a smaller, flexible space, and will allow the company to develop new programs such as readings, experimental work and an expanded teaching schedule.

Programs and services

Muny/Student Theatre Project; classes; internships; newsletter.

PRODUCTIONS 1981-82

Scapino!, Frank Dunlop and Jim Dale; dir: Courtney Flanagan
Butley, Simon Gray; dir: Fontaine Syer
Coming Attractions, Ted Tally; dir: Wayne Salomon
A Moon for the Misbegotten, Eugene O'Neill; dir: Fontaine Syer
Happy Birthday, Wanda June, Kurt Vonnegut, Jr.; dir: Courtney Flanagan
The Great Playground Plot, company-developed; dir: David Novak
The Matinee Kid, John Contini; dir: Courtney Flanagan
Marvelous Mo's Mysterious Show, Brian Hohlfeld; dir: Brian Hohlfeld
Killpoint, John Grassilli; dir: Courtney Flanagan
Shakespeare's People, adapt: Fontaine Syer; dir: Fontaine Syer
All Aboard the Orient Express, Brian Hohlfeld and David Novak; dir: Brian Hohlfeld
Great Religions, Great Stories, adapt: Courtney Flanagan; dir: Courtney Flanagan
In the Beginning, adapt: Courtney Flanagan; dir: Courtney Flanagan

PRODUCTIONS 1982-83

Bleacher Bums, Organic Theater Company; dir: Wayne Salomon
Bent, Martin Sherman: dir: Fontaine Syer
A Toby Show, Aurand Harris; dir: David Novak
Sister Mary Ignatius Explains It All for You, Christopher Durang; dir: Brian Hohlfeld
The Sea Horse, Edward J. Moore; dir: John Grassilli
Working, book adapt: Stephen Schwartz, from Studs Terkel; music and lyrics: Stephen Schwartz, et al.; dir: Courtney Flanagan
Arthur and Merlin, Brian Hohlfeld; dir: Brian Hohlfeld
Brothers, John Contini; dir: Courtney Flanagan
Shrew!, adapt: David Novak; dir: Fontaine Syer
Marvelous Mo's Mysterious Show
The Five Freedoms Revue, Susan M. Greenberg; dir: Courtney Flanagan
All Aboard the Orient Express
Great Religions, Great Stories
Explorers, David Novak and Courtney Flanagan; dir: Courtney Flanagan

DESIGNERS

Sets: Hunter Breyer, Jim Fay, Jay Ferger, Bill Schmiel, Kay Webb.
Costumes: Elizabeth Eisloeffel, Mary Ann Grothe, Kim Gruner, Lanette Marquardt, Kay Webb.
Lights: Daniel V. Belfontaine, Jim Greer, Christine E. Smith, Craig VanTassel, Deirdre A. Taylor.

NORMA YOUNG
Artistic Director

JAC ALDER
Executive Producer-Director

MICHAEL BARLERIN
Board Chairman

2800 Routh St.
Dallas, TX 75201
(214) 651-7225 (business)
(214) 871-3300 (box office)

FOUNDED 1961
Norma Young

SEASON
October-August

SCHEDULE
Evenings
Tuesday-Sunday

Matinees
Sunday

FACILITIES
Seating capacity: 242
Stage: arena

FINANCES
September 1, 1982-August 31, 1983
$741,000 operating expenses
$448,000 earned income
$313,000 grants/contributions

AUDIENCE
Annual attendance: 52,381
Subscribers: 3,900

TOURING CONTACT
Jac Alder

BOOKED-IN EVENTS
Theatre, dance, mime

AEA LORT (D) contract

Theatre Three was named by its founder, Norma Young, for the three basic elements of the theatrical experience: the script, the production and the audience. Young's aim has been to create an artistic environment in which each of these elements makes an equal contribution.

Theatre Three. Sweeney Todd. *Photo: Andy Hanson.*

At Theatre Three, audiences bring their temperaments and their senses of time and place to bear on an eclectic play selection. Recognizing the varied constituencies within the audience—and within the arts community—the range includes plays on the black experience, plays with music, works of new playwrights, classics, staples of academic study and a special series of children's plays.

The physical style of Theatre Three's productions reflects the characteristics of the modified arena space — designed for the company—which it occupies. Guest directors and designers augment the standing staff, in order to ventilate the theatre's artistic approach. Programming is augmented through the presentation of such artists as Marcel Marceau, Emlyn Williams and Hal Holbrook in their one-man shows.

Theatre Three pursues a relationship with sister arts organizations; joint productions have been presented with minority arts companies and musical organizations around Dallas. The theatre is also linked to a network of health/welfare organizations and educational institutions, which it serves with a variety of programs. This in turn helps the theatre to define its own role in the community.

Programs and services

Children's theatre; internships; newsletter and other publications; staged readings.

PRODUCTIONS 1981-82

Working, book adapt: Stephen Schwartz, from Studs Terkel; music and lyrics: Stephen Schwartz et al.; dir: Jac Alder
The Physician in Spite of Himself, Molière; adapt: Jac Alder; dir: Jac Alder
The Gondoliers, book and lyrics: W.S. Gilbert; music: Arthur Sullivan; dir: Jack Eddleman
The Second Stage Festival:
   Eden Court, Murphy Guyer; dir: Laurence O'Dwyer
   The World of Paul Crume, adapt: Jerry Haynes and Laurence O'Dwyer; dir: Laurence O'Dwyer
   Splendid Rebels, Ernest Joselovitz; dir: Charles Howard
Design for Living, Noel Coward; dir: Laurence O'Dwyer
Close of Play, Simon Gray; dir: Norma Young
Billy Bishop Goes to War, John Gray and Eric Peterson; dir: Jac Alder

PRODUCTIONS 1982-83

Rejoice, Dang It, Rejoice!, adapt: Jerry Haynes and Laurence O'Dwyer; dir: Laurence O'Dwyer
Sweeney Todd, book: Hugh Wheeler; music and lyrics: Stephen Sondheim; dir: Jack Eddleman
She Stoops to Conquer, Oliver Goldsmith; dir: Norma Young
Morning's at Seven, Paul Osborn; dir: Charles Howard
Festival of New Playwrights:
   Quality of Mercy, David Hall; dir: Jimmy Mullen
   The Crashing of Moses Flying-By, Adam LeFevre; dir: Laurence O'Dwyer
True West, Sam Shepard; dir: Laurence O'Dwyer
Man and Superman, George Bernard Shaw; dir: Jac Alder
Don Juan in Hell, George Bernard Shaw; dir: Jac Alder
Tom Foolery, Tom Lehrer; dir: Laurence O'Dwyer

DESIGNERS

Sets: Charles Howard, Beverly Nachimson, Linda Williamson.
Costumes: Patty Greer McGarity, Danealia Maretka.
Lights: Shari Melde, Harland Wright, Michael Murray.

Theatre West Virginia

STUART B. GORDON
Administrative Director

JACK KEATLEY
Board President

Box 1205
Beckley, WV 25801
(304) 253-8317 (business)
(304) 253-8313 (box office)

FOUNDED 1961
Local citizens

SEASON
June-September

SCHEDULE
Evenings
Tuesday-Sunday

FACILITIES
Cliffside Amphitheatre
Grandview State Park, Beaver
Seating capacity: 1,374
Stage: proscenium

FINANCES
October 1, 1981-September 30, 1982
$598,000 operating expenses
$266,000 earned income
$252,000 grants/contributions

AUDIENCE
Annual attendance: 107,153
Subscribers: 459

TOURING CONTACT
Johanna Young

BOOKED-IN EVENTS
Theatre, music, dance

AEA letter of agreement, Outdoor Drama agreement and Theatre for Young Audiences contract

Theatre Arts of West Virginia, the Mountain State's only resident professional theatre, is located in the center of America's coal fields. Conceived in the late 1950s to produce two summer outdoor productions, Theatre Arts expanded in 1972 to a year-round operation with the establishment of its touring wing, Theatre West Virginia.

Since that time, Theatre West Virginia has toured with classics and contemporary works as well as original pieces for 33 weeks a year throughout West Virginia and 15 states in the midwest and Atlantic coastal region. The troupe is fully self-contained, carrying its own sets, lights, costumes and sound equipment. A separate touring unit of professional puppeteers presents full-scale marionette productions designed for children. The philosophy of Theatre West Virginia is firmly rooted in the belief that the arts should be available to all, and not reserved for the elite.

In addition to its performances, TWV offers workshops in all areas from improvisation and theatre games to audience development. Complete promotional kits are provided along with study guides for students and teachers, supplementing all performances.

Due to the current economic crunch and substantial reductions in state funding, TWV has been forced temporarily to reduce its programming. Although its annual summer productions will continue, along with additional summer programming, there will be no tour during the 1983-84 season. It is hoped that through increased fund-raising, the touring season will be reinstated for 1984-85.

The staff and board of trustees remain convinced of the need for the programs provided by Theatre West Virginia. They have dedicated themselves to providing a creative atmosphere in which theatre professionals can bring more theatre to more people.

Programs and services

West Virginia On Stage newsletter; workshops; speaker's bureau; internships.

Note: During the 1981-82 and 1982-83 seasons, John S. Benjamin served as artistic director.

PRODUCTIONS 1981-82

The Apple Tree: The Diary of Adam and Eve, book: Sheldon Harnick and Jerry Bock; music: Jerry Bock; lyrics: Sheldon Harnick; dir: John S. Benjamin
A Phoenix Too Frequent, Christopher Fry; dir: John S. Benjamin
Merlyn's Magic and *The Student King,* adapt: Donald C. Watkins; dir: John S. Benjamin
Hatfields and McCoys, book and lyrics: Billy Edd Wheeler; music: Ewel Cornett; dir: John S. Arnold
Honey in the Rock, book and lyrics: Kermit Hunter; music: Ewel Cornett and Jack Kilpatrick; dir: John S. Arnold
Even as the Sun, Warren Green; dir: John S. Benjamin
Alias Mark Twain, adapt: John S. Benjamin; dir: John S. Benjamin
Count Dracula, adapt: Ted Tiller; dir: John S. Benjamin

PRODUCTIONS 1982-83

Sleuth, Anthony Shaffer; dir: John S. Benjamin
Soldiering, Stephen Willems; dir: John S. Arnold

Theatre X

Gateway to Atlantis, Donald C. Watkins; dir: John S. Benjamin
Hatfields and McCoys
Honey in the Rock
Count Dracula, adapt: Ted Tiller; dir: John S. Arnold

DESIGNERS

Sets: Sandra Lee Marks, Terry Shutko, Thomas Peter Sarr, Donald C. Watkins.
Costumes: Susi Kwast, Thomas Peter Sarr, Suzanne Brown.
Lights: James Morris-Smith, Scott D. Cain, Tim Maloy, Stephen Woodring, Mark Shickel.

Theatre West Virginia. "Wall of Faces" in Gateway to Atlantis. *Photo: Betty Benjamin.*

JOHN D. SCHNEIDER
FLORA COKER
Associate Artistic Directors

SUSAN ESSER
Business Manager

R. MAX SAMSON
Board President

Box 92206
Milwaukee, WI 53202
(415) 278-0555

FOUNDED 1969
Conrad Bishop, Linda Bishop, Ron Gural

SEASON
September-July

SCHEDULE
Evenings
Thursday-Sunday

FACILITIES
Black Box Theatre
Lincoln Center for the Arts
820 East Knapp St.
Seating capacity: 150
Stage: flexible

FINANCES
September 1, 1982-August 31, 1983
$71,000 operating expenses
$23,000 earned income
$49,000 grants/contributions

AUDIENCE
Annual attendance: 12,500

TOURING CONTACT
Marcie Hoffman

BOOKED-IN EVENTS
Theatre, dance, performance art

"X" is a commonly used term in mathematics for the unknown factor in an equation, the factor which serves the immediate need. In 1969, this definition of "X" was adopted by a theatre company interested in freedom from a too-closely defined artistic identity, and it is still a valid representation of Theatre X today.

Theatre X is an ensemble whose core members have worked together for more than 11 years. The work directly reflects the intellectual, emotional, political and/or social needs of its members, and any form, technique, medium or play that might serve those needs is considered for production. Research and development are the methods used to mark personal and cultural changes. History is neither denied nor revered, but used to help communicate a response to what is happening now. Most of Theatre X's work is generated within the group, although Shakespeare, Ibsen, Beckett, Brecht, Handke and others have been produced at one time or another.

Theatre X is both an international and local theatre company; it has toured half of the United States and Canada and been to Europe five times, while maintaining a performing and programming schedule in Milwaukee. This duality, rather than being counter-productive, is rigorous and symbiotic because the resulting work is conceived and performed with a more universal focus and clarity.

The spirit of Theatre X might be compared to that of an explorer who, having dreamed well and prepared with discipline, sets off to see what is beyond the trees and over the hill. The adventure is in the journey: the wonders seen and the changes wrought from having seen them. There will be tales to tell. A few will listen, some will scoff and the truth remains hidden, but the spirit will shine in the telling.

Programs and services

Touring; High School Project: writing and rehearsing a play for and with students; staged readings in schools; apprenticeships.

PRODUCTIONS 1981-82

Under Milkwood, Dylan Thomas; dir: John Schneider
Kaspar, Peter Handke; dir: John Schneider
The Unnamed, John Schneider; dir: Daniel Holly
Tobacco Road, Jack Kirkland; dir: Eric Hill and John Kishline

Trinity Square Repertory Company

PRODUCTIONS 1982-83

An Interest in Strangers, John Schneider; dir: John Schneider

Sweet Dreams, Ritsaert ten Cate, John Schneider and David Brisbin; dir: Ritsaert ten Cate

Acts of Kindness, John Schneider; dir: John Schneider

I Used to Like This Place Before They Started Making All Those Renovations, John Schneider; dir: John Schneider

DESIGNERS

Sets: Ritsaert ten Cate, Michael Fortuna, John Kishline, David Rommel, John Schneider.
Costumes: Mary Piering, Carin Hartmann.
Lights: Michael Fortuna, John Kishline, John Ricker, David Rommel.

Theatre X. Deborah Clifton and Flora Coker in An Interest in Strangers.

ADRIAN HALL
Director/Board President

E. TIMOTHY LANGAN
Managing Director

201 Washington St.
Providence, RI 02903
(401) 521-1100 (business)
(401) 351-4242 (box office)

SEASON
Year-round

SCHEDULE
Evenings
Tuesday-Sunday

Matinees
Wednesday, Saturday, Sunday

FACILITIES
Upstairs Theatre
Seating capacity: 544
Stage: flexible

Downstairs Theatre
Seating capacity: 297
Stage: thrust

FINANCES
July 1, 1982-June 30, 1983
$2,276,000 operating expenses
$1,652,000 earned income
$ 625,000 grants/contributions

AUDIENCE
Annual attendance: 160,000
Subscribers: 17,300

TOURING CONTACT
E. Timothy Langan

BOOKED-IN EVENTS
Music, theatre, dance

AEA LORT (C) contract

Now entering its 20th year, Trinity Square Repertory Company, housed in a renovated downtown movie "palace," is a unique American ensemble: a permanent company of talented artists dedicated to learning about themselves through their art, and a permanent audience drawn from throughout the eastern United States. Since 1964, Trinity actors have worked continuously with founding director Adrian Hall. "Time is the most expensive thing," says Hall. "It usually takes 20 years for an actor to master his craft. The actors at Trinity are much more interested in process than in product. For that, a permanent company and a permanent audience are necessary."

Project Discover, which brings high school students to the theatre for daytime performances of all main-season productions, is a major source of new audiences. Originally funded by the National Endowment for the Arts and the U.S. Office of Education in 1966, this program has become an integral part of area educational systems.

Two projects initiated in 1978 continue successfully: Trinity Rep Conservatory, a full-time training program for actors, directors and playwrights, and a project sponsored by the Rhode Island Committee for the Humanities, offering audiences after-theatre symposia and scholarly essays relating to all eight main-season productions.

Trinity Square Repertory Company. Richard Ferrone (above), Peter Gerety, Richard Kavanaugh and Richard Jenkins in The Tempest. *Photo: Constance Brown.*

In 1981, Trinity Rep won the Antoinette Perry ("Tony") award for distinguished service to the American theatre, and performed John Steinbeck's *Of Mice and Men* and Sam Shepard's *Buried Child* on a five-week tour of India and Syria, sponsored by the U.S. International Communication Agency.

A new East/West dimension to the operation was launched in May 1983 when Adrian Hall assumed the dual artistic directorship of Trinity Square and the Dallas Theater Center.

Programs and services

Administrative internships; acting and directing conservatory; touring; films.

PRODUCTIONS 1981-82

The Elephant Man, Bernard Pomerance; dir: Peter Gerety
Talley's Folly, Lanford Wilson; dir: Melanie Jones
Of Mice and Men, John Steinbeck; dir: Adrian Hall
Buried Child, Sam Shepard; dir: Adrian Hall
L'Atelier, Jean-Claude Grumberg; trans: Marion Simon and Philip Minor; dir: Philip Minor
A Christmas Carol, adapt: Adrian Hall and Richard Cumming, from Charles Dickens; dir: Melanie Jones
A Flea in Her Ear, Georges Feydeau; trans: John Mortimer; dir: George Martin
Dead Souls, Nikolai Gogol; trans and adapt: Tom Cole; dir: Adrian Hall
5th of July, Lanford Wilson; dir: Philip Minor
The Gin Game, D.L. Coburn; dir: Philip Minor
The Hothouse, Harold Pinter; dir: Adrian Hall
True West, Sam Shepard; dir: David Wheeler

PRODUCTIONS 1982-83

Tintypes, music and lyrics: various; adapt: Mary Kyte, Mel Marvin and Gary Pearle; dir: Sharon Jenkins
The Crucifer of Blood, Paul Giovanni; dir: Philip Minor
13 Rue de l'Amour, adapt: Mawby Green and Ed Feilbert, from Georges Feydeau; dir: Philip Minor
The Web, Martha Boesing: dir: Adrian Hall
The Dresser, Ronald Harwood; dir: David Wheeler
Translations, Brian Friel; dir: Henry Velez
In the Belly of the Beast, adapt: Adrian Hall, from Jack Henry Abbott; dir: Adrian Hall
A Christmas Carol
The Front Page, Ben Hecht and Charles MacArthur; dir: Philip Minor
The Tempest, William Shakespeare; dir: Adrian Hall
Pygmalion, George Bernard Shaw; dir: Philip Minor
Mass Appeal, Bill C. Davis; dir: Peter Gerety

DESIGNERS

Sets: Eugene Lee, Robert D. Soule.
Costumes: William Lane.
Lights: John F. Custer, Eugene Lee.

Victory Gardens Theater

DENNIS ZACEK
Artistic Director

MARCELLE McVAY
General Manager

ARNOLD WINFIELD
Board President

2257 North Lincoln Ave.
Chicago, IL 60614
(312) 549-5788 (business)
(312) 871-3000 (box office)

FOUNDED 1974
Cecil O'Neal, Cordis Fejer, David Rasche, Warren Casey, Stuart Gordon, Roberta Maguire, June Pyskacek, Mac McGinnes

SEASON
September-June

SCHEDULE
Evenings
Tuesday-Saturday

Matinees
Sunday

FACILITIES
Mainstage
Seating capacity: 195
Stage: thrust

Studio
Seating capacity: 60
Stage: flexible

FINANCES
July 1, 1982-June 30, 1983
$445,000 operating expenses
$304,000 earned income
$140,000 grants/contributions

AUDIENCE
Annual attendance: 35,000
Subscribers 3,341

TOURING CONTACT
Marcelle McVay

AEA Chicago Off Loop Theatre contract

Victory Gardens Theater celebrated its 10th season in 1984. Founded to promote and develop Chicago's professional theatre artists, Victory Gardens is unique in the city for its long-standing commitment to writers from various racial and cultural backgrounds. Under the artistic direction of Dennis Zacek since 1977, the theatre has expanded its programming to include five-play seasons in each of its theatres; Theater Center training for more than 700 students; Readers Theater Series and touring productions.

Victory Gardens has received numerous Joseph Jefferson Awards for its productions, and many of the writers it showcases have gone on to be nationally recognized.

Last season, Victory Gardens was one of five theatres chosen nationwide to participate in the 1984 FDG/CBS New Plays Program. With special funding from CBS in 1980, it developed the first professional Latin ensemble in Chicago, which has since successfully begun production on its own. In keeping with its role as a developmental theatre, Victory Gardens has recently added both a playwright-in-residence and a literary manager to its staff.

On the mainstage, the focus is on new work. Usually, three shows per season are world premieres, selected for their appeal to Chicago audiences. At least one play by a black playwright is produced each year. Special attention is also given to the work of Midwest writers.

In the Studio Theater, a season of new plays or plays geared toward a more limited audience are produced. *The Artaud Project,* a unique stage-video presentation, was a recent artistic and commercial success, as was the innovative *Einsteins,* a mask piece combining mime, music and dialogue. Three Studio plays per year feature students from the Theater Center, where classes are geared both to the novice and the professional in eight-week sessions.

The Readers Theater Series showcases—free-of-charge—an average of 20 new scripts per season in staged readings, offering local writers the opportunity for development. Discussions between the company and the audience follow each reading.

Programs and services

Theater Center classes; Readers Theater Series; high school and statewide touring.

Victory Gardens Theater. Shelley Berman and Jill Holden in The Value of Names. *Photo: Jennifer Girard.*

Virginia Museum Theatre

PRODUCTIONS 1981-82

Stops Along the Way and *Routed*, Jeffrey Sweet; dir: Dennis Zacek
Daughters, Martin Jones; dir: David Perkins
Clown, Richard Strand; dir: Dennis Zacek
Cait, Janice Finney; dir: Greg Vinkler
Close Ties, Elizabeth Diggs; dir: Sandy Shinner
Blind Mice, Dennis Ryan; dir: James Roach
Shadows, Steve Carter; dir: Chuck Smith
Einsteins, Steven Ivcich; dir: Steven Ivcich
Clara's Play, John Olive; dir: Dennis Zacek

PRODUCTIONS 1982-83

Old Times, Harold Pinter; dir: Dennis Zacek
Niagara Falls, Victor Bumbalo; dir: Sara Connor
Your Move, music and lyrics: John Karraker and Jeffrey Berkson; dir: Dennis Zacek and James Corti
Wonderful, Wonderful Siberia, Felix Leon; dir: Arnold April
Daddy's Seashore Blues, Farrell J. Foreman; dir: Chuck Smith
George's File and *The Value of Names*, Jeffrey Sweet; dir: Sandy Shinner
Buddies, Mary Gallagher; dir: Sandy Shinner
The Whales of August, David Adams Berry; dir: Dennis Zacek

DESIGNERS

Sets: Nels Anderson, Jeffery Bauer, James Boley, Jef Finger, Carl Forsberg, Mary Griswald, Patrick Kerwin, Michael Mortimer, John Paoletti, John Story.
Costumes: Kate Bergh, John Brooks, Kerry Fleming, Cookie Gluck, Ellen Gross, Marsha Kowal, Jordon Ross.
Lights: Robert Christen, Jef Finger, Roma Flowers, Dawn Hollingsworth, Michael Mortimer, Chris Phillips, Rita Pietraszek, John Rodriguez, Robert Shook, Michael Winter.

TOM MARKUS
Artistic Director

IRA SCHLOSSER
Managing Director

CHARLES L. REED, JR.
President, Virginia Museum

Boulevard and Grove Aves.
Richmond, VA 23221
(804) 257-0840 (business)
(804) 257-0831 (box office)

FOUNDED 1955
Virginia Museum of Fine Arts

SEASON
October-May

SCHEDULE
Evenings
Tuesday-Sunday

Matinees
Wednesday, Saturday, Sunday

FACILITIES
Seating capacity: 500
Stage: proscenium

FINANCES
July 1, 1982-June 30, 1983
$868,000 operating expenses
$609,000 earned income
$259,000 grants/contributions

AUDIENCE
Annual attendance: 80,800
Subscribers: 10,712

BOOKED-IN EVENTS
Film

AEA LORT (C) contract

Virginia Museum Theatre, for 29 years a division of the Virginia Museum of Fine Arts, is guided by the museum's mission to provide a wide range of theatrical fare aimed at improving the quality of life of a local, statewide and national audience through the development, interpretation and creation of theatre. This mission is filtered through the vision of Tom Markus, VMT's artistic director since 1978: "The theatre is where a community gathers to celebrate its strength and to confront its problems. It is a public arena in which the major questions of our culture may be considered. Sometimes these are philosophical, sometimes political, sometimes social. Some of the questions have eternal qualities and others are intensely temporal. Sometimes they are of local interest only and sometimes they are universal in scope. But the theatre is—in addition to a place for entertainment — *a place for thought.*"

This philosophy guides VMT towards a style which is more theatrical than realistic or psychological (though such plays are occasionally included to insure a healthy diversity). Musicals include the likes of *Candide* and *Never the Twain*, the American premiere of a Kipling/Brecht compendium; contemporary selections lean toward the presentational style of *Talley's Folly* and Samm-Art Williams' *Home*; classics are commonly reworked as with the expressionistic versions of Strindberg's *The Father* and Ibsen's *Ghosts*; and premieres are most typically of a political nature as in Robert Potter's *Just Across the Border*, Alfred Drake's *The Hiding Place* and Margaret Dukore's *Move*.

The 1982-83 10-play season drew the largest subscription audience in VMT's history, suggesting that the community does indeed "gather to celebrate" at Virginia Museum Theatre.

Programs and services

Production, design and administrative apprenticeships; film series; student matinees; Sunday seminars; VMT Guild.

PRODUCTIONS 1981-82

Count Dracula, Ted Tiller; dir: Tom Markus
Tintypes, music and lyrics: various; adapt: Mary Kyte, Mel Marvin and Gary Pearle; dir: Darwin Knight
A Christmas Carol, adapt: Tom Markus, from Charles Dickens; dir: Terry Burgler
Talley's Folly, Lanford Wilson; dir: Terry Burgler

Virginia Stage Company

The Father, August Strindberg; adapt: Tom Markus; dir: Tom Markus

Candide, book adapt: Hugh Wheeler, from Voltaire; music: Leonard Bernstein; lyrics: Richard Wilbur; dir: Darwin Knight

Move, Margaret Mitchell Dukore; dir: Tom Markus

Never the Twain, adapt: John Willett; dir: Wal Cherry

Just Across the Border, Robert Potter; dir: Tom Markus

PRODUCTIONS 1982-83

The Play's the Thing, Ferenc Molnar; trans: P.G. Wodehouse; dir: Tom Markus

The Hiding Place, Alfred Drake; dir: Alfred Drake

A Christmas Carol

The Lion in Winter, James Goldman; dir: Tom Markus

The Gin Game, D.L. Coburn; dir: Terry Burgler

Haven't a Clue, Douglas Watson; dir: Tom Markus

Dames at Sea, book and lyrics: George Haimsohn and Robin Miller; music: Jim Wise; dir: Darwin Knight

Home, Samm-Art Williams; dir: Woodie King, Jr.

A Stretch of the Imagination, Jack Hibberd; dir: Tom Markus

Billy Bishop Goes to War, John Gray and Eric Peterson; dir: Terry Burgler

DESIGNERS

Sets: Neil Bierbower, Charles Caldwell, C. Jane Epperson, Susan Senita, Tom Targownik, Joseph A. Varga.

Costumes: Carol H. Beule, Bronwyn Jones Caldwell, Thomas W. Hammond, Julie D. Keen, Rebecca Senskc, Susan Tsu.

Lights: F. Mitchell Dana, Richard Devin, Lynne M. Hartman, Richard Moore, Kevin Rigdon.

Virginia Museum Theatre. Robert Gerringer, Patricia Falkenhain and Todd Taylor in The Lion in Winter.

CHARLES TOWERS
Artistic Director

RANDY ADAMS
Managing Director

PAMELA D. ETHERIDGE
Board President

108 East Tazewell St.
Norfolk, VA 23510
(804) 627-6988 (business)
(804) 627-1234 (box office)

FOUNDED 1979
Community Members

SEASON
October-May

SCHEDULE

Evenings
Tuesday-Saturday

Matinees
Wednesday, Saturday, Sunday

FACILITIES
Seating capacity: 700
Stage: modified thrust

FINANCES
July 1, 1982-June 30, 1983
$927,000 operating expenses
$550,000 earned income
$345,000 grants/contributions

AUDIENCE
Annual attendance: 78,500
Subscribers: 6,137

BOOKED-IN EVENTS
Theatre

AEA LORT (C) contract

With the 1983-84 season, Virginia Stage Company enters a new phase of operation. Building on four seasons of rapid institutional growth and unprecedented community support, VSC is currently sharpening its policies to emphasize artistic programming and development. This process, initiated by the board of trustees, includes the

Virginia Stage Company. Lynn Eldredge, Alison Fraser and Robert Stoeckle in Charlotte Sweet. *Photo: Susan Best.*

division of the company's producing directorship into an artistic director/ managing director team, and the sharpening of an artistic vision that acknowledges and challenges the reciprocal relationship of the theatre and its audiences.

Components of VSC's current artistic policy include:
1) Clearer articulation of the theatre's philosophy and a commitment to challenging and innovative work;
2) Renewed concentration on mainstage work, through setting program priorities which directly support the creative process;
3) Establishment of an artistic development program which incorporates new artistic associates into the process of project, script and playwright development;
4) Establishment of new audience development programs to enhance the public's understanding of the art form, and to take the first steps toward deepening the theatre's role in the community;
5) New focus on shaping a flexible, creative environment through exploring innovative producing concepts.

Housed in the Wells Theatre, a National Historic Landmark in downtown Norfolk, Virginia Stage Company plays an integral part in the redevelopment of the inner city and waterfront. Serving the eight-city area of Hampton Roads, whose population base is 1.2 million, VSC has quickly established itself as one of Virginia's leading cultural institutions.

Programs and services

Internships; staged readings; student matinees.

Note: During the 1981-82 and 1982-83 seasons, Robert W. Tolan served as producing director.

PRODUCTIONS 1981-82

The Gin Game, D.L. Coburn; dir: Robert Tolan
A Christmas Carol, adapt: Barbara Field, from Charles Dickens; dir: Michael Hankins
Thérèse Raquin, adapt: Stephen Willems, from Emile Zola; dir: Stephen Willems
Leavings, Michael Richey; dir: Robert Tolan
Whatever Became of Love?, Edward Myerson; dir: Stephen Willems
Strider, book: Mark Rozovsky; lyrics: Uri Riashentsev and Steve Brown; adapt: Robert Kalfin and Steve Brown; music: Mark Rozovsky, S. Vetkin and Norman L. Berman; dir: Lynne Gannaway
Charley's Aunt, Brandon Thomas; dir: Michael Hankins
Gemini, Albert Innaurato; dir: Robert Tolan

PRODUCTIONS 1982-83

Talley's Folly, Lanford Wilson; dir: Michael Hankins
The Crucible, Arthur Miller; dir: Robert Tolan
A Christmas Carol
Vanities, Jack Heifner; dir: Robert Tolan
High-Rolling, Robert Litz; dir: Michael Hankins
Tiovivo, Mary St. Cloud; dir: Robert Tolan
The Hazard County Wonder, Bruce Peyton; dir: Michael Hankins
Tartuffe, Molière; trans: Richard Wilbur; dir: Israel Hicks
Charlotte Sweet, book and lyrics: Michael Colby; music: Gerald Jay Markoe; dir: Edward Stone

DESIGNERS

Sets: Duke Durfee, James Morgan, Neil Peter Jampolis, Joe Ragey.
Costumes: Carrie Curtis, Ann Wallace, Anne-Marie Wright.
Lights: Ted Bartenstein, Bonnie Brown, Joe Ragey.

Westport Country Playhouse

JAMES B. McKENZIE
Executive Producer

Box 629
Westport, CT 06881
(203) 227-5138 (business)
(203) 227-4177 (box office)

FOUNDED 1931
Laurence Langner

SEASON
June-September

SCHEDULE

Evenings
Monday-Saturday

Matinees
Wednesday, Saturday

FACILITIES
25 Powers Court
Seating capacity: 800
Stage: proscenium

FINANCES
November 1, 1982-October 31, 1983
$1,006,000 operating expenses
$ 991,000 earned income
$ 15,000 grants/contributions

AUDIENCE
Annual attendance: 73,500
Subscribers: 2,100

TOURING CONTACT
James B. McKenzie

BOOKED-IN EVENTS
Theatre, music

AEA Council on Resident Stock Theatre contract

Westport Country Playhouse. Noel Harrison and Cloris Leachman in The Housekeeper.
Photo: Ivan Kellogg.

The Westport Country Playhouse is, by a half-century of tradition, a summer theatre producing 12 plays in the 12 weeks of each summer, with an artistic approach similar to the time-honored methods of Broadway.

Each play is cast separately by the director and producer and productions are usually planned around a recognized leading actor or actress. Its proximity to New York City gives the Playhouse an almost infinite variety of talent to work with.

Rehearsals are held in New York City for two-to-four weeks before a one-week performance run at Westport, and often at several other theatres.

Plays are selected for their mutual interest to the audiences and the actors and directors. New plays, musicals and plays from recent Broadway history are considered for the repertoire, as well as plays of historic or classical interest.

In addition to its regular season, Westport presents a series of nine children's plays and several special Sunday evening concerts or one-person shows.

The theatre maintains a veteran professional support staff of 42 people with an average tenure of more than five years at Westport, creating a distinct continuity of administration. Concurrent with the performing season is an intensive 14-week hands-on intern training program for 12 college seniors. Each department head is responsible for tutorials in his or her discipline.

Of the more than 570 plays produced at Westport, 76 have been world premieres.

The theatre plans to continue in its present mode, producing good plays with leading directors and actors under conditions less confining than those found in the commercial theatre.

Programs and services

Internships; tutorials; children's theatre; concerts.

PRODUCTIONS 1982

Morning's at Seven, Paul Osborn; dir: Burry Fredrik
The Supporting Cast, George Furth; dir: Tom Troupe
The Elephant Man, Bernard Pomerance; dir: Kevin Conway
They're Playing Our Song, book: Neil Simon; music: Marvin Hamlisch; lyrics: Carole Bayer Sager; dir: Peter B. Mumford

The Whole Theatre Company

Lunch Hour, Jean Kerr; dir: Jack V. Booch
The Subject Was Roses, Frank D. Gilroy; dir: Jack V. Booch
What I Did Last Summer, A.R. Gurney, Jr.; dir: Melvin Bernhardt
Mass Appeal, Bill C. Davis; dir: Geraldine Fitzgerald
Children of a Lesser God, Mark Medoff; dir: Gordon Davidson
Ain't Misbehavin', music and lyrics: Fats Waller, et al.; adapt: Richard Maltby, Jr.; dir: Richard Maltby, Jr.

PRODUCTIONS 1983

Deathtrap, Ira Levin; dir: John Cullum
Twice Around the Park, Murray Schisgal; dir: John Vivian
Clara's Play, John Olive; dir: Burry Fredrik
I'm Getting My Act Together and Taking It on the Road, book and lyrics: Gretchen Cryer; music: Nancy Ford; dir: Word Baker
Beyond Therapy, Christopher Durang; dir: Jerry Zaks
Crimes of the Heart, Beth Henley; dir: Jack V. Booch
84 Charing Cross Road, adapt: James Roose-Evans; dir: Edward Hastings
The Housekeeper, James Prideaux; dir: John Tillinger
Annie, book: Thomas Meehan: music: Charles Strouse; lyrics: Martin Charnin; dir: Robert Fitch
The Dining Room, A.R. Gurney, Jr.; dir: Porter Van Zandt
The Best Little Whorehouse in Texas, book: Larry L. King and Peter Masterson; music and lyrics: Carol Hall; dir: Jack V. Booch

DESIGNERS

Sets: Anne Gibson, Ron Naversen, Robert Thayer, James Tilton.
Costumes: Randy Barcelo, Ruth Morley, Alvin Perry, Garland Riddle, Noel Taylor, Constance R. Wexler.
Lights: James F. Franklin, Ron Naversen, Ruth Roberts, Robert Thayer.

The Whole Theatre Company. Marat/Sade. Photo: Robert I. Faulkner.

OLYMPIA DUKAKIS
Artistic Director

ARNOLD MITTELMAN
Producer/Director

BERNARD S. BERKOWITZ
Board Chairman

544 Bloomfield Ave.
Montclair, NJ 07042
(201) 744-2996 (business)
(201) 744-2989 (box office)

FOUNDED 1973

SEASON
October-May

SCHEDULE
Evenings
Tuesday-Sunday

Matinees
Saturday, Sunday

FACILITIES
Seating capacity: 200
Stage: flexible

FINANCES
July 1, 1982-June 30, 1983
$960,000 operating expenses
$470,000 earned income
$490,000 grants/contributions

AUDIENCE
Annual attendance: 40,000
Subscribers: 5,000

TOURING CONTACT
Linda Cane

AEA LORT (D) contract

Now in its 11th year of operation, the Whole Theatre Company has evolved from a resident company founded by 16 professional

Williamstown Theatre Festival

theatre artists performing in a church, to a fully professional theatre with an operating budget of $960,000, employing more than 100 actors, directors, teachers and administrators.

About 50 percent of the budget is met through ticket sales, education fees, tours and other special projects; the remainder is raised through the activities of the Whole Theatre Company Foundation which provides fiscal stability by seeking contributions from the surrounding communities. In addition to grants from government agencies, corporations and foundations, donations come from the theatre's boards of advisors and trustees, and from more than 500 individuals.

Over 32,000 people attended WTC productions last season, reflecting its remarkable growth since a decade ago, when a little more than one-tenth that number attended. This season, subscriptions have surpassed 5,000.

The theatre presents a 25-week season of five plays, beginning in the fall and ending in the spring. Traditional and innovative interpretations of classics as well as new plays by developing and well known playwrights are included in the repertoire. The WTC's comprehensive training program is the largest professional arts training center of its kind in New Jersey. In addition, it offers a series of nationally recognized social services in settings that range from public schools to community agencies.

The WTC was founded on a dream, with the determination that if the work was attempted with integrity, talent and critical self-awareness, quality would prevail. The founders have endeavored to follow what their hearts, minds and energies dictated: to share with their audience those visions drawn from the deepest part of their imaginations and creative strength.

Programs and services

Professional and non-professional training; Arts Alternatives program; internships.

PRODUCTIONS 1981-82

The Cherry Orchard, Anton Chekhov; dir: Austin Pendleton
A Kurt Weill Cabaret, adapt: Alvin Epstein and Martha Schlamme
Marat/Sade, Peter Weiss; trans: Geoffrey Skelton; adapt: Adrian Mitchell; dir: Arnold Mittelman
The USO Show, music and lyrics: various; adapt: Philip Polito; dir: Philip Polito
Off Broadway, Norman Krasna; dir: Jose Ferrer

PRODUCTIONS 1982-83

Uncle Vanya, Anton Chekhov; dir: Olympia Dukakis
All Dressed Up, book, music and lyrics: Leslie Eberhard and David Levy; dir: Tony Stevens
A Touch of the Poet, Eugene O'Neill; dir: Arnold Mittelman
Angel Street, Patrick Hamilton; dir: Austin Pendleton
Alone Together, Lawrence Roman; dir: Arnold Mittelman

DESIGNERS

Sets: Jack Chandler, Paul Dorphley, Raymond C. Recht, Loren Sherman.
Costumes: Joseph G. Aulisi, Ann Emonts, Galen M. Logsdon, Sigrid Insull.
Lights: Jamie Gallagher, David Noling, Carol Rubinstein, David F. Segal, Loren Sherman, Marshall Spiller, John L. Tissot.

NIKOS PSACHAROPOULOS
Artistic/Executive Director

GARY S. LEVINE
Managing Director

WILLIAM H. EVERETT
Board President

Box 517
Williamstown, MA 01267
(413) 458-8145

FOUNDED 1955
Nikos Psacharopoulos, David Bryant

SEASON
July-August

SCHEDULE

Evenings
Tuesday-Saturday

Matinees
Thursday, Saturday

FACILITIES

Mainstage
Seating capacity: 479
Stage: proscenium

Other Stages
Seating capacity: 100
Stage: flexible

FINANCES
December 1, 1981-November 31, 1982
$754,000 operating expenses
$473,000 earned income
$265,000 grants/contributions

AUDIENCE
Annual attendance: 40,000

TOURING CONTACT
Kay Matschullat

AEA Council on Resident Stock Theatre contract

In its 29-year history, the Williamstown Theatre Festival has become known as an artist's theatre. Under the continuous leadership of artistic director Nikos Psacharopoulos, a number of theatre professionals who began their careers at WTF return year

Williamstown Theatre Festival. Dianne Wiest, Sigourney Weaver and Edward Herrmann in Old Times.

after year to enrich the Festival. These include Austin Pendleton, Santo Loquasto, Laurie Kennedy, John Conklin, Christopher Reeve, Sigourney Weaver and Zeljko Ivanek, to name a few. Many established artists consider themselves members of the WTF "family" as well, including Edward Herrmann, Carrie Nye, Maria Tucci, George Morfogen, Frank Langella, Pat Collins, Peter Hunt, Richard Dreyfuss and Blythe Danner.

For 11 weeks each summer, these actors, directors and designers collaborate to mount the modern classics. Productions such as the American premiere of *The Greeks, Cyrano de Bergerac, Tennessee Williams: A Celebration* (a collage of all 29 of Williams' works created with the playwright in residence), *Arturo Ui, Summerfolk* and *The Seagull* are representative of the scope and style of the WTF repertoire. The Festival's 29-year commitment to the works of Chekhov, Gorky and Brecht have made them "popular" playwrights there, playing to capacity audiences.

In 1983, WTF made a concerted effort to bring new playwrights into its growing artistic family, with exciting results. Two playwrights were in residence for the season, a new play was produced on the mainstage for the first time, three new plays were mounted by the second company Other Stages and seven new plays were given staged readings.

Each season the Festival mounts five or six mainstage productions, four cabaret revues, seven literary events, four Other Stages productions, a new play reading series, acting projects and more. All told, some 220 performances are offered during July and August by a company of 250 individuals, including 30-40 professional actors, 15 directors and designers, 25 non-professional actors, a staff of 40, 30 interns and 90 apprentices.

As it looks ahead to its 30th season, Williamstown continues to strive to be an artistic home where young artists can emerge, and where more established theatre professionals can stretch and take chances in a supportive, talented ensemble.

Programs and services

Training program; apprentice workshop; internships; non-Equity acting company; play readings; cabaret.

PRODUCTIONS 1982

Tennessee Wiliams: A Celebration, adapt: Jean Hackett, Steve Lawson and Nikos Psacharopoulos, from Tennessee Williams; dir: Nikos Psacharopoulos
Room Service, John Murray and Allen Boretz; dir: Ken Frankel
Enemies, Maxim Gorky; trans: Margaret Wettlin; dir: Austin Pendleton
A Life in the Theater, David Mamet; dir: Stan Wodjewodski, Jr.
Trelawny of the 'Wells', Arthur Wing Pinero; dir: Nikos Psacharopoulos
Gideon's Point, Tennessee Williams; dir: Steven Schacter
Theatre of the Film Noir, George F. Walker; dir: Gregory Boyd
Melody of a Glittering Parrot, Tom Eyen; dir: Sharon Ott

PRODUCTIONS 1983

Holiday, Philip Barry; dir: Nikos Psacharopoulos
Ivanov, Anton Chekhov; trans: Jeremy Brooks and Kitty Hunter Blair; dir: John Madden
Old Times, Harold Pinter; dir: Alvin Epstein
A Knife in the Heart, Susan Yankowitz; dir: Nikos Psacharopoulos
Present Laughter, Noel Coward; dir: Stan Wodjewodski, Jr.
Lives and Deaths of the Great Harry Houdini, David Ives; dir: Kay Matschullat
The Mandragola, Niccolo Machiavelli; dir: Richard Hamburger
Love Gifts, Charles Traeger; dir: Steven Schacter
Digging to China, Kathleen Tolan; dir: Claudia Weill

DESIGNERS

Sets: Zack Brown, Kalina Ivanov, Andrew Jackness, John Kasarda, Hugh Landwehr, G.W. Mercier, Kevin Rigdon, Kevin Rupnik, Tony Straiges.
Costumes: Jess Goldstein, Kalina Ivanov, Dunya Ramicova, Kevin Rigdon, Rita Ryack, Rita B. Watson.
Lights: William Armstrong, Pat Collins, Arden Fingerhut, Paul Gallo, Christina Giannelli, James F. Ingalls, Jack Jacobs, Roger Meeker, Kevin Rigdon.

Wisdom Bridge Theatre

ROBERT FALLS
Artistic Director

JEFFREY ORTMANN
Executive Director

DIANE GOLDIN
Board President

1559 West Howard St.
Chicago, IL 60626
(312) 743-0486 (business)
(312) 743-6442 (box office)

FOUNDED 1974
David Beaird

SEASON
September-June

SCHEDULE

Evenings
Wednesday-Sunday

Matinees
Sunday

FACILITIES

Mainstage
Seating capacity: 196
Stage: proscenium

Training Center
Seating capacity: 24
Stage: proscenium

FINANCES
August 1, 1982-July 31, 1983
$673,000 operating expenses
$422,000 earned income
$250,000 grants/contributions

AUDIENCE
Annual attendance: 46,000
Subscribers: 3,200

BOOKED-IN EVENTS
Theatre

AEA Chicago Off Loop Theatre contract

Wisdom Bridge Theatre was founded in 1974 by David Beaird, a young director/writer/actor who, after scraping the chewing gum off stolen movie theatre seats, proceeded to present a season of offbeat and striking reinterpretations of the classics alternating with his own original scripts. Wisdom Bridge exploded with youth, originality and inventiveness — all of which were necessary in lieu of financial support from its home city.

In the nine years since, the theatre has replaced the gum-plagued chairs, plastered and painted the ailing walls and recruited a sophisticated staff of artists and administrators, and become a center for the performing arts with a special commitment to the development of new plays and playwrights, and the training of theatre artists.

Wisdom Bridge derives its name from an obscure Belgian painting that once visited Chicago's Art Institute and had as its legend, "The bridge to wisdom is in the continual asking of questions." Company members ask a lot questions of themselves: Why? How? When? Should we have? Why did we? What does it mean? This questioning has led to the desire to challenge — first of all, the company itself — and then the artists involved in each work; and finally, the audience.

The theatre's approach is to present an eclectic season with a strong, personal point of view bolstered by imaginative designs. It attempts to explore classic material with the freshness and bravado usually reserved for new plays, and to produce world premieres with the respect and care usually lavished on the classics. Nowhere in the Wisdom Bridge repertoire have these goals been realized more fully than in the back-to-back presen-

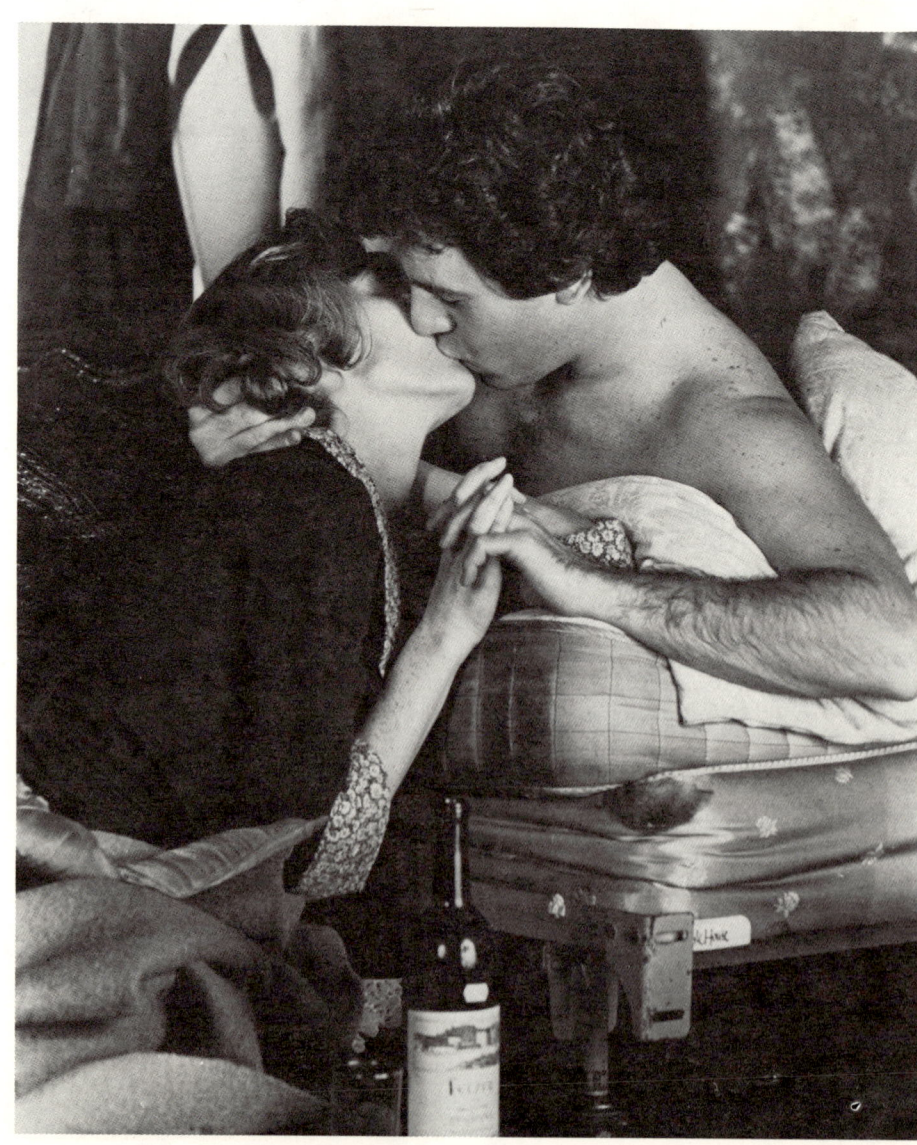

Wisdom Bridge Theatre. Kit Flanagan and Robert Neches in Standing on My Knees. *Photo: Jim Goodpasture.*

The Wooster Group

tations of *Macbeth* filtered through the imagination of Japanese artist Shozo Sato and rechristened *Kabuki Macbeth,* and John Olive's *Standing on My Knees,* a new play of unusual sensitivity and power which went on to a successful New York run.

Programs and services

Theatre Training Center; internships.

PRODUCTIONS 1981-82

Kabuki Macbeth, William Shakespeare; adapt: Shozo Sato; dir: Shozo Sato
Standing on My Knees, John Olive; dir: Robert Falls
A Streetcar Named Desire, Tennessee Williams; dir: Robert Falls
Sister Mary Ignatius Explains It All for You and *The Actor's Nightmare,* Christopher Durang; dir: Robert Falls
Sizwe Bansi Is Dead, Athol Fugard, John Kani and Winston Ntshona; dir: Jim O'Connor
The Island, Athol Fugard, John Kani and Winston Ntshona; dir: Jim O'Connor

PRODUCTIONS 1982-83

Princess Grace and the Fazzaris, Marc Alan Zagoren; dir: Allen R. Belknap
Awake and Sing!, Clifford Odets; dir: Edward Kaye-Martin
We Won't Pay! We Won't Pay!, Dario Fo; adapt: R.G. Davis; dir: Robert Falls
Losing It, Jon Klein; dir: Robert Falls
Clarence Darrow, David W. Rintels; dir: Lou Salerni

DESIGNERS

Sets: Jeffery Bauer, Gary Baugh, David Emmons, John Murbach, Jim O'Connor, Chris Phillips, Shozo Sato.
Costumes: Gary Baugh, Julie Keen, Douglas J. Koertge, Tom McKinley, Kaye Nottbusch, Jordan Ross, Shozo Sato.
Lights: Mary M. Badger, Ron Greene, Gary Heitz, Dan Kobayashi, Robert Shook.

The Wooster Group. Willem Dafoe and Ron Vawter in Route 1 & 9. *Photo: Bob van Dantzig.*

ELIZABETH LeCOMPTE
Artistic Director/Board President

LYNN RUBLEE
Administrator

Box 654
Canal Street Station
New York, NY 10013
(212) 966-9796 (business)
(212) 966-3651 (box office)

FOUNDED 1967
Richard Schechner

SEASON
Year-round

SCHEDULE
Evenings
Monday-Sunday

FACILITIES
The Performing Garage
33 Wooster St.
Seating capacity: 100
Stage: flexible

FINANCES
July 1, 1982-June 30, 1983
$199,000 operating expenses
$122,000 earned income
$ 78,000 grants/contributions

AUDIENCE
Annual attendance: 30,000

TOURING CONTACT
Jeffrey M. Jones

BOOKED-IN EVENTS
Theatre, dance, performance art, music

The Wooster Group is a six-member experimental theatre collective consisting of Jim Clayburgh, Willem Dafoe, Spalding Gray, Elizabeth LeCompte, Kate Valk and Ron Vawter. In recent years, the Group has principally been engaged in the ongoing creation of two bodies of thematically interrelated work: the multi-media, abstract theatre pieces created by the Group under the direction of Elizabeth LeCompte; and the autobiographical monologues and interview pieces of Group member Spalding Gray.

Worcester Foothills Theatre Company

The Wooster Group owns and operates The Performing Garage in New York City as the home base for its own seasons as well as a Visting Artists Season which it sponsors. Recent visiting companies and performers include SOON 3, Kei Takei's Moving Earth, Fiona Templeton, Laura Farabough's Nightfire Company and the Antenna Theater Company. The Group also conducts American and international tours.

Programs and services

Visiting Artists Season; children's workshops; touring; films, videotapes and recordings.

PRODUCTIONS 1981-82

Hula, company-developed; dir: Elizabeth LeCompte
In Search of the Monkey Girl, Spalding Gray; dir: Spalding Gray
Route 1 & 9, company-developed; dir: Elizabeth LeCompte
47 Beds, Spalding Gray; dir: Spalding Gray
Nayatt School, company-developed; dir: Elizabeth LeCompte
Point Judith, company-developed; dir: Elizabeth LeCompte

PRODUCTIONS 1982-83

Spalding Gray Retrospective, dir: Spalding Gray:
  Sex and Death to the Age 14
  Booze Cars and College Girls
  India and After (America)
  Nobody Wanted to Sit Behind a Desk
  A Personal History of the American Theatre
  47 Beds
  In Search of the Monkey Girl
  Interviewing the Audience
LSD: Part I, company-developed; dir: Elizabeth LeCompte

DESIGNERS

Sets: Jim Clayburgh, Elizabeth LeCompte.
Costumes: Peyton Smith, Kate Valk.
Lights: Jim Clayburgh, Elizabeth LeCompte.

Worcester Foothills Theatre Company. Rose Dresser and Wyman Kane in On Golden Pond. *Photo: Lindon Rankin.*

MARC P. SMITH
Artistic Director/Executive Producer

JOHN W. CURTIS
Board President

Box 236
Worcester, MA 01602
(617) 754-3314 (business)
(617) 754-4018 (box office)

FOUNDED 1974
Marc P. Smith

SEASON
September-May

SCHEDULE
Evenings
Wednesday-Sunday

Matinees
Thursday, Saturday, Sunday

FACILITIES
22 Front St.
Seating capacity: 200
Stage: thrust

FINANCES
June 1, 1981-May 31, 1982
$251,000 operating expenses
$188,000 earned income
$ 66,000 grants/contributions

AUDIENCE
Annual attendance: 33,000
Subscribers: 2,500

TOURING CONTACT
Thomas Vance

Worcester Foothills Theatre Company has operated on its philosophy of being "more than a theatre" since its founding in 1974. It seeks its meaning from the history and aspirations of the community in which, and from which, it lives.

Plays are selected or developed that will engage audiences in a dialogue of artistic expression. Whether a play's form is comedic or dramatic, its body classical or contemporary, its voice subtle or direct, it must stand as only one partner in a give-and-take discussion of ideas, issues and methods of presentation. The core company in residence must be involved in the community-at-large and these contacts—as well as lobby contact between the producing staff and the audience — provide a healthy conduit between company and audience. This relationship has fostered a broadly based audience that has taken the company to its heart as its "home town team."

New ideas are infused into the company from the visiting actors, directors and designers which comprise some 60 percent of the season's artistic staff.

The company's commitment to the community is also reflected in its special outreach programs for senior citizens, youth and the handicapped. Its props, sets and costumes are available for loan to a wide geographical area, and the company is officially represented in the activities of cultural and educa-

tional institutions, social service organizations and city agencies.

Worcester Foothills also participates in teaching, radio and television productions, film projects, new play development and sponsorship of guest productions. This total involvement in the community truly makes it "more than a theatre."

Programs and services

Conservatory; internships; apprenticeships; touring; costume and prop loan program; performances for the hearing-impaired; lobby gallery.

PRODUCTIONS 1981-82

Private Lives, Noel Coward; dir: Jack Magune
The Murder Game, Constance Cox; dir: Rose Dresser
On Golden Pond, Ernest Thompson; dir: Jeff Meredith
Commedia Tonight (Mistress of the Inn), Carlo Goldoni; dir: Tom Panko
Go Back for Murder, Agatha Christie; dir: James Moran
The Sunshine Boys, Neil Simon; dir: Jack Magune
Ladies of the Stage (The Holy Terrors), Jean Cocteau; dir: Mick Denniston
The Brewster Papers, Marc P. Smith; dir: Marc P. Smith

PRODUCTIONS 1982-83

Don Juan in Hell, George Bernard Shaw; dir: James David Moran
A Renaissance Revue, James David Moran; dir: James David Moran

DESIGNERS

Sets: William John Aupperlee, N. Taylor Blanchard, Tom Newman, Lindon Rankin, Don Ricklin.
Costumes: Deborah Bock, Wyman Kane, Leslie Murtha.
Lights: N. Taylor Blanchard, Richard Lund, August Piazza.

WPA Theatre

KYLE RENICK
Artistic Director/Board President

WENDY BUSTARD
Managing Director

138 Fifth Avenue
New York, NY 10011
(212) 691-2274

FOUNDED 1977
Howard Ashman, Craig Evans, Edward T. Gianfrancesco, Kyle Renick, Stephen G. Wells, R. Stuart White

SEASON
September-June

SCHEDULE
Evenings
Tuesday-Sunday

Matinees
Sunday

FACILITIES
Seating capacity: 98
Stage: proscenium

FINANCES
July 1, 1982-June 30, 1983
$189,000 operating expenses
$ 84,000 earned income
$ 65,000 grants/contributions

AUDIENCE
Annual attendance: 8,600
Subscribers: 435

AEA Showcase code and letter of agreement

Since its re-opening on lower Fifth Avenue in 1977, the WPA Theatre has been dedicated to neglected American classics and new American plays in the realistic idiom. In acting, writing, directing and design, the focus of its work is on the detailed examination of man in his everyday environment, with careful attention to the specifics of his moral, emotional and physical conditions.

It is a theatre of microcosm, and Ameri-

WPA Theatre. Hy Anzell, Lee Wilkof and "Audrey II" in Little Shop of Horrors. *Photo: Peter Cunningham.*

can theatre history is a testament to its viability. The WPA showcases a uniquely American acting style—derived from Stanislavski and nurtured by the Group Theatre—which was developed specifically to meet the demands of our great realistic writers. This acting style is taught across the nation: the WPA Theatre, through the revival of neglected plays which have helped to shape this style, and through the development and production of new works which grow out of the style, is an ongoing celebration of American theatrical tradition.

Programs and services

Phase One Series of new play readings; internships.

PRODUCTIONS 1981-82

Big Apple Messenger, Shannon Keith Kelley; dir: Stephen Zuckerman
Ghosts of the Loyal Oaks, Larry Ketron; dir: Amy Saltz
The Whales of August, David Berry; dir: William Ludel
What Would Jeanne Moreau Do?, Elinor Jones; dir: R. Stuart White
Little Shop of Horrors, book and lyrics: Howard Ashman; music: Alan Menken; dir: Howard Ashman

PRODUCTIONS 1982-83

Back to Back, Al Brown; dir: Douglas Johnson
A Different Moon, Ara Watson; dir: Sam Blackwell
Vieux Carré, Tennessee Williams; dir: Stephen Zuckerman
Asian Shade, Larry Ketron; dir: Dann Florek

DESIGNERS

Sets: Terry Ariano, James Fenhagen, Edward T. Gianfrancesco, Jim Steere, Ross A. Wilmeth.
Costumes: Judy Dearing, Sally Lesser, Mimi Maxmen, David Murin, Don Newcomb, Anne Watson.
Lights: Charles Cosler, Craig Evans, Phil Monat.

Yale Repertory Theatre

LLOYD RICHARDS
Artistic Director

BENJAMIN MORDECAI
Managing Director

222 York St.
New Haven, CT 06520
(203) 436-1589 (business)
(203) 436-1600 (box office)

FOUNDED 1966
Robert Brustein

SEASON
October-May

SCHEDULE
Evenings
Monday-Saturday

Matinees
Saturday

FACILITIES
1120 Chapel St.
Seating capacity: 491
Stage: thrust

University Theatre
222 York St.
Seating capacity: 684
Stage: proscenium

FINANCES
July 1, 1982-June 30, 1983
$1,577,000 operating expenses
$ 448,000 earned income
$1,078,000 grants/contributions

AUDIENCE
Annual attendance: 75,000
Subscribers: 6,850

AEA LORT (C) contract

Since the arrival of Lloyd Richards as artistic director in 1979, three elements have been central to each Yale Repertory Theatre season: William Shakespeare, Athol Fugard and the Winterfest of New Plays. This combination illustrates the guiding aesthetic of the theatre: an allegiance to the masters of dramatic literature; a commitment to the most eloquent of today's playwrights; and a conviction that tomorrow's playwrights must see their work produced.

Uniting these three elements makes the theatre a forum for emotion informed by thought, idea transfigured by feeling—and the recognition of the playwright as wellspring.

Such focus is appropriate to a theatre whose companion institution, the Yale School for Drama, was founded on the strength of George Pierce Baker's legendary "Playwrights Workshop," the course which (almost 60 years later) remains at the core of YSD's graduate training program.

The Rep/Drama School relationship provides the Rep a context of history and tradition, constantly reminding those associated with it of the standard of excellence set by the School's accomplished alumni, and of a far more extensive legacy as heirs to artists who extend from Aeschylus through the ages.

The Yale Repertory Theatre is a professional company daily aware of the never-ending processes of mastering craft and gaining an understanding of art.

Programs and services

Theater magazine: cabaret; technical internships.

PRODUCTIONS 1981-82

Uncle Vanya, Anton Chekhov; trans: Constance Garnett; dir: Lloyd Richards
Mrs. Warren's Profession, George Bernard Shaw; dir: Stephen Porter
Rip Van Winkle, or The Works, Richard Nelson; dir: David Jones
Winterfest of New Plays:
  Beef, No Chicken, Derek Walcott; dir: Walton Jones
  Flash Floods, Dare Clubb; dir: Dennis Scott
  Going Over, Stuart Browne; dir: Jim Peskin
  The Man Who Could See through Time, Terri Wagener: dir: David Hammond
Master Harold . . . and the boys, Athol Fugard; dir: Athol Fugard
Johnny Bull, Kathleen Betsko; dir: Lloyd Richards
Love's Labour's Lost, William Shakespeare; dir: Mladen Kiselov

Yale Repertory Theatre. Cecilia Rubino, Becky London, Kate Burton and Melissa Smith in Love's Labour's Lost. *Photo: Gerry Goodstein and Kirsten Beck.*

PRODUCTIONS 1982-83

A Doll House, Henrik Ibsen; trans: Rolf Fjelde; dir: Lloyd Richards

Hello and Goodbye, Athol Fugard; dir: Tony Giordano

The Philanderer, George Bernard Shaw; dir: David Hammond

Winterfest of New Plays:
  Astapovo, Leon Katz; dir: Lawrence Kornfeld
  Coyote Ugly, Lynn Siefert; dir: Christian Angermann
  Playing in Local Bands, Nancy Fales Garrett; dir: William Ludel

Much Ado About Nothing, William Shakespeare; dir: Walton Jones

About Face, Dario Fo; trans: Charles Mann and Dale McAdoo; dir: Andrei Belgrader

A Touch of the Poet, Eugene O'Neill; dir: Lloyd Richards

DESIGNERS

Sets: Christopher H. Barreca, Jane Clark, Joel Fontaine, Alison Ford, Philipp Jung, Wing Lee, G.W. Mercier, Ricardo Morin, Douglas O. Stein, Tony Straiges, Robert M. Wierzel, Michael H. Yeargan.

Costumes: Jane Clark, Quina Fonseca, Philipp Jung, Gene K. Lakin, Wing Lee, Richard Mays, Sheila McLamb, G.W. Mercier, Ricardo Morin, Dunya Ramicova, Connie Singer, Donna Zakowski, Catherine Zuber.

Lights: Andrew Carter, Timothy J. Hunter, Peter Maradudin, David Noling, Laurence F. Schwartz, Stephen Strawbridge, Jennifer Tipton, William B. Warfel, Robert M. Wierzel.

Appendices

Theatre Chronology

The following is a chronological list of founding dates for the theatres included in this book, and is intended to chart the growth of the nonprofit professional theatre movement in America. Years refer to dates of the first public performance, or, in a few cases, the company's formal incorporation.

1896
Hudson Guild Theatre

1915
Cleveland Play House

1925
Goodman Theatre

1928
Berkshire Theatre Festival

1931
Westport Country Playhouse

1933
Barter Theatre

1934
Paper Mill Playhouse

1935
Oregon Shakespearean Festival

1937
Old Globe Theatre

1946
Stage One: The Louisville Children's Theatre

1947
Alley Theatre

1949
New Dramatists

1950
Arena Stage

1951
Circle in the Square

1954
Milwaukee Repertory Theater
New York Shakespeare Festival

1955
Honolulu Theatre for Youth
Virginia Museum Theatre
Williamstown Theatre Festival

1956
Academy Theatre
Philadelphia Drama Guild

1957
Detroit Repertory Theatre

1959
Dallas Theater Center

1960
Asolo State Theater
Cincinnati Playhouse in the Park

1961
The Children's Theatre Company
Theatre West Virginia
Theatre Three

1962
Great Lakes Shakespeare Festival

1963
Center Stage
The Guthrie Theater
New Jersey Shakespeare Festival
Periwinkle Productions
Seattle Repertory Theatre

1964
Actors Theatre of Louisville
The American Place Theatre
Hartford Stage Company
Missouri Repertory Theatre
O'Neill Theater Center
South Coast Repertory
Theatre by the Sea
Trinity Square Repertory Company

1965
A Contemporary Theatre
American Conservatory Theatre
Cumberland County Playhouse
Detroit Repertory Theatre
East West Players
El Teatro Campesino
The Julian Theatre
Long Wharf Theatre
Looking Glass Theatre
Roundabout Theatre Company
Studio Arena Theatre

1966
Arizona Theatre Company
INTAR
The Living Stage Theatre Company
Repertory Theatre of St. Louis
Yale Repertory Theatre

1967
CSC Repertory
Magic Theatre
Mark Taper Forum
Puerto Rican Traveling Theatre Company
StageWest
The Wooster Group

1968
Berkeley Repertory Theatre
The Changing Scene
National Black Theatre
Odyssey Theatre Ensemble
Ontological-Hysteric Theatre
Playhouse on the Square

1969
Alliance Theatre Company/Atlanta Children's Theatre
AMAS Repertory Theatre

Body Politic Theatre
Circle Repertory Company
The First All Children's Theatre Company
Omaha Magic Theatre
Organic Theatre Company
Repertorio Español
Theatre X

1970

American Theatre Company
BoarsHead: Michigan Public Theatre
Folger Theatre
Interart Theatre
Mabou Mines
Manhattan Theatre Club
Medicine Show Theatre Ensemble
Music-Theatre Group/Lenox Arts Center
New Federal Theatre
The Street Theater
Theater for the New City

1971

The Cricket Theatre
Dell'Arte Players Company
The Empty Space
Ensemble Studio Theatre
Jean Cocteau Repertory
The Old Creamery Theatre Company
Playwrights' Center
Playwrights Horizons

1972

The Acting Company
Alabama Shakespeare Festival
GeVa Theatre
Indiana Repertory Theatre
Intiman Theatre Company
McCarter Theatre Company
New American Theater
New Playwrights' Theatre
Theater of the Open Eye

1973

Florida Studio Theatre
The Hippodrome State Theatre
L.A. Public Theatre
The Whole Theatre Company

1974

American Jewish Theatre of the 92nd St Y
Berkeley Shakespeare Festival
Berkeley Stage Company
The Clarence Brown Company
George Street Playhouse
Germinal Stage Denver
Hartman Theatre Company
Illusion Theatre
The Independent Eye
Jewish Repertory Theatre
L.A. Theatre Works
North Light Repertory Company
The People's Light and Theatre Company
Portland Stage Company
Roadside Theater
Syracuse Stage
Victory Gardens Theater
Wisdom Bridge Theatre
Worcester Foothills Theatre Company

1975

American Stage Festival
Boston Shakespeare Company
Caldwell Playhouse
Fairmount Theatre of the Deaf
Los Angeles Actors' Theatre
Nassau Repertory Theatre
Pittsburgh Public Theater
The Road Company
Soho Repertory Theatre
Theatre Project Company

1976

Alaska Repertory Theatre
American Theatre Arts
Arkansas Repertory Theatre
The Attic Theatre
Dorset Theatre Festival
Empire State Institute for the Performing Arts
The Great-American Children's Theatre Company
Nebraska Theatre Caravan
One Act Theatre Company of San Francisco
PlayMakers Repertory Company
San Diego Repertory Theatre
Steppenwolf Theatre Company

1977

Actors Theatre of St. Paul
Coconut Grove Playhouse
Horse Cave Theatre
North Carolina Shakespeare Festival
Pennsylvania Stage Company
WPA Theatre

1978

Crossroads Theatre Company
The American Theater Company in Aspen
Round House Theatre
Tacoma Actors Guild

1979

The American Stage Company
Delaware Theatre Company
Manhattan Punch Line Theatre
Merrimack Regional Theatre
The Second Stage
Virginia Stage Company

1980

American Repertory Theatre
Capital Repertory Company
Denver Center Theatre Company
San Jose Repertory Company

1981

L.A. Stage Company

1982

Huntington Theatre Company

Regional Index

ALABAMA

Alabama Shakespeare Festival

ALASKA

Alaska Repertory Theatre

ARIZONA

Arizona Theatre Company

ARKANSAS

Arkansas Repertory Theatre

CALIFORNIA

American Conservatory Theatre
American Theatre Arts
Berkeley Repertory Theatre
Berkeley Shakespeare Festival
Berkeley Stage Company
Dell'Arte Players Company
East West Players
El Teatro Campesino
Eureka Theatre Company
The Julian Theatre
L.A. Public Theatre
L.A. Stage Company
L.A. Theatre Works
Los Angeles Actors' Theatre
Magic Theatre
Mark Taper Forum
Odyssey Theatre Ensemble
Old Globe Theatre
One Act Theatre Company of San Francisco
San Diego Repertory Theatre
San Jose Repertory Company
South Coast Repertory

COLORADO

American Theater Company in Aspen
The Changing Scene
Denver Center Theatre Company
Germinal Stage Denver

CONNECTICUT

Hartford Stage Company
Hartman Theatre
Long Wharf Theatre
O'Neill Theater Center
Westport Country Playhouse
Yale Repertory Theatre

DELAWARE

Delaware Theatre Company

DISTRICT OF COLUMBIA

Arena Stage
Folger Theatre
Living Stage Theatre Company
New Playwrights' Theatre

FLORIDA

The American Stage Company
Asolo State Theater
Caldwell Playhouse
Coconut Grove Playhouse
Florida Studio Theatre
The Hippodrome State Theatre

GEORGIA

Academy Theatre
Alliance Theatre Company/Atlanta Children's Theatre

HAWAII

Honolulu Theatre for Youth

ILLINOIS

Body Politic Theatre
Goodman Theatre
New American Theater
North Light Repertory Company
Organic Theater Company
Steppenwolf Theatre Company
Victory Gardens Theater
Wisdom Bridge Theatre

INDIANA

Indiana Repertory Theatre

IOWA

The Old Creamery Theatre Company

KENTUCKY

Actors Theatre of Louisville
Horse Cave Theatre
Roadside Theater
Stage One: The Louisville Children's Theatre

MAINE

Portland Stage Company

MARYLAND

Center Stage
Round House Theatre

MASSACHUSETTS

American Repertory Theatre
Berkshire Theatre Festival
Boston Shakespeare Company
Huntington Theatre Company
Lenox Arts Center/Music-Theatre Group
Merrimack Regional Theatre
StageWest
Williamstown Theatre Festival
Worcester Foothills Theatre Company

MICHIGAN

The Attic Theatre
BoarsHead: Michigan Public Theater
Detroit Repertory Theatre

MINNESOTA

Actors Theatre of St. Paul
The Children's Theatre Company
The Cricket Theatre
The Guthrie Theater
Illusion Theater
Playwrights' Center

MISSOURI

Missouri Repertory Theatre
Repertory Theatre of St. Louis
Theatre Project Company

NEBRASKA

Nebraska Theatre Caravan
Omaha Magic Theatre

NEW HAMPSHIRE

American Stage Festival
Theatre by the Sea

NEW JERSEY

Crossroads Theatre Company
George Street Playhouse

McCarter Theatre
New Jersey Shakespeare Festival
Paper Mill Playhouse
Whole Theatre Company

NEW YORK

The Acting Company
AMAS Repertory Theatre
American Jewish Theatre of the 92nd St. Y
American Place Theatre
Capital Repertory Theatre
Circle in the Square
Circle Repertory Company
Cocteau Repertory
CSC Repertory
Empire State Institute for the Performing Arts
Ensemble Studio Theatre
The First All Children's Theatre
GeVa Theatre
Hudson Guild Theatre
INTAR
Interart Theatre
Jewish Repertory Theatre
Mabou Mines
Manhattan Punch Line
Manhattan Theatre Club
Medicine Show Theatre Ensemble
Music-Theatre Group/Lenox Arts Center
Nassau Repertory Theatre
National Black Theatre
New Dramatists
New Federal Theatre
New York Shakespeare Festival
O'Neill Theater Center
Ontological-Hysteric Theatre
Periwinkle Productions
Playwrights Horizons
Puerto Rican Traveling Theatre Company
Repertorio Español
Roundabout Theatre Company
The Second Stage
Soho Repertory Theatre
The Street Theater
Studio Arena Theatre
Syracuse Stage
Theater for the New City
Theater of the Open Eye
The Wooster Group
WPA Theatre

NORTH CAROLINA

The North Carolina Shakespeare Festival
PlayMakers Repertory Company

OHIO

Cincinnati Playhouse in the Park
The Cleveland Play House
Fairmount Theatre of the Deaf
The Great Lakes Shakespere Festival

OKLAHOMA

American Theatre Company

OREGON

Oregon Shakespearean Festival

PENNSYLVANIA

The Independent Eye
Pennsylvania Stage Company
The People's Light and Theatre Company
The Philadelphia Drama Guild
Pittsburgh Public Theater

RHODE ISLAND

Looking Glass Theatre
Trinity Square Repertory Company

TENNESSEE

The Clarence Brown Company
Cumberland County Playhouse
Playhouse on the Square
The Road Company

TEXAS

Alley Theatre
Dallas Theater Center
Theatre Three

VERMONT

Dorset Theatre Festival

VIRGINIA

Barter Theatre
Virginia Museum Theatre
Virginia Stage Company

WASHINGTON

A Contemporary Theatre
The Empty Space
Intiman Theatre Company
Seattle Repertory Theatre
Tacoma Actors Guild

WEST VIRGINIA

Theatre West Virginia

WISCONSIN

The Great-American Children's Theatre Company
Milwaukee Repertory Theater
Theatre X

Syracuse Stage. Michael Tolaydo and Jay Patterson in K2. Photo: Susan Piper Kublick.

Index of Names

A

Aaron, Jules, 196
Abady, Josephine, 19, 39, 40, 53, 134
Abbott, Charles, 12, 14, 99
Abbott, George, 21
Abbott, Jack Henry, 215
Abels, Gregory, 32, 199
Abraham, D.E., 208
Accardo, Jon R., 143
Achziger, Lowell, 54, 131
Ackerman, Robert Allan, 149, 153
Adair, Lach, 86
Adams, Abigail, 167
Adams, Betsy, 126, 166
Adams, Lee, 67
Adams, Randy, 218
Adamson, Eve, 61
Adshead, Pat, 88, 170
Adzima, Nanzi, 131, 204
Agazzi, James J., 24
Ahlert, Richard, 145
Ahrens, Judith, 3
Aibel, Douglas, 82
Ain, Noa, 138
Akalaitis, JoAnne, 123, 124, 149
Aladdin, Naila, 123
Albano, John, 207
Albee, Edward, 12, 22, 28, 39, 92, 112, 131, 152, 159, 171
Albers, Kenneth, 59
Albrezzi, Steven D., 6, 82, 167
Alcott, Louisa May, 76, 209
Alder, Jac, 210, 211
Aldredge, Theoni, 150
Aldrich, Amanda, 126
Aldridge, Amanda, 23, 134
Alegria, Alonso, 128, 189
Alexander, Len, 107
Alexander, Robert, 118
Alexander, Rod, 163
Allan, Squeak, 204
Allen, Billie, 15, 19
Allen, John, 39
Allen, Michael, 159
Allen, Peter W., 163
Allen, Ralph G., 56
Allen, Ross, 87
Allen, Woody, 159
Allison, Jack, 206
Allison, John, 153, 196
Almada, Carlos, 109
Almquist, Gregg, 174
Alonso, Luis, 208
Altman, Peter, 104
Altmann, Vivian, 83
Alvarez, Lynne, 144
Amdahl, Gary, 106
Amendola, Tony, 36
Amendolia, Don, 116, 200
Ammirati, John, 125
Amorose, Wendy, 190
Anania, Michael, 134
Anderson, Cordelia, 106
Anderson, David R., 118
Anderson, George, 12
Andersen, Hans Christian, 11, 40, 50
Anderson, Jill, 208
Anderson, Lindsay, 186
Anderson, Nels, 152, 217
Anderson, Robert, 120
Anderson, Tom, 154
Andrus, Dee, 75
Andrus, T.O., 74
Angel, Anthony, 208
Angell, Gene, 36, 38, 39, 83, 190
Angermann, Christian, 229
Anouilh, Jean, 45
Anstedt, Brian A., 22
Anthony, Earl, 145
Anton, Robert, 79
Antoon, A.J., 40, 202
Antrim, Donald, 12
Aoki, Yoichi, 69
Appelt, Joseph, 17, 95, 137
April, Arnold, 217
Apt, Joan, 170
Arakawa, Tetsuo, 135
Aranha, Ray, 14
Arbuzov, Aleksei, 152
Arcenas, Loy, 39
Archer, Deborah Atkins, 143
Archer, Julie, 124, 149
Archer, William, 139
Archibald, William, 69, 137
Argus, Camille, 153
Arhelger, Joan, 19, 36
Ariaho, Terry, 228
Ariel, 39
Ariosa, David, 53
Aristophanes, 153
Arkin, Jonathan, 171
Arlen, Harold, 53, 79
Armstrong, Alan, 156
Armstrong, William, 23, 54, 91, 96, 108, 128, 138, 170, 193, 223
Arndt, Denis, 163
Arnold, Barry, 53, 186, 199
Arnold, John S., 212
Arnold, Kenneth, 196
Arnold, Vickie, 187
Arnone, John, 19, 28, 56, 96, 150, 177, 194, 202
Aronson, Frances, 19, 28, 108, 131, 150, 177, 193
Aronson, Linda, 135
Aronstein, Martin, 57, 130, 186
Arrabal, Fernando, 109, 180
Arrick, Larry, 73, 170, 171
Artau, Estrella, 180
Ashley, George, 161
Ashman, Howard, 172, 227
Askins, Sally, 69
Assad, James, 137
Asse, Carlos, 100
Aston, Mary-Anne, 91, 95, 166
Aswegan, Jared, 30, 51, 96
Atkinson, Clinton J., 138, 139
Atkinson, Nancy, 35
Atlas, Larry, 6, 167
Auletta, Robert, 21
Aulisi, Joseph G., 222
Aupperlee, William John, 76, 227
Austin, Lyn, 137
Austin, Paul, 54, 88, 123
Austin-Olson, Sean, 204
Averill, Richard, 26
Averyt, Bennett, 32, 35, 82, 91
Avni, Ran, 112, 113
Axelrod, George, 134
Axtell, Barry, 194
Ayckbourn, Alan, 8, 12, 13, 24, 43, 46, 59, 86, 131, 143, 187, 192, 202, 205
Ayrton, Norman, 186

B

Babcock, Dennis A., 170
Babe, Thomas, 150, 200
Baboff, Alan, 15
Badger, Mary M., 43, 225
Baer, Tom, 49
Bafaloukos, Eugenie, 208
Bafalous, Eugenie, 208
Bagarella, Sam, 32
Bagdasian, Harry M., 147, 148
Bagnold, Enid, 17, 186
Baierlein, Ed, 89
Bailey, Elizabeth, 43
Bailey, Frederick, 153
Bailley, Randall J., 3
Baily, Charles Howard, 211
Baizley, Doris, 59, 116, 117
Baker, Cliff F., 30, 31
Baker, Don, 185
Baker, Georgia, 35
Baker, Laurence S., 200
Baker, Margaret, 184
Baker, Mark-Linn, 21
Baker, Paul, 67, 68
Baker, Word, 84, 221
Balderston, John L., 101
Baldori, Bob, 41
Baldwin, James 48, 64
Baldwin, Patricia, 86
Balfior, Joseph, 79
Balis, Andrea, 207
Ball, William, 15
Ballard, Clint, Jr., 12
Ballard, Orville, Jr., 115
Ballard, William C., Jr., 6
Ballouzole, Joelle, 208
Balson, Carl, 143
Bamman, Gerry, 178
Banbury, Frith, 60
Bangs, Don, 84
Baraka, Amiri, 145
Baral, Vicki, 116, 117
Barbosa, James, 131, 132
Barcelo, Randy, 11, 109, 150, 221
Barclay, Bill, 88
Barclay, Susan E., 138
Barclay, William, 19, 91, 126
Bard, Martha, 132, 208
Bardo, Dagmar, 166
Barer, Marshall, 45, 155
Barker, Howard, 128
Barkla, Jack, 5, 30, 51, 96
Barlerin, Michael, 210
Barnard, Judith, 142
Barnes, Paul, 163
Barnes, Peter, 159
Barnes, Theo, 206
Barnes, Tom, 15
Barnett, Robert, 91, 108
Barnhart, Dale, 24
Barr, Richard, 165
Barranger, Milly S., 173
Barreca, Christopher H., 229
Barrie, James M., 17, 26, 53, 186
Barrosse, Paul A., 168
Barrows, Harold W., 26
Barry, B.H., 12
Barry, Ellen, 146
Barry, Paul, 146, 147
Barry, Philip, 40, 120, 152, 190, 223
Barsha, Tony, 194
Bartelt, Bill, 92
Bartenieff, George, 206
Bartenstein, Ted, 219
Barthelme, Donald, 19
Bartlett, Bridget, 45
Bartlett, Jeff, 106
Barton, John, 4, 98, 151, 174
Barton, Samuel, 64
Bartsch, Hans, 120
Baruti, Osayanda, 15
Bass, Elizabeth, 148
Bass, Eric, 207
Bateman, Lane, 95
Bauer, Jeffery, 43, 217, 225
Bauer, Wolfgang, 125
Baugh, Gary, 91, 152, 225
Baum, Faith, 208
Baum, L. Frank, 53, 68, 79
Bauman, Larry, 59
Bautista, Michael, 26
Baxandall, Lee, 153
Bay, Jim, 138
Beaird, David, 224
Beals, Howard P., Jr., 70
Beals, Teri, 70
Beaman, Don, 99
Beard, Larry, 125
Beardslee, Christopher, 4
Beattie, Kurt, 80
Beatty, Charles, 35
Beatty, John Lee, 56, 96, 128, 130
Beaumarchais, Pierre, 96
Beautyman, William, 138
Beaver, Jim, 6
Beavers, Virgil, 69
Beccio, Barbara, 23
Bechtold, Michelle, 137
Beck, Carl, 141
Beck, Nancy, 205
Beck, Peter Dean, 32
Beckerman, Adam, 132
Beckett, Nancy, 106
Beckett, Samuel, 5, 21, 30, 92, 95, 123, 124
Beckner, Jay, 148
Beckos, Barbara, 203
Becvar, William, 204, 205

Beecroft, Jeffrey, 83, 91, 177
Beer, Lenny, 115
Beesely, Christopher, 30, 51, 63
Behan, Brendan, 73, 153
Behn, Aphra, 87
Behrangi, Samad, 207
Behrman, S.N., 153
Beistle, Michael, 100
Belasco, David, 32
Belden, Ursula, 73, 166, 171
Belfontaine, Daniel V., 210
Belgrader, Andrei, 21, 229
Belknap, Allen, R., 10, 144, 225
Bell, Barbara A., 60, 92
Bell, John Terry, 23
Belli, Keith, 13
Belov, Yuri, 207
Bendall, Joellen, 134
Benedetti, Robert, 163
Benedict, Paul, 126
Benjamin, John S., 212
Benmussa, Simone, 128
Bennett, Alan, 89, 147
Bennett, Frank, 45
Bennett, John, 50, 86
Bennett, J.C., 190
Bennett, Michael, 56, 149
Bennett, Patrick, 117
Bennett, Peter, 151, 205
Bennett, Sid, 91, 99, 166, 206
Bennett, Suzanne, 19
Bensmore, Joy Barrett, 135
Benson, Martin, 195, 196
Bentley, Eric, 89, 153
Bentley, Jeffrey, 151
Berendes, David, 155
Berenguer, Angel, 180
Beresford-Howe, Constance, 43
Berezin, Tanya, 55
Berg, Stephen, 135
Berger, Adam, 56
Berger, John, 180
Berger, Naomi, 113
Bergh, Kate, 152
Bergh, Kate, 217
Berkoff, Steven, 117, 130
Berkowitz, Bernard S., 221
Berkson, Jeffrey, 217
Berlin, Brenda, 113
Berlin, Pamela, 46, 67, 82, 106, 167, 168
Berliner, Charles, 59
Berman, Marc B., 82
Berman, Martin, 39
Berman, Norman L., 219
Berman, Paul, 35
Bermel, Albert, 20, 92
Berney, William, 32
Bernhard, Thomas, 96
Bernhardt, Gene, 26
Bernhardt, Melvin, 221
Bernstein, Leonard, 28, 143, 218
Berrigan, Daniel, 190
Berry, David, 228
Berry, David Adams, 217
Berry, Gabriel, 15, 109, 208
Berthelot, Larry, 36
Besier, Rudolf, 45

Bethel, Todd, 147
Betsko, Kathleen, 160, 228
Betti, Ugo, 54, 70
Beule, Carol H., 112, 218
Bick, Kristine, 171
Biel, Nicholas, 145
Bierbower, Neil, 151, 218
Bigelow, Dennis, 163
Bill, Mary, 94
Birch, Patricia, 79
Birkhead, Vada, 103
Birnbaum, Rhonda, 83, 159
Birnbaum, Steven L., 194
Birney, Juli, 158
Bisha, Robin, 86
Bishop, Andre, 176
Bishop, Bonnie B., 26
Bishop, Conrad, 6, 106, 107, 213
Bishop, Cynthia, 116
Bishop, John, 56
Bishop, Linda, 106, 213
Black, Bill, 57
Black, G. David, 59
Black, Lewis, 149
Black, William "Electric", 209
Blackman, Robert, 13, 17, 36, 73, 130, 192
Blackwell, Sam, 6, 70, 228
Blackwell, Vera, 8
Blahnik, Jeremy, 117
Blair, Kitty Hunter, 223
Blake, Kathleen, 147
Blake, Kathy, 18
Blake, Paul, 27
Blanchard, N. Taylor, 227
Blanche, Michele Jo, 123
Blank, Lenore, 48
Blase, Linda, 69, 103
Blau, Eric, 166, 173
Blau, Frances, 59
Blaustein, Richard, 184
Blecher, Hilary, 138
Blessing, Lee, 6, 106, 160, 174
Bliss, Matthew, 134
Blitzstein, Mark, 68, 183
Blizzard, John E., 2
Bloch, Alan, 121
Block, Richard, 6
Bloodgood, William, 13, 80, 112, 163
Bloom, Ken, 148
Bloom, Michael, 194
Bloom, Sidney S., 169
Blue, Adrian, 84
Boak, Mike, 150
Bobceam, Janet, 151
Bobrick, Sam, 64, 155
Bock, Deborah, 227
Bock, Jerry, 79, 173, 212
Boehlke, Bain, 50
Boesing, Martha, 215
Boley, James, 217
Bolger, T. Michael, 134
Bolinger, Don, 67
Bologna, Joseph, 159
Bolt, Jonathan, 32, 56
Bolt, Robert, 79, 143
Bond, Edward, 48, 128

Bonifay, Randy, 68, 69
Bonnard, Raymond, 69
Bono, Ray, 79
Booch, Jack V., 221
Booker, Margaret, 111, 112
Bookman, Kirk, 95
Bookwalter, D. Martyn, 115
Booth, David, 204
Boothe, Power, 138, 209
Boraas, Judith, 159
Borden, William, 7, 49
Boretz, Allen, 96, 142, 223
Borkhuis, Charles, 209
Boros, Frank J., 199
Boruzescu, Miruna, 5
Boruzescu, Radu, 5
Bos, John, 13
Bosakowski, Phil, 144
Bosch, Mark, 17, 36
Botts, Ed, 83
Bouchard, Bruce, 45, 46
Bourcier, Gerard P., 139
Bournival, Richard D., 133
Bovasso, Julie, 159
Bowen, Ann, 36
Bowen, John, 24
Bowles, Anthony, 194
Bowmer, Angus L., 162
Bowne, Alan, 160
Boyd, George, 153
Boyd, Gregory, 36, 95, 173, 223
Boyd, Julianne, 82
Boyer, Mike, 113
Boylan, Ann, 3
Boylen, Daniel, 131
Bozark, Kim, 182
Bozzone, Bill, 82
Braden, John, 15
Bradford, Dennis, 13, 23, 112, 134
Brady, James Edmund, 92
Bragg, Floyd H., 164
Brailsford, Pauline, 43
Braito, Andreas, 112
Bramble, Mark, 99
Bramon, Risa, 82
Brancale, Joan, 206
Brandeis, Irma, 209
Brandon, Johnny, 166
Brandstein, Eve, 115
Brassard, Gail, 23, 82
Brauner, Leon I., 108
Brechner, Stanley, 17, 18
Brecht, Bertolt, 24, 36, 39, 68, 89, 112, 137, 153, 183
Brecht, Mary, 208
Breed, Donna, 106
Breindel, Scott, 209
Brel, Jacques, 173
Brennan, Timothy, 195
Brentano, James, 38, 83
Brenton, Howard, 183, 202
Breuer, Lee, 100, 123, 124, 149
Brewer, David, 117, 173
Brewer, William P., II, 36
Brewster, Karen, 141
Breyer, Hunter, 210
Briggle, Gary, 51

Briggs, Jody, 4
Briggs, John, 67, 133
Brill, Michael, 102
Brink, Robert, 18, 23, 112
Brion, Mary, 167
Brisbin, David, 214
Brisler, Phil, 117
Brisson, Bruce, 159
Britton, Robert, 64, 88
Broad, Jay, 4, 30
Broadhurst, Kent, 6, 7, 168
Brockway, Adrienne J., 209
Brockway, Amie, 208, 209
Broden, Noel, 28
Brodsky, Larry, 109
Brody, Leslie, 159
Brogger, Erik, 115, 174
Brohan, Paul, 34
Brolaski, Carol, 115, 196
Bromberg, Conrad, 82
Bronte, Charlotte, 69
Bronte, Emily, 7
Brooker, Bob, 15
Brookhart, Laura, 67
Brooks, Alfred, 48, 49
Brooks, Colette, 110
Brooks, Donald, 208
Brooks, Jeremy, 95, 223
Brooks, John, 217
Brooks, Mel, 22
Brooks, Michael, 34
Brooks, Scott, 208
Brooks, Stuart, 150
Brooks, Tim, 208
Brothers-Lowry, Deborah, 36, 197
Broun, Nathan Kwame, 67
Broverney, Dan, 135
Brown, Al, 114, 228
Brown, Alain, 44
Brown, Arvin, 115, 119, 120
Brown, Bonnie Ann, 48, 199, 219
Brown, Claudia, 18
Brown, Dorothy J., 74
Brown, Martin, 132
Brown, Pat, 11, 12
Brown, Paul, 10
Brown, Roberta, 40
Brown, Steve, 141, 219
Brown, Suzanne, 213
Brown, Zack, 28, 223
Brown, Zoe, 40
Browne, Roscoe Lee, 19
Browne, Stuart, 228
Browne, Wynyard, 186
Brozgold, Lee, 132
Bruneau, Ainslie G., 13
Brustein, Robert, 19, 20, 228
Bryan, Wayne, 199
Bryant, David, 222
Buch, Rene, 65, 135, 180, 181
Buchholz, Fred, 150
Buchman, Nanrose, 4, 11, 196
Buchner, Georg, 65
Buchwald, Janet, 43
Buck, Gene Davis, 30, 51
Buckley, Candy, 68
Buckley, Peter, 190

Buckshi, Ken, 207
Budenholzer, Joe, 158
Budin, Rachel, 70, 91, 92, 108, 109, 135, 177, 208
Bullard, Thomas, 7, 53, 128, 143
Bullins, Ed, 114
Bumbalo, Victor, 217
Bunnin, Brad, 37
Bunt, George, 53
Burbridge, Edward, 130
Burgler, Terry, 217
Burk, Richard D., 155
Burke, Martha, 17, 163
Burner, Bill, 160
Burns, Helen, 17
Burrows, Abe, 31, 66
Burrows, Jeffrey, 121
Burton, Jim, 41
Burton, Richard, 6
Bush, Barbara, 38, 39, 74, 75, 83, 125, 190
Bush, Jay, 51
Bush, Jim, 155
Bushnell, Bill, 121, 123
Bushnell, Herb, 67
Bushor, Geoffrey, 164
Bustard, Wendy, 227
Butler, David, 205
Butler, Martha, 34
Butler, Rick, 65, 208
Butsch, Tom, 51
Butt, Dan, 209
Butterworth, Oliver, 98
Button, Jeanne, 98
Buzinski, Richard, 34
Bynum, Margaret, 15
Byrne, Kathy, 69
Byrne, Peter, 194

C

Caballero, Alberto, 179
Cabrujas, Jose Ignacio, 180
Cada, James, 8, 9
Cain, Candice, 163
Cain, Scott D., 213
Cain, William, 43, 44
Calderon, Ian, 104
Calderon de la Barca, Pedro, 135, 180
Caldwell, Ben, 145
Caldwell, Bronwyn Jones, 218
Caldwell, Charles, 218
Caldwell, Herb, 155
Caldwell, James R., 44
Call, Edward Payson, 73
Callego, Bobjack, 208
Callender, Eugene, 140
Calumet, Leslie, 150
Calvert, Lorraine, 126
Cambridge, Edmund J., 123
Cameron, Ben, 108
Cameron, Charles, 44
Cameron, Lisa Martin, 131
Cameron-Webb, Gavin, 44
Campbell, Clayton, 209
Campbell, Cyndy, 31
Campbell, Jane, 101
Campbell, Joseph, 208
Cane, Linda, 221
Cannan, Denis, 170
Cannon, Richard E., 184
Cantrell, Ruth, 68
Capecce, Victor, 99
Capen, Deborah, 159
Capone, Clifford, 193
Carballido, Emilio, 180
Carey, Mary, 59
Cariello, Thomas Michael, 32, 199, 202
Carlin, Joy, 4, 36
Carlisle, Barbara, 40, 41
Carlson, Harry G., 112
Carlson, James R., 22
Carlson, Roberta, 51
Carmichael, Linda, 6, 27
Carmichael, Patricia, 144, 176
Carmichael, Steve, 26
Carmines, Al, 187
Carney, Ben, 61
Carney, Georgia, 199
Carney, Kay, 110
Carothers, Charles O., 52
Carpenter, Larry, 22, 23, 134, 206
Carrington, Frank, 164
Carroll, Fred, 124
Carroll, Lewis, 51
Carroll, Mary Beth, 4
Carson, Heather, 208
Carson, Jo, 184
Carter, Andrew, 229
Carter, Randolph, 7
Carter, Ron, 49
Carter, Steve, 123, 217
Cartier, Jacques, 97, 105
Cascio, Anna Theresa, 160
Case, Suzanne, 101
Casella, Martin, 115
Casey, Lawrence, 96, 138
Casey, Michael, 17
Casey, Warren, 216
Cassella, Matt, 116, 117
Castellino, Bill, 153
Castle, Nancy, 125
Castrigno, Tony, 18
Castro, Elizabeth Olson, 153
Cate, Donald, 114, 153
Cate, Regina, 114
Cathcart, Thom, 124
Cavaco, Manny, Jr., 208
Cavander, Kenneth, 4, 70, 85, 98, 174
Celli, Tom, 206
Cesaitis, Edward, 23, 134, 206
Chabay, Gregory, 18, 126
Chaikin, Joseph, 149
Chaikin, Shami, 207
Chalem, Denise, 135
Chambers, David, 5, 28, 92, 96
Chambers, Jane, 110, 177
Chamberlain, Marisha, 51, 106
Chambers, Richard, 206
Chandler, Jack, 222
Chapin, Harry, 14
Chapman, Gerald, 56
Chapot, John, 125
Chappell, Fred, 13, 14, 35
Chappell, Tobey, 148
Chappell, Wallace, 183
Charlap, Jule, 53
Charlap, Mark, 26
Charles, Jill, 75, 76
Charles, Valerie, 64
Charnas, Fran, 32
Charnin, Martin, 67, 128, 221
Chase, Mary, 76, 103
Chayefsky, Paddy, 18
Chayes, Antonia, 19
Chekhov, Anton, 9, 10, 17, 21, 30, 36, 56, 65, 73, 112, 113, 120, 128, 131, 135, 137, 159, 167, 183, 187, 222, 223, 228
Cherry, Wal, 218
Chester, Daniel, 39
Chester, Nora, 33
Chiang, Dawn, 73, 135
Chiarelli, Randall G., 4
Childress, Alice, 98
Childs, Casey, 143, 144
Chiment, Marie Anne, 28, 178
Chin, Daryl, 207
Chioles, John, 149
Chirino, Carmen, 180
Chlarson, Linder, 194
Choate, Mabel, 39
Chorpenning, Charlotte E., 12
Choset, Chuck, 207, 208
Christen, Robert, 92, 217
Christian, C. Russell, 160
Christie, Agatha, 6, 7, 12, 24, 35, 53, 59, 60, 68, 134, 139, 202, 205, 227
Chuang, Fred, 123
Chugg, Eliza Dietsch, 83, 206
Chukram, Dru-ann, 124
Chulak, Armando, 180
Churchill, Caryl, 4, 83, 116, 150, 200
Cibula, Nan, 21, 92, 98, 128, 193
Ciulei, Liviu, 5, 95, 96
Cizmar, Paula, 19, 178, 189
Clark, Brian, 14, 100, 143, 202
Clark, Cullen, 3
Clark, Don, 44
Clark, Dru Minton, 44
Clark, James A., 203
Clark, Jane, 104, 209, 229
Clark, Ron, 64, 155
Clark, Terrie, 69
Clark, Walter, 39
Clarke, Leo J., 190
Clarke, Martha, 138
Clay, Burial, I, 145
Clay, Diskin, 135
Clayburgh, Jim, 150, 193, 226
Claymore, Cindy, 72
Clayson, Laurel, 174
Clements, Jill, 3
Cleveland, Celeste, 80
Cleveland, Margaret, 43
Cleveland, Sally, 30, 156
Clifton, John, 32
Clinton, Edward, 100
Cloud, Darrah, 82
Clough, Peter H., 45, 46
Clubb, Dare, 6, 228
Cluchey, Rick, 92
Clugstone, Scott, 194
Coates, Norman, 174
Coates, Thom, 14
Coberg, Wally, 48, 148, 199, 202
Coburn, D.L., 4, 17, 22, 26, 30, 31, 41, 63, 68, 86, 91, 100, 134, 143, 155, 156, 166, 215, 218, 219
Cochran, Randal R., 197
Cochrane, Steve, 165
Cochren, Felix E., 92
Cockburn, Barrie, 126
Cocke, Dudley, 184, 185
Cocteau, Jean, 227
Coen, Dana, 209
Cogo-Fawcett, Robert, 135
Cohen, Alice Eve, 207
Cohen, Arthur, 64
Cohen, Edward M., 113
Cohen, Geoffrey, 88
Cohen, Joel, 113
Cohen, Madeline, 82
Cohen, Marvin, 150
Cohen, Neil, 113
Cohen, Norman, 115
Cohen, Shura, 138
Coker, Flora, 213
Colavecchia, Franco, 5, 105
Colbron, Grace I., 120
Colby, Michael, 143, 219
Cole, Mark, 49
Cole, Nancy, 22
Cole, Tom, 135, 215
Coleman, Kevin, 22
Coleman, Marilyn, 123
Collins, Kathleen, 19, 101, 102
Collins, Pat, 11, 98, 99, 120, 128, 170, 193, 223
Collins, Sheryl, 80
Colman, Richard, 56
Colling, Brenda, 208
Colton, John, 108
Comden, Betty, 26, 53
Commire, Anne, 115, 160
Comunale, Frank, 56
Condon, Frank, 27, 153
Cone, Harriet, 84
Cone, Tom, 170, 177
Conklin, John, 98, 115, 120, 170
Conly, Sarah G., 186
Connell, David, 59
Connolly, Karen, 183
Connor, Sara, 217
Contaxis, Patricia, 207
Contessa, Maria Ferreira, 180, 181
Contini, John, 210
Conway, Jeremy, 91, 152
Conway, Kevin, 220
Conwell, Charles, 167
Cook, Divina, 33
Cook, Jon'Paul, 71
Cook, Margaret Van D., 103

Cook, Michael, 38, 190
Cook, Peter, 147
Cook, Reagan, 67, 126, 180, 208
Cook, Roderick, 155
Cook, Stoney, 209
Cooke, Thomas, 57
Cooper, Cindy, 174
Cooper, Gary D., 180
Cooper, Susan, 96
Cooper, Judith, 51
Copple, Mary, 200
Corbett, Nancy, 101
Corcoran, Hugh, 93
Corcoran, Tom, 155
Corey, Irene, 69, 103
Corey, Orlin, 103
Corley, Hal, 66
Cornell, Edward, 108
Cornett, Ewel, 6, 93, 212
Cornwell, Bruce, 99
Cort, Bill, 24
Corti, James, 217
Corwin, Walter, 207
Corzatte, Clayton, 4
Cosler, Charles, 204, 228
Coss, Claire, 110, 208
Costelloe, Paul, 95
Costigan, Ken, 35
Costin, James, 136
Cothran, Robert, 57
Cottrell, Marion Hill, 4, 205
Cottrell, Richard, 135
Couch, Guy, 30
Coulter, Alan, 113
Covay, Cab, 114
Covey, Elizabeth, 53, 131, 135, 199
Coward, Noel, 9, 14, 31, 35, 36, 44, 54, 60, 67, 112, 131, 137, 139, 143, 155, 163, 165, 166, 178, 183, 211, 223, 227
Cowart, Kate, 187
Cox, Barbara, 196
Cox, Constance, 227
Cox, Joe, 68
Cox, Susan, 10
Crabtree, Amelie, 67
Crabtree, Ann, 67
Crabtree, James R., 66, 67
Crabtree, Mary, 66, 67
Crabtree, Paul, 67
Cramer, Aileen, 53
Creevey, Rae, 77
Cranney, Jon, 8, 30, 96
Crinkley, Richmond, 87
Cristofer, Michael, 54, 56, 120, 190
Crofford, Keith, 3
Cromwell, David, 187
Cronyn, Hume, 96
Crouch, J.H., 163
Crouse, Russell, 132
Crow, Laura, 56, 80, 130, 192
Crowe, George, 113
Crowell, Richard, 173
Crowther, Paulette, 109
Cryer, Gretchen, 53, 221
Crystal, Raphael, 113

Cuddy, Mark, 73
Culbert, Bobbi, 30
Cullinan, Francis, 44, 144
Cullum, John, 221
Culman, Peter W., 47
Cumming, Douglas A., 187
Cumming, Richard, 2, 215
Cunliffe, Shay, 4, 208
Cunningham, Geoffrey T., 120
Cunningham, Julia, 41
Curcio, John, 189
Curfman, Bashie, 56
Curran, Leigh, 178
Curreri, Alan, 114
Currie, Richard, 208
Curtis, Carrie, 219
Curth, Michael, 209
Curtis, John W., 226
Curzon, Daniel, 159
Custard, William A., 67
Custer, John F., 215
Custer, Marianne, 57
Czeski, Patrick, 75

D

Dachs, Josh, 126
Dafoe, Susan, 43
D'Agostino, Joseph, 15
Dahdah, Robert, 207
Dahlstrom, Robert, 4, 112, 192
Daines, Gary, 78, 190
Dale, Jim, 31, 187, 210
Dale, Paul, 18
Dallas, L.B., 123, 124, 208
Dallas, Walter, 14, 48
Damashek, Barbara, 73, 171
Dambach, Steve, 75
Dana, F. Mitchell, 53, 92, 131, 150, 165, 170, 218
Dancy, Virginia, 135
D'Andrea, Paul, 114, 144
Danforth, Roger, 86
Daniels, Paul S., 176
Dante, Nicholas, 149
Dansicker, Michael, 128, 206
Darbon, Leslie, 68
D'Arcy, Oliver, 126
Darion, Joe, 22, 165, 205
Darnelle, Jeanne, 41, 46
Darnutzer, Don, 30
Darrow, Harry, 208
Datil, Leonor, 109
David, Narsai, 35
Davidson, Bob, 204
Davidson, Gordon, 56, 120, 128, 129, 221
Davidson, Jeannie, 36, 173
Davidson, John B., 51
Davidson, Michael, 80
Davila, Raul, 145
Davis, Aubrey, 3
Davis, Bill C., 7, 10, 27, 30, 45, 53, 88, 91, 156, 165, 166, 199, 206, 215, 221
Davis, David S.S., 86

Davis, Donald, 120
Davis, Edgar G., 107
Davis, Heidi Helen, 82
Davis, Jeff, 23, 40, 53, 104, 105, 145, 187
Davis, John Henry, 202
Davis, Judith, 68
Davis, Lindsay W., 197
Davis, Montgomery, 93
Davis, Owen, 120
Davis, Peter, 30, 73
Davis, R.G., 100, 122, 204, 225
Davis, Russell, 48, 160, 184
Davis, Ted, 134, 177
Davis, William, 87
Deak, Rose, 79
Dean, Jeff, 32
Dean, Megan, 80
Dean, Phillip Hayes, 39, 64
Dean, Tom, 93
Deane, Hamilton, 101
Dearing, Judy, 15, 19, 64, 88, 92, 99, 128, 130, 145, 150, 202, 228
de Barbieri, Mary Ann, 87
deBoeuf, Marsha, 164
de Bruyn, Judith, 61
de Cecco, Sergio, 180
Deckel, Larry, 6, 7
Decker, Ed, 159
Decker, Gary, 34
DeCuir, L.J., 57
Dee, Peter, 144
Deegan, John Michael, 5
De Fazio, Marjorie, 110
De Filippo, Eduardo, 205
de Forest, Marian, 76
Degan, Diane, 158
de Ghelderode, Michele, 113
Deitcher, Jordan, 104
de Jongh, James, 19
DeLaurier, Peter, 69, 70, 167
DeLieto, Leon R., 44
Del Rossi, Angelo, 164
Delu, Dahl, 51
Deluxe, Dolores, 153
Dembo, Royce, 194
de Molina, Tirso, 78
Dempster, Curt, 81
Denham, Reginald, 67
Denney, Felecia, 69
Dennis, Rick, 61
Denniston, G.H., Jr., 81
Denniston, Mick, 154, 227
Denson, Cheryl, 69
dePaola, Tomie, 51
Depenbrock, Jay, 53
De Priest, Margaret, 77
de Pury, Marianne, 158
Desmond, Patrick, 202
Detweiler, Lowell, 23, 53, 73
Devin, Richard, 13, 218
Devine, Jerry, 84
Devine, Michael, 115, 130, 196
De Volder, Max, 183
De Voss, David, 123
Deyonker, Deni, 34
Dezseran, Catherine, 197
Diament, Mario, 123

Diamond, Michael, 87
Diamond, Sallie, 89
di Canzio, William, 160
DiCrescenzo, Louis, 200
Dick, Ming, 196
Dickens, Charles, 2, 4, 7, 11, 17, 22, 30, 31, 41, 51, 59, 60, 68, 69, 92, 95, 96, 99, 100, 108, 131, 135, 137, 141, 151, 183, 189, 196, 204, 215, 217, 219
Dietz, Jed, 203
Dietz, Susan, 115, 116
DiGabriele, Linda M., 31
Dignan, Joe, 125
Diggs, Elizabeth, 12, 82, 115, 196, 217
Dillon, John, 120, 134, 135
Dilliard, Marcus, 44
Dimock, George E., Jr., 131
Dimont, Igor, 153
Dimou, Fotini, 61
Dingle, Michael, 114
Dinsmore, Susan, 168
Di Quinzio, Mark, 46
Dixon, Beth, 91
Dixon, Michael Bigelow, 196
Dobbins, Ray, 207
Doctorow, E.L., 89
Dodd, Joseph D., 102
Dodge, Norman B., Jr., 168
Doepp, John, 32, 178, 204, 206
Dolan, Judith, 5, 137, 186
Donahue, John Clark, 50, 51
Dondlinger, Mary Jo, 194
Donnelly, Mark, 36, 156, 189, 196
Donnelly, Peter, 190
Donoghue, Judy, 114
D'Orazi, Deborah Capen, 125
Dorfman, Richard, 126, 147
Dorlang, Arthur, 31
Dorphley, Paul, 222
Dorsey, Kent, 30, 73, 156, 196
Dorton, Moses, 66
Dos Passos, John, 36
D'Ovidio, David L., 116
Dowling, Vincent, 94, 95, 137
Downey, Roger, 80
Doyle, Arthur Conan, 32, 59, 187
Doyle, John H., 114
Drabent, Eugene, 49
Drabik, Robert, 86
Drake, Alfred, 218
Draper, Ruth, 40
Drawbaugh, Laura, 113
Dresser, Rose, 227
Dretsch, Curtis, 166
Dreyfuss, Randolph, 153
Driver, Donald, 202
Driver, John, 14, 36, 59
Drummond, Josiah H., Jr., 177
Dryden, Deborah M., 13, 36, 156, 163, 186
Dryden, John, 87
Duarte, Derek, 36, 38, 159
DuBois, Barbara, 36
DuBrock, Neal, 201
Duckert, Katherine E., 135
Duckworth, Stuart, 163

Duer, Fred, 189
Duff, Jonathan, 13
Duffy, Robert, 69
Duffin, Shay, 153
Dukakis, Olympia, 221, 222
Duke, Stuart, 40, 108, 152
Dukore, Margaret Mitchell, 218
Dumas, Alexandre, 6, 61, 68, 99
Dunbar, Geoffrey, 82
Duncan, A. Clark, 123, 153
Duncan, William B., 14
Dunham, Bill, 184
Dunleavy, Timothy, 104, 128
Dunlop, Frank, 31, 187, 210
Dunn, Glenn, 183
Dunn, James, 156
Dunn, Margaret Anne, 125
Dunn, Nell, 99
Dunn, Thomas G., 143
Durang, Christopher, 21, 36, 41, 80, 91, 100, 116, 177, 210, 221, 225
Durfee, Duke, 134, 194, 219
Durrenmatt, Friedrich, 12, 114
Dworsky, Richard, 51

E

Eakeley, Douglas S., 146
Eastman, Donald, 208
Ebb, Fred, 14, 173
Eberhard, Leslie, 222
Ebrahimian, Ghasem, 208
Eck, Marcia Louis, 79
Eckhart, Gary, 59, 202
Eddelman, William, 39, 83, 190
Edelstein, Gordon, 143, 145, 178
Eddleman, Jack, 211
Edgar, David, 83, 95, 137, 153, 179
Edgar, Miriam Colon, 179
Edgecomb, Bonnie, 208
Edmonds, Robert, 145
Edmondson, James, 17
Edmunds, Kate, 21, 108, 110, 128, 160, 192
Edwards, Andrea, 49
Edwards, Ben, 57
Edwards, Cathleen, 38
Edwards, Gus, 144
Edwards, Jack, 96
Edwards, John, 187
Edwards, Richard, 4, 205
Edwards, Sherman, 173
Effron, Ed, 79
Egan, Patricia, 177
Egan, Robert, 192
Ehman, Don, 131
Eich, Stephen B., 199
Eichman, Mark, 121
Eickhoff, Philip, 92
Eigsti, Karl, 28, 53, 56, 96, 120
Einhorn, Susan, 27, 207
Eis, Joel, 114
Eisenberg, Deborah, 193
Eisenberg, Herbert, 43

Eisenman, Nancy Dunn, 153
Eisloeffel, Elizabeth, 210
Eitner, Don, 23, 24
Ekstrom, Peter, 6, 143
Elder, Eldon, 170
Eliasberg, Jan, 183
Elisha, Rina, 207
Elkjer, Thom, 159
Ellerby, Harry, 35
Elliott, John Lovejoy, 103
Elliott, Marianna, 115, 123, 130
Elliott, William, 149
Ellis, Greg, 122
Ellis, Emily, 76
Ellis, Richard, 26
Ellis, Sheila, 122
Elmendorf, Ray, 123
Elmer, J. Patrick, 205
Elmer, Todd, 82
Elspas, Stephen, 159
Emmes, David, 195, 196
Emmons, Beverly, 124, 150, 208
Emmons, David, 91, 92, 128, 152, 225
Emonts, Ann, 138, 156, 177, 193, 222
Enderle, Douglas, 137
Enea, John, 15
Engel, Lisa, 208
Engelbach, Jerry, 193, 194
Engelgau, Fred, 41
Engels, Robert, 115, 144
Engles, Judy, 167, 168
English, Gary, 180
Engquist, Richard, 88, 113
En Yu Tan, Victor, 11, 53, 85, 150, 193, 208
Epstein, Alvin, 21, 186, 222, 223
Epstein, David, 7
Epstein, Martin, 75, 125
Epstein, Natalie, 94
Epton, Paul, 34
Epp, Steven, 106
Epperlin, Karin, 125
Epperson, C. Jane, 218
Epperson, Dirk, 17
Eppling, Sandy, 22
Epps, Sheldon, 32, 128
Erdman, Jean, 208, 209
Erickson, David Michael, 49
Erickson, Ron, 80, 205
Ernotte, Andre, 92, 109, 128, 170, 177
Ervin, Denise, 141
Esparza, Phil, 77
Espinosa, Victoria, 180
Esser, Susan, 213
Esslin, Martin, 125
Esslin, Renata, 125
Estrin, Jonathan, 153
Etheridge, Pamela D., 218
Ettinger, Daniel H., 35, 139, 165
Euripides, 4, 53, 57, 131
Eustis, Oskar, 93
Evangelatos, Spyros, 131
Evans, Craig, 227, 228
Evans, Don, 64, 99, 145
Evans, John Morgan, 59, 170

Evans, Tom, 148
Everett, Claudia, 163
Everett, William H., 222
Everhart, Gail, 126
Ewaskio, Henri, 91
Ewen, Bruce, 24
Ewin, Paula, 121
Eyen, Tom, 223
Ezell, John, 32, 95, 137

F

Fabricant, Gwen, 128
Fagin, Paul W., 82
Faison, Keibu, 140
Faison, Nabii, 140
Falabella, John, 23, 99, 170
Fallon, Richard, 31
Falls, Gregory A., 3, 4, 102
Falls, Robert, 7, 128, 224, 225
Falquez-Certain, Miguel, 109
Falzone, Ron, 92
Farley, Robert J., 10, 11
Farrell, Bernard, 196
Farrell, Patty Ann, 125
Farrington, Ann, 124
Farris, Cathy, 168
Fassler, Gary, 64, 88
Fassman, Jessica, 113, 208
Fast, Howard, 18
Faulkner, Cliff, 196
Faulkner, William, 96
Faust, Nick, 135
Fay, Jim 210
Fayad, Samy, 114
Fears, William, 26
Federico, Robert Weber, 65, 181
Fehr, Frankie, 170
Feiffer, Jules, 56, 130, 163
Feilbert, Ed, 215
Feinberg, Stephen, 7
Feiner, Harry, 137
Feingold, Michael, 19, 36, 153
Feinsod, Arthur, 104
Feist, Gene, 185, 186
Fejer, Cordis, 216
Felder, Eve, 157
Feldshuh, David, 96, 106, 144
Felix, Edmund, 208
Fen, Elisaveta, 137
Fendel, Dan, 153
Fenhagen, James, 228
Ferber, Betty, 24
Ferber, Edna, 137
Ferenz, George, 145, 204
Ferger, Jay, 210
Ferguson, Margaret, 2, 3
Ferguson-Acosta, Dennis, 109
Fergusson, Honora, 124
Ferra, Max, 109, 180
Ferraro, Craig R., 45
Ferraro, Jaclyn, 64
Ferraro, John, 56
Ferrer, Herbert, 33
Ferrer, Jose, 59, 60, 222

Feydeau, Georges, 17, 112, 129, 151, 190, 215
Fiala, Jeffrey A., 199
Fichandler, Thomas C., 27
Fichandler, Zelda, 27, 28
Fichter, Thomas M., 4
Field, Barbara, 7, 92, 96, 137, 174, 219
Field, Crystal, 206. 207
Fielding, Henry, 171, 194
Fields, Dorothy, 67, 160
Fields, Herbert, 67, 132
Fields, Michael, 71, 72
File, Claude, 41
Filgmiller, John, 68
Fineberg, Larry, 43
Finger, Jeff, 155, 217
Fingerhut, Arden, 19, 28, 48, 98, 128, 130, 135, 150, 178, 193, 223
Finkelstein, Linda, 118
Finkelstein, Richard, 79
Finn, William, 34
Finneran, Alan, 125
Finneran, Bean, 125
Finney, Janice, 217
Fire, Richard, 34, 164
Firestone, Ann, 53
Fischer, Correy, 122
Fischer, Stephen, 153
Fisher, Elizabeth, 131, 168
Fisher, Linda, 11, 40, 48, 98, 120, 128, 135, 170
Fitch, Robert, 221
Fitzgerald, Geraldine, 165, 221
Fitzgibbons, Mark, 5, 59
Fitzhugh, Ellen, 177
Fitzpatrick, Jane P., 39
Fitzpatrick, John, 184
Fjelde, Rolf, 65, 75, 96, 229
Flakes, Susan, 61
Flamer, Meg, 158
Flanagan, Courtney, 210
Flannery, Peter, 114
Flatt, Robyn, 68, 69
Fleisher, Yolanda, 33
Fleming, Conn, 12
Fleming, Joyce, 45
Fleming, Kerry, 43, 217
Fleming, Sam, 23, 135
Fletcher, Allen, 17, 192
Fletcher, John, 61
Fletcher, Robert, 27, 73, 99
Flodin, Lucinda, 184
Flones-Czeski, Anne-Kristiine, 75
Florek, Dann, 128, 228
Flower, C. Stanley, 205
Flower, Pat, 205
Flowers, Roma, 217
Flynn, William J., 21
Fo, Dario, 100, 122, 123, 130, 204, 225, 229
Foeller, Bill, 21
Folden, Lewis, 87, 148
Foley, Rosemary, 209
Fond, Miriam, 19
Fondaw, Ron, 60
Fonner, Fred, 3

Fonseca, Quina, 229
Fontaine, Joel, 229
Foote, Horton, 126
Forbes, Barbara, 35, 46, 60, 70, 134
Forbes, John B., 30, 156
Forbes, Joseph, 139
Ford, Alison, 4, 53, 229
Ford, Anne-Denise, 3, 4
Ford, Barbara, 141
Ford, Brad, 172, 173
Ford, Nancy, 53, 221
Ford, Peter, 169
Foreman, Farrell J., 217
Foreman, Richard, 96, 149, 150, 161
Forman, Lorraine, 36
Fornes, Maria Irene, 80, 109, 207, 208
Forrester, William, 4, 80
Forsberg, Carl, 217
Forsyth, Stephen, 173
Forsythe, Eric, 168
Forte, Johanna, 34
Forte, Randall, 34
Fortuna, Michael, 214
Fosse, Bob, 173
Foster, Paul, 126, 207
Fowler, Gene, 98
Foy, Kenneth, 18, 54, 186
Frame, Donald M., 96, 149, 161, 196
France, Richard, 77
Franchini, Bruce, 122
Frank, David, 201, 202
Frankel, Jerry, 153
Frankel, Kenneth, 120, 223
Frankel, Richard, 55
Franklin, James F., 13, 221
Franklin, Lester, 2016
Frankonis, W.A., 79
Frayn, Michael, 70
Frazier, Breton, 172
Frazier, Kermit, 82, 135
Frazier, Lynn, 30
Frederick, Dennis K., 184
Fredericks, K.L., 19
Fredrick, Marcia, 190
Fredrik, Burry, 220, 221
Freedman, Donald, 123
Freedman, Gerald, 99
Freimann, John Raymond, 36
Freeman, David, 190
French, Larry, 36
Fried, Martin, 28
Friedman, Alan Foster, 145
Friedman, Kim, 115
Friedman, Leah, 207
Friel, Brian, 34, 43, 59, 105, 137, 192, 215
Friml, Rudolf, 99
Frisch, Norman, 43
Frisch, Peter, 40
Fruchter, Danny S., 167
Fruchter, Margaret E., 167
Fruchter, Megan, 168
Fry, Christopher, 212

Fry, Ray, 6, 7
Fry, Ronald Scott, 51
Fryar, Steven, 3
Fuentes, Carlos, 21
Fugard, Athol, 2, 28, 31, 36, 44, 48, 53, 64, 68, 70, 74, 103, 108, 114, 129, 135, 167, 178, 196, 199, 225, 228, 229
Fukuda, Tsuneari, 135
Fulgenzi, Ben, 49
Fuller, Barry, 173
Fuller, Charles, 4, 92, 130
Fuller, Elizabeth, 6, 107
Fulton, Larry, 15, 206
Funicello, Ralph, 17, 130, 192, 196
Furth, George, 220
Futterman, Enid, 145
Fyffe, Dennie, 84

G

Gabbert, John, 187
Gabor, Nancy, 125
Gabrielson, Frank, 53
Gaburo, Ken, 39
Gaffney, Floyd, 189
Gaines, Frederick, 30, 68
Galantiere, Lewis, 73
Gale, Brian, 115
Gale, Zona, 135
Gallagher, Jamie, 120, 222
Gallagher, Mary, 82, 98, 217
Gallo, Paul, 54, 92, 98, 120, 130, 177, 223
Galloway, Terry, 19
Gannaway, Lynne, 219
Gant, Richard, 145
Gardner, Herb, 40, 103, 143
Gardner, Lewis, 27
Gardner, Michelle M., 196
Gardner, Rob, 41
Gardner, Worth, 53
Garnett, Constance, 187, 228
Garrett, Nancy Fales, 125, 160, 229
Garrison, Peter, 114
Gaskill, William, 186
Gatling, Helen, 18
Gatrell, Claire, 60
Geer, Richard Owen, 73, 163
Geisel, Theodor, 51
Gelbart, Larry, 30, 189
Gelber, Jack, 82, 180
Geller, Donald, 112
Gellerstedt, Lawrence L., III, 2
Gems, Pam, 17
Genet, Jean, 39, 51
Geoly, Guy, 165
George, Nathan, 145
George, Phillip T., 59
Gerety, Peter, 215
Gerlach, Robert, 155
Germack, Victor, 127

Gershman, Richard, 196, 199
Gerson, Karen, 7, 61
Getty, Peter, 56
Gianelli, Christina, 223
Gianfrancesco, Edward T., 228
Giannini, A. Christina, 186
Giardina, Anthony, 128
Gibson, Anne, 221
Gibson, Greg, 158
Gibson, Martha, 18
Gibson, Mary, 156, 189
Gibson, Philip, 151
Gibson, William, 18, 22, 40, 67, 68, 134, 187, 206
Giebel, Douglas, 113
Gigere, E.D., 126
Giguere, Edi, 104
Gilbert, Charles, Jr., 70
Gilbert, W.S., 4, 15, 23, 51, 57, 149, 108, 211
Gilg, Joseph, 143
Gilhooley, Jack, 144
Gilleland, Louanne, 194
Gilles, John Ivo, 196
Gillette, William, 32
Gillis, Joseph, 33
Gilman, Charlotte Perkins, 106
Gilroy, Frank D., 8, 221
Gimpel, George, 138
Gingold, Alfred, 22
Giomi, Rita, 115
Giordano, Tony, 56, 98, 110, 170, 170, 229
Giovanni, Paul, 112, 199, 215
Girardeau, Frank, 69
Giron, Arthur, 106
Gisondi, John, 23, 91, 134, 150, 177
Gisselman, Gary, 29, 30, 96
Gitter, Chaim, 194, 208
Gjelsteen, Karen, 4, 36, 80, 112, 163, 205
Glass, Joanna M., 34, 91, 199
Glass, Philip, 123
Glassco, Bill, 31, 152
Glasser, D. Scott, 106
Glazer, Benjamin F., 79
Gleason, John, 56, 130
Glenn, David M., 174
Glover, Eleanor, 73
Gluck, Cookie, 34, 164, 217
Godin, William E., 201
Goeller, Bill, 138
Goethe, Johann Wolfgang Von, 65
Goetz, Augustus, 35, 45, 103
Goetz, Ed, 15
Goetz, Ruth, 35, 45, 103
Gogol, Nikolai, 215
Gohr, Deb, 200
Going, John, 11, 53, 79, 204
Gold, Lloyd, 53
Goldberg, Dick, 12
Goldberg, Gayle, 113
Goldberg, Moses, 196, 197
Goldemberg, Rose Leiman, 39, 123

Golden, Ardyss, 56, 125, 159
Golden, John, 143
Golden, Norman, 17
Goldin, Diane, 224
Goldin, Toni, 79, 95
Goldman, Harris, 98
Goldman, James, 134, 173, 190, 218
Goldoni, Carlo, 5, 96, 170, 227
Goldsby, Robert W., 38, 39
Goldsmith, Clifford, 126
Goldsmith, Oliver, 87, 91, 103, 108, 112, 202, 211
Goldstein, Benjamin, 85
Goldstein, David Ira, 9
Goldstein, Debbi, 51
Goldstein, Nancy, 44
Gonzales, Keith, 18, 76
Gonzalez, Magda, 123
Goodman, David, 60
Goodman, Jeff, 160
Goodman, Robert, 135
Goodman, Robyn, 192
Goodrich, Francis, 36, 102, 170
Goodwin, Richard R., 48
Gordon, Dale, 145
Gordon, Denise, 110
Gordon, Ruth, 89
Gordon, Stuart B., 34, 163, 164, 212, 216
Gordone, Charles, 64
Gorky, Maxim, 223
Gornel, William, 49
Goss, Bick, 166
Goss, Robert, 114
Gotanda, Philip Kan, 77
Gottlieb, Alex, 155
Gotwald, David, 88
Gould, Peter David, 174
Gould, Richard, 59
Goya, Tito, 207
Graffy, Kurt, 159
Graham, Robert, 13, 104
Graham, W. Steven, 137
Graham-Lujan, James, 153
Grahame, Kenneth, 51, 79, 93, 167
Grainer, Ron, 165
Gralen, Paul, 22
Granata, Dona, 48
Grand, Sandra, 92
Granger, Percy, 54, 82, 94
Grant, Matthew, 13
Grant-Phillips, John, 21
Grantham, Ken, 125
Grassilli, John, 210
Gray, Amelia Cobb, 207
Gray, Amlin, 8, 12, 41, 83, 91, 115, 135, 153, 178
Gray, John, 7, 14, 63, 108, 156, 204, 211, 218
Gray, Kathy, 31
Gray, Rick, 194
Gray, Simon, 120, 152, 167, 210, 211
Gray, Spalding, 226
Green, Adolph, 26, 53

Green, Benny, 59, 66
Green, Dennis, 61
Green, Emily, 184
Green, Joann, 21
Green, Mawby, 215
Green, Michael, 126
Green, Robert, 24
Green, Warren G., 51, 212
Green-Caldwell, Lauren, 154
Greenberg, Albert, 122
Greenberg, Edward M., 109
Greenberg, James, 169
Greenberg, Rocky, 92
Greenberg, Susan M., 210
Greene, Ron, 225
Greenleaf, Jamie, 11
Greenwald, Robert, 117
Greenwood, Jane, 5, 54, 57, 99, 120, 150, 186
Greer, Jim, 210
Gregg, Susan, 7, 144, 167
Gregory, Andre, 138
Grey, Clifford, 99
Grey, Liebe, 117
Griffin, Tom, 120
Griffith, Trevor, 126
Griggs, Michael, 78
Griswold, Mary, 164, 217
Grob, Geoffrey B., 185
Gromet, Maryclare, 148
Gropman, David, 92, 150, 165
Grosbard, Ulu, 98
Gross, Ellen, 217
Gross, Gerald, 104
Gross, Robert F., 26
Gross, Theodore Faro, 125
Grossman, Dagmar, 153
Grossman, Lisa, 208
Grossmann, Suzanne, 129, 190
Grothe, Mary Ann, 210
Grout, Donna, 4
Grove, Barry, 127
Gruenewald, Thomas, 32, 35, 91, 95, 104, 105, 144, 166, 168
Grundmann, Tim, 148
Grunen, Gerta, 14
Gruner, Kim, 210
Grumberg, Jean-Claude, 31, 48, 120, 215
Guardino, Jerome, 103, 204
Guare, John, 12, 40, 92, 115, 128, 178
Guenther, James, 9, 96
Gumpper, Ann E., 147
Gunn, Don, 164
Gunn, L.B., 189
Gunter, John, 150
Gural, Ron, 213
Gurney, A.R., Jr., 4, 12, 13, 30, 32, 35, 41, 56, 59, 92, 100, 105, 143, 152, 156, 177, 178, 221
Guskin, Harold, 145
Gustafson, Otis, 139, 206
Guthrie, Pat, 66
Guthrie, Tyrone, 73, 95
Gutierrez, Gerald, 156, 177
Guttmann, Karl, 68

Guyer, Murphy, 7, 167, 168, 211
Guzik, Jeff, 34
Gwartney, Richard, 26
Gyorgyey, Clara, 24

H

Haak, Dianne, 24, 116, 117
Haas, Jeannine, 110
Haas, Karl, 7
Haas, Sue, 106
Haas, Tom, 107, 108
Haatainen, Christina, 73
Hackett, Albert, 36, 102, 170, 197
Hackett, Jean, 223
Hackler, Ewald, 38, 39
Haddow, Jeffrey, 14, 36, 59
Hage, George S., 8
Hagen, Kris, 195
Hague, Nola, 39
Hahn, Jessica, 152, 186
Hahn, Kenneth E., 138
Hailey, Oliver, 204
Haimes, Todd, 185
Haimsohn, George, 218
Haines, Fred, 123
Halac, Ricardo, 109
Halcott, Gary, 14
Hale, Sandra J., 95
Hall, Adrian, 2, 20, 67, 214, 215
Hall, Bob, 41, 88, 91
Hall, Carol, 82, 221
Hall, David, 211
Hall, Geoffry, 113
Hall, Hugh F., 11
Hall, Jeffrey, 126
Hall, Michael P., 44, 45
Hall, Nick, 199
Hall, Oakley, III, 45, 46
Hall, Peter J., 130
Hall, Randy, 173
Hall, Robert, 144, 167
Hall, Thomas, 155
Hallberg, Judy, 197
Hallick, Ned, 199
Halliwell, David, 200
Hally, Martha, 82
Halpern, Martin, 73
Halpern, Michael, 3
Hamburger, Richard, 223
Hames, Peter, 105
Hamilton, Jill, 9
Hamilton, Patrick, 9, 174, 222
Hamilton, Rob, 126, 207
Hamilton, William, 17, 152
Hamlisch, Marvin, 149, 220
Hammack, Warren, 102, 103
Hammer, Philip, 189
Hammer, Scott L., 69
Hammerstein, James, 82
Hammerstein, Oscar, II, 143, 165
Hammond, David, 228
Hammond, Thomas W., 218
Hample, Stuart, 91, 171

Hampton, Christopher, 36, 48, 98, 112, 129, 192, 199
Handel, Beatrice, 67
Handel, George Friedrich, 20
Handke, Peter, 213
Handman, Wynn, 18
Haniuk, Marc, 24
Hankins, Michael, 6, 53, 103, 219
Hanley, William, 155, 159
Hansberry, Lorraine, 64, 88, 202
Hansen, Michael L., 9
Hansen, Thomas Carl, 61
Harburg, E.Y., 53, 79
Harden, Richard, 70
Harders, Robert, 123
Hardison, O.B., 87
Hardman, Laura, 13
Hardwick, Mark, 207
Hardy, David, 124
Hardy, Joseph, 156
Hardy, Marsha, 60
Hare, David, 150, 194
Hariton, Gerry, 116, 117
Hariton, Renee, 78
Harley, Margot, 4
Harman, Leonard, 57
Harnick, Sheldon, 79, 99, 173, 212
Harper, Raynard, 69
Harris, Albert J., 57
Harris, Aurand, 141, 210
Harris, Bill, 145
Harris, James Berton, 11, 53, 63, 204
Harrison, Alfred, 106, 130, 166
Harrison, Lew, 145
Harrison, Margaret Keyes, 66
Harshaw, Robert, 84
Harsini, Manuchehr, 207
Hart, Judith, 64
Hart, Lorenz, 21, 108, 120
Hart, Moss, 11, 26, 35, 45, 79, 108, 143, 151, 165
Hartinian, Linda, 150
Hartman, Lynne M., 218
Hartmann, Carin, 214
Hartwell, Peter, 150
Harvey, Cameron, 196
Harwood, Ronald, 4, 26, 43, 53, 60, 69, 215
Haskell, Judith, 59, 171
Haskle, Kay, 87
Hasnain, Arif, 134
Hasson, Dana, 82
Hastings, Edward, 17, 73, 99, 192, 221
Hastings, Paul, 168
Haufrecht, Marcia, 82
Haugen, Kristine, 204
Hauger, Kerry, 26
Haughton, Linda E., 135
Hauptman, Barbara, 192
Hausch, Gregory, 99, 100
Hausch, Mary, 99, 100
Hauser, Frank, 98
Hauser, Lucille, 49
Havard, Lezley, 7

Havel, Vaclav, 8
Havens, Neil, 12
Havergal, Giles, 87
Hawkanson, David, 29
Hay, David, 27
Hay, Richard L., 17, 146, 163
Hayden, Jeffrey, 152, 186
Hayes, Catherine, 128
Hayes, Denis, 153
Hayes, Mary L., 194
Haynes, Isyla, 140
Haynes, Jerry, 211
Haynes, Randall, 151
Haynes, Tim, 69
Hays, Mary, 15
Hays, Stephen E., 198, 199
Hayter, Pearl, 34
Hebert-Slater, Marilee, 6
Hecht, Ben, 92, 98, 120, 174, 192, 215
Hedstrom, Cynthia, 124
Heefner, David Kerry, 103, 104
Heeley, Desmond, 5, 131
Heffernan, Maureen, 88
Heggen, Thomas, 173
Heifetz, Harold, 77
Heifner, Jack, 88, 144, 184, 204, 219
Heiman, Betsy, 153
Hein, Keith, 13, 196
Heitz, Gary, 225
Held, Dan, 18, 147
Hellermann, William, 132
Hellman, Lillian, 14, 17, 33, 173, 192
Helton, Ingrid, 189
Hemenway, Audrey, 208
Hemphill-Burns, Lisa, 168
Hemsley, Gilbert V., Jr., 156, 183
Henderson, Luther, 15
Henderson, Martin, 201
Henderson, Russell, 69
Hendren, Mark, 166
Henley, Beth, 3, 4, 41, 56, 76, 98, 200, 202, 221
Hennequin, Maurice, 9, 135
Hennes, Tom, 109
Henry, O., 6, 70, 143
Henshaw, Wandalie, 56, 57
Henson, John, 69
Henson, Van Emden, 49
Herman, George, 102
Herman, Jerry, 14
Herochik, John, 88
Heron, Nye, 186
Herrera, Shizuko, 77
Herrick, Lynn, 158
Herring, Zak, 69
Herrmann, Edward, 178
Hersey, John, 12
Hewitt, Kenneth R., Jr., 75
Heymann, Jerry, 126
Hibbard, Allen, 69
Hibberd, Jack, 218
Hicken, Donald, 199
Hickey, John, 126, 139
Hickok, John, 44

INDEX OF NAMES 243

Hicks, Israel, 108, 219
Hicks, Munson, 126
Hieronymous, Richard, 186
Higgins, Dave, 7
Hilbert, Kathryn, 142
Hilferty, Susan, 91, 92, 108, 128, 193
Hill, David, 144
Hill, Eric, 135, 213
Hill, Gary Leon, 7
Hill, Jeff, 7
Hill, Kelly R., Jr., 184
Hill, Kenneth, 69
Hill, Rob, 4
Hilton, Paul, 100
Hirsch, John, 129
Hirschfeld, Susan, 14
Hirshbein, Omus, 17
Hirson, Roger O., 15, 67, 206
Hischak, Thomas, 70
Hitchcock, Jane Stanton, 19
Hite, Michaele, 105
Hladsky, Barbara, 104
Ho, Alvin, 208
Hoag, Everett, 169
Hobbs, James Albert, 148
Hobson, Richard, 131
Hochwalker, Fritz, 18
Hoffman, Marcie, 213
Hofsiss, Jack, 144
Hogya, Giles, 61
Hohlfield, Brian, 210
Holamon, Monty Philip, 12
Holcomb, Barbara, 34
Holden, Charles I., Jr., 99
Holden, Vicki, 32, 86
Holder, Laurence, 15
Holdgriewe, David, 53
Holister, David, 194
Holkeboer, Katherine S., 34
Holland, Mara, 24
Holland, Sharon, 50, 51
Hollingsworth, Dawn, 152, 217
Hollis, Jesse, 36, 38
Hollis, Stephen, 120
Hollmann, Heide, 19, 46, 139, 147, 178
Holloway, Victoria, 21, 22
Holly, Daniel, 213
Holly, Dianne, 156
Holm, Klaus, 79
Holm, Peter, 112
Holman, Robert, 104
Holme, Christopher, 96
Holmes, Dolly, 208
Holmes, M.L., 131
Holmes, Ralph, 150
Holms, John Pynchon, 12, 88, 149
Holt, Christopher, 208
Holt, Stephen, 207
Holte, Phil, 205
Holzberg, Roger, 115
Honegger, Gitta, 28, 96, 209
Hong, James, 76
Hooker, Brian, 12
Hooper, Arthur W., 98
Hooven, Valentine, 159
Hoover, Richard, 91

Hopkins, John, 120
Hopkins, Kaki Dowling, 69
Hopkins, Richard, 22, 86
Hornung, Richard, 18, 54
Horovitz, Israel, 51, 123
Horton, Paul J., 199
Horwitz, Murray, 11, 166
Hoshi, Shizuko, 77
Hoskins, Jim, 32
Houghton, Norris, 7, 32
Hould-Ward, Ann, 28, 98, 126, 177
House, George, 159
Houseman, Arthur L., 173
Houseman, John, 4
Houtz, Stephen, 12
Howard, Charles, 211
Howard, Ed, 98
Howe, Tina, 193
Howell, Penny, 145
Hoyle, Geoff, 36
Hoyle, Mary Lou, 69
Huberman, Jeffrey, 57
Huddle, Elizabeth, 17
Huddleston, Will, 190
Hudgens, Bruce, 110
Hudson, Ken, 69
Hughes, Alice S., 147
Hughes, Allen Lee, 28, 73, 92, 171
Hughes, Douglas, 128, 177
Hughes, Kevin M., 79
Hulce, Thomas, 177
Hulett, Michael, 49
Hume, Michael J., 46
Hummel, Karen, 18, 113, 126
Hundley, C.L., 35
Hunecki, Durin, 110
Hunt, Pamela, 35
Hunter, Kermit, 212
Hunter, Timothy J., 229
Hurson, Michael, 149
Hurst, Gregory S., 165, 166
Hussein, Waris, 54
Hussey, Nora, 134
Hutchings, Robert S., Jr., 51
Hwang, David Henry, 63, 149

I

Iannicelli, Kathie, 206
Ibsen, Henrik, 8, 11, 20, 22, 26, 35, 65, 73, 75, 89, 96, 99, 112, 139, 183, 229
Idoine, Christopher M., 115, 135, 153
Ilson, Carol, 207
Infante, Jan, 121
Ingalls, James F., 21, 92, 98, 138, 177, 192, 223
Inge, William, 35, 137, 139
Ingham, Rosemary, 13
Innaurato, Albert, 39, 69, 170, 177, 219
Insull, Sigrid, 35, 222
Ionazzi, Danny, 73
Irvine, Daniel, 86

Irving, Washington, 68
Irwin, Bill, 19
Irwin, Catherine, 27, 118
Irwin, James, 59
Isaac, Alberto, 77
Isaackes, Richard, 44, 91, 99, 105
Israel, Robert, 124, 150
Ito, Teiji, 209
Ivanov, Kalina, 194, 223
Ivcich, Steven, 217
Ives, David, 223

J

Jack, Angel, 208
Jacker, Corinne, 56
Jackins, Brian, 67
Jackness, Andrew, 98, 120, 138, 177, 180, 223
Jackson, Bruce, 205
Jackson, Nagle, 17, 112, 130, 131, 135
Jacobs, Douglas, 188, 189
Jacobs, Jack, 223
Jacobs, Sally, 56, 150, 208
Jacobsen, John E., 148
Jacques, David Martin, 60
Jaimes, Jaime, 123
Jaggar, Franz, 147
Jakes, John, 79
Jamal, 114
James, Julie, 4, 205
James, Henry, 69, 137
James, Lonnie, 201
James, Luther, 39, 114
James, Morgan, 31
James, Robert, 43
Jampolis, Neil Peter, 53, 219
Jared, Robert, 73, 95, 98, 108, 137, 171, 202
Jarrell, Randall, 131
Jarry, Alfred, 132
Jasien, Deborah, 151
Jaster, Mark, 187
Jeffcoat, A.E., 127
Jeffers, Robinson, 57
Jeffrey, Lynn, 21
Jellicoe, Ann, 186
Jenkin, Len, 194
Jenkins, David, 54, 120, 130, 135, 150
Jenkins, Ken, 6, 88, 166, 167, 204
Jenkins, Paulie, 115, 153, 196
Jenkins, Sharon, 215
Jennings, John, 24
Jensen, John, 13, 53, 91, 92, 120, 131, 170, 171
Jensen, Julie, 33
Jerrold, Michael, 168
Jezewski, Steve, 115
Jilg, David, 173
Johanson, Robert, 165
John, Flozanne A., 171
John, Mary, 134
John, Tom H., 183
Johns, Andrew, 4, 41, 68, 135

Johns, Beth, 155
Johnson, Bernard, 166
Johnson, Claudia, 100
Johnson, Chris, 9
Johnson, David, 86
Johnson, Douglas, 228
Johnson, Edouard, 24
Johnson, Grey, 44
Johnson, Jerry, 49
Johnson, Joanne, 22
Johnson, Lisa, 63
Johnson, Loren, 51
Johnson, Myron, 51
Johnson, Stephanie, 83
Johnson, Thomas Peter, 154, 155
Johnson, Trish, 6, 7, 41
Jonathan, Brother, O.S.F., 82
Jones, Allen H., 93
Jones, Andrew Earl, 139
Jones, B.J., 143
Jones, B. Jack, 69
Jones, Barbara, 140
Jones, Charles, 141
Jones, Cliff, 153
Jones, Davey Marlin, 87
Jones, David, 228
Jones, Eleanor, 141
Jones, Elinor, 228
Jones, Gary, 120
Jones, Howard, 137
Jones, Jeffrey M., 82, 225
Jones, John-Frederick, 10, 117
Jones, Martin, 217
Jones, Mary Sue, 69
Jones, Melanie, 215
Jones, Preston, 7
Jones, Tom, 66, 139, 173
Jones, Walton, 11, 128, 160, 228
Jones, William M., 58
Jordan, Dale F., 46, 82, 178
Jordan, Glenn, 99
Jory, Jon, 6, 7, 119, 128, 184
Joselovitz, Ernest, 148, 211
Joubert, Elsa, 138
Joy, James Leonard, 40, 99, 104, 105
Joyaux, Simone, 120
Joyce, William, 62
Jozwick, Tim, 183
J'te, 190
Jung, Philip, 229
Jurasas, Jonas, 207

K

Kabakov, Joel, 196
Kacir, Marylynn, 75
Kaczorowski, Peter, 125
Kafka, Franz, 130, 138
Kageyama, Rodney, 77
Kahn, Michael, 4, 5, 109, 193
Kaikkonen, Gus, 41, 91, 152
Kajiwara, Ron, 208
Kalcheim, Lee, 104
Kalevas, Paula, 34

Kalfin, Robert, 145, 219
Kalmar, Bert, 28
Kamlot, Robert, 148
Kammer, Karen, 79
Kammer, Nancy, 41
Kandel, Gregory, 151
Kander, John, 14, 173
Kane, Eileen, 159
Kane, Wyman, 227
Kanee, Stephen, 171
Kani, John, 225
Kanin, Garson, 53, 135, 147, 166, 190
Kanter, David Robert, 60
Kaplan, David, 46
Kaplan, Shirley, 82
Kaplan, Stan, 194
Kaplan, Steve, 126
Kaplan, Trina, 188
Karchmer, Charles I., 23, 82, 170
Karp, Marshall, 23
Karraker, John, 217
Kasarda, John, 40, 91, 192, 223
Kashkin, Esther, 153
Katen, James, 76, 148
Kates, Roderick, 84
Katz, Gene, 172
Katz, Karen M., 115, 153
Katz, Leon, 229
Katz, Natasha, 88, 95
Katz, Stephen, 91
Kauffman, John, 80, 101
Kaufman, AnnaBelle, 115, 130
Kaufman, George S., 11, 26, 28, 79, 106, 108, 126, 132, 137, 165
Kaufman, Mark, 133, 134
Kaushansky, Larry, 9
Kava, Caroline, 91
Kavelin, John, 115
Kayden, Mildred, 153
Kaye-Martin, Edward, 225
Keathley, George, 98
Keatley, Jack, 212
Keats, Ezra Jack, 85
Kechely, Gary, 88
Keeffe, Barrie, 83, 104, 194
Keeler, Richard L., 167, 168
Keeling, Madeline, 3
Keen, Julie D., 218, 225
Keilstrup, Margaret, 104
Keim, Lisa, 208
Keller, Bruce, 84
Keller, John-David, 196
Keller, Mark, 8
Keller, Thomas, 166
Kelley, Shannon Keith, 228
Kellman, Barnet, 104, 160
Kellogg, Marjorie Bradley, 23, 54, 85, 99, 120, 178, 183, 193
Kelly, Casey, 70, 166
Kelly, David H., 165
Kelly, George, 32, 36
Kelly, Martha, 108
Kelly, Patrick, 186
Kelly, Paul, 104
Kelly, Tim, 173
Kemenes, Fanny, 79
Kempinski, Tom, 120, 152, 186

Kendall, Libby, 208
Kenna, Peter, 59
Kennedy, Craig, 208
Kennedy, Dennis, 41
Kennedy, Jimmy, 34, 163
Kennedy, Margaret, 127
Kennedy-Paulsen, Rick, 80
Kennon, Skip, 95, 177
Kent, Steven, 128
Kenyon, Neal, 183
Kepros, Nicholas, 63
Kern, Holly, 159
Kerner, Susan, 166
Kerr, Jean, 221
Kerr, Philip, 183
Kerr, Tom, 99
Kershen, Ed, 169
Kerwin, Patrick, 217
Kerwin, Shawn, 152
Kesey, Ken, 44
Kesselman, Wendy, 6, 7, 14, 82, 138, 144, 193
Kesselring, Joseph, 67, 156, 172
Ketron, Larry, 27, 228
Key, Tom, 14
Keyes, Daniel, 197
Khan, Rick, 63, 64, 88
Kilian, Charles, 10
Kilpatrick, Brian, 83
Kilpatrick, Jack, 212
Kilpatrick, Jackie, 84
Kilty, Jerome, 17, 99, 112, 186, 190
Kim, June, 76
Kim, Kwang Lim, 77
Kim, Mara, 14
Kim, Sora, 158
Kim, Sukman, 77
Kim, Willa, 150
Kimbell, Jon, 205
Kimmel, Alan, 53
King, Catherine, 32
King, Diane, 196
King, Helen, 34
King, Larry L., 221
King, Woodie, Jr., 53, 59, 144, 145, 171, 199, 218
Kinghorn, Deborah, 69
Kinghorn, Jeffrey, 68
Kinnaird, Donald, 158
Kinney, Alex, 36
Kinney, Terry, 199, 200
Kinsley, Dan, 113
Kipnis, Claude, 73
Kipphardt, Heinar, 18, 114, 153, 189
Kirkland, Christopher D., 175
Kirkland, Jack, 213
Kirkland, James, 32
Kirkpatrick, Sam, 130, 156
Kirkwood, James, 149
Kiselov, Mladen, 228
Kishline, John, 213, 214
Kissel, David, 165
Kissman, Katha, 118
Kleban, Edward, 149
Kleiman, Harlan, 119
Klein, Amanda J., 150

Klein, Jon, 225
Klein, Leslie, 100
Klein, Maxine, 19
Kline, Linda, 113
Klingensmith, Robin, 49
Klonsky, Kenneth, 113
Kluga, Raymond, 194
Knerly, Mary, Johnson, 83
Knight, Darwin, 217
Knott, Frederick, 13, 35, 155
Kobayshi, Dan, 225
Koelb, Clayton, 24
Koertge, Douglas J., 225
Kolsby, Marion, 45
Kondoleon, Harry, 128, 160, 177
Kone, Randy, 78
Kopit, Arthur, 48, 156, 163
Kopperl, Paul B., 127
Korie, Michael, 95
Kornfeld, Lawrence, 35, 206, 229
Koron, Barry, 194
Korsby, Kenneth, 100
Kos, Sally, 32
Kotlowitz, Dan J., 135
Kotze, Sandra, 138
Kotzwinkle, William, 164
Kowal, Marsha, 92, 217
Kowsar, Mohammad, 114
Kozak, Ellen, 91, 135
Kramer, Carla, 125
Kramer, Sherry, 144
Krashyasky, Anatol, 153
Krasna, Norman, 63, 222
Kraus, Arnold, 29
Krausnick, Dennis, 22
Krchelich, David, 106
Krebs, Eric, 88
Kripal, Janet, 158
Kroetz, Franz Xaver, 80, 83
Kubicki, Jan, 189
Kuhling, David, 150
Kuhling, Michael, 124
Kuklenski, Montgomery, 31
Kunz, Carol, 134
Kurland, Rachel, 35, 105, 120, 178
Kurtz, Kenneth N., 60
Kurtz, Penny, 79
Kwast, Susi, 213
Kyte, Mary, 6, 30, 35, 59, 63, 68, 70, 88, 134, 141, 155, 171, 177, 189, 196, 199, 215, 217

L

Labiche, Eugene, 126
La Bon, Curtis, 208
Lacey, Jackson, 197
Lagamarsino, Ron, 53
LaGue, Michael, 12
Lahr, John, 130
Laird, Gregory W., 61
Lakesmith, John, 208
Lakin, Gene, 95, 108, 194, 229
Lambert, Steve, 60
Lambeth, Jeanine, 115
Lamos, Mark, 97, 98

Lampell, Millard, 12
Lamude, Terence, 134
Lanchester, Robert, 95, 131
Landesman, Heidi, 5, 21, 28, 61, 150, 193
Landis, Joseph C., 61
Landisman, Eric, 38
Landisman, Kurt, 38, 39, 56, 83, 125, 159
Landon, John, 69
Landow, Brett, 208
Landrum, Baylor, 52
Landwehr, Hugh, 11, 48, 56, 105, 120, 135, 192, 223
Lane, William, 215
Langan, E. Timothy, 214
Langer, Laurence, 220
Langham, Michael, 17
Langman, Donna, 202
Langmead, Joseph M., 47
Lanier, Sidney, 18
Lansbury, Edgar, 4, 76
Lapidus, Jerry, 14
LaPierre, Billings, 14
Lapine, James, 22, 149, 177
LaPlatney, Martin, 33, 34
Larche, Gene, 155
Lardner, Ring, 132
Larkins, Grady, 7, 202
Larrance, John C., 35
Larsen, Lori, 80
Larson, James, 158
Lasakow, Paul, 3
Lashley, Edith, 23
Latouche, John, 28
Latta, Rich, 34
Laufer, Ken, 169
Laughead, Scott, 169
Laurents, Arthur, 56
Lauro, Shirley, 82, 120, 167, 170
Laveria, Tato, 145
Lavery, Emmet, 137
Laville, Pierre, 92
Lavino, Steve, 123, 153, 189, 196
Lawless, James, 63
Lawless, Sarah, 50
Lawless, Sue, 18, 19, 88, 166
Lawrence, D.H., 166, 186
Lawrence, Jerome, 14, 23, 53, 141, 163
Lawson, Steve, 223
Layton, Ed, 115
Layton, Peter, 36, 38
Lazar, Cathy, 208
Lazarus, Paul, 76
Leach, Wilford, 149
Leake, Damien, 145
Learning, Walter, 68
Leathers, Scott, 67
LeBar, Tom, 207
LeCompte, Elizabeth, 225, 226
Lederman, Fred, 15
Lee, Dana, 77
Lee, Eugene, 138, 215
Lee, Franne, 92, 150
Lee, Fred, 148
Lee, Guy, 76
Lee, Harper, 173

Lee, Margaret, 23, 199
Lee, Ming Cho, 28, 108
Lee Myrna Colly, 145
Lee, Paul, 59
Lee, Robert E., 14, 23, 53, 141, 163
Lee, Wing, 229
Leerhoff, Dick, 9
Leeson, George, 61
Leeson, Sylvia, 61
Lefever, John D., 106
LeFevre, Adam, 211
Le Gallienne, Eva, 99
Leggett, Joe, 26
Legrand, Michel, 99
Lehman, Susan, 46
Lehrer, Tom, 28, 59, 211
Leibert, Michael W., 35, 36
Leigh, Carolyn, 26, 53
Leigh, Dan, 79
Leigh, Mitch, 165, 205
Leigh, Rowland, 76
Leigh, Thomas, 103
Leighton, Kat, 205
Leipart, Charles, 167
Leipzig, Adam, 123
Leivick, H., 61
Lemos, David, 189
LeNoire, Rosetta, 14, 15
Leo, Veronica, 112
Leon, Felix, 217
Leonard, Amy, 121
Leonard, Jim, Jr., 14, 34, 148, 196
Leonard, Hugh, 4, 35, 60, 134, 143, 196
Leonard, Robert H., 183, 184
Leonardo, Joseph, 167
Leong, David, 121
Lepre, Steve, 208
Lerner, Alan J., 14
Leroux, Gaston, 51
Lessac, Michael, 73
Lesser, Gene, 171
Lesser, Sally, 145, 204, 228
Lessing, Gotthold Ephraim, 194
Lester, Hugh, 28, 87
Levenson, David S., 31
Levi, Stephen, 144
Levin, Ira, 35, 67, 76, 100, 134, 166, 187, 202, 204, 206, 221
Levine, Gary S., 222
Levitow, Roberta, 204
Levit, Ben, 91, 177
Levitt, Bruce, 82
Levy, David, 222
Levy, Simon, 159
Levy, Jacques, 28
Lewis, C.S., 69
Lewis, C.S. III, 25
Lewis, Ira, 27
Lewis, Irene, 11
Lewis, John, 99
Lewis, Karen L., 209
Lewis, Mary, 102
Lewitin, Margot, 110, 208
Leyasmeyer, Archibald I. 174
Li, Pat, 76
Libin, Paul, 53

Lichtenstein, Todd, 166
Liebentritt, Dan, 163
Liepart, Charles, 70
Life, Regge, 19, 64
Lifson, David, 114
Lim, Ginny, 145
Lindeman, Gregory, 154
Lindgren, Astrid, 51
Lindfors, Viveca, 123
Lindsay, Eleanor, 68, 69
Lindsay, Howard, 132, 143
Lindsay, Kate, 153
Lines, Janice I., 202
Ling, Barbara, 115, 123
Link, Peter, 41
Link, Ron, 207
Linn-Baker, Mark, 149
Linnerson, Beth, 50
Linney, Romulus, 3, 63, 74, 75, 82, 144, 196
Lion, John, 124, 125
Lippa, Louis, 82, 167, 168
Lippmann, Zilla, 143
Lipschultz, Carole Harris, 105
Lipscomb, Edward, 13
Lipsky, John, 40
Littlewood, Joan, 31
Litz, Robert, 160, 174, 219
Lleo, Vicente, 180
Llosa, Mario Vargas, 109
Loadholt, Anthony, 3
Lobel, Adrianne, 28, 96, 128
Lock, Kevin, 86
Lock, Yet, 76
Lockner, David, 134
Lockpez, Inverna, 193
Loesser, Frank, 66
Loewe, Frederick, 14
Loewenberg, Susan Albert, 117
Logan, John, 69
Logan, Joshua, 173
Logsdon, Galen M., 222
Lomaka, Christine, 153
Lone, John, 63, 145, 149
Lonergan, Kenneth, 56
Long, Joseph W., 199.
Long, Kathryn, 202
Long, William Ivey, 92, 150, 165, 177
Look, Phyllis, 102
Loomer, Lisa, 19
Loos, Anita, 139
Loosemore, Lisa, 84
Loper, Robert, 192
Lopez, Jose, 78
Lopez-Morillas, Julian, 38, 163
Loquasto, Santo, 96, 98, 128, 177
Lorca, Federico Garcia, 153, 180
Lorca, Monica, 208
Lord, Robert, 144
Lorden, Terry C., 22
Lounsbury, Loren, 10
Lovaglia, Toni, 36
Loveless, David, 104
Loven, John, 167, 168
Lowry, Deborah Brothers, 125
Loy, Myrna, 18
Lubell, Bernie, 125

Lubelski, Abe, 125
Lucas, Terri, 208
Luce, William, 36, 66, 76, 155, 199
Luckham, Claire, 110
Luczak, James Edward, 160
Ludel, William, 91, 120, 131, 160, 228, 229
Ludwick, Ruth, 137
Ludwig, Karen, 207
Ludwig, Kenneth, 23
Lujan, James Graham, 180
Lund, Richard, 82, 227
Lundell, Kert, 56
Lutgenhorst, Manuel, 150
Luypers, Maggie, 31
Lynch, Francis, 13
Lynch, Michael, 125, 159
Lynch, Peter, 68, 69
Lynch, Tom, 21, 28, 79, 108, 130, 177
Lyon, Ned, 44

M

MacAdam, Will, 144
MacArthur, Charles, 92, 120, 174, 192, 215
Mace, Mimi, 72
MacDermot, Galt, 109
MacDonald, Bruce, 196
MacDonald, Ginny, 143
MacDonald, Robert David, 67
MacDougall, Robert, 39
MacFarlane, Pamela, 187
Machado, Eduardo, 82
Machiavelli, Niccolo, 153, 223
Mack, Carol, 19, 40, 82
Mack, Reuben, 121
MacKecknie, Donald, 53
Mackintosh, Cameron, 28, 59
MacLaughlin, Wendy, 137
MacLean, Ross, 207
MacLeish, Archibald, 89
MacPherson, Gregory, 5, 126
Macy, W.H., 82
Madden, Donald, 32
Madden, John, 130, 223
Maddox, Diana, 130
Madeira, Marcia, 99, 150
Maggio, Michael, 30, 59, 92, 151
Maguire, Roberta, 216
Magune, Jack, 227
Magwili, Dom, 77
Maher, William Michael, 15
Mailand, Robert, 8
Major, Anthony, 201
Mako, 76, 77
Makovsky, Judianna, 35, 108, 126
Malave, Efraim, 180
Malcolm, David, 38
Maleczech, Ruth, 123, 124
Malizia, Lester, 207
Malkovich, John, 152, 199, 200
Malleson, Miles, 48, 103, 143, 156

Maloney, Peter, 82, 167
Maloy, Tim, 213
Maltby, Richard, Jr., 11, 23, 31, 128, 166, 221
Mamet, David, 51, 53, 63, 82, 92, 120, 187, 193, 223
Manarik, Laurie, 114
Manassee, Jackie, 83, 138
Mancinelli, Margaret, 459
Mandel, Frank, 165
Mandell, Alan, 121, 123
Manet, Eduardo, 109
Manheim, Ralph, 39, 137
Manim, Mannie, 80
Manion, Robert C., 182
Manis, Ruby K., 24
Manley, James, 189
Mann, Charles, 229
Mann, Edward, 53
Mann, Emily, 7, 28, 80, 83
Mann-Day, Willa, 189
Manners, J. Hartley, 70, 76
Manulis, John, 56
Maradudin, Peter, 229
Marchand, Shoshana, 56
Marchese, Fred, 194
Marchetta, Anthony L., 88
Maretka, Danealia, 211
Margulies, Donald, 113
Marie-Cocuzzo, Leslie, 187
Marini, Ken, 167
Marki, Csilla, 130
Markle, Christopher J., 5, 96
Markoe, Gerald Jay, 219
Markow, Gerald A., 143
Marks, Gayle, 117
Marks, Gerald, 150, 194
Marks, Sandra Lee, 213
Markus, Tom, 31, 217, 218
Marlay, Andrew Blackwood, 202
Marley, Donovan, 72, 73
Marlin-Jones, Davey, 202
Marlowe, Christopher, 57
Marowitz, Charles, 123

Marquardt, Lanette, 210
Marques, Rene, 180
Marren, Howard, 145
Marrero, Maria, 60, 204
Marriner, Greg, 15, 178
Marriott, B. Rodney, 55, 56, 205
Marsden, Susan, 83
Marsh, Frazier W., 6, 7
Marshall, Barry, 207
Marshall, Dorothy L., 183
Marshall, Gay, 95
Marshall, Victoria, 137
Martell, Leon, 159
Martin, Brian, 19, 64, 82, 131
Martin, Christopher, 61, 64, 65, 147
Martin, Dan J., 64
Martin, George, 215
Martin, James O., 51
Martin, Jane, 6, 7, 128, 167
Martin, Manuel, Jr., 109
Martin, Mary, 123
Martin, Nell, 189

Martin, Scott, 51
Martinez, Eddie, 78
Martinez, Marc, 173
Marvin, Jim, 68
Marvin, Mel, 6, 30, 35, 59, 63, 68, 70, 88, 91, 134, 141, 155, 171, 189, 196, 199, 215, 217
Marz, Charles, 43
Maso, Michael, 104
Mason, Marshall W., 55, 56, 96, 129
Mason, Mary, 82
Mason, Richard G., 102
Mason, Timothy, 7, 50, 51
Massee, Michael, 64
Masteroff, Joe, 14, 173
Masterson, Kathleen, 46
Mastrosimone, William, 7, 92
Matalon, Vivian, 104
Mather, Ada Brown, 35
Mathiesen, Paul, 204
Matschullat, Kay, 222
Matthews, Dakin, 17, 37, 38
Matthews, Edward E., 130
Matthews, Karen, 91, 109, 138, 177
Matura, Mustapha, 64
Maugham, W. Somerset, 63, 108
Maultsby, Sara, 117
Maurer, Karl, 153
Maurer, Laura, 120, 135
Maxmen, Mimi, 19, 228
May, Elaine, 92, 159
May, Henry, 36
Mayer, Gene, 61
Mayer, Jerry, 12
Mays, Richard, 229
Mazer, H. Paul, 60
Mazor, Jeff, 15
Mazzone-Clementi, Carlo, 71
Mazzone-Clementi, Joan, 71
McAdoo, Dale, 229
McAdoo, Harper Jane, 59
McAlister, Tom, 110
McAnuff, Des, 149, 150
McBride, Donald, 84
McBride, Vaughn, 6, 17, 128
McBroom, Robert, 70
McCall, Charles, 189
McCarry, Charles, 126
McCarthy, Celia, 39
McCartney, Ellen, 178
McCleary, Dan, 153
McClellan, Colbert, 158
McClelland, Jo, 26
McClendon, David, 156
McClure, James, 131
McCord, Stella, 69
McCoy, Loette, 208
McDermott, Tom, 159
McDevitt, Mary, 106
McDonald, James, 155
McDonald, LeRoy, 115
McDonald, Peggy, 38, 39, 83, 159
McElrath, Randy, 93
McElroy, Colleen, 138
McElroy, Evie, 59
McEntire, Joanne, 110

McEwen, Robbie, 148
McGarity, Patty Greer, 211
McGinnes, Mac, 216
McGourty, Patricia, 56, 128, 150
McGovern, Dennis, 169
McGregor, Dion, 131
McGuire, Mitch, 126
McIlrath, Patricia, 136
McIntyre, Dennis, 144
McIntyre, Jane, 200
McIntyre, Ron, 15
McKay, Anthony, 113
McKay, Gardner, 9, 39, 46, 59
McKay, Hugh, 87
McKeaney, Grace, 48, 159
McKeen, Elaine, 125
McKellar, John, 131
McKenna, David, 14
McKenney, Kerry, 99, 100
McKenzie, James B., 16, 220
McKeown, Douglas, 61
McKinley, Tom, 13, 225
McKinnon, Frederick, 15
McKnight, Jack, 89
McLachlan, Jo, 24
McLain, John, 54, 99, 156
McLamb, Sheila, 229
McLean, Jason, 51
McLure, James, 6, 7, 12, 155, 159
McNally, Terence, 126
McNamara, John, 56
McNaughton, Anne, 38, 39, 190
McNeill, Brian, 114
McNellis, Patrick, 51
McPherson, Fillmore, 34
McVay, Julie, 155
McVay, Marcelle, 216
McWest, Dan, 205
Meadow, Lynne, 127, 128
Means, Richard K., 170
Meares, James, 110
Medak, Susan, 165
Medoff, Mark, 27, 100, 189, 206, 221
Meehan, Thomas, 221
Meeker, Roger, 99, 105, 223
Mehrten, Greg, 123, 124, 150
Meister, Arthur, 13
Melde, Shari, 211
Melfi, Leonard, 109
Mellon, Karen Sparks, 23, 67
Menken, Alan, 172, 228
Mercier, G.W., 223, 229
Merckens, Meg, 154
Meredith, Jeff, 227
Merriam, Eve, 56, 128, 189
Merrill, Bob, 67
Merritt, Michael, 43, 92, 152
Merritt, Wayne, 59
Mertz, LuEsther T., 148
Merwin, W.S., 131
Meryash, Arthur, 104
Merzel, Anita, 159
Messina, Cedric, 137
Messner, John, 188
Messore, Pamela, 120
Metcalf, Jo Anne, 158
Metcalfe, Stephen, 41, 53, 128

Metheny, Russell, 87, 108, 148
Meyer, Michael, 186
Meyers, Patrick, 28, 204
Mgcina, Sophie, 138
Michel, Marc, 126
Mickelsen, David Kay, 30
Mickle, Shelley, 100
Micunis, Gordon, 32
Midlin, Ilya, 153
Mikiver, Lilian, 187
Mikulewicz, Bil, 135
Milano, Albert, 67
Miles, Carol, 67, 68, 69
Miles, Julia, 18
Militello, Ann, 208
Millan, Bruce E., 74, 75
Millar, Ronald, 165
Miller, Allan, 116, 186
Miller, Arthur, 11, 18, 32, 36, 40, 53, 67, 73, 113, 120, 134, 166, 170, 171, 189, 192, 204, 219
Miller, Craig, 48, 56, 96, 108, 124, 128, 150, 156
Miller, Edward, 137
Miller, Glenn, 194
Miller, Jason, 204
Miller, Jonathan, 21, 147
Miller, Lauren MacKenzie, 10, 11
Miller, Lawrence, 104
Miller, Leslie, 199
Miller, Marcie, 169
Miller, Michael, 13, 49, 54, 112
Miller, Robin, 218
Miller, Susan, 193
Miller, Wade, 164
Milliken, Christopher, 116
Millman, Howard J., 90, 91
Milner, Ron, 145
Milton, David Scott, 153
Milton, Jim, 144, 149, 150
Min, Susan, 4, 205
Miner, Jan, 8
Miner, Michael Andrew, 8, 9
Minor, Philip, 215
Minter, Patti, 200
Mintzer, William, 28, 53, 105, 128
Miralda, Antoni, 132
Mitchell, Adrian, 95, 100, 222
Mitchell, David, 150
Mitchell, Julian, 120
Mitchell, Loften, 15
Mitchell, Peter, 117
Mitsui, Janet, 76
Mittelman, Arnold, 221
Mitze, Teri Solomon, 93
Mitze, Thomas C., 93
Mockus, Tony, 92
Modereger, Jeff Robin, 173, 202
Moiseiwitsch, Tanya, 51
Moliere, 5, 8, 20, 28, 46, 48, 54, 68, 69, 72, 73, 80, 88, 91, 92, 96, 98, 103, 108, 130, 143, 149, 156, 159, 161, 167, 171, 183, 186, 190, 196, 202, 211, 219
Moll, James, 36, 163
Molnar, Ferenc, 79, 120, 196, 218
Monet, Phil, 19, 88, 91, 104, 113, 209, 228

Mongold, Mark S., 164
Monk, Isabell, 6
Monk, Meredith, 149
Monk, Robby, 128, 202
Monroe, Mary F., 152
Montez, Paul-Felix, 208
Montgomery, Bruce, 84
Montgomery, Robert, 194
Montilino, John, 105
Montresor, Beni, 21, 96
Moon, Gerald, 23
Moon, Lynbn, 69
Mooney, Roger, 104, 170, 186
Moore, Barry, 115
Moore, Benjamin, 16
Moore, Brian, 99
Moore, Carman, 138
Moore, Dudley, 147
Moore, Edward, 22, 41, 167, 178, 210
Moore, Randy, 69
Moore, R. Raymond, 183
Moore, Richard, 131, 148, 218
Moore, Tom, 17, 21, 129, 130, 156
Morales, Jacobo, 180
Moran, James, 33, 227
Morath, Max, 183
Mordecai, Benjamin, 107, 228
Morgado, Robert J., 78
Morgan, Bayard Quincy, 194
Morgan, Darlene, 24
Morgan, James, 100, 165, 219
Morgan, John A., 136
Morgan, Robert, 17, 36, 156, 202
Morgan, Roger, 95
Moriarty, Michael, 149
Morin, Michael, 167
Morin, Ricardo, 229
Moritz, Susan Trapnell, 3
Morley, Jay, 116
Morley, Ruth, 221
Morong, David, 26
Morris, Aldyth, 39
Morris, Bonnie, 105, 106
Morris, Cleveland, 69, 70
Morris-Smith, James, 213
Morrison, Jan, 199
Morrison, John, 76
Morrison, Malcolm, 150, 151
Morrison, Monica, 208
Morriss, Bruce K., 206
Morrissey, Eamon, 95
Mortimer, John, 17, 151, 215
Mortimer, Michael, 217
Morton, Mark, 14
Mosel, Tad, 66
Moser, Nina, 82
Moses, Gilbert, 28
Moses, Marysue, 106
Mosher, Gregory, 91, 92
Moss, Robert, 61, 63
Moss, Sylvia, 116
Mosse, Spencer, 11, 53, 93, 135, 150, 192
Mostel, Josh, 126
Motyka, Bill, 64
Moyer, Lavinia, 33, 34

Mozzi, Leonard, 53
Mroczka, Paul, 67
Mrozek, Slawomir, 104
Mrozik, Susanne, 139
Msomi, Welcome, 138
Mtumi, Andre, 128
Mtwa, Percy, 80
Murdock, Christine, 184
Mueller, Lavonne, 19
Muir, Keri, 137
Mulcahy, Lance, 131
Mullen, Jimmy, 211
Mumford, Peter B., 220
Munch, Allen E., 99
Munger, Paul, 68, 69
Munier, Leon, 177
Munt, Maxine, 48
Muramoto, Betty, 77
Murbach, John, 225
Murdock, David, 104
Murin, David, 23, 56, 98, 99, 170, 228
Murphy, Dallas, Jr., 144
Murphy, Eileen MacRae, 4
Murphy, John T., 190
Murphy, Michael, 80, 205
Murphy, Peter, 56
Murphy, Sean, 13, 131
Murphy, Thomas, 6
Murray, Brian, 5, 135
Murray, John, 96, 142, 223
Murray, Michael, 31, 52, 53, 211
Murray, Robert, 151
Murray-Walsh, Merrily, 98, 196
Murrell, John, 4, 8, 200
Murtha, Leslie, 227
Murton, Susan, 208
Muscha, Colleen, 59, 135, 166, 168
Muschamp, George, 51
Mussenden, Isis, 82
Musser, Tharon, 130
Myers, Jas, 45
Myerscough-Walker, Robin, 150
Myerson, Edward, 219

N

Nachimson, Beverly, 211
Nachtmann, Rita, 19
Naftel, Joseph D., 189
Nagrin, Lee, 110
Nakahara, Ron, 102
Namanworth, Philip, 85
Nanus, Susan, 159
Nash, Michael, 167
Nash, N. Richard, 30, 96, 205
Nass, Elyse, 189
Nassivera, John, 75, 76, 148
Nathanson, Donald, 201
Naversen, Ron, 221
Near, Timothy, 183, 199
Neff, Jill, 39
Nelke, Karolyn, 170
Nell, Christof, 112
Nelson, Doug, 39

Nelson, Gene, 24
Nelson, Richard, 5, 80, 92, 96, 228
Nelson, Richard (lighting designer), 54, 79, 104, 150, 177, 192
Nemiroff, Robert, 64, 88
Nestor, Lee, 45
Nestor, Marilyn, 45
Netzel, Sally, 68, 69
Neumann, Alfred, 67
Neumann, Frederick, 123, 124
Neville, Michael, 6
Neville-Andrews, John, 87
New, Marshall, 99, 100
Newcomb, Don, 228
Newcott, Rosemary, 3
Newkirk, Ricky G., 26
Newman, Molly, 73, 171
Newman, Betsy, 207, 208
Newman, Naomi, 122
Newman, Phyllis, 104
Newman, Tom, 227
Newton, Talmage, 209
Newton-Brown, Michael, 60, 204
Ney, Diane, 148
Ngema, Mbongeni, 80
Nichols, Ellen, 207
Nichols, Jackie, 172
Nichols, Mike, 31
Nichols, Peter, 120
Nicholson, James, 144, 160
Nicholson, Paul, 162
Nicola, James, 28, 148
Nicolaeff, Ariadne, 152
Nie, Carol, 42
Nieboer, Roger, 125
Nieminski, Joseph, 92
Nieves, Miriam, 56, 65
Nininger, Susan, 115, 153
Noe, Glenn, 49
Noel, Craig, 155, 156
Nolan, Victoria, 47
Noling, David, 194, 222, 229
Nolte, Charles, 50, 60, 174
Noonan, John Ford, 14, 26, 33, 41, 53, 60, 86
Nordan, Dale, 208
Norgard, Richard G., 36
Norland, Timothy C., 90
Norman, Marsha, 17, 21, 56, 178
Normoyle, Jeanne, 93
Norris, William J., 34, 164
Nottbusch, Kaye, 164, 225
Novak, David, 210
Nowak, Christopher, 170, 177
Ntshona, Winston, 225
Nugent, Elliott, 32
Nyberg, Peter, 190

O

Oberlin, Richard, 58
O'Brien, Adale, 6, 7
O'Brien, Jack, 155, 156
O'Brien, Terry, 159

O'Casey, Sean, 12, 159, 171, 194
Occhiogrosso, Peter, 207
O'Connel, Richard L., 153, 180
O'Connor, Jim, 225
O'Connor, Michael, 19
O'Connor, Sara, 31, 48, 134, 135
O'Dea, Marcia, 124
Odets, Clifford, 3, 22, 40, 113, 139, 192, 225
Oditz, Carol, 5, 120, 135, 150
Odle, Dwight Richard, 196
Odle, Robert L., 20, 26
Odom, Bary Allen, 87
O'Donnell, Mark, 177
O'Donnell, William, 44
O'Dowd, Donald D., 45
O'Dwyer, Laurence, 211
O'Flaherty, Liam, 6
Ofner, David, 91
Ogus, Carol, 9
Oh, Soon-Teck, 77
O'Hara, John, 108, 120
O'Harra, Michela, 143
Okazaki, Alan K., 156
O'Keeffe, John, 65, 125, 142, 147
Okun, Alex, 19
Oldenburg, Wendy, 200
Oleska, 126
Oleson, Dot, 158
Olexzczuk, Barbara, 34
Olich, Michael, 13, 17, 163
Olive, John, 6, 128, 143, 174, 205, 217, 221, 225
Oliver, Stephen, 95
Oliver, William, 159, 180
Olon, John, 35, 123
Olsen, Michael, 27
Olson, James, 131
Olson, Thomas W., 51
O'Morrison, Kevin, 23, 155
Oms, Alba, 180
O'Neal, Cecil, 216
O'Neal, Cynthia, 104
O'Neil, Raymond, 58
O'Neill, Eugene, 3, 17, 21, 22, 60, 76, 108, 151, 163, 166, 174, 186, 196, 200, 204, 210, 222, 229
Oppenheim, Irene, 159
Opitz, Lary, 46, 79
Orchard, Robert J., 19
Ordway, Sally, 110
O'Reilly, James, 42, 43
O'Reilly, Terry, 123
Orion, Elisabeth, 34
Orkeny, Istvan, 24, 28
Orlock, John, 106
Ormes, Vance G., 12
Orr, Leslye, 51
Ortmann, Jeffrey, 224
Orton, Joe, 17, 30, 88, 96, 163
Ortwein, Terrence, 143, 160
Osborn, M. Elizabeth, 144
Osborn, Paul, 17, 76, 98, 100, 143, 192, 220
Osborne, John, 35, 49, 163, 186
Oskarson, Peter, 112
Oster, Al, 13, 35

Osterweis, Steven L., 17
Ostroff, Elaine, 120
Ostroushko, Peter, 51
Ostwald, David, 83
Othuse, James, 141
Ott, Carolyn D., 67
Ott, Sharon, 4, 9, 91, 128, 135, 223
Overmyer, Eric, 123
Owen, Bobbi, 174
Owen, Paul, 7
Owens, Rochelle, 125, 153
OyamO, 128
Ozker, Eren, 178
Ozols, Karlis, 51, 96

P

Pace, Atkin, 128
Packard, Stephen, 205
Pagano, Chris, 114
Page, Anthony, 186
Paigen, Susan, 114
Painter, Estelle, 59, 95
Pair, Steve, 173
Paisley, E.J., 150
Palacios, 180
Palas, Lisa, 197
Palmer, Elizabeth P., 73, 166, 171
Palmer, Ruth A., 75
Palter, Lewis, 116
Panko, Tom, 227
Paoletti, John, 164, 217
Papandreas, Johniene, 82, 126
Papp, Joseph, 148, 150
Pardee-Holz, Rosemary, 187
Parichy, Dennis, 5, 56, 96, 128, 130, 170, 171
Paris, Ronnie, 106
Parke, April, 10
Parker, Lance, 117
Parker, Stewart, 34, 163
Parnell, Peter, 155, 177
Parrish, David, 9
Parrish, Donna, 197
Parsons, Sally Ann, 110
Partington, Rex, 34, 35
Partington, Tony, 35
Partlan, William, 160
Partyka, John, 67
Pasquier, Marie-Claire, 161
Pasquin, John, 120, 160
Passage, Charles E., 6a
Passman, Elizabeth, 43
Patch, Jerry, 196
Patinkin, Sheldon, 199
Paton, Angela, 38, 39
Paton, William T., 204
Patrick, John, 7
Patrick, Robert, 207, 208
Patsas, Giorgos, 131
Patton, Caymichael, 56
Patton, Pat, 163
Patton, William W., 162
Paul, Bobby, 18

Paul, Kent, 104, 205
Paul, Rick, 34, 164
Paulsen, Albert, 153
Peakes, John, 40, 41
Pearle, Gary, 6, 28, 30, 35, 59, 63, 68, 70, 88, 134, 141, 155, 171, 189, 196, 199, 215, 217
Pearson, Steven, 63
Pearson, Sybille, 128
Peaslee, Richard, 85
Peck, Tracey, 151
Pecktal, Lynn, 35
Peden, Margaret, 180
Pellerin, Bobby, 190
Pellicciaro, Elena, 194
Pelton, Jack, 115
Pendleton, Austin, 200, 222, 223
Penker, Ferdinand, 125
Penningroth, Phillip, 160
Penny, Rob, 145
Pennywitt, Christopher, 67
Pentecost, James, 104
Pepper, Pamela K., 166
Percy, Edward, 67
Perez, Gloriamalia Flores, 77
Perez, Judith, 78
Perez, Severo, 78
Perhonis, Peter, 148
Perkins, David, 217
Perkoff, Rachel, 116
Perlman, Bill, 110
Perlman, Liz, 21
Perloff, Carey, 194
Perrault, Charles, 50
Perrin, 180
Perry, Alvin, 221
Perry, Jeff, 200
Perry, Karen, 145
Perry, Shauneille, 145
Pertalion, Albert, 137
Peskin, James, 134, 228
Peters, Williams, 108, 149
Petersen, Linden, 14
Peterson, Eric, 7, 14, 63, 108, 156, 205, 211, 218
Peterson, Margie, 139
Peterson, Robert, 17, 36, 112, 156, 163, 205
Peterson, Steven B., 30
Peterson, Susan, 40
Petlock, Martin, 32
Petrie, Daniel, 129
Pettigrew, Craig, 159
Peyton, Bruce, 219
Phalen, Jane Schloss, 148
Phelan, Ceal, 69
Phetteplace, Gordon, 41
Philippi, Michael S., 143
Phillips, Bob, 35, 56, 208
Phillips, Chris, 43, 217, 225
Phillips, Sharon, 42
Phillips, Tim, 208
Phippin, Jackson, 48
Piazza, August, 227
Pickette, Walter, 46
Picklin, Don, 227
Piddock, Jim, 114
Pielmeier, John, 7

Piering, Mary, 135, 214
Pietraszek, Rita, 92, 217
Pifer, Drury, 38, 70
Pike, Frank, 51
Pike, Rick, 91
Pilditch, Charles, 180
Pilgram, Geraldine, 150
Pine, Larry, 138
Pinero, Arthur Wing, 99, 223
Pinero, Miguel, 123, 207
Pinner, David, 59
Pintauro, Joe, 56
Pinter, Harold, 53, 59, 63, 86, 88, 171, 174, 186, 196, 199, 204, 205, 215, 217, 223
Pipan, Doug, 51
Pirolo, Mark, 151, 206
PiRoman, John Faro, 40, 41
Piscator, Erwin, 67, 68
Pissarro, Jorge, 208
Pitek, Michael P., III, 201
Plachy, William, 208
Placzek, Ron, 11, 104, 139
Plant, Alfred L., 112
Plath, Sylvia, 39
Platt, Martin L., 9, 10, 11
Pleyer, Douglas, 208
Pliska, Steven, 116
Poe, Edgar Allan, 132
Poggi, Gregory, 107, 169
Poindexter, Elizabeth, 13
Polan, Lynn, 113, 178
Policoff, Stephen P., 132
Polito, Philip, 222
Pollak, Lucy, 152
Pollak, Sam, 34
Pollock, Sharon, 104
Polovko-Mednikov, Vera, 63, 95
Pomerance, Bernard, 12, 41, 45, 173, 215, 220
Pond, Helen, 165
Pope, Jerald D., 25, 26
Porcher, Nananne, 165
Poretz, Doraine, 24
Porter, Bruce, 194
Porter, Cole, 31, 59, 76, 132
Porter, Stephen, 54, 186, 228
Porterfield, Donna, 184
Porterfield, Robert, 34
Porto, Gary C., 165
Potter, John H., 174
Potter, Robert, 218
Pottlitzer, Joanne, 109
Potts, David, 19, 40, 53, 56, 98, 128, 134, 137, 166
Potts, Nancy, 99
Poul, Alan, 113
Povod, Ray, 207
Powell, A.L., Jr., 50
Powell, Mary Ann, 28, 148
Powers, Dennis, 17
Pratt, Ron, 36, 38, 39, 83, 190
Pratt, Susan, 168
Prendergast, Shirley, 64, 88, 145, 202
Pressner, Stan, 85
Price, Seth, 208
Prida, Dolores, 109

Prideaux, James, 76, 221
Pridham, Robert, 85
Priestley, J.B., 105
Prince, Neil, 46
Prindle, Ric, 158, 159
Proett, Daniel, 64, 88
Promislo, Daniel, 169
Prufer, Guntram, 68
Pryor, Deborah, 148
Psacharapoulous, Nikos, 222, 223
Pucci, Robert, 132
Pugh, Caroline, 30
Pulver, Gerald, 59
Pulvers, Roger, 77
Purdy, William, 162
Purdy-Gordon, Carolyn, 163
Pursley, David, 68, 69
Pyle, Russell, 27, 78, 123, 153
Pyne, James F., Jr., 168
Pyskacek, June, 216

Q

Quayle, Anthony, 56
Quintero, Joaquin Alvarez, 159
Quintero, Jose, 53
Quintero, Serafin, 159
Quo, Beulah, 76

R

Raaberg, Marianne Scozzari, 72
Rabassa, Gregory, 180
Rabb, Ellis, 156, 165
Rabe, David, 149
Rabkin, Nick, 163
Raby, Peter, 6, 68
Rackoff, Louis, 178
Raftery, Suzanne, 159
Ragey, Joseph, 168, 219
Ralph, Steve, 123
Rame, Fanca, 123
Ramey, Nayna, 9
Ramicova, Dunya, 11, 21, 92, 98, 128, 130, 223, 229
Ramos, Richard Russell, 73, 82, 196
Rampino, Lewis A., 95
Rampino, Lewis D., 202
Rand, Ayn, 51
Randolph, Clemence, 26, 108
Ranelli, J., 19
Rankin, Lindon, 227
Ranney, Celestine, 39
Ranson, Rebecca, 184
Ranson, Ron, 189
Raoul, Bill, 4
Rappaport, David, 145
Rasa, Maria, 207
Rasch, Sunna, 168, 169
Rasche, David, 216
Rasmuson, Judy, 11, 48, 120, 186, 204

Rasmussen, Tom, 13, 36, 196
Rathman, John, 125
Rattigan, Terence, 32, 186
Ravitts, Ricki G., 143
Ravitz, Jeff, 164
Ray, Joe, 208
Ray, Reggie, 84
Ray, Robin, 28, 59
Raymond, William, 123, 124
Rea, Oliver, 95
Reader, Peter, 70
Reale, Willie, 82
Reaves-Phillips, Sandra, 15
Reber, James, P., 189
Recht, Raymond C., 46, 67, 166
Reck, Don, 123
Reddin, Keith, 160
Reed, Charles L., Jr., 217
Reed, Dennis, 103
Reed, Henry, 54
Reed, Ishmael, 138
Reed, Lynne, 145
Reeht, Raymond C., 222
Rees, Herbert L., 90
Reeves, Geoffrey, 125
Regina-Thon, Stephan, 39
Regnier, Michael G., 83
Rehlkopf, Brian, 3
Rehn, Steven, 114
Reich, Catherine B., 202
Reich, John, 137
Reid, Kathryn 209
Reiff, Linda, 85
Reilly, Charles Nelson, 183
Reimer, Adrienne, 168
Reineccius, Richard, 113
Reiner, Carl, 193
Reis, Jemi, 128
Reis, Kurt, 170
Reisch, Michele, 126
Reiser, Sheila, 106
Reisman, Jane, 170
Reisz, Karel, 128
Remsen, Penny, 13
Renard, Joe, 207
Renault, Mary, 164
Renfield, Elinor, 19, 56, 82, 105, 125, 153, 177
Renick, Kyle, 227
Rennagel, Marilyn, 99, 130, 138
Rennerfeldt, Noel, 173
Rennie, Debbie, 84
Revenal, Cornelia, 148
Rey, Stephan, 102
Reynolds, Jonathan, 28, 73, 159, 177
Reynolds, Leah, 121
Reynolds, Linda, 88
Reynolds, Roger, 39
Rheaume, Susan, 10, 131
Rhys, William, 59
Riashentsev, Uri, 141, 219
Ribman, Ronald, 19, 20, 177
Riccio, Tom, 59
Rice, Michael, 98, 132
Rice, Tim, 154
Richards, Charles F., Jr., 69
Richards, James, 34

Richards, Lloyd, 159, 228, 229
Richards, Randy, 83
Richardson, Howard, 32
Richardson, James G., 82
Richardson, L. Kenneth, 63, 64
Richardson, Sally, 4, 80, 192, 205
Richey, Michael, 219
Richmond, David, 91
Ricker, John, 214
Rickett, Charles, 3
Riddell, Richard, 96
Riddle, Garland, 221
Rider, Ivan, Jr., 12, 68
Ridge, John David, 5, 73, 170, 186, 204
Ridley, Arthur, 9
Rieck, Margaret, 170
Riestenberg, Nancy, 106
Riford, Lloyd S., III, 79, 102
Rigdon, Kevin, 92, 200, 218, 223
Riggs, Austin, 39
Riggs, Jon, 159
Riley, James, 60
Riley, Norman, 145
Rimer, Thomas, 135
Rimmer, David, 51, 155
Rintell, David W., 63, 225
Rioja, Pilar, 181
Risberg, Del, 40, 48
Risser, Patricia M., 135
Ritman, William, 104
Rivera, Jose, 82
Rizik, Raoul, 109
Roach, James, 217
Robbins, Carrie, 130
Robbins, Jeff, 80
Robbins, Kenneth, 69
Robbins, Sanford, 10, 162
Robels, Frank, 109
Robero, Gary, 15
Roberts, Eve, 156
Roberts, Kitty, 25
Roberts, Ruth, 126, 221
Robertson, Patrick, 21
Robertson, Toby, 5, 61, 105
Robertson, Wil, 169
Robins, Michael, 105, 106
Robinson, Betsy Julia, 160
Robinson, David, 61, 126
Robinson, Dorothy Marie, 35
Robinson, Irwin, 144
Robinson, John, 125
Robinson, Mabel, 15
Robinson, Mary B., 82, 98
Robinson, Matt, 145
Robinson, Robert, 125
Robison, Barry, 51
Robles, Elsa, 109
Robman, Steven, 144
Rockafellow, Charles I., 82
Rodack, Soretta, 208
Rodale, Anna, 165
Rodger, Carolyn M., 145
Rodgers, Anton, 68
Rodgers, Lou, 194
Rodgers, Mary, 45, 155
Rodgers, Richard, 21, 67, 108, 120, 143

Rodriguez, Diane, 78
Rodriguez, Nelson, 180
Rodriguez, John, 43, 217
Roethler, Ginny, 51
Rogers, David, 197
Rogers, Rich, 208
Rogers, Roxanne, 159
Rogin, Deborah, 159
Rohrer, Sue Ellen, 209
Roman, Lawrence, 222
Romano, Denis, 56
Romberg, Sigmund, 165
Romberger, Judy, 6
Romero, Federico, 181
Romero, Frances, 78
Rommel, David, 214
Roos, Elaine Yokoyama, 79
Roose-Evans, James, 221
Rosa, Dennis, 59, 145
Rose, Lee, 123
Rose, Lloyd, 148
Roseman, Ralph, 185
Rosen, Irene, 114
Rosen, Sally, 124, 150
Rosen, Sheldon, 51
Rosen-Thomas, Sally, 189
Rosenak, David S., 81
Rosenbaum, Robert A., 154
Rosenblatt, Marc, 159
Rosenberg, Joe, 135
Rosenblum, M. Edgar, 119
Rosenfeld, Hilary, 79, 150
Rosenstock, Jeffrey, 205
Rosenthal, Fran, 139
Rosenthal, Sandy, 29
Roslevich, John, Jr., 183
Rosoff, Barbara, 19, 23, 177, 178
Ross, Carolyn, 137, 183
Ross, Jordan, 152, 217, 225
Ross, Sandra, 19, 145
Ross, Tavis, 189
Rossi, Al, 122
Rostand, Edmond, 12
Rotenberg, David, 108, 174
Roth, Ann, 40, 54, 56, 120, 128, 156
Roth, Bernard, 208
Rothchild, Ken, 113
Rothe, Sharon, 88
Rothman, Carole, 56, 144, 192, 193
Rothman, Stephen, 91, 166
Roudebush, William, 59
Rourke, Michael, 43
Rowland, L. Susan, 6
Royce, Jim, 38, 80
Rozovsky, Mark, 141, 219
Rubenstein, Alice, 110
Rubenstein, Lee G., 27
Rubin, Charles, 177
Rubin, Leon, 137
Rubin, Steven, 108, 120, 156
Rubinstein, Carol, 222
Rublee, Lynn, 225
Rubsam, Scott, 144
Ruby, Harry, 28
Ruch, John, 56
Rudd, Paul, 196

Rudolph, Stephanie, 124
Ruibal, Jose, 180
Runyan, James E., 26
Rupnik, Kevin, 11, 21, 98, 223
Ruscio, Beth, 159
Rush, David, 113
Rusika, Tom, 36
Ruskin, Joseph, 24
Russell, Brad, 86
Russell, Brian, 159
Russell, Douglas, 38
Russell, Gael, 114, 125, 159
Russell, John, 53
Russell, Mike, 184
Russell, Willy, 4, 14
Rustan, John, 148
Ruta, Ken, 17
Rutherford, Carolyn, 141
Ruzika, Donna, 196
Ruzika, Tom, 196
Ryack, Rita, 21, 128, 177, 223
Ryan, Dennis, 217
Ryan, Gail, 209
Ryan, Ralph, 190
Rydberg, Steven M., 50, 51
Ryskind, Morrie, 28

S

Sabato, John, 208
Saburo, 77
Sachs, Nelly, 96
Sackett, Christopher, 27
Sager, Carol Bayer, 220
Sahl, Hans, 18
St. Clair, Charles, 83
St. Cloud, Mary, 219
St. Edmund, Bury, 34
Sakamoto, Edward, 77
Sakash, Evelyn, 82
Saklad, Steve, 40
Sale, James E., 11, 13, 17, 112, 163, 192
Salerni, Lou, 4, 60, 62, 63, 225
Sales, Mitzi, 35
Salisbury, Evelyn, 102
Salk, Evelyn, 151
Salomon, Wayne, 210
Saltz, Amy, 7, 53, 160, 228
Sammons, Larry, 44
Samson, R. Max, 213
Samuelson, David, 51
Sanchez, Jaime, 123
Sanchez, John, 200
Sanderson, Barbara, 69
Sandler, Ellen, 126
Sandrow, Nahma, 113
Sanford, Beth, 12, 13
Sanford, Davis, 159
Sangmeister, Harry, 70
Sankowich, Lee, 196
Sannes, Loyd, 206
Santander, Felipe, 135
Sardou, Victorien, 147
Sargent, Peter E., 183

Sarr, Thomas Peter, 213
Sartre, Jean Paul, 61, 98
Sarvis, Carla, 159
Sato, Shozo, 225
Satter, Carolyn, 189
Saunders, Anne, 75
Saunders, James, 196
Saussotte, Elaine, 116
Savin, Marcia, 189
Sawyer, Cathey, 173
Scales, Robert, 112
Scardino, Don, 126
Scassellati, Vincent, 137
Schacter, Steven, 128, 170, 204, 223
Schade, Camilla, 107
Schaeffer, Eric, 168
Schaeffer, Louis, 46
Scharfenberger, Paul, 9, 51, 96
Schary, Dore, 40
Schay, Daniel L., 133
Schechner, Richard, 225
Scheeder, Louis W., 87
Scheeler, Bob, 64
Scheffler, John, 27, 67, 145
Schein, Gideon Y., 91
Schell, Pamela, 111
Schenck, C. Newton, 119
Schenkar, Joan, 49, 144
Schenker, Diane, 80
Schenkkan, Robert, 6, 82, 167, 202
Scherer, Susan, 169
Schermer, Phil, 4
Schermer, Shelley Henze, 4
Schertler, Nancy, 28
Scheuerlein, Elizabeth, 158
Schielke, Joanna, 208
Schier, Ernie, 167
Schierhorn, Paul, 21
Schiffman, Jean, 158
Schiller, Friedrich von, 61
Schiowitz, Josh, 115
Schirle, Joan, 71
Schisgal, Murray, 204, 221
Schissler, Jeffrey, 180
Schlamme, Martha, 186, 22
Schlesinger, Sarah, 128, 206
Schlosser, Ira, 217
Schmidman, Jo Ann, 157, 158
Schmidt, Carl, 93
Schmidt, Douglas, 150, 156
Schmidt, Harvey, 66, 139, 173
Schmidt, Sue, 109
Schmiel, Bill, 210
Schnautz, Robert, 49
Schneider, Alan, 4, 5, 92, 96
Schneider, Barbara, 7
Schneider, Bekki Jo, 6
Schneider, Betty, 36
Schneider, Jeffrey, 113
Schneider, John D., 107, 213, 214
Schnitzler, Arthur, 28, 139, 159
Schochen, Seyril, 89
Schoenbaum, Donald, 95
Schofield, B-St. John, 123, 124, 150
Scholtz, Christa, 40, 92, 128

Schons, Alain, 71, 72
Schoonmaker, Charles, 145
Schraeder, Thomas H.,, 70
Schreiber, Terry, 204
Schroder, William, 11, 53, 166, 171, 204
Schubert, Fannie, 14
Schuenke, Jeff, 39
Schuler, Duane, 17, 51, 96
Schulfer, Roche, 91
Schulman, Charlie, 56
Schultz, Karen, 150
Schultz, Norman D., 69
Schulz, Karen, 63, 92, 98, 108, 170
Schuman, Mort, 173
Schwab, Brenda, 67
Schwab, John, 82
Schwab, Lawrence, 165
Schwab, Terry, 67
Schwartz, Bruce D., 19
Schwartz, Delmore, 113
Schwartz, Gil, 126
Schwartz, Joel, 153
Schwartz, Laurence F., 229
Schwartz, Robert Joel, 61
Schwartz, Stephen, 15, 34, 67, 85, 155, 206, 210, 211
Schwesinger, Edmund, 61
Schwolow, Julie, 126
Scofield, Ann, 209
Scofield, Pamela, 91
Scott, Dennis, 160, 228
Scott, George C., 54
Scott, Harold, 64, 145, 199, 202
Scott, Stephen, 92
Scott, Walter, 38
Scudday, Michael, 68
Scudder, Antoinette, 164
Seale, Douglas, 60
Sears, Joe, 98
Seder, Robert, 132
Sedgwick, Dan, 11
Segal, David F., 186, 222
Segal, David G., 156
Segal, Sondra, 100
Seger, Richard, 17, 156
Sehnert, Paul, 49
Seifer, Bobbie, 22
Seifter, Harvey, 144, 206
Seiler, Hariette, 196
Selden, Cynthia, 90
Selden, William, 90
Sellars, Peter, 20, 43
Sellby, Karen, 209
Seltzer, Daniel, 130
Semans, William H., 62
Semerano, Frank, 148
Senita, Susan, 218
Senn, Herbert, 165
Senske, Rebecca, 53, 171, 199, 218
Senters, Marquetta, 155
Serban, Andrei, 20, 92, 96, 149
Serlin-Cobb, Fran, 134
Serrano, Lynette, 56, 169
Serries, Michelle O., 49
Sestrap, Kathryn, 80
Seuss, Dr., 51

Seyd, Richard, 83, 114
Shabazz, Jeffrey, 75
Shaffer, Anthony, 76, 88, 212
Shaffer, Henry, 148
Shaffer, Nancy J., 24
Shaffer, Peter, 17, 45
Shaffer, Steve, 155
Shain, Charles Edward, 144
Shaiman, Marc, 128
Shakespeare, William, 5, 7, 10, 14, 17, 21, 26, 28, 30, 32, 33, 35, 36, 38, 43, 44, 48, 53, 54, 56, 57, 59, 61, 65, 67, 68, 73, 79, 87, 89, 92, 95, 96, 97, 101, 103, 105, 108, 124, 130, 137, 141, 147, 149, 150, 151, 155, 156, 162, 163, 166, 167, 171, 173, 174, 183, 189, 190, 192, 196, 204, 215, 225, 228
Shaktman, Ben, 170, 171
Shalansky, Ruby, 120
Shallat, Lee, 196
Shamus, Laura, 27, 49
Shange, Ntozake, 14
Shank, Adele Edling, 7, 125, 193
Shank, Terrence, 6
Shank, Theodore, 7, 125
Shanley, John Patrick, 82, 143, 144, 160
Shanto, Anne, 204
Shapiro, Mel, 130
Sharkey, Jack, 154
Sharp, Mrs. Dudley C., 11
Sharp, Michael, 109, 147, 186
Sharp, Richard, 163
Shaughnessy, Patrick, 96
Shaw, Barnett, 68
Shaw, Christopher H., 35
Shaw, Deborah, 82, 109, 177, 180, 199
Shaw, George Bernard, 3, 7, 10, 11, 30, 32, 36, 44, 45, 54, 61, 70, 73, 89, 96, 99, 112, 120, 128, 131, 132, 139, 156, 159, 163, 167, 174, 186, 187, 189, 190, 192, 196, 199, 206, 211, 215, 227, 228
Shaw, Guillermo Fernandez, 181
Shaw, Robert, 18
Shaynes, Nancy, 33
Sheehan, John, 158
Sheffer, Isaiah, 18
Sheffield, Don, 208
Shein, Brian, 113
Shellene-Jans, June, 164
Shelley, Mary, 26, 46, 173
Shelton, Debbie, 13
Shelton, Sloan, 177
Shena, Lew, 144
Shengold, Nina, 46
Shenk, Tom, 137
Shepard, Sam, 21, 28, 46, 51, 56, 63, 73, 125, 135, 183, 189, 196, 200, 202, 204, 211, 215
Shepherd, David M., 194
Sheridan, Richard Brinsley, 12, 21, 61, 156, 205
Sherin, Edwin, 98, 99

Sherman, Arthur, 99
Sherman, Geoffrey, 18, 104, 186, 202
Sherman, Loren, 109, 177, 180, 222
Sherman, Martin, 80, 210
Sherman, Roger, 38, 190
Sherman, Tracey, 208
Sherriff, R.C., 30
Sherrin, Ned, 23, 35, 199
Sherwood, Madeline Thornton, 82
Sherwood, Richard E., 128
Shevelove, Bert, 30, 153, 189
Shickel, Mark, 213
Shinner, Sandy, 217
Shiomi, R.A., 77
Shire, David, 31
Shook, Robert, 152, 217, 225
Shook, Warner, 116
Shookhoff, David, 103, 106
Shorr, William, 26, 27
Short, Ron, 185
Shortt, Paul, 59
Shrawder, Mel, 173
Shroder, William, 113
Shuang, Fred, 77
Shue, Larry, 14, 135
Shugg, Eliza, 38
Shuler, Duane, 73
Shulz, Karen, 177
Shumate, Peggy, 83
Shutko, Terry, 213
Shyre, Paul, 36
Sibbald, George, 196
Sicangco, Eduardo, 26
Sidlow, Chuck, 84
Siegl, Simon, 111
Siefert, Lynn, 160, 229
Sierra, Ruben, 115
Sigel, Steve, 158
Sills, Paul, 84
Silva, Chris, 82
Silva, Pedro, 150, 151
Silver, Joan Micklin, 82
Silverman, Stanley, 138, 161
Silverstein, Shel, 82, 92, 116
Simmons, Pat, 60
Simmons, Stanley, 14
Simms, Willard, 153
Simo, Ana Maria, 109
Simon, Barney, 80
Simon, Kim, 27
Simon, Lisa, 207
Simon, Marion, 215
Simon, Mayo, 123
Simon, Neil, 11, 35, 84, 86, 99, 100, 155, 199, 220, 227
Simon, Roger Hendricks, 27, 87, 144
Simonds, Will, 159
Simone, Carmine, 205
Simons, David, 209
Simons, Ken, 196
Simons, Kim, 78
Simpson, Bland, 174, 204
Simpson, Dorothy L., 190
Simpson, James A., 82

Simpson, Leslie, 205
Simpson, Paul, 75
Sims, Jack, 169
Sims, James, 39
Singelis, James, 139
Singer, Connie, 229
Singer, Raymond, 82
Sinise, Gary, 199, 200
Sinisi, Rosaria, 138
Size, Dennis M., 70, 126
Skaggs, Calvin, 126
Skannal, Lesley, 48
Skelton, Buck, 24
Skelton, Geoffrey, 222
Skelton, Tom, 150
Skeoch, Skipper, 196
Skinner, Doug, 19
Skipitares, Theodora, 132
Sklar, Roberta, 110
Slade, Bernard, 23, 143, 155, 159, 172
Slaiman, Marjorie, 28, 96
Sloane, Hilary, 116
Smart, Jeffrey M., 59, 100
Smeeth, Barrie, 106
Smith, Baker, 44, 137
Smith, Bradley Rand, 56
Smith, Christine E., 209, 210
Smith, Chuck, 217
Smith, Craig, 20, 61
Smith, Dick, 75
Smith, Doug, 49
Smith, Ernest Allen, 170, 193
Smith, Esther K., 209
Smith, Glenn Allen, 68
Smith, Gray, 200
Smith, James, 33, 34
Smith, Marc P., 226, 227
Smith, Mavis, 85
Smith, Michael, 31, 113
Smith, Oliver, 85
Smith, Patricia K., 41, 201
Smith, Patti, 73
Smith, Peyton, 226
Smith, Robert Lewis, 15, 31
Smith, Roger, 99
Smith, Russell, 173
Smith, Tarant, 194
Smith, Victoria, 36
Smithee, Debbie, 13
Smitherman, Robert, 24
Smittle, Grover, 155
Smythe, Robert, 168
Smull, Jeff, 22
Snipper, Rossi, 62
Snyder, Patricia B., 78
Soeder, Fran, 88
Sokolov, Elliot, 209
Solly, Bill, 93
Soloway, Norman P., 22
Somers, Arnold, 14
Sondheim, Stephen, 14, 23, 28, 30, 35, 143, 153, 177, 189, 199, 211
Sonnenberg, Craig, 44
Soon, Terrence Tam, 77
Sophocles, 60, 61, 70, 79, 135
Sossi, Ron, 152, 153

Soule, Don, 21
Soule, Robert D., 53, 215
South, Frank, 75, 167
Southworth, John, 198
Spain, Craig, 173
Spatz-Rabinowtiz, Elaine, 21
Specktor, Mira, 207
Speer, Alexander, 6
Spencer, Sara, 196
Spencer, Stuart, 82
Spencer, Thomas, 59
Spera, Robert, 7
Spesert, Douglas, 115
Spewak, Bella, 196
Spewak, Sam, 196
Spiller, Marshall, 186, 222
Spisak, Neil, 165
Spivak, Alice, 27
Spray, Tom, 11
Spyri, Johanna, 12
Stabile, Bill, 204
Stacklin, Andrew, 56, 125
Stafford-Clark, Max, 150
Stahlhuth, Gayle, 166
Stalzer, William, 79
Stames, Penny, 89
Stancil, William 135
Stanford, Gully, 72
Stanley, Florence, 113
Stapleton, Christopher, 180
Stapleton, Tim, 41
Staris, Stanley, 109
Stark, Robert, 15
Stark, San, 172
Stauffer, Michael, 10, 14, 73
Steadman, Jan, 114
Steblay, Tony, 50
Stecker, Robert D., Sr., 67
Steckman, Larry, 208
Steere, Jim, 23, 134, 228
Stegenga, Penny, 138
Stein, Anthony, 85
Stein, Daniel A., 31, 48, 93, 135
Stein, Deborah, 139
Stein, Debra, 109
Stein, Douglas, 108, 156, 177, 186, 193, 229
Steiner, George, 98
Stein, Gertrude, 132, 138, 161, 187
Stein, Jan Alois, 183
Stein, Joan, 39
Stein, Joseph, 79, 173
Stein, June, 46, 56, 82
Stein, Mark, 6, 128, 167, 168
Stein, Meridee, 11, 84, 85
Steinbach, Victor, 143, 144
Steinbeck, John, 6, 68, 73, 88, 151, 170, 200, 202, 205, 215
Steinberg, Mike, 41
Steiner, Eric, 152
Steinman, Barry, 59
Steitzer, Jeff, 4, 8, 80
Stephens, Ann, 69
Stephens, John, 3
Stephens, Kent, 14, 60, 100
Stern, Edward, 59, 95, 107, 204
Stevens, Emily, 53

Stevens, Hank, 208
Stevens, John Wright, 126
Stevens, Tony, 222
Stevenson, Clay, 98
Stevenson, Robert Louis, 141
Stewart, C. William, 97
Stewart, Cheryl, 159
Stewart, Jack, 61, 139
Stewart, Michael, 67
Stewart, Wenton, 31
Stipe, Sally Carlson, 184
Stix, John, 186
Stockdale, Muriel, 139, 208
Stockenstrom, Truda, 51
Stockton, Frank, 48
Stoker, Bram, 84, 101
Stolzberg, Jon, 207
Stone, Arnold M., 123
Stone, Edward, 48, 219
Stone, Harold, 96
Stone, John Hieronymus, 115
Stone, Peter, 67, 173
Stone, Rocky, 15
Stoppard, Tom, 28, 44, 105, 159
Storch, Arthur, 203, 204
Storer, Stephen, 189
Storey, John, 43, 217
Strachen, Alan, 59, 66
Strahs, James, 124
Straiges, Tony, 21, 28, 48, 98, 128, 177, 223, 229
Strand, Richard, 217
Strane, Robert, 31, 91
Stratman, Daniel, 64, 88
Stratton, Allan, 166
Strauch, Claire, 79
Strauss, Botho, 123, 149, 161
Strauss, Johann, 161
Strawbridge, Stephen, 229
Streeter, Elizabeth A., 59
Strege, Gayle M., 135
Strehlich, Thomas, 24, 69
Strindberg, August, 61, 65, 112, 163, 186, 218
Strock, William C., 205
Stroheier, Robert F., 204
Strouse, Charles, 11, 15, 67, 79, 85, 221
Strout, Benjamin, 84
Struckman, Jeffrey, 199
Sturchio, Malcolm, 46, 56, 82
Styne, Jule, 26, 104
Suarez, Roberto Rodriguez, 180
Sullivan, Arthur, 14, 15, 23, 51, 57, 108, 149, 211
Sullivan, Daniel, 190, 192
Sullivan, Greg, 13, 36, 73, 112, 115, 196
Sullivan, J.R., 142, 143
Sullivan, J. Stacey, 155
Sullivan, John Carver, 13, 112, 137, 183, 199
Sullivan, Kenneth, 23
Sullivan, Mike, 208
Sullivan, Patrick, 132
Summers, Caley, 53
Sunde, Karen, 61, 65
Supervielle, Jules, 209

Suro, Teresita Garcia, 92
Sutton, Phoeff, 100
Swados, Elizabeth, 85, 149, 153
Swan, Matt, 143
Swartz, Marlene, 193, 194
Swee, Daniel, 103
Sweet, Jeffrey, 6, 7, 82, 167, 217
Sweet, Sam, 110
Swerling, Jo, 66
Syer, Fontaine, 209, 210
Synge, John Millington, 43, 95
Szogyi, Alex, 65

T

Tabachnick, Ken, 124
Tabori, George, 183
Taccone, Anthony, 82, 83, 190
Taikeff, Stanley, 144
Tait, Pam, 150
Takazauckas, Albert, 36, 38, 125
Talbot, Craig, 187
Talesnik, Ricardo, 181
Tallman, Randolph, 68
Tally, Ted, 26, 48, 63, 100, 104, 108, 137, 156, 196, 199, 210
Talmadge, Clyde, 183
Talpers, Danny, 208
Tam Soon, Terrence, 130
Tandet, Joseph, 127
Tannen, Christina, 99
Tansy, June, 145
Targownik, Tom, 218
Tarver, Ben, 32
Taylor, C.P., 200
Taylor, David, 153
Taylor, Deborah, 84
Taylor, Dierdre A., 165, 210
Taylor, Frolic, 189
Taylor, James, 103
Taylor, James J. 187,
Taylor, Leslie, 19, 46, 82, 178, 208
Taylor, Linwood, 174
Taylor, Noel, 183, 221
Taylor, Renee, 159
Taylor, Stephen, 59
Taylor-Dunn, Corliss, 15
Taymor, Julie, 19, 150
Tebelak, John-Michael, 155
Teer, Barbara Ann, 140
Teitel, Carol, 120
Teitel, Nathan, 18
Temperley, Stephen, 104
ten Cate, Ritsaert, 214
Ten Eyck, Lee, 208
Tenney, Del, 98
Tenney, Margot, 98
Terkel, Studs, 34, 210, 211
Terrel, Elwin Charles, III, 208
Terrill, Ken, 197
Terry, Keith, 36
Terry, Megan, 100, 158
Tesich, Steve, 26, 48, 189
Thacker, Cheryl, 82, 109, 128
Tharp, Twyla, 138

Thatch, Robert, 136
Thatcher, Maggie, 41
Thayer, Gloria Muzio, 46
Thayer, Robert, 46, 98, 166, 221
Theoktisto, Pete, 99
Thies, Howard, 208
Thirkield, Robert, 55
Thomas, Brandon, 32, 139, 183, 205, 219
Thomas, Brett, 202
Thomas, Chris, 145
Thomas, Crispin, 117
Thomas, Donald Edmund, 48, 128
Thomas, Dylan, 95, 213
Thomas, Eberle, 31, 91
Thomas, Isa, 32
Thomas, Lisette, 196
Thomas, Quentin, 202
Thomas, Robin, 124
Thomas, Tim, 135
Thomas, Vida, 165
Thompson, Bill, 70
Thompson, Darrell, 177
Thompson, Ernest, 35, 41, 98, 142, 159, 227
Thompson, Jay, 45, 155
Thompson, Kay, 121
Thompson, Kent, 44
Thompson, Peter, 19
Thompson, Sherry, 115
Thompson, Tommy, 174
Thomsen, Richard, 40, 41
Thomson, Virgil, 138
Thorne, Joan Vail, 68
Thornton, Clarke W., 23
Thun, Nancy, 21, 88, 180
Thurber, James, 32
Tigar, Kenneth, 24
Tiller, Ted, 212, 217
Tillinger, John, 23, 120, 221
Tillman, Ellis, 60
Tilton, James, 165, 204, 221
Tine, Hal, 204
Tipton, Jennifer, 21, 92, 96, 128, 150, 229
Tissot, John, 48, 180, 222
Titus, Hiram, 50, 51
Tobias, Nancy, 126
Tofteland, Curt L., 197
Tolan, Kathleen, 7, 223
Tolan, Michael, 18
Tolaro, Robert, 84, 134, 173, 219
Tolstoy, Leo, 68
Tomlinson, Charles, 196
Toner, Don, 53
Topor, Tom, 12, 116
Torbett, David, 56
Torg, Arthur, 120
Torsek, Dierk, 7
Toser, David, 166, 171, 204
Touliatos, George, 73
Tourneur, Cyril, 61
Tovatt, Patrick, 6, 7, 93
Towers, Charles, 205, 218
Traeger, Charles, 223
Traister, Andrew J., 155, 156
Tramutola, Franklin C., 15

Trapp, Pat, 44
Travis, Warren, 36, 38, 39, 163
Tremblay, Michel, 31, 152, 204
Treyz, Russell, 7, 14
Trigger, Ian, 183
Trimble, David, 60
Tripp, Peter, 158, 159
Tronto, Rudy, 165
Trotter, Kim A., 59
Troupe, Tom, 220
Trow, George W.S., 39
Trow, JD, 159, 190
Troxler, June, 183
Truitt, Quay, 145
Trumbo, Dalton, 56
Tschetter, Dean, 88, 104, 150
Tschida, Chris, 96
Tsu, Susan, 93, 112, 170, 218
Tucci, D. Albert, 93
Tucker, Patrick, 38
Tucker, Sylvia, 113
Tugwell, Colin, 63
Tuohy, Susan, 196
Tulchin, Deborah, 15
Turbitt, Christine, 151
Turgenev, Ivan, 130
Turnage, Cyndy, 153
Turner, Jerry, 162, 163
Tuso, Fred, 15
Tutino, Tom, 44
Tutor, Rick, 204, 205
Twain, Mark, 51, 115, 164, 167

U

Udoff, Yale, 160
Uhrman, Walter R., 91, 186
Uhry, Alfred, 59, 100
Ulmer, John, 31, 32, 204

V

Vadeboncoeur, Clare, 121
Valdez, Luis, 77, 78
Valdez, Socorro, 78
Valency, Maurice, 12
Valk, Kate, 226
Valone, Ginger, 89
Valoris, Paul, 10, 151
Valtin, Jan, 88
Vanase, Paul, 153
Van Burek, John, 31, 152, 204
Vance, Nina, 11
Vance, Thomas, 226
Vandenburg, P.C., 34
Vander Voort, Jo, 68
Van Druten, John, 17, 27
van Itallie, Jean-Claude, 21, 31, 120, 128
Van Keyser, William, 35
Van Landingham, Michael, 45
Vann, Barbara, 131, 132

Van Peebles, Melvin, 145
van Roden, Mary E., 167
VanTassel, Craig, 210
Van Zandt, Porter, 221
Varga, Joseph A., 218
Vargas, Joseph, 126
Vartorella, Rick, 82
Vassar, Heather Lee, 76
Vaughan, Stuart, 32
Veber, E.P. 135
Veber, Pierre, 9
Vega, Rosa, 192
Velez, Henry, 215
Vennerstrom, Michael, 9, 30, 51, 63
Vercheski, Linn, 13
Vercoe, Rosemary, 21
Verheyen, Mariann, 13, 104, 105, 137, 163, 193
Vernacchio, Dorian, 194
Vetkin, S., 141, 219
Vick, Susan, 82
Vida, Bernadine, 34
Vida-Darrell, Bernadine, 75
Vigdor, Linda, 113
Vigna, John, 69
Vincent, Dennis, 68, 69
Vinkler, Greg, 217
Viscasillas, Manuel Power, 180
Vives, Amadeo, 181
Vivian, John, 221
Voelpel Fred, 79, 160, 206
Voltaire, 28, 218
Volz, Jim, 9
von Brandenstein, Patrizia, 79
Von Horvath, Odon, 153
von Mayrhauser, Jennifer, 54, 56, 96, 98, 99, 170
Vonnegut, Kurt, 172, 210
Vos, David, 155
Vos, Donna, 199
Vos, Erik, 137
Vreeke, John, 12, 13
Vukovich, Ted, 72
Vyzga, Bernard, 36

W

Waas, Cinthia, 46
Wachholtz, Becky, 173
Wachholtz, Ron 172, 173
Wade, Janet, 58
Wade, Kevin, 7, 59, 86, 100
Wagener, Terri, 6, 196, 228
Wager, Douglas C., 28
Wagner, Robin, 99
Waite, Ralph, 121
Waiwaiole, Lloyd K., 46
Walcott, Derek, 9, 59, 91, 92, 98, 100, 228
Waldman, Robert, 59, 100
Walker, Bill, 108, 120, 202
Walker, M. Burke, 4, 79, 80
Walker, George F., 34, 43, 80, 149, 223

Wall, Cheryl, 63
Wall-Asse, Marilyn, 100
Wallace, Ann, 13, 99, 105, 219
Wallach, Ira, 45
Wallach, Jason, 115
Walach, Jeffrey, 208
Wallace, Peter, 181
Wallace, Ronald, 120, 171, 186
Waller, Fats, 11, 23, 166, 221
Walsh, Addie, 183
Walsh, Charles, 102
Walsh, Thomas A., 73, 130, 171, 196
Wangh, Steven, 40
Wann, Jack, 103
Wann, Jim, 6, 184, 204
Wanshel, Jeff, 138
Ward, Donald, 93
Ward, Douglas Turner, 4, 92, 98, 130
Ward, R. Thomas, 26
Warfel, William B., 229
Warrilow, David, 92, 123
Warshaw, Sheldon, 100
Washington, Nancy, 24
Wasserman, Dale, 44, 165, 175, 205
Wasserstein, Wendy, 82, 116
Wasson, James, 3
Waters, Les, 150
Waterstreet, Edmund, 79, 206
Watkins, Donald C., 212
Watkins, Katja, 123
Watson, Anne Thaxter, 98, 199, 228
Watson, Ara, 6, 228
Watson, Douglas, 218
Watson, Michael Orris, 14, 151, 202
Watson, Rita B., 223
Watson, Walter, 36
Watson, Whitney, 159
Watters, Hilleary, 89
Watts, Jacqueline, 48
Waugh, Brenda, 153
Way, Brian, 115
Way, Jeff, 132
Wayne, Philip, 65
Webb, Charles D., 55
Webb, Elmon, 135
Webb, Kay, 210
Webber, Andrew Lloyd, 154
Weber, Larry, 153
Wedekind, Frank, 106
Weeks, Alan, 23
Weiant, Ted, 40, 108, 199
Weidner, Paul, 131
Weill, Claudia, 205, 223
Weill, Kurt, 36, 68, 153, 183
Weinstein, Jo, 3
Weinstein, Judith, 14
Weisman, Jael, 71, 72
Weiss, Barbara, 18, 139
Weiss, David, 110, 177, 194
Weiss, Joan E., 56, 104, 139
Weiss, Julie, 54, 130
Weiss, Marc B., 128, 131, 204
Weiss, Peter, 222

Weist-Hines, Marsha, 51
Weldin, Scott, 4, 80, 192, 205
Weldman, John, 82
Weller, Michael, 14, 137, 196, 200
Welles, Orson, 156
Wells, Ruth A., 98
Wells, Stephen, G., 227
Welsh, Stephen, 60
Wendelin, Karl, 134
Wengrow, Arnold, 3
Wensinger, A.S., 139
Weppner, Christina, 19, 110, 180, 208
Wesbrooks, Bill, 169
West, Robert, 3
West, Tom, 44
West, Virginia, 102
Westaway, Laurellee, 18
Wettlin, Margaret, 223
Wexler, Bradley, 15
Wexler, Constance R., 221
Wexler, Peter, 130
Wexler, Robert, 15
Wharton, Edith, 120
Wharton, John, 143
Wheeldon, Carole, 163
Wheeldon, Steven, 141
Wheeler, Billy Edd, 212
Wheeler, David, 21, 215
Wheeler, Hugh, 14, 28, 79, 143, 211, 218
Whelan, Ray, 123
Whelan, Richard, 6
Whiddon, Jerry, 187
Whisenand, Charles E., 155
Whitburn, Denis, 108
White, Ben, 135
White, Dale, 13
White, Diane, 121
White, George C., 159
White, Joshua, 85
White, Michael Franklin, 44
White, Pamela, 102
White, Richard E.T., 38, 83
White, J. Steven, 190
White, R. Stuart, 98, 227, 228
White, Stuart, 56, 76
White, Susan A., 95, 137, 194
Whitehead, Paxton, 129, 156, 190
Whitehead, Robert, 57
Whitehead, William M., 12
Whitlock, Lewis, 30, 63
Whitmore, Sally, 79
Whittemore, Cate, 51
Whittlesey, Peregrine, 127
Whyte, Ron, 9
Wicks, Debra, 209
Wierzel, Robert M., 229
Wiesel, Elie, 149
Wilbur, Richard, 5, 28, 46, 54, 69, 73, 98, 108, 130, 143, 167, 171, 186, 190, 202, 218, 219
Wilcox, Michael, 104
Wilcox, Richard, 7
Wilde, Oscar, 23, 44, 53, 57, 156, 167, 190
Wilde, Peter R. 97
Wilder, Ann G., 176

Wilder, Thornton, 35, 46, 96, 147, 156, 163
Wilensky, Jane, 40
Wiley, Kevin, 166
Wilhelm, Kurt, 7, 11, 53, 95, 96, 112, 135
Wilkins, Sophie, 149
Wilkins, Suzanne Y., 174
Willems, Stephen, 204, 212, 219
Willett, John, 218
Williams, Bill, 99
Williams, Carol, 160
Williams, Christopher, 51
Williams, Clifford, 95
Williams, Emlyn, 35, 99
Williams, Jaston, 98
Williams, Jerry, 63
Williams, Marshall, 145, 207, 208
Williams, Matt, 34
Williams, Robert, 74
Williams, Samm-Art, 14, 53, 64, 108, 115, 43, 145, 171, 199, 218
Williams Tennessee, 3, 22, 24, 27, 36, 46, 61, 67, 92, 98, 99, 103, 131, 135, 139, 147, 152, 159, 171, 174, 178, 187, 190, 199, 204, 205, 223, 225, 228
Williamson, Laird, 17
Williamson, Linda, 211
Williamson, Nicol, 54
Willis, Joanna, 159
Wills, J.C., 205
Wilmeth, Ross A., 228
Wilson, Andrea, 99
Wilson, August, 160
Wilson, Lanford, 11, 12, 14, 35, 41, 46, 53, 56, 59, 60, 69, 70, 80, 86, 96, 103, 129, 134, 137, 143, 147, 154, 156, 170, 199, 200, 204, 215, 217, 219
Wilson, Richard, 26
Winfield, Arnold, 216
Wingate, Peter, 18
Wingate, William P., 128
Wingreen, Jason, 53
Winkler, Richard, 23, 87

Winograd, Judy, 3
Winters, Michael, 17, 217
Winters, Nancy, 99
Wise, Jim, 218
Wise, William, 82
Wishengrad, Morton, 3
Witt, Andrew M., 13
Wittenberg, Eric, 195
Wittich, Ina, 153
Wittman, Scott, 128
Wittop, Freddy, 99
Wittow, Frank, 2, 3
Wittstein, Ed, 48
Wodehouse, P.G., 99, 196, 218
Wofford, Pam, 3
Wojewodski, Robert, 48, 120, 178, 192
Wojewdoski, Stan, Jr., 47, 48, 223
Woldin, Judd, 64, 88
Wolf, Sheldon, 198
Wolff, Art, 82
Wolff, Egon, 180
Wolk, James, 143
Wollner, David, 27
Wollner, Donald, 126, 144
Wolshonak, Derek, 70
Wondisford, Diane, 137
Wong, Andrew, 76
Wong, Joni, 19, 208
Wonsek, Paul, 18, 104, 165, 166, 199, 202
Wood, Binky, 51
Wood, G., 155
Wood, John, 28
Woodbridge, Patricia, 23, 40, 109, 128, 134, 170, 178, 199, 204
Woodhouse, Sam, 188, 189
Woodman, William, 23, 131, 170
Woodring, Stephen, 213
Woodruff, Robert, 82, 92, 152
Woods, Mark, 150
Woods, Steve, 67
Woolard, David, 19, 177, 194, 202
Woolever, Mary, 155
Woolf, Steven, 182
Woppat, Christine, 19

Worman, Martin, 208
Woronicz, Henry, 44
Worrell, Marily, 138
Worsley, Dale, 124
Wortman, Bryna, 19
Wouk, Herman, 99
Wray, Elizabeth, 39
Wright, Anne-Marie, 219
Wright, Bagley, 190
Wright, Barbara, 128
Wright, Garland, 5, 28, 56, 96
Wright, Harland, 211
Wright, Michael, 148
Wright, Robert, 80
Wrightsen, Ann, 18, 19, 48, 91, 110, 128, 160, 170, 177, 178
Wrona, Maciej, 104
Wrona, Teresa, 104
Wulp, John, 40
Wurtzel, Stuart, 79, 128, 150
Wycherley, William, 5

X

Xoregos, Shela, 79

Y

Yabara, Yoshio, 150
Yafa, Stephen, 125
Yaffee, James, 14
Yaji, Shiegeru, 77
Yamaguchi, Eiko, 15
Yamauchi, Wakako, 77
Yanik, Don, 31
Yankowitz, Susan, 160, 223
Yeargan, Michael, 5, 21, 92, 96, 108, 120, 145, 160, 229
Yegen, Christian C., 185
Yellusich, Andrew 112
Yerxa, Alison, 124
Yeuell, Michel, 108

Yodice, Robert, 115, 150
Yokoyama, Elaine, 78
York, John, 123
Yorkin, Peg, 114
Yoshimura, James, 110, 144, 160
Yost, Linda A., 187
Young, Johanna, 212
Young, Norma, 210, 211
Young, Robert H., 187
Yount, Kenneth M., 70, 166
Yuen, Roberta, 39, 125
Yulin, Harris, 120, 193
Yunker, Don, 9, 30, 51
Yurgaitis, Daniel, 33, 34

Z

Zabriskie, Nan, 43, 152
Zacek, Dennis, 59, 216, 217
Zagoren, Marc Alan, 225
Zajchowski, Michael, 168
Zakowski, Donna, 229
Zaks, Jerry, 82, 170, 177, 221
Zalamea, Pilar, 180
Zaldivar, Gilberto, 180
Zaloom, Paul, 207
Zaltzberg, Charlotte, 64, 88
Zeder, Suzan, 69, 197
Zeisler, Peter, 95
Zerbe, Anthony, 19
Ziehe, Lynne, 43
Zigun, Dick D., 83, 144
Zimmerman, Carol, 37
Zindel, Paul, 3, 60
Zingarelli, Vito, 190
Zipprodt, Patricia, 96, 150, 177
Zirkenbach, Parris, 184
Zirm, Fred, 148
Zola, Emile, 219
Zuber, Catherine, 229
Zubrick, Joe, 34
Zuckerman, Jill Young, 60
Zuckerman, Stephen, 228

Index of Titles

A

Able-Bodied Seaman, The, 160
Aboriginal Sin, 207
About Face, 228
Absence of a Cello, 45
Absent Friends, 12, 24
Absurd Person Singular, 8, 202, 205
Accident, The, 114
Accidental Death of an Anarchist, 130
Accounts, 104
Action News, 107
Actors and Actresses, 99
Actor's Nightmare, The, 41, 80, 116, 177, 225
Acts of Kindness, 107, 214
Adam, 145
Adaptation, 159
Admirable Crichton, The, 17
Admit One, 189
Advances, 158
Adventures of Hercules, The, 197
Adventures of Huckleberry Finn, The, 164
Adventures of Tom Sawyer, The, 51
After Magritte, 159
After the Fall, 36, 113
After the Rain, 24
Age of Invention, The, 132
Ah, Wilderness, 91, 163, 186, 191
Ain't Misbehavin', 11, 23, 166, 221
Aladdin and the Magic Lamp, 4
Album, 51
Alias Mark Twain, 212
Ali Baba and the 40 Thieves, 102
Alice in Wonderland, 51
Aliens under Glass, 158
All Aboard the Orient Express, 210
All Dressed Up, 222
All in Favour Said No!, 196
All My Sons, 170
All Night Strut!, The, 32
All's Well That Ends Well, 10, 38, 87
All-Time Good-time Knickerbocker Follies, The, 79
All the Way Home, 66
Alms for the Middle Class, 91, 171
Alone Together, 22
Alterations, 178
Amen Corner, The, 48, 64
America Hurrah, 31
America Kicks Up Its Heels, 177
America Was, 144
Americana, 143
America, Yes!, 169
American Buffalo, 63
American Dream, The, 12
American Garage, 167
American Primitive, 67
Am I Blue, 56, 98
Amorous Flea, The, 84
An American Dream, 159
And a Nightingale Sang, 200
And I Ain't Finished Yet, 128
"and if that Mockingbird don't sing . . .", 12
Androcles and the Lion, 73
And They Dance Real Slow in Jackson, 148
An Enemy of the People, 73, 75
Angel and Dragon, 69
Angel Street, 9, 56, 174, 222
Animal Crackers, 28
Animal Kingdom, The, 40
An Interest in Strangers, 214
An Introduction to Paperwork Management, 66
Annie, 221
Annie Get Your Gun, 67
Another Country, 120
Another Part of the Forest, 14, 17, 192
Antigone, 73, 79, 149
Antony and Cleopatra, 38, 97, 137
Appearances, 82
Appear and Show Cause, 59
Apple Tree: The Diary of Adam and Eve, The, 212
April Show, 144, 196
Arabian Nights, The, 6
archy and mehitabel, 22
Aristotle Said, 144
Arms and the Man, 10, 73, 131, 167, 199, 206
Arsenic and Old Lace, 67, 156, 172
Artaud at Rodez, 123
Arthur and Merlin, 210
Artichoke, 91, 199
Art of Self Defense, The, 7
Arts & Leisure, 173
Astapovo, 228
Asian Shade, 228
As You Like It, 30, 36, 95, 96, 132, 141, 155
At Fifty, She Discovered the Sea, 135
At This Evening's Performance, 131
Audience, The, 194
Augustus Does His Bit, 159, 187
Autumn Ladies, 159
Autumn Portraits, 207
Awake and Sing!, 22, 113, 192, 225
AWOL, 160

B

Baby with the Bathwater, 21
Back to Back, 114, 228
Baden Teaching Play, The, 153
Badgers, 126
Ballad of Dexter Creed, The, 149
Balloon, 65
Balm in Gilead, 200
Bandido!, 78
Barbarians, 194
Barretts of Wimpole Street, The, 45
Bartok as Dog, 7
Basement Tapes, The, 115
Bathers, The, 143, 144
Bea, Frank, Richie and Joan, 159
Beauty and the Beast, 3, 79, 197
Beaux Arts Ball, The, 208
Becoming Memories, 106
Bedroom Farce, 143, 192
Bedtime Story, 12, 159
Beef, No Chicken, 228
Before She Is Even Born, 207
Behind a Mask, 209
Behind the Broken Words, 19
Belder and the Bloom, 75
Bella Figura, 82
Belle of Amherst, The, 36, 66, 76, 155, 199
Bent, 80, 210
Beowulf—Nocturnal Solstice, 68
Bert, 106
Beside the Seaside, 104
Best Little Whorehouse in Texas, The, 221
Betrayal, 53, 59, 63, 86, 88, 171, 174, 196, 204, 205
Between Daylight and Boonville, 34
Between Mouthfuls, 12
Beyond Here Are Monsters, 144
Beyond the Fringe, 147
Beyond Therapy, 36, 100, 221
Big Apple Messenger, 228
Billy Bishop Goes to War, 7, 14, 63, 108, 156, 205, 211, 218
Birthday Present, The, 56
Bits & Bytes, 196
Black and Blues, 207
Black Angel, 56
Black Coffee, 59
60, 68
Black Comedy, 17
Black Peoples Party, 145
Blanco!, 95
Bleacher Bums, 210
Blind Desire, 184
Blind Mice, 217
Blithe Spirit, 67, 131, 163, 166
Blonde Leading the Blonde, The, 207
Blood Knot, The, 64, 196
Bloodlines to Oblivion, 114
Blood Relations, 104, 148
Bluffing, 56
Bodies, 196
Body to Light, 24
Boesman and Lena, 135
Bonesongs, 138
Bonjour, la, Bonjour, 31
Boogey Man, The, 100
Book of Job, The, 103
Booze Cars and College Girls, 226
Born Yesterday, 53, 135, 145, 166, 190
Boy and Tarzan Appear in a Clearing, 145
Boy Meets Girl, 196
Boy Meets Girl Meets Shakespeare, 197
Boys from Syracuse, The, 21
Boys Own Story, The, 114
Breakfast with Les and Bess, 104
Brecht Meets the House Un-American Activities Committee, 153
Brecht on Brecht, 183
Brewster Papers, The, 227
Brigadoon, 14
Broken and the Beautiful, The, 40
Brother Jack, 186
Brothers, 196, 210
Brothers, The, 19
Bronx Zoo, The, 56
Browning Version, The, 17, 186
Buck, 19, 177
Buddies, 82, 217
Bully, 144
Bunkhouse, The, 143, 160
Buried Child, 28, 135, 183, 215
Buried Inside Extra, 150
Burnish Me Bright, 41
Burrhead, 148
Bus Stop, 35, 139
Butterfingers Angel, The, 187, 206
Butley, 210
Butter and Egg Man, The, 126
Butterfly, Marguerite, Norma . . . and Irma Jean, 6
Bye Bye Birdie, 67
Byron's Ghost, 75

C

Cabaret, 14, 173
Cafe Amerique, 161
Caine Mutiny Court Martial, The, 99
Cait, 217
Calls from a Curious Planet, 107
Cameo, The, 7
Can Can, 31
Candida, 3, 28, 54, 190
Candide, 143, 218
Canterbury Tales, 3
Captivity of Pixie Shedman, The, 74
Caretaker, The, 186
Carmone Brothers' Italian Food Products Corp's Annual Pasta Pageant, The, 120
Carnival, 67
Cash, 82
Cat Among the Pigeons, 17
Catholics, 99
Cat on a Hot Tin Roof, 103, 147, 187, 204
Catsplay, 24
Cemetery Man, 6, 88, 167
Chalk Garden, The, 17, 186
Champeen, 145
Chapter Two, 199
Charley's Aunt, 32, 139, 183, 205, 218
Charlotte Sweet, 218
Chekhov in Yalta, 14, 36, 59
Cherry Orchard, The, 36, 65, 120, 222
Chicago, 173

Chicken Skin, 102
Childe Byron, 63
Child of the Sun, 145
Children, 152
Chidren's Crusade, The, 85
Children of a Lesser God, 100, 189, 206, 221
Child's Christmas in Humboldt County, A, 72
Child's Christmas in Wales, A, 95
Chinamen, 70
'Chines, 201
Chinese Coffee, 27
Chinese Viewing Pavilion, The, 41
Chopin in Space, 144
Chorus Line, A, 149, 150
Christmas Carol, A, 2, 3, 4, 7, 17, 22, 26, 30, 31, 41, 59, 60, 68, 69, 92, 96, 99, 100, 108, 131, 135, 137, 141, 151, 183, 189, 196, 204, 215, 217, 218, 219
Christmas Firebird, 197
Christmas in Camp, 77
Christmas on Mars, 177
Christmas Tapestry, A, 183
Chucky's Hunch, 125, 153
Chug, 88
Circus of Sings, 84
Cisterns, 33
City Games, 132
Civilization and Its Malcontents, 144
Clap Your Hands, 156
Clara's Play, 143, 217, 221
Clara Toil, 160
Clarence Darrow, 63, 225
Class, 40
Class Reunion, 82
Classy Comics, 132
Closely Related, 196
Close of Play, 211
Close Ties, 12, 115, 217
Closing Notice, 167
Cloud 9, 4, 83, 116, 200
Clown, 217
Clown of God, The, 51
Clowns, 102
Clown Show, The, 80
Club, The, 189
Clucks, 7
Coach with the Six Insides, The, 209
Coarse Acting Show, The, 126
Cocanuts, 106
Code Breaker, The, 115
Cold Harbor, 124
Cole, 59, 66
Come and Go, 124
Comedians, 126
Comedy of Errors, The, 10, 87, 163, 173
Coming Attractions, 108, 196, 210
Coming from a Great Distance, 122
Commedia Tonight (Mistress of the Inn), 227
Commercial Theater, 207
Como Ser Una Buena Madre, 181
Companions of the Crossed Swords, 3
Company, 124

Complex Pleasures, 132
Condemned of Altona, The, 61
Confessions of an Irish Rebel, 153
Confluence, 56
Confusions, 43
Constance and the Musician, 91
Constant Wife, The, 63
Contest, The, 170
Continental Drift, 39
Cookie Jar, The, 51
Corn is Green, The, 35
Corpse, 23
Cotton Patch Gospel, 14
Count Dracula, 212, 217
Countertalk, 135
Count of Monte Cristo, The, 61
Country Wife, The, 5
Coup, 7
Coupla White Chicks Sitting Around Talking, A, 14, 26, 33, 41, 53, 60, 86
Courage, 7
Cowboys!, 67
Coyote Ugly, 160, 228
Crashing of Moses Flying-By, The, 211
Crime Don't Pay No Wages, 201
Crime on Goat Island, 70
Crimes of the Heart, 4, 221
Crisp!, 109
Crock of Gold, A, 207
Crossing Niagara, 18, 128
Crowd of Two, A, 19
Crown of Thorn, 137
Crucible, The, 67, 218
Crucifer of Blood, The, 112, 199, 215
Curse of the Starving Class, 125
Cymbeline, 28, 163
Cyrano de Bergerac, 12

D

Da, 4, 35, 60, 134, 196
Daddy, 114
Daddy's Seashore Blues, 217
Dame Lorraine, 123
Dames at Sea, 218
Damien, 39
Dance and the Railroad, The, 63, 149
Daniel in Babylon, 116, 117
Danny and the Deep Blue Sea, 160
Danton's Death, 65
Danube, The, 208
Dark of the Moon, 32
Dark Ride, 194
D'Art, 51
Daughters, 59, 170, 217
David and Paula, 18
Day in the Death of Joe Egg, A, 120
Day of the Picnic (The Witch Doctor's Revenge), The, 160
Day out of Time, A, 145
Day, the Night, The, 138

Day They Shot John Lennon, The, 131
Dead End Kinds, 124
Dead Souls, 215
Dead Wrong, 199
Dear Daddy, 170
Dear Dragon, 3
Dear Liar, 17, 112, 186, 190
Dear Ruth, 63
Death of a Miner, The, 19, 178, 189
Death of a Salesman, 189, 192, 204
Death of Galatea, The, 49
Death of Von Richthofen as Witnessed from Earth, The, 150
Deathtrap, 35, 67, 76, 100, 166, 187, 202, 204, 206, 221
Debt, The, 125
Decrescendo, 159
Delicate Balance, A, 22, 28, 112, 131
Delmore, 113
Delusions of a Government Witness, 82, 167
Derelict, 202
Desert Fire, 115
Desert in Flower, 51
Desert Weather, 159
Design for Living, 211
Desire Under the Elms, 108, 166, 204
Dessie, 107
Destiny with Half Moon Street, A, 60
Dialectic of Enlightenment, The, 207
Dial M for Murder, 35
Diamond Studs: The Life of Jesse James, 204
Diary of Anne Frank, The, 36, 102, 170, 197
Did You Ever See a Unicorn?, 116, 117
Die Fledermaus, 161
Different Moon, A, 6, 228
Digging to China, 223
Dinah Washington Is Dead, 135
Dingaling, 158
Dining Room, The, 4, 13, 30, 32, 35, 92, 100, 105, 143, 156, 177, 178, 221
Disability: A Comedy, 9
Disappearance of the Jews, The, 92
Distilled Spirits, 201
Ditch, The, 209
Diviners, The, 14, 34, 196
Division Street, 26, 48, 189
Doctor Faustus, 57
Doctor in Spite of Himself, The, 88
Doctor's Dilemma, The, 120
Dog Eat Dog, 98
Doll House, A, 228
Do Lord Remember Me, 19
Dolorosa Sanchez, 144
Dolphin Position, The, 82
Domestic Issues, 56
Dona Francisquita, 181
Dona Rosita, La Soltera, 180
Don Carlos, 61
Don Juan, 96, 149, 161

Don Juan Comes Back from the War, 153
Don Juan in Hell, 89, 132, 163, 211, 227
Dracula, 84, 101, 163
Dramatic License, 23
Dream of Kitamura, The, 77
Dream Home, The, 167
Dreamhouse, 163
Dreamplay, A, 112
Dresser, The, 4, 26, 43, 53, 60, 69, 215
Drinks Before Dinner, 89
Dr. Faustus Lights the Lights, 161
Dr. Rat, 164
Duet for One, 152, 186
Dumping Ground, 82
Dungeons and Gryphons, 14

E

Early Warnings, 128
Eccentricities of a Nightingale, The, 139
Ecco!, 178
Eden Court, 7, 211
Edmond, 92
Educating Rita, 14
Edward IV, 147
Effect of Gamma Rays on Man-in-the Moon-Marigolds, The, 3
Egyptology (My Head Was a Sledgehammer), 150, 161
Eh Joe, 92
Eighties or Last Love, The, 135
84 Charing Cross Road, 221
Einsteins, 217
Einstein: The Man Behind the Genius, 153
Elastic, 169
Elba, 128
El Dia Que Me Quieras, 180
Elephant Man, The, 12, 41, 45, 173, 215, 220
Elephants, 113
Eli: A Mystery Play of the Sufferings of Israel, 96
Elizabeth Dead, 39
Elmo and June Confront Concepts Much Larger Than Themselves, 167
Eloise at Christmastime, 121
Embarcadero Fugue, 24, 69
Emigres, 104
Eminent Domain, 54
Emma Rothstein, 159
Emperor's New Clothes, The, 14
Endings, 207
Enemies, 223
Enormous Egg, The, 98
Entertainer, The, 163, 186
Entertaining Mr. Sloane, 96
E/R Emergency Room, 164
Erma's Dream, 51
Ethan Frome, 120

Eulogy, 32, 148
Eve, 43
Even as the Sun, 212
Even in Laughter, 45
Eve of Retirement, 96
Exception and the Rule, The, 153
Exiles, 109
Explorers, 21
Extended Attack, 117
Extraordinary Histories, 132
Extravagant Triumph of Jesus Christ, Karl Marx, and William Shakespeare, The, 109
Extravaganza, 169
Eye of the Beholder, The, 6

F

Face It Baby, It's Really Your Show!, 140
Faces of Love, 122
Fall Down Go Boom, 106
Fallen Angels, 9, 35, 60
Fall Guy, The, 135
False Colors, 49
Falsies, 207
Falstaff, 44
Familiar Faces/Mixed Feelings, 123
Families, 107
Family Business, 12
Family Devotions, 149
Fanshen, 194
Fantasticks, The, 139, 173
Fantod: A Victorian Reverie, 153
Farewell Supper, The, 159
Fast Woman, 82
Father, The, 163, 218
Faust, Parts I and II, 65
Feathers, 41, 46
Feelers, 208
Fefu and Her Friends, 80
Female Parts, 123
Fen, 150
Fences, 160
Ferocious Kisses, 126
Fiddler on the Roof, 79, 173
Fiddler's Rock, 3
Fifteen Million Fifteen Year-Olds, 158
5th of July, 12, 14, 59, 60, 86, 143, 147, 215
Fifty Million Frenchmen, 132
Filthy Rich, 80, 152
Filumena, 205
Fine-Feathered Review, A, 93
Finer Points of the Situation, The, 148
Fire at Luna Park, 125
First Draft, 160
Fisher Wedding, The, 82
Fish Riding Bikes, 110
Fisherman and His Wife, The, 75
Fitness Game!, The, 196
Fits and Starts, 159
Five Finger Exercise, 45
Five Freedom Revue, The, 210
500 Hats of Bartholomew Cubbins, The, 51
Five Points, 15
Five Unrelated Pieces, 892
Flame Keepers, 201
Flash Floods, 228
Flea in Her Ear, A, 129, 151, 190, 215
Flies in the Buttermilk, 144
Flight Lines, 7
Flirtations, 139
Flowering Peach, The, 3
Flowers for Algernon, 197
Flux, 193
Flying Lemon Circus, The, 184
Fog, 82
Food, 110
Food from Trash, 7
Fool for Love, 56, 125
Fools, 11
Footfalls, 31, 123
Forbidden Copy, 98
Forced Marriage, The, 159
Foreigner, The, 135
Forest Lawn Diet, The, 82
Fortress of Solitude, The, 82
47 Beds, 226
Fox, The, 116, 186
Foxfire, 96
Frankenstein, 26, 46, 173
Free and Clear, 120
Fridays, 4, 41, 135
Friends Too Numerous to Mention, 113
Frogs, The, 153
Front Page, The, 92, 120, 174, 192, 215
Fuhrer is Still Alive, The, 135
Full Circle of the Traveling Squirrel, The, 144
Full Hookup, 6
Full Length Portrait of America, A, 114
Funny Thing Happened on the Way to the Forum, A, 30, 189
Further Adventures of Sally, The, 160, 184

G

Gandhiji, 123
Gardenia, 92, 128, 178
Gardens of Eden, 144
Gateway to Atlantis, 212
Gemini, 69, 170, 218
Geniuses, 28, 177
Gentleman and a Scoundrel, A, 154
Geoff Hoyle Meets Keith Terry, 36
George's File, 217
Getting Out, 178
Ghost Dancing, 160
Ghosts, 20, 125, 139
Ghost Sonata, 65
Ghosts of the Loyal Oaks, 228
Ghost Tales of the South, 121
Gideon's Point, 223
Gift of the Magi, The, 6, 7, 70, 143
Gigi, 139
Gin Game, The, 4, 17, 22, 26, 30, 31, 41, 63, 68, 86, 91, 100, 134, 143, 155, 156, 166, 215, 218, 219
Girl of the Golden West, 32
Girl Who Ate Chicken Bones, The, 194
Glass Menagerie, The, 3, 22, 27, 36, 67, 98, 135, 152, 174, 178, 190
Go Back for Murder, 227
God, 159
God Bless You, Mr. Rosewater, 172
Godspell, 155
Going Over, 228
Gold Dust, 184
Golden Girl, 207
Golem, The, 61
Gondoliers, The, 211
Goodbye Freddy, 196
Goodbye, Howard, 82
Goodnight, Ladies, 150
Good Old Boy, 7
Good Person of Szechwan, The, 137
Good Time, A, 159
Good Woman of Setzuan, The, 89
Goona Goona, 158
Goose and Tomtom, 149
Gorilla, 92
Government Man, The, 135
Grace, 19
Grand's Finale, 70
Great American Family, The, 51
Great Confession, The, 180
Great Days, 19
Great Divide, 160
Greater Tuna, 98
Great Gorilla Musical, The, 144
Great Grandson of Jedidiah Kohler, 56
Great Magoo, The, 98
Great Playground Plot, The, 210
Great Religions, Great Stories, 210
Greek, 117
Greeks, The, 4, 98, 174
Griffin! Griffin!, 48
Groves of Academe, The, 128, 167
Growing Up, 201
Growing Up Gothic, 110, 208
Grown Ups, 130
Guardsman, The, 120
Guess Again, 85
Guys and Dolls, 66

H

Habeas Corpus, 89
Habitual Acceptance of the Near Enough, The, 7, 167
Haggadah, The, 149
Hajj, 124
Half A Lifetime, 41, 128
Half Fare, 56
Halfway There, 169
Hamlet, 10, 38, 44, 108, 131, 150, 163
Hand in Hand, 51
Hansel and Gretel, 68
Happy Birthday, Wanda June, 210
Happy End, 36
Happy Landings, 17
Happy Worker, The, 7
Hard Look at Old Times, A, 76
Harvey, 76, 103
Hasty Heart, The, 7
Hatfields and McCoys, 212
Haven't a Clue, 218
Have You Anything to Declare?, 9, 135
Have You Heard, 77
Hay Fever, 31, 35, 112, 137
Hazard County Wonder, The, 218
Heartbreak House, 36, 96
Heart of a Dog, 19
Hedda Gabler, 8, 26, 35, 89, 99, 183
Heidi, 12
Heiress, The, 35, 45, 103
Heist, The, 114
Hello and Goodbye, 199, 228
Henry V, 95, 163
Henry IV, Part 1, 44, 149, 156, 196
Henry IV, Part 2, 44
Henry VI, 147
Herringbone, 177
Herself As Lust, 177
Hidden Parts, 144
Hidden Place, The, 102
Hiding Place, The, 218
High & Dry, 3
High-Rolling, 218
His Master's Voice, 144
History of the American Film, A, 91
Holdup, The, 17, 56
Hold Me!, 163
Holiday, 120, 223
Hollow Crown, The, 151
Holly and the Ivy, The, 186
Holy Ghosts, 13, 75
Holy Mary, 41
Home, 14, 53, 64, 108, 115, 143, 145, 171, 189, 199, 218
Homesteaders, 46
Honey in the Rock, 212
Hooters, 104
Horizontal White II, 207
Horsepower An Electric Fable, 184
Hoss Drawin', 159
Hostage, The, 73
Hothouse, The, 215
Hot l Baltimore, The, 11
Hotline, 92
House, The, 200
House Across the Street, The, 82
Houseguest, 123
Housekeeper, The, 221
House Music, 18
House Not Meant to Stand, A, 92
House of Blue Leaves, the, 12, 40

House of Ramon Iglesia, The, 82
How He Lied to Her Husband, 186
How I Got That Story, 8, 12, 41, 83, 91, 115, 178
How the Other Half Loves, 187
Hughie, 21
Hula, 226
Hundred Years' War, The, 159
Hypochondriac, The, 41

I

I Am a Woman, 123
I Am Waiting, 100
Igugu Lethu, 114
Il Campiello—a Venetian Comedy, 5
I Love You, I Love You Not, 7, 82
Imaginary Invalid, The, 28, 103, 196
I'm Almost Famous, 41
I'm Getting My Act Together and Taking It on the Road, 53, 221
I'm Happier Than You, 158
Immorality Play, 14
Imperial Valley, 77
Importance of Being Earnest, The, 23, 44, 53, 57, 156, 167, 190
Impromptu of Outremont, The, 152, 204
I'm Tired and I Want to Go to Bed, 56
In a Northern Landscape, 7
In a Very Special House, 102
In Celebration of Ruth Draper, 40
In Circles, 187
Increased Difficulty of Concentration, The, 8
Incredible Feeling Show, The, 85
Independence, 160
Indian and After (America), 226
Indian Wants the Bronx, The, 51
Inferno, 144
Inherit the Wind, 23, 53, 163
Innocents, The, 69, 137
Inquisition, 180
In Search of the Monkey Girl, 226
Interlude, The, 167
International Folk Tales, 3
Interrogation, The, 167
Interviewing the Audience, 226
In the Bag, 7
In the Beginning, 210
In the Belly of the Beast, 215
In the Garden of Eden, 167
In the Jungle of Cities, 112
In the Matter of J. Robert Oppenheimer, 18, 114, 153, 189
In the Sweet Bye and Bye, 202
Intrigue at Ah-Pah, 72
I/O: A Ritual for 23 Performers, 39
Ionescopade, 153
I Ought to Be in Pictures, 35, 86, 100
Iphigenia in Aulis, 131

I Remember Mama, 17
Island, The, 114, 225
Islands—Further, Farther, and Beyond, 102
Isle is Full of Noises, The, 98
Italian Strawhat, The, 126
It's Only a Play, 126
It's Time for a Change, 56
I Used to Like this Place Before They Started Making All These Renovations, 214
Ivanhoe, 38
Ivanov, 113, 223
I Want to Be an Indian, 7

J

Jacinta, 144
Jacques Brel Is Alive and Well and Living in Paris, 173
Jail Diary of Albie Sachs, The, 83
Jane Eyre, 69
Jazz Set, 145
J.B., 89
Jemima Boone, 197
Jesse and the Bandit Queen, 190
Jessie's Land, 148
Johnny Bull, 228
Johnny Got His Gun, 56
Joseph and the Amazing Technicolor Dreamcoat, 154
Josh, 41
Journey of the Fifth Horse, The, 20
Journey's End, 30
Julius Caesar, 7, 44, 57, 87, 162, 167
Juniper Tree, A Tragic Household Tale, The, 138
Jungle Coup, 92
Juno and the Paycock, 171
Just Across the Border, 218
Just a Song at Twilight, 189
Just Between Ourselves, 131

K

Kabuki Macbeth, 225
Kaspar, 213
Katmandu, 158
Kean, 98
Keeper, 124
Keeper, The, 170
Keep Truckin', 207
Kegger, 158
Kenneth and Barbara's Musical Dreamhouse, 41
Keyboard, 145
Key Exchange, 7, 59, 86, 100
Keymaker, The, 18
Keystone, 131
Kidnapped in London, 50
Kid Purple, 144
Kids and Dogs, 144

Kid Twist, 194
Killpoint, 210
Kilo, 82
Kingdom Come, 135
King John, 38, 151
King Lear, 10, 65
King Must Die, The, 164
Kiss Is Just a Kiss, A, 126
Knack, The, 186
Knife in the Heart, A, 160, 223
K2, 28, 204, 205
Kudzu, 177
Kurt Weill Cabaret, A, 186, 222

L

La Belle Au Bois, 209
La Bodega Sold Dreams, 207
La Chafa, 145
La Corte de Faraon, 180
Ladies in Retirement, 67
Ladies of the Stage (The Holy Terrors), 227
Lady and the Clarinet, The, 120
Ladyhouse Blues, 23, 155
Lady of the Castle, 207
Lady or the Tiger, The, 82
Lady Speaks Her Mind, 207
Lakeboat, 92, 120
Langston Speaks, 15
La Pastorela, 78
La Ronde, 86
Las Quiero a Las Dos, 181
Last Call, 159
Last Latin Lover, 109
Last Looks, 48
Last Monthly Meeting of the Brothers Westmoreland, The, 154
Last Night's Lightning, 49
Last of Hitler, The, 48
Last of Mrs. Lincoln, The, 76
Last on the List, The, 93
Last Prostitute, The, 49
Last Slumber Party, The, 49
Last Tape (and Testament) of Richard M. Nixon, 123
Last Vision of Paddy O'Sheen, The, 3
Last Yiddish Poet, The, 122
L'Atelier, 215
Laughter in the Far Dark, 39
Laundry Hour, The, 149
La Vida Es Sueno, 181
La Virgen del Tepeyac, 78
L Zapatera Prodigiosa, 181
Learned Ladies, The, 186
Leavings, 218
Le Cabaret de Camille, 107
Legend of Sleepy Hollow, The, 68
Les Belles Soeurs, 152
Lesson from Aloes, A, 2, 28, 36, 44, 48, 53, 68, 70, 74, 103, 108, 129, 167, 178, 183
Let's Get a Divorce, 147
Letters Home, 39

Letters to Ben, 207
Liberty Call, 145
Lids, 51
Life, A, 143
Life and Adventures of Nicholas Nickleby, The, 95, 137
Life in the Theatre, A, 53, 187, 223
Life on the Mississippi, 174
Lifesaver, 107
Light Up the Sky, 45, 151
Limb King, The, 160
Limited Edition Ronald Firbank, The, 117
Lion in Winter, The, 134, 173, 190, 218
Lion, the Witch and the Wardrobe, The, 69
Little Black Fish, The, 207
Little Chicago, 184
Little Eyolf, 22
Little Foxes, The, 173
Little Mahagonny, The, 153
Little Match Girl, The, 50
Little Night Music, A, 14
Little Shop of Horrors, 228
Little Victories, 19
Little Women, 76
Lives and Deaths of the Great Harry Houdini, 223
Lives of the Great Composers, The, 148
Livin' Dolls, 128
Local Dilemma, A, 15
Lone Star, 155
Long Day's Journey into Night, 151
Long Goodbye, The, 159
Long Journey of Poppie Nongena, The, 138
Loose Ends, 14, 137, 196, 200
Loot, 17, 88
Lorenzo, 88
Los Corridos, 78
Losing It, 225
Lost Ones, The, 124
Louisiana Summer, 15
Love, 145
Love Gifts, 223
Love of Don Perlimplin and Belisa in the Garden, The, 180
Love's Labour's Lost, 35, 48, 228
Lovesong for Miss Lydia, A, 64
LSD: Part I, 226
Lucky Lindy, 83
Ludlow Ladd, 143
Lullabye and Goodnight, 149
Lunchbreak, 167
Lunch Hour, 221

M

Macbeth, 33, 38, 53, 54, 68, 103, 137, 156
Madame Adare, 161
Mad World, My Masters, A, 83
Maggie Magalita, 144

Magic Word, The, 169
Magistrate, The, 99
Magnificent Yankee, The, 137
Mahalia, 99
Maids, The, 39, 51
Majestic Kid, The, 27
Major Barbara, 11, 28, 192, 196
Male Animal, The, 32
Maledetto, 39
Malpractice, or Love Is the Best Doctor, 72
Malvey, 167
Mame, 14
Man and Superman, 163, 211
Man and the Fly, The, 180
Mandate, 159
Mandragola, The, 223
Mandrake, The, 153
Man for All Seasons, A, 143
Man Friday, 100
Man of Destiny, The, 187
Man of La Mancha, 165, 205
Man Who Became a Woman, The, 208
Man Who Came to Dinner, The, 11
Man Who Could See Through Time, The, 196, 228
Man Who Had Three Arms, The, 92
Man Who Killed Buddha, The, 75
Man with a Load of Mischief, 32
Many Happy Returns, 82
Ma Rainey's Black Bottom, 160
Marat/Sade, 222
March of the Falsettos, 34
Marine Tiger, 180
Mark and Samuel and the Frog, 197
Mark Twain Today, 92
Marriage à la Mode, 87
Marriage of Figaro, The, 96
Marriage Proposal, The, 167
Martha Rose and the Miners, 122
Marvelous Mo's Mysterious Show, 210
Mary Barnes, 153
Masque of Beauty and the Beast, The, 102
Mass Appeal, 7, 10, 27, 30, 45, 53, 86, 88, 91, 156, 165, 166, 199, 206, 215, 221
Master Harold . . . and the boys, 228
Matchmaker, The, 35, 163
Matinee Kid, The, 210
Medea, 53, 57
Medea/Sacrament, 107
Medieval Christmas Pageant, The, 87
Medusa, 85
Meetings, 65
Melody of a Glittering Parrot, 223
Melody Sisters, 160
Mensch Meier, 80
Mercenaries, 110
Merchant of Venice, The, 26, 87, 204
Merely Players, 51
Merlin, 93
Merlin and Arthur, 68

Merlyn's Magic and the Student King, 212
Merry Wives of Windsor, The, 95
Messiah, 208
Metamorphosis, 130
Metamorphosis in Miniature, A, 138
Middle Ages, The, 59
Midnight Cabaret, 154
Midsummer Night's Dream, A, 5, 14, 28, 32, 67, 101, 108, 149, 171
Midwinter Night's Dream: Lester and the Winter Vistors, A, 143
Mikado, The, 15, 57
Millionairess, The, 99
Millionaire y el Pobrecito, The, 115
Mine, 7
Miracle Man, 207
Miracle Worker, The, 68, 134
Misalliance, 7, 30, 32, 45, 112, 156
Miser, The, 58, 54, 69, 98, 130, 143, 156
Miss Firecracker Contest, The, 3, 41, 67, 200, 202
Miss Julie, 186
Miss Lulu Bett, 135
Miss Waters, To You, 15
Mister Roberts, 173
Miyako, 194
Mobile Hymn, 174
Moby Dick Rehearsed, 156
Modern Ladies of Guanabacoa, The, 82
Mojo, 98
Molly, 120
Molly Bailey's Traveling Family Circus—Featuring Scenes from the Life of Mother Jones, 158
Mother Courage, 39
Mother Figure, 12
Mother Goose, 197
Mother of Us All, The, 138
Mound Builders, The, 46
Mountain Tales and Music, 186
Mourning Becomes Electra, 17
Monkey, Monkey, 141
Month in the Country, A, 130
Moon for the Misbegotten, A, 3, 60, 76, 174
Morning's at Seven, 17, 100, 143, 220
Mousetrap, The, 35, 134, 205
Move, 218
Mr. Lion, 194
Mr. Pickwick's Christmas, 51
Mrs. Dally Has a Lover, 159
Mrs. Warren's Profession, 32, 189, 228
Much Ado About Nothing, 38, 44, 48, 73, 163, 228
Mummers' Play, The, 132
Murder at the Howard Johnson's, 155
Murder at the Vicarage, 7
Murder Game, The, 227
Murder Is Announced, A, 24, 68
My Heart is in the East, 113
My Heart is in Your Shoes, 207
My Sister in This House, 14, 193

N

Nabakov, 153
Na Keiki Haku Mele O Ka Aina (The Children of the Land Are Poets), 102
Name of the Game is 'Ben', The, 144
Nathan the Wise, 194
Native Speech, 123
Nayatt School, 226
Necessary Ends, 150
Ned and Jack, 51
Needle's Eye, The, 39
Neither Fish nor Fowl, 83
Neutral Countries, 7
Never Say Never, 148
Never the Twain, 218
Nevis Mountain Dew, 123
New Approach to Human Sacrifice, A, 56
New Client, A, 49
New, Improved Bride of Sirocco, The, 148
New Moon, 165
Niagara Falls, 217
Nzice People Dancing to Good Country Music, 7
Night and Day, 105
Nightclub Cantata, 153
Night in Bulgaria, A, 159
Nightingale, The, 11, 15, 79, 85
Nightmare!!, 148
'night Mother, 21
Night Must Fall, 99
Night of January 16th, 51
Night of the Iguana, The, 131
Night Thoreau Spent in Jail, The, 141
Nobody Wanted to Sit Behind a Desk, 226
No Easy Answers, 106
No End of Blame, 128
No Man's Land, 199
No Place to Be Somebody, 64
Norman, Is That You?, 64
No Scratch, 153
No Smile for Strangers, 77
Not So Silent Night, A, 153
Number Our Days, 129
Nurse Jane Goes to Hawaii, 166
Nuts, 12, 116

O

Odd Couple, The, 84
Oedipus Project, The, 135
Oedipus Rex, 60
Off Broadway, 222
Off Center, 125
Of Mice and Men, 68, 73, 88, 151, 170, 200, 202, 205, 215
Oh, Coward!, 155
Ohio Impromptu, 92, 123

Ohio Tip-Off, 144, 160
Oh, My Irish Ancestors, 132
Oh, What a Lovely War, 31
Oldest Living Graduate, The, 7
Old Explorers, 8
Oldtimer's Game, 6
Old Times, 217, 223
On Borrowed Time, 76, 98
Once Upon A Mattress, 45, 155
One Flew Over the Cuckoo's Nest, 44
One for the Road, 183
110 in the Shade, 66
One Potato, Two, 184
On Golden Pond, 35, 41, 142, 227
On the Razzle, 28
On the Swing Shift, 128
On Trial, 115
Open Admissions, 82, 120
Open Heart, 160
Opening Night, 15
Operetta, My Dear Watson, 108
Orchids in the Moonlight, 21
Ord-Way, Ames-Gay, 82
Orlando, 20
Othello, 44, 89, 103, 151, 162
Our Town, 96, 147
Out of the Night, 88
Out of the Reach of Children, 148
Outpost, 144
Overland Rooms, The, 131
Overruled, 139
Owl Was a Baker's Daughter, The, 207
Oxcart, The, 180
Oz—Land of Magic, 68, 69
Ozma of Oz, 197

P

Painting Churches, 193
Palace of Amateurs, The, 40
Pal Joey, 108, 120
Pantagleize, 113
Panto, 92
Pantomime, 9, 59, 91, 100
Paper Angel, 145
Paper Flowers, 180
Paradise, 12
Paris, 132
Park Your Car in the Harvard Yard, 123
Partial Objects, 144
Partners, 7
Passing Shots, 125
Passione, 39
Passion of Dracula, The, 91
Pastorale, 193
Pastoral or Recollections of Country Life, 82
Patti's Poem to Sam, 73
Paul Robeson, 39, 64
Peer Gynt, 65, 96
Peg O' My Heart, 70, 76
Pentecost, The, 135

INDEX OF TITLES 259

Performance Anxiety, 72
Period of Adjustment, 24
Pericles, 5
Personal History of the American Theatre, A, 226
Peter Pan, 26, 53
Phallacies, 148
Phantom Limbs, 209
Phantom of the Opera, 51
Philadelphia Story, The, 190
Philanderer, The, 228
Philoctetes, 61, 70
Phoenix Too Frequent, A, 212
Physician in Spite of Himself, The, 211
Piaf: La Vie l'Amour, 95
Picnic, 137
Piece of Monologue, A, 92
Pie Rate's Off, The, 100
Pigeons on the Walk, 68
Pilgrimmage, 77
Pinocchio: Evviva!, 12
Pippi Longstocking, 51
Pippin, 15, 67, 206
Pirates of Penzance, The, 14, 149, 150
Play, 5
Playboy of the Western World, The, 43, 95
Playground, 201
Playing in Local Bands, 125, 160, 228
Playing with Fire, 186
Play's the Thing, The, 196, 218
Plenty, 150
Plymouth Rock Isn't Pink, 152
Point Judith, 226
Poisoner of the Wells, 82
Poppa, 160
Portage to San Cristobal of A. H., The, 98
Portrait of Jennie, 145
Possum Song, 125
Postcards, 82
Potato-Faced Blindman and Other Stories, 117
Potsdam Quartet, The, 59
Powder, 167
Power Lines, 153
Prayer for My Daughter, A, 200
Precious Blood, 75, 167
Prelude to Death in Venice, A, 124
Present Laughter, 54, 183, 223
Present Tense, 56
Pretty Passion, A, 110
Price, The, 18, 53, 134, 166, 171
Pride of the Brittons, The, 69
Primary English Class, The, 123
Prince and the Pauper, The, 12
Princess Grace and the Fazzaris, 225
Private Life of the Master Race, 24
Private Lives, 14, 44, 139, 143, 178, 227
Promise, The, 152
Proprietor, The, 167
Proud Flesh, 160
Punch with Judy, 209

Push-Ups, 106
Puss in Boots, 50
Puss N. Boots, 68
Put Them all Together, 115
Pvt. Wars, 12, 159
Pygmalion, 174, 215

Q

Quality of Mercy, 211
Quannapowitt Quartet, The, 123
Quartermaine's Terms, 120
Queen and the Rebels, The, 54
Quilters, 73, 171

R

Ragged Dick, 207
Rain, 26, 108
Rainmaker, The, 30, 96, 205
Raisin, 64, 88
Raisin in the Sun, A, 202
Range, 110
Rape Upon Rape, 194
Raspberry Picker, The, 18
Rattlesnake in a Cooler, 75
Ready or Not, 166
Rear Column, The, 152, 167
Red and Blue, 149
Red Bluegrass Western Flyer Show, The, 12
Red Fox/Second Hangin', 186
Red, Hot & Blue, 132
Red Rain, 125
Red River, 92
Regard of Flight, The, 19
Rejoice, Dang It, Rejoice!, 211
Relatively Speaking, 86
Release of a Live Performance, The, 144
Relics, 106
Renaissance Radar, 125
Renaissance Revue, A, 227
Rennings Children, The, 56
Rent, 207
REO/Internal Combustion, 41
Requiem for a Nun, 96
Restaurant, or Your Goose is Cooked, The, 207
Resurrection of Lady Lester, The, 128
Return of Pinocchio, The, 80
Revenger's Tragedy, The, 61
Rhino Fat from Red Dog Notes, 202
Ribadier System, The, 112
Rich and Famous, 115
Richard II, 17, 56
Richard III, 130, 147, 163
Rip Van Winkle, or The Works, 228
Rise and Rise of Daniel Rocket, The, 177

Rise of David Levinsky, The, 18
Rivals, The, 12, 156, 205
Riverwind, 24
Roads to Home, The, 126
Robber Bridegroom, The, 59, 100
Robert & Elizabeth, 165
Rockaby, 21, 123
Rocket to the Moon, 139
Rogue of Seville, The, 78
Romance, 167
Romantic Comedy, 143, 159
Romeo and Juliet, 10, 38, 44, 59, 79, 151, 163, 183, 192
Room Service, 96, 142, 223
Room 17C, 158
Rope Dancers, The, 3
Rosa, 159
Rosario and the Gypsies, 82
Rosencrantz and Guildenstern Are Dead, 44
Routed, 82, 217
Route 1 & 9, 226
Rover, The, 87
Royal Family, The, 137
Rumpelstiltskin, 197
Rundown, 21
Running Gag, 158
Rupert's Birthday, 6, 88, 167
Russian Strip, 70

S

Saddest Summer of Val, The, 144
Safe Place, A, 40
Saint and the Football Players, The, 100
Saint Joan, 44, 61
Salad Days, 189
Sally and Marsha, 128
Sam Patch & Company, 121
Same Time, Next Year, 23
Sand Castles, 7, 125
Sanibel and Captiva, 100
San Joaquin Blues, 159
Savages, 36, 48, 192, 199
Scapino, 31, 187, 210
Scenes from American Life, 12, 41
Scenes from La Vie de Boheme, 128
School for Scandal, The, 21, 61
Screenplay, 28
Schubert's Last Serenade, 159
Seagull, The, 9, 56, 112
Sea Horse, The, 22, 41, 167, 178, 210
Sea Marks, 9, 39, 46, 59
Seascape, 39
Second Chance, 189
Second Prize: Two Months in Leningrad, 41
Secret Injury, Secret Revenge, 135
Secret Numbers, 125
Secreto Agravio, Secreta Venganza, A, 181

Seige of Frank Sinatra, The, 108
Self-Begotten, The, 82
Selma, 207
Senorita from Tacna, The, 109
September Song, 155
Serious Bizness, 19
Sermon, A, 82
Servant of Two Masters, 170
1776, 173
Seven Year Itch, The, 134
Sex and Death to the Age 14, 226
Sganarelle, an Evening of Moliere Farces, 20, 92
Shadow Box, The, 190
Shadows, 217
Shakespeare's People, 210
Sharing, 121
Shay, 115
She Also Dances, 196
Sheen's Outside, 207
Sherlock Holmes, 32
Sherlock Holmes and the Curse of the Sign of Four, 59
She Stoops to Conquer, 87, 91, 103, 108, 112, 202, 211
She, That One, He and the Other, 180
Shim Sham, 166
Short Stuff, 155
Short Wave Man, The, 106
Showdown, The, 100
Show Off, The, 32, 36
Shrew!, 210
Side by Side by Sondheim, 23, 35, 199
Sign of Four, The, 187
Signs of Life, 144
Silver Screen, The, 67
Silver Tassie, The, 194
Singapore Sling, 125
Sin, Sex and Cinema, 125
Singular Life of Albert Nobbs, The, 128
Sister Mary Ignatius Explains It All for You, 41, 80, 116, 177, 210, 225
Sizwe Bansi Is Dead, 114, 225
Skin, 153
Skin of Our Teeth, The, 46, 156
Skirmishes, 128
Sky Blue Pink, 144
Slacks and Tops, 128
Sleeparound Town, 177
Sleep Beauty, 104
Sleepover, 106
Sleuth, 76, 88, 212
Slow Dance on the Killing Ground, 155
Slow Drag, Mama, 6
Sneakers, 14
Snow Orchid, 56
Soldierboy, 78
Soldiering, 212
Soldier's Play, A, 4, 92, 130
Solo: The Subject Animal, Sidekick, 6
Some Rain, 160

Something Cloudy, Something Clear, 61
Something Different, 193
Something's Afoot, 155
Something's Rockin' in Denmark, 153
Something Unspoken, 159
Song of Myself, 166
Songs of A Mermaid, 41
Sore Throats, 183
Sorrows of Stephen, 155
Soul Fusion II, 140
Southgate Porter, The, 167
South of the Mountain, 186
Speakeasy: An Evening Out with Dorothy Parker, 19
Specimen Days, 149
Spider's Web, The, 6, 139
Splendid Rebels, 211
Spokesong, 34, 163
Spring Awakening, 106
Squabbles, 23
Stopover on Whitney Street, 148
Stage that Walks, The, 19
Standing on My Knees, 128, 205, 225
Stars in the Sky, The, 121
Starting Here, Starting Now, 31
Starting Tomorrow, 3
Station J: An American Epic, 77
Starz, Stripes . . . Forever, 39
Steaming, 99
Step on a Crack, 69
Still Life, 28, 83
Stitchers and Starlight Talkers, 160
Stone Soup, 121
Stops Along the Way, 217
Stories, 167
Story of Don Cristobal, The, 180
Storytellers, The, 169
Story Theatre, 84
Strange Snow, 41, 53, 128
Streetcar Named Desire, A, 46, 99, 160, 171, 199, 205, 225
Stretch of the Imagination, A, 218
Strider, 141, 218
Stuck, 125
Sty of the Blind Pig, The, 64
Subject Animal, The, 167
Subject to Fits, 194
Subject Was Roses, The, 8, 31, 221
Suicide in B Flat, 73
Suite in Two Keys, 165
Sullivan and Gilbert, 23
Summer, 128
Summer People, The, 60
Summer Vacation Madness, 96
Sun Always Shines for the Cool, The, 123
Sunday in the Park with George, 177
Sun Gets Blue, The, 209
Sunny Morning, A, 159
Sunrise at Campobello, 40
Sunshine Boys, The, 155, 227
Supporting Cast, The, 220
Survivalist, The, 6, 82, 167
Sus, 104

Swan, The, 79
Swan Song, 159
Swanwhite, 61
Sweeney Todd, 211
Sweet Basil, 53
Sweet Dreams, 214
Swing Shift, 206

T

Table Manners, 46
Table Settings, 22
Taking Steam, 113
Taing Steps, 13, 43, 192
Tale of Two Cities, A, 59, 183
Tales from Hollywood, 129
Tales of Scheherazade, 3
Tale Told, A, 129
Talking With, 6, 128, 167
Tallahassee, 167
Talley's Folly, 12, 35, 41, 53, 59, 60, 69, 70, 80, 86, 96, 103, 134, 137, 143, 154, 156, 170, 199, 204, 215, 217, 218
Taming of the Shrew, The, 10, 43, 73, 105, 156, 190
Tangled Snarl, The, 148
Tantalizing, A, 7
Taps at 8:23, 159
Tartuffe, 5, 8, 46, 68, 73, 80, 108, 167, 171, 183, 190, 202, 218
Tartuffe: Alias "The Preacher", 9
Te Juro Juana Que Tengo Ganas, 180
Temperance!, 67
Tempest, The, 73, 87, 96, 124, 149, 156, 215
Tenants, The, 207
Tender Offer, 82
Tenement, 144
Ten Little Indians, 53
Tennessee, USA!, 67
Tennessee Williams: A Celebration, 223
Tenth Man, The, 18
Ten Times Table, 59
Teoria y Juego del Duende, 181
Terra Nova, 26, 48, 63, 100, 137, 156, 199
Territorial Rites, 19
Thanksgiving, 71
That Championship Season, 204
That's All Folks!, 177
Theatre Festival of New Music I, 39
Theatre of the Film Noir, 223
Therese Raquin, 219
These Men, 123
They're Playing Our Song, 220
Think Piece, A, 56
Third Street, 56
13 Rue de l'Amour, 215
This Story of Yours, 120
This Wooden 'o', 151

Thousand Clowns, A, 40, 103, 143
Threads, 56
Three Acts of Recognition, 149, 161
3 by Beckett, 123
Three Musketeers, The, 68, 99
Threepenny Opera, The, 68, 183
Three Sisters, The, 17, 21, 73, 128, 131, 187
Three Sisters Who Are Not Sisters, 132
Through the Leaves, 80
Thwarting of Baron Bolligrew, The, 79
Thymus Vulgaris, 56
Time and the Conways, 105
Timon of Athens, 149
Tintypes, 6, 30, 35, 59, 63, 68, 70, 88, 134, 141, 155, 171, 189, 196, 199, 215, 217
Tiovivo, 218
Titus Andronicus, 189
Tobacco Road, 213
To Be Young, Gifted and Black, 64
Toby Show, A, 210
Toda Desnudez Sera Castigada, 181
Today's Special, 135
To Grandmother's House We Go, 34
Tomfoolery, 28, 59, 211
Tom Jones, 171
To Kill a Mockingbird, 173
Tonight at 8:30, 36
Topeka Scuffle, 69
Top Girls, 150
Touch, 106
Touch Black, 82
Touch of the Poet, A, 22, 222, 228
Towards Zero, 24
Transfiguration of Benno Blimpie, The, 177
Translations, 34, 43, 59, 105, 137, 192, 215
Treasure Island, 141
Trelawny of the 'Wells', 223
Trespassers Will Be Prosecuted, 59
Trial by Jury, 51
Trial of the Catonsville Nine, The, 190
Trials and Tribulations of Staggerlee Booker T. Brown, The, 64
Tribute, 155, 172
Tricycle Trail, 27
Trio, 138, 145
Trip, The, 85
Tristan and Isolt, 187
Trojanshorse and Other Conundrums, 49
Trouble Begins at Eight, 96
True West, 21, 46, 63, 189, 196, 200, 202, 211, 215
Tooth of Crime, The, 204
Tu-Be, 49
Tuesday's Child, 121
Twelfth Night, 5, 10, 14, 44, 147, 149, 156, 174
12-1-A, 77
Twelve-Pound Look, The, 186
24 Inches, 207

Twice Around the Park, 204, 221
Twinkle, Twinkle, 98
Two American Families, 132
Two by A.M., 120
2 by South, 75
Two by Two, 67
Two for the Seesaw, 18, 22, 40, 134
Two Gentlemen of Verona, The, 38, 57, 151, 166, 192
Two Hot Dogs with Everything, 82
Two Noble Kinsmen, The, 61
Two Pieces of Silver, 75
Two Tigers, The, 114

U

Ubu Revue, The, 132
Umbrellas, Bicuspids and Angels, 207
Unauthorized Autobiography of "Kid Purple" Schwartz, The, 27
Uncle Vanya, 10, 17, 30, 135, 222, 228
Uncommon Women and Others, 116
Undefeated Rhumba Champ, The, 70, 82
Under Distant Skies, 68
Under the Ilex, 183
Undiscovered Country, 28
Unexpected Guest, The, 12
Unicorn Song, 27
Union City Thanksgiving, 109
Unnamed, The, 213
Unseen Hand, The, 51
Upper Depths, The, 145
U.S.A., 36
USO Show, The, 222

V

Vagabond Stars, 113
Value of Names, The, 7, 167, 217
Vamps and Rideouts, 104
Vanities, 88, 45, 184, 204, 218
Vasilisa, 197
Velveeta Meltdown, 158
Veronica's Room, 134
Vienna Notes, The, 39
Vieux Carre, 228
View from the Bridge, A, 32, 40, 120
Village Wooing, 70, 139, 159
Vinegar Tree, The, 192
Virginia Behind the Cotton Wool, 106
Visit, A, 207
Visit, The, 12
Voice of the Turtle, The, 27
Voodoo Automatic, 125

INDEX OF TITLES 261

W

Wait Until Dark, 13, 155
Waiting for Godot, 5, 21, 30, 95
Waiting for Lefty, 40
Waiting for the Parade, 4, 8, 200
Wake of Jamey Foster, The, 98
Wall, The, 12
Waltz of the Toreadors, 45
War and Peace, 67
Warp I, II, III, 34
Watch on the Rhine, 33
Way Upstream, 12
We Won't Pay! We Won't Pay!, 100, 122, 204, 225
Weapons of Happiness, 202
Web, The, 215
Weehawken Castle, 27
Weekend Near Madison, A, 7
Welcome to the Moon, 82
Welfare Lady, 167
Whale Concerts, The, 117
Whales of August, The, 217, 228
What a Life, 126
Whatchamacallums & Thingamajigs, 40
What I Did Last Summer, 56, 221
What the Babe Said, 73
What the Butler Saw, 30, 163
Whatever Became of Love?, 218
What Would Jeanne Moreau Do?, 228
When Hell Freezes Over, 208
White Linen, 41
Who Loves the Dancer, 145
Whorl, 110
Who's Afraid of Virginia Woolf, 152, 171
Whose Life Is It Anyway?, 14, 100, 143, 202
Who's Happy Now?, 204
Wild Duck, The, 112
Wilderness of Shur, 145
Wild Gardens of Loup Garou, The, 138
Wild Oats, 65, 142, 147
Wild Rose Branches, 100
Will They Ever Love Us on Broadway?, 15
Willa, 106
Wind in the Willows, The, 51, 79, 93, 167
Winds of Change, The, 15
Wings, 48, 156, 163
Winners, 186
Winslow Boy, The, 32
Winterfire, 144
Winterplay, 193
Winter's Tale, The, 38
Wisteria Bush, The, 68
Witches, 3
Without Willie, 126
Witness for the Prosecution, 60, 202
Wizard of Oz, The, 53, 79
Woman, The, 48
Wonderful, Wonderful Siberia, 217
Wonderland, 104
Woods, The, 51, 193
Woolen Sox, 169
Woolgatherer, The, 92
Working, 34, 210, 211
Workroom, The, 31, 48, 120
World of Ben Caldwell, The, 145
World of Paul Crume, The, 211
Woza Albert!, 80
Wrong Guys, 124
Wuthering Heights, 7

Y

Yamashita, 77
Yankee Wives, 155
Yanks 3, Detroit 0, Top of the Seventh, 73, 159
Years Ago, 89
Yeast Beast, 201
Yellow Fever, 77
Yellow Wallpaper, The, 106
Yerma, 153
Yes, I Can!, 48
You Can Be Replaced, 72
You Can't Take It with You, 26, 35, 79, 108, 165
you know Al he's a funny guy, 12
You Never Can Tell, 199
You Never Know, 76
Your Move, 217

Z

Zaloominations, 207
Zastrozzi, 34, 43, 149
Zeks, 207

New York Shakespeare Festival. Marcell Rosenblatt and William Hurt in A Midsummer Night's Dream. *Photo: Martha Swope.*

About TCG

Theatre Communications Group, the national organization for the nonprofit professional theatre, was founded in 1961 to provide a national forum and communications network for the then-emerging nonprofit theatres, and to respond to the needs of both theatres and theatre artists for centralized services.

Today, TCG is a unique national arts organization, creatively combining the activities of both service organization and national professional association by addressing artistic and management concerns, serving artists and institutions, and acting as advocate and provider of services for a field diverse in its aesthetic aims and located in every part of this country. TCG's 222 Constituent and Associate theatres, as well as thousands of individual artists, participate in nearly 30 programs and services. TCG participants encompass artistic and managing directors, actors, playwrights, directors, designers, literary managers, trustees and administrative personnel. Institutions and individuals are served through casting and job referral services, management and research services, publications, literary services, conferences and seminars, and a wide variety of other programs.

TCG's goals are to foster cross-fertilization and interaction among different types of organizations and individuals that comprise the profession; to improve the artistic and administrative capabilities of the field; to enhance the visibility and demonstrate the achievements of the American theatre by increasing the public's awareness of theatre's role in society; and to encourage a nationwide network of professional theatre companies and individuals that collectively represent our "national theatre."

Theatre Communications Group, Inc.
355 Lexington Avenue
New York, NY 10017
(212) 697-5230

Peter Zeisler, *Director*
Lindy Zesch, *Associate Director*

BOARD OF DIRECTORS

Alan Schneider, President
Richard Nelson, Vice President
Alison Harris, Secretary/Treasurer

Peter Culman
Robert Falls
Edes Gilbert
Spalding Gray
Adrian Hall
John Jensen

James Earl Jones
Rosetta LeNoire
Romulus Linney
William Ludel
Mako
Emily Mann
Des McAnuff
David Ofner
Harold Prince
Lloyd Richards

Barbara Rosoff
Donald Schoenbaum
Stanley Silverman
Daniel Sullivan
Patrick Tovatt
M. Burke Walker
Michael Weller
Peter Zeisler

CSC Repertory. Christopher Martin in Faust. *Photo: Gerry Goodstein.*

Other TCG Publications

American Theatre

Recently expanded from *TheatreCommunications,* the national monthly forum for news, features and opinion.

Theatre Directory

The annual pocket-sized contact resource of theatres and related organizations.

Subscribe Now!

Danny Newman's landmark work on building arts audiences through dynamic subscription promotion.

New Plays USA 1

TCG's 1982 collection of current scripts from America's professional theatres includes *A Prelude to Death in Venice,* by Lee Breuer; *Dead Souls,* adapted by Tom Cole; *FOB,* by David Henry Hwang; *Still Life,* by Emily Mann; *The Resurrection of Lady Lester* by OyamO; and *Winterplay,* by Adele Edling Shank.

New Plays USA 2

The second volume of this series of anthologies includes *Secret Honor,* by Donald Freed and Arnold M. Stone; *Food from Trash,* by Gary Leon Hill; *Mensch Meier,* by Franz Xaver Kroetz, translated by Roger Downey; *Buck,* by Ronald Ribman; and *Mercenaries,* by James Yoshimura.

Plays in Process

A subscription service providing immediate circulation of new plays, translations and adaptations produced at theatres across America.

Computers and the Performing Arts

The special report on TCG's 1980 National Computer Project for the Performing Arts.

Dramatists Sourcebook

The guide to opportunities for playwrights, translators, composers, lyricists and librettists.

Theatre Facts

The annual report on the economic health of the nonprofit professional theatre in the United States.

Graphic Communications for the Performing Arts

A richly illustrated compendium of outstanding examples of graphic design for the performing arts.

ArtSEARCH

The bi-monthly national employment bulletin for the performing arts.

Performing Arts Ideabooks

A series of monographs by working professionals outlining innovative approaches to telemarketing, touring and volunteer groups.

The Hartman Theatre. Donalyn Petrucci and David Garrison in The Three Musketeers. *Photo: Martha Swope.*